INTERPERSONAL

COMMUNICATION

A GOALS-BASED APPROACH

THIRD EDITION

DANIEL J. CANARY
Arizona State University

MICHAEL J. CODY
University of
Southern California

VALERIE L. MANUSOV
University of Washington

BEDFORD / ST. MARTIN'S
BOSTON · NEW YORK

For Bedford/St. Martin's

Editor: Michael Bagnulo
Associate Editor, Publishing Services: Maria Teresa Burwell
Production Supervisors: Tina Cameron, Jennifer Wetzel
Marketing Manager: Richard Cadman
Project Management: Books By Design, Inc.
Cover Design: Lucy Krikorian
Cover Art: Poetry Reading by Milton Avery, 1957. Oil on canvas, 43¾" × 56", Munson-Williams-Proctor Arts
    Institute, Museum of Art, Utica, New York. Museum purchase. Copyright © 2002 Milton Avery Trust/Artist
    Rights Society (ARS), New York. Photo by G. R. Farley-Photography.
Composition: Books By Design, Inc.
Printing and Binding: Haddon Craftsmen, an RR Donnelley & Sons Company

President: Joan E. Feinberg
Editorial Director: Denise B. Wydra
Publisher for History and Communication: Patricia A. Rossi
Director of Marketing: Karen R. Melton
Director of Editing, Design, and Production: Marcia Cohen
Manager, Publishing Services: Emily Berleth

Library of Congress Control Number: 2002106323

Manufactured in the United States of America.

8 7 6 5 4 3
f e d c b

For information, write:
Bedford/St. Martin's, 75 Arlington Street, Boston, MA 02116   (617-399-4000)

ISBN: 0–312–25895–X

PREFACE

As interpersonal scholars and practitioners, we are committed to providing a text that combines research on interpersonal communication with the everyday practices communicators undertake. This new edition, our third, continues this commitment to integrating research and application, as well as featuring goals as an important, useful framework for understanding the complexities of interpersonal communication. In our opinion, few things can be as important to students as learning how communication helps or hinders them in working toward life objectives. Providing both theory and personal application is our primary means for helping students in this process.

This edition of *Interpersonal Communication: A Goals-Based Approach* continues the approach of the first two versions, with an emphasis on three often interrelated goals:

1. *Self-presentation goals:* how people use communication as they present an image of themselves.

2. *Relational goals:* how communication is tied to the escalation, maintenance, de-escalation, and possible termination of relationships.

3. *Instrumental goals:* how people use communication in their attempts to obtain personal favors or resources.

We have enhanced this edition in a number of ways. First, we have provided important new material. Chapter 1 includes a more contemporary presentation of what is involved in the interpersonal communication process. Our updated definition of communication includes understanding that communication occurs between people, changes over time, and depends on the use of culturally based symbols. We introduce early on the importance of understanding that interpersonal communication — particularly when used in the pursuit of goals — calls upon communicators to think about the ethical implications of their decisions. We include discussion of interpersonal communication as an ethical practice in our introductory pages.

We have also included a new chapter on listening, Chapter 3, because of the importance of this process in the pursuit of goals. Students are encouraged to understand the range of processes involved in listening, to see the role of listening in a range of relationship contexts (including education and organizations), to link listening with other important interpersonal goals, and to learn about the characteristics typically involved in effective listening.

Another new chapter, Chapter 14, entitled "Interpersonal Goals over Time," illustrates well how goals change over the life span. We cover theories that explain the developmental nature of goals and provide research and applications of communicating across generations, turning points in long-term relationships, and the negotiation of identities across time and relationships. This chapter presents additional material on families and friendships.

Reflecting the development in information technology that has occurred since the book's last edition, there is new coverage throughout the book on the many ways new technologies affect interpersonal communication. New research in the area of computer-mediated communication (CMC) has offered us an opportunity to see how some interpersonal processes, such as self-disclosure and nonverbal communication, may be changed or enhanced when they occur via new technologies. To our benefit, Dr. Joseph Walther, a leading authority of the interpersonal uses of CMC, provided much of this material.

This edition also includes "Student as Observer" exercises in each chapter, a new feature designed to encourage students to become actively engaged in the text material. These quick exercises allow the students to test their observations of day-to-day interactions against the scholarly research presented in the chapter.

OVERVIEW OF THE BOOK

The purpose of this text is to present research on interpersonal communication so that students can see the relevance of communication as they pursue personal goals. This pursuit does not mean that we adopt a skills-based approach or that we want students to manipulate others. Instead, it reflects our belief that communication processes are essential to everything we do when we engage with others to fulfill our goals. Understanding the complexities of the communication process allows people to undertake the pursuit of their goals with a better picture of what is involved.

The third edition of this book is structured into five parts. The organization of the parts is based on the three primary goals mentioned earlier — self-presentation, relational, and instrumental — with the middle three parts of the book concentrating on these goals specifically. The first part provides a foundation for understanding the nature of the communication processes that shape the pursuit of interpersonal goals, and the final part presents students with the bigger picture of a goal-oriented approach to interpersonal communication.

Taken together, the five parts will provide the reader with a relatively complete picture of interpersonal communication. Part I begins this picture by presenting the fundamentals of interpersonal communication. Chapter 1 offers a definition of interpersonal communication and some of the ethical considerations that are a part of interacting with others. This definition relies on understanding that interpersonal communication involves the interaction among many people, all of whom are pursuing their goals in relationship to one another. It also reviews the importance, variety, and nature of interpersonal goals. Chapter 2 examines the role of perception in shaping interpersonal communication and discusses how some of the things that go on inside people's heads influence how they act with others. Chapter 3 explores the nature of listening, the importance of listening in various contexts, and the characteristics of effective listeners. Chapter 4 reviews some of the vast literature on language and the different ways that people exchange verbal messages. Chapter 5 complements the introduction of the verbal code (language) with discussion of the characteristics and importance of the nonverbal code for communicating.

Part II addresses self-presentation goals. Chapter 6 discusses what is meant by self-presentation and focuses on the primary means through which people present themselves to others. Chapter 7 examines the nature of self-disclosure as one of the ways in which we express who we are to others. Chapter 8 concerns the defense of our public or self-images in cases when those images are questioned. Special attention is given to accounting as a means of restoring the images we wish to convey.

Part III focuses on relational goals. Chapter 9 includes material on how relationships develop, with particular emphasis on the importance of attraction in the process of relationship initiation. Chapter 10 discusses relational maintenance — why and how we sustain our personal relationships and the specific strategies that are available to us for doing so. Chapter 11 considers relational decay and termination, exploring the reasons for breakups and other relational endings, the ways that people separate from one another, and the emotional consequences that may occur because of relational termination.

Part IV covers instrumental goals. Chapter 12 addresses the basic principles underlying the influence or compliance process. It looks at the research on compliance-gaining and compliance resistance strategies and tactics. Chapter 13 concerns conflict: how conflicts emerge, strategies for managing conflict interactions, and the potential effects of conflict. Chapter 14 looks at goals across time and place to provide a picture of the changing, evolving nature of interpersonal communication and the pursuit of goals.

Part V focuses on factors related to achieving interpersonal competence. Chapter 15 reviews research relevant to individual factors that affect our interactions with others. Chapter 16 closes the text by reviewing research on communication competence — what it means to be an effective and appropriate communicator. A person's degree of competence — in self-presentation, in relationships, and instrumentally — is often based on an understanding and integration of the communication principles discussed throughout this text.

ACKNOWLEDGMENTS

Numerous people deserve our thanks. Several people at Bedford/St. Martin's, in particular, were instrumental as catalysts for the third edition. Patricia Rossi, Jennifer Bartlett, Marcia Cohen, Emily Berleth, and, most notably, Michael Bagnulo all worked to get us started — and to keep us on track — that we might offer a new and exciting version of the text. We would also like to thank Nancy Benjamin, of Books By Design, for her help in producing our book.

Next, several reviewers gave us important evaluations on the second edition so that we can provide even more of what instructors and students need from a revised text. This review team was made up of Patricia Amason, Julie Burke, Pamela Cooper, Stephanie Coopman, Joy Hart, John Makay, Steve McCornack, Juliann Scholl, and Harry Weger.

Several people also provided important substantive matter for this book. As mentioned, Joe Walther from Rensselaer Polytechnic Institute provided us with excellent material regarding computer-mediated communication, which we incorporated throughout this text. As well, Sandi Lakey, from the Pennsylvania College of Technology, revised the instructor's manual to complement the new material in this version.

Several colleagues provided important help and advice on ideas and projects for the book over the years. These include Deborah Dunn, Steve Phillips, John Seiter, Michelle Tennebruso-Gradis, and Sandra Petronio.

We also know that getting the time to read, think, and write this edition depended on the support of our friends and family. In this group, we include Susan Messman, Julia Cody, and Chuck McSween, and we thank them for understanding why we needed time to be away from our interpersonal relationships to write about interpersonal communication.

Daniel J. Canary
Michael J. Cody
Valerie L. Manusov

C O N T E N T S

PREFACE   iii

PART I   FUNDAMENTALS OF INTERPERSONAL COMMUNICATION   1

CHAPTER 1   THE IMPORTANCE OF INTERPERSONAL COMMUNICATION IN PURSUING PERSONAL GOALS   2

Defining Interpersonal Communication   4

The Nature of Goals   9

Types of Interpersonal Goals   11

    Self-Presentation Goals   11

    Relational Goals   13

    Instrumental Goals   17

Chapter Summary and Book Overview   18

KEY TERMS   19   •   EXERCISES FOR FURTHER DISCUSSION   19

SUGGESTED READING   20   •   REFERENCE LIST   21

CHAPTER 2   PERCEPTION AND INTERPERSONAL PROCESSES   24

Knowledge Structures and Communication   26

Four Important Cognitive Processes   27

    Interpersonal Expectancies   28

    Attributions   32

    Person Perception   36

    Stereotypes   39

Expectancies, Attributions, Person Perception, and Stereotypes On-Line   42

Chapter Summary   44

KEY TERMS   44   •   EXERCISES FOR FURTHER DISCUSSION   44

SUGGESTED READING   45   •   REFERENCE LIST   46

CHAPTER 3   LISTENING   50

Listening Defined   51

Contexts of Listening   55

    Marriage   55

    Organizations   56

Medical Contexts   57
Education   59

Dialogue/Listening as Dyadic   60

Important Interpersonal Communication Processes Associated
with Listening   62

Social Support   62
Empathy   63
Competence   65

Listening Styles   66

Effective Listening   67

Chapter Summary   70

KEY TERMS   70   •   EXERCISES FOR FURTHER DISCUSSION   70

SUGGESTED READING   71   •   REFERENCE LIST   72

CHAPTER 4   FUNDAMENTALS OF VERBAL COMMUNICATION   76

Verbal Communication Codes   77

Semantic Code   77
Syntactic Code   78
Pragmatic Code   80

Verbal Communication and Goals   80

Grice's Principle of Cooperation   81
Illocutionary Acts and Pair Parts   82
Staying on Topic and Changing Topics   83
Confirming and Disconfirming Messages   85

Culture and Verbal Communication   87

Individualism-Collectivism   87
Communication Accommodation Theory   88

Individual Factors and Verbal Communication   92

Message Design Logics   92
Self-Construals   94
Life-Span Issues   95

Chapter Summary   96

KEY TERMS   97   •   EXERCISES FOR FURTHER DISCUSSION   98

SUGGESTED READING   98   •   REFERENCE LIST   99

CHAPTER 5   FUNDAMENTALS OF NONVERBAL COMMUNICATION   102

What Is Nonverbal Communication?   104

Facial Expressions and Gaze   104
Kinesics   105
Haptics   105

Vocalics   107
Proxemics   107
Physical Appearance   108
Chronemics   108
The Environment   109
Misconceptions about Nonverbal Communication:
Intentionality and Culture   109
Functions of Nonverbal Behavior   113
Expressing Emotion   114
Expressing Affection   116
Impression Formation/Identity Management   117
Deception   118
Conversation Management   121
Relational Messages   122
Nonverbal Ability   126
Chapter Summary   128
KEY TERMS   128   •   EXERCISES FOR FURTHER DISCUSSION   129
SUGGESTED READING   129   •   REFERENCE LIST   130

PART II   PURSUING SELF-PRESENTATION GOALS   135

CHAPTER 6   PRESENTING THE SELF   136
What Is Self-Presentation?   137
The Nature of Self-Presentation   138
The Nature of Interpersonal Self-Presentation   141
Monitoring Self-Presentation   147
Self-Identity and Self-Presentation   148
Indicators of Attainment   150
Direct Strategies of Self-Presentation   151
Ingratiation   151
Intimidation   158
Self-Promotion   158
Exemplification   161
Supplication   162
Indirect Strategies of Self-Presentation   163
Roles, Gender, Personality, and Culture   166
Chapter Summary   170
KEY TERMS   170   •   EXERCISES FOR FURTHER DISCUSSION   171
SUGGESTED READING   172   •   REFERENCE LIST   173

CHAPTER 7   DISCLOSING THE SELF   178

The Nature of Self-Disclosure   179
   Types of Self-Disclosure   179
   Social Penetration Theory   180

Factors Affecting Self-Disclosure Choices   183
   The Norm of Reciprocity   183
   Reasons for Not Disclosing   185
   Self-Disclosure and Privacy   186

Factors Affecting the Manner of Self-Disclosure   190
   Sex Differences   190
   Nature of the Relationship   191
   Cultural Factors Affecting Self-Disclosure   192

Factors Affecting the Perception of Self-Disclosure   193
   Amount of Disclosure   193
   Reciprocity   194
   Valence   196
   Honesty   196
   Timing   197

Chapter Summary   198
KEY TERMS   198   •   EXERCISES FOR FURTHER DISCUSSION   198
SUGGESTED READING   199   •   REFERENCE LIST   200

CHAPTER 8   DEFENDING THE SELF   204

What Are Accounts?   207
   Types of Accounts   208
   An Expanded Typology of Accounts   210
   The Functions Served by Accounts   213
   Goals Achieved through the Communication of Accounts   214
   Facework and Politeness Theory   214

Culture and the Communication of Accounts   223

Attribution Theory and the Communication
   of Accounts   225
   Credibility of Excuses   227
   Control of Emotions   228

The Triangle Model of Responsibility   230

Impression Management   232
   Public Images   234

A Note on Forgiveness   239

Chapter Summary   239

KEY TERMS   240   •   EXERCISES FOR FURTHER DISCUSSION   240
SUGGESTED READING   242   •   REFERENCE LIST   243

PART III   PURSUING RELATIONAL GOALS   247

CHAPTER 9   ESCALATING RELATIONSHIPS   248

Features of Relational Escalation   249
  Advantages of Escalating Relationships   250
  Disadvantages of Escalating Relationships   251
Interpersonal Attraction: The Catalyst of Escalation   252
  Anthropological Class: Physical Beauty   253
  Reinforcement Class: Supportiveness   253
  Cognitive Class: Attitude Similarity   254
  Structural Class: Communication Behaviors   255
Increasing Intimacy during Interaction   256
  Behaviors That Communicate Liking and Intimacy   256
  Courtship and Quasi-Courtship Behaviors   257
  Cognitive Valence Theory   259
Relational Development Processes   263
  Social Penetration Revisited   263
  Developing Relationships On-Line   264
  Stages of Relational Escalation   265
  Research on Relational Escalation   267
  Turning Points   268
Chapter Summary   272
KEY TERMS   273   •   EXERCISES FOR FURTHER DISCUSSION   274
SUGGESTED READING   274   •   REFERENCE LIST   275

CHAPTER 10   MAINTAINING RELATIONSHIPS   280

Relational Maintenance and Equity   282
Relational Maintenance Strategies   285
  Positivity   286
  Openness   287
  Assurances   288
  Social Networks   290
  Sharing Tasks   290
Relational Dialectics   291
  Dialectical Tensions   292
  Responding to Dialectical Tensions   292

Maintaining Platonic Friendships   293

Maintaining Different Types of Romantic Relationships   298

Love Styles and Love Ways   298

Fitzpatrick's Marital Typology   302

Differences in Communication among Marital Types   302

Chapter Summary   305

KEY TERMS   305   •   EXERCISES FOR FURTHER DISCUSSION   306

SUGGESTED READING   307   •   REFERENCE LIST   308

CHAPTER 11   DE-ESCALATING RELATIONSHIPS   314

Why Break Up?   316

Confronting Relational Unhappiness: The Four Phases
of Disengagement   319

The Importance of Equity, Commitment, and Rewards   325

Reasons for Disengagement and Termination   327

Attribution Theory   331

The Valence and Frequency of Problems   332

The Dark Side of Relationships: Power, Control,
and Infidelity   333

The Cascade Model of Dissolution   336

Methods Used in Relational Disengagement   337

Tactics Used in Relational Disengagement   337

Facework and Politeness Theory   342

The Consequences of Relational Disengagement   345

Emotional Consequences   347

Staying Friends   348

Grave Dressing and Adjustment   348

Chapter Summary   353

KEY TERMS   354   •   EXERCISES FOR FURTHER DISCUSSION   354

SUGGESTED READING   356   •   REFERENCE LIST   356

PART IV   PURSUING INSTRUMENTAL GOALS   361

CHAPTER 12   PRINCIPLES OF INFLUENCE   362

Compliance and Compliance-Gaining Messages   364

Why People Agree to Do Things   364

Anchors and Contrast Effects   365

Reciprocity   366

Reciprocal Concessions or Guilt?   368

Commitment   369

Liking   371
Social Proof or Social Validation   372
Authority   373
Scarcity   374

What Are Compliance-Gaining Messages?   376
Marwell and Schmitt's Typology   376
Falbo's Power Tactics   380
Bisanz and Rule's Persuasion Schema   383

When People Use Tactics   387
Social Power   388
Politeness Theory and Image Concerns   390
Attribution Theory Revisited   393

Compliance-Resisting Tactics   394

Culture and Compliance   396

Chapter Summary   398
KEY TERMS   399   •   EXERCISES FOR FURTHER DISCUSSION   399
SUGGESTED READING   401   •   REFERENCE LIST   402

CHAPTER 13 MANAGING INTERPERSONAL CONFLICT   408

Why Study Conflict?   410

Defining Conflict   411

Conflict Styles   412

Choices in Managing Conflict   414
Confront or Avoid?   414
Cooperate or Compete?   415

Conflict Strategies and Patterns   417
Conflict Strategies   417
Conflict Patterns   417

Managing Relational Problems   424

Consequences of Conflict Behaviors   427
Attributions   427
Relational Consequences   429

Chapter Summary   430
KEY TERMS   431   •   EXERCISES FOR FURTHER DISCUSSION   431
SUGGESTED READING   432   •   REFERENCE LIST   433

CHAPTER 14 INTERPERSONAL GOALS OVER TIME   438

Interpersonal Relationships in Families and Beyond   440
Attachment Theory   440
Intergenerational Solidarity Theory   445

A Comment on Families   448
Turning Points in Family Relationships   448
Consequences of Divorce   451
Turning Points after Divorce   453
Communication Processes in Becoming a Family   455
Socioemotional Selectivity Theory   458

Self-Presentation in Later Years   460

Self-Presentation and Negotiated Identities in Intergenerational
    Conversations   460

Intergenerational Friendships   464

Friends and Mentors   464

Chapter Summary   469

KEY TERMS   469   •   EXERCISES FOR FURTHER DISCUSSION   470

SUGGESTED READING   471   •   REFERENCE LIST   471

PART V   PERSONALITY AND INTERPERSONAL COMPETENCE   479

CHAPTER 15   INDIVIDUAL DIFFERENCES AND INTERPERSONAL
                COMMUNICATION   480

The Importance of Knowing about Individual
    Differences   482

Factors Affecting Individual Differences   483

Machiavellian Behavior   483
Self-Monitoring Behavior   486
Locus of Control   488
Cognitive Complexity   491
Argumentativeness   496
Communication Apprehension   499
Loneliness   500

Chapter Summary   508

KEY TERMS   508   •   EXERCISES FOR FURTHER DISCUSSION   508

SUGGESTED READING   510   •   REFERENCE LIST   511

CHAPTER 16   IMPLICATIONS FOR INTERPERSONAL COMMUNICATION
                COMPETENCE   516

A Component Model of Competence   518

Motivation   518
Knowledge   519
Skill   519

Criteria for Assessing Competence   520
    Adaptability   520
    Conversational Involvement   521
    Conversational Management   521
    Empathy   521
    Effectiveness   522
    Appropriateness   523
Assessing Your Own Interpersonal Communication
    Competence   523
Implications for Competence: A Review   525
    Fundamentals of Communication Competence   527
    Competence in Self-Presentation   528
    Competence in Relational Development   528
    Competence in Instrumental Objectives   531
    Personality and Competence   532
Final Comments   532
    KEY TERMS   533   •   EXERCISES FOR FURTHER DISCUSSION   533
    SUGGESTED READING   534   •   REFERENCE LIST   534

NAME INDEX   537
SUBJECT INDEX   545

FUNDAMENTALS OF INTERPERSONAL COMMUNICATION

Part I of this book presents our approach for understanding interpersonal communication and discusses essential concepts. In Chapter 1 we discuss the goals-based approach, what constitutes interpersonal goals, and our definition of interpersonal communication. In Chapter 2 we emphasize how people's perceptions affect their understanding of interpersonal communication. We discuss the importance of the listening process in Chapter 3. Chapters 4 and 5 elaborate on the nature of verbal and nonverbal communication, respectively. In Chapter 4 we discuss the features of language, stressing how people must cooperate in order to carry on a conversation. In Chapter 5 we stress the functions of nonverbal messages, showing how nonverbal behaviors help express emotions, form impressions of ourselves, and develop relationships.

C H A P T E R   1

THE IMPORTANCE

OF INTERPERSONAL

COMMUNICATION

IN PURSUING

PERSONAL GOALS

DEFINING INTERPERSONAL
COMMUNICATION

THE NATURE OF GOALS

TYPES OF INTERPERSONAL GOALS
Self-Presentation Goals
Relational Goals
Instrumental Goals

CHAPTER SUMMARY AND
BOOK OVERVIEW

Alex wanted to add a particular class. If he could add it, he would be able to graduate before summer; if he couldn't, he would have to take a different early morning class, reshuffle his tight schedule, and possibly take a summer school course. He had already e-mailed the professor to introduce himself and indicate his interest in the course. But the professor was noncommittal and advised Alex to attend the first session. So here he was, and all the seats were taken. Students were actually standing in the back of the room, so clearly not everyone would get in. When the professor asked for a show of those who still wanted to be considered for the class, Alex raised his hand. Alex decided that he would act positive and polite — but he would definitely pitch his case.

Years from now you will recall your college experience. You will have engaged in many conversations, attended thousands of classes, taken hundreds of tests, and purchased a great number of books. Naturally you will recall best those memories and experiences that are relevant and important to you. That being the case, the ideas in this course on interpersonal communication should leave a lasting impression on you. Why? Because few things are as important as achieving personal goals through interpersonal communication.

This text is about how we use interpersonal communication to pursue our personal goals. Pursuing goals is perhaps so common that we don't stop to reflect on how often we do it. For example, you want someone to deliver a message for you; you need help when you move into a new apartment; you want to initiate or to terminate a relationship; you want to be seen as honest, sincere, and capable. All of these concerns are personal goals that people pursue daily. Note that all of these goals are interpersonal — people attempt to achieve a significant number of their personal goals in concert with other people. It follows, then, that interpersonal communication is a critical part of achieving our goals. The way we communicate with other people directly affects whether or not we achieve our desires.

When we study interpersonal communication, it is important to study the driving component of communication, our personal goals, as well. First, doing so can help us understand social action in general because people's behaviors are goal-driven (Berger, 1997). Consider the story at the introduction of this chapter. We can appreciate the delicate balancing act that Alex has to perform — he cannot appear pushy, yet he must make a clear case in a situation that gives him little opportunity to do so. Second, we best understand communication in the context of communicators' goals. As Sanders (1991) observes, "A concern with goals is unavoidable in studies of human

3

communication. The proposition that what actors say and do in any instance is contingent on their goals is true by definition, insofar as we regard human communication as a form of social action" (p. 186). Moreover, being sensitive to the other person's goals increases that person's perceptions that we are appropriate and effective communicators (Lakey & Canary, 2001). In this light, it would be smart to examine the types of goals that people pursue. Finally, we emphasize goals because we are most interested in goal-related behaviors. Goals indicate what we generally seek to accomplish in our daily lives; events related to our goals are more important to us than events that are unrelated to our goals (Lavallee & Campbell, 1995).

In this chapter, we look first at the concept of interpersonal communication, and within that context we consider six assumptions that underlie our conceptualization of interpersonal communication processes. We follow that material with an in-depth look at the nature of goals in general and then, more specifically, at types of interpersonal goals that focus our communication.

DEFINING INTERPERSONAL COMMUNICATION

Interpersonal communication is "the exchange of symbols used, at least in part, to achieve interpersonal goals." This definition is based on six assumptions.

ASSUMPTION 1: INTERPERSONAL COMMUNICATION REQUIRES AN EXCHANGE BETWEEN PEOPLE. We can think of interpersonal communication as an exchange, and we can look at the exchange in three ways: act, interact, and transact. At a minimum, one person sends a message to a second person. In very basic terms, that is an **act,** or one behavior. This act is then followed by a second act, and so on. In short, we can examine the communication process as a series of acts that one person performs in context with another person. Importantly, we can examine the effects of particular message behaviors. For example, Dainton (2000) examined how the use of relational maintenance strategies can affect how relationships are sustained.

A second view of the communication exchange focuses on the **interact** as the unit of analysis. An interact involves two behaviors: one person's act coupled with the second person's act. For example, the verbal acts "What do you want to do?" and "I don't care, whatever you want to do" combine to form the interact. In this case, both persons want the other to take control of the situation, so they mirror the other's submissive behavior (Millar & Rogers, 1976, 1987). Using the interact, scholars have been able to identify patterns of interaction, such as the demand-withdrawal pattern (that is, where one person demands change and the partner tries to avoid the issue; Caughlin & Vangelisti, 1999).

A third way to examine the communication exchange is to think of it as the simultaneous sending and receiving of messages. This unit of message analysis is referred to as a **transact.** At a minimum, transactional analysis requires a focus on both actors, regardless of whose turn it is. A transact also refers to both actors' simultaneous experience of the communication event. For example, Gottman (1982) showed how partners' physiological reactions were strongly associated with each other when they communicate.

Each unit of analysis brings a different insight to the communication process, and these insights help scholars and students translate different kinds of research into meaningful, real-life portrayals of interpersonal communication processes.

ASSUMPTION 2: INTERPERSONAL COMMUNICATION OCCURS BETWEEN PEOPLE WHO ARE THEMSELVES DEVELOPING. Communication scholars assume that communication occurs between individuals who both are changing (Brockriede, 1978). This assumption entails three important elements. First, it means that people change over the life cycle, and their interpersonal communication reflects those changes (Nussbaum, Pecchioni, Robinson, & Thompson, 2000). Second, it suggests that people are searching for meaning and develop strategies for adapting to their social world. Third, it implies that the communication exchanges we have now, as fleeting as they are, can never be replicated exactly. When we try to repeat certain memorable communication episodes (such as a heart-to-heart talk or a particular discussion at a party), they are just not the same and may be quite disappointing.

The changing nature of people and communication is not always evident to us, however. Indeed, we often communicate *in order to* provide stability and structure to our lives. Storytelling is one such means through which we give a framework to the things that we have done. Most people have stories about important events in their lives and about memorable experiences that typify a relationship such as a family (Koenig, 2002; Koenig & Manusov, in press), and our putting those memories into words through a story may seem to make them more stable. Ironically, though, our telling of stories actually transforms the experiences, because we choose what parts of the event get told to others (Bochner, 1994). According to Rosenwald, "life experience is larger and more ambiguous than any of its [stories] . . . not only does the past live in the present, but it also appears different at every new turn we take" (1992, p. 275).

ASSUMPTION 3: INTERPERSONAL COMMUNICATION INVOLVES THE USE OF SYMBOLS. Interpersonal communication occurs because people have created socially understood symbols for communicating their ideas. **Symbols** include verbal and nonverbal representations of ideas, emotions, objects, or events. Burgoon (1985) identified symbols as "behaviors that are typically sent with intent, used with regularity among members of a social community, and have consensually recognizable interpretations" (p. 348). Meaning is given to symbols by the people who use them.

Certainly, other behaviors occur in interpersonal interactions that are not symbolic but may be important. Information may be conveyed through behaviors that have a direct relationship with their meaning, and the behaviors reflecting this type of information have been referred to as **symptoms** (Cronkhite, 1986). For example, a growling stomach is symptomatic of hunger. The meaning of symptoms does not have to be agreed on by the people who use it; rather, the source of the meaning has a direct connection to the behavior that reflects it.

Although symptoms are important sources of meaning, symbols are typically more meaningful in interpersonal interaction. Because they are created between the people who use them and by their larger social or cultural groups, symbols are more likely to reflect what is important to those groups, the particular ways that they frame the world, and the choices they make about how they want to interact with one another. Unlike the information derived from symptoms, the meaning of symbols "is not simply a magical assignment of content to concept but represents a *choice* of something and a simultaneous rejection of something else" (Duck, 1994, p. 55). Symbols reflect the messages people choose as part of communication, whether reflected in a facial expression or in words.

ASSUMPTION 4: INTERPERSONAL COMMUNICATION IS STRATEGIC. We use the term **strategic** in a broad sense to refer to all goal-relevant communication behavior (Berger, 1997). As Kellermann (1992) observed, "Communication is selected, structured, and patterned; it is not random, unrestrained, and lawless; it is voluntary, controllable, directional, chosen, and purposeful" (p. 292).

Some people will not admit to being strategic. They do not think that they manipulate others or control others through communication. Granted, in some instances, people may behave without any clear goal in mind (Langer 1989), such as in routine interactions or when the person's goals are distal or unclear. At other times, our strategic interaction doesn't appear to us to be very strategic, because our communication has largely become routine (Berger, 1997). For example, we may decide in advance that we won't bargain to lower the price of a stereo, only that we'll simply ask the salesperson once to reduce the price. Such behavior is still strategic to the extent that a message was constructed to achieve a goal. Kellermann (1992) has further argued that strategic behavior is often used implicitly; that is, our strategies are not always processed consciously.

Much of our behavior is quite strategic. Many people have plans for arranging a particular schedule of courses, getting into law school, finding a job, getting into a fraternity or sorority, being introduced to a particular potential mate, getting to the church on time, and so forth. In addition, most conversations are strategic. That is, people seek assistance from friends, attempt to clarify ideas, want others to like them and share activities with them, and the like. In other words, we all have goals that we pursue, and we use communication strategies to help us achieve those goals.

ASSUMPTION 5: COMMUNICATORS MUST BE COMPETENT IN USING INTERPERSONAL COMMUNICATION IN ORDER TO ACHIEVE THEIR GOALS. Much research has focused on what it means to be a competent communicator (e.g., Parks, 1985; Spitzberg & Hecht, 1984; Wiemann & Backlund, 1980). Specifically, scholars have researched the behavioral properties of **communication competence,** including such factors as empathy, interaction management, and involvement (Spitzberg & Cupach, 1989), and most would agree that it involves two fundamental properties: effectiveness (achieving our goals in the conversation) and appropriateness (maintaining the situational rules or expectations) (Spitzberg & Cupach, 1984).

To be optimally competent, a person typically must be both appropriate and effective. This means that optimal competence involves obtaining goals while upholding the expectations of your partner in a particular situation. Deceiving, controlling, coercing, degrading, and other forms of manipulating one's partner clearly do not uphold the partner's desired goals and expectations. Anyone who has experienced these behaviors knows they are not appropriate, and their use reflects a lack of understanding of the interdependent and transactional nature of communication.

In most situations, competent communicators meet the dual requirements of appropriateness and effectiveness when pursuing their goals. However, there are rare situations in which people are primarily concerned about one goal at the expense of other important goals or the appropriateness of their strategies. The deceptive or coercive manipulation of others for personal gain raises an ethical question: Should

We often plan how to make a favorable impression on others. Sometimes, however, our plans do not work out as expected.

we study how communication functions to achieve goals strategically without any principled guidance? We think not.

ASSUMPTION 6: PEOPLE SHOULD CONSIDER HOW THEIR COMMUNICA-TION AFFECTS OTHERS.   Ethical concerns are pivotal to any exploration of how communication connects people to their personal goals. More precisely, ethics are part and parcel of interpersonal communication. *Ethics* concerns the use of principles to guide action. Such principles are often based on moral codes that one obtains in the home, church, school, or other institutions. In terms of interpersonal communication, ethics involves more than not doing another person harm and performing mutual aid (Englehardt, 2001). That is, people should avoid hurting others and assist them when needed. According to Englehardt (2001), people are *obligated* to treat each other with good intentions based on a number of philosophical reasons. More precisely, individual codes, rights, utilitarian considerations, virtues, and relational concerns represent alternative reasons that require that people consider how their behaviors affect others.

From an ethical viewpoint, competent interaction requires an agreement that each party is equally deserving of respect. As Cupach and Canary (1997) state, "Fostering mutual respect and meeting minimal expectations for appropriate behavior promotes collaboration that is necessary to sustain civilized interaction" (p. 235). In other words, civility in interpersonal communication depends on the presumption of each person's value and worth. To take advantage of an interaction derails the very process of interpersonal communication. And, as mentioned, people who are sensitive to the goals and desires of others in interaction are more likely to obtain what they want (Lakey & Canary, 2001).

Most of us have either seen or had some experience with incompetent communication, and we realize it is neither appropriate nor effective. Much of the controlling, abusive dialogue that one hears on talk shows represents a lack of mutual respect. Ridicules, put-downs, and sarcastic references to other people's values clearly illustrate what not to do. Television shows involving social disputes, situation comedies where actors brutally insult one another, and any number of movies show inappropriate behaviors designed to shock or amuse. They are entertainment, not reality. We might be amused by harsh statements and put-downs *because* they are inappropriate and violate our expectations. Some of us might wish we could say and do some of these things in real life, but doing so would actually result in the loss of friendships, dismissal from employment, lawsuits for creating a hostile work environment, and more. According to Parks (1994), "We can agree that it is a mark of incompetence when . . . self-esteem is damaged, and when physical health is threatened. We can also agree that socially inappropriate and violent behavior is usually undesirable" (p. 589).

In sum, exchange, change, symbols, strategy, competence, and ethics are features of every goal-directed interpersonal interaction. Within each interaction, each individual has many choices that are guided by ethical considerations — to balance the individual's own needs and desires, on the one hand, and to uphold the expectations of one's partner in the interaction for fair and considerate treatment, on the other. We turn now to the driving force underlying interpersonal communication — goals.

THE NATURE OF GOALS

A goal is a state you want to achieve. As Cody, Canary, and Smith (1994) note, goals have both cognitive and emotional elements; they combine thoughts and feelings. An **interpersonal goal** is a goal you want that is linked to another person's thoughts, feelings, or actions. People who share interpersonal goals are interdependent (Kelley, 1979). Scholars have identified several important properties of goals (e.g., Pervin, 1989; Tracy, 1991). Seven general properties of goals are relevant to interpersonal communication.

1. *Goals Vary in Their Degree of Abstractness.* Relying on the research of Cantor and Mischel (1979; and also Cantor, Mischel, & Schwartz, 1982), we classify goals into three levels of abstraction: supraordinate, basic, and subordinate. **Supraordinate goals** are general and inclusive. "Be friendly," "be strong," and "be a winner" reflect supraordinate goals. **Basic goals** provide more specificity in terms of actors' motives and relationships. For example, the goal "to share an activity" identifies the motive for interacting (to go out and do something) as well as the role relationship with the other (friend or peer). Finally, **subordinate goals** are very specific and are quite distinct from other goals. For example, the goal "to get Kathy to go shopping on Friday night" is different from "to ask John to shoot baskets on Saturday afternoon," though both are specific instances of the basic goal of "to share an activity."

2. *Goals Differ in Clarity.* It appears obvious that the more specific the goal, the clearer it tends to become, and people are more motivated to achieve clear goals than ambiguous ones. Also, different goals sometimes have overlapping properties (Cody et al., 1994) and can lead to the same kinds of behavior (for example, wanting to appear competent and likable will help you obtain the job promotion you want and win the approval of co-workers). Clear goals indicate standards that help us realize when our goals have been reached (Bandura, 1989). For example, the goal "to do well in this class" is not as clear as "to get an A in this class." Knowing exactly what you want helps you achieve exactly what you want. As the saying goes, "You can't get what you want until you know what you want."

3. *Goals Vary in Their Degree of Challenge.* Some goals are more difficult to achieve than others. Some require a strong sense of determination and effort. According to Bandura (1989), people attempt to pursue challenging goals because they believe that they can succeed at reaching their goals — a property that Bandura calls *self-efficacy.* According to Bandura, a person with high self-efficacy persists in achieving challenging goals, even in the face of failures, and is more likely to achieve those goals. People who have little self-efficacy do not pursue challenging goals, nor do they achieve challenging goals. In other words, self-efficacy is crucial in determining the success you experience in achieving challenging goals.

4. *People Often Engage in Multiple Goals.* Dillard, Segrin, and Harden (1989) separate goals into primary and secondary types. **Primary goals** are the most important to the communicator; **secondary goals** are less important to the communicator, but they function to constrain the primary goals. For example, imagine that you are caught speeding in a school zone. Your primary goal may be to avoid getting a traffic ticket. So you quickly decide what you'll say when the police officer knocks on your car window. But because you also want to be seen as honest and responsible, you decide not to lie or argue. These secondary goals thus moderate your communication behavior that is motivated only by your primary goal. So instead of lying or arguing, you explain why you were speeding ("I was not paying attention to the changes in zones"), and you apologize for speeding (see also Chapter 8).

5. *Goals Vary in Terms of Immediacy.* Goals that occur in the immediate future are called **proximal goals;** those that must be realized in the distant future are called **distal goals.** In many instances, the more proximal the goal, the more salient it is. That is, you are more likely to focus on proximal than distal goals, although the distal goals may be more important to you. For example, you may have the goal "to marry next year." But despite this goal's importance to you, you also want to have a good time now. So instead of pursuing a particular relationship, you prefer to date two or three people. In short, proximal goals may seem more urgent and may motivate us more than distal goals.

6. *People's Goals Are Affected by the Communication Event Itself.* According to Hocker and Wilmot (1991), goals can be modified or changed during interaction. Hocker and Wilmot call these **transactive goals** (pp. 55–58; see also Berger, 1986). The following example shows how Sandy's goal "to seek assistance from a peer" is transformed into the goal "to defend oneself."

Sandy:	Hey, Chris, what are you doing Tuesday afternoon?
Chris:	Why? What do you need?
Sandy:	Well, I really need a babysitter. I know it's short notice and all.
Chris:	Why is it that you only come around here when you need a favor or something?
Sandy:	What?
Chris:	Well, it seems that all I'm good for is babysitting.
Sandy:	*(defensively)* I can't believe this! Forget it. I thought you were a friend.

7. *Goals Prompt Plans for Action.* Planning consists of producing one or more mental models, detailing how you might achieve your goal through interaction (Berger, 1997; Dillard, 1990). Plans differ in complexity and completeness.

People typically use communication plans that have been stored in memory and can be activated with ease (Berger, 1997). According to Berger, people use more complex plans when their goals are important or are blocked. For example, imagine that you ask your roommate to pay for several long-distance telephone calls you know you did not make. You would probably rely on a strategy that you have used in the past, such as a simple request ("Can you pay me this week for these calls?"). But if your roommate refuses, you would need to create a more complex strategic plan ("I will call this one number and ask who lives there, then I can confront my roommate with the fact that this call is his").

Plans that incorporate a number of elements, contingencies, and sequences are more complex than plans involving only a single message tactic. You may generate a complex plan by considering the many ways in which you can change an undesirable behavior, how the other person may resist changing, and how the resistance can be overcome. Complex plans, however, are not always the best ones. As researchers have found, overly complex plans may actually lead to communication problems (such as speech dysfluencies; see Berger, 1997; Greene & Ravizza, 1995).

In addition, plans vary in the degree to which they are complete. Communicators may have a general idea about talking with their friends and "working things out" or "compromising" or "resolving our differences." But such plans are incomplete until communicators flesh out in more detail which topics need to be addressed, how they will actually work out details, what exactly they would be willing to compromise, and how they plan to search for common interests in order to resolve differences.

This book focuses on the communication behaviors that people use to pursue their interpersonal goals. Many of these interaction behaviors will sound familiar, probably because you or others you know have used them. Yet many of the ideas presented in this book will be new to you. As you will see, interpersonal communication behaviors vary according to the types of goals we routinely seek.

TYPES OF INTERPERSONAL GOALS

Researchers have uncovered three general types of goals that people seek through interpersonal communication (Clark & Delia, 1979; Dillard, 1990; Dillard et al., 1989; Hecht, 1984; O'Keefe & McCornack, 1987; Tracy, Craig, Smith, & Spisak, 1984; Wilson, 1990). First, in the **self-presentation goal** (also called *identity management*), we communicate an image of who we are and how we want to be perceived. Second, in the **relational goal,** we develop relationships and then maintain or neglect those relationships. Third, in the **instrumental goal,** we try to get others to do us a favor or offer some kind of resource. These three types of goals form the organizational core of this text. We examine them in brief here and return to each of them in Parts II, III, and IV, respectively, for an in-depth look at how people use interpersonal communication to achieve their important goals.

Self-Presentation Goals

We use interpersonal communication to present an image of who we are, to create an impression of ourselves for other people to believe (Tedeschi & Norman, 1985).

People's self-presentation goals may differ a great deal. For example, some people may wish to be perceived as competent, while others may prefer to be seen as more friendly and likable.

Joel Gordon

Goffman (1971) has also argued that we are strategic in the presentation of who we are. That is, we perform what he calls *facework* to make others see us in the way in which we want them to see us. Our public image is something we work on every day.

By and large, we want to appear competent. That is, we want to seem intelligent, capable, expert, and effective. However, people may differ a great deal in their preferred public image. For instance, when asking questions, we want to present an image of self as intelligent and knowledgeable (Tracy & Naughton, 1994). Whereas some want to be perceived as competent, others prefer a public image as being friendly and likable. These two self-presentation styles, competence and friendliness, involve using different communication tactics. Competent people often try to show others that they know what is best and that they are better trained and more capable. They talk more about themselves and their achievements, and they engage in behaviors that draw attention to themselves. Friendly communicators do not want to show others up, and they try to get along without "rocking the boat." These communicators smile and nod more often, frequently express agreement with others, and find more sources of similarity with others (see Chapter 6).

Other communicators may want to appear weak and indecisive. By appearing helpless, such people get their friends to help them with their homework, car repairs, errands, and other tasks. And they might receive emotional support, sympathy, and attention. Still other communicators may want to appear assertive and strong (or even intimidating) or to appear to be more dedicated and worthy than others (e.g.,

Jones & Pittman, 1982). As we shall see in Chapters 6, 7, and 8, people use communication differently, depending on their desire to project a certain public image. For now, see Table 1.1 for some examples of self-presentation goals.

On the Internet, people often engage in *selective self-presentation*. O'Sullivan (2000) has argued that computer-mediated communication (CMC) helps people control how their own communication conveys their self-presentation, especially when one wants to define a relationship. When using e-mail, people know that others cannot see their physical and nonverbal responses, especially when they are not on-line at the same time (Walther & Burgoon, 1992). Using e-mail, communicators are better able to plan, self-censor, reflect, and edit their messages before sending them (Walther & Burgoon). In this manner, people communicating on e-mail can utilize messages to reflect a generally more likable image.

Relational Goals

Nothing brings us more joy or sadness than our personal relationships. We spend significant amounts of time, energy, and emotion in the pursuit of quality relationships. The feelings of love and sharing we experience as a daughter or a son, a friend, and a romantic partner are unobtainable anywhere but in these relationships. Yet we also experience pain due to our interpersonal involvements. Every relationship eventually ends. Some seem to end naturally; others seem to end prematurely. Certain

Table 1.1
SELF-PRESENTATION GOAL EXAMPLES

Goal	Example
To present oneself to a peer	You want to appear friendly and intelligent to someone in class.
To present oneself to a superior	You want your supervisor to believe that you are reliable and honest.
To prolong an obligation	You want to postpone a debt of $50 that you owe a friend.
To defend oneself	You want to defend yourself against someone who likes to talk about you behind your back.
To protect a right	You want to make sure your roommate gives you your telephone messages.

Source: Adapted from Canary, Cody, & Marston, 1987; Canary, Cunningham, & Cody, 1988; Cody, Canary, & Smith, 1994.

GOALS IN FILMS: THE CASE OF *L.A. STORY*

Self-presentation goals are pursued when communicators use tactics to offer a desired public image, usually to appear competent or friendly. But sometimes people want to appear weak or intimidating. One extreme type is the person who constantly adapts to others, projecting a different image to different audiences. An example of this is seen in the film *L.A. Story*. Throughout the film, Steve Martin, as a Los Angeles TV weatherman, conforms to what others are doing. He has a twist of lemon when everyone else has a twist of lemon, he consistently agrees with what others are saying, and he even gets an enema when his date gets an enema.

One scene illustrates how abruptly some communicators alter their public image. Martin's girlfriend (played by Marilu Henner) admits to having an affair:

Martin:	How long has this been going on?
Henner:	Three years.
Martin:	Three years!
Henner:	I'm sorry.
Martin:	This has been going on since the eighties?

Martin appears to be in a state of shock and disbelief. Looking weak and vulnerable and about to cry, he says, "I'm sorry — I just can't be here right now."

We see Martin walk sadly down the stairs to the street, at first with heavy footfalls. But as he leaves the woman behind, his posture changes, and he starts to dance. He ceases to appear sad; he dances in the street. He screams with happiness, "Yes, yes, L.A. I love you. I'm out of my relationship, I'm out of the agency, and I only had to look like a jerk for three years. Now if I can just get out of doing the weather."

These last lines also reveal the three different types of goals people pursue: self-presentation ("I only had to look like a jerk for three years"); relational de-escalation ("I'm out of my relationship"), and instrumental ("Now if I can just get out of doing the weather"). Martin, the "L.A. yuppie," had learned to adapt strategically to his various audiences, presenting a self that was appropriate or desirable for particular audiences and situations (for a fuller discussion of self-presentation, see Chapter 6).

Whereas Martin's character in *L.A. Story* achieves what he wants by constantly adapting to others, Robin Williams's in *The Dead Poets Society* tells his students not to conform to others. This character, Mr. Keating, advises his students: "Now we all have a great need for acceptance. But you must trust that your beliefs are unique, your own, although others may think of them as unpopular, even though the herd may go, 'That's baaaaad.'"

We can contrast the many ways in which self-presentation, relational, and instrumental goals are pursued by looking at ourselves or others or by taking examples from the media (newspapers and films). Think about films like *The Firm, Unforgiven, When Harry Met Sally, A Beautiful Mind*, and hundreds of others as stories that show how people want and set out to obtain their important personal goals.

Excerpts from *L.A. Story* by Steve Martin. Reprinted by permission of Steve Martin.

relationships stagnate and continue at a very basic level of social survival. Whether for joy or for sorrow, our interpersonal relationships are important to us. As several scholars have shown (e.g., Duck, 1994), communication defines our personal relationships.

Relationships are the products of our interpersonal communication, and how we communicate depends in turn on the nature and quality of our relationships (Miller, 1976; Montgomery, 1988). For example, it is possible that you and your partner discuss how you will spend time with each other in the future (whose in-laws to visit at

People have different goals in their various relationships. These goals involve escalating, maintaining, or de-escalating relationships.

Joel Gordon

Christmas, where to vacation next summer, where to apply to school or seek a job, and the like). Such statements about the future might increase the level of commitment between the two of you; they assure you that the relationship will continue for a length of time. In turn, increases in levels of commitment allow you to think about the future and discuss plans with your partner. In other words, interpersonal communication both reflects and affects the nature and quality of our relationships.

One useful way to look at relational goals is to break them into three types: escalating, maintaining, and de-escalating. Escalating a relationship involves learning more about one another and growing more intimate or more interdependent. Maintaining a relationship refers to activities and communication behaviors used to sustain various close relationships as we want them to be sustained. De-escalating a relationship deals with how friends and lovers drift away from each other (or how relationships suddenly "explode") and how communication with these former friends and intimates decreases or ceases entirely. We will return to these three types of relational goals in Chapters 9, 10, and 11; for now, see Table 1.2 for some examples of common relational goals.

Table 1.2
RELATIONAL GOAL EXAMPLES

Goal	Example
To share an activity	You want your friend to go with you to a party.
To initiate a relationship	You decide to ask a person in your class for a date.
To escalate a relationship	You want a more permanent commitment from your partner.
To maintain a relationship	You want to keep in touch with your friends from high school or from a previous job.
To de-escalate a relationship	You discover a friend of yours is not dependable, so you want to stop making plans to see that person.
To give advice to a peer	You want your sister to seek the advice of a counselor because she has been depressed lately.
To give advice to a parent	You want your parents to take a vacation and relax a little more.

Source: Adapted from Canary, Cody, & Marston, 1987; Canary, Cunningham, & Cody, 1988; Cody, Canary, & Smith, 1994.

Instrumental Goals

We also rely on interpersonal communication to achieve our instrumental goals. These goals refer to desires for self-advancement, and they usually involve some resource or favor; they also include everyday events, such as getting a ride to school, obtaining particular vacation time, or persuading someone to help you print something from the computer. In North America, instrumental goals may be the most salient during interaction, followed by self-presentation and relational goals (e.g., Cody et al., 1986; Dillard et al., 1989). However, in cultures where people are more sensitive to face than to instrumental goals (e.g., Southeast Asian countries), self-presentation goals are probably more salient. The point is that each of us has instrumental goals, and we rely on our interpersonal communication to achieve these goals, as we shall see in detail in Chapters 12 and 13. For now, see Table 1.3 for some examples of instrumental goals.

Communicators sometimes pursue one type of goal at the expense of other goals. For example, it may be more important for you to accept a job out of state than to keep dating a particular person. Alternatively, you might decide against taking the job in order to maintain your relationship at its current level of interdependence. In a majority of situations, however, we try to present ourselves favorably and seek satisfying relationships while we pursue our instrumental goals (you might accept the job and attempt to maintain a long-distance relationship).

Table 1.3
INSTRUMENTAL GOAL EXAMPLES

Goal	Example
To seek assistance from a peer	You want a friend to help you with a task.
To seek assistance from a parent	You want to borrow $50 from your parents so that you can pay some bills.
To gain permission from a parent	You want permission to borrow the family car for a special night out.
To elicit support from a peer	You want your brother's friend to advise your brother to seek counseling.
To change a habit	You want your roommate to stop smoking.
To change an opinion	You want your friend to vote for a particular candidate in an upcoming election.

Source: Adapted from Canary, Cody, & Marston, 1987; Canary, Cunningham, & Cody, 1988; Cody, Canary, & Smith, 1994.

STUDENT AS OBSERVER: INTERPERSONAL GOALS IN DAILY INTERACTIONS

In the past twenty-four hours, you have probably tried to achieve a number of self-presentation, relational, and instrumental goals. In no more than four pages, complete the following:

a. Think of as many instances as you can in which you tried to achieve each type of goal and provide an example for each.
b. Write down the communication you used to obtain these goals.
c. Were these strategies effective? Why or why not?
d. Were you aware of and did you show sensitivity to the other person's goals?

In sum, people use interpersonal communication to obtain three types of goals: self-presentation, relational, and instrumental. We present an image of who we are through our interpersonal communication. Most of the time we want to be seen as competent and likable, though people differ in preferences for how they are viewed publicly. Our interpersonal communication also affects and reflects the very nature of our relationships. We use communication to develop, maintain, and de-escalate our relationships with others. Finally, we use interpersonal communication to achieve our instrumental goals. While pursuing instrumental goals, we typically also attempt to keep our self-presentation and relational goals intact.

CHAPTER SUMMARY AND BOOK OVERVIEW

This book is concerned with how individuals use interpersonal communication to pursue different goals in their interactions with others. Two key features are presented in this introductory chapter. The first key feature, the six assumptions about interpersonal communication, includes discussion of the requirement of an exchange between people who are in a constant state of change, the strategic use of symbols, and competence. The second key feature is a discussion of goals and how goals differ in abstractness, degree of challenge, and other ways.

Using recent theory and research on goals provides a powerful tool for understanding human behavior generally and interpersonal communication specifically. People communicate to achieve multiple goals. Of course, during interpersonal interaction, two people are simultaneously communicating to achieve their goals. We can verify from the research as well as experience that people use self-presentation goals to present a desired image of who they are to others. In addition, people use relational goals to define or redefine their relationships with others. People also use instrumental goals to persuade others to do them a favor or provide some resource. These three goal types form the foundation for understanding much of what occurs during interaction between two people.

Part I of this book, which includes this chapter as well as Chapters 2–5, discusses the fundamental features of interpersonal communication: perception (Chapter 2), listening (Chapter 3), verbal messages (Chapter 4), and nonverbal messages (Chapter 5). Parts II through IV detail how people use interpersonal communication to achieve their important self-presentation goals (Chapters 6–8), relational goals (Chapters 9–11), and instrumental goals (Chapters 12–14). Part V shows how differences in personality are manifested in interpersonal communication (Chapter 15) and how people assess each other's competence as communicators (Chapter 16).

Throughout this book we hope to provide you with insights regarding the powerful ways in which communication operates in interpersonal settings, in particular, how communication relates to your valued goals.

KEY TERMS

▼

act, p. 4
basic goals, p. 9
communication competence, p. 6
distal goals, p. 10
instrumental goal, p. 11
interact, p. 4
interpersonal communication, p. 4
interpersonal goal, p. 9
primary goals, p. 10
proximal goals, p. 10

relational goal, p. 11
secondary goals, p. 10
self-presentation goal, p. 11
strategic [communication], p. 6
subordinate goals, p. 9
supraordinate goals, p. 9
symbols, p. 5
symptoms, p. 5
transact, p. 4
transactive goals, p. 10

EXERCISES FOR FURTHER DISCUSSION

▼

1. Consider the ethical principles that guide your own interpersonal behavior.
   a. Write down your ethical principles.
   b. Do these principles pertain to not doing harm to others and helping others?
   c. Are these principles based on a utilitarian base or some other base (e.g., individual rights)?
   d. Do other people you know share these principles?

2. Look again at Tables 1.1, 1.2, and 1.3.
   a. Think of several self-presentation goals that you could add to Table 1.1.
   b. Think of several relational goals that you could add to Table 1.2.
   c. Think of several instrumental goals that you could add to Table 1.3.
   d. Discuss the goals you have written down with other class members, and create a list of goals for your reference that includes as many different examples of each type of goal as possible.
3. Consider the types of thinking and behavior that a goals-based approach to interpersonal communication encourages.
   a. Does a goals-based approach stress self-conscious, rational aspects of behavior more than unconscious, irrational aspects of behavior?
   b. When you think about your own behavior, do your goals involve feelings as well as rational thoughts?
   c. What do you think the benefits of a goals-based approach to interpersonal communication would be? What would be the drawbacks?
4. Think of people you know well and consider whether or not they seem to be aware of their goals.
   a. Are most of the people you know aware of their goals? Or are most of the people you know unaware of their goals?
   b. Do you think that people you know who are goal-directed are more effective communicators than those who do not have a clear sense of their own goals?

SUGGESTED READING

▼

Berger, C. R. (1997). *Planning strategic interaction: Attaining goals through communicative action*. Mahwah, NJ: Erlbaum. Berger presents his most recent theory on interpersonal communication, linking goals to planning and strategic communication. Studies that support his theory are reported in detail.

Cody, M. J., Canary, D. J., & Smith, S. W. (1994). Compliance-gaining goals: An inductive analysis of actor's goal types, strategies, and successes. In J. Wiemann & J. Daly (Eds.), *Communicating strategically*. Hillsdale, NJ: Erlbaum. This chapter shows how we derive several of the goals presented in this book. Although this chapter focuses on interpersonal influence, virtually all of the principles can be extended to cover other types of interpersonal communication.

Dillard, J. P. (1990). Primary and secondary goals in interpersonal influence. In M. J. Cody & M. L. McLaughlin (Eds.), *Psychology of tactical communication*. Clevedon, England: Multilingual Matters. Dillard presents a model of how goals lead to interpersonal communication. In addition, Dillard shows the relationship between primary and secondary goals.

Pervin, L. A. (Ed.). (1989). *Goal concepts in personality and social psychology*. Hillsdale, NJ: Erlbaum. This anthology offers some of the best thinking on the topic by social psychologists. Pervin's introductory chapter offers an excellent overview of the study of goals in social psychology.

Tracy, K. (Ed.). (1991). *Understanding face-to-face interaction: Issues linking goals and discourse.* Hillsdale, NJ: Erlbaum. Tracy provides a forum for scholars in communication to discuss how goals are related to communication behaviors. Several different approaches are offered. Virtually all, however, focus on microscopic levels of discourse.

REFERENCE LIST

▼

Bandura, A. (1989). Self-regulation of motivation and action through internal standards and goal systems. In L. A. Pervin (Ed.), *Goal concepts in personality and social psychology* (pp. 19–85). Hillsdale, NJ: Erlbaum.

Berger, C. R. (1986). Planning, affect, and social action generation. In H. Sypher & E. T. Higgins (Eds.), *Communication, social cognition, and affect* (pp. 76–87). Hillsdale, NJ: Erlbaum.

Berger, C. R. (1997). *Planning strategic interaction: Attaining goals through communicative action.* Mahwah, NJ: Erlbaum.

Bochner, A. P. (1994). Perspectives on inquiry II: Theories and stories. In M. L. Knapp & G. R. Miller (Eds.), *Handbook of interpersonal communication* (pp. 21–41). Thousand Oaks, CA: Sage.

Brockriede, W. (1978). The research process. *Western Journal of Speech Communication, 42,* 3–11.

Burgoon, J. K. (1985). Nonverbal signals. In M. L. Knapp & G. R. Miller (Eds.), *Handbook of interpersonal communication* (pp. 344–390). Beverly Hills, CA: Sage.

Cantor, N., & Mischel, W. (1979). Prototypes in person perception. In L. Berkowitz (Ed.), *Advances in experimental social psychology* (Vol. 12, pp. 4–52). Orlando, FL: Academic.

Cantor, N., Mischel, W., & Schwartz, J. (1982). A prototype analysis of psychological situations. *Cognitive Psychology, 14,* 45–77.

Caughlin, J. P., & Vangelisti, A. L. (1999). Desire for change in one's partner as a predictor of the demand/withdraw pattern of marital communication. *Communication Monographs, 66,* 66–89.

Clark, R. A., & Delia, J. (1979). Topoi and rhetorical competence. *Quarterly Journal of Speech, 65,* 187–206.

Cody, M. J., Canary, D. J., & Smith, S. W. (1994). Compliance-gaining goals: An inductive analysis of actor's goal types, strategies, and successes. In J. Wiemann & J. Daly (Eds.), *Communicating strategically* (pp. 33–90). Hillsdale, NJ: Erlbaum.

Cody, M. J., Greene, J. O., Marston, P. J., Baaske, E., O'Hair, H. D., & Schneider, M. J. (1986). Situation perception and the selection of message strategies. In M. L. McLaughlin (Ed.), *Communication yearbook 8* (pp. 390–420). Newbury Park, CA: Sage.

Cronkhite, G. (1986). On the focus, scope, and coherence of the study of human symbolic activity. *Quarterly Journal of Speech, 72,* 231–246.

Cupach, W. R., & Canary, D. J. (1997). *Competence in interpersonal conflict.* New York: McGraw-Hill.

Dainton, M. (2000). Maintenance behaviors, expectations for maintenance, and satisfaction: Linking comparison levels to relational maintenance strategies. *Journal of Social and Personal Relationships, 17,* 827–842.

Dillard, J. P. (1990). Primary and secondary goals in interpersonal influence. In M. J. Cody & M. L. McLaughlin (Eds.), *Psychology of tactical communication* (pp. 70–90). Clevendon, England: Multilingual Matters.

Dillard, J. P., Segrin, C., & Harden, J. M. (1989). Primary and secondary goals in the production of interpersonal influence messages. *Communication Monographs, 56,* 19–38.

Duck, S. (1994). *Meaningful relationships: talking, sense, and relating.* Thousand Oaks, CA: Sage.

Englehardt, E. E. (2001). Introduction to ethics in interpersonal communication. In E. E. Englehardt (Ed.), *Ethical issues in interpersonal communication: Friends, intimates, sexuality, marriage, and family.* Orlando, FL: Harcourt College.

Goffman, E. (1971). *Relations in public: Microstudies of the public order.* New York: Harper & Row.

Gottman, J. M. (1982). Emotional responsiveness in marital conversations. *Journal of Communication, 32,* 108–120.

Greene, J. O., & Ravizza, S. M. (1995). Complexity effects on temporal characteristics of speech. *Human Communication Research, 21,* 390–421.

Hecht, M. L. (1984). Persuasive efficacy: A study of the relationship among type and degree of change, message strategies, and satisfying communication. *Western Journal of Speech Communication, 48,* 373–389.

Hocker, J. L., & Wilmot, W. W. (1991). *Interpersonal conflict* (3rd ed.). Dubuque, IA: Brown.

Jones, E. E., & Pittman, T. S. (1982). Toward a general theory of strategic self-presentation. In J. Suls (Ed.), *Psychological perspectives on the self* (pp. 231–263). Hillsdale, NJ: Erlbaum.

Kellermann, K. (1992). Communication: Inherently strategic and primarily automatic. *Communication Monographs, 59,* 288–300.

Kelley, H. H. (1979). *Personal relationships: A theory of interdependence.* New York: Wiley.

Koenig, J. L. (2002). *Family ties: Identity, process, and relational qualities in joint family storytelling.* Unpublished dissertation, University of Washington.

Koenig, J. L., & Manusov, V. (in press). What's in a story? The relationship between narrative completeness and tellers' adjustment to relational dissolution. *Journal of Social and Personal Relationships.*

Lakey, S. G., & Canary, D. J. (2001, May). *Actor goal achievement and sensitivity to the partner as critical factors in understanding interpersonal competence and conflict strategies.* Paper presented at the International Communication Association conference, Washington, DC.

Langer, E. J. (1989). *Mindfulness.* Boston: Addison-Wesley.

Lavallee, L. F., & Campbell, J. D. (1995). Impact of personal goals on self-regulation processes elicited by daily negative events. *Journal of Personality and Social Psychology, 69,* 341–352.

Millar, F. E., & Rogers, L. E. (1976). A relational approach to interpersonal communication. In G. R. Miller (Ed.), *Explorations in interpersonal communication* (pp. 87–103). Newbury Park, CA: Sage.

Millar, F. E., & Rogers, L. E. (1987). Relational dimensions of interpersonal dynamics. In M. E. Roloff & G. R. Miller (Eds.), *Interpersonal processes: New directions in communication research* (pp. 117–139). Newbury Park, CA: Sage.

Miller, G. R. (1976). Introduction. In G. R. Miller (Ed.), *Explorations in interpersonal communication.* Newbury Park, CA: Sage.

Montgomery, B. M. (1988). Quality communication in personal relationships. In S. W. Duck (Ed.), *Handbook of personal relationships* (pp. 343–359). New York: Wiley.

Nussbaum, J. F., Pecchioni, L. L., Robinson, J. D., & Thompson, T. L. (Eds.). (2000). *Communication and aging*. Mahwah, NJ: Erlbaum.

O'Keefe, B. J., & McCornack, S. A. (1987). Message logic design and message goal structure: Effects on perceptions of message quality in regulative communication situations. *Human Communication Research, 14*, 68–92.

O'Sullivan, P. B. (2000). What you don't know won't hurt me: Impression management functions communication channels in relationships. *Human Communication Research, 26*, 403–431.

Parks, M. R. (1985). Interpersonal communication and the quest for personal competence. In M. L. Knapp & G. R. Miller (Eds.), *Handbook of interpersonal communication* (pp. 171–201). Newbury Park, CA: Sage.

Parks, M. R. (1994). Interpersonal communication and the quest for personal competence. In M. L. Knapp & G. R. Miller (Eds.), *Handbook of interpersonal communication* (2nd ed., pp. 598–618). Thousand Oaks, CA: Sage.

Pervin, L. A. (1989). Goal concepts in personality and social psychology: A historical analysis. In L. A. Pervin (Ed.), *Goal concepts in personality and social psychology* (pp. 1–17). Hillsdale, NJ: Erlbaum.

Rosenwald, G. (1992). Conclusion: Reflections on narrative understanding. In G. Rosenwald & R. Ochberg (Eds.), *Storied lives: The cultural politics of self-understanding* (pp. 265–289). New Haven, CT: Yale University Press.

Sanders, R. E. (1991). The two-way relationship between talk in social interactions and actors' goals and plans. In K. Tracy (Ed.), *Understanding face-to-face interaction: Issues linking goals and discourse* (pp. 167–188). Hillsdale, NJ: Erlbaum.

Spitzberg, B. H., & Cupach, W. R. (1984). *Interpersonal communication competence*. Newbury Park, CA: Sage.

Spitzberg, B. H., & Cupach, W. R. (1989). *Handbook of interpersonal competence research*. New York: Springer-Verlag.

Spitzberg, B. H., & Hecht, M. L. (1984). Component model of relational competence. *Human Communication Research, 10*, 575–599.

Tedeschi, J. T., & Norman, N. M. (1985). Social power, self-presentation, and the self. In B. R. Schlenker (Ed.), *The self and social life* (pp. 293–322). New York: McGraw-Hill.

Tracy, K. (Ed.). (1991). *Understanding face-to-face interaction: Issues linking goals and discourse*. Hillsdale, NJ: Erlbaum.

Tracy, K., Craig, R. T., Smith, M., & Spisak, F. (1984). The discourse of requests: An assessment of compliance-gaining requests. *Human Communication Research, 10*, 513–538.

Tracy, K., & Naughton, J. (1994). The identity work of questioning in intellectual discussion. *Communication Monographs, 61*, 283–302.

Walther, J. B., & Burgoon, J. K. (1992). Relational communication in computer-mediated interaction. *Human Communication Research, 19*, 50–88.

Wiemann, J. M., & Backlund, P. (1980). Current theory and research in communication competence. *Review of Educational Research, 50*, 185–199.

Wilson, S. R. (1990). Development and test of a cognitive rules model of interaction goals. *Communication Monographs, 57*, 81–103.

C H A P T E R   2

PERCEPTION AND

INTERPERSONAL

PROCESSES

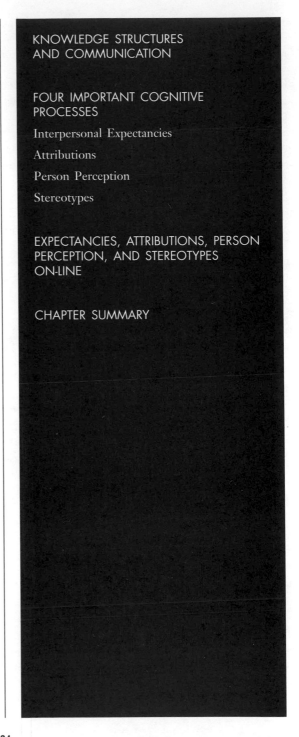

KNOWLEDGE STRUCTURES
AND COMMUNICATION

FOUR IMPORTANT COGNITIVE
PROCESSES
Interpersonal Expectancies
Attributions
Person Perception
Stereotypes

EXPECTANCIES, ATTRIBUTIONS, PERSON
PERCEPTION, AND STEREOTYPES
ON-LINE

CHAPTER SUMMARY

In the film *He Said/She Said,* two directors portray the relationship of Lorie Bryor and Dan Hanson, one from the perspective of Lorie and the other from the perspective of Dan. The portrayal follows the opening scene in which Lorie throws a coffee mug at Dan on their TV show, "He Said/She Said." Dan, who believes that the mug-throwing incident is "just the way we are," presents a very positive — almost perfect — view of their relationship. Lorie, who feels their relationship is over, gives a less glowing view; she talks about Dan as an unreliable womanizer and herself as an insecure individual who thinks marriage will help quiet her fears. At the end of the film, the audience is left guessing whose version of events is more accurate.

As discussed in Chapter 1, many researchers believe that people are relatively strategic in their communication with others. Being able to strategize about our interpersonal communication implies that we are able to think about our behaviors, at least at some level of awareness. To better understand the dynamics of interpersonal communication, it is helpful to know more about how the mind works when people interact with others and when they think about their own behavior. To do this, we focus in this chapter on **social cognition** (the mental processes and structures used to make sense of, remember, and think about people and interactions). These cognitive processes are important because they (a) can influence our interactions with others, even when we are not aware of them, (b) guide our behaviors, and (c) influence what we perceive, how we interpret interpersonal actions, and what we recall from our interactions with others.

In the fictional example that opened this chapter, two characters, Dan and Lorie, were looking back on their relationship in very different ways. Dan, who did not want the relationship to end, remembered events in one way. Lorie, who was very unhappy at the time, remembered the same events quite differently. Their memories — one of the cognitive processes important to interpersonal communication — were affected by their feelings, backgrounds, personalities, fears, and goals. Each had remembrances of a very different reality. What *really* happened was probably not exactly what either of the characters recalls because we tend to remember very selectively. Indeed, we remember only certain parts of events or only some events and not others. In addition, what we do remember tends to be in a different form than what may have happened originally. We may do this because we are not able to notice everything and must make choices (usually unconsciously) about what we will focus our attention on. This is known as **selective attention.**

The operation of selectivity in perception is important, because it shows that we each interact with others and with the world in a way that is different from how others perceive the world. This is natural yet inherently problematic. Because no two people will ever perceive events or situations in exactly the same way, the discrepancy has the potential to increase communication errors. Our goal in this chapter is to explain some of the perception processes that we all use in our interpersonal interactions as we attempt to achieve our communication goals. We hope that a better understanding will make the influences of those processes more apparent.

KNOWLEDGE STRUCTURES AND COMMUNICATION

When people communicate with others or try to make sense of their own behavior, they do so within the constraints of a certain way of viewing the world. Over their lifetimes, people develop knowledge structures — or **schemata** — that they carry with them. These structures help them interpret, remember, and organize new information. Schemata are influenced by the culture in which people live (see the box on *The Gods Must Be Crazy* for an example) and the personal experiences people have. When you see someone act in a certain way, you process the observations through your existing schemata. You are likely to take something that was potentially ambiguous such as the observed behavior and make sense of it with an already established way of viewing the world.

On the first day of class, for example, you probably entered your classroom, sat down in a seat, and waited for the instructor. You may have talked to others in the class whom you knew already or asked other students you did not know brief questions about the class. It is likely that your instructor distributed a syllabus and talked

THE GODS MUST BE CRAZY

In the film *The Gods Must Be Crazy*, a pilot drops a soda bottle out the window of his small plane as he flies over an African desert. The bottle falls to the ground near where a group of Bushmen live. One member of the tribe finds the bottle and brings it back to the group. Having never seen a glass bottle before, the tribe members try to figure out what it is. They assume it was sent by the gods for a purpose, as that belief is consistent with their world view. And because they think all things must be useful to their everyday way of life (the gods would never give them something that was not), they use the bottle for many of the tasks they perform (e.g., drying snake skins, pounding food, making music). Eventually the members start to fight over the bottle. This conflict is something new for the tribe and is inconsistent with how they define themselves as a group. They value harmony with one another more than they value personal possessions, and so they decide to get rid of the bottle. The rest of the movie portrays one group member's quest to throw the bottle off the end of the world.

about what the class would involve. Without knowledge structures, you would not have known how to act, and little of what your instructor did would have made any sense. Instead, however, you relied on established schemata to help you process the situation and communicate with others.

Different types of schemata exist. Fiske and Taylor (1984) discuss four:

1. Self-schemata reflect peoples' views of themselves and guide how they process information about themselves. These are discussed later in this chapter.

2. Event schemata, also called scripts, help people recognize the typical ways in which a sequence of actions tends to unfold (e.g., the particular events that are likely to occur on the first day of a class and the order in which they occur).

3. Role schemata provide information about appropriate behavior based on social categories (e.g., age, race, sex, and occupation) (Fiske & Taylor, 1984). Scholars often refer to these as stereotypes.

4. Person schemata reflect peoples' understanding of individuals they know (e.g., "my husband Chuck") and/or particular types of people (e.g., happy people). This knowledge guides interactions with others.

Planalp (1985) argues that people also have a fifth schemata, a relational schemata, to make sense of love, friendship, family, and work bonds. Relational schemata help people predict, interpret, expect, and remember things for these different types of relationships. Fitzpatrick and Ritchie (1994) describe some of the relational schemata that are particular to families and their communication patterns. According to Fitzpatrick and Ritchie, people form one of the following schemata about what families are or should be like: pluralistic families, in which communication is open and discussion is encouraged; consensual families, in which there is strong pressure toward agreement and children are supposed to be involved in the family without disturbing the family's power structure; laissez-faire families, in which little direction comes from parents to children and children are influenced more by people outside the family; and protective families, in which obedience is highly valued and the family is focused internally. It is likely that your view of your own family falls into one of these categories. Like the other types of knowledge structures, family schemata are thought to affect the ways in which people think and communicate.

Schemata, or knowledge structures, play out in a number of different types of social cognition. The next section focuses on certain types of cognition that are likely to be particularly important as we pursue goals in interpersonal interactions.

FOUR IMPORTANT COGNITIVE PROCESSES

Researchers have identified some important processes involved when people communicate that are connected to knowledge structures. Four particularly important processes for understanding how people communicate and achieve their interpersonal goals are (1) interpersonal expectancies, (2) attributions, (3) person perception, and (4) stereotyping.

Interpersonal Expectancies

When people communicate with others, they usually bring along a set of interpersonal expectations for how they think the interaction (or the relationship they have or hope to have with another) will proceed. Like relational schemata, expectancies guide our communication with others; but expectancies focus particularly on *how we think people will or ought to communicate with us.* That is, we have expectations for what a teacher may say on the first day of class, what people should (and should not) talk about on a date, what we can only say to a close friend. Interpersonal expectancies may also be reflected in our behavior as we act in ways that adapt to the expectations we have for others. In turn, our behaviors may affect others' communication.

One of the best-known interpersonal expectancies is the **self-fulfilling prophecy,** discussed originally by Merton in 1948: "[A] self-fulfilling prophecy is, in the beginning, a false definition of the situation evoking a new behavior which makes the originally false conception come true" (p. 195). Thus, if you believed, incorrectly, that another student was not likely to be friendly, you may have acted toward him or her as if he or she were unfriendly. A self-fulfilling prophecy would have occurred if that student reacted in an unfriendly way rather than how he or she might have otherwise. Because of your actions, you brought about what you had expected would occur. Merton also discussed the self-disconfirming prophecy. This happens when the beliefs that we have about others make them act in ways that would counter the expectancy (e.g., they would act particularly friendly). If another responds to our friendliness with friendliness — and this is not how he or she would have behaved had we not acted as we did — a self-disconfirming prophecy would have occurred. Our "opposite" behaviors helped bring about behaviors that went against how we expected the other to act.

Another type of prophecy effect is the **Pygmalion effect.** According to this prophecy, if people believe something will take place, they behave in ways that ensure that it will occur. Rosenthal and Rubin (1978) first used the term to define the potential influence of teachers' expectancies on students' performance. According to Miller and Turnbull (1986), in Rosenthal and Rubin's initial study,

> Teachers in an elementary school were told that a new IQ test administered to their students indicated that certain students, "bloomers," should show a marked increase in intellectual competence over the course of the school year. In actuality, the label "bloomer" was assigned randomly by the researchers. All students were given an IQ test at both the beginning and the end of the school year. The results indicated that students labeled "bloomers" showed a significantly greater gain in IQ than other pupils. (p. 235)

People are likely
to judge others
differently if they
have the opportu-
nity to interact
with them.

Sven Martson/The Image Works

Rosenthal and Rubin concluded that the expectancies the teachers had for the students affected how the teachers treated the students. This treatment in turn had significant outcomes: higher IQ scores. Although subsequent studies have found mixed
support for the Pygmalion effect (and for the other types of prophecies), there has
been enough research to document that sometimes expectancies have an effect on another's behavior.

Expectancies are important for us in a number of other contexts, most notably our
personal relationships. One such type of expectancy entails how a romance should
develop. Honeycutt and his colleagues concluded that people have a knowledge
structure that reflects their expectations for how they think a relationship is likely to
grow. In one study (Honeycutt, Cantrill, & Greene, 1989), participants read stories
about couples whose relationships moved toward marriage. The readers typically divided the stories into six phases, reflecting their beliefs about the common "path"
that relationships take (i.e., a form of script). The first phase or "scene" was called
initiation and involved the characters' meeting. The second scene, intensifying, included dating, sharing time, and showing affection. Scene three, self-disclosure,
included talks about matters that are important to each couple member, and it was
followed by scene four, sexual intercourse, in which the couple made love. Scene five,
integrating, involved meeting one another's families and making a verbal commitment; and scene six, bonding, included actually getting married. Honeycutt (1995)

found that peoples' awareness of how they think relationships ought to progress affects the ways in which they practice or "imagine" future interactions with their partner. A more recent study shows that people also use their expectancies of a romance to determine what compliance-gaining strategies they might use to convince their partner to move forward to another stage (Honeycutt, Cantrill, Kelly, & Lambkin, 1998).

People in relationships also develop expectancies for the actual and desired behaviors they think or want their romantic partners to use with them. Kelley and Burgoon (1991) proposed that people enter relationships with **relational expectancies,** knowledge structures that mirror the beliefs we have for how our interaction partner should act (see Table 2.1 for an assessment tool for some of these expectancies). As will be discussed in Chapter 10, people's communication reflects the kind of relationship that they have with one another. For instance, if a relationship is defined to be unequal, such as when one person has more power, this inequality may be shown through the behaviors used. An example of this would be when one person speaks more and takes control of the conversation.

Like the imagined interactions discussed earlier, relational expectancies become particularly important for communication because they may influence how we act with others. A study by Manusov, Trees, Liotta, Koenig, and Cochran (1999) showed, for example, that relational expectancies affected whether married couples reciprocated or compensated their partners' behaviors (see Chapter 5 for more information on reciprocity and compensation of nonverbal cues). Specifically, when one couple member expected the other to act dominantly, he or she was more likely to compensate (act different from) the partner. When high levels of intimacy were expected, some reciprocity of intimacy cues was most likely. This is a clear case of how expectancies can affect communication behavior because the nature of the expectancy was mirrored in the behaviors used by those who held the expectations.

STUDENT AS OBSERVER: THE PATH TOWARD MARRIAGE?

Write down a description of your view of the most common path toward marriage that people take (starting with meeting one another and ending with marriage—or beyond). Ask five friends to do the same. Then compare the stages you and your friends reported with the stages proposed by Honeycutt and his colleagues. Did your answers match up? If there was variation, what do you think might have caused it? Do your descriptions of the most common paths mirror your view of the "best" path? What other movement-toward-marriage models do you know from other cultural or social groups? What would you like to see be different, if anything, in the "common path toward marriage" within your culture?

Table 2.1

SELECTED ITEMS FROM KELLEY AND BURGOON'S (1991) MEASURE OF RELATIONAL EXPECTANCIES

On a scale of 1 (strongly disagree) to 7 (strongly agree), indicate the extent to which you agree that a partner should/my partner will:

Dominance:

1. Try to control the interaction
2. Act more powerful than me
3. Dominate the conversation
4. Have the upper hand during our conversations
5. Be in control of the relationship
6. Be assertive with me

Intimacy:

1. Be interested in talking with me
2. Be willing to listen to me
3. Establish rapport with me
4. Desire further conversation with me
5. Be interested in what I have to say
6. Treat me like a good friend
7. Like me
8. Be open to my questions
9. Show affection to me

Informality:

1. Keep our discussions formal
2. Make the conversation informal
3. Not attempt to influence me

Source: Adapted from D. L. Kelley & J. K. Burgoon, Understanding marital satisfaction and couple type as functions of related expectations in *Human Communication Research* (pp. 40–69). Reprinted by permission of Oxford University Press (UK).

The preceding studies demonstrate that we have expectancies and that we act in ways that are influenced by our expectancies for other people. Of course, those others do not always act as we expect them to. When people notice that someone has violated their beliefs about how they thought the other would act, they try to make sense of the violation (Burgoon & Hale, 1988). One way that people do this is to consider the person who committed the violation. Burgoon and Hale argue that, when we think about others and try to determine why they acted in a certain way, we judge them based on how many positive or negative judgments we can make about them. Using Burgoon and Hale's terms, we think of those who have many positive judgments as being "high reward," because we are likely to benefit from knowing them. We are likely to think of others as "low reward" if we see largely negative attributes or costs associated with another. When another person violates our expectations, and we have judged that person to be "high reward," we are likely to assume that he or she violated our beliefs for a good reason. This judgment actually makes us evaluate the violator better than if he or she had acted normally. If we judge another to be "low reward," however, the violation of expectations results in a lower evaluation than would have occurred if she or he had not committed the violation. Thus, violations of expectations can actually help our judgment of people we have labeled as rewarding, but they will likely hurt our perceptions of those we had already seen as less rewarding to us.

Although the influence of expectancies is quite strong, it is important to note that what people think will occur in an interaction is not the only factor that influences their judgments and behaviors. How other people act in interactions may prove even more important than expectancies for how people think about them. We will return to this point in the section on stereotypes.

Attributions

When we perceive others and make judgments about them or about ourselves, we are making **attributions** about their behavior. The term attribution refers to assessments of the cause of an action or behavior (i.e., our thoughts about why someone acted as he or she did or what caused us to act in a certain way) or the degree of responsibility that someone or something had for the action.

Fritz Heider (1958) was one of the first researchers to study attributions in any depth. He asserted that people act as "naive scientists," untrained but active psychologists, who study others' (and their own) actions in order to determine why people behave in certain ways. Finding a cause, even an incorrect one, helps put unexpected behavior in order and make sense of the world. Causes can be either internal to a person, such as a person's disposition, mood, or other character trait, external to him or her, like environmental or situational factors, or both internal and external. Heider called these dimensions of attributions **causal loci** or the sources of observed behavior. For example, if you see someone who is walking across campus suddenly trip, you may attribute the cause to the person ("She fell because she's clumsy"), to something outside of the person ("A crack in the pavement must have caused her to fall"), or to a combination ("There must be a crack, but only clumsy people would trip on cracks"). As we will see in Chapter 8, other dimensions besides causal locus differentiate attributions (e.g., responsibility for and stability of the cause), and these factors help reflect the great variety of causes that can be found for any communication behavior.

In an extension of Heider's work, Jones and Davis (1965) argued that human behavior has the potential to be more or less meaningful depending on the level of intention inferred for a behavior. Accordingly, one of the most important considerations for making an attribution is deciding whether or not another person acted with intent. Those behaviors judged to be intended are thought to say more about the person (i.e., to be more meaningful) than those thought to have occurred without intent (i.e., on a whim or under conditions that could not have been controlled). Importantly, Jones and Davis argued that people will judge a behavior to be intended under specific conditions: (1) the other had knowledge about the potential effects of his or her action, and (2) he or she had the ability to enact the actions.

Vangelisti (2001) discussed a series of studies that she and her colleagues have performed specifically looking at attributions of intent behind hurtful messages. "In these investigations, people were asked to describe and evaluate an interaction when someone said something to them that was extremely hurtful and to note whether the individual who hurt them did so intentionally" (p. 43). Across her studies, Vangelisti found that people who attributed intent to the other person also reported that they distanced themselves from the other and their relationship.

What else beyond level of intention determines our attributions of actions to internal or external causes? Three features of observing others may influence such judgments: distinctiveness, consistency, and consensus (Kelley, 1973). *Distinctiveness* is whether or not a person's behavior is clearly different in one situation than in other situations. For example, if a friend of yours got good grades in all of her classes but one, you are likely to make an external attribution: The one class is too difficult or is taught poorly. However, if your friend received poor grades in all her classes, you would be more likely to make an internal attribution: She is not very smart and/or she is not very motivated.

Consistency is the extent to which a person's behavior is the same over time. Highly consistent behavior means, using the preceding example, that your friend has always received high grades or has always received low grades. If your friend has in the past demonstrated the ability and motivation to get good grades, you would probably look for external causes for a recent bout of bad grades. Perhaps this semester she had tough professors, or other things going on in her life are distracting her from her coursework.

Consensus is the perception of similar others in similar situations, such as how well your friend is doing in one class relative to other similar students in the same class. High consensus means that all students in particular classes receive poor grades. When all students get poor grades, you would probably attribute your friend's poor grades to an external cause, such as the professor's grading or the difficulty of the material. Consensus is low, however, when other students are receiving high marks, but your friend is one of the few who are not. Overall, according to Kelley, people are likely to believe that a person's behavior is caused by external factors when distinctiveness, consistency, and consensus are high.

The preceding determinants of attributions assume a relatively logical approach toward deciding the cause of another's (or one's own) behavior. That is, they assume that people can and will go through the steps of making a sound attribution. Other researchers have shown that people do not always use rational processing when they try to figure out what caused something to occur, however. Instead, several **attribution biases** are involved in our attempts to determine the causes of behavior. Table 2.2 summarizes these biases.

The fundamental attribution error, for instance, suggests that people are more likely to assume that another's actions were caused by something internal rather than external (Ross, 1977). Rather than going through the steps of one of the attribution models listed earlier, a person may just believe that some personality trait or intention was the cause of the action. This may occur because it is easier to find an internal cause — there are fewer of them and the observer is already focused on the person. The ultimate attribution error asserts that peoples' tendency to assume another's actions were caused by something internal is particularly likely when another's behavior is negative. Conversely, people are less likely to assume an internal explanation with positive behaviors. So, if a stranger acted nice to you, you might assume that he was just following social rules, which is an external explanation. If he acted rudely, you would be more likely to think that his actions were due to something about him ("he's a snob").

Other errors or biases depend on our place in an interaction. The actor-observer bias refers to people's tendency to see their own behaviors as less negative overall than they see others' actions (Jones & Nisbett, 1972). For example, if you decided to turn down a job, you could easily say that the cause of your behavior was your belief that taking the job would hurt your school performance. If someone else had done the same thing, however, you might attribute his or her actions to laziness ("He or she didn't want to have to work hard").

The negativity and positivity biases (Kellermann, 1984) are also due to one's perspective in an interaction. If people are watching someone from afar, they tend to make relatively negative judgments of the other's actions (the negativity bias) at least when compared to what they do when they try to make sense of the same behavior while interacting with that person. It appears that having a chance to actually talk with another person helps us focus on more positive attributes (positivity bias). Some researchers say that we do this because we can now be seen as the cause of the other's actions ("She acted that way because she likes me"). We may label other people and/or their behavior positively (rather than negatively as we do with strangers) because we want to think that we would cause others to take only positive actions.

Attributions may also be biased by peoples' feelings for each other. In one study, Manusov (1990) had couples play the game "Trivial Pursuit." One of the couple members had been asked to become a part of the study, and his or her cards were marked. About a third of the way into the game, the "informed" couple member received a marked card that told him or her to start acting unusually positive or negative. Watching the videotape of the interactions after they were complete, the "naive" partner was asked to explain any unusual behaviors. Manusov found that, for most couples, negative behaviors were more likely to prompt attribution-making than were

Table 2.2

ATTRIBUTION ERRORS OR BIASES COMMON TO INTERPERSONAL COMMUNICATION

Term	Definition
Fundamental Attribution Error	The tendency to assume others' behaviors were caused by internal rather than external factors
Ultimate Attribution Error	The tendency to assume that others' negative behaviors, in particular, were caused by internal rather than external factors, while making more external than internal attributions for their positive behaviors
Negativity Bias	The tendency to make more negative than positive judgments about others when we do not have the chance to interact with them
Positivity Bias	The tendency to make more positive than negative judgments about others when we do have the chance to interact with them
Distress-Maintaining Bias	The tendency for unhappy couples to attribute their partners' negative behaviors to internal causes and to attribute their positive behaviors to external causes
Relationship-Enhancing Bias	The tendency for happy couples to attribute their partners' positive behaviors to internal causes and to attribute their negative behaviors to external causes

positive behaviors (not all behaviors make us think about their causes). For positive behaviors, however, the nature of the attributions differed based on couples' satisfaction level. Couples who were happy with one another attributed positive behaviors to something internal to their partner, whereas unhappy couples made more external attributions.

Manusov's study was only one of many that have looked for biases in the attributions made by couples. Indeed, it is so common for unhappy couples to assume that their partners are responsible for negative actions and for happy couples to attribute internal causes for positive behaviors that these tendencies have names. The tendency for unhappy couples to "see the worst" is known as the distress-maintaining bias; whereas the inclination for happy couples to "see the best" is called the relationship-enhancing bias (Holtzworth-Munroe & Jacobson, 1985). Attributions that are distress-maintaining give people responsibility for having behaved badly ("It was his fault/a result of his personality/his intention to not do the chores that I asked him to do") but not for positive behavior ("She just acted nice to me because her parents could hear us"). Attributions that reflect a relationship-enhancing bias do the opposite. People are seen to be the cause of and responsible for positive, but not negative, actions. In both cases, however, couples are not necessarily seeing their partners' behaviors for what they are, but rather for what they expect them to be. Both of these biases reflect a tendency to view the world in a particular way, which may or may not conform to reality. Couples are then likely to communicate with one another based on their biases. Ways to increase the accuracy of attributions exist, such as assessing distinctiveness, consistency, and consensus, but because people see causes through the lenses of existing knowledge structures, the attributions they provide are often biased. Importantly, studies that look at attributions over time suggest that the nature of attributions early in relationships are likely to affect the degree to which partners are happy in their relationships later on (Johnson, Karney, Rogge, & Bradbury, 2001).

Attributions are important for understanding interpersonal communication in that the causes we give for behaviors are part of the meaning we derive from them. This meaning is a fundamental part of what is communicated in an interpersonal interaction. As well, the attribution we decide on for another's behavior helps influence how we communicate with him or her.

Person Perception

The positivity and negativity biases just discussed reflect a larger social cognition process: **person perception.** Every day, as we communicate with others, we attempt to determine what others are like and whether we like them. Person perception is therefore both a communicative goal in itself and a skill used to pursue other goals. For example, we try to figure out what someone is like in order to know best how to ask them to comply with a request.

As noted earlier, people create person schemata that guide their actions and thoughts regarding (1) people they know, and (2) certain types of people (such as people who are in particular groups with characteristics people think they can identify). Schemata for specific friends, family, and co-workers (e.g., the authors have schemata for one another) and for types of people such as friends, family, and co-workers (e.g., the authors have schemata for what co-authors are like) are both part of person perception. People also have general person schemata that are based on personality traits such as shyness, humorousness, and kindness. These are called **prototypes.**

Sometimes general perception categories are very broad and influenced by factors out of our awareness. Monahan (1998) argues that people make quick and often automatic judgments of whether another person is good or bad. Interestingly, these views of others can be instigated in a number of ways. Monahan had her participants watch some slides prior to viewing a videotape of a young man whom they were going to judge. Some of the participants saw presentations that included subliminal (quickly shown, out of awareness) slides of the young man smiling. Those participants, who had been "primed" to see the young man positively, evaluated him as more attractive and more likable than did those who did not receive the subliminal slides. Further, those who saw the slides evaluated others more positively as well. Monahan suggests that person perception processes may also be affected by factors unknown to the perceiver (e.g., mood, temperature, and even time of year).

Once we've established a way of thinking about someone, we tend to hold onto it. This may be why we are often advised about the importance of first impressions. It appears to be very difficult to let go of an image of someone once it is formed. However, this occurs more consistently when we form an impression of someone but then do not interact with that person (a more likely outcome when our first impression is not positive). When we actually have the chance to interact with another person, we may be inclined to use "individuating information" (Fiske & Neuberg, 1990) or knowledge that comes from learning about a person's particular characteristics as compared to information that is part of a general category or prototype. Thus, how an individual acts may prove more important than how we thought he or she would act.

In addition to the perceptions we form of others, we also have self-perceptions and generally work equally hard to maintain them. Swann (1987) explains that, as part of their primary task of making sense of the world, children watch their own behavior, see how others react to them, and use those reactions to form a view of self. As their self-views become clearer, children try to find ways to maintain them, even if the self-perceptions are negative. According to Swann (1990), "people want to confirm their self-views not as an end in itself, but as a means of bolstering their perception that the world is predictable and controllable" (p. 414). We tend to seek out, notice, and remember those things that are consistent with our self-views. These "stabilizing processes" cause us often to have what Swann calls a "chronic view of self," one that is particularly unlikely to change.

People do not create their self-concepts in isolation, however. Rather, self-perception is very much a result of interpersonal communication. For a long time researchers argued that a primary means for creating self-perceptions was due to reflected appraisal, also known as the reflected or looking-glass self (Cooley, 1902). Reflected appraisal is the part of the self-concept that we may develop because of how we seem to be to others. That is, we may see others' perception of us in their actions toward us. So, if your sister acted bored around you, she may have been "mirroring" back to you that you are a dull person.

Researchers argue that a primary means of creating our self-perceptions is reflecting the appraisals of others.

Jodi Jacobson/Peter Arnold

McCall (1987), however, shows that reflected appraisals may not be as notable as once thought. He asserted that "[i]n social life, . . . people do not usually communicate their appraisals of others to those others directly. Relationships with significant others are hedged about with tact, discretion, and deference. . . . These and other barriers to communication reduce the accuracy of reflected appraisals by distorting the looking-glass process, leading to self-conceptions that are idiosyncratic and idealized" (p. 67). Instead of being the result only of others' perceptions of us, McCall argues that self-perception is more likely to result from the give-and-take between individuals and others. Over time, he argues, people present themselves in certain ways to others (see Chapter 6 for more on self-presentation). This occurs largely through their conversations with others. As long as the others do not disagree with the image presented, a "working agreement" exists between them as to their accepted identity. Thus, our self-views are based largely on the degree to which others accept our reflections of self rather than on the degree to which we see ourselves in others' behavior toward us.

Despite its origins, how we view ourselves is important for several reasons. First, who we see ourselves to be and how we evaluate ourselves — our degree of self-esteem — likely influences what goals we set and whether or not we pursue them. Second, self-views affect the choices of others with whom we wish to interact or form relationships. Third, the way we see ourselves is also likely to influence how we interpret others' behaviors in regard to us and our relationship with them. So, in *He Said/She Said*, the example at the beginning of this chapter, Lorie's view of her relationship with Dan was made more negative by her own belief that she was largely unlovable. As was seen, however, Dan's view reflected a very different reality: that Lorie was interesting and dynamic and a person whom he could love.

In addition to perceptions of others and perceptions of ourselves, we also have **metaperceptions.** According to Sherman and colleagues (2001), metaperceptions are our beliefs about how *others* perceive us, and we are accurate in our metaperceptions to the degree that they match others' actual views of us. In a particularly interesting study, Sherman and colleagues compared the metaperception accuracy of people who presented themselves on a Web page and those who met others face-to-face. The researchers found that people who created on-line self-displays believed, wrongly, that others perceived them as favorably as they viewed themselves and in a way that was consistent with their own self-perception. Those who met others face-to-face were much more likely to form the same impression of a conversational partner as the partner had for him or herself. The researchers speculate that there are many reasons for the greater accuracy of face-to-face interactions. Among these, "[b]ecause creators of homepages seldom receive feedback regarding the reactions of others . . . they have no corrective mechanism for adjusting the impression they may be giving" (p. 128). This helps show the interconnectedness between communication and person perception.

The processes of person perception are key to our communication. Our perceptions of others affect how we will communicate with them — or even if we will communicate with them at all. Our perceptions of self also influence how we will communicate and in what contexts as well as the types of relationships we develop.

Stereotypes

In addition to creating a view of ourselves (and of those around us), we also tend to use categories for others. Lakoff (1987) states that,

> [T]here is nothing more basic than categorization to our thought, perception, action, and speech. Every time we see something as a kind of thing, for example, a tree, we are categorizing. Whenever we reason about kinds of things — chairs, nations, illnesses, emotions, any kind of thing at all — we are employing categories. (pp. 5–6)

When categories are about people and are based on their group membership, they are called **stereotypes.** People categories may include ethnic or cultural groups, gender groups, and social groups, and stereotypes include beliefs about the characteristics common to all members of that group ("All basketball players are tall"). As Lakoff suggests, stereotypes, as a type of categorization, *are a common way to make* *sense of people and objects and in this regard are thought of as important to communication.* Stereotypes, however, are also sometimes incorrect and always only partially reflect the complexities of the group; thus they may hurt our ability to communicate with others.

As a type of category or knowledge structure, stereotypes help people process information. When one person sees another person act in a particular way, the observer may do so in light of a stereotype of the other person's group. But using a stereotype, like any other form of perception, means that people see things in a certain way, and that way is usually consistent with the stereotype they hold. For example, if you notice someone from another group (e.g., you are a college student and you are watching someone who is not a student), and that person is doing something that does not fit your stereotype (e.g., reading a textbook), you probably will not even notice the behavior because it doesn't fit with your image of things. If you do pay attention to it (this is more likely if the behavior seems extraordinary), you probably will try to make it fit with your existing stereotype. You may say that the person you observed was an exception or that he or she was enacting the behavior for a reason that allows it to fit with your view. For example, you may offer an external attribution that means something else besides that the person was responsible for the behavior. In other words, you will usually try to make what you observe fit with your preexisting views if possible.

It is important to remember that stereotyping is one of the "normal" ways that our minds process information, and it benefits us by making sense of things more easily. It also helps us guide our behaviors so that we can communicate with some degree of competence. Brown (1995) notes the following example in support of this: "[S]uppose I visit some foreign city and I need to find my way to some famous landmark. It is much more useful for me to be able to recognize particular categories of people (for example, police, taxi drivers, local residents) to ask for directions than simply to ask the first person I meet (usually a lost fellow tourist)" (pp. 41–42).

It is equally important to realize, however, that stereotypes can lead us to act in ways that are prejudiced negatively by the beliefs that accompany the stereotypes. Sometimes the negative discrimination that occurs because of stereotyping happens quickly and only as a result of separating people into groups. In two well-known experiments by Rabbie and Horwitz (1969; Horwitz & Rabbie, 1982), school children in the Netherlands, who did not yet know one another, were divided randomly into two groups. One group was called the "green" group, and the other was labeled "blue." The children were told that this division was made solely to help the administration of the school. Just putting the children into two groups encouraged the children to evaluate those in their own group (their "in-group") more favorably than they evaluated the other group (their "out-group"). This finding was exaggerated when the groups were told that only one group would be able to get an award for an upcoming activity.

In a related set of experiments, Tajfel, Flament, Billig, and Bundy (1971) confirmed that the mere act of putting people into groups made people act with negative discrimination. Specifically, the people in the study were asked to divide up a sum of money between members of their own group and members of the other group. In their study, the experimental participants did not meet the others to whom they were "giving money" so could not base their prejudice on anything other than group membership. Indeed, others were identified only by a number and by their membership in one's own group or another group. When no directions were given as to how to divide up the money, the researchers found that, although often people gave money evenly to members of the out-group and the in-group, many others gave more money to the members who were in their own group. In some experimental trials, the researchers gave the participants a chance to (a) give everyone an equal amount of money, such as $5, or (b) give the in-group members less (only $4, for example), so that the out-group members would get even less (only $2, for instance). Many people chose the latter alternative. According to Brown (1995), "this apparently spontaneous discrimination is entirely consistent with the more general differentiation phenomena associated with the categorization process" (p. 47).

Much of the time the ways that stereotypes play out in behavior are relatively subtle. Manusov and Hegde (1993) paired undergraduate students from the United States with graduate students from India. The videotapes of the interactions were looked at for a number of behaviors. As well, the U.S. students' views of how much they knew about people from India were assessed. Those who claimed to know a lot and to have neutral or positive evaluations of the culture acted in ways that were more familiar than those without fully formed stereotypes. For example, they asked more open questions and appeared more engaged in the interaction. In this case, the actions were relatively positive, showing that discrimination that follows from stereotypes may be favorable as well as unfavorable. But it also shows that something as general as believing we know something about a person's culture makes us act differently than do those who do not have any established stereotype for another group.

Importantly, however, people may let go of stereotypes to some degree when they get a chance to interact with someone from another group or culture. Manusov, Winchatz, and Manning (1997), for instance, paired up students from the United States with students from other countries. Before interacting, the authors asked the participants to evaluate how positively or negatively they viewed people from the other group. After talking for ten minutes, some residual, or leftover, effects of the initial stereotype remained (e.g., if participants expected a positive interaction, they judged their partner more positively no matter how the partner behaved). Still, it was clear that in the majority of the evaluations people made, how their partner actually acted influenced participants' assessments more strongly. So, even if the initial stereotype led them to think that they would not enjoy the conversation, if they thought their partner acted positively, the study participants were likely to evaluate their partners well. As well, if they had high expectations that were not met, they judged their partners more negatively than their initial stereotype would have led them to do.

As noted, however, the stereotype-based expectancies did influence judgments somewhat. The expectations participants had also influenced their own behavior to a certain degree (e.g., gazes, leans, head nods, body orientation, and behavioral congruence were used somewhat differently by participants with positive versus negative stereotypes for their partner's culture), and these even had some effects on how their partner acted. The behavioral manifestations were relatively small. But, as Jussim (1990) asserted after conducting a series of studies in this area, "even relatively modest expectancy effects may contribute to social problems in important ways" (p. 9), and thus they should not be overlooked. It is clear, then, that stereotypes as a form of knowledge structure are likely to influence our evaluations and our behavior toward others.

EXPECTANCIES, ATTRIBUTIONS, PERSON PERCEPTION, AND STEREOTYPES ON-LINE

As cognitive processes, all of the topics we have talked about work in tandem in our interactions. One model helps to show some of the ways that this integration occurs, and it has been applied specifically to explain computer-mediated communication. Lea and Spears's (1992; Spears, Postmes, Lea, & Watt, 2001) "SIDE" is an acronym for their Social Identity model of Deindividuation Effects. SIDE assumes that communicators may have different identities, or aspects of selves, that "come out" in different situations because certain situations make particular identities more or less salient. That is, one role you play in life may be more important at one moment while others are in the background. If you list, for example, twenty self-descriptors, it is likely that certain of them are more key to you in the part of your life where you are a student. Others may be more vital to you at home or at work.

Many of these aspects of the self are not really personal descriptors but rather pertain to the social categories one may occupy: a student at an American university, a communication major, a daughter in a particular family, a member of a particular organization. At times, we see the world and behave toward others on the basis of one of these social categories (Tajfel, 1978; Turner, Hogg, Oakes, Reicher, & Wetherell, 1987). When this occurs, we assume that other members of the same social category are similar to us, and this seeming similarity helps create a certain level of social attraction. This attraction is one of the effects of social categories.

When you are communicating over the Internet, in a chat system or something similar, there is an added dimension: The lack of nonverbal cues — primarily those signaling individual differences such as physical appearance and vocal qualities — submerges the communicator in what Lea and Spears (1992) call **deindividuation.** Rather than perceiving individual differences among others or the self, the invisibility of the interaction often causes people to cling more tightly to whatever salient identity is most available. The same process may occur when people are in "off-line" groups and individual identities become secondary to group affiliations (Spears et al., 2001).

Thus, when a social identity is operating, and the communication channel promotes relating to others on the basis of categories rather than as unique individuals, interpretations and evaluations of other people are altered. The results, according to these theorists, include overattributions, making exaggerated or more certain judgments about others based on minimal information. This is one way that people on-line "fill in the gaps" about what they don't know about each other. Drawing on assumed similarities, they fill in what they don't know by drawing on stereotypes about the group.

One experiment that was designed to test SIDE illustrates the point very well. Lea and Spears (1992) assigned students majoring in psychology into groups of three and had them communicate using a computer chat system. Some groups were prompted to think about their partners as "students in a psychology course," whereas others were encouraged to try to think about the ways that their partners were unique individuals; this constituted making salient a social or an individual/personal identity. Moreover, half of each of these groups sat between partitions blocking their view of one another, while the other groups could see their partners.

Within each group, one member was actually a confederate, who, at a certain point, included intentional misspellings, abbreviations, and exaggerated punctuation marks in each message (e.g., hellooooooo!!!!!!!). The SIDE dynamics accounted for the results in people's judgments about or perceptions of their partners. When partners could see each other and were therefore *individuated*, average ratings were ascribed to their partners (presuming that they liked some of their partners fairly well, and disliked some somewhat, in ways that averaged out). When partners could not see one another, however, the salient identity made a big difference. Students who presumed they were all the same via a salient social identity, such as all psychology students in some experiment, liked the confederate *more* when she altered spelling and punctuation. When instructed to look for inter-individual differences — finding ways that the partner is different than oneself — the students rated those confederates who used the altered writing style as much less likable and more negative overall than those who used a more "normal" style.

These results show two important issues. First, we judge others not only on who they are in their own right but also on the basis of their presumed social categories and whether or not we share them. Second, one of the compelling features about computer-mediated communication is that the presumptions we make about the similarity and attractiveness of others may be exaggerated when we cannot see or hear our partners, causing us to interpret the same behaviors in more extreme ways.

As can be seen from the preceding examples, cognitive processes help people make sense of their social world, but they may also hamper people's ability to see behaviors and people accurately. These biases can influence people to see things and act more negatively, or more positively, than reality would suggest. Importantly, however, social actors are likely to be more accurate and to be less influenced by others' expectations under certain conditions. For instance, Jussim (1990) reviews work that shows that when people's goals are to be accurate, they are more likely to make judgments consistent with reality. More often, however, judgments of one's self and others are affected by other goals (e.g., self-enhancement and the desire to hold certain beliefs) that may actually harm the accuracy of social cognitions because they distract people from making careful assessments of others. In our everyday communication with others, we are likely to pursue multiple goals. Thus we will probably be less accurate than we could be in judging others, and our communication with them will be based on these biased assessments.

CHAPTER SUMMARY

People notice, remember, and interpret things through the knowledge structures or schemata that they develop over time. These schemata are part of a larger process of social cognition and exist to help people understand themselves, other people, events, categories, and relationships. To some degree, these schemata bias what people see and influence how people act.

Social cognition includes **interpersonal expectancies** (the beliefs people have of what will or should happen in interactions), attributions (how people determine what caused behaviors to occur), person perception, and stereotyping. Stereotypes are a particular form of schemata used to help organize information about groups of people.

KEY TERMS

attribution biases, p. 34
attributions, p. 32
causal loci, p. 32
deindividuation, p. 42
interpersonal expectancies, p. 44
metaperceptions, p. 39
person perception, p. 36
prototypes, p. 37

Pygmalion effect, p. 28
relational expectancies, p. 30
schemata, p. 26
selective attention, p. 25
self-fulfilling prophecy, p. 28
social cognition, p. 25
stereotypes, p. 39

EXERCISES FOR FURTHER DISCUSSION

1. In a group of three or four, complete the following activity:
    a. Go to a place on campus where you can watch people unobtrusively.
    b. Choose a person to watch.

  c. Privately, each person in your group should assess his or her impression of that person and try to decide what led to that impression.

  d. Group members should then discuss their perceptions to find areas of similarity and difference in their evaluations.

2. Think about your beliefs about what a best friend should be like.

  a. How should a best friend communicate with you? Why?

  b. Where do you think these interpersonal expectancies came from?

3. Try to think of a time recently when you made an attribution for someone else's communication behavior.

  a. Analyze the way you decided how to attribute the cause to the behavior. Might other factors have caused the behavior?

  b. Share this experience with others in class to see if they can offer suggestions for possible causes.

4. What is a common stereotype that you tend to use? Think about how it would be if you no longer used that stereotype.

  a. What, if anything, would take its place?

  b. How would your way of communicating be affected?

  c. How do you think it affected the way your friends communicated with you?

5. Watch your own behavior when you communicate on-line with someone you have not met.

  a. What beliefs, if any, do you have about what he or she is like?

  b. How may those beliefs affect your on-line behavior toward him or her?

  c. Are there aspects of the other person's on-line communication that have helped you form the view you have of that other person?

SUGGESTED READING

▼

SCHEMATA AND EXPECTANCIES

Fitzpatrick, M. A., & Ritchie, L. D. (1994). Communication schemata within the family: Multiple perspectives on family interaction. *Human Communication Research, 20,* 275–301.

Honeycutt, J. M., Cantrill, J. G., Kelly, P., & Lambkin, D. (1998). How do I love thee? Let me consider my options: Cognition, verbal strategies, and the escalation of intimacy. *Human Communication Research, 25,* 39–63.

Kelley, D. L., & Burgoon, J. K. (1991). Understanding marital satisfaction and couple type as functions of relational expectations. *Human Communication Research, 18,* 40–69.

Planalp, S. (1985). Relational schemata: A test of alternative forms of relational knowledge as guides to communication. *Human Communication Research, 12,* 3–29.

Rosenthal, R., & Rubin, D. B. (1978). Interpersonal expectancy effects: The first 345 studies. *Behavioral and Brain Sciences, 3,* 377–415.

ATTRIBUTIONS

Heider, F. (1958). *The psychology of interpersonal relations.* New York: Wiley.

Johnson, M. D., Karney, B. R., Rogge, R., & Bradbury, T. N. (2001). The role of marital behavior in the longitudinal association between attribution and marital quality. In V. Manusov & J. H. Harvey (Eds.), *Attribution, communication behavior, and close relationships* (pp. 173–192). Cambridge, England: Cambridge University Press.

Kelley, H. H. (1973). The processes of causal attribution. *American Psychologist, 28,* 107–128.

Manusov, V. (1990). An application of attribution principles to nonverbal behavior in romantic dyads. *Communication Monographs, 57,* 104–118.

STEREOTYPES AND PERSON PERCEPTION

Jussim, L. (1990). Social reality and social problems: The role of expectancies. *Journal of Social Issues, 46,* 9–34.

Lea, M., & Spears, R. (1992). Paralanguage and social perception in computer-mediated communication. *Journal of Organizational Computing, 2,* 321–341.

Manusov, V., Winchatz, M. R., & Manning, L. M. (1997). Acting out our minds: Incorporating behavior into models of stereotype-based expectancies for cross-cultural interactions. *Communication Monographs, 64,* 119–139.

Spears, R., Postmes, T., Lea, M., Watt, S. E. (2001). A SIDE view of social influence. In J. P. Forgas & K. D. Williams (Eds.), *Social influence: Direct and indirect processes* (pp. 331–350). Philadelphia: Psychology Press-Taylor and Francis Group.

Swann, W. B. (1987). Identity negotiation: Where two roads meet. *Journal of Personality and Social Psychology, 53,* 1038–1051.

REFERENCE LIST

▼

Brown, R. (1995). *Prejudice: Its social psychology.* Oxford, England: Blackwell.

Burgoon, J. K., & Hale, J. L. (1988). Nonverbal expectancy violations: Model elaboration and application to immediacy behaviors. *Communication Monographs, 55,* 58–79.

Cooley, C. H. (1902). *Human nature and the social order.* New York: Scribners.

Fiske, S. T., & Neuberg, S. L. (1990). A continuum of impression formation, from category-based to individuating processes: Influences of information and motivation on attention and interpretation. In M. P. Zanna (Ed.), *Advances in experimental psychology* (Vol. 23, pp. 1–74). San Diego, CA: Academic.

Fiske, S. T., & Taylor, S. E. (1984). *Social cognition.* New York: Random House.

Fitzpatrick, M. A., & Ritchie, L. D. (1994). Communication schemata within the family: Multiple perspectives on family interaction. *Human Communication Research, 20,* 275–301.

Heider, F. (1958). *The psychology of interpersonal relations.* New York: Wiley.

Holtzworth-Munroe, A., & Jacobson, N. S. (1985). Causal attributions of married couples: When do they search for causes? What do they conclude when they do? *Journal of Personality and Social Psychology, 48,* 1398–1412.

Honeycutt, J. M. (1991). Imagined interactions, imagery, and mindfulness/mindlessness. In R. Kunzendorf (Ed.), *Mental imagery* (pp. 121–128). New York: Plenum.

Honeycutt, J. M. (1995). Predicting relational trajectory beliefs as a consequence of typicality and necessity rating of relationship behaviors. *Communication Reports, 12,* 3–14.

Honeycutt, J. M., Cantrill, J. G., & Greene, R. W. (1989). Memory structures for relational escalation: A cognitive test of the sequencing of relational actions and stages. *Human Communication Research, 16,* 62–90.

Honeycutt, J. M., Cantrill, J. G., Kelly, P., & Lambkin, D. (1998). How do I love thee? Let me consider my options: Cognition, verbal strategies, and the escalation of intimacy. *Human Communication Research, 25,* 39–63.

Honeycutt, J. M., & Eidenmuller, M. E. (2001). Communication and attribution: An exploration of the effects of music and mood on intimate couples' verbal and nonverbal conflict resolution patterns. In V. Manusov & J. H. Harvey (Eds.), *Attribution, communication behavior, and close relationships* (pp. 21–37). Cambridge, England: Cambridge University Press.

Honeycutt, J. M., & Wiemann, J. M. (1999). Analysis of functions of talk and reports of imagined interactions (IIs) during engagement and marriage. *Human Communication Research, 25,* 399–419.

Horwitz, M., & Rabbie, J. M. (1982). Individuality and membership in the intergroup system. In H. Tajfel (Ed.), *Social identity and intergroup relations* (pp. 241–274). Cambridge, England: Cambridge University Press.

Johnson, M. D., Karney, B. R., Rogge, R., & Bradbury, T. N. (2001). The role of marital behavior in the longitudinal association between attribution and marital quality. In V. Manusov & J. H. Harvey (Eds.), *Attribution, communication behavior, and close relationships* (pp. 173–192). Cambridge, England: Cambridge University Press.

Jones, E. E., & Davis, K. (1965). From acts to dispositions: The attribution process in person perception. In L. Berkowitz (Ed.), *Advances in experimental social psychology* (Vol. 2, pp. 219–267). New York: Academic.

Jones, E. E., & Nisbett, R. E. (1972). The actor and the observer: Divergent perceptions of the causes of behavior. In E. E. Jones, D. E. Kanouse, H. H. Kelley, R. E. Nisbett, S. Valins, & B. Weiner (Eds.), *Attributions: Perceiving the causes of behavior* (pp. 79–94). Morristown, NJ: General Learning.

Jussim, L. (1990). Social reality and social problems: The role of expectancies. *Journal of Social Issues, 46,* 9–34.

Kellermann, K. (1984). The negativity effect and its implications for initial interaction. *Communication Monographs, 51,* 37–55.

Kelley, D. L., & Burgoon, J. K. (1991). Understanding marital satisfaction and couple type as functions of relational expectations. *Human Communication Research, 18,* 40–69.

Kelley, H. H. (1973). The processes of causal attribution. *American Psychologist, 28,* 107–128.

Lakoff, G. (1987). *Women, fire, and dangerous things: What categories reveal about the mind.* Chicago: University of Chicago Press.

Lea, M., & Spears, R. (1992). Paralanguage and social perception in computer-mediated communication. *Journal of Organizational Computing, 2,* 321–341.

Manusov, V. (1990). An application of attribution principles to nonverbal behavior in romantic dyads. *Communication Monographs, 57,* 104–118.

Manusov, V., & Hegde, R. (1993). Communicative outcomes of stereotype-based expectancies: An observational study of cross-cultural dyads. *Communication Quarterly, 41,* 338–354.

Manusov, V., Trees, A. R., Liotta, A., Koenig, J., & Cochran, A. T. (1999, May). *I think therefore I act: Interaction expectations and nonverbal adaptation in couples' conversations.* Paper presented to the Interpersonal Division of the International Communication Association, San Francisco.

Manusov, V., Winchatz, M. R., & Manning, L. M. (1997). Acting out our minds: Incorporating behavior into models of stereotype-based expectancies for cross-cultural interactions. *Communication Monographs, 64,* 119–139.

McCall, G. J. (1987). The self-concept and interpersonal communication. In M. E. Roloff & G. R. Miller (Eds.), *Interpersonal processes: New directions in communication research* (pp. 63–76). Newbury Park, CA: Sage.

Merton, R. K. (1948). The self-fulfilling prophecy. *Antioch Review, 8,* 193–210.

Miller, D. T., & Turnbull, W. (1986). Expectancies and interpersonal processes. *Annual Review of Psychology, 37,* 233–356.

Monahan, J. L. (1998). I don't know it but I like you: The influence of nonconscious affect on person perception. *Human Communication Research, 24,* 480–500.

Planalp, S. (1985). Relational schemata: A test of alternative forms of relational knowledge as guides to communication. *Human Communication Research, 12,* 3–29.

Rabbie, J. M., & Horwitz, M. (1969). Arousal of ingroup-outgroup bias by a chance win or loss. *Journal of Personality and Social Psychology, 13,* 269–277.

Rosenthal, R., & Rubin, D. B. (1978). Interpersonal expectancy effects: The first 345 studies. *Behavioral and Brain Sciences, 3,* 377–415.

Ross, L. (1977). The intuitive psychologist and his shortcomings: Distortions in the attribution process. In L. Berkowitz (Ed.), *Advances in experimental social psychology* (Vol. 10, pp. 173–220). New York: Academic.

Sherman, R. C., End, C., Kraan, E., Cole, A., Campbell, J., Klausner, J., & Birchmeier, Z. (2001). Metaperception in cyberspace. *CyberPsychology & Behavior, 4,* 123–129.

Spears, R., Postmes, T., Lea, M., Watt, S. E. (2001). A SIDE view of social influence. In J. P. Forgas & K. D. Williams (Eds.), *Social influence: Direct and indirect processes* (pp. 331–350). Philadelphia: Psychology Press-Taylor and Francis Group.

Swann, W. B. (1987). Identity negotiation: Where two roads meet. *Journal of Personality and Social Psychology, 53,* 1038–1051.

Swann, W. B. (1990). To be adored or to be known: The interplay of self-enhancement and self-verification. In E. T. Higgins & R. M. Sorrentino (Eds.), *Handbook of motivation and cognition: Foundations of social behavior* (Vol. 2, pp. 408–448). New York: Guilford.

Tajfel, H. (1978). Interindividual behaviour and intergroup behaviour. In H. Tajfel (Ed.), *Differentiation between groups: Studies in the social psychology of intergroup relations* (pp. 27–60). London: Academic Press.

Tajfel, H., Flament, C., Billig, M. G., & Bundy, R. P. (1971). Social categorization and intergroup behaviour. *European Journal of Social Psychology, 1*, 149–178.

Turner, J. C., Hogg, M. A., Oakes, P. J., Reicher, S. D., & Wetherell, M. S. (1987). *Rediscovering the social group: A self-categorisation theory*. Oxford: Basil Blackwell.

Vangelisti, A. L. (2001). Making sense of hurtful interactions in close relationships: When hurt feelings create distance. In V. Manusov & J. H. Harvey (Eds.), *Attribution, communication behavior, and close relationships* (pp. 38–58). Cambridge, England: Cambridge University Press.

C H A P T E R   3

LISTENING

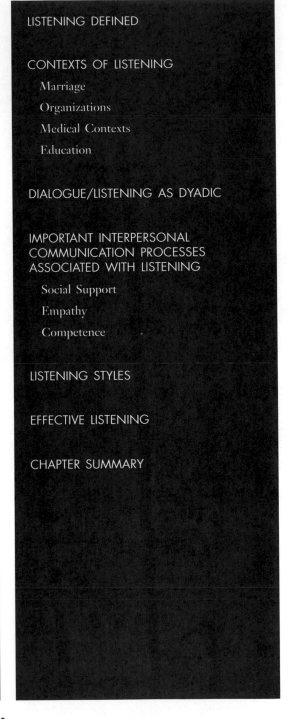

LISTENING DEFINED

CONTEXTS OF LISTENING
  Marriage
  Organizations
  Medical Contexts
  Education

DIALOGUE/LISTENING AS DYADIC

IMPORTANT INTERPERSONAL
COMMUNICATION PROCESSES
ASSOCIATED WITH LISTENING
  Social Support
  Empathy
  Competence

LISTENING STYLES

EFFECTIVE LISTENING

CHAPTER SUMMARY

"[A]lmost everything that gives us pleasure in the communicative interaction is due to the listening process." (Bostrom, 1990, p. 2)

"[O]ne common weakness of many executives is the failure to recognize that listening is equal in importance to talking." (Haas & Arnold, 1995, p. 125)

"Positive and responsive listening behavior benefits marital interaction." (Pasupathi, Carstensen, Levenson, & Gottman, 1999, p. 173)

"Among the basic skills we need for success in life, listening is primary." (Purdy, 1991, p. 4)

"[A]ll conversation lives in the listening of its participants." (Hyde, 1994, p. 179)

These quotes demonstrate that many people have strong beliefs about the importance of listening as part of interpersonal communication. The quotes also show certain ideas about listening. For example, many people believe that some types of listening are better than others, that listening as a practice is often overlooked, that listening is fundamental to communication and to success. What do you think? What do you mean when you say that someone is a good (or poor) listener?

Johnson (1996) reports people spend between 45% and 70% of their time every day listening to others. Although listening is such a common — and important — activity, as a fundamental communication process it has received much less attention than what people do when they are the ones who are doing most of the speaking. Parents and teachers instruct children on grammar, speaking, poise, and manners, but not on listening well. In fact, some of the people reading — and writing — this book may have actually learned their *poor* listening habits from their parents! This chapter is designed to highlight some of the key issues surrounding listening as a communicative process. Through this discussion, we hope to show that listening itself may be an important interpersonal goal. It is also part of many other goals we may pursue and therefore particularly necessary to understand. To help show listening's role in pursuing goals, we start with a discussion of what's involved when people listen.

LISTENING DEFINED

Most of us have an idea of what listening is, and therefore the thought that it needs to be defined may seem odd. Listening, however, is a multifaceted process, and defini-

Most of the research on listening has focused on the cognitive processes going on inside people's heads when they are (or are not) listening.

tions provide a way to understand better those things we do each day. Listening is also a necessary part of interpreting others' messages, an important goal of interpersonal communication. Communicators often assume mistakenly that their messages are interpreted exactly as they were intended. However, the way people listen affects their message interpretations.

According to Bostrom and Waldhart (1988), "[e]arly researchers assumed that the retention of information presented orally was the obvious operational definition of successful listening. Those who retain many facts were assumed to be good listeners, and those who retained only a few were assumed to be poor listeners" (p. 1). However, retention — or how much we remember — may be more a product of intelligence than it is an outcome of listening (Bostrom, 1990). The limits to a listening-equals-retention view led researchers to try to find a more accurate model of listening in interpersonal interactions. From this greater investigation, researchers have found three processes that are part of listening, each of which is multifaceted: *cognition* (discussed in the last chapter), *affect*, and *behavior* (discussed in the next two chapters) (for a review, see Coakley, Halone, & Wolvin, 1996).

Most research attention has been given to what goes on inside people's heads as they are (or are not) listening. Researchers have identified several cognitive processes involved in listening: (1) signal acquisition/hearing; (2) selection/attending to a signal; (3) literal processing/interpretation or decoding; (4) retention/memory; and (5) comprehension/understanding (Bostrom, 1990). Each of these processes is itself quite complex. For example, there are different types of memory, such as short and long term, and what is selected for retention may be influenced by the nature of the message or signal itself (i.e., some things are more likely to be noticed).

Taking a different perspective on listening, Halone and Pecchioni (2001) asked their participants to describe what is involved in **relational listening,** or listening as it is enacted with a particular friend, romantic partner, or relative. As part of a larger model of relational listening, the authors noted seventeen different cognitive processes described by participants as part of the cognitive aspect of listening. These processes included understanding, paying attention, focusing, concentrating, observing, and evaluating. For a full list, and a model of relational listening, see Table 3.1.

Table 3.1
HALONE AND PECCHIONI'S (2001) THEORETICAL MODEL OF RELATIONAL LISTENING

Macro (large)-level Processes

Pre-Interaction	*During Interaction*	*Post-Interaction*
Hear	(Not) just listen	Remember the conversation
Put own thoughts aside	To respond	Act on it
Be open-minded	To not interrupt	
Be there	To talk freely	
Make a conscious effort	To offer feedback	
Take time	Be together	
Do it even if you don't want to	To acknowledge	
Sit down	To give input	
Willingness	To share	
	Attend to verbal cues	
	To interact	
	To participate	
	Attend to nonverbal cues	
	To be involved	

(Continued)

(Table continued from previous page)

Micro (small)-level Processes

Cognitive	*Affective*	*Behavioral*
To understand	To sympathize	To (not) give advice
To pay attention	To empathize	To (not) give opinion
To take in	To care	To ask questions
To comprehend	To listen with your heart	To tell them how you feel
To get the meaning		To ask for clarification
To see it from their point of view		Make eye contact
To focus		Silence
To think about what they are saying		Nod
To know what they mean		To help
To concentrate		To (not) problem solve
To process what they say		To listen to feelings
To consider		To show interest
To interpret		To support
Observe nonverbal cues		To show compassion
To evaluate		To show concern
To not judge		
To assimilate		

As we interact with others we may not be able to know whether these cognitive processes are indeed occurring. Consequently, the behavioral processes associated with listening have become an area of investigation for communication scholars. Thomas and Levine (1994), for example, noted short verbalizations known as **backchannels,** such as "uh huh" and "ummm," as well a range of nonverbal behaviors that are associated with people who are listening actively. Such cues include nodding, smiling, and posture adjustment. Pasupathi and colleagues (1999) likewise view listening as a behavioral response to what another is saying, which may involve actions such as emotional facial expressions and forward lean. In Halone and Pecchioni's model (2001) the behaviors included verbal cues such as advice-giving, nonverbal cues like making eye contact, and interactive cues such as helping or showing interest. All of these cues show attentiveness to the other person, an important part of many successful interpersonal interactions. Indeed, if you think about what makes someone a "good listener," it is likely that your judgment is based at least somewhat on how that person acts.

Finally, though not as often articulated, Halone and Pecchioni (2001) also argue that listening involves affective processes (also see Coakley et al., 1996). In particular, their participants noted four primary affective or emotional responses that relational listeners experience. These processes are as follows: to sympathize, to empathize, to care, and to listen to your heart. Each of these processes reflects internal states that may well emerge in listeners' behaviors.

With all this in mind, perhaps the best definitions of listening are those that incorporate what is going on in people's minds, in their emotions, *and* in their behavior when listening. These **definitions of listening** (such as "how individuals perceive, interpret, evaluate, and respond to oral messages," Kirtley & Honeycutt, 1996, p. 174, and "listening is where the 'rubber' of perception meets the 'road' of communication," Stewart & Logan, 1998, p. 166) help show the way thoughts, feelings, and behaviors work together as part of what is involved when people listen — or do not listen — to one another. Listening also involves some level of activity or choice on the part of the listener to perform the needed cognitive and behavioral processes involved. Thus, listening is not just hearing: It involves choice-making and motivation on the part of the listener to be a part of the communicative interaction (Brownell, 1985).

CONTEXTS OF LISTENING

Despite recognition of its importance and its complex nature, listening remains a relatively under-investigated area of study in interpersonal communication. There are, however, particular interpersonal contexts in which listening processes have received greater attention. These contexts include listening and how it occurs in marriage, work, medical interactions, and education. Looking at some of the research in these contexts also reveals further the ways in which people define and think about what listening involves.

Marriage

Much of the research that has been done in the context of marriage (or other intimate relationships) reflects a belief that listening can be done poorly and that poor listening habits are likely to have adverse effects on relationships. The idea that poor listening may have adverse effects on relationships has been referred to as a **"deficit" model** of listening. In 1990, for example, Vangelisti (cited in Beatty & Dobos, 1993) surveyed marriage counselors and found that a common problem that the counselors perceived for unhappy couples was the inability or unwillingness of husbands and wives to take the other's perspective when listening. Indeed, much of the literature on listening in the context of intimate couples has to do with the tie between satisfaction (happiness or unhappiness) with the relationship and perception of listening ability and/or motivation.

Beatty and Dobos make the argument that one reason some couples may have listening problems can be traced to the husbands'/boyfriends' relationship with their fathers. They propose that these males received disconfirming messages from their fathers as they were growing up. As a result, some of these males may believe that their fathers did not respect them and/or that their fathers showed a lack of interest in them. These men may end up with a listening style that is similarly disconfirming. That is, they do other things while listening, or they forget what their wives/girlfriends have said. These disconfirmation behaviors tend to make the wives/girlfriends feel more uncomfortable with interactions with their partners than they might otherwise feel. Importantly, such discomfort may in turn make the women not want to interact with their partners, resulting in a potential negative cycle.

Both the way people listen and the effects of listening habits may change over the course of a relationship. Although some studies find few differences between newly married and long married couples, others have shown differences. Gould and Dixson (cited in Pasupathi et al., 1999), for instance, found that recently married couples used more vocal backchannels than did longer married couples. While it is easy to think that the longer married couples were not listening as well, Pasupathi et al. (1999) noted the same relationship (less "generic listening behavior" such as backchannels) only for those older couples that reported being happily married. The authors argue that the results of their study "[reflect] differing levels of need for the listener to demonstrate comprehension and attention, based on increased familiarity with the . . . topic in long-married couples" (p. 185).

The research on listening within the marital context shows that poor listening may be tied to potential marital problems. In some ways, good listening is thought of as a commodity, with more of it occurring within and leading to satisfied relationships. This literature also suggests, however, that what may be defined as "good" may change over the lifetime of a relationship.

Organizations

Within the organizational context, listening is typically thought of and investigated as a skill. Indeed, Seibert (1990), in a review of twenty-five different studies "seeking to identify the most frequently necessary employment skills" (p. 121), noted that listening skill or ability was mentioned most often. Along with the tendency to identify listening as an important organizational skill, however, Seibert noted a clear concern that people in organizations do not listen well enough, despite the important perceived role that listening has in a person's success in the organization.

Quite a lot of research points toward the belief that listening is important in organizations. For example, Goby and Lewis (2000) investigated the importance of listening skills for 125 people in Singapore's insurance industry. The authors found that, across organizational positions (managers, agents, policyholders, nonpolicyholders), listening skills were ranked as more important than other communicative abilities (such as writing and speaking). Further, of the five elements of listening represented in their survey (focus, comprehension, nonverbal cues/body language, objectivity, and manners), focus — a cognitive process — and manners — a behavioral process — were perceived as the most important to good listening. The concern that listening is an important (and underdeveloped) skill in business contexts has led to tremendous efforts within and across organizations to heighten people's ability to listen through workshops and models of good listening (Wolvin & Coakley, 1991).

Interestingly, research evidence has only recently been provided to show (1) the actual detriments of poor listening in organizations (or the benefits of good listening) and (2) that training works to improve people's performance in their organizations. Haas and Arnold (1995) found support for the benefits of good listening or at least perceived listening ability. People perceived to be better listeners were rated more highly by their co-workers, which is one measure of success, than those perceived to be poor listeners. Brownell (1990) learned that subordinates who thought their managers were good listeners were also more satisfied in their jobs and with their managers.

Brownell also found that subordinates whose managers were taking courses on listening judged them to be better listeners than those whose managers were not enrolled in the courses. More notably, Papa (1989) provided evidence for the actual effects of listening training in his investigation of the relationship between listening, a measure of communicator competence, and employees' ability to perform well with new computer technologies. His experiment showed that those insurance claims adjustors who received "communicator competence training" and were trained to be good listeners were much more productive in their use of the new technologies than those who did not get training. Together, these studies provide some support for the effort to increase listening ability in organizational contexts.

Medical Contexts

People in the medical professions are also concerned about the effects of listening skills. In fact, Thompson (1994) found that listening was on every list of valuable skills for health care providers. Most commonly, work on listening in this context has focused on the affective or emotional responses patients may have when a medical professional, particularly a doctor, appears to listen well or poorly. Mechanic and Meyer (2000) found that patients were more likely to trust their physicians when they also perceived that the doctors showed "interpersonal competence." Such competence was defined as the degree to which the physicians cared and had compassion for their patients. Listening was the central focus in the patients' assessments of such competence. As in the case within organizations, patients also saw listening as a learnable skill and not just a reflection of the physician's personality.

The medical context, however, may sometimes provide a challenge for the health care provider who wishes to be perceived as being a good listener. Ruusuvuori (2001) noted that the doctors' necessary "shift of focus from interaction with the patient toward reading or writing the medical records is received as problematic. It is suggested that disengaging from interaction and engaging in studying the medical records may leave the patient puzzled about whether the doctor is listening or not"

Research shows that listening was the central focus in patients' assessment of health care providers' interpersonal competence.

© Susie Fitzhugh

(p. 1093). Indeed, doctors typically have other goals that they are pursuing in addition to listening to their patients, and a potential problem to listening well (or being perceived as listening well) is the pursuit of other interaction goals.

Bethea and Travis (2000) recently argued that health care providers might also miss opportunities for listening in information interviews with patients. Following in-depth analyses of twenty-three interviews between care providers and elderly patients, the researchers noted that certain behaviors provide information that the patient has more to say. It is often up to the health care provider to notice or "listen to" these cues and probe the patient for further information. Bethea and Travis noted that "[s]uch conversational cues as changes in vocalics or pitch, laughter, stuttering, pausing, use of metaphorical language, humor, self-disclosure, narratives, and anecdotes may indicate patient fears, hopes, goals, and other factors that aid caregivers in diagnoses. Heath care professionals and researchers who are able to recognize and listen to such patient cues . . . will likely gain valuable information that could easily be lost" (p. 73). This claim is supported by Wolff, Marsnik, Tacey, and Nichols (1983), who noted that people who have undergone a difficult medical procedure, a mastectomy in their example, often show verbal and nonverbal glimpses of their emotional state. But the patients may only discuss their feelings if the health care provider "picks up on" or listens to the behavior and asks about its source.

Besides the desire to be listened to, patients also are involved in listening themselves. Many of the studies on doctor-patient communication revolve around concerns with getting patients to comply with "doctors' orders." According to Ray and Bostrom (1990), patient recall of a doctor's prognosis and treatment recommendations may be as low as 37% of what the doctor actually communicated. Recall, a cognitive component of listening, may be lessened further with extensive medical jargon, severity of illness, and sex of the doctor (males tend to be listened to more than females, although in Ray and Bostrom's study, male patients remembered the least from male doctors).

Like the other contexts we reviewed, studying listening in the medical context helps show the potential consequences of good and bad listening. It also, however, highlights the importance of contextual needs to pursue other goals (like physical examinations and record writing) and shows how all interactants may play the role of listener.

Education

Coakley and Wolvin (1991) also provide a useful discussion for seeing how all of the "players" in the education context have, at least at times, the role of listener.

> Into the educational environment come the three major participants: the teacher, the student, and the parent. . . . Each of the three participants comes with a primary purpose [goal]: [T]he teacher comes primarily to teach, the student comes primarily to learn; and the parent comes primarily to determine the learning success of the student. . . . The participants attempt to accomplish their purpose by means of communication — through speaking, listening, reading, writing, and engaging in nonverbal cues. But, of all the forms for verbal and nonverbal communication, the communication form that is most basic, most utilized, and most central to the student's learning success at all levels is *listening*. (p. 162)

Despite the recognition of the importance of listening for all people in the educational context, students are particularly likely to spend a great deal of their time listening (Barker, Edwards, Gaines, Gladney, & Holley, 1980) and have been the focus of most of the listening research done within the educational context. One of the most important findings from this research is that listening poorly may be linked more forcefully to failing a class than either reading skills or general academic aptitude (Conaway, 1982). Fortunately, students who learn and choose to listen well can make up in some ways for mental or physical limitations, like hearing impairments, that they may have (Legg, 1971).

Within the educational context, listening is in some ways thought of as a performance. That is, listening may be something that can be measured, learned, and even "graded." Rubin and Hampton (1998) make the argument that listening performance ought to be encouraged as part of the K–12 curriculum and can be measured validly and authentically to assess how well students listen. The researchers state that students can keep a portfolio of their communicative performance, including notes taken while listening to a lecture, drawings that capture something learned while watching a film, and other artifacts of listening. Rubin and Hampton's suggestion not only shows the importance of listening across a range of activities, but it also enlarges the ways in which we typically think about reflections of listening well.

DIALOGUE/LISTENING AS DYADIC

Our discussion of some of the contexts in which listening occurs shows that, in all cases, every member of an interaction (husband/wife, employee/employer, doctor/patient, teacher/student/parent) plays the role of listener. In Chapter 1 we also made a related claim about interpersonal communication: It involves multiple people simultaneously engaged in pursuing their goals. This becomes particularly clear when we talk about listening. It is somewhat erroneous, although we have done so repeatedly in this chapter, to refer to people as speakers *or* as listeners. In most of our interpersonal interactions, we are engaged in both speaking *and* listening. Even when listening is our primary interpersonal activity, we are likely to be engaged actively in the outcome of the interaction, as in the medical interviews we mentioned earlier.

But this view of "involved listeners" is not usually how listening is discussed. According to Bavelas, Coates, and Johnson (2000), "listeners are [often] considered nonexistent or irrelevant" (p. 941) in work on interpersonal communication processes. At best, many people think of the listener or message receiver as a speaker-in-waiting (i.e., a person who is there but important only in that he or she will be involved as the speaker as soon as it is his or her "turn") and not as an active participant in the outcome of the interaction. Even the term *listener backchannel*, introduced earlier in this chapter, was created *in relation to the speaker* who "owns the *main* channel" in conversation (Bavelas et al., 2000, p. 942, emphasis added).

Discussions on interpersonal communication as **dialogue** (rather than monologue) or collaboration help to show the important role that the listener plays in conversations (see Stewart & Zediker, 2000, for an excellent review of dialogue research). According to Bavelas at al. (2000) referring to work by Clark (1996), "dialogue is a joint activity. The actions that make up dialogue are not engaged in independently but rather require constant coordination; dialogue is a duet and not two solos" (p. 942). A typical interpersonal interaction may have one person as the primary speaker, a person seeking social support or advice, or one who wants to tell the other about something that happened, for example. The other interactant, the listener, though, uses nonverbal cues or language that may shape what the other person's talk looks like.

For example, Manusov and Trees (in press) investigated the role that listeners may play in accounting (accounting will be discussed more fully in Chapter 8; for now, though, accounting can be defined as the ways in which people offer explanations to others for things, especially negative things, that have happened). In taped interactions between pairs of friends or of strangers, one person, the listener, had the goal

---

STUDENT AS OBSERVER: LISTENING ON REALITY TV

All of the "reality-based" television shows available for viewing right now give us ample evidence of the ways in which listeners shape the conversation. Choose an episode of any one talk or reality-based show and tape it (use the tape only for this purpose and then erase it). Choose those parts of the tape that include a conversation between people and do the following:

1. Identify the primary speaker and the listeners for that part of the episode.
2. Watch and listen to the listeners' behaviors.
3. Observe any ways in which the speaker appears to alter his or her behavior because of what the listeners are doing.
4. In what ways do these observations verify or change your view of what is involved in the listening process?

---

of getting the other person to offer an account. The speakers' account types (such as excuses, justifications, and apologies) were coded as were the nonverbal behaviors used by the speaker. The authors found that several sets of vocalic and facial cues appeared to lead the speakers to offer certain forms of accounts. For example, when any of a range of negative meanings such as negative affect/emotion, confusion, uncertainty, disagreement, or disbelief were expressed on the face or in the vocal qualities of the listener, people were most likely to use account forms such as justifications and external excuses. These account forms can be seen as aggravating responses and may mirror the tone set by the nonverbal cues. In cases when greater certainty was expressed by the listener, concessions were a common form of account. The positive nature of the concessions also seems to follow from the positive nature of the listeners' nonverbal behaviors. These observations show clearly how the nonverbal cues used by listeners as they evoked an explanation from their conversational partner helped influence the use of certain types of verbal explanations by the speaker.

In addition to listeners' nonverbal cues affecting the speakers' talk, the listeners' own talk is also typically important for the development of a conversation. Listeners ask brief questions, show agreement or disagreement verbally, provide encouragement to keep talking, and indicate confusion or understanding through their own brief utterances. Bavelas et al. (2000) argue that listener talk, including verbal and nonverbal cues, tends to take one of two forms: generic (backchannels or other cues that show one is listening generally) and specific (utterances that are "tightly connected to what the narrator is saying at the moment," p. 943). Specific responses are important because they allow listeners to become "co-narrators who illustrate or add to the story" (p. 944).

A particularly good example of the ways in which listeners shape conversation was discussed by Mandelbaum (1989). In an example of a group of friends, where one is telling a potentially embarrassing story to another member in the group, Mandelbaum helps show that listeners "have resources with which they may actually initiate and work through with the teller [speaker] a change in the nature of a storytelling, while the storytelling is in progress" (p. 114). In one particular instance, one of the friends, Vicki, starts to tell a story about Shawn, who is also a listener in the group. It begins to be clear from her conversation that Vicki plans to make Shawn the "butt" of her story. At this point, Matthew, one of the listeners, speaks briefly in such a way that Shawn is rescued from being embarrassed in the telling. Just as Vicki is about to talk more about what Shawn did, Matthew asks about a related issue ("Was it a whole lobster?") that takes the focus off of Shawn's potentially embarrassing action. With additional follow-up questions that direct the story to be about the lobster rather than Shawn, Matthew successfully changes the direction of the conversation and shows the dialogic or collaborative nature of talk/listening.

IMPORTANT INTERPERSONAL COMMUNICATION PROCESSES ASSOCIATED WITH LISTENING

The view of listening as part of a larger dialogue helps reveal more about the embedded nature of listening in interpersonal communication. Listening is also interconnected with a range of other important processes involved in our pursuit of interpersonal goals. Think, for example, of why you tend to like good listeners. Those people who have listened to you probably made you feel supported and understood. You likely also thought they were good communicators or they had "communication competence." To fully understand listening and its role in interpersonal communication, it makes sense that we look briefly at how listening processes tie into other goals and outcomes. The primary areas that have been identified as listening-related are social support, empathy, and perceptions of competence.

Social Support

From Thomas and Levine's (1994) study, we saw that the behaviors listeners enact (head nods, gaze at speaker) are important aids to listening well. These cues, primarily nonverbal behaviors, are also important to speakers, as they show that the other is (or appears to be) paying attention to what a speaker is saying and provide information for the speaker.

One of the reasons speakers find listeners' behaviors to be important in interpersonal interactions is that certain listener cues can provide **social support** for the speakers. According to Trees (2000), "social support refers to verbal and nonverbal cues communicating affirmation, caring, and/or assistance to an individual dealing with a problem or stressful event" (p. 240). Often our goal in seeking out and talking to another person is to receive support from him or her. We are likely to feel more supported when our listener acts in ways that signal that he or she is sensitive to what we are discussing.

In an investigation of mothers talking to and providing support for their adult children, Trees found a number of cues that the mothers (listeners) did to help their children feel particularly supported. Vocal warmth and interest, physical attentiveness like sitting forward, and moving "in sync" with their children were cues that were tied to higher levels of perceived supportiveness. More notably, Trees found that listening cues, defined broadly, were seen as particularly appropriate in support situations, and the increase in such "appropriate behaviors" also led to an increase in children's perceptions of being supported by their mothers. Thus, one of the outcomes of others' listening behaviors may be feeling the support we may desire in certain interactions.

Support doesn't just occur with people whom we know well. Another study by Passman and Gangestad (2001) investigated the ways in which the listening behaviors of athletic trainers affected injured athletes' perception of the trainers' social support. Based on actual interactions between trainers and athletes, the researchers found that trainers who "responded well" and showed that they were listening were perceived as more supportive than those who seemed more distracted. Interestingly, however, trainers tended to think of themselves as less skilled listeners than the athletes judged them to be.

Empathy

When we seek out others to listen to us, we often do so because we want to feel that our needs and concerns are understood. As Weaver and Kirtley (1995) note, "[I]t has long been argued that an effective listener must be appreciative of, discriminative toward, and responsive to the thoughts, feelings, and emotions of others. . . . The ability to respond to others empathically, in particular, has been proposed as the crucial emotive dimension of effective communication . . . in general, and listening . . . in particular" (p. 131). In one of the effective listening styles discussed in the final section of this chapter, empathic listening is considered most likely to be successful (but for some important arguments about the assumptions of empathic listening, see Arnett & Nakagawa, 1983; Stewart, 1983).

Like listening, **empathy** is a multidimensional process. Richendoller and Weaver (1994) identified three interrelated aspects of being empathic: responding empathically, taking the other's perspective, and responding sympathetically. Doing any of these functions or goals requires listening to others. Table 3.2 provides the questionnaire used to assess people's empathy styles.

People may be more or less inclined toward being empathic by virtue of how they prefer to listen. Those people who are more people-oriented listeners and are concerned internally with others' feelings and welfare appear, not surprisingly, more concerned externally with others. Such people are more likely to respond

Table 3.2

EMPATHY MEASURE

Use the following scale to answer each of the items below: never, 0; infrequently, 1; sometimes, 2; frequently, 3; always, 4.

1. I don't get upset just because a friend is acting upset. (ER)
2. Before criticizing someone, I try to imagine how I would feel if I were in their place. (PT)
3. I am the type of person who is concerned when others are unhappy. (SR)
4. When I see someone being treated unfairly, I sometimes don't feel very much pity for them. (SR)*
5. I cannot continue to feel okay if people around me are depressed. (ER)
6. I become nervous if others around me seem nervous. (ER)
7. I sometimes try to understand how people feel by looking at things from their perspective. (PT)
8. The people around me have a great influence on my moods. (ER)
9. I sometimes don't feel very sorry for people when they are having problems. (SR)*
10. When someone else is upset, I almost always try to console them. (SR)
11. I sometimes find it difficult to see things from the other person's perspective. (PT)*
12. I am able to remain calm, even though those around me worry. (ER)*
13. I try to look at everybody's side of a disagreement before I make a decision. (PT)
14. When I'm upset at someone, I usually try to "put myself in his or her shoes" for a while. (PT)
15. Other people's misfortunes do not usually disturb me a great deal. (SR)*
16. I tend to get emotionally involved with a friend's problems. (SR)
17. When I see someone who badly needs help in an emergency, I go to pieces. (ER)
18. I often have tender, concerned feelings for people less fortunate than me. (SR)
19. Hearing about someone else's misfortune makes me feel sad. (SR)
20. When I see someone get hurt, I tend to remain calm. (ER)*

Scoring: On each of the above items that is starred (*), reverse the rating you used. So, if you scored a 0, change this to a 4. Cross out or discard your old score. If you scored a 3, change it to a 1, etc. Next, add up your total score for each of three scales: Sympathetic Responsiveness (SR), Emotional Responsiveness (ER), and Perspective-Taking (PT). The range of scores possible for the SR empathy style scale is 0 (not descriptive of your empathy style) to 32 (very descriptive of your empathy style). The range for the ER style is 0 (not descriptive of you) to 28 (very descriptive of you). The range for the PT style is 0 (not descriptive) to 20 (very descriptive). Do you see one style that is more predominant for you? Are you high — or low — on all of the measures?

Source: Weaver & Kirtley, 1995, pp. 131–140.

sympathetically than are those with other listening styles. Interestingly, though, people-oriented listeners are not necessarily likely to respond *empathically* (Weaver & Kirtley, 1995). Their concern with offering assistance and looking sympathetic may in fact make them *less* likely to really understand or be empathic and react to the other's emotions.

In addition to people being more or less empathic when listening, certain listening responses may be seen as more or less empathic. In their work, Bavelas and her colleagues (Bavelas, Black, Lemery, & Mullett, 1986; Bavelas & Chovil, 1997) identified a particular kind of listener reaction that they labeled **motor mimicry.** Motor mimicry includes certain facial or other movements that reflect that the listener understands what the speaker is feeling. So, for example, if a friend is talking to you about a ski accident she was in, and you make a face that reflects how painful the accident must have felt, you would be engaged in motor mimicry. According to Bavelas and her colleagues, motor mimicry counts as a specific listener response (as opposed to a generic one, as we discussed earlier) reflecting that the listener understands or empathizes with the speaker.

Competence

When somebody acts appropriately for a particular context, as in the Trees' study discussed earlier, we often also judge that other person as interpersonally competent (see Chapter 1 and Part 5 for more detailed discussions of the importance of **competence** in pursuing interpersonal goals). Indeed, in his study on communicator competence and employee performance, Papa (1989) listed listening as one of three interpersonal competence skills, along with message clarity and interpersonal skills. For Haas and Arnold (1995), "listening ability, or the perception of effective listening, is inextricably linked to effective individual performance in organizations" (p. 124). In fact, in their study of employees at a newspaper company, these researchers showed that listening behavior was responsible for about 33% of the competence judgments the employees made about their fellow workers.

Listening is not only linked to perceptions of competence. People may indeed *be* more or less competent listeners. Clark (1989) found that listening comprehension, as one form of competence, was affected by other communicator characteristics. Clark noted that students' willingness to communicate and communication apprehension scores helped predict how well people listened, with less willing and more apprehensive communicators less likely to be competent listeners. Interestingly, those who were more communicatively apprehensive were better listeners when "good listening" was assessed based on their ability to understand the emotional content of messages (delivered largely through nonverbal, vocalic cues such as tone and pitch) rather than to understand the informational content of the verbal message (comprehension). Clearly, listening is often an important part of our judgments that others are — or are not — competent communicators.

LISTENING STYLES

It is clear from our discussion that we all listen differently from one another in our interactions and that such differences may have effects on how well we achieve our interpersonal goals. Research shows that, despite our ability to listen in different ways in different situations, we are more likely to form a preference for a particular **listening style.** Weaver and Kirtley (1995) identified four common listening styles or preferences: people, action, content, and time-oriented. Weaver and Kirtley refer to the people style as one that emphasizes concern for others' feelings. Action-style listeners prefer others to speak concisely and with few errors and may become frustrated with disorganized presentations. A content preference includes an interest in hearing complex information that needs to be analyzed carefully before responding. A time-oriented style listener tends to like quick interchanges with others. Each of these preferences may be associated with different outcomes (e.g., relational satisfaction) and personality types (e.g., neuroticism).

As noted, we each tend to have a style of listening that we use most frequently as our "default" mode of listening. Kiewitz, Weaver, Brosius, and Wiemann (1997) were interested in whether cultures also have preferred listening styles. In their survey of 1,821 students from the United States, Germany, and Israel, they found students from the United States were more likely than the other two groups to have a preference for the people style of listening or for the time-oriented listening style. That is, the U.S. group showed particular concern with the social aspects of interaction and how much time was devoted to analysis. German students were more likely than Americans or Israelis to prefer the action listening style. According to Kiewitz and colleagues, "Germans approach communication with a very active, inquisitive, and direct style that focuses primarily on rhetorical considerations to arbitrate or negotiate interpersonal interactions" (p. 239). Israelis, on the other hand, preferred the content style more than did the other two groups, with a greater tendency to deliberate and analyze information.

EFFECTIVE LISTENING

It is clear that, for many of us, listening is synonymous with effective listening. **Effective listening** can enhance communication and increase the likelihood of achieving interpersonal goals by raising our sensitivity to others' wants and needs, by giving us insight into problems and solutions, and by garnering feedback regarding behaviors. In addition, good listening can provide some access to other people's thoughts and feelings, allowing us to understand them better and connect with them. Further, effective listening may influence others' views of us, because people tend to like us better when we listen to them.

One of the primary aims of this chapter is to show the complexity involved in listening processes. Despite the many influences on listening, however, it is still, as noted earlier, thought of as a skill in many contexts. The assumption with skills is that they can be taught; thus a great deal of work has gone into creating courses and categories of effective listening. This literature reflects at least three kinds of approaches or strategies that may be effective, although they appear to be more or less effective in particular contexts: empathic, deliberative, and active listening.

Empathic listening involves associating with the speaker's cognitions and emotions and trying to interpret the message "as if" you were the speaker (Stiff, Dillard, Somera, Kim, & Sleight, 1988). Empathic listening promotes maximal understanding of communication from the speaker's perspective. According to McComb and Jablin (1984), several behaviors are typically associated with empathic listening: using silence as a response and not interrupting, asking probing questions, providing verbal encouragement, restating the other's message, and seeking clarification. Dansereau and Markham (1987) found that empathic listening is one of the behaviors that people view as part of what makes someone a good supervisor.

Deliberative listening entails evaluating the message's logic and support according to one's own position. Deliberative listening increases interpretation of a message from the listener's own perspective. Behaviors associated with deliberative listening include a predisposition to criticize, making internal summaries during a message, evaluating the message, and agreeing or disagreeing with the speaker during and following the message (Kelly, 1972). Deliberative listening is thought to be crucial in discussions requiring advocacy and critical analysis.

Active listening involves providing feedback to help the speaker clarify his or her message (Cooper, 1995; Johnson, 1996). Feedback can take many forms, including such behaviors as advising and evaluating, analyzing and interpreting, reassuring and supporting, questioning and probing, and paraphrasing and understanding. These

Deliberative listening occurs when listeners evaluate a speaker's message in terms of its own logic, regardless of whether they agree with it or not. Journalists practice deliberative listening when listening to politicians.

Ron Edmonds/AP/Wide World Photos

behaviors do not appear to be those associated with listening (except when conversation is defined dialogically), but they do highlight the interactive nature of all communication. These behaviors may be particularly useful when one's goal is to help or support someone else and are often a part of marital therapy.

Although, as noted earlier, we do tend to have preferred listening styles, we can choose from a larger repertoire of possibilities. The selection of an effective listening strategy likely depends on the goal that is most salient to the listener and/or the speaker during the conversation, and "[r]esearchers have discovered that the best listeners modify their listening behavior to meet the constraints of given situational contexts" (Kirtley & Honeycutt, 1996, p. 175). It is also possible to use a combination of listening approaches. For example, you can first listen for interpretation from the other speaker's perspective so that you can understand the message from that viewpoint; to do so, you can ask him or her questions or paraphrase the speaker's ideas; then you can respond from your own perspective.

Despite these potentially effective listening styles, people can act in a number of ways that make them less effective listeners or, at least, make them seem like poor listeners. McComb and Jablin (1984), for instance, looked at the behaviors used by interviewers and related them to how the behaviors were judged by their interviewees. The strongest negative influence was the number of interruptions used by the listener. Interruptions are also likely to affect the degree to which physicians are able to gain necessary information in conversations with patients (Nyquist, 1996). Golen (1990), in a survey of business college students, also found six common "listening hindrance factors." The most notable of these involved people listening mainly for details or facts (and ignoring other important social information), becoming distracted by environmental noises, and thinking about other things/daydreaming.

Fortunately, researchers have also noted several methods for becoming a more effective listener. These are listed in Table 3.3. Most of us can use these to help us do a better job at this important interpersonal communication task.

One final idea that may help us improve, or at least help us understand, listening comes from Halone and Pecchioni (2001). In their study of 246 relational partners who were asked what was involved in listening, the researchers learned that people appear to see listening as occurring at several different times across an interactional context. More specifically, they note that listening — or its related processes — can occur prior to an interaction, during an interaction, and after an interaction. They note that listeners can do several things prior to an interaction occurring that can make them better listeners. These pre-interaction processes (or those things that people can "bring with them" into a conversation) include being open-minded, being there for another, sitting down, and being willing. The processes that good listeners can do during the interaction involve not interrupting, offering feedback, sharing, participating, and attending to nonverbal cues. Finally, after or post-interaction processes are two-fold: remembering the conversation and acting on it. For Halone and Pecchioni's participants, these listening behaviors are linked with positive relational outcomes.

Table 3.3
IDEAS FOR IMPROVING LISTENING SKILLS

1. Stop talking as necessary.
2. Listen for ideas.
3. Ask questions.
4. Listen for unexpected situations.
5. Avoid arguing until you comprehend the other person's points.
6. Avoid distractions.
7. Remove physical barriers to listening.
8. Focus on the speaker's main idea.
9. Listen for intent as well as content.
10. Give the other person a full hearing.
11. Try to overcome your emotional reactions to words.
12. Concentrate on the other person as a human being.

Source: Adapted from Cooper (1995) and Gross & O'Hair (1988).

CHAPTER SUMMARY

The goal of this chapter is to show what is involved in listening during interpersonal interaction. Listening is composed of both cognitive and behavioral elements and can best be seen as part of an ongoing dialogue between interactants. Indeed, listeners are likely to shape the interaction in a number of important ways.

Listening is related to other vital constructs in interpersonal communication: social support, empathy, and competence. The degree to which they work effectively in interactions depends on our view of what counts as good listening. Research supports several models of good or effective listening, but the effectiveness of these models appears to be dependent on the nature and goals of the interaction. Finally, listening processes may also occur prior to and after an interaction takes place.

KEY TERMS

active listening, p. 67
backchannels, p. 54
competence, p. 65
deficit model, p. 55
definitions of listening, p. 55
deliberative listening, p. 67
dialogue, p. 60

effective listening, p. 67
empathic listening, p. 67
empathy, p. 63
listening style, p. 66
motor mimicry, p. 65
relational listening, p. 53
social support, p. 62

EXERCISES FOR FURTHER DISCUSSION

1. Next time you are in class, look around at other students.
   a. Do they seem to be listening?
   b. What are the behaviors that you used to decide if they were or were not listening?
   c. Can people actually be listening (cognitively) without appearing (behaviorally) to listen?
2. Pay attention to a time when you are not listening to someone else.
   a. Change your behavior to make it appear that you are listening.
   b. Did the change in behavior also affect the degree to which you paid attention to what the other person was saying?

3. Choose a listening style. The next time a friend calls, try to use that style carefully.
   a. What type of effects do you think it had on your ability to understand what your friend was saying?
   b. Why was it easy or difficult to perform?
   c. How do you think it affected the way your friend communicated with you?
4. Think about why we are not always very good listeners. What keeps us from using some of the suggestions for improved listening?
5. What is your view of what makes someone a good listener?
   a. How many of the elements in your description are cognitive (such as "a good listener remembers what I tell him/her") and how many are behavioral (for example, "a good listener stops doing other things when I am talking to him or her")?
   b. Does your definition of listening change when you explore the potential complexities of the processes involved in listening?

SUGGESTED READING

▼

DEFINITIONS AND MODELS OF LISTENING

Bostrom, R. N. (1990). *Listening behavior: Measurement and application.* New York: Guilford.

Conaway, M. S. (1982). Listening: Learning tool and retention agent. In A. S. Algier & K. W. Algier (Eds.), *Improving reading and study skills* (pp. 51–63). San Francisco: Jossey-Bass.

Halone, K. K., & Pecchioni, L. L. (2001). Relational listening: A grounded theoretical model. *Communication Reports, 14*, 59–71.

Purdy, M. (1991). What is listening? In D. Borisoff & M. Purdy (Eds.), *Listening in everyday life: A personal and professional approach* (pp. 3–19). Lanham, MD: University Press of America.

RELATIONAL CONTEXTS OF LISTENING

Cooper, P. (1995). *Communication for the classroom teacher* (5th ed.). Scottsdale, AZ: Gorsuch Scarisbrick.

Goby, V. P., & Lewis, J. H. (2000). The key role of listening in business: A study of the Singapore insurance industry. *Business Communication Quarterly, 63*, 41–50.

Ray, E. B., & Bostrom, R. N. (1990). Listening to medical messages: The relationship of physician gender, patient gender, and seriousness of illness on short- and long-term recall. In R. N. Bostrom (Ed.), *Listening behavior: Measurement and application* (pp. 128–143). New York: Guilford.

Richendoller, N. R., & Weaver, J. B. (1994). Exploring the links between personality and empathic response style. *Personality and Individual Differences, 17,* 303–311.

LISTENING AS DIALOGUE

Bavelas, J. B., Coates, L., & Johnson, T. (2000). Listeners as co-narrators. *Journal of Personality and Social Psychology, 79,* 941–952.
Mandelbaum, J. (1989). Interpersonal activities in conversational storytelling. *Western Journal of Speech Communication, 53,* 114–126.

INTERPERSONAL PROCESSES ASSOCIATED WITH LISTENING

Clark, A. J. (1996). Communication confidence and listening competence: An investigation of the relationships of willingness to communicate, communication apprehension, and receiver apprehension to comprehension of content and emotional meaning in spoken messages. *Communication Education, 38,* 237–248.
Stewart, J. (1983). Interpretive listening: An alternative to empathy. *Communication Education, 32,* 379–391.
Trees, A. R. (2000). Nonverbal communication and the support process: Interactional sensitivity in interactions between mothers and young adult children. *Communication Monographs, 67,* 239–261.

LISTENING STYLES

Kirtley, M. D., & Honeycutt, J. M. (1996). Listening styles and their correspondence with second guessing. *Communication Research Reports, 13,* 174–182.

EFFECTIVE LISTENING

Brownell, J. (1985). A model for listening instruction: Management applications. *The Bulletin of the Association for Business Communication, 57,* 39–44.
Golen, S. (1990). A factor analysis of barriers to effective listening. *The Journal of Business Communication, 27,* 25–37.

REFERENCE LIST

▼

Arnett, R., & Nakagawa, G. (1983). The assumptive roots of empathic listening: A critique. *Communication Education, 32,* 368–378.
Barker, L., Edwards, R., Gaines, C., Gladney, K., & Holley, F. (1980). An investigation of proportional time spent in various communication activities by college students. *Journal of Applied Communication Research, 8,* 101–110.
Bavelas, J. B., Black, A., Lemery, C. R., & Mullett, J. (1986). "I *show* how you feel": Motor mimicry as a communicative act. *Journal of Personality and Social Psychology, 50,* 322–329.

Bavelas, J. B., & Chovil, N. (1997). Faces in dialogue. In J. A. Russell & J. M. Fernandez-Dols (Eds.), *The psychology of facial expression* (pp. 334–346). New York: Cambridge University Press.

Bavelas, J. B., Coates, L., & Johnson, T. (2000). Listeners as co-narrators. *Journal of Personality and Social Psychology, 79,* 941–952.

Beatty, M. J., & Dobos, J. A. (1993). Mediated effects of adult males' perceived confirmation from father on relational partners' communication apprehension. *The Southern Communication Journal, 58,* 207–215.

Bethea, L. S., & Travis, S. S. (2000). The research interview: Listening for the communicative signals of humor, narrative, and self-disclosure in the caregiver–care-recipient interview. *The Gerontologist,* Oct. 15, 73.

Bostrom, R. N. (1990). *Listening behavior: Measurement and application.* New York: Guilford.

Bostrom, R., & Waldhart, E. (1988). Memory models and the measurement of listening. *Communication Education, 37,* 1–18.

Brownell, J. (1985). A model for listening instruction: Management applications. *The Bulletin of the Association for Business Communication, 57,* 39–44.

Brownell, J. (1990). Perceptions of effective listeners: A management study. *The Journal of Business Communication, 27,* 401–416.

Clark, A. J. (1989). Communication confidence and listening competence: An investigation of the relationships of willingness to communicate, communication apprehension, and receiver apprehension to comprehension of content and emotional meaning in spoken messages. *Communication Education, 38,* 237–248.

Coakley, C. G., Halone, K. K., & Wolvin, A. D. (1996). Perceptions of listening ability across the life-span: Implications for understanding listening competence. *International Journal of Listening, 10,* 21–48.

Coakley, C., & Wolvin, A. (1991). Listening in the educational environment. In D. Borisoff & M. Purdy (Eds.), *Listening in everyday life: A personal and professional approach* (pp. 161–200). Lanham, MD: University Press of America.

Conaway, M. S. (1982). Listening: Learning tool and retention agent. In A. S. Algier & K. W. Algier (Eds.), *Improving reading and study skills* (pp. 51–63). San Francisco: Jossey-Bass.

Cooper, P. (1995). *Communication for the classroom teacher* (5th ed.). Scottsdale, AZ: Gorsuch Scarisbrick.

Dansereau, F., & Markham, S. E. (1987). Superior-subordinate communication: Multiple levels of analysis. In F. M. Jablin, L. L. Putnam, K. H. Roberts, & L. W. Porter (Eds.), *Handbook of organizational communication: An interdisciplinary perspective* (pp. 343–388). Newbury Park, CA: Sage.

Goby, V. P., & Lewis, J. H. (2000). The key role of listening in business: A study of the Singapore insurance industry. *Business Communication Quarterly, 63,* 41–50.

Golen, S. (1990). A factor analysis of barriers to effective listening. *The Journal of Business Communication, 27,* 25–37.

Gross, B., & O'Hair, H. D. (1988). *Communicating in interpersonal relationships.* New York: Macmillan.

Haas, J. W., & Arnold, C. L. (1995). An examination of the role of listening in judgments of communication competence in co-workers. *The Journal of Business Communication, 32,* 123–140.

Halone, K. K., & Pecchioni, L. L. (2001). Relational listening: A grounded theoretical model. *Communication Reports, 14*, 59–71.

Hyde, R. B. (1994). Listening authentically: A Heideggerian perspective on interpersonal communication. In K. Carter & M. Presnell (Eds.), *Interpretive approaches to interpersonal communication* (pp. 179–195). Albany, NY: SUNY Press.

Johnson, D. (1996). Helpful listening and responding. In K. M. Galvin & P. Cooper (Eds.), *Making connections: Readings in relational communication* (pp. 91–97). Los Angeles: Roxbury.

Kelly, L. (1972). Empathic listening. In J. Stewart (Ed.), *Bridges not walls: A book of interpersonal communication* (pp. 222–227). Reading, MA: Addison-Wesley.

Kiewitz, C., Weaver, J. B., Brosius, II-B., & Wiemann, G. (1997). Cultural differences in listening style preferences: A comparison of young adults in Germany, Israel, and the United States. *International Journal of Public Opinion Research, 9*, 233–248.

Kirtley, M. D., & Honeycutt, J. M. (1996). Listening styles and their correspondence with second guessing. *Communication Research Reports, 13*, 174–182.

Legg, W. B. (1971). Listening, intelligence, and school achievement. In S. Duker (Ed.), *Listening: Readings II* (pp. 121–133). Metuchen, NJ: Scarecrow Press.

Mandelbaum, J. (1989). Interpersonal activities in conversational storytelling. *Western Journal of Speech Communication, 53*, 114–126.

Manusov, V., & Trees, A. R. (in press). "Are you kidding me?" The role of nonverbal behaviors in the verbal accounting process. *Journal of Communication.*

McComb, K. B., & Jablin, F. M. (1984). Verbal correlates of interviewer empathic listening and employment outcomes. *Communication Monographs, 51*, 353–371.

Mechanic, D., & Meyer, S. (2000). Concepts of trust among patients with serious illness. *Social Science & Medicine, 51*, 657–669.

Nyquist, M. (1996). Learning to listen. In K. M. Galvin & P. Cooper (Eds.), *Making connections: Readings in relational communication* (pp. 98–100). Los Angeles: Roxbury.

Papa, M. J. (1989). Communicator competence and employee performance with new technology: A case study. *The Southern Communication Journal, 55*, 87–102.

Passman, J. L., & Gangstead, S. K. (2001). An analysis of perceived and observed support behaviors exhibited by athletic trainers during rehabilitation. *Journal of Athletic Training, 36*, 1–80.

Pasupathi, M., Carstensen, L. L., Levenson, R. W., & Gottman, J. M. (1999). Responsive listening in long-married couples: A psycholinguistic perspective. *Journal of Nonverbal Behavior, 23*, 173–194.

Purdy, M. (1991). What is listening? In D. Borisoff & M. Purdy (Eds.), *Listening in everyday life: A personal and professional approach* (pp. 3–19). Lanham, MD: University Press of America.

Ray, E. B., & Bostrom, R. N. (1990). Listening to medical messages: The relationship of physician gender, patient gender, and seriousness of illness on short- and long-term recall. In R. N. Bostrom (Ed.), *Listening behavior: Measurement and application* (pp. 128–143). New York: Guilford.

Richendoller, N. R., & Weaver, J. B. (1994). Exploring the links between personality and empathic response style. *Personality and Individual Differences, 17*, 303–311.

Rubin, D. L., & Hampton, S. (1998). National performance standards for oral communication K-12: New standards for speaking/listening/viewing. *Communication Education, 47*, 183–193.

Ruusuvuori, J. (2001). Looking means listening: Coordinating displays of engagement in doctor-patient interaction. *Social Science & Medicine, 52,* 1093.

Seibert, J. (1990). Listening in the organizational context. In R. Bostrom (Ed.), *Listening behavior: Measurement and application* (pp. 119–127). New York: Guilford.

Stewart, J. (1983). Interpretive listening: An alternative to empathy. *Communication Education, 32,* 379–391.

Stewart, J., & Logan, C. (1998). *Together: Communicating interpersonally* (5th ed.). Boston: McGraw-Hill.

Stewart, J., & Zediker, K. (2000). Dialogue as tensional, ethical practice. *Southern Communication Journal, 65,* 224–242.

Stiff, J. B., Dillard, J. P., Somera, L., Kim, H., & Sleight, C. (1988). Empathy, communication, and prosocial behavior. *Communication Monographs, 55,* 198–213.

Thomas, L. T., & Levine, T. R. (1994). Disentangling listening and verbal recall: Related but separate constructs? *Human Communication Research, 21,* 103–127.

Thompson, T. (1994). Interpersonal communication and health care. In M. L. Knapp & G. R. Miller (Eds.), *Handbook of interpersonal communication* (pp. 696–725). Beverly Hills, CA: Sage.

Trees, A. R. (2000). Nonverbal communication and the support process: Interactional sensitivity in interactions between mothers and young adult children. *Communication Monographs, 67,* 239–261.

Weaver, J. B., & Kirtley, M. D. (1995). Listening styles and empathy. *The Southern Journal of Communication, 60,* 131–140.

Wolff, F. I., Marsnik, N. C., Tacey, W. S., & Nichols, R. G. (1983). *Perceptive listening.* New York: Holt, Rinehart & Winston.

Wolvin, A., & Coakley, C. G. (1991). A survey of the status of listening training in some Fortune 500 corporations. *Communication Education, 40,* 154–162.

C H A P T E R   4

FUNDAMENTALS

OF VERBAL

COMMUNICATION

VERBAL COMMUNICATION CODES

Semantic Code

Syntactic Code

Pragmatic Code

VERBAL COMMUNICATION AND GOALS

Grice's Principle of Cooperation

Illocutionary Acts and Pair Parts

Staying on Topic and Changing Topics

Confirming and Disconfirming Messages

CULTURE AND VERBAL
COMMUNICATION

Individualism-Collectivism

Communication Accommodation Theory

INDIVIDUAL FACTORS AND VERBAL
COMMUNICATION

Message Design Logics

Self-Construals

Life-Span Issues

CHAPTER SUMMARY

(1) Gene: Nice work.

(2) Jesse: Thanks, got it done not too long ago.

(3) Gene: Not at some chop shop, eh.

(4) Jesse: Naw, a custom studio.

(5) Gene: Nice, the guy was an artist.

(6) Jesse: Yeah, I am thinkin' 'bout getting some new ink.

(7) Gene: Where you gonna put it?

(8) Jesse: Don't know yet, but I've got some clean spots.

(9) Gene: Lookin' good, see ya. (From Ellis, 1992a, p. 8)

This brief exchange illustrates some useful information about the nature of verbal messages. First, we can deduce the general goal of the conversation: Gene wants to compliment Jesse. At least, that appears to be Gene's goal on the surface. Second, we can see that two issues — admiration of work done by an artist (turns 1–5) and future work is planned (turns 6–8) — were discussed as part of the compliment. Next, we find a cooperative give and take, where every statement relates to the previous statement. Fourth, the conclusion to the conversation appears natural; it summarizes the event and leaves no unresolved questions to be addressed (turn 9). Finally, of course, the cultural context of the conversation helps us understand the meaning of the exchange. In this case, the conversation took place between two men in a tattoo shop.

This chapter concerns how people use verbal messages. People use words to create ideas, inspire action, and win hearts. People also use words to confuse issues, postpone obligations, and end relationships. This chapter will show how verbal messages are used to achieve goals, whatever they may be. Furthermore, we shall see that the process of exchanging words is linked to the way language reflects people's goals as well as to cultural and individual factors that affect its use.

VERBAL COMMUNICATION CODES

Verbal messages consist of words or everyday language codes. Verbal messages reflect three different types of codes: semantic, syntactic, and pragmatic.

Semantic Code

Semantics refers to the study of the meaning of words. Words have both denotative and connotative meanings. Denotative meaning refers to the primary and literal meaning of a word, whereas connotative meaning refers to the secondary meanings that a word might convey. For instance, when you say someone is "bad," the primary literal meaning indicates that the person or object has malicious beliefs or behaviors. However, secondary meanings of "bad" include that the person or object might be sarcastic, nasty, powerful, athletic, or even good.

How can words have such variability when it comes to their literal meaning? The answer lies in realizing that people create and change language. Words are arbitrary metaphors. They are arbitrary in that they are created by people for any number of reasons. There is no deterministic reason why a person, event, or object is named what it is. *Metaphors* are symbols; they serve as substitutes for the person, event, or object. Accordingly, words are not reality; they merely represent reality.

Many years ago, Ogden and Richards (1927) proposed the semantic triangle, a model showing the relationship between words and the reality that words represent (for a brief review, see Foss, Foss, & Trapp, 1991). In each corner of the triangle is a necessary element of meaning. In one corner is the thought or thing being perceived (a person, an event, or an object), which is called the **referent.** In the second corner is the word, or the **symbol** of what is perceived. In the third corner is your collective image of the class of the perceived person, event, or object, which is the **reference.** The reference is composed of your previous experience. Figure 4.1 illustrates how the semantic triangle shows the relations among words, referents, and references.

Meanings of messages depend on the communicators' use of shared symbols for the same referents using similar references. People often confuse meanings because their symbols, referents, or references are not similar. For instance, two people can have very different references for an apparently simple symbol, such as a fur coat (see Figure 4.1). One person might think of a fur coat as an elegant and effective means of dressing for cold weather, whereas a second person might think of a fur coat as an excessive waste of money and animal life. People have different associations for other words and phrases as well — "connecting," "hooking up," and "meeting for drinks" can imply having a date or simply meeting another person. In short, words have semantic content, but that content can reflect different realities (e.g., "connecting" can mean simply meeting another person or making a commitment as boyfriend and girlfriend). Likewise, people may use different words to represent the same reality (e.g., film, movie, show, flick). Of course, the picture can become more confused with more abstract symbols or separately experienced references (e.g., freedom, love, lies).

Syntactic Code

The **syntactic code** has its roots in how people have examined logic and literacy, largely in the written word (Ellis, 1992a, 1992b). Words are used in precise and conventional ways. People rely on grammatical rules to construct sentences that make sense.

One way to show how words can be understood at the syntactical level simply involves changing the order of words used in a sentence. When we change the order of

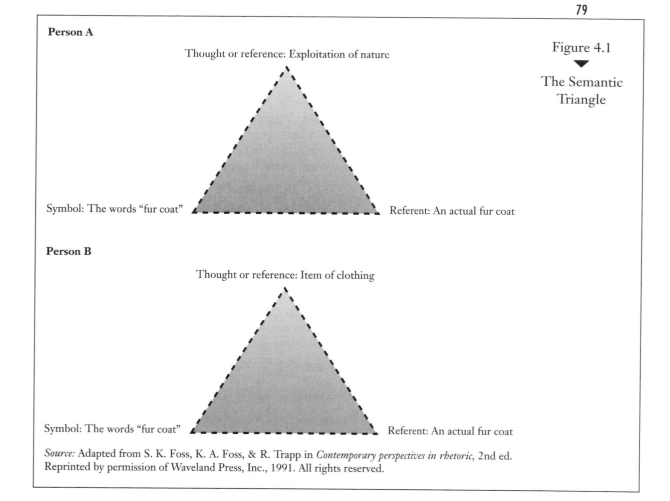

Person A

Thought or reference: Exploitation of nature

Symbol: The words "fur coat"

Referent: An actual fur coat

Person B

Thought or reference: Item of clothing

Symbol: The words "fur coat"

Referent: An actual fur coat

Figure 4.1

The Semantic Triangle

Source: Adapted from S. K. Foss, K. A. Foss, & R. Trapp in *Contemporary perspectives in rhetoric,* 2nd ed. Reprinted by permission of Waveland Press, Inc., 1991. All rights reserved.

words, we can see how they can reflect a deeper structure that people use to make sense of verbal messages. Compare the following (rather famous) sentences that have little semantic meaning (as cited in Jacobs, 1994, p. 208):

a. Colorless green ideas sleep furiously.
b. Furiously sleep ideas green colorless.

The first sentence appears to make sense because its syntax is correct for English speakers, whereas the second sentence lacks proper syntax and therefore makes even less sense than the first (nonsensical) sentence. Let's consider four sentences that contain semantic meaning, but again reveal how meaning is dependent on proper use of syntax:

a.   I want to go to the party.
b.   To the party, I want to go.
c.   Go to want I party the to.
d.   Party the to to go want I.

Examples a and b have acceptable syntax (although b switches the noun and object), whereas examples c and d show how the meaning of the words is jeopardized because the communicator did not use proper syntax.

Pragmatic Code

The **pragmatic code** concerns how people coordinate actions and activities during real-time communication (Ellis, 1992a, 1992b, 1995). People have experiences and tendencies that they use to interpret words. People do not talk as they write; words are often used in imprecise and haphazard ways to convey meaning. Using the pragmatic code, communicators rely on context and their mutual interdependence to interpret the meaning of language (e.g., "Hand me that, uh . . ." [the woman gives her husband the spatula]).

According to Jackson and Jacobs (1980; Jacobs & Jackson, 1983a; Jacobs, 1994), we see the relationships among words because they serve a pragmatic purpose for the communicator. Both speakers and listeners link messages to the communicator's goals and understand messages according to their **pragmatic connectedness,** or the degree to which the words are relevant to a goal. Pragmatic connectedness lends coherence to words. As Jacobs and Jackson (1983b) argued, "Coherent conversation requires that each player's contributions bear a rational relation to some goal. That is part of what it means for an utterance to be coherent: it ought to have a point" (p. 53). In other words, people use and interpret verbal messages on the basis of their connection to the communicator's goals.

In sum, verbal communication can be examined for the meaning at three different levels: the semantic, the syntactic, and the pragmatic. Although people use and make sense of messages at each of these levels, how words work to achieve personal goals represents the communicative feature of language, more than the study of **semantics** or syntax (Ellis, 1992a, 1995). The pragmatic nature of verbal messages is evident when two people jointly produce verbal messages to coordinate their actions and activities.

VERBAL COMMUNICATION AND GOALS

For people to use messages for pragmatic purposes, at least two people have to participate in the same conversation. For two people to participate jointly in the same conversation, they must be in **alignment,** which refers to the degree to which both parties share in the construction of the interaction. Alignment does not mean that two people must agree on the issues they discuss; rather, alignment "involves fitting lines of action into a set" of sequences that involve both parties (Jacobs & Jackson, 1983b, p. 34). To fit their lines of action together, the two people must cooperate.

Grice's Principle of Cooperation

Paul Grice (1975, 1989), an English philosopher who examined social interaction, contends that when people use words, they do so for a purpose. Grice stated that conversations "are characteristically, to some degree at least, cooperative efforts; and each participant recognizes in them, to some extent, a common purpose or set of purposes, or at least a mutually accepted direction" (1989, p. 26). Based on this observation, Grice offered the Cooperative Principle, which we summarize as follows: Contribute what is required to keep your conversation progressing so it meets both parties' pragmatic objectives (Grice, 1989, p. 26).

Grice then presented four **conversational maxims** that provide direction regarding how one fulfills the Cooperative Principle. These maxims are quantity, quality, relation, and manner. Quantity refers to providing as much information as is needed, but no more than is required, to keep the conversation running smoothly. Quality, which Grice claimed was the most critical maxim, concerns not stating falsehoods nor making assertions for which you know you lack sound evidence. The maxim of relation refers to being relevant, a point covered later in the discussion of changing topics. The maxim of manner concerns being clear and avoiding obscure expressions.

Grice (1989) indicated that when two people in a conversation fulfill these four maxims, they accomplish certain things: The two parties share a common goal; their contributions are sequentially ordered; and they continue to communicate in a suitable way until both people decide to end the conversation. However, if one of these maxims is not met, for instance, when one person is not truthful or does not offer sufficient information, the conversational partner needs to search for reasons why the other person stopped cooperating.

Indeed, research by McCornack and colleagues (McCornack, 1992; McCornack, Levine, Solowczuk, Torres, & Campbell, 1992) has shown that deception might be indicated if a communicator violates Grice's maxims. That is, the deceiver deliberately violates the maxim of quality by stating what he or she knows to be false (for example, in covering up a lie that a previous lover dropped into town and they had a romantic evening), does not provide enough information ("A friend and I just went out"), is vague about certain events ("Who? Oh, just someone I used to go to school with. Where? Some restaurant downtown"), or changes the subject ("By the way, where were you last night?"). The point is that Grice's maxims specify how the assumption of cooperation is fulfilled. When people refuse to follow the maxims, they indicate that they are not cooperative in constructing the conversation and are out of verbal alignment.

Grice noted that words are said for an intended purpose, and (importantly) they imply a desired way for the other person to respond conversationally and perhaps otherwise. Linguists label **speech acts** that have intended effects on the listener as **illocutionary acts** (Searle & Vandervenken, 1985). Illocutionary acts have a prominent place in the research on language, and they combine into pair parts to reveal further how partners cooperate in making conversation.

Illocutionary Acts and Pair Parts

Bach and Harnisch (1979) identified four types of illocutionary acts: constatives, directives, commissives, and acknowledgements (Bach & Harnisch, 1979; see also Searle & Vandervenken, 1985). *Constatives* reflect the intention that the speaker wants the listener to believe something. Assertions (where one claims something exists), predictions, descriptions (such as classification systems like this one), information (including giving advice), and disputations (where one disagrees with a point of view), are examples of constatives. *Directives* concern affecting the probable behavior of the listener. Such speech acts include requests, requirements (e.g., prescribe something), prohibitions (forbidding), and permissions.

Whereas these first two types of illocutionary acts concern affecting the partner's behavior, the latter two regard one's own behavior. *Commissives* concern obligating oneself, and two major forms occur here: promises to negotiate a contracted agreement, to guarantee that something will occur, or to bet on the future; and offers to engage in future behavior. Finally, *acknowledgments* express one's feelings for the listener, and several types have been uncovered. Apologies, condolences (commiserations), congratulations (including compliments), greetings, thanks, biddings (wishing one well), acceptances (including mere acknowledgement of the other person's point), and rejections (refusals) all indicate our attitudes toward another person (Bach & Harnisch, 1979).

Illocutionary acts do not occur in isolation. Rather, people engage in exchanges of messages, in sequences of illocutionary acts, to construct a series of conversational moves (Jacobs & Jackson, 1983b). When people respond to one another, they engage in at least one sequence of two consecutive messages, or **pair parts** (e.g., "Hi, how are you?" "Fine, how are you?"). It is reasonable to assume that people want and expect cooperative responses. One way to show their cooperation through conversation involves the use of preferred pair parts (Jacobs, 1994). A preferred pair part refers to how a person wants you to respond to his or her initial statement (or first pair part). Imagine the following situation, where Tom tries to reach Harry on the telephone, but Dick answers:

(1) Dick: Hello?
(2) Tom: Is Harry there?
(3) Dick: May I ask who is calling?
(4) Tom: Yes, this is Tom.
(5) Dick: Hold on — let me see if he is still here.

In this example, we see the use of pair parts, first in turns 2 and 5 and then in turns 3 and 4. Referring to the type of illocutionary speech acts reviewed earlier, Tom offers a typical request in turn 2. However, in turn 3 Dick presents a prerequisite — that Tom identify himself — before Dick provides him the preferred pair part (compliance with the request). Tom offers the preferred pair part to Dick's prerequisite (turn 4), and Dick then offers the preferred pair part in turn 5 to Tom's initial request back in turn 2.

The cooperative ebb and flow of even mundane conversation can come quickly to a frustrating halt when the person does not ever respond in a desired manner (with preferred pair parts). That is, people might choose to violate Grice's maxim of cooperation and provide a dispreferred pair part — a statement that does not validate the previous illocutionary act (Jacobs, 1994; Jacobs & Jackson, 1983b). Consider the same situation in which the telephone rings and Dick answers but with the following exchange:

(1) Dick: Hello?
(2) Tom: Who is this?
(3) Dick: Who is this?
(4) Tom: Is Harry there?
(5) Dick: May I ask who is calling?
(6) Tom: That is not necessary. Let me talk to Harry.
(7) Dick: I'm sorry, but you'll need to identify yourself before I check.

This example shows how communication can go awry when people neglect to reply in a preferred manner to a previous speech act. After Dick answers the telephone, Tom responds with an unconventional request in turn 2 (because the burden to identify oneself normally falls on the person making the call). But Dick does not acknowledge the request in turn 3 and instead requires that Tom identify himself. In turn 4, Tom ignores Dick's request and asks for Harry's whereabouts, to which Dick (turn 5) implies that Tom really must meet the requirement stated earlier (to identify himself). Tom responds to this requirement with a disputation and a command (turn 6). Dick offers a polite acknowledgment in turn 7 and restates the requirement.

Staying on Topic and Changing Topics

When people cooperatively engage in conversation, they remain on topic as long as it is necessary to allow both parties to make their desired points. Chapter 3 concluded with different listening strategies, which are relevant when thinking about why people change topics (e.g., they do not listen very well). But some forms of topic change appear more suitable than others.

People remain on topic in two ways — by being event-focused and by being issue-focused (Tracy, 1983). **Event-focused messages** concern the broader, underlying topic of discussion, and **issue-focused messages** relate to the precise content under discussion at that particular conversational turn. Recall the example offered at the beginning of this chapter:

(1) Gene: Nice work.
(2) Jesse: Thanks, got it done not too long ago.
(3) Gene: Not at some chop shop, eh.
(4) Jesse: Naw, a custom studio.
(5) Gene: Nice, the guy was an artist.
(6) Jesse: Yeah, I am thinkin' 'bout getting some new ink.
(7) Gene: Where you gonna put it?
(8) Jesse: Don't know yet, but I've got some clean spots.
(9) Gene: Lookin' good, see ya. (From Ellis, 1992a, p. 8)

This example illustrates both event-focused and issue-focused topical replies. Gene in turn 3 does not respond to the topic issue in the immediately preceding statement (in turn 2, regarding recency). Rather Gene points out that the tattoo was done at a quality studio ("not at some chop shop"). Jesse responds to that issue (turn 4), which Gene elaborates (turn 5). In turn 6, Jesse changes the issue but not the event ("getting some new ink"), to which both Gene and Jesse comment in turns 8 and 9. Clearly, Gene and Jesse demonstrate how to remain on topic using both event-focused and issue-focused language. In short, people can show that they are cooperating in extending the conversation in the direction that the other person desires by talking about the overriding concern or by responding to the content in the immediately preceding statement.

Changing topics can be a delicate practice, a communicative art. In one study of the types of messages that reveal topic shifts, Crow (1983) examined five satisfied couples' behaviors. Although a vast majority of the responses stayed on topic, Crow found that topics changed every 48 seconds, on the average. Crow found both coherent and noncoherent topic shifts. Coherent topic shifts occurred when the response somehow tied the new topic into the previous topic. Noncoherent shifts occurred when there was no transition from one topic to the next.

One common coherent topic shift device involved topic shading, where the person explicitly, though perhaps awkwardly, attempts to link a new topic to the current topic ("Speaking of the weekend, have you thought about taking golf lessons?"). A second coherent topic shift involves an explicit pre-act, or a message that explicitly bounds to the next topic. Pre-act bounding includes the following examples: "Before I forget, I need to talk to you about something, ..."; "By the way, ..."; and "Listen to this . . . ." (Crow, 1983, p. 142). Crow also found that people changed the topic in a coherent manner when they would recall a former topic, or what he called renewal (e.g., "Like I was saying, ..."; "Where were we? Oh yeah, I remember. . . ..").

Noncoherent topic shifts tend to be unannounced, sounding abrupt because they do not provide any bounding or shading into the new topic (Crow, 1983, p. 148). For example, consider the following example in which the male abruptly changes topics in turn 2.

(1)	Female:	And they were telling about a show, a new movie, with a guy who was in Howard Hughes's will or something. Just an ordinary . . .
(2)	Male (interrupting):	Did you want to cut your hair? And make it look short?
(3)	Female:	I wasn't planning to but I feel like it. (from Crow, 1983, p. 147)

Such abrupt topic shifts appear to throw the conversation out of alignment because one person, in this case, the male, does not cooperate in discussing the female's topic.

As Crow points out, people also engage in **sin licenses** that function to obtain permission to change the topic (e.g., "I don't mean to change the topic, but . . ."; "This might not relate entirely to what you were saying, but . . ."; "You might think I am coming from left field because I want to mention that . . .") (p. 147). The function of a sin license is to obtain permission for being inappropriate without really asking. People use sin licenses to get away with a number of messages. For example, when introducing an obscene joke, a person might begin with "I heard this one from my sister-in-law. . . ." or "Don't think I am being rude, but have you heard the one about . . . ?" or "I never tell dirty jokes, but this one is cute. . . ."

In brief, staying on topic provides one clear way for people to fulfill Grice's Cooperative Principle. Besides revealing how cooperative a person is, verbal messages show the extent to which one person confirms or disconfirms the very existence of the other person.

Confirming and Disconfirming Messages

Verbal messages impart how you feel about your partner on two levels. First, messages indicate positive or negative reactions to another person's ideas or proposals (positive reactions such as "Great!" and "That sounds good"; negative reactions such as "I don't think so" and "No way"). Second, messages convey an evaluation of your partner and the relationship. Recall from Chapter 1 that communication functions to achieve three types of goals: self-presentation, relational, and instrumental. Your messages confirm or disconfirm the other person's self-presentation and definition of the relationship, in addition to indicating your attitude toward the other's ideas.

Sieburg (1976) specifies how messages confirm or disconfirm others. According to Sieburg, a **confirming message** contains the following elements:

1. Recognition of your partner's existence
2. Recognition of your partner as a unique individual
3. Expression of your partner's significance
4. Acceptance of your partner's way of experiencing life
5. Expressions of concern and willingness to become involved with your partner.

These elements are indicated by showing yourself as involved in what the other person is saying. Indeed, showing that you are conversationally involved is a primary criterion of communication competence (see Part 5). You do not necessarily have to agree with your partner's opinions to be confirming and positive. Simple messages such as "I see" and "I understand" indicate your positive regard for your partner without expressing agreement with the ideas expressed.

A **disconfirming message,** by contrast, conveys a negative evaluation of your partner and the relationship. According to Sieburg (1976), disconfirming messages fall into three categories: indifference, imperviousness, and disqualification. Indifference means disconfirming the other through silence (not giving a sound or an utterance), through absent (mindless) responses, or by interrupting or disrupting what the partner is saying. Imperviousness involves being inattentive to the other's thoughts and feelings, as if the person did not matter. Impervious responses reflect this lack of attention ("Yeah, uh, what?"; "Say that again — I wasn't listening") and are often accompanied by nonverbal responses showing lack of involvement (e.g., blank gaze, lack of movement). Disqualification entails being unaware of the other. Disqualification is exhibited as monologues, wherein one person talks endlessly about his or her own concerns. Irrelevant responses to messages ("So, do you think I should take that job offer?"; "Let's get an ice cream.") or tangential responses, whereby the communicator responds incidentally to the issue and then proceeds with a different thought ("So, do you think I should take that job offer?"; "Who knows? Let's get an ice cream.") also fall into the category of disqualification.

People must cooperate with each other if they are to achieve their interpersonal goals, which reflects the pragmatic nature of verbal communication. Cooperation is conveyed in Grice's maxims and how partners align their messages to each others'. Cooperation is further demonstrated in the use of preferred pair parts. Likewise, cooperation is seen in the way that people stay on topic and shift topics. How we respond to the other person indicates our recognition of the value of the other person, through confirming or disconfirming messages.

In computer-mediated communication such as e-mail, chat, instant messages, and the like, people rely on verbal communication codes almost exclusively. Nonverbal messages (see Chapter 5) are almost nonexistent. Accordingly, the connotation of the message and whether or not you anticipate communicating with an individual again become important factors that predict how we communicate. In on-line encounters, such as chat rooms or interest lists, people correctly believe that they will never encounter the people who posted comments. However, communicators on-line who expect to converse again look for cues in each others' messages that say who the other is, make more of an effort to get to know one another, and act more friendly with one another, than those who expect that their on-line interaction is a one-time chance encounter (Walther, 1994). In computer-mediated communication and in face-to-face communication, knowing that we are going to interact with someone again promotes the use of positive and confirming messages (Kellermann & Reynolds, 1990; Walther, 1994).

STUDENT AS OBSERVER: FAILING TO COOPERATE

Reconstruct a recent conversation you had with someone (or that you observed) that involved a lack of cooperation. Describe the conversation in detail in terms of the following:

1. What was the conversation about? What were the goals in conflict (recall Chapter 1)?
2. How did the communication reflect a lack of cooperation in terms of the maxims of quantity, quality, relation, and manner? Recall precisely the parts of the conversation that reflected a violation of these maxims.
3. Recall and list the preferred and dispreferred pair parts. Were there more preferred or dispreferred pair parts?
4. Did the parties try to change the topic or recast the topic in terms of their own positions?
5. How did the communicators confirm or disconfirm the other person in the conversation? What were the types of confirming and disconfirming messages that were used?

The pragmatic nature of language helps us see the extent to which we rely on other people in our conversations with them. Besides the other person, additional influences on our language exist. These influences are discussed within two broad categories — cultural factors and individual differences.

CULTURE AND VERBAL COMMUNICATION

Culture is one of the most important influences on language use. We begin by discussing the most critical dimension of cultural differences related to verbal messages. Then we present a comprehensive theory regarding how culture affects conversational management.

Individualism-Collectivism

Perhaps the most important difference between cultural systems for language use concerns whether the culture is individualistic or collectivistic (Gudykunst & Ting-Toomey, 1988). Individualism refers to the tendencies of people in some cultures to emphasize their individual selves over their group memberships, personal rights and responsibilities over group rights, and personal gains over group gains (Ting-Toomey, 2000, p. 125). In **individualistic cultures,** people tend to develop personal identities that focus on obtaining personal rewards, avoiding personal costs, and viewing people and organizations in terms of their personal relevance for gain. Examples of such societies include the United States, Germany, and Australia.

On the other hand, collectivism concerns how people in some cultures tend to stress group identity over individual identity, group rights over individual rights, and group needs over individual needs (Ting-Toomey, 2000, p. 125). In such cultures, people are concerned with the well-being, harmony, and outcomes for one's important social groups. Such groups include one's family, extended family, school, and company. Interdependent cultures include Japan, Korea, the Philippines, and Mexico.

As one might expect, variation in individualism and collectivism affects how people use verbal messages. At a very general level, individualistic people tend to use words explicitly to convey meaning, so they use more direct terms, more complete elaborations and explanations, more precise terms, more dramatic and exaggerated stories, and fewer forms of indirect communication (Gudykunst et al., 1996). Again, at a very general level, people in **collectivistic cultures** tend to rely more on context for meaning, so they use more indirect language, more listening and other signs of being sensitive, less openness, fewer words to confront another person in public, and words that show sensitivity to the self-presentation of group members (Gudykunst et al., 1996).

Naturally, cultural differences lead to difficulties in communicating, especially if the parties to the conversation fall victim to ethnocentrism. **Ethnocentrism** refers to the extent to which we judge other people's cultures by our own cultural standards. For example, some Americans can be intolerant of visitors who do not speak English. Yet these same people can be upset when they visit Europe or Asia and a resident cannot speak English. At a more subtle level, we can impose our sense of correct cultural rules when we communicate with people from other cultures (e.g., "I wish she would give me a direct response"; "I can never tell what they really mean"). Of course, people from other cultures might be dismayed by U.S. preferences for open and honest communication, especially when such communication might lead to a loss of face (see Chapter 6).

What happens when people from different cultures or subcultures communicate? Clearly a degree of accommodation must occur. One or both parties will need to alter their communication behavior to adapt to the messages of the other person. A general theory that helps us understand the process of intercultural adaptation is the Communication Accommodation Theory.

Communication Accommodation Theory

Language systems obviously occur within particular cultures and subcultures, and many, if not most, countries have multiple languages. Perhaps more important, culture and language are closely linked — culture defines how language should be used, and language helps to create and preserve the culture (Giles & Coupland, 1991). Furthermore, language and ethnicity are closely related in several ways; according to Giles and Coupland, "Language is often a criterial attribute of group membership, an important cue for ethnic categorization, an emotional dimension of identity, and a means of facilitating ingroup cohesion" (p. 96). The box "Taggers' Codes" provides one set of words that indicates to graffiti artists (or taggers) that they have an established subculture. A tagger would use such words and others to identify with other taggers. Relationships can also be conceived as subcultures that have their own

TAGGERS' CODES

In Los Angeles, teenagers who make it a business to paint graffiti on street signs, walls, and other visible backdrops are called *taggers*. Regardless of how we might feel about graffiti, taggers are a good example of a group that has its own subculture, complete with a set of common codes. These codes illustrate how words can serve as arbitrary metaphors. Here is a sample of terms taggers use.

- Tag: Your graffiti signature.
- Crew: Your tagging group — also known as a posse, mob, or tribe.
- Homies: Fellow members of your crew.
- Kicking it: To relax with your homies.
- Toy: A novice, amateurish tagger.
- Ranker: A person who chickens out, doesn't defend his tag.
- Slipping: Being caught by rival taggers without homies to back you up.
- Mob: To hit a target with graffiti.
- Kill: To completely cover with graffiti.
- Seek and destroy: To tag everything in sight.
- Map the heavens: To tag hard-to-reach freeway overhead signs.
- To be down: To be a dedicated tagger, accepted by your crew.
- Buster: Someone who claims he's down but isn't.
- To get up: To spread your tag in as many places as possible.
- To battle: To go up against another crew to see who gets up the most.
- To be rank: To have the privileges of deciding who is in and out of your crew.
- Hero: An adult who would turn in a tagger.
- Landmark: A prime spot where a tag won't be erased.
- To be buffed: To have a tag cleaned off by authorities.
- To be crossed out: To have a tag erased by a rival tagger.

Source: "Leaving Their Marks: Youths Risk Everything to Tag Walls, Buses and Traffic Signs with Graffiti," by John Gilonna. Copyright © 1993, *Los Angeles Times*. Reprinted by permission.

uses for language. Friends and partners in romantic relationships often develop their own codes, as do members of particular groups.

Communication Accommodation Theory (CAT) specifies how two people from different cultures interact in ways that reflect their personal goals as well as cultural identity. Although we are not aware that we alter our behaviors, several verbal and nonverbal behaviors may be involved in the accommodation, including the use of different languages, speech rate, volume, and other message behaviors.

Imagine that Amy is a likable person from Great Britain and Beth is a U.S. exchange student trying to obtain information about where to live in London. As Beth talks to Amy, you might notice a change in Beth's communication style. Beth attempts to use British terms, and she speaks at her slightly faster rate, nods more frequently (like Amy), and adopts her English accent. Beth has accommodated to Amy's speech pattern by altering her usual manner of speaking to converge toward Amy's pattern. At another party, you see Beth conversing with someone who speaks with a very different accent, one you have never heard before. Here you notice that Beth diverges from the speech pattern of the stranger. Beth speaks more slowly and loudly, articulating and pronouncing her words carefully, employing standard American English.

Table 4.1 outlines why speakers converge or diverge in their communication behaviors. We often converge when we want approval (when we want to make a good

---

Table 4.1
SUMMARY OF COMMUNICATION ACCOMMODATION THEORY

Causes of Speech Convergence

1. Communicators will attempt to converge toward the speech and nonverbal patterns *believed* to be characteristic of their fellow interactants when communicators seek
   (a) social approval
   (b) a high level of efficiency
   (c) a sense of oneness with other interactants
   (d) appropriate situational or identity definitions

   Further, communicators will attempt to converge toward the speech and nonverbal patterns of others when
   (e) the target or targets of the convergence employ expected speech patterns
   (f) speech is positively valued (nonstigmatized)
   (g) the speech style is appropriate for all parties

2. The *magnitude* of speech convergence will be a function of
   (a) the extent to which a communicator has the ability to use a particular repertoire of speech behaviors
   (b) situational factors that may increase the need for social approval, efficiency, or social comparison

Causes of Speech Divergence

3. Speakers will attempt to maintain their communication patterns or even diverge from the speech and nonverbal behaviors of the recipients of their message when they
   (a) seek to communicate a contrastive self-image
   (b) seek to dissociate personally from the interactants or from the interactants' definition of the situation
   (c) define the encounter in intergroup or relational terms with communication style being a valued dimension of their situationally salient in-group or relational identities
   (d) wish to change interactants' speech behavior, for example, moving it to a more acceptable level

   Further, communicators will attempt to diverge from other interactants' speech behavior when the interactants
   (e) exhibit a stigmatized form of speech, one that deviates from a valued norm
   (f) fail to meet the speakers' expectations regarding their performance
4. The magnitude of such divergence will be a function of factors similar to those cited in point 2.

Source: Adapted from Speech Accommodation Theory: The first decade and beyond by H. Giles. Published in *Communication Yearbook 10* (1987), pp. 13–48, edited by M. L. McLaughlin. Copyright © by Sage Publications, Inc. Reprinted by permission.

first impression, have an enjoyable date, and so on), when we want to be efficient (for example, sales clerks often converge when they try to sell us items), and when we desire either a shared identity with others or a particular identity of our own. For example, members of social groups (from country clubs to street gangs) exhibit some convergence in speech patterns when they meet. The more valued the speech pattern, the more likely it is that people will converge. Stigmatized speech patterns prompt speakers to diverge.

Communicators exhibit **mutual accommodation** when they both switch their speech styles to move toward the partner's use of language and nonverbal behaviors. Accommodation can also be nonmutual, as in the previous example when Beth accommodated to the speech style of Amy, who was from Great Britain, but Amy did not reciprocate — she did not accommodate to Beth's American style of speaking. Many reasons exist for mutual and nonmutual accommodation. One reason deals with our abilities to employ a particular repertoire of speech behaviors. Some people are not confident in their abilities to speak second languages, to alter spoken dialects, or to increase gestures and speaking rate, and such people are unlikely to show any convergence toward the style of their partners. Both speakers have to be motivated and skilled for mutual convergence to occur. (For more on the speech accommodation theory, see Giles & Coupland, 1991; Giles, Coupland, & Coupland, 1991; Giles, Mulac, Bradac, & Johnson, 1987.)

Of course, individuals within cultures vary in their use of language. Some people are very direct, whereas other people are indirect; some people use highly charged and intense language, whereas others are more reserved and cautious. You can think of your own relationships as subcultures, complete with special uses of language. Friends and partners in romantic relationships often develop their own codes, as do members of particular groups. What words have special, perhaps unique, meanings in your relationships?

INDIVIDUAL FACTORS AND VERBAL COMMUNICATION

In Chapter 2, we discussed the role of individuals' perceptions in interpersonal communication. Here we examine how people's use of words reflects three key individual differences that are probably just as relevant as culture: message design logics, self-construals, and life-span issues.

Message Design Logics

Although people relate language to the communicator's goals, people may hold different conceptions of how language should be used. O'Keefe and associates (O'Keefe, 1988; O'Keefe & McCornack, 1987; O'Keefe & Sheppard, 1987) present a theory of communication that explains why people use various messages based on underlying beliefs about communication. These beliefs are called **message design logics.** There are three types of message design logics: expressive, conventional, and rhetorical.

An **expressive message design logic** refers to the belief that communication functions primarily to express ideas and feelings. People who adopt the expressive logic present their ideas and feelings as they are experienced, without much editing, not really discriminating between thoughts and feelings (O'Keefe, 1988).

A **conventional message design logic** refers to the view that communication is a kind of game with commonly understood rules (conventions). People who use this logic are concerned with both expression and achieving their goals within the boundaries of social appropriateness; communication functions primarily to uphold social conventions.

A **rhetorical message design logic** refers to the belief that communication functions primarily to create a person's social world. People who adopt the rhetorical logic believe that self-expression and social conventions can be used or changed to meet their interpersonal objectives.

As the above descriptions suggest, the personal theories that people have regarding how to use communication influences their selection of messages (O'Keefe, 1988). For example, Bill is an Expressive — he discloses his dreams and looks forward to hearing about other people's lives; if someone disappoints Bill, he lets them know in clear terms without much regard for the final outcome of the conversation. Ken is a Conventional — he attempts to meet other people's expectations by appearing agreeable; he also points out what he considers to be appropriate behavior and holds others to the same standards. Newt is a Rhetorical — he discloses at times and at other times does not disclose or does so with a twist. Newt is well aware of social conventions and uses them to his advantage; if such conventions present an obstacle he questions and tries to redefine those norms.

According to O'Keefe (1988), when goals are easily achieved by simply expressing our needs, all three message design logics lead to similar kinds of communication. But when situations become more complex due to competing goals, differences in logics lead to differences in message use. You also can hold portions of all these message design logics; that is, your beliefs can be part expressive, part conventional, and part rhetorical, though you probably lean toward one logic over the other two.

O'Keefe demonstrates how verbal messages reflect these three logics within the context of problem solving. An expressive message typically is not edited, nor does it necessarily conform to social norms or apply to the partners' current activities. For example, imagine that you are in a work group and one of the members has not performed his assignment. You might hear one group member offer this expressive message:

> Ron, you lazy idiot! Did you think we wouldn't notice you were this far behind? All you have is a rough draft! I can't believe it. I am so mad! I'm getting you out of our group because I don't want a bad grade. (adapted from O'Keefe, 1988)

Such a message primarily expresses the frustration of the communicator but does little to change the situation. A conventional message implies appropriateness norms and links a person's goal to the fulfillment of these norms; for example:

> Ron, you owe it to us to get your job done because each of us has spent a lot of time and energy to make an excellent presentation. You must know that the

teacher will see who has spent the most effort during the presentation, so I doubt that your grade will be very good. (adapted from O'Keefe, 1988)

A rhetorical message would use the conditions and information in the situation to persuade others; for example:

> Ron, I'm sorry you're not prepared for tomorrow. Can you think of some reason why you are so unprepared? Both the group and the teacher will want to know. You also need to see how your personal problems affect others. I sympathize with you, but you must help us out right now with all you've got. So get as ready as you can by tomorrow. (adapted from O'Keefe, 1988)

Knowledge of these message design logics makes it possible for you to choose which logic to adopt in a given situation. O'Keefe's theory implies that the rhetorical logic is superior. Our view is that the most sophisticated communicators can become aware of and use all three logics and corresponding messages to achieve their most important goals.

Self-Construals

Earlier we mentioned how people from various cultures use language differently. People in individualistic cultures tend to be more direct, for example, than are people in collectivistic cultures. Although this sweeping generalization is valid for noting differences in group tendencies, individuals within different cultures adopt their own personal identities and values that affect how they communicate with others. In other words, individuals vary in their personal styles, which changes the ways that their culture influences their behaviors (Gudykunst et al., 1996).

According to various scholars, people have different **self-construals** or ways of thinking of themselves and what brings them happiness (e.g., Kim et al., 1996; Markus & Kitayama, 1991; Oetzel, 1998; Ting-Toomey, 2000). According to the research, two self-construals, independent and interdependent, in particular highlight variation within cultures. Individuals holding an independent self-construal see themselves as unique from others, as having a stable personality, as having the ability to take care of themselves, and so forth. People adopting an interdependent self-construal see themselves as willing to sacrifice their own interests for the sake of others, as avoiding arguments with their own group, as remaining in the group when they want to leave, and the like. This research shows that these self-construals predict communication behavior (e.g., independence associates positively with being clear about one's own concerns, whereas interdependence correlates positively with concern for others' feelings).

Moreover, this research indicates that these self-construals can filter out the effects of culture on interpersonal communication. That is, culture affects communication through a person's beliefs regarding their interdependence and independence

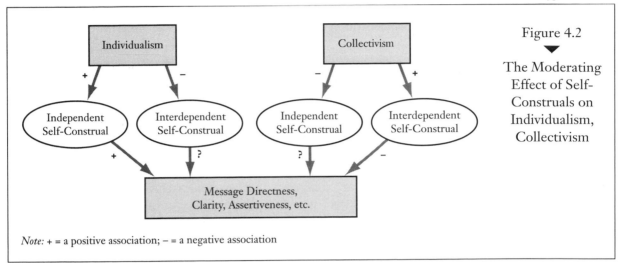

Figure 4.2

▼

The Moderating Effect of Self-Construals on Individualism, Collectivism

Note: + = a positive association; – = a negative association

(Kim et al., 1996). Figure 4.2 illustrates how self-construals moderate the effect of culture on interpersonal communication and that broad-based cultural differences are further affected by individual differences to affect language use.

Life-Span Issues

People use communication differently over their life span (Nussbaum, 1989). Although we address life-span issues in-depth in Chapter 14, we want to highlight a few concepts here. For example, 18- to 21-year-olds (versus older people) appear to use communication behavior for a wider latitude of reasons, including for the sheer fun of it (Rubin, Perse, & Barbato, 1988).

Sillars and Wilmot (1989) reviewed how interpersonal communication between spouses changed from young couple stages (honeymoon through early marriage), through middle age (launching and empty nest periods), to older couples (retirement and beyond). Sillars and Wilmot succinctly summarized the research on life-span differences. Their conclusions are as follows:

1. Young couples appear to be "more expressive, conflictive, and intense than older couples, by philosophy as well as circumstance" (p. 235). For example, younger couples disclose more verbal messages and use words more frequently to say what is on their minds.

2. Middle-age couples engaged in less disclosure and intensity, and they appear to be brief, direct, and analytical in their conversations (pp. 238–239). For ex-

ample, middle-age couples attempt to face the issue and solve the problem directly without much demonstration of feelings.

3. Older couples appear to take on one of two primary message profiles. The more common message profile presents a very efficient and subdued picture, where "implied meanings increasingly substitute for words, where interactions are stable and repetitious and where background assumptions are closely in alignment, conditions that particularly describe older couples" (p. 242). The second message profile is one of constant bickering — where older couples relate to each other often through disagreement (e.g., the elderly miracle maker and his wife in the film *The Princess Bride*).

People use verbal messages within different cultural systems, and to understand how words work, we must acknowledge that each of these systems colors how we create and use words. As well, individual differences contextualize and indicate to us how we should use verbal messages.

CHAPTER SUMMARY

Verbal messages can be understood at three levels: semantic, syntactic, and pragmatic. At the semantic level, words are arbitrary metaphors created by people to represent the real world. People sometimes refer to different realities when using the same word, and people often use different words to refer to the same reality. At the syntactic level, words make sense when they are combined using rules of grammar. Words that are combined outside of grammatical rules can reflect a lack of cohesion. As a pragmatic activity, verbal messages operate to achieve goals of the conversational parties. Acknowledging the pragmatic function of language helps us to interpret the meaning and implications of verbal messages.

To engage another person in a goal-directed conversation involves cooperation between two people regarding how the conversation proceeds. Grice formulated maxims that act as general guidelines for cooperation. In addition, cooperation is reflected in the way in which people use preferred or dispreferred pair parts, how they extend the topic of conversation, and whether or not they confirm their conversational partners.

Verbal communication does not occur in a vacuum. Differences in culture can affect how verbal messages are used and interpreted. Individualistic and collectivistic cultural tendencies reveal how people from different cultures might value certain forms of verbal messages over others, with individualistic people being more direct and open. Communication Accommodation Theory provides a rich, general theory that helps explain why a member from one culture might adapt to a member from a different culture.

Differences within the individual affect verbal messages. The beliefs that people hold with regard to the function of communication — or their message design logic — began our discussion of individual differences. With an earnest self-assessment, people can better understand their implicitly held beliefs about the role of communication in their lives. Individuals also vary in their self-construals. For example, people with an interdependent self-construal tend to engage in more cooperative messages even if they live in an individualistic society and people with independent self-construals might behave more competitively, regardless of the larger cultural norm to be sensitive to the other person's self-presentation needs. Because individuals change over their life span, what they want out of life at any one time depends on the stage of life at which they find themselves. And, as we maintain in this book, how you communicate depends on what you want out of life.

Naturally verbal messages present only part of the picture with regard to how people communicate with each other. Chapter 5 provides an overview of the way in which people send and receive messages using nonverbal messages.

KEY TERMS

▼

alignment, p. 81
collectivistic cultures, p. 88
Communication Accommodation
    Theory (CAT), p. 90
confirming message, p. 85
conventional message design
    logic, p. 93
conversational maxims, p. 81
disconfirming message, p. 86
ethnocentrism, p. 88
event-focused messages, p. 83
expressive message design logic,
    p. 92
illocutionary acts, p. 82
individualistic cultures, p. 87
issue-focused messages, p. 83

message design logics, p. 92
mutual accommodation, p. 92
pair parts, p. 82
pragmatic code, p. 80
pragmatic connectedness,
    p. 80
reference, p. 78
referent, p. 78
rhetorical message design
    logic, p. 93
self-construals, p. 94
semantics, p. 80
sin licenses, p. 85
speech acts, p. 82
symbol, p. 78
syntactic code, p. 78

EXERCISES FOR FURTHER DISCUSSION

▼

1. First write down a definition for each of the following words: commitment, love, successful, open, family values. Then compare your definitions with those written by another class member.
   a. Are there any differences in the definitions that you came up with?
   b. Can you think of any situations in which the differences in definitions could lead to misunderstandings?
   c. Have you had experiences in which an underlying difference in the definition of a word led to a misunderstanding?
   d. What do you do when such misunderstandings occur?
2. We generally understand how people use words because of the pragmatic connectedness of the words (that is, their relationship to an interaction goal).
   a. Have you ever misinterpreted someone by attributing a goal that the person did not in fact have?
   b. Has anyone recently misinterpreted your words by not accurately perceiving your goal?
   c. Have you ever had trouble interpreting someone's words because you were unsure of that person's goals? If so, did you do?
3. Think of someone you know who is very confirming to be with and another person whom you find disconfirming to be with.
   a. What communication behaviors does the confirming person use that make you feel that he or she is confirming?
   b. What communication behaviors does the disconfirming person use that make you feel that he or she is disconfirming?
4. Consider any intercultural communication you have had that stands out in your mind.
   a. Did you notice wondering whether you were right or wrong in interpreting the situation?
   b. Did you try to accommodate more, or did the other person, or was there mutual accommodation?
   c. In what ways did you accommodate or not accommodate to each other?

SUGGESTED READING

▼

Ellis, D. G. (1992). *From language to communication*. Hillsdale, NJ: Erlbaum. Using a chronological review of the ways that language has been studied, Ellis provides an excellent review of the scholarly literature and then presents a theory on the ways that pragmatic and syntactical features combine to form meaning.

Giles, H., & Coupland, N. (1991). *Language: Contexts and consequences*. Pacific Grove, CA: Brooks/Cole. Giles and Coupland show how people accommodate to each other by using language.

Jacobs, S. (1994). Language and interpersonal communication. In M. L. Knapp & G. R. Miller (Eds.). *Handbook of interpersonal communication* (2nd ed., pp. 199–228). Thousand Oaks, CA: Sage. A very good overview of various approaches to the study of language in interpersonal contexts.

REFERENCE LIST

▼

Bach, K., & Harnisch, R. M. (1979). *Linguistic communication and speech acts*. Cambridge, MA: MIT Press.

Clark, R. A. (1979). The impact of self-interest and desired liking on selection of persuasive strategies. *Communication Monographs, 46,* 257–273.

Crow, B. K. (1983). Topic shifts in couples' conversations. In R. T. Craig & K. Tracy (Eds.), *Conversational coherence: Form, structure, and strategy* (pp. 136–156). Beverly Hills, CA: Sage.

Ellis, D. G. (1992a). *From language to communication*. Hillsdale, NJ: Erlbaum.

Ellis, D. G. (1992b). Syntactic and pragmatic codes in communication. *Communication Theory, 2,* 1–23.

Ellis, D. G. (1995). Fixing communicative meaning: A coherentist theory. *Communication Research, 22,* 515–544.

Foss, S. K., Foss, K. A., & Trapp, R. (1991). *Contemporary perspectives in rhetoric* (2nd ed.). Prospect Heights, IL: Waveland.

Giles, H., & Coupland, N. (1991). *Language: Contexts and consequences*. Pacific Grove, CA: Brooks/Cole.

Giles, H., Coupland, J., & Coupland, N. (1991). *Contexts of accommodation*. Cambridge, England: Cambridge University Press.

Giles, H., Mulac, A., Bradac, J. J., & Johnson, P. (1987). Speech accommodation theory: The first decade and beyond. In M. L. McLaughlin (Ed.), *Communication yearbook 10* (pp. 13–48). Newbury Park, CA: Sage.

Grice, P. C. (1975). Logic and conversation. In P. Cole & J. L. Morgan (Eds.), *Syntax and semantics, Volume 3: Speech acts*. New York: Academic.

Grice, P. C. (1989). *Studies in the ways of words*. Cambridge, MA: Harvard University Press.

Gudykunst, W., & Ting-Toomey, S. (1988). *Culture and interpersonal communication*. Newbury Park, CA: Sage.

Gudykunst, W. B., Matsumoto, Y., Ting-Toomey, S., Nishida, T., Kim, K., & Heyman, S. (1996). The influence of cultural individualism-collectivism, self construals, and individual values on communication styles across cultures. *Human Communication Research, 22,* 510–543.

Jackson, S., & Jacobs, S. (1980). Structure of conversational argument: Pragmatic bases for the enthymeme. *Quarterly Journal of Speech, 66,* 251–265.

Jacobs, S. (1985). Language. In M. L. Knapp & G. R. Miller (Eds.), *Handbook of interpersonal communication* (pp. 313–343). Newbury Park, CA: Sage.

Jacobs, S. (1994). Language and interpersonal communication. In M. L. Knapp & G. R. Miller (Eds.), *Handbook of interpersonal communication* (2nd ed., pp. 199–228). Thousand Oaks, CA: Sage.

Jacobs, S., & Jackson, S. (1983a). Strategy and structure in conversational influence attempts. *Communication Monographs, 50,* 285–304.

Jacobs, S., & Jackson, S. (1983b). Speech act structure in conversation: Rational aspects of pragmatic coherence. In R. T. Craig & K. Tracy (Eds.), *Conversational coherence: Form, structure, and strategy* (pp. 47–66). Beverly Hills, CA: Sage.

Kellermann, K., & Reynolds, R. (1990). When ignorance is bliss: The role of motivation to reduce uncertainty in uncertainty reduction theory. *Human Communication Research, 17,* 5–75.

Kim, M. S., Hunter, J. H., Mirahara, A., Horvath, A. M., Bresnahan, M., & Yoon, H. J. (1996). Individual- vs. culture-level dimensions of individualism and collectivism: Effects of preferred conversational styles. *Communication Monographs, 63,* 29–49.

Markus, H., & Kitayama, S. (1991). Culture and the self: Implications for cognition, emotion, and motivation. *Psychological Review, 98,* 224–253.

McCornack, S. A. (1992). Information manipulation theory. *Communication Monographs, 59,* 1–16.

McCornack, S. A., Levine, T. R., Solowczuk, K., Torres, H. I., & Campbell, D. M. (1992). When the alteration of information is viewed as deception: An empirical test of information manipulation theory. *Communication Monographs, 59,* 17–29.

Nussbaum, J. F. (Ed.). (1989). *Life-span communication: Normative issues.* Hillsdale, NJ: Erlbaum.

Oetzel, J. G. (1998). The effects of self-construal and ethnicity on self-reported conflict styles. *Communication Reports, 11,* 133–144.

Ogden, C. K., & Richards, I. A. (1927). *The meaning of meaning: A study of the influence of language upon thought and of the science of symbolism* (2nd rev. ed.). Orlando, FL: Harcourt Brace.

O'Keefe, B. J. (1988). The logic of message design: Individual differences in reasoning about communication. *Communication Monographs, 55,* 80–103.

O'Keefe, B. J., & McCornack, S. A. (1987). Message design logic and message goal structure: Effects on perceptions of message quality in regulative communication situations. *Human Communication Research, 14,* 68–92.

O'Keefe, B. J., & Sheppard, G. J. (1987). The pursuit of multiple objectives in face-to-face persuasive interaction: Effects of construct differentiation on message organization. *Communication Monographs, 54,* 396–419.

Rubin, R. B., Perse, E. M., & Barbato, C. A. (1988). Conceptualization and measurement of interpersonal communication motives. *Human Communication Research, 14,* 602–628.

Searle, J. R., & Vandervenken, D. (1985). *Foundations of illocutionary logic.* New York: Cambridge University Press.

Sieburg, E. (1976). Confirming and disconfirming organizational communication. In J. L. Owens, P. A. Page, & G. I. Zimmerman (Eds.), *Communication in organizations* (pp. 129–149). St. Paul, MN: West.

Sillars, A. L., & Wilmot, W. W. (1989). Marital communication across the life span. In J. F. Nussbaum (Ed.), *Life-span communication: Normative issues* (pp. 225–253). Hillsdale, NJ: Erlbaum.

Ting-Toomey, S. (2000). Intercultural conflict competence: A cultural variability perspective. In W. R. Cupach & D. J. Canary, *Competence in interpersonal conflict* (pp. 120–147). Prospect Heights, IL: Waveland.

Tracy, K. (1983). The issue-event distinction: A rule of conversation and its scope condition. *Human Communication Research*, *9*, 320–334.

Walther, J. B. (1994). Anticipated ongoing interaction versus channel effects on relational communication in computer-mediated interaction. *Human Communication Research*, *40*, 473–501.

C H A P T E R 5

FUNDAMENTALS

OF NONVERBAL

COMMUNICATION

WHAT IS NONVERBAL
COMMUNICATION?

Facial Expressions and Gaze

Kinesics

Haptics

Vocalics

Proxemics

Physical Appearance

Chronemics

The Environment

MISCONCEPTIONS ABOUT NONVERBAL
COMMUNICATION: INTENTIONALITY
AND CULTURE

FUNCTIONS OF NONVERBAL BEHAVIOR

Expressing Emotion

Expressing Affection

Impression Formation/Identity Management

Deception

Conversation Management

Relational Messages

NONVERBAL ABILITY

CHAPTER SUMMARY

Sarah Conner stood silently, smoking, watching a video recording that she had made months earlier. In the recording, she talked about how the world was going to come to an end and everyone would die. After the television screen froze on Sarah's expression of anger, she spoke up. Without any vocal enthusiasm, she dryly, almost sadly stated, "I feel better. . . . Things are clearer." Later Sarah sat across from her psychiatrist and tried to convince him that she was making progress and that she should be able to see her son. When the therapist asked Sarah questions about the "terminator," she denied that he existed. As she did, her face was tense, and her vocal tone was forced, controlled, constrained, and lacking in emotion. Her body also became rigid as she leaned forward and held her hands together on her lap. The therapist heard her verbal message and considered her nonverbal performance. After a pause, he decided that Sarah really wasn't well, hadn't made progress, and was lying.

This story, representing a few scenes in the movie *Terminator 2*, highlights several features of interpersonal communication. The story deals with the importance of nonverbal cues as part of the interpersonal communication process. In this scene, a decision about what is true is based not on what Sarah Conner says but on how she acts, which is inconsistent with the words she says. The therapist believes that Sarah's tense posture and voice reflect that she is not feeling better, despite what she claims verbally. The story also illustrates a variety of nonverbal cues that may be meaningful in interpersonal interactions and shows how these behaviors often work together. The therapist relies on his observations of Sarah's facial expression, posture, hands, and vocal tone to judge her progress. The story exhibits clearly that nonverbal cues are at work in our attempts to fulfill our communicative goals. For Sarah, the goal is to send emotions and beliefs that she didn't have. For the therapist, the nonverbal cues are used to determine whether or not Sarah was using deception.

To understand how such processes work, we must look more closely at nonverbal ways of communicating. This chapter extends the observations apparent in the example by discussing behaviors and other indicators that count as nonverbal cues, revealing some of the misconceptions concerning the nature of those behaviors (particularly those about the intentionality of nonverbal behavior and its cross-cultural consistency), and showing how nonverbal cues help us perform our communicative functions or goals. The chapter ends with a review of models predicting the dynamic nature of nonverbal cues as they occur between people in interactions.

WHAT IS NONVERBAL COMMUNICATION?

Nonverbal communication involves the creation of meaning through cues other than the words that we use. This relatively simple definition hides the complexity of the nonverbal system, however. Unlike language, which is highly symbolic and rule-governed, nonverbal cues can take various forms. Remland (2000), basing his discussion on work by Ekman and Friesen (1969), argues that there are at least three types of nonverbal codes: intrinsic, iconic, and arbitrary. **Intrinsic** cues include behaviors that have a direct relationship to a biologically shared signal system. Such cues would likely be used and understood by anyone at any time, because they are created by innate mechanisms. **Iconic** cues are those behaviors that stem from this biological base but are used purposefully or in some modified way. Liska (1993) referred to such cues as *semblances* or "signs that resemble their referents [but] are expressed voluntarily" (Remland, 2000, p. 13). Finally, **arbitrary** cues are created within a social or cultural group to convey meanings specific to that group. These cues are often referred to as symbols, and we argue later that the symbolic potential of nonverbal cues is often overlooked.

Nonverbal means of communicating are rich and varied not only by their nature but also in the kind of cues that count as part of these nonverbal codes. In this section we examine some of the behaviors and other cues that are part of the nonverbal communication system.

Facial Expressions and Gaze

When many people think about the nonverbal cues that they use in interpersonal interactions, they often think of how people use their **facial expressions** and their eyes to communicate. Cues that occur in and around the face are so important in our interactions that researchers created the term *facial primacy* to indicate that facial cues rank first among all forms of communication in their influence on initial impressions (Knapp & Hall, 2002).

Facial cues can come in several different forms. For example, we use static facial features, such as skin color, nose size, and bone structure, to make assessments of attractiveness, a key determinant in the overall judgments we make of others. More importantly, we use dynamic or changeable facial features, such as a person's degree of expressiveness, to decide what someone is communicating and to evaluate what that person is like. Similarly, we use many aspects of the eyes in communicating with another. The direction, duration, and accompanying muscular movement of the eyes are likely to be used to communicate different messages or to provide information. For example, in reviewing research on depression, Segrin and Abramson (1994) found that, despite the association we often make between squinting and concentration, there is also a relationship between squinting or closed eyes, among other nonverbal cues, and depression. The researchers also found that people were more likely to reject others whom they thought were depressed, highlighting the importance of these nonverbal cues.

Kinesics

Facial and eye movements are part of a larger category of nonverbal cues called **kinesics,** which refers to any movements we make with our bodies (Birdwhistell, 1970). Kinesic cues encompass the way we sit, walk, gesture, shake hands, and orient our bodies as we engage in interactions with others. They are the cues most typically associated with the unfortunate term *body language.*

Perhaps the most well known kinesic behaviors are gestures, and gestures alone have a lot of variety. When we use our body to communicate something that can also be communicated with words (e.g., waving "hello") we are using gestures as **emblems** (Ekman, 1976). Like language, emblems are created and given meaning by a culture, although interestingly, most cultures have gestures for the same types of meanings. For example, most cultures have gestures for greetings, gestures for profanity, and so on. We can also use our gestures as **illustrators** by providing a visual image of something we are saying or to which we are referring — such as showing someone where the door is located or how small something is — or as **regulators** to punctuate the rhythm or importance of what we are saying such as accentuating a point by hitting the table as we speak about it. Although gestures are often associated with a particular culture, Morris, Collett, Marsh, and O'Shaughnessy (1979) noted interesting patterns in the ways such gestures "moved" across national boundaries and were adopted in the repertoires of other, neighboring groups.

Haptics

A special category of kinesic behavior involves touches, and its study and use are known as **haptics.** Touches can vary based on their duration, location, and strength, and these varieties of touch influence the meanings that we give to touches (Floyd, 1999). After asking people to keep a record of their daily touches, Stanley Jones (1994) looked at the functions that were most common to everyday touches and showed the tremendous variety of messages that touch alone communicates. For instance, he defined touch types as positive, sexual, playful, control, ritual, greeting or departure, task-related, accidental, or hybrid (multi-meaning) in nature.

There also appears to be a lot of variety in individuals' use of touch. In particular, some people are more touch avoidant in general than are others (Andersen, 1999). Floyd (2000) also reviewed the finding that U.S. women are more likely to touch than are U.S. men in general and that same-sex touch is considered more positive and expected when it occurs between women than it is when it occurs between men. Although there are a number of theories attempting to explain these differences, Floyd specifically tested a position by Derlega, Lewis, Harrison, Winstead, and Costanza (1989) that stated that men in general engage in less same-sex touching because of a concern with being perceived as homosexual, whereas women are less likely to have this concern. In his study of participants looking at photographs of same-sex pairs hugging, Floyd (2000) found that the degree to which a person fears being seen as homosexual *did* predict more negative judgments of same-sex touch except when told

STUDENT AS OBSERVER: KEEPING A TOUCH DIARY

Although we are often unaware of them, touches occur more (or less) than we think. To get a better sense of how many and what types of touches you give or receive on an average day, use Jones's diary form to record all of the touches of which you are a part over the course of one day.

a. What types of touches (e.g., handshakes, pats, etc.) were most common? Least common?
b. What were some of the most common functions the touches seemed to serve?
c. Were you more likely to give or receive touches?
d. Compare your diary to others in the class. Were you more or less involved in touching than others? Why?

RECORDING FORM FOR TOUCHES

Directions: Circle the appropriate response or responses under each category. Write your answers in the designated areas.

Incident # _____ Date: _____ Time: _____ Circle: AM or PM

Initiator:

a. Me   b. Other   c. Mutual

Type of touch: (main body parts involved: _____ to _____)

a. frontal hug   b. side hug   c. hold   d. caress   e. press against   f. spot touch
g. handshake   h. pinch   i. punch   j. pat   k. squeeze   l. other _____

Relationship of other to you: (initials/name of other: _____)

a. romantic intimate   b. close friend   c. friend (not close)
d. acquaintance   e. stranger   f. relative (specify _____)

Meaning of the touch: _____

Response to the touch:

a. accepted by me   b. accepted by other   c. rejected by me   d. rejected by other

If rejected, tell why (taboo violation?): _____

Circumstances influencing the touch or the reaction (explain): _____

Source: Adapted from *The right touch: Understanding and using the language of physical contact* by S. E. Jones. Reprinted by permission of Hampton Press.

that the embraces were specifically nonsexual. Given that more men than women are likely to fear being seen as homosexual, his study provides support for this concern being one reason for less same-sex touch between men than between women.

Vocalics

In addition to how we use our bodies to communicate, we may also employ components of our voice to fulfill our interpersonal communication goals. Referred to as **vocalics** or **paralanguage,** vocal cues include the rate, pitch, character, volume, and amount of variation used as we speak. Vocalics may even involve the way we don't speak or our use of silence.

It is easy to overlook vocal behaviors as part of the nonverbal system, because they are so closely tied to language. Cues such as silence, groans, and laughter can exist separately from or substitute for words we might have said. We use such cues for many goals, including determining what another person is like. Indeed, we often use vocal stereotypes to assess another's personality, depending on the sound, tone, and character of his or her voice. If we determine that a person's voice is attractive because it is calm, less monotonous, less nasal and shrill, we are also likely to judge that person as extraverted, open, and conscientious (Andersen, 1999; Zuckerman, Hodgins, & Miyake, 1990). In addition, vocalics are often necessary for determining the meaning of the words others say. Researchers such as Blanck and Rosenthal (1982) have looked at the importance of vocalics in understanding when a message is meant to be sarcastic. They found that knowing when a verbal message is not meant to be taken literally depends on understanding the accompanying vocal cues. For example, vocalics are crucial to determining the real message of the words, "I'm sorry."

Proxemics

Proxemics refers to our use of personal space when communicating with others. Edward Hall (1966) pioneered work in this area and concluded that people tend to have four physical distance zones. These are, in order from close to far, distances for interacting with intimates (often 0 to 18 inches in the United States), casual-personal distances (about 1 to 4 feet), impersonal or social-consultative distances (from 4 to 12 feet typically), and public distances (past 12 feet). These distances reflect the nature of the relationship we have with another person.

Most cultures and ethnic groups have distance zones, but the size of those zones varies. For example, African Americans tend to use the largest impersonal spaces, followed by European Americans, with Latin Americans using the smallest conversational (casual-personal) space (Halberstadt, 1985). Some sex differences in the use of space are notable. One review of literature found that females are likely to use less space and to stand or sit closer to others than are males (Hall, 1985), at least in situations perceived as friendly. Arguments over the reason for this distinction separate researchers, however. According to Knapp and Hall (2002), the different distances kept by males and females may be the result of diverse socialization when we are young. It may also be based on differences in social power. People with more power tend to use greater space than do those with less power. Henley (1977) argued that the differences between the sexes in their use of space reflects a social imbalance in the power given to males and females in many cultures.

Physical Appearance

Several features of **physical appearance** may play a role in our communication with others. Skin and hair color, body type, clothing choices, and unique physical characteristics all help us make choices about what another person is like (although, as will be discussed later, we are often incorrect in the personality judgments we make about others). Most notably, however, we use our own or others' physical attractiveness in our communication (this can be based on the facial expressions discussed earlier).

An attractive person tends to find it easier to reach his or her goals in large part because people tend to assume that attractive people also have other positive characteristics. In the United States, attractive people are likely thought to be more honest, intelligent, sexual, and socially skilled than are unattractive people. Different characteristics are tied to attractiveness in other cultures; for example, in Korea attractiveness has been linked to integrity and concern for others (Wheeler & Kim, 1997). Few, if any, actual links exist between attractiveness and most of these characteristics, however. Some ties exist between attractiveness and social skills, and these may be due to the fact that attractive people may have more opportunities to interact. One study by Herman, Zanna, and Higgins (1986) found that physically attractive people are sought out for interaction more often than are unattractive people. The chance to interact more may increase the social skills of attractive people.

Chronemics

Although different in nature than the cues already mentioned, we may also use **chronemics,** or time, as a medium of communication. Like the other cues, however, chronemics includes several characteristics such as rules of time (e.g., how late to arrive), rhythms (e.g., body cycles), and how many activities we perform at one time. And although we don't think of it very often, time is not real in that the meanings that we assign to time are not inherent to time itself. Rather our use of time is very much dictated by the values and lifestyles of a particular culture or group (Levine, 1997).

Many goals can be achieved through chronemics, although we are not always aware of them. For example, we can communicate our preferences based on how much time we spend with another person. One investigation by Word, Zanna, and Cooper (1974) studied how long interviewers spent with interviewees of their own race (white) and of another (black) race. The interviewers (all white in this study) tended to interview other whites for longer periods than they interviewed black interviewees. The length of time spent may have communicated the degree of comfort the interviewers felt with the interviewees, their beliefs about how much they had in common, or other effects of racial stereotyping. The reason for the different interview lengths was not made clear, however.

The Environment

As with the preceding cues, certain features of our **physical environment** affect our communication, although this cue is different in nature than the other nonverbal behaviors listed earlier. The amount of noise, the physical structure, the temperature, and even the color of our environment may alter our communication. We talk more quietly in some places such as a temple or a library than we do in others, and the rules for our talk are dictated by our knowledge of the environment. Environment cues can also make statements about people and their relationship to others. For instance, the person with the largest, most centrally located office is likely to be the person with the highest status in an organization.

Though we are often unaware of the effects of our environments on our behavior, factors such as temperature and color can have a large influence. One researcher's review of this literature found that aggressiveness is linked, in part, to climate, with "[h]otter regions of the world yield[ing] more aggression . . . and [hotter] years, quarters of years, and seasons, months, and days, all yield[ing] relatively more aggressive behaviors" (Anderson, 1989, p. 93). As for color, Pelligrini and Schauss (1980) found that pink walls reduced aggressiveness; however, when a prison followed this guideline and painted the interior a shade of hot pink, aggression actually increased substantially (Knapp & Hall, 2002).

MISCONCEPTIONS ABOUT NONVERBAL COMMUNICATION: INTENTIONALITY AND CULTURE

As can be seen, many nonverbal cues can be part of our communicative attempts. Although we have talked about them here separately from one another, most of the time the cues work together to fulfill communicative ends. Even though nonverbal cues are potentially an important part of interaction, misconceptions persist about how they work to help us accomplish our goals. Two such misconceptions are

1. Nonverbal cues are largely natural, unintentional, and out of our control and awareness.
2. Nonverbal cues make up a universal language and have cross-cultural consistency.

Many people are more likely to believe nonverbal behaviors when they contradict what we say verbally, because people often assume that we do not have as much control over our nonverbal cues as we have over our verbal cues. But this is not necessarily the case. Although many nonverbal behaviors are out of our awareness and are linked directly to largely uncontrollable, innate, intrinsic systems, some nonverbal cues are easier to control than others; for example, the face is more readily controllable than the body, which is easier to control than vocal cues (DePaulo & Rosenthal, 1979). And situations often arise in which we think about and use our nonverbal cues with **intentionality.** When we want to deceive others, for instance, we try to seem sincere by looking another directly in the eye. When we want to impress others, we alter our appearance to look our best. When we want to show our interest in what someone is saying, we make sure to nod our head as he or she speaks.

We also try to make all of our behaviors send the same message by being consistent with one another. Such **channel consistency** usually helps us send a clear, credible message. **Channel discrepancy** occurs when some behaviors seem to say one thing, and others (including language) appear to communicate a different message (as Sarah Conner's behaviors did in the opening example). Unintended discrepancy may make us appear dishonest or not credible. Intended discrepancy can make our communication purposefully ambiguous and is often necessary, such as when we are trying to be sarcastic or evasive.

All these examples show that nonverbal cues are sometimes a conscious part, at least to some degree, of how we go about communicating and pursuing our goals. Other people are likely to be aware that our behaviors can be intentional at times. Manusov and Rodriguez (1989) had their research participants go into banks to talk to employees about opening an account. The researchers found that the participants were more likely than not to assume that the employees used their nonverbal behaviors purposefully to show the participants that they wanted (or in some cases did not want) their business. Likewise, married couples often attribute intent to their spouses' nonverbal behaviors. When a behavior is important enough to catch their attention, couples may be more likely than not to assume their spouses acted intentionally, especially if the behavior is consistent with how they expect their spouse to act (Manusov, 1995). Couples who are happy in their relationship are more likely to assume positive behaviors are intentional. Unhappy couples are more inclined to think negative behaviors are intentional.

The studies mentioned earlier looked only at the person deciding whether another's nonverbal behaviors were intended. Other researchers have investigated whether intentionally sent cues appear different from those sent without intent. Ekman and his colleagues (Ekman, Friesen, & O'Sullivan, 1988), for example, looked at the physical distinctions between "felt" (i.e., real and not sent intentionally) and "false" smiles (those used to cover up another feeling). They found that felt smiles involved different muscles, and more of them, and therefore looked different than false smiles. Other research has noted that intended (but not necessarily deceptive) nonverbal behavior tends to be easier to read, more redundant with other cues, and somewhat more exaggerated than unintended nonverbal cues. For example, Motley and Camden (1988) learned that posed emotional expressions are much more likely to communicate a clear meaning than are spontaneous expressions. This is in part because posed messages are more consistent with stereotypical facial expressions.

Motley (1986) argues that "the difference between intended and unintended behaviors is, in communication, *a vital difference*" (p. 5, emphasis his), and other researchers have also clarified a distinction between different "origins" of nonverbal cues. For example, Buck (1988) discusses those nonverbal cues that are unintended or spontaneous. He argues that some nonverbal cues are used automatically and have a natural, intrinsic relationship with a certain meaning. For example, a sigh can reflect a feeling of fatigue, and this is likely a universal, biologically based behavior. Conversely, cues such as those discussed earlier can be seen as purposeful and other-directed (Motley, 1990). They are intended, rule-governed behaviors that are designed to send a message to another. These two varieties of nonverbal behavior are probably best seen as the end points of a continuum of cues, with many of the behaviors we use falling between the extremes: having some intent and purpose and some more natural, unintended basis. Whether there are two forms or many points on a continuum, however, what is most important is that we understand that nonverbal cues may have very different origins.

In addition to the belief that nonverbal cues are always out of our awareness and control, another misconception about nonverbal behaviors is that they make up a universal language. Although people from all nations may be able to read some basic facial expressions and other intrinsic codes, much of our nonverbal language is tied to cultural rules. Jones (1994), for example, reports that handshakes, although used in most societies, vary significantly from one country to another. In Columbia, for example, handshakes tend to be longer than in other countries. "In France, India, and Japan, the hand grip may be much less firm than Americans are used to" (Jones, 1994, p. 229).

The distance we stand from others, the amount and direction of our gaze, the form of our buildings and landscapes, and the number of activities we perform at once are all tied to our culture and/or our ethnicity. Ekman and Friesen (1969) refer to these cultural variations and the prescriptions that underlie them as **display rules,** indicating that they are learned behaviors dictated in large part by the community in which they exist. What is acceptable in one culture — such as sitting with crossed legs and showing the underside of the foot in the United States — is often taboo in other cultures. In Thailand, for example, showing the sole of one's foot is a great insult. Being able to achieve interaction goals depends on knowing (and usually, but not always, following) the rules.

Andersen (1999) recently discussed some differences in cultural evaluations of physical appearance. He noted,

> There is some cross-cultural similarity in what constitutes an attractive face, but little else is similar. Ubangi women insert pieces of wood into their mouths to create lips ten inches in diameter. In China during much of this century, women often had their feet bound and deformed, which prevented them from walking outside the home. . . . The amount of body hair that is desirable also varies greatly from culture to culture. American advertisers have been quite successful in convincing women that hair on their legs or underarms is unsightly. . . . By contrast, European women are much less likely to remove the hair. (pp. 79–80)

112

These examples are important because they show that what we evaluate and how we communicate nonverbally is, in many cases, very much a part of the culture in which we live. Besides some basic facial expressions (see Figure 5.1 for six emotional expressions thought to be universal) and cues that reflect our moods, many of the nonverbal cues we come to accept as natural and universal are rather specific to, or culturally bound with, the communication system of the cultural group in which they occur. Indeed, they are so important that they actually may help to define a culture or ethnic group (Levine, 1997). If we think about our own or another's cultural heritage,

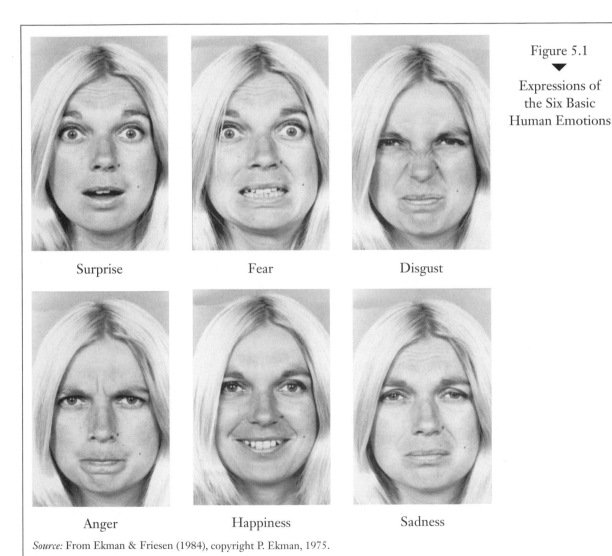

Figure 5.1

▼

Expressions of the Six Basic Human Emotions

Surprise   Fear   Disgust

Anger   Happiness   Sadness

Source: From Ekman & Friesen (1984), copyright P. Ekman, 1975.

much of what we think of are the ways people look and act. These appearances and actions are often made up of the nonverbal cues discussed earlier.

The idea that the use and meaning of many nonverbal cues are culturally bound suggests that these cues are part of a larger culturally created symbol system. The idea that nonverbal cues may have a range of symbolic meanings across (and within) groups has not been lost on several researchers. Holman (1979), for example, investigated the communicative value of clothing and found that "[t]he 'language' of clothing use in one social system, one situation, and one role was partially decoded and its meaning explained in terms of attributions made to a user" (p. 372). That is, one of the most important symbolic values of clothing within a social system is to help others make attributions about the characteristics of the person wearing the clothes. Importantly, however, those attributions varied based on the social group of the attributor, emphasizing their **symbolic,** arbitrary, and assigned nature.

Marcus (1995) researched extensively the meanings people give to the environment of their home (see Csikszentmihalyi & Rochberg-Halton, 1981, for a similar discussion of the home's contents). For Marcus, the home's primary symbolic value is, not the perception of *another's* character, but rather the presentation of one's own and the playing out of one's self. For some, building (or tearing down) a house can be symbolic. As one of her participants noted, "[w]ith a sledgehammer, my son David destroyed some of the old walls in the house. Not vindictively, as some children destroy houses because they don't like them, but creatively" (Marcus, 1995, p. 53).

For others, the home's importance and its furnishings may reflect some aspects itself. As an example, Marcus tells the story of Angela. Angela "had recently broken up with her lover Eileen. . . . She started to tell me about her lover's ability to create a home, and her own lack of ability — or refusal — to participate in the process" (p. 54). According to Angela,

> Eileen was always very home-oriented and wanted a home very much, while I had always placed myself in dingy kinds of inexpensive places. When we began to live together, she started to organize the apartment and always wanted me to participate, and I would never bring myself to do that . . . I think it was partly because I always knew that someday I would leave. (Marcus, 1995, p. 54)

In interesting ways, Marcus's work explores "the symbolic role of the house as an expression of the social identity we wish to communicate" (p. 12), and she found tremendous variety in the ways such expressions emerged.

FUNCTIONS OF NONVERBAL BEHAVIOR

From the previous discussion, it is obvious that nonverbal cues — whether unintended or intended, universal or culturally bound — play a significant role in our interactions with others. We might say that nonverbal cues perform a range of **communicative**

functions, or tasks; they allow us to try to fulfill a number of our interpersonal goals. Such a functional approach to nonverbal behaviors makes two assumptions. First, it assumes that clusters of behaviors are used together to communicate a function; although a single behavior such as gaze may fulfill a function, it is more common for cues, including language, to work together. Second, the functional approach assumes that any one behavior can be used, alongside other cues, to communicate any of several functions. Proxemics, for example, may be a part of communicating a liking for another person or it may be an indication of the amount of power one person has over someone else.

Expressing Emotion

For many people, the most obvious functions of nonverbal cues are to communicate how we feel and to reveal how others are feeling. In particular, the term *facial expression* shows the inherent connection often made between certain behaviors and their meanings. Although the previous discussion warning against assuming an automatic, natural connection between behaviors and their meanings is important to keep in mind, nonverbal cues are a vital part of emotional expressions. When we are trying to understand what others are feeling, for example, we look at their face and their posture and listen to their vocal tone. When we want to communicate our feelings to others, we are inclined to do so nonverbally. But the relationship between nonverbal cues and emotional expression is complex, in large part because emotions themselves are complex.

Some researchers argue that **emotional expressions** reflect an area of universal communication that can be used and understood by all. To provide evidence for this, they point to studies that show that people from a range of cultures can recognize the emotions reflected in certain photographs (Ekman & Friesen, 1969). The similarity between the expressions used by humans and those used by other primates (e.g., showing aggression or sadness) also reflects that some expressions may have biological and evolutionary origins. However, most of the emotional expressions we actually use are modified through our culture's display rules. We learn, for example, how to show sadness, happiness, and anger in ways appropriate to our culture. In the United States, for example, we would likely show grief on our faces and in the quietness of our voices. We also behave according to chronemic rules, which regulate when a grieving period should be complete. In several African cultures, however, the way to show grief is through loud wailing for extended periods. The same emotion is reflected in different behaviors as dictated by the culture in which they occur. Contexts also affect the display of emotions, for example, a new vocabulary for displaying emotions on-line has developed. See the box "Emoticons" for more on this.

Other work limits the extent to which emotional expressions form a simple, universal set of messages. Motley's (1993) studies revealed that most emotional expressions used in everyday conversations cannot be interpreted outside of the conversation in which they occur. Seldom do we use the kind of exaggerated expressions that led Ekman and Friesen (1969) to conclude that everyone can read emotional messages.

EMOTICONS

It is often said that one of the ways that Internet communication differs from face-to-face interactions is that there are no nonverbal cues on-line. One of the ways users have tried to overcome this is through the use of typed-out faces: typographic symbols which, when turned sideways, look like facial expressions, known as *emoticons* (emotional icons) or *smileys*. There are hundreds if not thousands of these little symbols on various lists of emoticons floating around the Internet (see what a Yahoo.com search for "smileys" renders, http://dir.yahoo.com/Arts/Visual_Arts/Computer_Generated/ASCII_Art/Smileys/). Emoticons range from the simplest facial expressions, such as :-) (happy), :-((sad), and ;-) (winking), to elaborate and obscure constructions (among which 8-{} representing "someone wearing glasses, a moustache, and beard," is a relatively mild one!). Commentators and researchers who have discussed these all seem to agree that they are used to convey emotion the way that nonverbal cues function in other settings (Rezabek & Cochenour, 1998). But do they?

Walther and D'Addario (2001) conducted an experiment to see if they really do, and if so, in what ways. These researchers reviewed nonverbal communication research to see what was previously known about the impact of visual, especially facial, displays of emotion, in combination with verbal cues in face-to-face settings. They hypothesized based on these findings that emoticons might have additive effects (e.g., a positively valenced verbal statement, plus a :-) should be doubly positive, whereas a positively valenced statement plus a :-(should be less positive than the same verbal statement with no emoticon); or that emoticons could have a primacy effect (e.g. a negative verbal message with a :-) could be interpreted as positive). A mixed message effect of :-) plus a negative statement might result in an interpretation of sarcasm, as could a wink ;-) if the latter has iconic effects. The research presented one of eight mock-up e-mail messages to each subject, with a particular message-plus-emoticon embedded in the message, or with no emoticons, as a control condition.

The range of variations included these combinations:

That econ class you asked me about, it's a joy. I wish all my classes were just like it. :-)

That econ class you asked me about, it's a joy. I wish all my classes were just like it. :-(

That econ class you asked me about, it's a joy. I wish all my classes were just like it. ;-)

That econ class you asked me about, it's a joy. I wish all my classes were just like it.

That econ class you asked me about, it's hell. I wish I never have another class like it. :-)

That econ class you asked me about, it's hell. I wish I never have another class like it. :-(

That econ class you asked me about, it's hell. I wish I never have another class like it. ;-)

That econ class you asked me about, it's hell. I wish I never have another class like it.

Subjects completed a questionnaire in which they rated the message on the sender's happiness/sadness, sarcasm, ambiguity, and reported their attitude toward the course. In a separate part of the questionnaire they were asked to match the three basic emoticons with a list of emotion labels.

(Continued)

(Box continued from previous page)

Although the level of consensus on what emoticons match which emotions was as high or higher than that obtained in research on actual human facial expressions, the impact of the emoticons in the messages were very few. In general, Walther and D'Addario found there was a "negativity effect"; if there was *any* negative element in the message — either the verbal portion or the "frownie" — the message was interpreted as negative. A double negative (negative statement plus frownie) was no more negative than just one negative element, but emoticons in general had less impact than the simple variations in attitude conveyed by the valence of the verbal statements. It seems true that, as Marvin (1995) characterized the on-line environment, virtual interaction comprises "worlds made of words."

Sources: Marvin (1995); Rezabek & Cochenour, 1998; Walther & D'Addario, 2001.

Instead, most of the movements that our faces make in our conversations with others act as interjections (e.g., communicating the equivalent of "gosh," "geez," "really," or "oh, please") and make sense only when we have also heard the topic being discussed. Thus, although nonverbal behavior is an important component of emotional expression, any particular cue (e.g., a facial expression) is likely to need other behaviors (such as language or vocal cues) to be interpreted accurately.

Expressing Affection

In addition to expressing emotions, people express other needs through their nonverbal (and verbal) cues. One of these needs or goals is the communication of affection for others. According to Floyd (1997), "**affectionate communication** is critical for the development and maintenance of personal relationships" (p. 68). Being able to show others you care about them (and having them show they care about you) is a particularly important interpersonal goal and communicative function. Affectionate nonverbal behaviors include hugs, kisses, holding hands, and putting one's arm on another's shoulder (Floyd, 1994; Floyd & Morman, 1998; Greenbaum & Rosenfeld, 1980).

Despite its importance to overall relational health, Floyd argues, however, that "communicating affection is not a wholly risk-free endeavor" (1997, p. 68). Particularly in certain relationships, such as between male siblings, communicating affection may not be easy, and expectations for how much affection is expected or normal influences the expression of actual affection. These expectations, and some of the possible biological or evolutionary bases for them, led Floyd (2001) to develop an Affection Exchange Theory (AET). In AET, affection is thought of as an adaptive behavior, helpful to human long-term survival by promoting bonding and its subsequent increased access to resources. If AET is correct, affection ought to increase as its ability to enhance survival also increases. In particular, parents should be likely to be more affectionate with those children who are able to carry on their reproductive lines. In an interesting test of the theory, Floyd measured several variables that could be linked to adaptation or long-term survival and looked at their association with reported affection. He made the argument that fathers with fewer children would show more affection to their offspring than would fathers with many children, as the need to pass on affectionate (and ultimately reproductive) ability decreases with more offspring. As well, fathers would likely express more affection to heterosexual sons than to homosexual sons, again to facilitate greater reproductive ability in the future. Although there was no support for a link between the number of offspring and the amount of affection displayed by fathers, Floyd did find that males who reported being homosexual or bisexual also reported receiving less affectionate behavior from their fathers. "AET explains this difference as a function of parents investing discriminately in their children so as to maximize the likelihood that grandchildren will be produced. According to the theory, children who are less likely to reproduce biologically will receive, on average, fewer resources from their parents than children who are likely to reproduce, and affection is one such resource" (Floyd, 2001, p. 46).

Impression Formation/Identity Management

Emotion and affection expression are important not only for the information they convey; we also make evaluations of the expressor based on his or her expressiveness, and this reflects our reliance on nonverbal cues for assessing what another person is like. The process of person perception was discussed in Chapter 2. In this section, the focus is on showing not only how nonverbal cues work as part of person perception (**impression formation**), but also the ways in which people work to get others to see them in a certain way (**identity management**).

Many of the examples given up to this point already highlight how important nonverbal cues are for judging others. Berry and Zebrowitz-McArthur (1988) showed not only the link between nonverbal cues and impressions but also the important effects that such impressions may have. These researchers used a simulated courtroom trial to study the effects of physical attractiveness; in particular, they looked at the importance of facial maturity on perceptions and on trial outcomes. Berry and Zebrowitz-McArthur found that "babyfaced" adults are thought to be more honest than adults with more mature facial features. Because of this, the babyfaced adults in the mock trial were seen to be less likely to have intentionally committed a crime, and they subsequently received shorter criminal sentences.

Berry and Zebrowitz-McArthur's study helps show the series of links that people tend to make when judging others through nonverbal means. We see one or more behaviors or cues (e.g., little gaze or physical attractiveness) and assume that the person has certain characteristics (e.g., shyness). We may then treat that person in a particular way because we believe he or she has certain characteristics; this treatment may actually help bring around those qualities, creating a self-fulfilling prophecy. More likely, as discussed in Chapter 2, we tend to notice those behaviors that are consistent with the beliefs we have about another and ignore those that are inconsistent. Because of this process, we come to believe that we have made the right judgment of another.

Importantly, however, research has revealed very few reliable personality characteristics that are revealed through nonverbal means (Burgoon, Buller, & Woodall, 1996).

People still rely on nonverbal cues, despite the potential errors, when judging what others are like. For instance, besides helping us try to figure out what another person is like, we also reflect aspects of our own identity (or desired identity) through nonverbal means. Others are likely to know our sex or ethnicity by observing our physical features. This ability to reflect certain aspects of ourselves to others is linked with others' ability to make judgments of us. In her discussion of Tajfel's research on how we reflect our social identities to others, Burgoon (1994) says that,

> Manifest indications of one's cultural, social, demographic, and personal characteristics serve as "identity badges," enabling individuals to project their own identification with various personal and social categories while simultaneously enabling observers to use the same cues as an instant means of classification. Thus, not only may individuals rely on their own nonverbal behavior as affirmation or self-verification of their identities . . . but others may also treat such information as outward reflections of the inner self. (p. 245)

Deception

When people think of impression management, they sometimes think only of reflecting aspects of themselves that are inaccurate or exaggerated (e.g., acting smart or kind; see Chapter 6). Although many of our self-reflections are true, others, particularly those that depend on nonverbal cues, may have an element of deception in them. **Deception** is the deliberate attempt to foster a false belief.

People usually behave differently when they lie than when they tell the truth, although not reliably and not always in the ways others expect (for the best indicators, see Table 5.1). According to Leathers (1986), most people use a "liar stereotype" to decide when someone else is lying to them. They assume that a person who is lying will gaze less often, move his or her body frequently, and appear anxious. But researchers have found no consistent association between gaze or amount of movement and lying, making liar stereotypes hurtful to attempts to figure out if someone else is lying. A liar may only appear anxious if he or she is concerned about the lie or about getting caught. If the lie is unimportant, a communicator may instead be relaxed and controlled, but he or she may be lying nonetheless. Further, someone accused of lying but who is, in fact, telling the truth may still show signs of anxiety.

Most of our attempts to deceive or to detect deception occur with others, and our relationship with those others works to affect the deception process. Interpersonal Deception Theory (IDT) tries to take various aspects of relationships into account. In a review of her theory, Burgoon (1994) lays out several of the theory's assumptions. One assumption is that the deception that occurs when people are interacting with others differs in form from that which occurs outside of interpersonal contexts, such as in a taped deposition. During interaction, for example, people have the chance to show their suspicion and to probe for more information. Probing has been linked

"I knew the suspect was lying because of certain telltale discrepancies between his voice and nonverbal gestures. Also his pants were on fire."

Sometimes people are obviously lying. But most of the time we have to look at subtle nonverbal behaviors associated with deception to discover someone is lying.

with more effective deception detection in other studies. Interestingly, however, deception that occurs in interaction during dialogue with another also allows the deceiver to better manage his or her deceptive behavior, resulting in *less* accurate judgments about another's deception when compared to judgments made from another's monologue (Burgoon, Buller, & Floyd, 2001). While it is clear, then, that deception that occurs in interaction differs from that outside it, it is less clear which context allows ultimately for greater deception or detection accuracy! White and Burgoon (2001) offer an extensive discussion of what interaction deception looks like.

Another assumption of IDT is that familiarity with another "moderates the behaviors, perceptions, and interpretations" (Burgoon, 1994, p. 261) that people use when lying and when deciding if a partner is lying. For instance, if one of your primary goals is to keep a relationship intact, you may not see behaviors in your partner that could indicate that he or she is lying to you. Conversely, knowledge of a partner's typical or baseline behavior may help a person detect unusual cues (e.g., excessive blinking) that may denote deception. In any case, however, IDT helps reveal how the interpersonal nature of most deception alters the deception process and shows the complexity of the communication that occurs during deception.

Table 5.1

SUMMARY OF NONVERBAL BEHAVIORS ASSOCIATED WITH DECEPTION

The following behaviors have been examined by researchers and found to be relatively (but not completely) reliable indicators of deception.

Channel	Behavior
Face	
Pupil dilation	A liar's pupils may dilate when lying.
Blinking	Liars engage in more frequent blinking when lying.
Body	
Adaptors	Liars tend to engage in some type of adapting, such as rubbing hands or arms together.
Vocalics	
Response length	Liars usually speak for briefer time durations than do truth tellers.
Speech errors	Liars usually communicate messages containing more speech errors, such as mixing present and past tenses.
Speech hesitations	Liars usually communicate messages containing more pauses and filled pauses (e.g., "ah," "err," "humm"). A liar's speech may therefore not be as fluent as a truth teller's.
Pitch	Liars usually communicate messages with a tone of voice higher in pitch than they do when telling the truth.
Verbal	
Negative statements	Liars frequently include some negative statement, like "I was afraid you'd ask" or "I hated it," when lying.
Irrelevant statements	Liars frequently include some irrelevant statement in the lies they communicate; e.g., when asked, "What is it like working in the governor's office?" a liar might talk about politics or about his or her own work habits.

Channel	Behavior
Immediacy statements	Liars frequently include some expression on non-immediacy (noninvolvement) in the lies they communicate; e.g., they say things like "that girl over there" rather than the more immediate expression "this girl."
Leveling terms	Liars frequently include more vague terms such as "the usual stuff" or "the typical things" and "you know" (as in "you know what I mean"). Leveling terms also include universal expressions: "all," "every," and "none."
Channel discrepancy	At least one channel (face, body, vocalic, or verbal) fails or even contradicts the message communicated in other channels.

The following behaviors have been examined by scholars and have been found *not* to be reliable indicators of deception: gaze frequency, smiling, head movements, illustrators or other gestures, shrugs, foot/leg movement, postural shifts, response latency (the length of time it takes to answer a question; the hesitation that occurs between when a question is asked and an answer provided), speech rate, and self-references (the number of times someone refers to the self, "I," "my," "me," and "mine," etc.).

Source: Based on analysis and review by Zuckerman & Driver (1985). Used with permission of the publisher, Lawrence Erlbaum Associates, Inc.

Conversation Management

Although this chapter focuses primarily on what nonverbal cues allow us to do, often separate from what we say, our ability to have conversations with others depends, ironically, on nonverbal behaviors. The way in which nonverbal cues allow for the structuring of conversation is known as **conversation management.**

Many examples show the role of nonverbal cues in facilitating conversations (e.g., we gesture to make points and use high levels of gaze to show we are listening to another), but one of the most notable is how the behaviors help people take turns in their conversation (i.e., to know when it is our time to speak and to know when it is our conversational partner's time). According to Burgoon (1994), "[n]onverbal cues are the lubricant that keeps the conversation [turn-taking] machine well-oiled" (p. 268).

Research has identified that speaker and listener behaviors determine whose turn it is to speak, auditor feedback cues that control speaker behavior, behaviors that mark changes in the tone and topic of interaction, the influence of interruptions and other dynamic cues on floor-holding and the flow of conversation, the role of distance and silence in maintaining engagement, and factors influencing the smoothness of interaction. (Burgoon, 1994, p. 268)

In most cases, good conversations include the smooth exchange of speaking turns; this is made possible largely through nonverbal cues such as eye behavior, vocal pitch and tone, rate of speech, and gestures. Cappella's work (reviewed in his 1994 chapter) refers to people's ability to keep the floor (i.e., to keep speaking when they want to, through both verbal and nonverbal means), and he has shown a strong link between holding the floor and others' assessments of the speaker's power and control. Those who are able to hold the floor by increasing vocal volume, gazing away, using gestures, and including vocal fillers between verbal statements tend to have more power than others have in a conversation. Not only are nonverbal cues important in how smoothly a conversation will flow, they are also vital in understanding the outcomes (e.g., perceived or actual power) of those conversations.

Relational Messages

Burgoon and Hale (1984, 1987) were some of the first researchers to discuss in-depth the ways in which nonverbal cues both denote and change the relationship we have with others. For them, **relational messages** include the amount of intimacy two people share, whether the power balance is matched or not between interactants, and the degree to which one's relationship with another person is formal or informal. Overall, "relational communication addresses the processes and messages whereby people negotiate, express, and interpret their relationships with one another" (Burgoon et al., 1989, p. 289), and such messages are typically sent nonverbally.

One of the ways in which people may reflect both intimacy and equality with one another is through the degree of behavioral **synchrony** that exists. Synchrony can occur in many forms (i.e., mirroring, mimicry, or behavioral meshing), but overall it refers to the amount of coordination in peoples' behaviors (i.e., two people move in the same ways and/or their behaviors fit with the other's behaviors). When two or more peoples' nonverbal cues are in sync with one another, the relational message sent is usually solidarity, agreement, support, and attraction.

Only behavior that appears to be naturally synchronous is likely to reflect positively on relationships. In one study, Manusov (1992) led some participants to believe that the person with whom they had interacted mirrored their behavior on purpose (the other person was actually a confederate in the study); she told others that the mirroring behavior was accidental, or she never discussed the behaviors (the control group). Those participants who were told that the behaviors were intentional judged the confederate to be less competent and attractive (and the behaviors as more disjointed and exaggerated) than they judged him or her to be when they were not led to think that the behaviors were purposeful, even though the confederate actually acted the same way each time. The negative evaluations were due in large part to

M. B. Duda/Photo Researchers

Liking can be communicated nonverbally through a wide range of behaviors, including close distance, forward leaning, pleasant facial expression, touch, open posture, eye gaze, and postural mirroring.

participants' beliefs that they were being manipulated by the confederate, a common outcome of synchrony perceived to be unnatural.

As noted, nonverbal cues can show the current state of a relationship or help interactants move to a different type of relationship. For example, Muehlenhard and his colleagues performed a series of studies relating specific behaviors with the intent to date (Muehlenhard, Koralewski, Andrews, & Burdick, 1986; Muehlenhard & McFall, 1981; Muehlenhard, Miller, & Burdick, 1983). Their participants watched videotapes of male-female interactions and rated the probability that the woman would accept if the man asked her for a date. Observers believed that the woman would be likely to accept a date if she maintained high levels of eye contact, smiled, leaned forward, leaned sideways, maintained a direct body orientation, moved closer to the man, touched him, and used animated speech, among other cues. Because these cues are often linked with desires to escalate a relationship, some subset of these cues is likely to help communicate that one person is ready for the relationship to change.

The process of moving from one level of relationship to another is often problematic, however, and this may be based in behavioral mistakes made in our quest to attain goals. Specifically, Abbey (1982) conducted a study in which male and female students engaged in a five-minute interaction while being observed from another room. After the conversation, both partners and the observers rated the extent to which the interactants were friendly, seductive, flirtatious, and promiscuous. Male and female observers saw the female interactants as friendly, but the male observers rated them as more seductive and flirtatious than did the female observers. Abbey concluded that males very often perceive a higher level of sexual intent than females do, and this could lead to different interpretations (i.e., mistakes) for the same actions. Shotland and Craig (1988) contend, however, that there are objective distinctions between seductive behavior (e.g., long eye contact, softer speaking patterns, many short smiles, and comments that the other has been noticed before) and friendliness (e.g., more frequent brief eye contact, taking longer speaking turns, being distracted by other activities).

The idea of relational messages also connotes that nonverbal cues allow us to relate in a general sense to others. A recent book illustrates this idea. Cole (1998) conducted a series of interviews with people who could speak but could not rely on faces to communicate (some had Möbius syndrome, in which the face is immobile, and others were blind and therefore could not see others' faces). He was able to show that, unless people find another means of connecting with others (e.g., through vocal characteristics such as tone and volume), they often feel at odds with the social world (see the box "About Mary" for a description of one of the people in this study). According to Cole, "without the feedback and reinforcement that facial gestures provide, there [is] little relatedness and engagement" (p. 10). This discussion shows just how profound social relationship to others is and highlights the importance of nonverbal cues in the process of engagement.

Certain aspects of relational messages have received extra attention by researchers from communication and psychology. In particular, a set of theories exists that help

ABOUT MARY

"[A] case of the neurological demonstration was wheeled into the lecture theatre. She sat on the chair impassively. She looked at our group of neurologists, students, and nurses, some interested, some bored. Before us was an elderly lady; we looked but could not work out how she felt. She seemed anxious and frightened; that much we knew, though it was not clear how we knew. . . . But what was immediately apparent was the lack of movement in her face. This disturbed us, for we could not gauge if our questions were being received with the sympathy with which they were asked, nor if she was cooperating in answering or even comprehending them. . . . Some wondered if she was also slightly demented, given her problem with comprehension and answering us." (p. 1)

Taken from Jonathan Cole's *About Face.* Used with permission from the publisher, Bradford/MIT Press.

to explain and predict one aspect of the relationship that can form between people: expressions of intimacy and of immediacy. **Intimacy** and **immediacy** are related messages, but they are not the same. Intimacy refers to the closeness that people feel for or express to one another. Immediacy is part of how actively engaged we are in an interaction. Both intimacy and immediacy rely on many of the same nonverbal cues, however, including increased gaze, more direct body orientation, greater facial and vocal pleasantness, closer proximity, and more touch.

The particular emphasis of the theories on intimacy and immediacy is on the ways in which changes in one person's behavior affect or are tied to changes in another's nonverbal cues. For example, if two people were on their first date, and one of them began acting more intimate or more immediate at some point in the evening (e.g., moved a bit closer to his date, talked with a softer vocal tone, and reached over to touch his date's hand), the date could respond in different ways. She could act exactly as she had been (a reaction called non-response or non-accommodation), act more intimately like her partner (**reciprocity**), or act less intimate than she had before (**compensation**). The theories that have been developed attempt to both predict which response is most likely to occur and to explain why such a response is most likely. Some of these theories are discussed briefly to help show how dynamic and unpredictable responses to behavioral changes can be.

The first researchers to discuss changes in intimacy in some depth were Argyle and Dean (1965). The primary thesis of their Equilibrium Theory was that people attempt to maintain a certain comfort balance in their interactions with others. When one person acts in a way that tips the balance — particularly by changing the amount of intimacy he or she expressed — the automatic response is to try to restore balance, or equilibrium. Argyle and Dean predicted that too much intimacy (or immediacy) by one person (e.g., sitting very close, gazing much of the time) would be met with a large decrease in intimacy (or immediacy) by the other (e.g., increased distance, less eye contact, or even cues like using a louder voice or talking about non-intimate topics). Conversely, too little intimacy leads to the other person's attempting to add more intimacy. In both cases, the predicted action would be compensation, at least in relationships that have already established a comfortable or acceptable intimacy level.

Other researchers used Argyle and Dean's initial model to propose theories that also incorporate times in which people use reciprocity or do not change their behaviors. For example, Andersen's (1985) Cognitive Valence Theory relies on the size of the change in behaviors (the "violation") and on how people label the behaviors. That is, whether we reciprocate or compensate another's behaviors depends on how much the other person changed the intimacy or immediacy balance (the size) and on how we interpret the motives or reasons underlying the behaviors (the label). With large violations, the most common response is to compensate without labeling, "[b]ecause steep increases in arousal are inherently stress- and fear-producing" (Andersen, Guerrero, Buller, & Jorgensen, 1998, p. 509). If a good friend all of a sudden sat so close to you that his leg touched yours, for example, this would likely be a large violation, and you would probably move away without having to think about it. Andersen

(1985) argues that with moderate changes in others' behaviors, on the other hand, we will feel either positive or negative, depending on a range of *valencers* about the other person and the environment. These valencers are (1) social or cultural norms, (2) interpersonal relationship history, (3) perceptions of the other person, (4) the environmental context, (5) the state (e.g., mood) of the other person, and (6) psychological or communicative traits of the other person. For example, if a friend leaned somewhat close to you, and you and she have a good relational history, you would be likely to valence her behavior positively. According to this model, compensation occurs with negative labeling, or valencing, and reciprocity follows positive labeling.

Andersen's model was an attempt to bring greater complexity — and reality — to the ways people respond to others' nonverbal behaviors. Burgoon, Stern, and Dillman's (1995) **Interaction Adaptation Theory** also adds some layers of detail to previous models of the ways people respond to changes in intimacy cues; it incorporates a large set of factors that may determine our reaction to another's change in behavior. The authors argue that, for biological reasons and because of social learning, we tend toward reciprocity. That is, we will match someone's behavior in most of our interactions. We use compensation only in a few instances, such as when the roles we are playing dictate that we do so (e.g., superior/subordinate interaction may prescribe that people act in complementary ways) or when a disliked other acts more immediate or involved than expected. For instance, if another student whom you do not like touches you briefly as you talk, you would be likely to compensate for the behavior by moving back or with some other non-intimate action. More complex ways of responding are likely to be based on three factors: (1) the required, (2) the expected, and (3) the desired level of interaction behaviors. These help make up one's "interactional position," and Burgoon and colleagues lay out how these influences are likely to work to predict behavioral adaptation.

As can be seen, many attempts have been made to understand and predict a certain set of behaviors: those that follow from another's changes in intimacy or immediacy cues. As also noted, there are some similarities and some differences in these theories. How do we decide which one is right? Andersen et al. (1998) specifically tested several of the models. The researchers "failed to find unequivocal support for a single theory" (p. 501). Instead, they argued that the best predictor of behavioral responses to changes in another's nonverbal behaviors may be a combination of the models. Guerrero, Jones, and Burgoon (2000), for example, found that compensation (through verbal behavior) is common only when another's intimacy is very low. More research will be needed to get a fuller picture of this complex area.

NONVERBAL ABILITY

To perform any of the functions just discussed, and to work toward achieving interpersonal goals, people need a certain degree of ability. Three primary nonverbal abilities have been identified: encoding skill, decoding ability or **sensitivity,** and skill in regulating or controlling nonverbal communication (Riggio, 1992). Encoding skills refer to the ability to enact the nonverbal cues that you wish to and to have them interpreted consistently with what you intended. Decoding (or receiving) skills are concerned with people's ability to pick up and interpret others' nonverbal cues as the others intended. This type of nonverbal sensitivity has been linked with the empathic skills discussed in Chapter 3. Finally, nonverbal control deals with one's ability to perform the function of conversation management referred to earlier. People who are high self-monitors and those who deceive well tend to be very skilled at nonverbal regulation.

Research has found that, in general, females are more skilled nonverbally than are males (Hall, 1985). In particular, females tend to be more nonverbally expressive (an encoding skill). Males, however, may be more able to control what they perceive as undesirable emotional displays and therefore show some greater ability in nonverbal regulation (Riggio, 1992). Females also tend to pick up on others' nonverbal behaviors more effectively, particularly to cues that they see such as facial cues (rather than vocalics, for example) and are typically thought to develop greater nonverbal sensitivity than do males overall. People in lower subordinate work positions also tend to have greater decoding accuracy (Hall, Carter, & Horgan, 2001).

These sex/status differences may have important consequences, as the implications of good nonverbal ability are quite profound. Hodgins and Belch (2000) argue that greater nonverbal ability has been linked with social adjustment, being perceived positively by others, greater interpersonal influence, and marital adjustment, among other things (see Miczo, Segrin, & Allspach, 2001 for more on the link between nonverbal skill and relational satisfaction and Carton, Kessler, & Pape, 1999 for the tie between skill deficit, depression, and lower relational well-being). For example, people who are more expressive nonverbally also "may have an advantage in forming interpersonal relationships . . . because they participate more in social encounters and make more favorable impressions on others" (Riggio, 1992, p. 15).

Greater nonverbal skill may be associated with one's upbringing and may also have significant influence on current or desired relationships. According the Halberstadt (1986), we learn encoding and decoding skills in different ways, however. Encoding skills (or deficits) tend to be developed (or not) by having others around who are more (or less) expressive. So, if your parents were particularly expressive, chances are you are also highly proficient in encoding skills. Decoding skills are more likely to develop when we do not have expressive families; it requires more expertise to read others' nonverbal cues when they are not good encoders.

Other influences in our upbringing may affect our ability to use nonverbal cues adequately and accurately. Most notably, the emotional tone of a home appears to influence nonverbal skills. Hodgins and Belch (2000) report that a positive home environment tends to foster greater encoding ability. Conversely, people exposed to domestic violence in their parents' homes are likely to have deficits in their encoding and decoding skills (Hodgins & Belch, 2000).

CHAPTER SUMMARY

Several cues may be used as part of how we communicate nonverbally. Those cues include both behaviors (e.g., gaze, body movements) and other cues (e.g., time, environment). Although we do not always realize it, we have the ability to control and use many nonverbal cues with intent. As well, nonverbal behaviors are often understood as having the meaning we intend them to within our own culture. Although sometimes cues reflect natural and universal meanings, at other times we may use our nonverbal behaviors with intention to fulfill our goals. Typically the cues work in groups to help serve a range of communicative functions. As well, people differ in their ability to use nonverbal cues to perform these functions.

The functions enacted nonverbally include emotional expression, affection expression, person perception, conversation management, deception and its detection, and relational messages. One type of relational message, the message of intimacy, is often ambiguous. A number of models try to predict how people will respond to changes in intimacy cues. Although no one model or theory is seen to be fully accurate, together they help to show the range of complexity of the nonverbal communication system.

KEY TERMS

▼

affectionate communication, p. 116
arbitrary, p. 104
channel consistency, p. 110
channel discrepancy, p. 110
chronemics, p. 108
communicative functions, p. 113
compensation, p. 125
conversation management, p. 121
deception, p. 118
display rules, p. 111
emblems, p. 105
emotional expressions, p. 114
facial expressions, p. 104
haptics, p. 105
iconic, p. 104
identity management, p. 117
illustrators, p. 105

impression formation, p. 117
intentionality, p. 110
Interaction Adaptation Theory, p. 126
intimacy/immediacy, p. 125
intrinsic, p. 104
kinesics, p. 105
nonverbal communication, p. 104
physical appearance, p. 108
physical environment, p. 109
proxemics, p. 107
reciprocity, p. 125
regulators, p. 105
relational messages, p. 122
sensitivity, p. 127
symbolic, p. 113
synchrony, p. 122
vocalics, or paralanguage, p. 107

EXERCISES FOR FURTHER DISCUSSION

▼

1. What physical characteristics are most common to physically attractive people, in your view? Why do you think these characteristics make people more or less attractive? What do you think are some other characteristics that attractive people are likely to have?
2. Choose a time when you had an important interpersonal interaction (e.g., a first date, meeting someone's family, a job interview, a speech).
   a. What nonverbal behaviors did you use with intent?
   b. How successful do you think you were at using them as intended?
   c. Was it easier to control, and therefore use, some of the behaviors rather than others?
3. List nonverbal behaviors that you think are universal. Make another list that includes behaviors that have certain meaning within your culture but perhaps not in other cultures. If you were talking to someone from another culture, how would you know when to interpret his or her seemingly unusual nonverbal behaviors as unique to, and therefore usual in, his or her culture or as just universally unusual?
4. Each person in a group should choose an emotion (e.g., fear, happiness, and sadness) to communicate while saying the words, "What's for dinner?" While each person is making the statement, watch the cues used to express the emotion.
   a. What nonverbal cues were involved? Did some surprise you?
   b. Were some emotions easier to read? Why?
   c. Was it easier to read the emotions of some people rather than others? Why?
   d. How typical is it to have to discern emotions from nonverbal cues alone, as you did in this exercise?
5. Choose a place where you can observe a lot of people. Watch anyone who is with someone else. Try to guess what type of relationship they have.
   a. Are they friends? Family? In love? Co-workers? Acquaintances? What nonverbal cues did you use to make this assessment?
   b. In any of the relationships you observed, do you think that one person was trying to change the nature of the relationship (e.g., make it more or less intimate)? If so, what cues did they use? What was the other person's reaction?

SUGGESTED READING

▼

NONVERBAL BEHAVIORS/CUES

Birdwhistell, R. L. (1970). *Kinesics and context*. Philadelphia: University of Pennsylvania Press.

Ekman, P., & Friesen, W. V. (1969). The repertoire of nonverbal behavior: Categories, origins, usage, and coding. *Semiotica, 1*, 49–98.

Hall, E. T. (1966). *The hidden dimension*. Garden City, NY: Anchor Books/Doubleday.

Jones, S. E. (1994). *The right touch: Understanding and using the language of physical contact*. Cresskill, NJ: Hampton.

NONVERBAL FUNCTIONS

Andersen, P. A. (1985). Nonverbal immediacy in interpersonal communication. In A. W. Siegman & S. Feldstein (Eds.), *Multichannel integrations of nonverbal behavior* (pp. 1–36). Hillsdale, NJ: Erlbaum.

Burgoon, J. K., & Hale, J. L. (1984). The fundamental topoi of relational communication. *Communication Monographs, 51*, 193–214.

Cappella, J. N. (1994). The management of conversational interaction in adults and infants. In M. L. Knapp & G. R. Miller (Eds.), *Handbook of interpersonal communication* (2nd ed., pp. 380–418). Thousand Oaks, CA: Sage.

DePaulo, B. M., & Rosenthal, R. (1979). Ambivalence, discrepancy, and deception in nonverbal communication. In R. Rosenthal (Ed.), *Skill in nonverbal communication: Individual differences* (pp. 204–248). Cambridge, MA: Oelgeschlanger, Gunn & Hain.

Floyd, K. (2001). Human affection exchange: I. Reproductive probability of men's affection with their sons. *The Journal of Men's Studies, 10*, 39–50.

NONVERBAL ABILITY

Hodgins, H. S., & Belch, C. (2000). Interparental violence and nonverbal abilities. *Journal of Nonverbal Behavior, 24*, 3–24.

Riggio, R. E. (1992). Social interaction skills and nonverbal behavior. In R. S. Feldman (Ed.), *Applications of nonverbal behavioral theories and research* (pp. 3–30). Hillsdale, NJ: Erlbaum.

REFERENCE LIST

▼

Abbey, A. (1982). Sex differences in attributions for friendly behavior: Do males misperceive females' friendliness? *Journal of Personality and Social Psychology, 42*, 830–838.

Andersen, P. A. (1985). Nonverbal immediacy in interpersonal communication. In A. W. Siegman & S. Feldstein (Eds.), *Multichannel integrations of nonverbal behavior* (pp. 1–36). Hillsdale, NJ: Erlbaum.

Andersen, P. A. (1999). *Nonverbal communication: Forms and functions*. Mountain View, CA: Mayfield.

Andersen, P. A., Guerrero, L. K., Buller, D. B., & Jorgensen, P. F. (1998). An empirical comparison of three theories of nonverbal immediacy exchange. *Human Communication Research, 24*, 501–535.

Anderson, C. A. (1989). Temperature and aggression: Ubiquitous effects of heat on occurrence of human violence. *Psychological Bulletin, 106,* 74–96.

Argyle, M., & Dean, J. (1965). Eye-contact, distance, and affiliation. *Sociometry, 28,* 289–304.

Berry, D. S., & Zebrowitz-McArthur, L. (1988). What's in a face? Facial maturity and the attribution of legal responsibility. *Personality and Social Psychology Bulletin, 14,* 24–33.

Birdwhistell, R. L. (1970). *Kinesics and context.* Philadelphia: University of Pennsylvania Press.

Blanck, P. D., & Rosenthal, R. (1982). Developing strategies for decoding "leaky" messages: On learning how and when to decode discrepant and consistent social communications. In R. S. Feldman (Ed.), *Applications of nonverbal behavioral theories and research* (pp. 89–115). Hillsdale, NJ: Erlbaum.

Buck, R. (1988). Nonverbal communication: Spontaneous and symbolic aspects. *American Behavioral Scientist, 31,* 341–354.

Burgoon, J. K. (1978). Attributes of a newscaster's voice as predictors of his credibility. *Journalism Quarterly, 55,* 276–281.

Burgoon, J. K. (1994). Nonverbal signals. In M. L. Knapp & G. R. Miller (Eds.), *Handbook of interpersonal communication* (2nd ed., pp. 229–285). Beverly Hills, CA: Sage.

Burgoon, J. K., Buller, D. B., & Floyd, K. (2001). Does participation affect deception success? A test of the interactivity principle. *Human Communication Research, 27,* 503–534.

Burgoon, J. K., Buller, D. B., & Woodall, W. G. (1989). *Nonverbal communication: The unspoken dialogue.* New York: HarperCollins.

Burgoon, J. K., Buller, D. B., & Woodall, W. G. (1996). *Nonverbal communication: The unspoken dialogue* (2nd ed.). New York: McGraw-Hill.

Burgoon, J. K., & Hale, J. L. (1984). The fundamental topoi of relational communication. *Communication Monographs, 51,* 193–214.

Burgoon, J. K., & Hale, J. L. (1987). Validation and measurement of fundamental themes of relational communication. *Communication Monographs, 54,* 19–41.

Burgoon, J. K., Stern, L. A., & Dillman, L. (1995). *Interpersonal adaptation: Dyadic interaction patterns.* Cambridge, England: Cambridge University Press.

Cappella, J. N. (1994). The management of conversational interaction in adults and infants. In M. L. Knapp & G. R. Miller (Eds.), *Handbook of interpersonal communication* (2nd ed.). Thousand Oaks, CA: Sage.

Carton, J. S., Kessler, E. A., & Pape, C. L. (1999). Nonverbal decoding skills and relationship well-being in adults. *Journal of Nonverbal Behavior, 23,* 91–100.

Cole, J. (1998). *About face.* Cambridge, MA: Bradford/MIT Press.

Csikszentmihalyi, M., & Rochberg-Halton, E. (1981). *The meaning of things: Domestic symbols and the self.* Cambridge, England: Cambridge University Press.

DePaulo, B. M., & Rosenthal, R. (1979). Ambivalence, discrepancy, and deception in nonverbal communication. In R. Rosenthal (Ed.), *Skill in nonverbal communication: Individual differences* (pp. 204–248). Cambridge, MA: Oelgeschlanger, Gunn & Hain.

Derlega, V. J., Lewis, R. J., Harrison, S. Winstead, B. A., & Costanza, R. (1989). Gender differences in the initiation and attribution of tactile intimacy. *Journal of Nonverbal Behavior, 13,* 83–96.

Ekman, P. (1976). Movements with precise meanings. *Journal of Communication, 26,* 14–26.

Ekman, P., & Friesen, W. V. (1969). The repertoire of nonverbal behavior: Categories, origins, usage, and coding. *Semiotica, 1*, 49–98.

Ekman, P., & Friesen, W. V. (1984). *Unmasking the face.* Palo Alto, CA: Consulting Psychologists.

Ekman, P., Friesen, W. V., & O'Sullivan, M. (1988). Smiles when lying. *Journal of Personality and Social Psychology, 54*, 414–420.

Floyd, K. (1994). *Gender and manifestations of intimacy among same-sex friends and same-sex siblings.* Paper presented at the 7th International Conference in Personal Relationships, Groningen, The Netherlands.

Floyd, K. (1997). Communicating affection in dyadic relationships: An assessment of behavior and expectancies. *Communication Quarterly, 45*, 68–80.

Floyd, K. (1999). All touches are not created equal: Effects of form and duration on observers' interpretations of an embrace. *Journal of Nonverbal Behavior, 23*, 283–299.

Floyd, K. (2000). Affectionate same-sex touch: The influence of homophobia on observers' perceptions. *The Journal of Social Psychology, 140*, 774–788.

Floyd, K. (2001). Human affection exchange: I. Reproductive probability of men's affection with their sons. *The Journal of Men's Studies, 10*, 39–50.

Floyd, K., & Morman, M. T. (1998). The measurement of affectionate communication. *Communication Quarterly, 46*, 144–162.

Greenbaum, P. E., & Rosenfeld, H. M. (1980). Varieties of touching in greetings: Sequential structure and sex-related differences. *Journal of Nonverbal Behavior, 5*, 13–25.

Guerrero, L. K., Jones, S. M., & Burgoon, J. K. (2000). Responses to nonverbal intimacy change in romantic dyads: Effects of behavioral valence and degree of behavioral change on nonverbal and verbal reactions. *Communication Monographs, 67*, 325–346.

Halberstadt, A. G. (1985). Race, socioeconomic status, and nonverbal behavior. In A. W. Siegman & S. Feldstein (Eds.), *Multichannel integrations of nonverbal behavior* (pp. 227–266). Hillsdale, NJ: Erlbaum.

Halberstadt, A. G. (1986). Family socialization of emotional expression and nonverbal communication styles and skills. *Journal of Personality and Social Psychology, 51*, 827–836.

Hall, E. T. (1966). *The hidden dimension.* Garden City, NY: Anchor Books/Doubleday.

Hall, J. A. (1985). Male and female nonverbal behavior. In A. W. Siegman & S. Feldstein (Eds.), *Multichannel integrations of nonverbal behavior* (pp. 195–225). Hillsdale, NJ: Erlbaum.

Hall, J. A., Carter, J. D., & Horgan, T. G. (2001). Status roles and recall of nonverbal cues. *Journal of Nonverbal Behavior, 25*, 79–100.

Henley, N. M. (1977). *Body politics: Power, sex, and nonverbal communication.* Englewood Cliffs, NJ: Prentice-Hall.

Herman, C. P., Zanna, M. P., & Higgins, E.T. (Eds.). (1986). *The Ontario symposium: Vol. 3. Physical appearance, stigma, and social behavior.* Hillsdale, NJ: Erlbaum.

Hodgins, H. S., & Belch, C. (2000). Interparental violence and nonverbal abilities. *Journal of Nonverbal Behavior, 24*, 3–24.

Holman, R. H. (1979). Clothing as communication: An empirical investigation. *Advances in Consumer Research, 7*, 372–377.

Jones, S. E. (1994). *The right touch: Understanding and using the language of physical contact.* Cresskill, NJ: Hampton.

Knapp, M. L., & Hall, J. A. (2002). *Nonverbal communication in human interaction* (5th ed.). Stamford, CT: Wadsworth/Thomson Learning.

Leathers, D. G. (1986). *Successful nonverbal communication: Principles and applications*. New York: Macmillan.

Levine, R. (1997). *A geography of time: The temporal misadventures of a social psychologist*. New York: Basic Books.

Liska, J. (1993). Bee dance, bird songs, monkey calls, and catacean sonar: Is speech unique? *Western Journal of Communication, 57*, 1–26.

Manusov, V. (1992). Mimicry or synchrony: The effects of intentionality attributions for nonverbal mirroring behavior. *Communication Quarterly, 40*, 69–83.

Manusov, V. (1995). Intentionality attributions for naturally occurring nonverbal behaviors in intimate relationships. In J. Aitken & L. J. Shedletsky (Eds.), *Reader in intrapersonal communication* (pp. 339–350). Plymouth, MI: Midnight Oil & Speech Communication Association.

Manusov, V., & Rodriguez, J. S. (1989). Intentionality behind nonverbal messages: A perceiver's perspective. *Journal of Nonverbal Behavior, 13*, 15–24.

Marcus, C. C. (1995). *House as a mirror of self: Exploring the deeper meaning of home*. Berkeley, CA: Conari.

Marvin, L. E. (1995). Spoof, spam, lurk and lag: The aesthetics of text-based virtual realities. *Journal of Computer-Mediated Communication* [On-line], 1. Available: http://www.ascusc.org/jcmc/vol1/issue2/marvin.html

Miczo, N., Segrin, C., & Allspach, L. E. (2001). *Relationship between nonverbal sensitivity, encoding, and relational satisfaction, 14*, 39–48.

Morris, D., Collett, P., Marsh, P., & O'Shaughnessy, M. (1979). *Gestures: Their origins and distributions*. New York: Stein and Day.

Motley, M. T. (1986). Consciousness and intentionality in communication: A preliminary model and methodological approaches. *Western Journal of Speech Communication, 50*, 3–23.

Motley, M. T. (1990). On whether one can(not) not communicate: An examination of traditional communication postulates. *Western Journal of Speech Communication, 54*, 1–20.

Motley, M. T. (1993). Facial affect and verbal content in conversation. *Human Communication Research, 20*, 3–40.

Motley, M. T., & Camden, C. T. (1988). Facial expression of emotion: A comparison of posed expressions versus spontaneous expressions in an interpersonal communication setting. *Western Journal of Speech Communication, 52*, 1–22.

Muehlenhard, C. L., Koralewski, M. A., Andrews, S. L., & Burdick, C. A. (1986). Verbal and nonverbal cues that convey interest in dating: Two studies. *Behavior Therapy, 17*, 404–419.

Muehlenhard, C. L., & McFall, R. M. (1981). Dating initiation from a woman's perspective. *Behavior Therapy, 12*, 682–691.

Muehlenhard, C. L., Miller, C. L., & Burdick, C. A. (1983). Are high-frequency daters better cue readers? Men's interpretation of women's cues as a function of dating frequency and SHI scores. *Behavior Therapy, 14*, 626–636.

Pelligrini, R. F., & Schauss, A. G. (1980). Muscle strength as a function of exposure to hue differences in visual stimuli: An experiential test of Kinesoid theory. *Journal of Orthomolecular Psychiatry, 2*, 144–147.

Remland, M. S. (2000). *Nonverbal communication in everyday life*. Boston: Houghton Mifflin.

Rezabek, L. L., & Cochenour, J. J. (1998). Visual cues in computer-mediated communication: Supplementing text with emoticons. *Journal of Visual Literacy, 18,* 210–215.

Riggio, R. E. (1992). Social interaction skills and nonverbal behavior. In R. S. Feldman (Ed.), *Applications of nonverbal behavioral theories and research* (pp. 3–30). Hillsdale, NJ: Erlbaum.

Segrin, C., & Abramson, L. Y. (1994). Negative reactions to depressive behaviors: A communication theories analysis. *Journal of Abnormal Psychology, 103,* 655–668.

Shotland, R. L., & Craig, J. M. (1988). Can men and women differentiate between friendly and sexually interested behavior? *Social Psychology Quarterly, 51,* 66–73.

Walther, J. B., & D'Addario, K. P. (2001). The impacts of emoticons on message interpretation in computer-mediated communication. *Social Science Computer Review, 19,* 323–345.

Wheeler, L., & Kim, Y. Y. (1997). What is beautiful is culturally good: The physical attractiveness stereotype has different content in collectivist cultures. *Personality and Social Psychology Bulletin, 23,* 795–796.

White, C. H., & Burgoon, J. K. (2001). Adaptation and communicative design: Patterns of interaction in truthful and deceptive conversations. *Human Communication Research, 27,* 9–37.

Word, C. O., Zanna, M. P., & Cooper, J. (1974). The nonverbal mediation of self-fulfilling prophecies in interracial interaction. *Journal of Experimental Social Psychology, 10,* 109–120.

Zuckerman, M., & Driver, R. E. (1985). Telling lies: Verbal and nonverbal correlates of deception. In A. W. Siegman & S. Feldstein (Eds.), *Multichannel integrations of nonverbal behavior* (pp. 129–147). Hillsdale, NJ: Erlbaum.

Zuckerman, M., Hodgins, H., & Miyake, K. (1990). The vocal attractiveness paradigm: Replication and elaboration. *Journal of Nonverbal Behavior, 14,* 97–112.

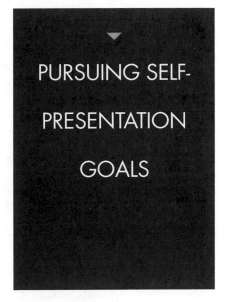

PURSUING SELF-PRESENTATION GOALS

In Part II, we look more closely at the goal of self-presenta-tion, one of the three fundamental goals discussed in Chapter 1. Chapter 6 discusses the nature of self-presentation: what it is, when we engage in it, how it relates to interpersonal communication, and how we make self-presentations believable. We also discuss various communicative strategies employed to create and maintain desired public images. Chapter 7 examines self-disclosure, or how we reveal ourselves to different people in different degrees and in different situations. We discuss factors that affect whether people will disclose, how they disclose, and how their disclosure is perceived. Chapter 8 focuses on how we defend ourselves in situations that are threatening to our self-identity, particularly how we use accounts to justify our behaviors.

C H A P T E R 6

PRESENTING

THE SELF

WHAT IS SELF-PRESENTATION?

THE NATURE OF SELF-PRESENTATION

THE NATURE OF INTERPERSONAL
SELF-PRESENTATION
Monitoring Self-Presentation
Self-Identity and Self-Presentation
Indicators of Attainment

DIRECT STRATEGIES OF
SELF-PRESENTATION
Ingratiation
Intimidation
Self-Promotion
Exemplification
Supplication

INDIRECT STRATEGIES OF
SELF-PRESENTATION

ROLES, GENDER, PERSONALITY,
AND CULTURE

CHAPTER SUMMARY

Personal Ad 1 | **Single Female,** 22, loves dancing, movies, moonlight drives, photography — and all outdoor activities, hiking, camping, snowboarding, all of it! Seeks really good guy, 21–27, big-hearted, fun, adventurous, humorous, and ready to take on life!

Personal Ad 2 | **Smart, witty, attractive, original** — what more could you want? Attractive Single Female, fit, kind, seeks similar male, 36–45. Hopefully, you're also adventurous, slightly zany, & occasionally walk on the wild side.

Personal Ad 3 | **Sexy and sensual.** Vertically independent, horizontally compliant, silky soft with laserlike mind, 48. Me: Intellectually challenging, creatively analytical, analytically incisive, politically astute, MENSA member seeks male of same qualities, interested in passion and passionate living. You: Professional, financially secure, brilliant and analytic, 45–55, non-smoker, fit, and please be good looking.

Personal Ad 4 | **Attention Drop Dead Gorgeous** ladies, 22–32. I am a handsome, marriage-minded Divorced Male, youthful 49, educated, romantic, slim, fit, athletic, sensual, gentle, funny, clean, good kisser, ready for Long Term Romantic liaison. You: slim, romantic, loyal, funny, sexy, gorgeous.

WHAT IS SELF-PRESENTATION?

When others first meet you, they form impressions of you based on your physical characteristics, what you say and how you say it, as well as your poise, posture, gesturing (or lack of), and other body movements. You may want to be liked by the people you meet, and try to be a likable person. They may consider you a truly likable person, or a phony who is trying too hard to be liked. You may want to be perceived as a competent, successful person, and others may think of you as a competent, successful person, or as a person who is a bragger, conceited, and stuck-up. When you groom a desired image, you are engaging in **impression management,** or **strategic self-presentation,** which is an individual's conscious attempt to exercise control over selected behaviors in order to make a desired impression (Schlenker & Pontari, 2000; Tice & Faber, 2001).

You have been doing this for years. In fact, modern technologies have made it possible for us to groom desired images on the Internet (by our e-mail or talking in chat rooms); by what we include and present on our Web sites; by our answering machines, personal advertisements, license plates, and stickers; and more. In grooming your image to the public at large, you may rehearse and rerecord the greeting on your answering machine, so that you speak more fluently, sound happy, or use a joke to show how likable and fun you are. Or, you may edit your e-mail in order to be friendly and engaging. You select photographs for your Web site to reveal what is more important to you or to show a particular aspect of yourself to others. In this chapter, we will first discuss the general nature of self-presentation and then discuss the significance of interpersonal self-presentations and how they are groomed and monitored. We focus attention on both direct and indirect strategies of self-presentation.

THE NATURE OF SELF-PRESENTATION

Over four decades ago, Erving Goffman (1959) coined the term *dramaturgy*, which is based on the view that the whole world is a stage, and we are all actors performing various roles (some more competently than others) (see Brissett & Edgley, 1990; Schlenker, 1986; Schlenker & Weigold, 1992). Goffman's notion of the presentation of self details the coordination of six elements: the actor, the audience, the stage, the script, the performance, and audience reactions.

1. *The Actor.*   It is assumed that we all play multiple roles in the "stage" of life — you may present one self to your parents, one to friends, one to co-workers, one to professors, one to your coach, and one to your significant other. Some elements of the selves may overlap (i.e., being witty, polite), but otherwise you adapt to being romantic, studious and serious, or zany, depending on the role you are adopting. We can legitimately claim a number of roles; we develop knowledge of these roles as we mature and gain feedback from others on performances from the past (like dancing, dating, kissing, etc.).

2. *The Audience.*   Most of us learn to "segregate" our audiences, and we come to know their status, power, attractiveness, familiarity, expectations, and what they value. We can best achieve any number of our interactional goals by performing appropriately to the audience. For example, if we are passing the patrol officer on his or her motorcycle, we monitor our behavior to ensure that we appear to be a good, safe

driver. Or, we act studious and serious around the professor from whom we will one day ask for a letter of recommendation. We may also say or do things we believe a desirable person wants to hear in order to get a date.

3. *The Stage.* Life is a series of stages — blind dates, double dates, classes, parties, interviews, work, meetings with a significant other's friends or family members, and so forth. Some of these have well-defined norms (lecture classes, work, eating out, shopping); others do not. Unless there is a rehearsal (like a wedding rehearsal), most of us engage in a scripted performance based on the norms for the situation. The stage idea is important because, as actors, we recognize different stage settings, and we know that different scripts and props are used for different stage settings.

4. *The Script.* We all have well-defined scripts for some events or rituals — grocery shopping, eating at a restaurant, perhaps attending classes, being at work, attending church services, funerals, etc. (see also Chapter 2). We hardly have to think about our performance, roles, or impression management concerns as we routinely act out the script (wait to be seated, the host seats us, we engage in small talk, look at menus, order beverages, etc.). For a number of events, we enter with a certain notion of what to expect, and/or we develop plans regarding how we will create our desired image. We usually try to be likable on a first date, or to self-promote on a job interview.

5. *The Performance.* The communication aspect of dramaturgy rests in our ability to combine behaviors that are verbal, vocal, and nonverbal in order to perform the role, on stage, to the particular audience and achieve the desired outcome. In a competent performance, we successfully achieve the goal of promoting the desired image, depending on our strategy. For example, we can appear likable or competent, and we avoid being perceived as a bragger, a conceited individual, and so forth.

6. *Audience Reactions.* We never merely perform a role without gaining feedback, and no one could develop a realistic sense of self without confirmation from others. Feedback can be positive, meaning the audience nods or vocalizes acceptance of our performance as likable, competent, and so on. Or, the feedback can be qualified and muted, which may prompt us to place greater effort in the performance or to rethink the performance for the next date or event. Negative feedback (boredom, rejection — "I don't think that is funny") provides greater impetus to rework our performance and perhaps emphasize different elements of the self. We depend on confirmation from others regarding major portions of our public self-presentations. We tend to be happy or gratified when they accept our presentation, and their rejection may entail altering our notions of self that we present to the public (i.e., "Maybe I am not that open-minded after all?").

The dramaturgical approach can be applied to a wide range of settings — organizational, political, interpersonal, and more. Communication scholars have also focused on preferences for particular communication channels for communicating particular impression management goals. Richer channels, ones involving access to words and nonverbal behaviors (tone of voice, speed of speech, gestures, and the like), such as face-to-face and telephone conversations, provide more information and feedback to both communicators (see O'Sullivan, 2000). Leaner channels are ones involving limited information, such as electronic mail and letters. Richer channels, relative to leaner ones, are considered more authentic and credible, and less controlled or contrived.

Communicators prefer to use richer channels when sharing positive information about the self (or when receiving positive information about a friend) because richer channels provide greater direct access to each person's positive reactions; people can see, hear, and feel positive information (praise, pride, happiness, etc.). A fuller range of emotions is experienced, and, relative to leaner channels, communicators can assess with a certain amount of clarity just how much each person shares the positive emotions. The advantages of leaner channels, however, rest in the extent to which a communicator can exert control over the message; there is greater ambiguity in the message when given access only to words, and emotional experiences are muted. In support of the claim about preferences, O'Sullivan (2000) concluded that communicators prefer to communicate positive information (for either self or other) in face-to-face settings, and to use mediated channels when communicating negative information. They prefer, in particular, to use mediated channels when the negative information threatens their self-presentation to others.

On-line messages and relationships also allow for communicators to edit and refine messages prior to sending them. It has been demonstrated that people spend more time backspacing, deleting, inserting, and rearranging their text when they wanted to impress the receiver (Walther, 1997). For example, female students edited more when they thought they were addressing a female professor, while males spent more time and effort crafting their message when communicating to female students. Edited messages were considered friendlier and conveyed greater receptivity to continued communication, compared to those receiving less editing. In studying the uses of computer-mediated communication, which was traditionally viewed as impersonal (i.e., a way of sending brief notes, reminders, memos, etc.), Walther (1996) found that selective self-presentation on-line is part of the process that can lead to "hyperpersonal" interaction. By this he meant that people who can competently use the Internet can communicate with others in ways that parallel or even exceed face-to-face messages in terms of friendliness, intimacy, and desirability. Communicators on-line can work to achieve impression management goals by editing messages to be more precise in what they say, and how they say it. They can reveal just as much information as they want to at any given time, and do so without a turn-taking, turn-yielding exchange in ongoing dialogue.

There is plenty of evidence to indicate that friends and acquaintances can be supportive and humorous and use relational maintenance strategies on-line. Bangerter (2000), on the other hand, examined strategic self-presentation in ongoing natural conversations, where one's self-presentation has to fit in with the conversational rules (see discussion of Grice's maxims in Chapter 4). In this context, or stage, effective self-presentation depends on building up intermediary links so that the self-presentational information is thematic to the conversation at hand, and partners may have to make explicit efforts to return to the topic of the conversation after one or more partners engage in self-presentation.

A special stage on which to present the self is the personal Web page, or home page (Arnold & Miller, 1999, 2000; Miller, 1995, 1999; Miller & Arnold, 2001; Miller & Mather, 1998). Some communicators use the *home* metaphor literally by including a front door, flower arrangements, and so forth. However, Miller (1995) notes that home pages, although not interactive, often invite comment from visitors and give visitors options for contacting the site owner, and operate, obviously, as a way to manage one's public image. Elements on Web sites may include personal touches ("This is me," "Here are my friends/friends' links"), associations to groups and others, links to social groups (a group photograph of sorority, baseball team, etc.), and attitudes ("This is what I think is cool"). These elements help make the owner appear likable, friendly, personable. Other elements may include a vita or resume, an advertisement for services the owner can perform, "cool stuff" that owner has achieved, references to accomplishments, or credentials. These elements help promote an image of the owner as a competent, effective, and achievement-oriented individual.

THE NATURE OF INTERPERSONAL SELF-PRESENTATION

Why do people engage in impression management? The three main reasons for managing impressions are self-glorification, self-consistency, and accuracy (Schlenker & Weigold, 1992). The first reason, self-glorification, simply reflects our desire to promote and maintain a positive image — many home pages show how friendly and sociable you are, and/or show your achievements and career plans, and the like. Because we cannot present whole home pages in a text like this, let's look at examples from another area relevant to self-presentation: personal ads. Take a look at the four personal ads that begin this chapter. In Ad 4 an individual bolsters a positive image by claiming to be a "youthful 49," while the person in Ad 3 claims to be "analytically incisive" or "sexy and attractive." We present a positive image of the self for a number of reasons: to feel good about ourselves, to attract more attention, to get more date offers, to get hired, to get promoted, and so on. However, a person may place too great an emphasis on self-glorification, and it may fail to resemble an accurate portrayal of the self. We know, for example, that individuals who place personal ads are primarily interested in gaining attention and getting date offers. In doing so, they emphasize what they believe members of the desired sex are seeking (Koestner & Wheeler, 1988), rather than focusing on accuracy. Heterosexual women are more likely to offer their weight (which they believe is of interest to men) and seek the height of men; men offer height (because they believe women prefer tall men) and seek information about women's weight. Women advertise themselves in more instrumental characteristics (energetic, adventurous, competent) and seek men who are expressive (warm, tender, sensitive). Men advertise themselves as expressive and seek women who are instrumental. Both men and women say things to look appealing, to report on information they think the other gender wants to hear, and to get more date offers.

The second reason, self-consistency, means that we try to create images of our self and our social environments that verify and maintain stable, consistent self-conceptions. Our sense of self is stable and consistent over time (months or years) and is stable and consistent across many situations — like the outgoing and active person in Personal Ad 1. Personal Web pages offer an advantage over personal ads in portraying a consistent image of the self because one can include photographs showing athletic ability, accomplishments, or fun activities spanning years.

The third reason for managing impressions is to communicate an accurate presentation of self. We would not want to say we are geniuses who are analytic, fit and trim, and friendly, when in fact we are not. The people we meet would reject our self-presentations and say we were dishonest, and we would not make any friends. Emphasis on self-glorification may gain more attention and date offers than modest and more accurate ones. However, it is reasonable to assume that more accurate messages (ads, Web pages, etc.) may prompt fewer but more genuine reactions. Nonetheless, for most people the chore is to portray a positive view of the self that is consistent over time and that fairly accurately reflects the true self.

Of course, people can lie about their self-presentations, just as they can during self-disclosure, reasons for rejecting dates, and reasons for coming home late. Deceptive self-presentations take a variety of forms. The most obvious is one in which the individual presents a view of self altered in some way to look more appealing to the target audience (as in personal ads). People prefer to date others who are beautiful, wealthy, friendly/humorous, kind, understanding, and intelligent. This leaves plenty of room for exaggeration; in fact, Rowatt, Cunningham, and Druen (1998) noted that in one of their earlier projects, 90% of college students admitted to telling at least one lie to a prospective date. What people lie or exaggerate about depends on their beliefs about what the audience expects and seeks in others. Further, the more desirable the potential date partner, the greater the motivation to fabricate or exaggerate (claim to be taller, richer, humorous). In order to appear more similar to the potential date partner or to what the date partner seeks, self-presenters will alter their descriptions of their personal characteristics or attitudes — a male may claim to be taller, a female may claim to be more traditional and nurturing, and so on.

A different approach to lying during self-presentations is called **sandbagging** (Gibson & Sachau, 2000). Sandbagging is a self-presentational strategy involving a false claim of your ability to perform a task, such as a sport or a test. Sandbaggers may possess certain skills and abilities, but communicate to others that they are less skillful, less competent, or less qualified than they are in real life. In order to sandbag, a person can fail strategically early in the performance, understate one's abilities, skills, or efforts, or simply make a false prediction of performance. Sandbagging is much more likely to occur if the sandbagger believes there is intense pressure to perform and that audience members have no or limited knowledge of his or her true skills (Gibson & Sachau, 2000). Why sandbag? First, it offers a competitive advantage. By claiming relatively low skills or abilities, one's rivals or opponents may not prepare or exert sufficient effort during an event, or earlier in the event. Further, there are psychological benefits to sandbagging. People with high levels of social anxiety or low levels of self-esteem may be more sensitive to stress or pressure and sandbagging helps to remove some of the pressure (since people won't have high expectations of their performance). Finally, there is a greater sense of achievement and praise from audience members if expectations were initially low, and the individual performed better than expected.

What are the desirable images people seek to communicate to others? Table 6.1 lists five common self-presentational strategies discussed in this chapter, along with the desirable images sought, the negative reaction from others if they fail to present the desired image, the desired emotion sought from others, and some of the verbal strategies employed. The **ingratiator** desires to be liked and to arouse the emotion of affection. The typical actions of the ingratiator (far right column in Table 6.1) include self-characterizations (see Chapter 7), conforming one's opinions to fit in with others. The individuals in Personal Ads 1 and 2 are ingratiators. An ingratiator engages in

Table 6.1
A TAXONOMY OF SELF-PRESENTATION STRATEGIES

Strategy	Desirable Image Sought	Negative Image Risked	Desirable Emotion Sought	Typical Actions
1. Ingratiation	likable	sycophant conformist obsequious	affection	self-characterization opinion conformity other enhancement favors
2. Intimidation	dangerous ruthless volatile	bombastic wishy-washy ineffectual	fear	threats anger (incipient) breakdown (incipient)
3. Self-promotion	competent effective successful	fraudulent conceited defensive	respect awe deference	performance claims performance accounts performances
4. Exemplification	worthy suffering dedicated	hypocritical sanctimonious exploitative	guilt shame emulation	self-denial helping militancy
5. Supplication	helpless handicapped unfortunate	stigmatized lazy demanding	nurturance obligation	self-deprecation entreaties for help

Source: Adapted from Jones & Pittman, 1982. Used with permission of the authors.

STUDENT AS OBSERVER: GENDER-BASED WEB SITE SELF-PRESENTATIONS

Do males and females really present themselves differently on-line? One way to assess this question is to perform a content analysis of Web sites. In completing a content analysis, you will first need to consider the variables based on self-presentational styles on which males and females are likely to differ. Women, in our society, are expected to be and are rewarded for being, personal, sociable, friendly, and status neutral. Men are expected to be and are rewarded for being strong, competent, achievement-oriented, competitive, and status-assertive. It is likely that men's and women's pages would differ substantially along two self-presentational strategies: ingratiation and self-presentation (although there could be differences in other self-presentational strategies).

Below is a list of ways in which the content on the Web sites may feature "ingratiator" or "self-promoter." Visit ten home pages, five of women and five of men, and count the number of times the Web pages present information or photographs involving ingratiation and self-promotion. Add a one-page summary of your findings to the count and compare the results with those of other students in your class.

I. Presentation of the self as likable, personal, sociable, friendly (i.e., an ingratiator)

Presence of (and number of) the following:

1. Disclosure of information of a personal nature: dreams, wishes, hopes.
2. Disclosure of descriptive information about past, present.
3. Explicitly welcomes you or greets you, invites comments.
4. Uses expressions of "you" and "we."
5. Provides information about popularity.

II. Presentation of the self as an accomplished individual, competent (i.e., self-promotion)

Presence of (and number of) the following:

1. Discloses information about achievements: National Merit Scholarship, grade point average, awards won, etc.
2. Lists places of employment. Includes on-line resume, work accomplishments.
3. Uses "I" and "me."
4. Discloses skills, such as playing instruments, competence at various computer programs, etc.
5. Lists important people met, favorite professional sports teams, celebrities.
6. Presents titles or credentials, such as president of fraternity, captain of baseball team, etc.

behaviors that make him or her appear friendly, helpful, kind, positive, and so forth. However, each strategy also involves risks, and being perceived as a conformist, or a manipulator, is a negative consequence the ingratiator risks.

The **self-promoter** wants to be seen as competent, successful, and talented, but he or she runs the risk of being perceived as conceited. The individuals in Personal Ads 3 and 4 are self-promoters: The female (Ad 3) emphasizes being "analytic" and asserts she is smarter than others (MENSA is an association for individuals who score high on IQ tests). The male (Ad 4) says a good deal about himself (slim, funny, etc.) but says nothing about his interests, profession, likes or dislikes, and so on. Self-promotion and ingratiation are the most common self-presentational strategies.

The **intimidator** seeks to be perceived as a dangerous, tough individual who wants to be feared and respected by others. People who are intimidators are often competitive athletes in sports, such as wrestling or football, or on the job (some police or guards, and so on). However, the intimidator runs the risk of being perceived as wishy-washy if unable to maintain the style fully, or as ineffectual if unable to follow through on the tough stance if someone calls his or her bluff. We offer no examples from personal ads, but a person who indicates he or she wants to dominate his or her partner in a personal ad or Web page would be an intimidator.

The **exemplifier** wishes to be viewed as dedicated, committed, and self-sacrificing, and engages in self-denial and helping others. An exemplifier is a person who lives his or her life based on certain values (pro-environment, salvation, pro-family, anti-globalization, etc.). A person who participates in "Heal the Bay" demonstrations, petition drives, and political campaigns is living a morally worthy life, and an exemplifier would like for others to copy his or her example. In some cases, an exemplifier may even engage in militant behavior, such as chaining oneself to trees or destroying sawing equipment. While some exemplifiers are successful in portraying themselves as worthy and dedicated, some fail in their self-presentational goal and are perceived as sanctimonious (better than others), hypocritical, and/or exploitative, prompting others, through guilt, to give to a charity, doing volunteer work, and so on.

The **supplicator** desires to be perceived as helpless and in need of nurturing; although there may be relatively few supplicators in college (relative to other forms of strategies), they depend on others for assistance, help, advice, nurturance. A supplicator grooms a dependence on another person, who feels some obligation to help the supplicator. A supplicator, however, runs the risk of being perceived as lazy and demanding and/or stigmatized as immature, a failure, someone to avoid.

Credible self-presentation strategies are those in which the elements can be verified or confirmed; when combined, the elements form a coherent, whole picture of the individual. Some elements of a presentation (fit, trim, extroverted, attractive, blonde, likes outdoor activities, etc.) can be verified or confirmed with one or two conversations or dates. Other elements cannot be so readily or easily verified. Elements such as intellectually challenging, analytically incisive, politically astute, and loyal require more effort to confirm or verify. Also the credibility of a self-presentation can be enhanced by including credentials, such as awards, memberships in organizations, and so forth. This is more easily done on personal Web pages (and links to other pages).

INTIMIDATING SCHOOL BULLIES EXPLOIT NEW TECHNOLOGIES

One of the most obvious examples of the intimidator style of self-presentation is the school bully, who asserts power and control over his (her) victims by use of threats, name calling, rumor-spreading, theft of belongings, and physical aggression. Recent surveys indicate that bullying has increased substantially over the years, and it is linked to a number of suicides by victims, and to brutal acts of revenge, as in the case of the Columbine massacre. School bullies, who are often popular among other boys at school (who are not victims) often prey upon those who are weaker, alone, smaller, or stigmatized in some way. Stammerers, for example, are routinely terrorized by bullies. Over 80% of adult stammerers surveyed said they were bullied in school — over 70% were bullied weekly, and nearly 20% were bullied daily. Being the victim of a bully can have a significant impact on the victim's level of self-esteem, and can affect one for life.

So problematic is bullying today in some areas of the world that schools have developed a "zero tolerance" rule — bullies are promptly suspended and then expelled. However, there has been an increase in bullying using technology — by text-messaging, e-mail, and verbally assaulting others in chat rooms. In Europe, where text messaging is extremely popular, one in six school children report receiving intimidating messages like, "I'm watching you," and " Tomorrow you'll get yours." This development means that victims no longer have a safe haven at home. They are at the mercy of the intimidator.

A number of Web sites offer aid to the victims and to the victim's parents. Some sites you might find useful include:

http://www.bullying.org/
http://www.bullying.co.uk/
http://www.bullydefense.com/fast_facts.htm
http://www.pta.org/programs/sycsch.htm
http://www.safechild.org/bullies.htm
http://www.mentalhealth.org/publications/allpubs/CA-0043/Default.asp

Also see:

Carvel, J. (June 4, 1999). "Stammerers targeted by school bullies," www.guardian.co.uk/uk_news/story/0,3604,292176,00.html

"High-tech school bullies work round the clock. Survey finds some kids plagued by online tormentors," www.cnn.com/2002/TECH/ptech/04/16/britain.bullying.reut.index.html

Prentice, K. (April 25, 2000). "School bullies are popular, study says," www.apbnews.com/safetycenter/family/2000/04/25/bullies0425_01.html

© Marilyn Humphreys/The Image Works

Exemplifiers live their lives based on certain values and would like for others to follow their example. When exemplifiers fail in their self-presentational goals, they are perceived as sanctimonious, hypocritical, or exploitative.

Monitoring Self-Presentation

Sometimes we consciously and deliberately work at making an impression on others. At other times, we hardly give any thought to the impressions we are creating as we routinely greet people, carry on conversations, and so forth. Self-presentational goals become relevant primarily when our social identity is subject to evaluation by others. At one point in time, as when having lunch with a friend, we may pay little attention to our presentational goals. However, when we notice our lunch partner yawning or looking around the room, we acknowledge that we may be boring or not paying enough attention to the friend's interest. Because we usually prefer not to be evaluated as boring or insensitive, our presentational goals immediately become important, and we pay closer attention to what we are doing and the impression that might be communicated.

Although we do not always think about presentational goals, our surroundings can quickly activate the need to monitor them. We continually monitor the success of our presentational goals at a pre-attentive, or nonconscious, level (Leary & Kowalski, 1990). When we are preoccupied with other goals involving work, relationships, listening to others, and so forth, our concerns about how we are being perceived are relegated to the back of our mind. However, at the pre-attentive, or nonconscious, level of awareness, we might still monitor how other people act or react toward us. When we believe that we are being evaluated in some way, most communicators can quickly recall from memory what they can and should do to promote a desirable image.

Self-Identity and Self-Presentation

There are many ways to view the self. Schlenker (1986) says this is because a person's identity is a "theory of self that is formed and maintained through" interpersonal communication and agreement (p. 23). Two important aspects of this definition are (1) our identity is a theory and is dependent on available evidence to be a credible or believable theory; and (2) our identity is based on interpersonal agreement and is therefore dependent on communication. Schlenker also notes that we strive to create an identity that is "personally beneficial"; that is, we groom an image as a person who has the skills needed to achieve a particular goal. For example, to project an image of "graduate school material," a student will groom a personally beneficial image that includes skills in writing and researching and other abilities judged as necessary for success in graduate school. Similarly, a woman who wants to be a successful, intimidating wrestling champion will also want to groom an image beneficial to this goal — being strong, having stamina, appearing imposing, displaying attitude, and so forth.

Any good theory of the self must be believable and must be based on sufficient evidence. If we do not believe that a given identity is true, we will not internalize it and claim it as our own. To be believable, an identity must explain, predict, and guide behavior.

First, an identity must explain our thoughts, feelings, and actions (Gergen, 1989). For example, Jack notices that he is very attracted to Jill, he enjoys going up the hill with her, and he thinks about Jill almost constantly throughout the day. Given these observations, Jack might conclude, "I'm in love with Jill." But what if Jack also notices that he really misses his ex-girlfriend Mary and wishes that they could get back together, and also that he would also like to date Diane? In this case, the identity "in love with Jill" is less believable; it doesn't do a very good job explaining Jack's thoughts, feelings, and actions. The strength of Jack's explanation is influenced by how inclusive and coherent it is. The inclusiveness of an explanation refers to the number of different thoughts, feelings, and actions for which it is able to account; the greater the number, the more inclusive it is. Coherence refers to how well the items we use to develop an identity fit together; the better they fit together, the more coherent the identity. Jack's first three observations fit together under the identity "in love with Jill"; the additional ones do not. If Jack believes in all of them, he can respond in at least three ways. First, he might attempt to explain all the relevant information and revise his identity; for example, after hearing popular talk shows, he might change his identity from "being in love with Jill" to "having a dependent personality." Second, he might maintain the identity of being "in love with Jill" but be less confident about it. Third, he might actually distort the available information or selectively attend to certain information, ignoring contradictory facts, in order to maintain the "I love Jill" belief.

The second purpose our identities must serve is to help us predict future thoughts, feelings, and actions. If Jack believes that he is in love with Jill, he can predict that he will enjoy studying with her this weekend. He can predict that Jill will be in his dreams, that the two of them have commonalities and share interests and hobbies. He can predict that he will ask her out for a romantic evening, that she will say yes, and that they will plan the evening.

The third purpose our identities must serve is to help guide our actions. If Jack were in love, he would show his devotion to Jill and not ask out, or flirt with, others. Because people in love do things together and celebrate events together, Jack might change his class schedule to take classes with Jill, share the same lunch break, arrange to spend more time with her off campus, and plan to spend an event together (Valentine's Day, etc.). He might show how romantic he is by having flowers delivered, dedicating songs to her on the radio, and so forth.

Our identities do not exist in isolation. We test them, develop them, and refine them using interpersonal communication. Jill may reciprocate Jack's interest in her, which would reinforce his theory and encourage him to reveal his love. His friends can support his theory or question it. They might ask Jack why, if he really loved Jill, he would flirt and spend time with Joanne. Jack's friends would provide a reality check on just how much Jack is "in love" — which could run the gamut from being insincere infatuation to puppy love to stalking behavior. Without confirmation from others, we would develop unrealistic, personally beneficial self-theories that have no basis in reality and limit our ability to function in society.

We have used an example of an identity "I'm in love with Jill" to illustrate the two main features of self-identity. First, we believe and adopt as our own an identity if there is sufficient available evidence. Second, we believe and adopt as our own an identity if it is confirmed and validated through communication with relevant others. The same process occurs for any identity to be adopted as our own. A person who believes he or she is likable can adopt this as part of a theory of self if there is convincing evidence that he or she is likable. To be believable, the theory must explain a set of behaviors that can all be viewed as representing the things that likable people do, and the explanation must be inclusive and coherent. The first condition involves the number of thoughts, feelings, and actions that an identity of being likable includes — greeting people, supporting others, comforting others, praising others, doing favors for others, and so forth. The more behaviors the person engages in that fall within "things that likable people do," the greater the believability. Second, the person is more likely to find the identity believable if the likable behaviors fit together coherently, without contradiction. If he or she behaves in a likable manner to everyone, the behaviors form a coherent picture of the self as likable. But if the person is likable only to attractive people of the opposite sex, he or she is not really likable, but is a flirt. If the person is likable only to those who have power and status, but does not behave in any friendly manner to co-workers or subordinates, he or she is not really likable, but a slimeball (or worse). If the person behaves in a likable manner only to people of his or her own race, he or she is not really likable but racist. Once a theory of self is capable of explaining a set of behaviors subsumed under the label *likable*, the theory is put to work predicting a person's future thoughts, feelings, and actions, and is used to guide behavior.

Without validation from others, however, our theory of self can be inaccurate. We could simply be biased in our recall of how friendly we are, ignoring the times when we are preoccupied and moody, even angry. We can fail in our attempt by trying too hard to be liked so that others actually see us as unlikable, as a conformist, or as obsequious. We need reality checks from others to confirm and validate our interpretation of behavior in public. We can then take on this identity as our own.

Indicators of Attainment

We have shown that to make our identity claims legitimate, we need to engage in communicative activities that will make them believable. These activities are what Gollwitzer (1986, p. 145) refers to as **indicators of attainment.** These indicators operate as symbols of the desired identity that communicates to ourselves and others that we have attained a particular identity. Taking the identity of student as an example, indicators of attainment could include fulfilling the responsibilities associated with being a student (attending class), displaying material symbols (wearing a school sweatshirt), meeting institutional requirements (paying student fees), or making verbal claims ("I am a student"). Such a person could legitimately claim to be a student. However, our identities lack a sense of completion until others acknowledge our possession of a desirable identity. Therefore, we develop ways of presenting ourselves to get the feedback desired to feel complete. The following conversation involved a student who desperately wanted to be seen as "graduate school material." It occurred two weeks before the semester was over and a paper was due. Notice how the student tries to indicate that he is a good student:

Professor: Hi, what's up?

Student: I need your help. Yesterday I spent seven hours in the library getting articles for my paper. [Spending long hours working symbolizes being a good student.]

Professor: You're not just getting started are you? [Good students do not put off papers to the last minute.]

Student: I couldn't think of anything to write on. But look how many articles I copied yesterday. This is a lot, huh? [I'm not a poor student because I have a good excuse for not starting earlier. Further, look at the sheer bulk of reading I plan to do. Only good students do this much work.]

Professor: What do you mean you couldn't think of anything? You've had over two months to work on this. Why did you put it off until now? [Your excuse is not legitimate.]

Student: I know I should have started earlier, but I really want to do a good job on this paper. This is really important to me. Will you show me which of these articles I should read and which ones I shouldn't? [I may be starting late, but I am a highly motivated student!]

The student continued to come up with new ways to assert his identity as a good student. Our desire to present ourselves as possessing a certain identity is often most acute when our identity has been challenged. We may resort to exaggerated verbal claims or increase performances related to proving the identity to ourselves and to others. Gollwitzer (1986) demonstrated this nicely in an experiment with medical students. Each student took a test that presumably measured whether or not he or she had the personality necessary to be a competent physician. Although the test was bogus, half the students received feedback that they possessed the personality of a successful physician; the other half were told that they did not. Later the students were asked to solve a set of medical problems. The ability to complete this test symbolized their ability to be a successful doctor. The results indicated that those who had been given the negative feedback tended to show their completed tasks to the experimenter, whereas those who were given the positive feedback did not. The students felt compelled to prove to the experimenter (and themselves) that they truly did have the skills necessary to be a good doctor.

The desire to create an acceptable identity can be so strong that it actually motivates us to engage in acts that are damaging to ourselves or to others. For example, Norman and Tedeschi (1989) found that the desire to create a personally beneficial identity was a significant factor in motivating adolescents to start smoking. Six months after attending an antismoking seminar, adolescents who had rated smoking as being "cool" and who wanted to see themselves as "cool" started smoking and believed their friends would approve. Finally, the desire to create a beneficial identity can be so powerful that it motivates people to engage in violent acts. Studies indicate that when an insult threatened an aspect of a person's personality that he or she thought was important, the person was more likely to respond aggressively, particularly in the presence of a same-sex audience (Felson, 1982; Harris, Gergen, & Lannamann, 1986). The insulted parties felt the need to protect their identity by attacking the other party.

DIRECT STRATEGIES OF SELF-PRESENTATION

When managing impressions, a communicator can use direct or indirect methods. Direct methods, which were discussed earlier (see Table 6.1), include the tactics used to ingratiate, intimidate, self-promote, supplicate, and exemplify. Indirect methods are used to bolster image and self-esteem.

Ingratiation

Communicators can ingratiate themselves to others in order to appear likable by being humorous, warm, charming, trustworthy, and so on. The choice to enact ingratiating behavior is influenced by three factors: incentive value, subjective probability of success, and perceived legitimacy. The first factor, **incentive value,** is associated

152

with being liked by a particular person (Jones & Pittman, 1982). As the value of being liked by a person increases, so does the incentive or motivation to engage in ingratiating behaviors.

An ingratiator, however, can have either illicit or authentic motivations. **Illicit ingratiation** is considered phony behavior targeted solely to get something from the other person in the interaction. It is used when people act friendly because they want something in return, because they have an ulterior motive to be friendly to you now so that you will buy something, donate something, or do them a favor later (see also Chapter 12 on compliance principles). A typical example is when a student says, "Professor, I really like your class. It's my favorite this semester. Do you think it would be possible for me to take a makeup because I have to be out of town during the next exam?" Though the student's primary goal is to persuade the professor to give a makeup exam, the student begins with a compliment. The success of the compliment depends on its being seen as honest feedback rather than apple-polishing. In any case, a person who, for ulterior motives, wants to be liked and employs illicit ingratiation runs the risk of being perceived as insincere.

Authentic ingratiation, by contrast, occurs when a person's primary motivation is to meet the demands of the situation. In this case, the reasons for engaging in the behavior are implicitly known by most people in the situation. The desire to be liked, though important, is secondary to other goals. For example, you may congratulate a classmate after a speech because she did a good job and deserves it. In this case, your congratulatory behavior may increase how much she likes you, but your primary motivation is to affirm her performance rather than meet your own personal needs. Our earlier example on self-identity shows that a person can legitimately claim the identity as a true likable person if he or she engages in a series of actions that reflect being likable, if he or she behaves that way uniformly with everyone, and if the identity predicts and guides future actions.

The second factor that influences the decision to ingratiate is the **subjective probability of success.** Prior to deciding to ingratiate, we tend to size up the situation to determine the likelihood of our success. This requires that we assess our own skills and resources as well as the probability that our tactics might fail. For example, a friend receives the lowest score on a test on which you receive the highest. In your effort to be a friend, what do you do? One possible tactic is to offer to let your friend borrow your notes before the next exam. This may be appropriate if you believe that your resources (the notes) will help your friend and that he will be receptive to your offer. But if you think your friend will interpret your offer as an implication that he is stupid, that you are condescending, or that you are implying he cannot get good grades on his own merits, you will probably not use the tactic.

Consider attending a social event and interacting with someone you want to like you very much — say a stunningly beautiful person whom you always imagined dating, or a highly successful and powerful executive who could help advance your career. In such a setting you are highly motivated to ingratiate in order to elicit liking from such desirable targets. Ironically, the **ingratiator's dilemma** (Jones & Wortman,

Ingratiators can have illicit or authentic motivations. This student could be genuine in her praise of her professor (authentic ingratiation), or she could just be softening him up to ask permission to take a makeup exam (illicit ingratiation).

K. Preuss/The Image Works

1974) may well come into play here: As the need to be liked by a particular target person increases, the probability of successful ingratiation decreases. Why? Because as your desire to be liked by a person increases, your ingratiation tactics become more salient (to target and observers), and there is an increase in the likelihood that you will be perceived as motivated by ulterior motives. The stunningly gorgeous or powerful person you want to like you will ask, "Is he (or she) for real, genuine and honest, or is he (or she) a suck up and someone who would say anything to impress me?" The advice generally given in such a setting is to gain ingratiation credits early (and indirectly, as with a carefully planted introduction by a third party), and to appear sincere.

The third factor affecting the decision to ingratiate is the **perceived legitimacy** of the ingratiating behavior. Each of us develops moral standards that govern whether we believe certain behaviors are appropriate or not, and any ingratiating behavior we choose must fit within those standards. Should you praise a friend's new haircut when she is desperate to hear words of approval, even though the haircut is awful? Perceived appropriateness strongly affects whether we ingratiate or not. People who are sufficiently motivated — who believe that they are likely to be successful and that certain ingratiation tactics are morally legitimate — usually choose to engage in one of several ingratiation tactics: complimenting, opinion conformity, rendering favors, or general affinity-seeking tactics.

COMPLIMENTING. One of the most commonly employed tactics, complimenting, involves expressing a positive evaluation of the target by drawing attention to the target's strengths and virtues: "You did very well on this test. You are so smart!" "Wow, you look great this evening!"

Our attraction tends to increase naturally toward those who compliment us. However, it is usually essential that the compliments be seen as genuine. Though this may seem simple, anyone who has tried it knows how difficult it can be. Consider the following situation. A friend tells you that she is worried about an exam because she desperately wants an A. Because you are confident of her abilities, you try to be reassuring: "I'm sure you will get one of the highest scores in the class. You always do." The complimentary nature of your response may seem obvious, but your response could be interpreted in five different ways (see Jones & Wortman, 1974):

1. You want something from her.
2. That's just the kind of person you are.
3. Your comment was triggered by the situation.
4. You are just trying to be nice.
5. You are being honest and sincere.

First, your friend could believe that you are complimenting her because you want something from her. Interpreted in this way, your comment is likely to boomerang on you and produce a decrease in liking. To guard against this, a successful complimenter would play down any perceived dependence on the friend; praising her and asking for a favor (to borrow notes) at the same time makes the dependence too obvious.

Alternatively, she may think, "That's just the kind of person you are. You always say nice things." A complimenter can avoid this interpretation by making it appear that he or she is a discerning complimenter who does, in fact, occasionally make negative statements about others. For example, the complimenter can blend a negative comment on one minor point ("You may not be the most efficient person I know at studying") with a positive comment on a major point ("but you always remember what is important").

Third, your comment may be perceived as purely normal; friends are obligated to reassure each other. Offering compliments in situations where they are considered normative may not increase liking, but failing to do so is likely to result in decreased liking. To derive the most benefit in such situations, the ingratiator should offer compliments that provide greater detail than usual. This could include not only expressing confidence in the friend's ability but also mentioning specific behaviors she engages in, such as "You study more than anyone I know. I've seen you get anxious about assignments in the past, yet you always seem to pull it off. I'm sure you will get one of the highest test scores."

Fourth, the friend might believe that you are "just trying to be nice." Your motives are good, but you are not being entirely honest in your estimation of her abilities. To avoid this, complimenters can provide proof concerning the positive evaluation. You could include reasons for your compliment, such as "I know some of the people in your class, and they're not putting nearly as much time into studying for this exam. Also, you had the same professor last semester and always did well on the exams."

Finally, your friend might conclude you are being honest and sincere, that you really do believe that she is competent and will do well on the exam. In this case, the ingratiation tactic is likely to be successful.

OPINION CONFORMITY. **Opinion conformity,** or simply agreeing with others, is based on the assumption that we tend to find people who are similar to us more attractive than those who are dissimilar. Similar others are often considered more attractive because they add support to the correctness of our world view, we expect them to be more cooperative, and we expect them to help us reach our goals. However, the value placed on independent thought and action makes opinion conformity a rather risky tactic. Communicators who are too quick to conform to others are often considered weak and indecisive or phony.

RENDERING FAVORS. Rendering favors communicates to other people that we respect them and are willing to help them pursue their goals. Like offering compliments, rendering favors is based on the principle that we reciprocate liking for people who like us. One of the ways to avoid the suspicion of ulterior motives is to only do favors that are considered appropriate for a given situation. A good example of doing favors beyond what was considered appropriate was reported in the *Los Angeles Times* ("Man spends $20,000 trying to win hand of girl who can say no"). After dating for two months, Keith, a 35-year-old stockbroker, proposed to Karine, a 20-year-old cocktail waitress, but Karine turned him down. Her refusal prompted a shower of gifts from Keith, including a Lear jet rental, a gold ring, a limousine waiting outside her door, $200 worth of champagne, 4,000 flowers, and musicians to serenade her. Karine was flattered but still said no. Keith's public image suffered.

Effective ingratiation through helping others depends on whom we are seen helping. Vonk (1998) studied people's reactions when workers were described as helpful to all employees (superiors and co-workers), compared to when workers were helpful to superiors and rude and unhelpful to co-workers, rude and unhelpful to superiors and helpful to co-workers, or rude and unhelpful to everyone. Workers were considered likable when helpful to all, or at least when helpful to co-workers. However, workers who were helpful to superiors and unhelpful to co-workers were rated as unlikable and untrustworthy; they were called "slimy," or "slimeballs."

AFFINITY-SEEKING. Bell and Daly (1984; Daly & Kreiser, 1994) explored the communication strategies specifically intended to increase liking for a communicator. They identified the twenty-five most commonly employed **affinity-seeking** strategies people claim to use when they want to get others to like them. Table 6.2 lists these strategies. The most frequently used affinity-seeking strategies were conversational rule keeping, self-concept confirmation, eliciting disclosures, nonverbal immediacy, self-inclusion, listening, facilitating enjoyment, openness, and altruism. The least used were conceding control, influencing perceptions of closeness, and assuming control.

Table 6.2

AFFINITY-SEEKING STRATEGIES

1. *Altruism.* Strive to be of assistance to the other in whatever he or she is doing (e.g., doing a favor).
2. *Assuming control.* Present yourself as someone in control (e.g., taking charge of activities).
3. *Assuming equality.* Strike a posture of social equality with the other person (e.g., avoid acting snobbish).
4. *Comfortable self.* Act comfortable and relaxed when around the other person.
5. *Conceding control.* Allow the other to assume control over relational activities (e.g., where to go for coffee).
6. *Conversational rule keeping.* Adhere closely to cultural rules for polite, cooperative interaction (e.g., act interested in what the other is telling you, even if you are not).
7. *Dynamism.* Present yourself as an active, enthusiastic person (e.g., although you are very tired, you answer the phone using an upbeat, energetic voice).
8. *Eliciting disclosures.* Encourage the other to talk by reinforcing his or her conversational contributions (e.g., ask the partner for opinions).
9. *Facilitating enjoyment.* Maximize the positiveness of relational encounters (e.g., participate fully in an activity you know the other enjoys).
10. *Inclusion of other.* Include the other in your social groups (e.g., ask this person to a party your friends will be attending).
11. *Influencing perceptions of closeness.* Engage in behaviors that imply that the relationship is closer than it is (e.g., use nicknames for other; refer to "us" and "we").
12. *Listening.* Listen actively to the other (e.g., be attentive; ask for clarification).
13. *Nonverbal immediacy.* Show interest in the other through various nonverbal behaviors (e.g., smile at the other).
14. *Openness.* Disclose personal information (e.g., "Don't be embarrassed, Sammy. I'm also afraid of Ferris wheels.").
15. *Optimism.* Present yourself as a positive person (e.g., offer positive comments about others).
16. *Personal autonomy.* Present yourself as independent and a free thinker (e.g., disagree with the other).
17. *Physical attractiveness.* Look and dress as attractively as possible (e.g., get rid of those sweats!).
18. *Presenting an interesting self.* Appear to be someone interesting to know (e.g., drop names of impressive people).

19. *Rewarding association.* Imply that you can reward the other (e.g., shower the other with gifts).
20. *Self-concept confirmation.* Show respect for the other and promote good feelings in the other (e.g., use compliments).
21. *Self-inclusion.* Arrange frequent contact with the other (e.g., show up where you know the other will be).
22. *Sensitivity.* Act warm and empathic (e.g., show your concern for the other).
23. *Similarity.* Convince the other about your similarity in interests (e.g., say that you really do like to go bowling).
24. *Supportiveness.* Support the other's social encounters (e.g., side with this person in an argument with a third party).
25. *Trustworthiness.* Present yourself as honest and reliable (e.g., fulfill commitments made to the other).

Source: Adapted from Bell & Daly, 1984, pp. 96–97. Copyright by the Speech Communication Association. Reprinted by permission of the publisher and the authors.

The use of these strategies can have a strong impact on the perceptions of liking and loving for the communicator. As a general rule, the more frequently a communicator employed the strategies listed in Table 6.2, the more liked, loved, and effective the communicator was rated. Bell, Tremblay, and Buerkel-Rothfuss (1987) also found that individuals who score high on the use of affinity-seeking strategies are perceived to be less lonely and apprehensive and more socially capable and assertive. A number of studies confirm that using affinity-seeking behaviors is important, from initial interactions (Martin & Rubin, 1998) through marriage (Bell, Daly, & Gonzalez, 1987; Daly & Kreiser, 1994). The use of affinity-seeking behaviors is linked to liking the communicator, communication competence, and quality of marriage. In extended families, however, the picture is more complex. Ganong, Coleman, Fine, and Martin (1999) found that stepparent-stepchild relationships characterized by liking and affection were ones in which the stepparent developed friendships with the stepchild through dyadic activities and various affinity-seeking behaviors, which continued after the stepparent moved in with the family. Poor step-relationships were characterized by competition from the nonresident parent, stepparents who wanted to take control of the family, and stepchildren who did not even recognize that stepparents were using affinity-seeking behaviors. It is important that the recipients of affinity seeking are aware that affinity-seeking behaviors are being used, and that they perceive them as sincere efforts to increase liking, rather than motivated by ulterior purposes. Also, we should note that humor can serve as an affinity-seeking behavior (Wanzer, Booth-Butterfield, & Booth-Butterfield, 1995). Finally, teachers increase their teaching effectiveness by using affinity-seeking behaviors (Roach & Byrne, 2001), and students use affinity-seeking behaviors with professors (Wanzer, 1998). Wanzer found that students rely on "conversational rule keeping," "eliciting disclosures," "nonverbal immediacy" (see Chapter 5), "self-inclusion" (having more contact with the professor), and fulfilling course requirements in a timely fashion.

Intimidation

The goal of an intimidator is to be seen as dangerous. Intimidators let it be known that they are both able and willing to inflict physical or psychological pain on anyone who gets in the way. In his research on criminal behavior, Toch (1969) found that intimidation was a common tactic among violent men. One out of four violent-prone men engaged in "self-image promoting," going out of their way to create the impression that they are formidable and fearless. Such men challenge other men who invade their space and territory. They worry that if they don't act first to create the image of an intimidator, they will be mistaken as weak or cowardly.

Though violent-prone men are the most extreme intimidators, others use this tactic as well. Many public figures and executives work hard on impression-management goals, including the perception of being intimidating. In some situations, intimidation is an important ingredient to success. Intimidation plays an important role in certain jobs, such as police officer, probation officer, collection agent, or athlete, in football, boxing, hockey, wrestling, and so forth. In many of these situations, the intimidation is part of a competitive relationship with a real opponent (crook, rival, dead-beat debtor, etc.). In various relationships, the individuals most likely to use bullying and strong tactics on others are those with greater resources (income, property, etc.) who are less dependent on their partner (Howard, Blumstein, & Schwartz, 1986). Intimidation is also related to more frequent expressions of negative emotions, as indicated in a recent study by Olson, Hafer, and Taylor (2001). Ingratiators expressed the least amount of negative emotions.

Self-Promotion

The goal of the self-promoter is to be seen as competent. A successful self-promoter is usually competent in a particular context or in a particular activity (sports, singing, dancing, etc.). Most of us realize that developing competence in one area requires a trade-off in another area. This leads to two implications for the potential self-promoter. First, self-promoting either too excessively or in the wrong context can lead to the attribution of incompetence. These self-promoters are like Cliff, the self-promoting mail carrier on reruns of "Cheers"; although he presents himself as an expert on almost every topic, to everyone else he is obviously self-deceived. Second, in some situations self-promoters can enhance others' attributions of their competence by declaring their incompetence in other areas. This not only makes a competent person seem more human but also reinforces the perception of competence by generating the additional attribution of accurate self-awareness.

The following story illustrates the use of self-promotion (Potter, 1962, p. 287). About the time when Harvard University administers extremely difficult midwinter examinations, one of the students, Fitzjames, disappeared from the college. His classmates struggled with mounds of reading materials and were anxious and worried about performing well on the important tests. When the tests were administered, all students were present in the lecture room except Fitzjames. When all others were furiously writing their answers, Fitzjames casually walked in five minutes late, well-tanned and wearing a light suit, strolling without an apparent care or worry in the world. He amusingly inspected the test questions and then began to write slowly. Later it became known that Fitzjames had received an A. What is your perception of Fitzjames? How competent is he? Consider the full story.

Fitzjames did not go to Florida to vacation, nor did he take the exams any less seriously than the other students. The truth was that he checked into a cheap room in Boston, surrounded himself with the entire reading assignment, and spent virtually every day and night for three weeks reading and preparing for the exams, sitting between two sunlamps.

Now what do you think of Fitzjames? Though he cannot be commended for his honesty, Fitzjames was a shrewd self-promoter. He understood the "attributional arithmetic" used to determine the meaning of an accomplishment and staged the situation to increase his perceived competence. According to Jones (1989), accomplishments are produced by a combination of natural ability, motivation, and effort. Earning a grade of A in a class, for example, requires a combination of intelligence (natural ability), a desire to get a grade of A (motivation), and studying (effort).

The component most closely associated with competence is natural ability. Natural ability is a stable factor, and the greater one's natural ability, the less one has to compensate with motivation and effort (both unstable factors). Therefore, the greater one's natural ability, the greater the potential for future success. Fitzjames disguised his degree of motivation and effort in the hope of appearing competent because of his natural ability.

Self-promotion can be a risky proposition. Research indicates that people often fail to self-promote successfully. They can make strategic blunders in deciding how to self-promote, such as listing too many accomplishments. They can also make mistakes in communicating their self-promotion strategies as the conversation unfolds, perhaps making a brash claim too early in the conversation or appearing arrogant, self-centered, and uninterested in their conversational partners (see Godfrey, Jones, & Lord, 1986).

Miller, Cooke, Tsang, and Morgan (1992) raised a fundamental issue: When do people perceive positive self-serving statements as "positive disclosures"; when do they see them as "brags"? Consider the following statements:

My softball team had its awards dinner last night. We had a good season and so everyone was in a great mood. I even got the most valuable player award. Boy, was I surprised. I played really hard this summer, but I did it for the fun and the exercise. So I was really pleased to get the award and the recognition. I was glad to help my team finish the season so well.

My softball team had its awards dinner last night. I had my best season yet, and so I was in a great mood. They gave me the most valuable player award. But that was no surprise because I was the leading player all summer. Actually, I'm the best all-around player this league has ever seen. I could have my choice to play on any team I want next year, so I may be changing to a better team.

Most people readily identify the first statement as a positive disclosure statement and the second as a boast or brag.

Miller and colleagues (1992) identified three elements that make a statement a brag. First, a bragging statement is one in which the communicator emphasizes a personal and chronic quality of power, status, or wealth. Second, brags involve exaggeration, emphasis, or elaboration of how the speaker accomplished the achievement with no effort or of how much the achievement benefited others. Third, statements are perceived as brags if the communicators emphasize that they are better than others at a skill or a task.

Miller and associates found that communicators who employed bragging statements were perceived as competent but less likable. However, they also argued that bragging is perceived as a masculine behavior, characteristic of male competitiveness. If you are a male and you want other males to think of you as competent, you might try to increase ratings of competence by bragging. However, you will probably be perceived as less likable. However, if you are a female and you want males to think of you as competent, bragging does not increase ratings of competence as much as making mere positive disclosures does. Further, females who brag received low ratings of likability.

Self-promoters may use a variety of tactics that help to create credible claims concerning their competence. Three are discussed here. First, self-promoters can have their accomplishments made known, perhaps by a third person, or when grades are posted as in the case of Fitzjames, and then try to emphasize the role of natural ability while de-emphasizing the role of effort or motivation. This is what Fitzjames attempted. Second, self-presentations can be made to appear credible and impressive by drawing attention to impediments that have been overcome. A third tactic, **self-handicapping,** is an individual's attempt to protect self-esteem and competence by pointing to something external to him or her as an excuse or causal explanation for any possible failure (Shepperd & Arkin, 1989). In other words, self-handicappers sabotage their own performance. A typical example is the student who comes to class the day of an exam and says, "My friends and I went out last night and I haven't studied for this test at all." On the surface, it may appear that self-handicapping would create an impression of incompetence, but actually it has the potential to create or maintain an impression of competence in two ways. First, if self-handicappers fail, their competence is protected because people attribute the failure to the obstacle. Second, if self-handicappers succeed, their natural ability is enhanced because they were able to overcome the obstacles. A growing literature base in sports (i.e., Ryska, Yin, & Boyd, 1999) examines who is likely to engage in self-handicapping. Ryska and associates found that athletes protect their self-concepts and cope with the threat of competition by self-handicapping (reducing effort to win, making up excuses for losing) if they are less competent but highly ego-involved athletes, or when they prefer to disregard self-improvement and skill mastery information.

Sandbagging (discussed earlier) may seem similar to handicapping, but it is not. People who sandbag are in fact relatively confident in their abilities to perform a task, while self-handicappers are often uncertain about their ability. Because they doubt their ability, they self-handicap in order to have an excuse for failure so their self-concept remains intact. A second difference is that sandbaggers may perform poorly at first or announce a lower skill level, but not actually place real impediments or obstacles in the way of winning. Self-handicappers are in fact more likely to skip practice, drink alcohol the night before an event, or stay up all night before a game or an important test so that they have an excuse for low performance already prepared.

Exemplification

Exemplifiers attempt to project the image of integrity and moral worthiness. They appear to deserve our respect because they apparently do what we wish we could do or know we should do. The exemplifier's social power is based on the ability to instill respect, admiration, or even guilt in the minds of others. Prototypical exemplifiers might include religious leaders who live a life of humility and self-sacrifice, political leaders who willingly endure hardship for the sake of their cause, and heroes who risk their lives for the good of others. Closer to home, parents typically try to be exemplifiers to their children. You may also find exemplifiers among some of your friends, co-workers, or even in members of a particular sorority or fraternity — each of them may try to be perceived as having high principles and high moral worth. If you watch "The Simpsons," you will recognize Homer Simpson's neighbor, the moralistic and eternally cheerful Mr. Flanders, as an exemplifier.

Gilbert and Jones (1986) attempted to determine the relative impact of moral failure on people's perceptions of an exemplifier compared with a moral pragmatist. Moral pragmatists do not maintain a stable, consistently applied set of moral principles; the decision regarding what is ethical varies from situation to situation. Exemplifiers, on the other hand, let it be known that they maintain high moral standards in all or most situations. The researchers gave participants self-presentation information about two hypothetical students (one exemplifier and one pragmatist) that the participants were led to believe participated in a similar study two years earlier. The exemplifier made the following series of claims: He thought honesty was extremely important in both politics and in interpersonal relationships; he liked only jokes that had no potential to hurt anybody; he felt that rules should not be bent; and he thought about going into the Peace Corps because he liked helping people. The pragmatist made different claims: He liked practical jokes and had pulled some on friends; he thought that politics and interpersonal relationships should be managed with diplomacy because being truthful all the time was unrealistic; he thought rules were made to be broken; and he claimed he was going to become a lawyer or a public relations agent.

After hearing these two descriptions, students were led to believe that the hypothetical characters had either cheated or resisted cheating on a test. The students

162

were then asked to indicate their perceptions of the cheater and the resister. The results indicated that when they cheated, the pragmatist and the exemplifier were both disliked, but for different reasons. The pragmatist was disliked because he was seen as exploitive, manipulative, and devious; in contrast the exemplifier was perceived as being a self-deceived hypocrite. In this study, the negative consequences of the fallen exemplifier were less severe compared to those of the cheating pragmatist because students saw the exemplifier's hypocrisy as pitiable but the pragmatist's deviousness as offensive.

Supplication

Communicators who attempt supplication base their self-presentation on the social norm that the strong are supposed to help the weak, and hence they attempt to create the impression of being weak or helpless. This style of self-presentation may not seem to augment power, but the supplicant often knows that many people who cannot be persuaded to act through reason alone can be moved to do so out of compassion or pity. Most people feel compelled to be supportive and encouraging when their friends are down. You may even have used this tactic yourself.

The potential danger associated with this tactic is adapted from a *Los Angeles Times* article headlined "Playing for Sympathy." The article tells the story of a 35-year-old corporate secretary named Anna.

Shortly after her fiancé broke off their relationship, Anna told her friends she had terminal breast cancer. She shaved her head to resemble the side effects of chemotherapy, wore a wig, lost twenty pounds, and avoided any social activity that required physical energy. She did not want to appear too healthy. She eventually joined a support group for women with breast cancer and began counseling others on coping with the illness.

Her friends and co-workers embraced her with warmth and sympathy, she was unconditionally accepted in the support group, and she eventually developed a close group of friends at the hospital even though she had always had a difficult time making friends. Later some of her friends began to wonder why she never got any worse, and they contacted her physician. They discovered that none of the doctors she had mentioned had any record of her. The leaders of the support group confronted her, and she confessed that she had been lying. The role had so overtaken her life that she had actually come to see herself as a cancer patient. She was eventually admitted to a psychiatric hospital to help with her recovery. Initially her thoughts and actions were governed by the identity of being a cancer patient. However, she was released after four weeks and promised to stop lying. By then, however, she had lost her job, and many of her friends had abandoned her.

Despite this last, extreme example, we need to emphasize the role of dependence when discussing the use of supplication. A supplicator may initiate and nourish a relationship and can become increasingly dependent on others. A typical supplicator wants attention and help from others. However, a supplicator runs the risk of appearing too needy, too demanding, and may be perceived as exploiting a relationship by being helpless. The work of Howard and associates (1986) indicates that the more dependent individual in a dating couple is likely to use supplication or manipulation (hinting, seduction, altering emotions).

INDIRECT STRATEGIES OF SELF-PRESENTATION

So far we have talked about how communicators go about directly and actively trying to create public images. However, communicators may also rely indirectly on associations with others in order to bolster their self-image or public image. Indirect self-presentation management tactics are based on the idea that when seeking to enhance a public image, a person can do so "not only by presenting information about his or her own traits, actions, and accomplishments," but also by presenting information "about the traits, actions, and accomplishments of his or her associates" (Cialdini, Finch, & De Nicholas, 1990, p. 195). Schutz (1998a) recently organized these tactics in terms of (a) looking good by making others look bad, and (b) looking good by making the self look good. Both of these strategies include a number of variations. We will talk generally here about attacking others, and then talk about the various indirect strategies for presenting a positive self-image.

The strategy "blasting the opposition" (Cialdini et al., 1990; Cialdini & Richardson, 1980; Richardson & Cialdini, 1981) is the same as "derogation of competitors" (Buss & Dedden, 1990). This strategy involves making negative statements and assertions of a rival group, school, team, or individual in order to tarnish the image of the opponent or rival and enhance the self-presenter's image by comparison. This tactic is indirect because the self-presenter is not directly claiming an identity, but blasting the image and/or reputation of others. The strategy varies in how blunt or obvious the self-presenter is when making the claims. According to Schutz, the political world is ripe with examples of a variety of tactics for attacking or blasting others, including outright negative evaluation of the opponent, setting for oneself a higher standard (and one-upping) than one's opponent, attacking others or groups linked to the opponent, and controlling the topics of discussion. The stiff competition for rewards, fame, and glory in Hollywood also provides an analysis by which people bring down their opponents, or at least gloat over the misfortunes of others (see the box "Where They Root for Failure").

Who uses blasting the opposition/derogating competitors and indirect ways of promoting the self, at the expense of opponents? People with lower self-esteem or threatened self-esteem are more likely to bask in reflected glory and boast (Cialdini et al., 1990). People promote a positive self-presentation and increase their own feelings of esteem by associating themselves with positive elements of their universities and teams, while lowering their evaluations of other universities and teams.

WHERE THEY ROOT FOR FAILURE

Taking pleasure from the misfortune of others may not be very nice,
but in Hollywood it's a way of life.

By PATRICK GOLDSTEIN

The other day *The Times'* Business section did a story about MGM reporting a loss of $61.3 million in its second-quarter. . . . But what really caught my eye was something studio chief Chris McGurk said at the end of the piece. After boasting that his current hit, "Legally Blonde," had already made more than $50 million at the box office, McGurk felt compelled to add that his movie "didn't have any $20-million actors with high-gross participation" in it.

It didn't take a genius to figure out that McGurk was taking a thinly veiled shot at "America's Sweethearts," the Julia Roberts–starring film from Revolution Studios that was ranked higher in this paper's Company Town Film Profit Report than "Legally Blonde." In other words, it was not enough to brag about his movie — he also had to question the profitability of a rival's movies.

The Germans have a word for it — schadenfreude, the pleasure one takes from the misfortune of others — and in Hollywood it's a way of life. If show business were a religion, its first commandment would be: Instead of enjoying your own success, take pleasure in others' failure. One producer I know used to go around his office chanting "OPMF." Translation: Other people must fail. As Ned Tanen, a former studio chief at Paramount and Universal, once put it: "The only words you need to know about Hollywood are 'negativity' and 'illusion.' Especially 'negativity.'"

Why do so many people in Hollywood root for everyone else to fail? You could chalk it up to jealousy and insecurity. You could say it's a telling example of Hollywood's spiritual emptiness. You could blame it on an insular culture that encourages cutthroat competition. Whatever the reason, schadenfreude is deeply imbedded in Hollywood culture. "This is a town filled with envy and jealousy," says "Tomb Raider" producer Larry Gordon, who's been a high-profile force in Hollywood for years. "You've got two kinds of people — the people who've made it who are angry that they're not more successful and the people who haven't made it who are angry because they think the other guy is a lucky [expletive]."

The equation is simple: Power + Success = Envy. In the 1980s, the backbiting focused on Creative Artists Agency czar Michael Ovitz, whose velvet glove grip on the industry inspired a storm of schadenfreude. When Michael Eisner let Ovitz go at Disney in 1996, there was dancing in the streets. When Mark Canton ran Sony in the early 1990s, he was a fat target: He made bad movies, kept people waiting forever in his office and paid Jim Carrey $20 million to star in "Cable Guy" at a time when studios were trying to hold the line on star salaries. Jealous of the adoring press DreamWorks got after its launch, many in Hollywood openly exulted when the studio's much-ballyhooed debut animation film, "The Prince of Egypt," failed to perform up to expectations.

Last year the sniping focused on Miramax chief Harvey Weinstein because the industry felt Weinstein's crafty "Chocolat" marketing blitz had won the lightweight romance an undeserved best picture Oscar nomination. When Disney's "Pearl Harbor" opened to withering reviews this summer, there was a tidal wave of gloating. . . . It's tempting to view some of this behavior as classic testosterone guy stuff, Hollywood being full of young men in a hurry, eager to get to the top. But women aren't so sure. "There's very little sisterhood in Hollywood — the cat claws come out when successful women meet other successful women," says screenwriter Leslie Dixon. "Most women perceive so little room at the top of the pyramid that they're suspicious of any woman who wants to get up there."

Schadenfreude is hardly confined to the movie business. Washington insiders were gleeful when Newt Gingrich fell from power and Hillary Clinton was beset by legal and marital woes. . . . People who handle power with grace and honor generally have few enemies — at least until they become too successful.

Copyright 2001 *Los Angeles Times.* Tuesday, August 7, 2001. Reprinted with permission. The full article can be downloaded by searching "Hollywood" August 7, 2001 at www.latimes.com.

Strategies for presenting a favorable image include a number of methods that vary subtly from one another:

1. *Basking in reflected glory* refers to the strategy of highlighting one's association with positively evaluated others (Cialdini & De Nicholas, 1989). Researchers found that, among other things, sports fans are more likely to wear clothing displaying their university's name or insignia on Mondays after the football team won than when the team lost or tied (Cialdini et al., 1976). People bask in the reflected glory (the achievements of others) because it increases their public image and also makes them feel better, a psychological boost stemming from being associated with winning. Hence, millions of people rally around the Yankees, Lakers, or their national soccer teams as a way to bask in the glory — if the teams win.

2. When using an *entitlement*, a person associates himself or herself with positive events (separate from teams or athletes winning competition) (Schutz, 1998a). People can enhance their public image by claiming "I was there" in the audience when David Letterman returned to the air after the September 11th tragedy, or I was there at Nirvana's last concert. Attendance at opening nights, movie premieres, or a performer's farewell tour are just a few of the events with which one can associate in order to enhance a public image (with a certain targeted audience).

3. When using an *enhancement*, a person who is already associated with an identity, group, or event may benefit from an increase in status of the group, identity, or event. Or, the person convinces others that membership in the group, event, etc., is more important than previously believed. For example, a person's friends may all know that she or he is from Scotland or Ireland, and the person's status is elevated when Riverdance, *Braveheart*, and

166

other Celtic-related movies and performances become popular. Membership in the Navy SEALS, the FBI Terrorist Task Force, the American Indian "code talkers," or other less well-known groups and organizations may not impress others adequately at first until they learn or are told how unique or important the groups have been and are today.

4. The strategy of *boosting* is similar to and is a variation of basking, using entitlements, or using enhancements. In boosting a person knows about or uncovers that s/he is associated with a negative event. Instead of allowing a negative association to tarnish a person's image, s/he could psychologically re-evaluate the event to which s/he was associated and make it less negative, even something positive. For example, people were led to believe that they shared the same birth date as Rasputin, the power-oriented crazed Russian monk (Cialdini et al., 1990; Finch & Cialdini, 1989). After hearing the news, people thought of good things to say about Rasputin (they "boosted their evaluation of Rasputin") and rated him less negatively.

5. Schutz (1998a) also includes *power display* as an assertive indirect strategy that communicates (via nonverbal means) one's sense of power, strength, and potential.

6. By *identification* Schutz (1998a) identifies how individuals exploit group membership to create or maintain a public image. Motor-biker's self-presentational tactics, for example, may include particular tatoos, clothing, artifacts, and verbal claims of self and one's particular kind of bike.

ROLES, GENDER, PERSONALITY, AND CULTURE

People in different occupations or roles use different self-presentational strategies. For example, Schutz (1997) examined the self-presentational styles of guests on talk shows and found that each type of guest worked to present a particular image to the audience members. Experts often present themselves as self-promoters (i.e., "I graduated highest in my law school"), and entertainers tend to present themselves as ingratiators, trying to appear likable by self-disclosing personal details of their lives and by appearing to be modest. In the latter case, entertainers would reveal personal stories and embarrassing moments in order to appear more human, more personal, down to earth, and amusing. Politicians might emphasize values and moral issues (i.e., "My parents taught me these values," "We have to defend personal freedom"). Schutz (1993, 1998b) examined how politicians employ self-presentation strategies and found that students rated politicians as less competent if they used overt self-enhancement statements (bragging) and heavy-handed negative statements about others. Politicians were also rated less competent if they behaved in an intimidating manner by interrupting or attacking their opponents. Politicians were rated more competent when they used moderate levels of self-enhancement.

Impression management strategies are, of course, important in organizational settings because they have an impact on perceived leadership abilities, perceived effectiveness, and worker satisfaction (Gardner & Avolio, 1998; Gardner & Cleavenger, 1998; Gardner & Martinko, 1988). Gardner and Cleavenger (1998) studied people's reactions to world class leaders and found that those who scored high on exemplification were perceived to be more charismatic, idealistic, intellectually stimulating, considerate, and effective and also led satisfied workers. Similarly, ingratiating, likable leaders also received high ratings in leadership and effectiveness. Intimidating leaders, however, were correlated negatively with leadership, effectiveness, and satisfaction, "presumably because coercion and manipulation inhibit, rather than promote, the empowerment and development of followers" (Gardner & Cleavenger, 1998). Self-promotion was also related negatively with leadership, effectiveness, and satisfaction. The authors note a "self-promoter's paradox," in that self-promotion can secure high ratings of competence and expertise, but when used to excess the self-promoter can be perceived as conceited, defensive, or promoting self-interest over concern for others (recall Table 6.1). Leaders who were perceived as supplicators (depending on others, being needy and helpless) were related to positive ratings of leadership qualities. A possible reason for this is that leaders who relied on supplication knew their limitations and hired (and rewarded) particular people who helped them. These results imply that in long term leader-follower relationships, it is best to be an exemplifier, or ingratiator, to know and fill one's weaknesses, while avoiding relying on (too much) self-promotion and intimidation.

As noted earlier, academic women and men's Web pages involved different presentational strategies. Arnold and Miller (1999; also see Arnold & Miller, 2000; Miller & Arnold, 2001) found that women's Web pages are friendlier than males', but women felt obligated to display credentials (more so than men) because they felt compelled to be professional in their self-presentation. Higher status men tended to be more self-effacing, and, while no female professional used jokey pictures of herself, some men did. In fact, using a photograph is problematic for women, since it raises the issue of the traditional judgments of women's images versus their achievements and abilities. Some women post photographs on the first page of the site, others present credentials and background information first and place photographs on later pages, and still others refuse to post photographs. Women also show more awareness of the reader in their use of language compared to men. Women are more likely to use "you," and to refer to the viewer/reader, while men use "I" more often (Miller & Arnold, 2001; Miller & Mather, 1998).

A number of studies find that women are more modest in public than men. There are several possible reasons for this; one of the best explanations focuses on the fact that during socialization women's identities and self-definitions are more likely to be connected with those of others (best friend(s), sports team members, sorority members, and so on). They are more sensitive to the feelings of others and are more collectivist, less individualistic, and more status neutralizing than men, who are more individualistic and status assertive (Brown, Uebelacker, & Heatherington, 1998; Deaux & Major, 1987; Eagly, 1987; Heatherington, Burns, & Gustafson, 1998; Jordan, Kaplan, Miller, Stiver, & Surrey, 1991). Women are more modest in public, especially if they are concerned with not appearing better than others. For example, women will report more modest grade point averages in public if they believe it will be heard by a person worried about grades (see Heatherington et al., 1998). They would rather be modest than increase status over another who might have hurt feelings. Other recent research has focused on women's use of exercise and diet as fulfilling self-presentational needs (see, for instance, Kashubeck-West, Mintz, & Saunders, 2001; Kowalski, Crocker, & Kowalski, 2001).

While we have much more to say about individual differences in Chapter 15, two personality concepts are strongly related to particular self-presentational strategies: Self-esteem and self-monitoring (Baumeister, Tice, & Hutton, 1989; Brown, Collins, & Schmidt, 1988; Schutz, 2001; Schutz & DePaulo, 1996). People who score high on self-esteem measures promote a more positive impression of the self and are more likely to take chances in promoting a positive image; they are also more confident in communicating negative evaluations of others. Low self-esteem scorers, however, often try to be positive and pleasant, try to avoid being negative or unpleasant, and try to be liked. That is, high self-esteem individuals are quite capable of engaging in self-promotion, while low self-esteem individuals focus on ingratiation (see Chapter 15 as well). Self-monitoring individual are ones who pay close attention to their own behavior and to that of others in social situations, and they behave appropriately for a given situation. They are referred to as *social chameleons*, blending in with their current environment. People scoring high on self-monitoring (see Chapter 15) are skilled impression managers, possessing high levels of acting ability, flexibility, and adaptability. While low self-monitors present themselves in ways that reflect their true, authentic attitudes, values, and beliefs, high self-monitors alter their impressions for different audiences, sometimes deceiving others. In fact, Rowatt and colleagues (1998) found that high self-monitors were more likely to alter their presentations to appear more similar to that of a desirable date prospect. They strategically altered their ratings on values, expectations, and so-called love attitudes in order to appear similar to, and more attractive to, a desirable date prospect. Further, they rated their own physical attractiveness higher in order to increase the likelihood of dating a desirable potential date. Another recent study found that high self-monitors are more effective than low self-monitors at managing impressions, especially using ingratiation, self-promotion, and exemplification (Turnley & Bolino, 2001).

Communication scholars have found significant differences in communication styles among those from collectivist cultures (Asia, Latin America, Africa) and individualistic cultures (Europe, United States) (Brewer & Gardner, 1996; Gardner, Gabriel, & Lee, 1999; Gudykunst et al., 1996; Kanagawa, Cross, & Markus, 2001; Markus & Kitayama, 1991; Park & Levine, 1999). As mentioned in Chapter 4, members of both types of cultures develop self-construals that represent ways of thinking of the self, which have an impact on ways of presenting the self. Members of collectivist cultures are socialized to and naturally present a view of the self that is connected with family, groups, and communities; they develop interdependent self-construals that reference relationships with others (see Ellis & Wittenbaum, 2000). Examples include "I am Chinese," "I am a first-born son," "My parents are the best," "My friends and I go snowboarding every weekend," "My friends and I like to party," "My parents work hard," "My father is stern, but supports me." Members of individualist cultures develop independent self-construals that focus on the self rather than others; in fact, when promoting the self, they may avoid reference to others intentionally. Self-promotional statements by independent self-construals include: "I attend college on a scholarship," "I am president of Lambda Pi Eta," "I am captain of the baseball team," "I am editor of a publication," "I clerked in a law office at age nineteen."

Ellis and Wittenbaum (2000) demonstrated how self-construal systems (interdependent vs. independent) influence how individuals self-promote. Individuals scoring high on interdependent and high on independent self-construal systems were asked to engage in an interview to win a student award, which would provide recognition and money. Individuals with independent self-construal systems provided significantly more self-promotional statements, focusing on the *self* and de-emphasizing *other* promotional statements (see Ellis & Wittenbaum, 2000). On the other hand, individuals with interdependent self-construal systems provided significantly more other promotional statements, focusing on family, friends, groups, and ethnic alliances and de-emphasizing self or individual achievements.

Kanagawa and associates (2001) had American and Japanese students describe themselves in several situations (alone, with a faculty member, with a peer, and in a group) and found that Americans relied more on psychological attributes and long-term dispositions when describing the self to others ("I am outgoing," "I'm sociable," "I'm friendly"). Also, Americans presented this stable, enduring presentation of self across the four situations. Japanese students, however, tended to describe themselves in terms of preferences ("I like to snowboard"), goals ("I plan to get married next year"), and behaviors or actions ("I laugh a lot during conversations"). Further, Japanese students varied their self-presentations substantially from one situation to another. They were more positive when describing themselves when alone, and generally altered their self-presentations to reflect salient social relationships and interdependence in the three situations involving others.

Members of Japanese, Chinese, and Korean societies are also more likely to make negative, self-effacing statements ("I'm so sorry to take up your time," "Sorry, I am not very smart," etc.) (Bond, Leung, & Wan, 1982; Kanagawa et al., 2001; Kitayama, Markus, Matsumoto, & Norasakkunkit, 1997; Yik, Bond, & Paulhus, 1998). Kanagawa and colleagues (2001) argue that the communication of self-critical, self-effacing statements does in fact improve the self-image by admitting to those present that the individual is aware of a socially shared standard of excellence that he or she could not achieve (otherwise, one would appear arrogant and presumptuous). "It is most likely that in any given instance a person will not be able to realize the cultural ideal or

170

meet the standard of appropriate behavior. Moreover, part of realizing the cultural ideal is to reflect on one's self modestly and to be very sensitive to the expectations of whatever in-group is constituted by the immediate situation. Therefore, Japanese people often will focus on negative aspects of themselves and their behavior in social situations" (Kanagawa et al., p. 100).

Most of the research on communication and self-presentation has focused on samples of members of collectivist cultures, and an emphasis has been placed on relatively direct ways of presenting an independent, stable, enduring self. Results of studies on cultural comparisons indicated that other self-related processes are involved, including different indirect means of self-presentation and self-enhancement, and people present a self appropriate to different cultural rules.

CHAPTER SUMMARY

Self-presentation is one of the most important and pervasive goals we pursue through interpersonal communication. Self-presentation can be used to enhance our sense of self-esteem and to increase our confidence in other desired attributes. The way others see us determines how they respond to us and therefore governs the opportunities available to us. Certainly people who are seen as hardworking and competent have different opportunities than those who are seen as lazy and incompetent. Five direct self-presentation strategies include presenting oneself as likable, dangerous, competent, morally worthy, and helpless. Each of these images implies a different type of relationship with others. Indirect self-preservation tactics include basking in the reflected glory of another person, blasting one's opposition, and boosting one's current associations. Finally, one's occupation, gender, personality, and culture strongly influence the nature of one's self-presentation.

KEY TERMS

affinity-seeking, p. 155
authentic ingratiation, p. 152
exemplifier, p. 145
illicit ingratiation, p. 152
impression management/strategic self-presentation, p. 138
incentive value, p. 151
indicators of attainment, p. 150
ingratiator, p. 143

ingratiator's dilemma, p. 152
intimidator, p. 145
opinion conformity, p. 155
perceived legitimacy, p. 153
sandbagging, p. 142
self-handicapping, p. 160
self-promoter, p. 145
subjective probability of success, p. 152
supplicator, p. 145

EXERCISES FOR FURTHER DISCUSSION

▼

1. Have everyone in class type out a personal ad. Collect all personal ads and create a directory to circulate in class (or on-line). See if class members can accurately match class members with their personal ads. What types of images do class members try to create? Are they credible? Do the advertisements bolster self-images, portray self-consistency, and/or represent honest portrayals of the self?

2. List five main characters from movies or television shows that you have watched recently. Then write down the self-presentation style of the main character.
   a. Is the self-presentation style presented in a positive or negative way?
   b. Does the self-presentation style allow the person to gain love, money, or other types of rewards?
   c. Does the self-presentation style of the person result in conflict with others?
   d. What does the movie or television show tell us about this type of self-presentation?

3. Think of situations in which you or people you know have engaged in self-handicapping strategies. Were these strategies effective in protecting your sense of competence?

4. Identify your own style of self-presentation.
   a. Are you a self-promoter? Ingratiator? Intimidator? Exemplifier? Supplicator?
   b. Are you a blend of more than one style? If so, which ones?
   c. Why do you think you tend to use this style or these styles?
   d. Do you think that being male or female affects the style you use?
   e. Is your style similar to or different from that of your parents or siblings?

5. Think of a situation in which you would want to ingratiate yourself with someone (the parents of a person you are dating, an instructor, someone you would like to become friends with).
   a. What behaviors would you use to try to be ingratiating?
   b. Have you tried to be ingratiating in similar situations and failed? If so, what would you change if you could do it over again?

6. Think of each type of self-presentation behavior and consider whether, in your own experience, men and women can successfully use the same tactics.
   a. Are women perceived in the same way as men when they try to be self-promoting? Ingratiating? Intimidating? Exemplifying? Supplicating?
   b. If they are not perceived in the same way, why not?

7. Discuss the case of Fitzjames. Can you devise ways in which you can use the "attributional arithmetic" in order to bolster an image of competence, or self-promotion?

SUGGESTED READING

▼

IMPRESSION MANAGEMENT

Brissett D., & Edgley, C. (Eds.). (1990). *Life as theater: A dramaturgical sourcebook* (2nd ed.). New York: Aldine de Gruyter. This book features a number of classic writings on dramaturgical studies and provides an excellent compilation of readings on all aspects of motivations, performances, rituals, and more.

Jones, E. E., & Pittman, T. S. (1982). Toward a general theory of strategic self-presentation. In J. M. Suls (Ed.), *Psychological perspectives on the self* (pp. 231–262). Hillsdale, NJ: Erlbaum. Jones and Pittman provide a thorough discussion of the five most fundamental strategies of self-presentation, including the competent communicator, the ingratiator (or likable communicator), the intimidator, the exemplifier, and the supplicator.

Jones, E. E., & Wortman, C. (1974). *Ingratiation: An attributional approach*. Morristown, NJ: General Learning. Jones and Wortman look at four basic strategies designed to derive liking from others: praising or flattering others, conforming one's opinions to fit in with others, rendering favors for others, and self-bolstering (in which the communicator attempts to increase his or her status, competence, and so forth).

Schlenker, B. R., & Pontari, B. A. (2000). The strategic control of information: Impression management and self-presentation in daily life. In A. Tesser, Felson, R. B., and Suls, J. M. (Eds.), *Psychological perspectives on self and identity* (pp. 199–232). Washington, DC: American Psychological Association. The authors provide a review of literature on impression management, with an emphasis on two topics: dispelling misconceptions about impression management and assessing motivations underlying impression management.

INDIRECT METHODS OF PRESENTING THE SELF

Cialdini, R. B., Finch, J. F., & De Nicholas, M. E. (1990). Strategic self-presentation: The indirect route. In M. J. Cody & M. L. McLaughlin (Eds.), *The psychology of tactical communication* (pp. 194–206). Clevedon, England: Multilingual Matters. Cialdini and his students review their work on indirect methods of presenting the self, including the work on basking in reflected glory (BIRGing), blasting the opposition, and boosting.

Finch, J. F., & Cialdini, R. B. (1989). Another indirect tactic of (self-)image management: Boosting. *Personality and Social Psychology Bulletin*, *15*, 222–232. Finch and Cialdini report on two of their studies on boosting, wherein an individual confronted with a personal connection to another, especially a negative other, elevates or boosts some aspect of the other.

REFERENCE LIST

▼

Arnold, J., & Miller, H. (1999, March). *Gender and Web home pages.* Paper presented as a poster at CAL99 Virtuality in Education, The Institute of Education, London, [On-line]. Available: http://ess.ntu.ac.uk/miller/cal99.htm

Arnold, J., & Miller, H. (2000, May). *Same old gender plot? Women academics' identities on the web.* Paper presented at Cultural Diversities in/and Cyberspace Conference, University of Maryland, Campus Park, Maryland, [On-line]. Available: http://ess.ntu.ac.uk/miller/cyberpsych/gendplot.htm

Bangerter, A. (2000). Self-representation: Conversational implementation of self-presentational goals in research interviews. *Journal of Language and Social Psychology, 19,* 436–462.

Baumeister, R. F., Tice, D. M., & Hutton, D. G. (1989). Self-presentational motivations and personality differences in self-esteem. *Journal of Personality, 57,* 547–579.

Bell, R. A., & Daly, J. A. (1984). The affinity-seeking function of communication. *Communication Monographs, 51,* 91–115.

Bell, R. A., Daly, J. A., & Gonzalez, M. C. (1987). Affinity-maintenance in marriage and its relationship to women's marital satisfaction. *Journal of Marriage and the Family, 49,* 445–454.

Bell, R. A., Tremblay, S. W., & Buerkel-Rothfuss, N. L. (1987). Interpersonal attraction as a communication accomplishment: Development of a measure of affinity-seeking competence. *Western Journal of Speech Communication, 51,* 1–18.

Berg, J. H., & Archer, R. L. (1982). Responses to self-disclosure and interaction goals. *Journal of Experimental Social Psychology, 18,* 501–512.

Bond, M. H., Leung, K., & Wan, K. (1982). The social impact of self-effacing attributions: The Chinese case. *The Journal of Social Psychology, 118,* 157–166.

Brewer, M. B., & Gardner, W. (1996). Who is this "we"? Levels of collective identity and self-representations. *Journal of Personality and Social Psychology, 71,* 83–93.

Brissett D., & Edgley, C. (Eds.). (1990). *Life as theater: A dramaturgical sourcebook* (2nd ed.). New York: Aldine de Gruyter.

Brown, J. D., Collins, R. L., & Schmidt, G. W. (1988). Self-esteem and direct versus indirect forms of self-enhancement. *Journal of Personality and Social Psychology, 55,* 445–453.

Brown, L., Uebelacker, L., & Heatherington, L. (1998). Men, women, and the self-presentation of achievement. *Sex Roles, 38,* 253–268.

Buss, D. M., & Dedden, L. A. (1990). Derogation of competitors. *Journal of Social and Personal Relationships, 7,* 395–422.

Cialdini, R. B., Borden, R. J., Thorne, A., Walker, M. R., Freeman, S., & Sloan, L. R. (1976). Basking in reflected glory: Three (football) field studies. *Journal of Personality and Social Psychology, 34,* 36–75.

Cialdini, R. B., & De Nicholas, M. E. (1989). Self-presentation by association. *Journal of Personality and Social Psychology, 57,* 626–631.

Cialdini, R. B., Finch, J. F., & De Nicholas, M. E. (1990). Strategic self-presentation: The indirect route. In M. J. Cody & M. L. McLaughlin (Eds.), *The psychology of tactical communication* (pp. 194–206). Clevedon, England: Multilingual Matters.

Cialdini, R. B., & Richardson, K. D. (1980). Two indirect tactics of image management: Basking and blasting. *Journal of Personality and Social Psychology, 39*, 406–415.

Daly, J. A., & Kreiser, P. O. (1994). Affinity-seeking. In J. A. Daly & J. M. Wiemann (Eds.), *Strategic interpersonal communication* (pp. 109–134). Hillsdale, NJ: Erlbaum.

Deaux, K., & Major, B. (1987). Putting gender into context: An interactive model of gender related behavior. *Psychological Review, 94*, 369–389.

Eagly, A. H. (1987). *Sex differences in social behavior: A social-role interpretation.* Hillsdale, NJ: Erlbaum.

Ellis, J. B., & Wittenbaum, G. M. (2000). Relationships between self-construal and verbal promotion. *Communication Research, 27*, 704–722.

Felson, R. B. (1982). Impression management and the escalation of aggression and violence. *Social Psychology Quarterly, 45*, 245–254.

Finch, J. F., & Cialdini, R. B. (1989). Another indirect tactic of (self-)image management: Boosting. *Personality and Social Psychology Bulletin, 15*, 222–232.

Ganong, L., Coleman, M., Fine, M., & Martin, P. (1999). Stepparents' affinity-seeking and affinity-maintaining strategies with stepchildren. *Journal of Family Issues, 20*, 299–327.

Gardner, W. L., & Avolio, B. J. (1998). The charismatic relationship: A dramaturgical perspective. *Academy of Management Review, 23*, 32–58.

Gardner, W. L., & Cleavenger, D. (1998). The impression management strategies associated with transformational leadership at the world-class level: A psychohistorical assessment. *Management Communication Quarterly, 12*(1), 3–41.

Gardner, W. L., Gabriel, S., & Lee, A. Y. (1999). "I" value freedom but "we" value relationships: Self-construal priming mirrors cultural differences in judgment. *Psychological Science, 10*, 321–326.

Gardner, W. L., & Martinko, M. J. (1988). Impression management: An observational study linking audience characteristics with verbal self-presentations. *Academy of Management Journal, 31*, 42–65.

Gergen, K. J. (1989). Warranting voice. In J. Shotter & K. J. Gergen (Eds.), *Texts of identity* (pp. 70–81). Newbury Park, CA: Sage.

Gibson, B., & Sachau, D. (2000). Sandbagging as a self-presentational style: Claiming to be less than you are. *Personality and Social Psychology Bulletin, 26*(1), 56–70.

Gilbert, D. T., & Jones, E. E. (1986). Exemplification: The self-presentation of moral character. *Journal of Personality, 54*, 591–615.

Godfrey, D. K., Jones, E. E., & Lord, C. G. (1986). Self-promotion is not ingratiating. *Journal of Personality and Social Psychology, 50*, 106–115.

Goffman, E. (1959). *The presentation of self in everyday life.* Garden City, NY: Doubleday.

Goffman, E. (1974). *Frame analysis: An essay on the organization of experience.* New York: Harper and Row.

Gollwitzer, P. M. (1986). Striving for specific identities: The social reality of self-symbolizing. In R. F. Baumeister (Ed.), *Public and private self* (pp. 143–159). New York: Springer-Verlag.

Gudykunst, W. B., Matsumoto, Y., Ting-Toomey, S., Nishida, T., Kim, K., & Heyman, S. (1996). The influence of cultural individualism-collectivism, self-construals, and individual values on communication styles across cultures. *Human Communication Research, 22*, 510–543.

Harris, L. M., Gergen, K. J., & Lannamann, J. W. (1986). Aggression rituals. *Communication Monographs, 53,* 252–265.

Heatherington, L., Burns, A. B., & Gustafson, T. B. (1998). When another stumbles: Gender and self-presentation to vulnerable others. *Sex Roles, 38,* 889–913.

Howard, J. A., Blumstein, P., & Schwartz, P. (1986). Sex, power, and influence tactics in intimate relationships. *Journal of Personality and Social Psychology, 51,* 102–109.

Jones, E. E. (1989). The framing of competence. *Personality and Social Psychology Bulletin, 15,* 477–492.

Jones, E. E., & Pittman, T. S. (1982). Toward a general theory of strategic self-presentation. In J. M. Suls (Ed.), *Psychological perspectives on the self* (pp. 231–262). Hillsdale, NJ: Erlbaum.

Jones, E. E., & Wortman, C. B. (1974). *Ingratiation: An attributional approach.* Morristown, NJ: General Learning.

Jordan, J. V., Kaplan, A. G., Miller, J. B., Stiver, I. P., & Surrey, J. L. (1991). *Women's growth in connections: Writings from the Stone Center.* New York: Guilford.

Kanagawa, C., Cross, S. E., & Markus, H. R. (2001). "Who Am I?" The cultural psychology of the conceptual self. *Personality and Social Psychology Bulletin, 27,* 2001, 90–103.

Kashubeck-West, S., Mintz, L. B., & Saunders, K. J. (2001). Assessment of eating disorders in women. *Counseling Psychologist Special Issue, 29,* 662–694.

Kitayama, S., Markus, H. R., Matsumoto, H., & Norasakkunkit, V. (1997). Individual and collective processes in the construction of the self: Self-enhancement in the United States and self-criticism in Japan. *Journal of Personality and Social Psychology, 72,* 1245–1267.

Koestner, R., & Wheeler, L. (1988). Self-presentation in personal advertisements: The influence of implicit notions of attraction and role expectations. *Journal of Social and Personal Relationships, 5,* 149–160.

Kowalski, N. P., Crocker, P. E., & Kowalski, K. C. (2001). Physical self and physical activity relationships in college women: Does social physique anxiety moderate effects? *Research Quarterly for Exercise and Sport, 72,* 55–62.

Leary, M. R., & Kowalski, R. M. (1990). Impression management: A literature review and two-component model. *Psychological Bulletin, 107,* 34–47.

Markus, H. R., & Kitayama, S. (1991). Culture and the self: Implications for cognition, emotion, and motivation. *Psychological Review, 98,* 224–253.

Martin, M. W., & Rubin, R. B. (1998). Affinity-seeking in initial interactions. *Southern Communication Journal, 63,* 131–143.

Miller, H. (1995, June). *The presentation of self in electronic life: Goffman on the Internet.* Paper presented at Embodied Knowledge and Virtual Space Conference, Goldsmiths' College, University of London, [On-line]. Available: http://ess.ntu.ac.uk/miller/cyberpsych/goffman.htm

Miller, H. (1999, September). *The hypertext home: Images and metaphors of home on World Wide Web home pages.* Paper presented at the Design History Society Home and Away Conference, Nottingham Trent University, [On-line]. Available: http://ess.ntu.ac.uk/miller/cyberpsych/homeweb.htm

Miller, H., & Arnold, J. (2001). Breaking away from grounded identity: Women academics on the web. *CyberPsychology & Behavior, 4,* 95–108.

176

Miller, H., & Mather, R. (1998, March). *The presentation of self in WWW Home Pages.* Paper presented at IRISS '98 Conference, Bristol, UK, [On-line]. Available: http://ess.ntu.ac.uk/miller/cyberpsych/millmath.htm

Miller, L. C., Cooke, L. L., Tsang, J., & Morgan, F. (1992). Should I brag? Nature and impact of positive and boastful disclosures for women and men. *Human Communication Research, 18,* 364–399.

Norman, N. M., & Tedeschi, J. T. (1989). Self-presentation, reasoned action, and adolescents' decisions to smoke cigarettes. *Journal of Applied Social Psychology, 19,* 543–558.

Olson, J. M., Hafer, C. L., & Taylor, L. I'm mad as hell, and I'm not going to take it anymore: Reports of negative emotions as a self-preservation tactic. *Journal of Applied Social Psychology Special Issue, 31,* 981–999.

O'Sullivan, P. B. (2000). What you don't know won't hurt me: Impression management functions of communication channels in relationships. *Human Communication Research, 26,* 403–431.

Park, H. S., & Levine, T. R. (1999). The theory of reasoned action and self-construal: Evidence from three cultures. *Communication Monographs, 66,* 199–218.

Potter, S. (1962). *Threeupmanship.* Austin, TX: Holt, Rinehart and Winston.

Richardson, K. D., & Cialdini, R. B. (1981). Basking and blasting: Tactics of indirect self-presentation. In J. T. Tedeschi (Ed.), *Impression management theory and social psychological research* (pp. 41–53). Orlando, FL: Academic.

Roach, K. D., & Byrne, P. R. (2001). A cross-cultural comparison of instructor communication in American and German classrooms. *Communication Education, 50,* 1–14.

Rowatt, W. D., Cunningham, M. R., & Druen, P. B. (1998). Deception to get a date. *Personality and Social Psychology Bulletin, 24*(11), 1228–1242.

Ryska, T. A., Yin, Z., & Boyd, M. (1999). The role of dispositional goal orientation and team climate on situational self-handicapping among young athletes. *Journal of Sport Behavior, 22,* 410–425.

Schlenker, B. R. (1986). Self-identification: Toward an integration of the private and public self. In R. F. Baumeister (Ed.), *Public and private self* (pp. 21–62). New York: Springer-Verlag.

Schlenker, B. R., & Pontari, B. A. (2000). The strategic control of information: Impression management and self-presentation in daily life. In A. Tesser, R. B. Felson, & J. M. Suls, (Eds.), *Psychological perspectives on self and identity* (pp. 199–232). Washington, DC: American Psychological Association.

Schlenker, B. R., & Weigold, M. F. (1992). Interpersonal processes involving impression regulation and management. *Annual Review of Psychology, 43,* 133–168.

Schutz, A. (1993). Self-presentational tactics used in a German election campaign. *Political Psychology, 14,* 469–491.

Schutz, A. (1997). Self-presentational tactics of talk-show guests: A comparison of politicians, experts, and entertainers. *Journal of Applied Social Psychology, 27,* 1941–1952.

Schutz, A. (1998a). Assertive, offensive, protective, and defensive styles of self-presentation: A taxonomy. *The Journal of Psychology, 132,* 611–628.

Schutz, A. (1998b). Audience perceptions of politicians' self-presentational behaviors concerning their own abilities. *The Journal of Social Psychology, 138,* 173–188.

Schutz, A. (2001). Self-esteem and interpersonal strategies. In J. P. Forgas, K. D. Williams, & L. Wheeler (Eds.), *The social mind: Cognitive and motivational aspects of interpersonal behavior* (pp. 157–176). Cambridge: Cambridge University Press.

Schutz, A., & DePaulo, B. M. (1996). Self-esteem and evaluative reactions: Letting people speak for themselves. *Journal of Research in Personality, 30,* 137–156.

Shepperd, J. A., & Arkin, R. M. (1989). Determinants of self-handicapping: Task importance and the importance of preexisting handicaps on self-generated handicaps. *Personality and Social Psychological Bulletin, 15,* 101–112.

Tice, D. M., & Faber, J. (2001). Cognitive and motivational processes in self-presentation. In J. P. Forgas, K. D. Williams, & L. Wheeler (Eds.), *The social mind: Cognitive and motivational aspects of interpersonal behavior* (pp. 139–156). Cambridge: Cambridge University Press.

Toch, H. (1969). *Violent men: An inquiry into the psychology of violence.* Hawthorne, NY: Aldine.

Turnley, W. H., & Bolino, M. C. (2001). Achieving desired images while avoiding undesired images: Exploring the role of self-monitoring in impression management. *Journal of Applied Psychology Special Issue, 86,* 351–360.

Vonk, R. (1998). The slime effect: Suspicion and dislike of likable behavior toward superiors. *Journal of Personality and Social Psychology, 74,* 849–864.

Walther, J. B. (1996). Computer-mediated communication: Impersonal, interpersonal, and hyperpersonal interaction. *Communication Research, 23,* 3–43.

Walther, J. B. (1997, November). *Selective self-presentation in computer-mediated communication.* Paper presented at the annual meeting of the National Communication Association, Chicago.

Wanzer, M. B. (1998). An exploratory investigation of student and teacher perceptions of student-generated affinity-seeking behaviors. *Communication Education, 47,* 373–382.

Wanzer, M. B., Booth-Butterfield, M., & Booth-Butterfield, S. (1995). The funny people: A source-orientation to the communication of humor. *Communication Quarterly, 43,* 142–153.

Yik, M. S. M., Bond, M. H., & Paulhus, D. L. (1998). Do Chinese self-enhance or self-efface? It's a matter of domain. *Personality and Social Psychology Bulletin, 24,* 399–406.

CHAPTER 7

DISCLOSING

THE SELF

THE NATURE OF SELF-DISCLOSURE

Types of Self-Disclosure

Social Penetration Theory

FACTORS AFFECTING
SELF-DISCLOSURE CHOICES

The Norm of Reciprocity

Reasons for Not Disclosing

Self-Disclosure and Privacy

FACTORS AFFECTING THE MANNER
OF SELF-DISCLOSURE

Sex Differences

Nature of the Relationship

Cultural Factors Affecting Self-Disclosure

FACTORS AFFECTING THE PERCEPTION
OF SELF-DISCLOSURE

Amount of Disclosure

Reciprocity

Valence

Honesty

Timing

CHAPTER SUMMARY

That Saturday night, John felt alone. Another weekend had come, and he couldn't get up the nerve to ask Julie for a date. She represented everything he wanted in a companion: She was positive, athletic, intelligent, and kind. But here he was again on a weekend night hanging out with Dave. John liked to hang out with Dave, but not all the time. John felt that if he could talk about Julie, he might feel better and get some advice about what to do next. Dave had been pretty trustworthy so far. So when the conversation topic turned to women, John decided to tell Dave what was bothering him.

THE NATURE OF SELF-DISCLOSURE

Self-disclosure is communication that offers information about oneself. Cozby (1973) defines self-disclosure as any information that one person offers another (p. 73). Pearce, Sharp, Wright, and Slama (1974) highlight the strategic nature of self-disclosure as follows:

> Self-disclosing communication occurs when a person intentionally tells some-thing about himself (herself) to another person. Thus defined, self-disclosure is best conceptualized as a subset of communication behavior involving specific types of speaker decisions about what and to whom to speak. (p. 5)

This chapter examines how people present themselves through self-disclosure. Al-though self-disclosure functions to develop relationships (as we discuss below) and to obtain instrumental goals, it most clearly works as a reflection of who we are.

Types of Self-Disclosure

Gilbert and Horenstein (1975) observe that disclosure is not simply divided between people who do and do not disclose. Instead, there are several types of disclosure. Per-haps the most critical distinction among types concerns whether the disclosure re-flects one's attitudes and values, or whether the disclosure represents a report of rather objective material (Dindia, Fitzpatrick, & Kenny, 1997). Disclosure that presents one's attitudes is called **evaluative intimacy,** and disclosure that conveys an objective obser-vation is called **descriptive intimacy** (Berg & Archer, 1982). For example, evaluative intimacy refers to disclosures that express an assessment about some thing, person, or event; for example, "I like Mozart," "He is a sexist pig," and "Florida beaches are better than California beaches" are evaluative disclosures. Descriptive intimacy refers to self-revelations, or personal information about yourself ("That's the third time she's broken a date with me," "I earned a letter in high school for wrestling"). The distinctions among types of disclosure can be important. For example, Berg and Archer found that evaluative disclosures are used when the communicator's goal is to create a favorable impression more than when the communicator's goal is to obtain information. Also, Dindia, Fitzpatrick, and Kenny (1997) found another distinction: People tend to reciprocate disclosures of evaluative intimacy but not disclosures of descriptive intimacy.

Social Penetration Theory

Perhaps the most cited theory regarding self-disclosure is **social penetration theory** (Altman & Taylor, 1973; see also Chapter 9). According to social penetration theory, each relationship is assessed in terms of its rewards and costs. If the rewards outweigh the costs, increases in intimacy are sought. For example, if an acquaintance has similar values, tells interesting stories, or can help you with your homework, you may want to learn more about this person and share more about yourself. If the costs outweigh the

Social penetration theory holds that we will become closer to individuals who are rewarding to be with. Over time, if the rewards continue to outweigh the costs, we tend to disclose more about ourselves.

Joel Gordon

rewards, no further intimacy is sought. Moreover, if the forecast for rewards is low relative to costs, the relationship may be downplayed or even terminated.

Altman and Taylor (1973) predict that self-disclosure is most prevalent during the initial acquaintance stages and becomes less frequent in later stages once the partners have learned more about each other. In addition, disclosure occurs along two dimensions. The first dimension is depth, or the level of intimacy of the disclosure. The second dimension is breadth, or the number of topics that are discussed. According to Altman and Taylor, people penetrate one another's individuality along various topics in different degrees of intimacy (hence, the expression *social penetration*), as the following scenario illustrates:

Kris Wilkins has many friends. Perhaps her best friend is John. John and Kris have known each other since the fifth grade. And although they thought about dating during high school, nothing serious ever came of that. Kris knows that John will support her, regardless of what she thinks or does. For example, last year Kris dated someone John thought was immature. Kris was being used, and most people guessed that. Still, throughout that relationship, and afterward, Kris knew she could count on John. It was during this period that Kris often confided in John, relating things about herself she never thought she could tell anyone. Besides telling John all about her relationships with men, she also shared plans for the future and personal opinions about almost everything. Kris implicitly trusts John and believes that he would never use this information to hurt her.

Another friend of Kris's is Julie. Julie is new to the school, having just transferred there from a two-year college. Kris met Julie while taking the same aerobics class, and they hit it off right away. Now, Julie and Kris usually go to aerobics together and hang out on weekdays. They talk about everything, but not at very deep levels. Although Julie "came out," neither one of them makes a big deal about Julie's sexual orientation. Although they feel comfortable talking about romantic relationships, one of them carefully changes the topic whenever the talk about relationships gets too personal.

And then there's Beth. Beth and Kris are both communication majors, so they have had several classes together. Beth is very popular and was elected president of her sorority. Because she has so many other friends, Beth hasn't gotten to know Kris very well. Kris doesn't belong to a sorority, and she feels out of place at sorority parties. So Beth knows to a moderate degree how Kris feels about schoolwork and career goals.

Altman and Taylor (1973) liken the social penetration process to peeling an onion: Penetration proceeds along breadth and depth dimensions, revealing various segments and layers of a person's personality. Figure 7.1 illustrates social penetration using the onion skin metaphor, with reference to Kris's relationship with her three friends, John, Julie, and Beth. More specifically, we illustrate how well each friend knows Kris in terms of depth and breadth in four topic areas: romantic relationships, college issues (such as grades), future plans and hopes, and personal opinions. These are common disclosure topics for college students (see Schmidt & Cornelius, 1987).

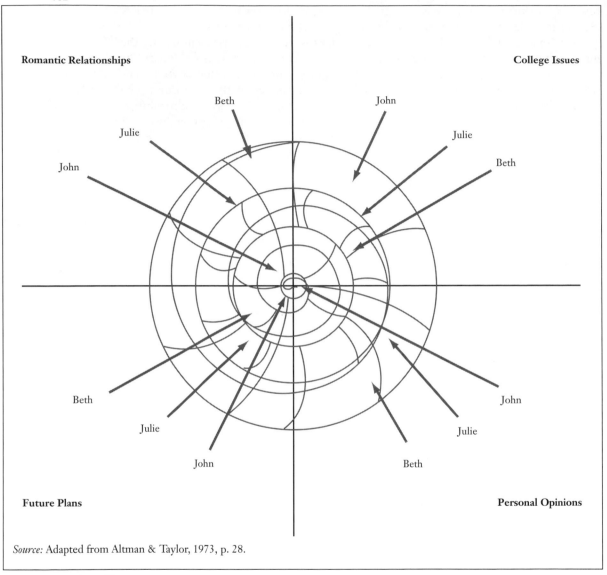

Romantic Relationships

College Issues

Beth

John

Julie

Julie

John

Beth

Beth

John

Julie

Julie

John

Beth

Future Plans

Personal Opinions

Source: Adapted from Altman & Taylor, 1973, p. 28.

Figure 7.1

▼

Social Penetration
of Kris by Three
Friends

As Figure 7.1 indicates, Kris allows three friends to penetrate her personality
along different topics (breadth) and to different levels of intimacy (depth). For example, John knows all about Kris's relational life, future plans, and personal opinions;
Julie has penetrated all four topic areas, but only superficially; and Beth knows Kris
moderately well only in terms of college issues and future plans. As this example indicates, social penetration theory is useful for understanding how people become more
intimate along the dimensions of breadth and depth.

FACTORS AFFECTING SELF-DISCLOSURE CHOICES

Dave raised the topic first. He said, "You know, getting together like this every Saturday is OK, but I could really use some company from a member of the female persuasion. I'd like to ask Beth out, but then so would every guy in town. Besides, she is so busy with her sorority these days, I don't know if she would find time for me." John replied, "Yeah, I know what you mean. I've been thinking of asking out Julie, you know, the transfer student who's been exercising with Kris. She is the most positive woman I know. But something tells me she's seeing another guy, you know, 'cause she doesn't flirt or anything. It drives me crazy — I think about her all the time. It bothers me that all I do is think about her."

People disclose to obtain various interpersonal goals. A person may disclose to get close to another person, to achieve catharsis, to present oneself as likable, to obtain information, to avoid rejection, to achieve acceptance, among other goals (Derlega, Metts, Petronio, & Margulis, 1993; Miller, 1990; Rosenfeld, 2000). These various reasons reflect the basic thesis of this book: that people disclose primarily to achieve interpersonal goals. Regardless of these reasons, disclosures always entail a concern for presenting an image of who we are.

Recent reviews regarding the consequences of disclosing secrets provide interesting observations (Kelly & McKillop, 1996; Pennebaker, 1997; Tardy, 2000). First, disclosing reduces psychological and physical problems. Not disclosing problems or traumatic events requires energy that drains the individual and tends to lead to health risks including cancer, hypertension, ulcers, and immune system breakdown (Pennebaker, 1989, 1997; Tardy, 2000). Disclosing to others reduces the "psychological work of inhibition" and "helps individuals to understand and ultimately assimilate" a negative or traumatic event (Pennebaker, 1989, p. 231). Second, revealing a secret avoids making the secret highly salient and accessible to others. "In keeping a secret, one must continually monitor information consistent with the state of mind one wants to maintain as well as monitor the information one wishes to hide from others" (Kelly & McKillop, 1996, p. 453). Paradoxically the suppression of information can make that information more salient to oneself and, eventually, to others. Ask someone not to think about some event or someone, and you will likely find that they cannot help but think and talk about that event or person. Third, revealing a secret helps people gain insights and thereby obtain a degree of control (Kelly & McKillop, 1996, p. 453). Disclosing helps people clarify their understanding and obtain feedback from others. And over time, disclosure can assist in the prevention of disease, even in cases where drug therapies are not effective (Tardy, 2000).

The Norm of Reciprocity

One of the most examined reasons for people's disclosure is the **norm of reciprocity.** A norm refers to a behavior so common that it is expected. The norm of reciprocity means offering a communicative response that matches the partner's previous communication. When applied to self-disclosure, the norm of reciprocity, or **dyadic effect,** as Jourard (1971) calls it, refers to the phenomenon of the communicator matching the partner's previous disclosure at a similar level of intimacy.

The norm of reciprocity is explained according to various theories, as Jones and Archer (1976) observe. First, you match disclosures because the other communicator cues you regarding what is appropriate in a particular context. Second, you might reciprocate behavior because you trust the other person, so you feel safe in risking a disclosure. Finally, you may feel compelled to exchange information so as not to be indebted. As Chaikin and Derlega (1974) indicate:

> The recipient to high disclosure who fails to reciprocate has put himself [or herself] and the discloser in an inequitable relationship. . . . Since inequity sets up tension which motivates behavior designed to reduce it, reciprocity in self-disclosure should be likely to occur. (p. 118)

But how strong is the reciprocity norm? Much of the research indicates that the norm of reciprocity has a strong influence on our self-disclosure behaviors (e.g., Shaffer & Ogden, 1986; for a solid review, see Dindia, 1982). Rosenberg and Mann (1986) found that children learn the norm of reciprocity for disclosure by the sixth grade. Ludwig, Franco, and Malloy (1986) reported that reciprocation of high or low disclosure was a powerful predictor of the communicator's level of disclosure, regardless of people's predispositions to monitor themselves. Likewise, Dindia, Fitzpatrick, and Kenny (1997) found that "within conversations, disclosure of highly intimate feelings was reciprocal. This was true regardless of the sex composition (same-sex male, same-sex female, opposite sex) or type of dyad (strangers or spouses)" (p. 408). In other words, the dyadic effect appears to be a major factor in explaining why people disclose what they do.

Other research has questioned the proposition that the norm of reciprocity leads to matching disclosure levels. Schmidt and Cornelius (1987) report that participants rated the other's behavior as the least important influence on their own self-disclosing behavior. Pearce and colleagues (1974) argue that self-disclosure is affected more by what people perceive as equivalent than what is actually equivalent: "From this perspective, we would expect persons to disclose in a way which is equivalent to what they think the other has disclosed to them rather than to the other's actual disclosure" (p. 8). Dindia (2000) summarized the differences between perspectives accordingly:

> Thus, there is overwhelming evidence that self-disclosure is reciprocal. The effect sizes range from moderately large to very large except for the studies employing sequential analysis. The degree to which self-disclosure is reciprocal depends on how reciprocity is tested . . . [and] on how self-disclosure is measured; perceptions of reciprocity exceed actual reciprocity. It also appears that while self-disclosure is not reciprocal on a turn-by-turn basis, there is some evidence that it is reciprocal within conversations. (pp. 27–28)

Table 7.1
FAMILY SECRETS

Type of Secret	Example
Taboo	
Substance abuse	Father is addicted to drugs or alcohol
Physical/psychological abuse	You hide bruises from beatings at home
Extramarital affairs	An aunt had an affair with a family friend
Mental health	A sister needs medication for schizophrenia
Illegalities	A brother has served time for stealing property
Finances	Mom has been laid off and needs financial help
Rule Violation	
Drinking/partying	You hide that you party hearty on weekends
Sexual relations	A brother does not discuss his sexual relationships
Cohabitation	Your sister lives with her boyfriend
Premarital pregnancy	You were born before your parents were married
Conventional	
Traditions/stories	Your family vacations together every summer
Death	Your brother committed suicide
Grades/school achievements	One family member earns exceptional grades
Dating partners	Your sister is dating someone twenty years older
Religion	You are Jewish and the rest of the family is atheist

Source: Adapted from "Family secrets: Forms, functions, and correlates," by A. Vangelisti in *Journal of Social and Personal Relationships, 11,* 1994, pp. 113–116. Reprinted by permission of Sage Publications Ltd. (UK).

not to self-disclose, we must assess how vulnerable we will become. Rawlins (1983) reports that tolerance of vulnerability is a function of two factors: the need to be open and the degree of trust in the other. Figure 7.2 shows how the need to be open and trust in the other interact to affect tolerance of vulnerability.

According to Figure 7.2, you would feel most at ease disclosing personal information in situations where you trusted the other party and felt a need to be open. Spouses, psychologists, clergy, and best friends can reassure us they can be trusted with intimate disclosures more easily than strangers, co-workers, or acquaintances can. You are most likely to conceal information from others when your need to be

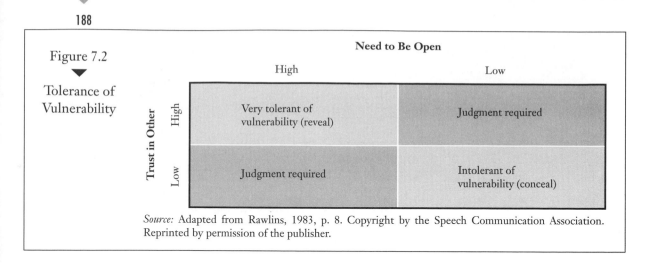

Figure 7.2

▼

Tolerance of
Vulnerability

Need to Be Open

Source: Adapted from Rawlins, 1983, p. 8. Copyright by the Speech Communication Association. Reprinted by permission of the publisher.

open is low and you do not trust the other party. But when either the need to be open or trust is low, you must judge the extent to which the disclosure is worth the risk. As Gilbert (1976b) postulates, security needs are balanced with intimacy needs. Sometimes you choose to maintain the status quo and not disclose, and other times you risk your security in order to increase intimacy.

LIKELIHOOD OF CANDOR. Rawlins (1983) also observes that the expressiveness/protectiveness decision is made on the basis of the **likelihood of candor,** the probability that you will make personal observations about your communication partner. The likelihood of candor comprises two factors: your perceived need to be honest about the issue at hand and your restraint or awareness that certain topics should be avoided.

Figure 7.3, which portrays how the need to be honest and restraint affect the likelihood of candor, indicates that you are most likely to disclose if you have a high need to be honest with your partner about the issue and restraint is not appropriate. For example, imagine that you have a friend who drinks so much that it is affecting his schoolwork, relationships, and physical health. Because you are friends, you feel compelled to be honest with him. According to Figure 7.3, you are least likely to be candid with your partner when you have a low need to be honest and the issue is a sensitive one. For example, you have an in-law who idolizes a TV evangelist you do not like, but your need to express this opinion is low. Judgment regarding candor is required when either the need to be honest or topic appropriateness is low. For example, do you disclose your honest impressions to a friend whose new expensive haircut is definitely not flattering?

PRIVACY BOUNDARY COORDINATION. Petronio (1991, 2000) offers insight into how relational privacy is achieved. Petronio's Privacy Boundary Coordination theory concerns the manner in which married couples coordinate their boundaries of

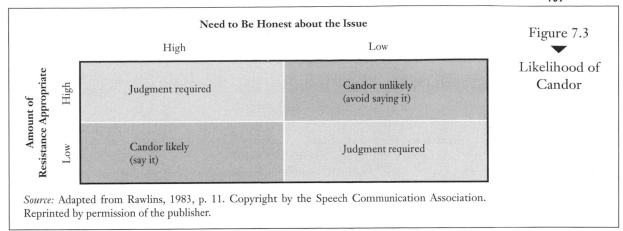

Need to Be Honest about the Issue

Figure 7.3

Likelihood of Candor

Source: Adapted from Rawlins, 1983, p. 11. Copyright by the Speech Communication Association. Reprinted by permission of the publisher.

privacy. As Petronio, Martin, and Littlefield (1984) note, disclosure functions to define the boundaries of privacy (p. 269). Petronio (2000) argues that people develop boundaries on several fronts; for example, people form rules for exchanging personal information, how such rules are used, and what methods exist for coordinating their messages. We develop this last point briefly at this juncture.

According to Petronio (1991), **boundary coordination** refers to the degree to which the explicit or implicit demand within a disclosure is met by an explicit or implicit response. Petronio reports four ways in which disclosure demands and responses are coordinated in daily life. First, a *satisfactory fit* involves a disclosure with an explicit, direct message and a response that is also direct. For example, the husband discloses, "I don't care for such parties," to which the wife replies, "I agree — they are too formal." Both messages are clear and reflect satisfactory boundary coordination. Second, *overcompensation* occurs when the disclosure is implicit and the response is explicit. For example, the wife says, "I happen to have the day off tomorrow," to which the husband responds, "There is no way that I can take a weekend trip until the first of the month." Clearly the second message provides more information than the first message demands.

A *deficient fit* takes place when the disclosure is explicit and the response is implicit. For example, the wife notices, "You never surprise me with cards or flowers anymore," to which the husband responds, "I never thought of that before." In this example, the husband evades the implied request for reasons for his not sending cards or flowers. Finally, an *equivocal fit* takes place when both the disclosure and the response are implicit or indirect. For example, the husband confides, "It was quite a day today," to which the wife replies, "How about I take you out to dinner?" In this case, neither wants to discuss the details of the husband's (rough) day, so both parties coordinate in an indirect manner the level at which the issue is discussed.

In sum, self-disclosure is understood in terms of pulls to express yourself versus desires to protect yourself. As Rawlins observes, needs for honesty and candor are balanced by how much you trust your partner and the sensitivity of the issues under discussion. In addition, privacy boundary coordination involves four types of responses to disclosures: satisfactory, overcompensatory, deficient, and equivocal.

FACTORS AFFECTING THE MANNER OF SELF-DISCLOSURE

What are the various influences on self-disclosure? Of course, people vary in their tendencies to communicate, as we discuss in Chapter 15. But what about sex differences in disclosure? Also, are people more likely to communicate in some relationships and cultures than in others? In addressing these questions, we discuss three factors that affect self-disclosure: sex differences, relationship type, and culture.

Sex Differences

Much of the research on self-disclosure reports differences between men and women. For example, Derlega, Durham, Gockel, and Sholis (1981) state that men may use a status-assertive disclosure style, hiding weaknesses and emphasizing successes, but women use an affiliative, or status-neutralizing, disclosure style. Also, Petronio and co-workers (1984) found that women place more importance on certain "prerequisites" for self-disclosure than men do. "Before women will disclose, they find it more important than do men that the receiver be discreet, trustworthy, sincere, liked, respected, a good listener, warm, and open" (p. 271). In other words, women emphasize personal features of the other person, whereas men emphasize situational norms. Consider the following example:

> Thus, if a husband and wife go shopping together and the wife wants to talk to her husband about their sexual relationship, her criteria is being met by being with someone she trusts, feels comfortable relating to, and knows will listen to her. She selects the department store to disclose because of convenience, but the situation is not important to the wife. As she makes this disclosure, the husband is mortified and looks around in every direction to see if other people are listening. (Petronio, 2000, p. 40)

The role of sex differences in disclosure has also been questioned. In an analysis of 205 studies on sex differences in self-disclosure, Dindia and Allen (1992) found that women tend to disclose more than men, but the differences were small. They also found that the composition of the dyad (i.e., same-sex male, same-sex female, mixed sex) affected the differences due to the communicator's sex. Specifically women are more likely to disclose to women and to members of the opposite sex (i.e., women are more likely to disclose to men than men are likely to disclose to women), but men are just as likely as women to disclose to other men (when comparing the mixed dyad conversations to the same-sex dyad conversations). Also, women are more likely to receive disclosure from both men and women. Recall too, people tend to reciprocate behavior; so sex differences are often outweighed by the actual give-and-take involved in reciprocity (Dindia et al., 1997). Thus it appears that when we discuss sex differences in self-disclosure, we should recognize that these differences are significant, though they are also small and dependent on the composition of the dyad. As Dindia (2002) concluded, "Although women disclose slightly more than men, and the disclosure-liking relation appears to be slightly stronger for female than male disclosures, in general, it appears that the process of self-disclosure is more similar than different for men and women" (p. 184).

Nature of the Relationship

As one might anticipate, the relationship between communicators affects their self-disclosure. Miller (1990) has demonstrated that we disclose to others because such disclosures are understood within the context of the relationship. She offers the following example: Mary may "respond with joy to Alice's teary-eyed disclosure [because] Alice's telling her this news fits with Mary's understanding that Alice has longed to see her beloved father again and has been worried about him" (p. 52). Relation-specific effects are gleaned from other studies. For example, Dickson-Markman (1986) found that disclosure tends to be more negative as the age group of friends increases.

Married couples also have marked disclosure patterns. For example, Burke, Weir, and Harrison (1976) reported that both husbands and wives most often selected their spouse as the person to whom they would disclose personal problems. These researchers also found that amount of disclosure was negatively associated with a person's age and length of marriage but that disclosing problems was positively associated with the spouse's helping (that is, as disclosure increased, so did actual helping behavior). Morton (1978) reports that married couples were likely to offer descriptive disclosures more than evaluative disclosures. Strangers, by contrast, were more likely to engage in evaluative disclosures. Overall, and remembering that spouses prefer to disclose to each other, the tendency in marriage is for the amount of disclosure to decrease, the disclosure to become more negative, and the type of disclosure to become more descriptive (and less evaluative) over time.

One study examined how getting acquainted over a computer-mediated chat system affected the presentation and evaluation of self-disclosure. Tidwell and Walther (2000) recognized a paradox: Although self-disclosure and asking personal questions are considered rather direct methods for getting to know someone face-to-face (vs. asking other people for information, such as "Is she dating anyone?"), in many on-line settings such as chat rooms and e-mail, offering disclosures and asking questions are the only means to exchange personal information. Accordingly, do people disclose more information on-line or do they prefer to be indirect like they would when talking face-to-face (even if disclosures are all they have to work with)?

Tidwell and Walther (2000) designed an experiment to address this question. Unacquainted partners were assigned to chat together face-to-face or from different rooms using a computer-based chat program, and were asked to try to get to know one another. After their conversations were over, they rated how well they had gotten to know their partners, and no differences were found between on-line and face-to-face conditions. Analysis of the partners' recorded messages, however, showed that the way they had achieved these impressions relied on different cue systems. The computer-based dyads exhibited *more* self-disclosures and personal questions than did the people who communicated face-to-face. Moreover, when the intimacy of disclosures was superficial, moderate, or deep, further analyses found that mediated partners exchanged more moderate-level disclosures, while face-to-face partners exchanged more superficial disclosures. This study suggests that users of computer-based communication systems adapt to the constraints of the medium when it comes to getting to know one another. In addition, the norms regarding disclosure are somewhat relaxed when ways of sharing information are less obvious and available than they are in face-to-face settings.

Cultural Factors Affecting Self-Disclosure

Gudykunst and Kim (1984, pp. 181–183) review the limited research related to cultural influences on self-disclosure. Generally Americans disclose more frequently than other cultural groups, with the exception of those in the Middle East (see also Gudykunst & Nishida, 1984). Nakanishi's (1986) review of the literature also suggests that, in general, Americans tend to disclose more than do Asians. For example, Japanese are less dependent than Americans on explicit symbols (e.g., self-disclosure) to infer personal characteristics, such as status. Nakanishi also reports that in his Japanese sample, high disclosers were held to be less socially attractive and less communicatively competent than moderate or low disclosers.

Likewise, Klopf (1998) asserts that different ethnic groups disclose more or less, with Euroamericans more likely to disclose than Hispanic and African Americans. Klopf also notes that Americans disclose more than Koreans, who disclose more than Japanese. Some of this may have to do with the degree to which a culture is high- or low-context. High-context cultures depend less on verbal explanation and so would not value or need disclosures. Low-context cultures (such as the United States) value and need explicit information and thus would be likely to disclose more.

In sum, we find a general, though weak, tendency on average for women to disclose more than men. Also, people appear to offer more disclosure (especially evaluative disclosure) to a certain point in relational development; then disclosure frequency and intensity declines (see also Chapter 9). Finally, it appears that Euroamericans tend to be relatively open in their disclosure behaviors. Although the preceding factors do not exhaust the many structural features that affect people's self-disclosure, they do indicate that disclosure occurs in particular contexts and among people with particular personalities.

FACTORS AFFECTING THE PERCEPTION OF SELF-DISCLOSURE

Clearly, when a person discloses, he or she is often evaluated by the other person hearing the message (Derlega, Winstead, Wong, & Greenspan, 1987). Your self-disclosure is viewed as appropriate or inappropriate in terms of its timeliness in the interaction, the overall communication episode, and the relationship. The exchange between Dave and John appears appropriate in terms of its timeliness, the episode, and their relationship. What and how you disclose to others can have a profound effect on your public image and your personal relationships. We can examine the consequences of self-disclosure in terms of its amount, reciprocity, valence, honesty, and timing.

Amount of Disclosure

Does the amount of self-disclosure, in terms of depth and breadth, affect your public image or personal relationships? This question does not have a simple answer. Chaikin and Derlega (1974) contend that "no simple relationship between level of disclosure and evaluation of the discloser exists" (p. 117). There are at least two competing hypotheses.

One hypothesis is that a positive and linear association should exist between disclosure and liking the discloser because disclosures are a reward for the recipient and lead to relational intimacy. Indeed, several studies have reported a positive and linear association between the amount of self-disclosure and liking or relational satisfaction (e.g., Hendrick, 1981; Worthy, Gary, & Kahn, 1969). In a meta-analysis (a statistical summary of statistical findings), Collins and Miller (1994) found a general tendency to like other people who disclose to us, though the effect is not very strong. Collins and Miller also found support for the view that we tend to disclose to others whom we like.

A second hypothesis, which has also received empirical support, is that a curvilinear association should exist between disclosure and liking the discloser (e.g., Cozby, 1972; Gilbert, 1976a). Liking rises with increased disclosures to a point; then liking decreases as disclosure continues to increase. Why would liking decrease if the communicator continues to disclose? One explanation is that too much disclosure causes anxiety in the listener (Cozby, 1973). For example, according to Jones and Archer (1976), too much disclosure embarrasses the listener without providing a means to cope with the embarrassment. Another explanation is that relationships function best when moderate disclosure, not total disclosure, is offered. In other words, total relational intimacy may be an ideal, but it is not functional or realistic (Gilbert, 1976a).

One answer to these contradictory results may be found in the difference between personalistic and general self-disclosure. **Personalistic self-disclosure** involves messages expressed because the particular relationship between the communicator and the recipient permits deep disclosures (Jones & Archer, 1976; Miller, 1990). **General**

self-disclosure involves messages sent to almost anyone — the discloser offers personal information to friends, acquaintances, Mom and Dad, Cousin Jack, and the pizza man. When people believe that a disclosure they are hearing is not targeted specifically for them, they regard the discloser as less well adjusted and less likable than the person who reserves the disclosure for a particular person (Falk & Wagner, 1985; Jones & Archer, 1976).

A second reason for the unclear association between depth of disclosure and liking is that other dimensions, such as reciprocity and valence, must be considered as well (see Gilbert, 1976a; Gilbert & Horenstein, 1975). It is possible that reciprocation or valence, more than the sheer amount of disclosure, affects our impressions of the communicator.

Reciprocity

Recall that one of the reasons people disclose has to do with the norm of reciprocity. We feel compelled to match the level of disclosure initiated by our conversational partner. If the norm of reciprocity guides expectations for appropriate disclosure, not reciprocating disclosures should lead to negative judgments about the communicator. This expectation has been tested in several experiments.

Chaikin and Derlega (1974) had participants watch a videotape of "Sue" as she offered either a high or a low disclosure in response to another person's initial high or low disclosure. That is, each participant was exposed to one treatment condition: a high or low disclosure followed by Sue's high or low response. Participants then rated Sue on several factors, including her perceived warmth, psychological adjustment, appropriateness, and desirability as a friend. According to the norm of reciprocity, participants should rate Sue most favorably in the condition where she offered a high disclosure in response to a high disclosure or when she offered a low disclosure in response to a low disclosure. Table 7.2 reports the relevant results of this experiment.

As the table reveals, when Sue offered a high-depth disclosure in response to a low-depth disclosure, participants rated her as warm but inappropriate, psychologically maladjusted, and undesirable as a friend. And when Sue offered a low-depth disclosure in response to a high-depth disclosure, participants rated her as psychologically well adjusted but cold. Finally, Table 7.2 supports the expectation that people who match low disclosure levels are perceived favorably, compared to those who do not match low disclosure levels. Chaikin and Derlega (1974) concluded that people are guided by two social norms: the norm of reciprocity and a norm of appropriateness that prescribes that people should not disclose too much information in most situations.

Support for variations on the reciprocity norm has been reported in other studies. Hosman (1987) found that a combination of breadth reciprocity and depth reciprocity was judged as competent. For example, if the communicator disclosed sensitive information on the same topic as an initial highly personal message, the communicator was perceived as socially competent, understandable, involved, attentive, and so forth.

Amount of Disclosure in Initial Message	Amount of Disclosure in Sue's Response	Measures			
		Warmth	Psychological Adjustments	Appropriateness	Desirability as a Friend
Low	Low	6.12	5.85	5.92	5.66
Low	High	6.35	3.85	3.00	4.41
High	Low	5.10	6.15	5.62	5.50
High	High	6.35	5.31	5.62	5.65

Table 7.2
RESULTS OF CHAIKIN AND DERLEGA'S (1974) STUDY

Note: The higher the number, the greater the perceived rating on a 9-point scale.
Source: Adapted from "Self-disclosure and liking" by A. L. Chaikin & V. J. Derlega in *Journal of Personality, 42,* 1974, pp. 117–129. Reprinted by permission of Blackwell Publishers.

Reciprocating the same depth of disclosure and topic in response to a low personal disclosure was also seen as socially competent (Hosman, 1987). Hosman's study is important because it suggests that we do not have to offer highly personal information to satisfy the reciprocity norm.

Likewise, Bradac, Hosman, and Tardy (1978) found that the intensity of language affects how people view others who deviate from the norm of reciprocity. Language intensity refers to the use of language that connotes emotional involvement rather than neutrality ("I feel fantastic" instead of "I feel fine"). In this experiment, participants were exposed to high or low disclosures offered with high-intensity or low-intensity language. Each of these four types of messages was shown as a response to either a high- or low-intimacy disclosure.

Consistent with the Chaikin and Derlega (1974) study, Bradac and colleagues (1978) found that communicators who mismatched both intimacy and intensity levels of disclosures were judged least favorably. They also found that participants judged the intimate message without intense language as the most favorable of all message combinations when the message responded to a low-intimacy, low-intensity message. It is easy to imagine how a friend can tell you something very personal in a low-key manner ("Yeah, I was once in a mental hospital"). In doing so, the intensity of the disclosure is minimized.

196

Valence

Valence refers to the positive or negative elements in a message. Research reveals that valence has a strong effect on perceptions of the communicator. More precisely, it indicates that communicators who offer negative disclosures ("I am so depressed," "I can't stand people like that") are seen in a negative light.

Negative disclosures tend to taint the conversation and the image of the communicator. Gilbert and Horenstein (1975) report that attraction for an individual was higher when that person offered a positive disclosure than when the person offered a negative disclosure, and intimacy level did not affect communicator attraction. Similarly, Hecht, Shepard, and Hall (1979) found that both positive and neutral messages, more than negative messages, were rated as satisfying to the receiver. For example, positive messages such as "I like working in groups" or neutral messages such as "Working in groups is sometimes kind of interesting" are more satisfying to hear than such messages as "I don't like working in groups" or "I get furious with people who don't show up for meetings."

Honesty

Honesty in self-disclosure refers to offering information that accurately reflects your thoughts and feelings. Is honesty the best policy? Not always, according to the research. It appears that honesty about personal experiences may at times hurt your public image. Derlega, Harris, and Chaikin (1973) found that people who disclosed personal deviant information were less liked than those who disclosed nonintimate information. Regardless of the value one places on honesty, some disclosures are viewed negatively (e.g., that you steal money from your parents).

STUDENT AS OBSERVER: RATING DISCLOSURES

Over the next week, take notes regarding disclosures that you hear as soon as possible after the fact. In particular, describe these disclosures in terms of the dimensions of depth, breadth, reciprocity, valence, honesty, and timing. Rate each disclosure using these dimensions. In other words, rate the disclosure for its depth (deep to superficial), breadth (a lot of topics/one topic), reciprocity (in response to something you said?), valence (positive or negative), and timing (early/late in the conversation). Which of these dimensions had the greatest impact on your perceptions of the people who disclosed to you? Do you think others would see the same messages in the same way using these dimensions? In other words, are your perceptions of these disclosures generalizable to other people? How do you think other people tend to see your disclosures according to these same dimensions?

Too much self-promotion by disclosing accomplishments and successes may adversely affect others' impressions and choices of companions. Schlenker and Leary (1982) found that accurate communicators were seen as more competent and sincere than boastful communicators when the participants knew of the communicators' performance. The implication of this study is that people should be honest when disclosing information if a conversational partner has potential knowledge of that information.

Timing

Is timing everything? Is it smart to offer a personal disclosure early in the conversation? Or should a person wait until later in the conversation to reveal something personal? Research indicates that people who immediately offer a personal disclosure are seen as more immature, phony, maladjusted, and insecure than those who wait several minutes (Wortman, Adesman, Herman, & Greenberg, 1976). As Wortman and colleagues explain:

> If an individual makes a highly personal remark to us early in a conversation, we may conclude that this remark has little to do with his or her feelings for us. Instead, we may infer that he or she is the kind of person who is disclosing to everyone. If someone makes a disclosing remark after he or she has been talking to us for a while, we may be more likely to take the remark personally and infer that it has positive implications for the relationship. (p. 185)

But on some occasions, a disclosure should be offered right away. One instance may be when accepting responsibility for an action. For example, Archer and Burleson (1980) found that accepting responsibility for a negative event early in the conversation rather than later led to social attraction. Imagine that you severely scratched your friend's car while attempting to park it. You suspect that she will discover that you are the responsible party. Because you are honest with your friends, you decide to tell her that you scratched the car. Archer and Burleson's study suggests that in such circumstances you should confess earlier rather than later.

In sum, the association between self-disclosure and liking for the communicator is not a simple one. Some observers have hypothesized a linear association, and others have hypothesized a curvilinear one. Perhaps more important than the amount of disclosure is how it is offered. Research reveals that people who reciprocate at the same level of depth or breadth are judged more favorably than those who do not reciprocate at the same level. The study by Bradac and co-workers suggests that how intensely you offer a disclosure affects how intimately it is perceived. In addition, the valence of the message affects the impression people have of the communicator: Positive messages lead to positive evaluations. Finally, in general, disclosures that are offered late (rather than early) in a conversation reflect more positively on the discloser.

CHAPTER SUMMARY

Self-disclosure is an important communication activity, although it may not occur as much as other types of communication (Duck, Rutt, Hurst, & Strejc, 1991). It is the most controllable method you have of indicating to others just who you are. You can present yourself as wise or foolish in the ways you disclose your feelings, attitudes, and behaviors. The research suggests that high self-disclosure should be reserved for particular situations with people you know and trust (Kelly & McKillop, 1996). Reciprocity should mark the disclosure (do not disclose if the other person withholds information). In addition, negative disclosures can adversely affect your public image. As the old song prescribes, you may want to "accentuate the positive and eliminate the negative" when disclosing information about yourself.

Of course, judgment is required in all disclosure situations. Both researchers and students need to be aware of the potential benefits (e.g., Tardy, 2000) as well as negative outcomes of self-disclosure (e.g., Parks, 1982). Inappropriate use of self-disclosure can handicap you in achieving your interpersonal goals. Wise use of self-disclosure can help you obtain your self-presentation, relational, and instrumental goals.

KEY TERMS

boundary coordination, p. 189
descriptive intimacy, p. 179
dyadic effect, p. 184
evaluative intimacy, p. 179
general self-disclosure, p. 193
likelihood of candor, p. 188

norm of reciprocity, p. 183
personalistic self-disclosure, p. 193
self-disclosure, p. 179
social penetration theory, p. 180
tolerance of vulnerability, p. 186

EXERCISES FOR FURTHER DISCUSSION

1. Think back to the last time you disclosed to someone. Try to recall the event as specifically as possible. Who was it? Where did it take place? When did it take place? What was the self-disclosure about? Now look again at the items in Table 7.1 and try to evaluate your self-disclosure. Was your self-disclosure an accurate reflection of who you are?

2. Recall the events immediately after the tragedy of 9/11. How did you cope with that terror and its resulting shock? Did you talk about the event with other people? Did you communicate how you felt emotionally (e.g., depressed, hurt, an-

gered)? Did you participate in any ceremonies that commemorated the victims (e.g., candlelight service)? Did you find that being with others and talking with others helped you deal with your negative reactions?

3. List five people to whom you recently disclosed or who disclosed to you.
   a. How many men are on the list? How many women?
   b. In your experience, do men or women disclose more?
   c. In your experience, do you find it easier to disclose to men or to women?

4. Think of a time when you thought someone was trying to use the norm of reciprocity to get you to disclose.
   a. What do you think the person's motives were? Did the person genuinely want to be intimate with you, or was the person trying to find out something from you?
   b. What was your reaction to the person's self-disclosure? Was it different from your reaction to other people's self-disclosures?
   c. What do you think would be a good strategy to use when you feel pressure to disclose but don't really want to?

5. List three suggestions you would give to someone regarding self-preservation through self-disclosure, based on the information in this chapter.

SUGGESTED READING

▼

SELF-DISCLOSURE THEORY

Altman, I., & Taylor, D. A. (1973). *Social penetration: The development of interpersonal relationships.* Austin, TX: Holt, Rinehart & Winston. This classic book links self-disclosure to relational development, showing how intimacy increases along the dimensions of breadth and depth. The authors specify propositions that predict when a relationship will escalate or de-escalate.

Gilbert, S. J. (1976). Empirical and theoretical extensions of self-disclosure. In G. R. Miller (Ed.), *Explorations in interpersonal communication* (pp. 197–215). Newbury Park, CA: Sage. Gilbert explores the premise that self-disclosure is related to liking in a linear fashion. She presents the hypothesis that the relationship between disclosure and liking is, instead, curvilinear.

REVIEWS

Cozby, P. C. (1973). Self-disclosure: A literature review. *Psychological Bulletin, 79,* 73–91. Few reviews on self-disclosure are as comprehensive as this one. Although much research on the topic has been presented since 1973, this review still discusses many current issues.

Derlega, V. J., Metts, S., Petronio, S., & Margulis, S. T. (1993). *Self-disclosure.* Thousand Oaks, CA: Sage. This is a very readable and interesting overview of how disclosure affects relational development, including discussions of sex differences, privacy regulation, and coping with stress.

Petronio, S. (Ed.). (2000). *Balancing the secrets of private disclosures.* Mahwah, NJ: Erlbaum. An intriguing anthology that reports how self-disclosure and privacy can be jointly considered.

SELF-DISCLOSURE AND LIKING

Collins, N. L., & Miller, L. C. (1994). Self-disclosure and liking: A meta-analytic review. *Psychological Bulletin, 116,* 457–475.

RECIPROCITY

Dindia, K. (1982). Reciprocity of self-disclosure: A sequential analysis. In M. Burgoon (Ed.), *Communication yearbook 6* (pp. 506–528). Newbury Park, CA: Sage. Dindia does an excellent job of reviewing the literature on reciprocity of disclosure. This article also examines reciprocity using observational data.

SEX DIFFERENCES

Dindia, K. (2000). Sex differences in self-disclosure, reciprocity of self-disclosure, and self-disclosure and liking: Three meta-analyses reviewed. In S. Petronio (Ed.), *Balancing the secrets of private disclosures* (pp. 21–35). Mahwah, NJ: Erlbaum.

Dindia, K., & Allen, M. (1992). Sex differences in self-disclosure: A meta-analysis. *Psychological Bulletin, 112,* 106–124. This review examines how sex differences affect disclosure. Over two hundred articles are included in this statistical analysis.

SELF-DISCLOSURE AND HEALTH

Tardy, C. H. (2000). Self-disclosure and health: Revising Sidney Jourard's hypothesis. In S. Petronio (Ed.), *Balancing the secrets of private disclosures* (pp. 111–122). Mahwah, NJ: Erlbaum.

REFERENCE LIST

▼

Altman, I., & Taylor, D. A. (1973). *Social penetration: The development of interpersonal relationships.* Austin, TX: Holt, Rinehart and Winston.

Archer, R. L., & Burleson, J. A. (1980). The effects of timing of self-disclosure on attraction and reciprocity. *Journal of Personality and Social Psychology, 38,* 120–130.

Bradac, J. J., Hosman, L. A., & Tardy, C. H. (1978). Reciprocal disclosures and language intensity: Attributional consequences. *Communication Monographs, 45,* 1–17.

Burke, R. J., Weir, T., & Harrison, D. (1976). Disclosure of problems and tensions experienced by marital partners. *Psychological Reports, 38,* 531–542.

Chaikin, A. L., & Derlega, V. J. (1974). Liking for the norm breaker in self-disclosure. *Journal of Personality, 42,* 117–129.

Collins, N. L., & Miller, L. C. (1994). Self-disclosure and liking: A meta-analytic review. *Psychological Bulletin, 116,* 457–475.

Cozby, P. C. (1973). Self-disclosure: A literature review. *Psychological Bulletin, 79,* 73–91.

Derlega, V. J., Durham, B., Gockel, B., & Sholis, D. (1981). Sex differences in self-disclosure: Effects of topic content, friendship, and partner's sex. *Sex Roles, 7,* 433–447.

Derlega, V. J., Harris, M. S., & Chaikin, A. L. (1973). Self-disclosure reciprocity, liking, and the deviant. *Journal of Experimental Social Psychology 9,* 277–284.

Derlega, V. J., Metts, S., Petronio, S., & Margulis, S. T. (1993). *Self-disclosure.* Thousand Oaks, CA: Sage.

Derlega, V. J., Winstead, B. A., Wong, P. T. P., & Greenspan, M. (1987). Self-disclosure and relationship development: An attributional analysis. In M. E. Roloff & G. R. Miller (Eds.), *Interpersonal processes: New directions in communication research* (pp. 172–187). Newbury Park, CA: Sage.

Dickson-Markman, F. (1986). Self-disclosure with friends across the life cycles. *Journal of Social and Personal Relationships, 3,* 259–264.

Dindia, K. (1982). Reciprocity of self-disclosure: A sequential analysis. In M. Burgoon (Ed.), *Communication yearbook 6* (pp. 506–528). Newbury Park, CA: Sage.

Dindia, K. (2000). Sex differences in self-disclosure, reciprocity of self-disclosure, and self-disclosure and liking: Three meta-analyses reviewed. In S. Petronio (Ed.), *Balancing the secrets of private disclosures* (pp. 21–35). Mahwah, NJ: Erlbaum.

Dindia, K. (2002). Self-disclosure research: Knowledge through meta-analysis. In M. Allen, R. W. Preiss, B. M. Gayle, & N. A. Burrell (Eds.), *Interpersonal communication research: Advances through meta-analysis* (pp. 169–185). Mahwah, NJ: Erlbaum.

Dindia, K., & Allen, M. (1992). Sex differences in self-disclosure: A meta-analysis. *Psychological Bulletin, 112,* 106–124.

Dindia, K., Fitzpatrick, M. A., & Kenny, D. A. (1997). Self-disclosure in spouse and stranger interaction: A social relations analysis. *Human Communication Research, 23,* 388–412.

Duck, S. W., Rutt, D. J., Hurst, M. H., & Strejc, H. (1991). Some evident truths about conversation in everyday relationships: All communications are not created equal. *Human Communication Research, 18,* 228–268.

Falk, D. R., & Wagner, F. N. (1985). Intimacy of self-disclosure and response processes as factors affecting the development of interpersonal relationships. *Journal of Social Psychology, 125,* 557–570.

Gilbert, S. J. (1976a). Empirical and theoretical extensions of self-disclosure. In G. R. Miller (Ed.), *Explorations in interpersonal communication* (pp. 119–215). Newbury Park, CA: Sage.

Gilbert, S. J. (1976b). Self-disclosure, intimacy, and communication in families. *Family Coordinator, 25,* 221–231.

Gilbert, S. J., & Horenstein, D. (1975). The communication of self-disclosure: Level versus valence. *Human Communication Research, 1,* 316–322.

Gudykunst, W. B., & Kim, Y. Y. (1984). *Communicating with strangers: An approach to intercultural communication*. Reading, MA: Addison-Wesley.

Gudykunst, W. B., & Nishida, T. (1984). Individual and cultural influences on uncertainty reduction. *Communication Monographs, 51*, 23–56.

Hecht, M., Shepard, T., & Hall, T. J. (1979). Multivariate indices of the effects of self-disclosure. *Western Journal of Speech Communication, 43*, 235–245.

Hendrick, S. S. (1981). Self-disclosure and marital satisfaction. *Journal of Personality and Social Psychology, 40*, 1150–1159.

Hosman, L. A. (1987). The evaluational consequences of topic reciprocity and self-disclosure reciprocity. *Communication Monographs, 54*, 420–435.

Jones, E. E., & Archer, R. L. (1976). Are there special effects of personalistic self-disclosure? *Journal of Experimental Social Psychology, 12*, 180–193.

Jourard, S. M. (1971). *The transparent self* (2nd ed.). New York: Van Nostrand.

Kelly, A. E., & McKillop, K. J. (1996). Consequences of revealing personal secrets. *Psychological Bulletin, 120*, 450–465.

Klopf, D. W. (1998). *Intercultural encounters: The fundamentals of intercultural communication*. Englewood, CO: Morton.

Ludwig, D., Franco, J. N., & Malloy, T. E. (1986). Effects of reciprocity and self-monitoring on self-disclosure with a new acquaintance. *Journal of Personality and Social Psychology, 50*, 1077–1082.

Miller, L. C. (1990). Intimacy and liking: Mutual influence and the role of unique relationships. *Journal of Personality and Social Psychology, 59*, 50–60.

Morton, T. L. (1978). Intimacy and reciprocity exchange: A comparison of spouses and strangers. *Journal of Personality and Social Psychology, 36*, 72–81.

Nakanishi, M. (1986). Perceptions of self-disclosure in initial interaction: A Japanese sample. *Human Communication Research, 13*, 167–190.

Parks, M. R. (1982). Ideology in interpersonal communication: Off the couch and into the world. In M. Burgoon (Ed.), *Communication yearbook 6* (pp. 79–107). Newbury Park, CA: Sage.

Pearce, W. B., Sharp, S. M., Wright, P. H., & Slama, K. M. (1974). Affection and reciprocity in self-disclosing communication. *Human Communication Research, 1*, 5–14.

Pennebaker, J. W. (1989). Confession, inhibition, and disease. In L. Berkowitz (Ed.), *Advances in experimental social psychology* (Vol. 22, 211–244). San Diego, CA: Academic.

Pennebaker, J. W. (1997). *Opening up: The healing power of expressing emotions*. New York: Guilford.

Petronio, S. (1991). Communication boundary management: A theoretical model of managing disclosure of private information between marital couples. *Communication Theory, 1*, 311–335.

Petronio, S. (2000). The boundaries of privacy: Praxis of everyday life. In S. Petronio (Ed.), *Balancing the secrets of private disclosures* (pp. 37–49). Mahwah, NJ: Erlbaum.

Petronio, S., Martin, J., & Littlefield, R. (1984). Prerequisite conditions for self-disclosure: A gender issue. *Communication Monographs, 51*, 268–273.

Rawlins, W. K. (1983). Openness as problematic in ongoing friendships: Two conversational dilemmas. *Communication Monographs, 50*, 1–13.

Rosenberg, K. J., & Mann, L. (1986). The development of the norm of reciprocity of self-disclosure and its function in children's attraction to peers. *Child Development, 57,* 1349–1357.

Rosenfeld, L. (1979). Self-disclosure avoidance: Why I am afraid to tell you who I am. *Communication Monographs, 46,* 63–74.

Rosenfeld, L. B. (2000). Overview of the ways privacy, secrecy, and disclosure are balanced in today's society. In S. Petronio (Ed.), *Balancing the secrets of private disclosures* (pp. 3–17). Mahwah, NJ: Erlbaum.

Schlenker, B. R., & Leary, M. R. (1982). Audiences' reactions to self-enhancing, self-denigrating, and accurate self-presentations. *Journal of Experimental Social Psychology, 18,* 89–104.

Schmidt, T. O., & Cornelius, P. R. (1987). Self-disclosure in everyday life. *Journal of Social and Personal Relationships, 4,* 365–373.

Shaffer, D. R., & Ogden, J. K. (1986). On sex differences in self-disclosure during the acquaintance process: The role of anticipated future interaction. *Journal of Personality and Social Psychology, 51,* 92–101.

Snyder, M. (1979). Self-monitoring processes. In L. Berkowitz (Ed.), *Advances in experimental social psychology* (Vol. 12, 85–128). Orlando, FL: Academic.

Tardy, C. H. (2000). Self-disclosure and health: Revising Sidney Jourard's hypothesis. In S. Petronio (Ed.), *Balancing the secrets of private disclosures* (pp. 111–122). Mahwah, NJ: Erlbaum.

Tidwell, L. C., & Walther, J. B. (2000, July). *Getting to know one another a bit at a time: Computer-mediated communication effects on disclosure, impressions, and interpersonal evaluations.* Paper presented at the International Conference on Language and Social Psychology, Cardiff, Wales.

Vangelisti, A. (1994). Family secrets: Forms, functions, and correlates. *Journal of Social and Personal Relationships, 11,* 113–135.

Worthy, W., Gary, A. L., & Kahn, G. M. (1969). Self-disclosure as an exchange process. *Journal of Personality and Social Psychology, 13,* 59–63.

Wortman, C. B., Adesman, P., Herman, E., & Greenberg, R. (1976). Self-disclosure: An attributional perspective. *Journal of Personality and Social Psychology, 33,* 184–191.

C H A P T E R   8

DEFENDING

THE SELF

WHAT ARE ACCOUNTS?

Types of Accounts

An Expanded Typology of Accounts

The Functions Served by Accounts

Goals Achieved through the
  Communication of Accounts

Facework and Politeness Theory

CULTURE AND THE COMMUNICATION
OF ACCOUNTS

ATTRIBUTION THEORY AND THE
COMMUNICATION OF ACCOUNTS

Credibility of Excuses

Control of Emotions

THE TRIANGLE MODEL OF
RESPONSIBILITY

IMPRESSION MANAGEMENT

Public Images

A NOTE ON FORGIVENESS

CHAPTER SUMMARY

One sunny spring day a patrolman in Indiana saw a driver of a station wagon speeding and driving erratically. The officer turned on his siren and flashers and pulled the driver over. As he examined the driver's license, the officer said, "Sir, is there some problem?"

"Well, officer, I know you think I broke the law, and I did. But I didn't mean to! You see, I am allergic to bee stings, and there was a bee in the car. At first I tried to roll down the windows and speed up to get it out of the car. Finally, I killed it with this newspaper." The driver then displayed a folded-over newspaper on the passenger's seat and pointed to a dead bee on the dashboard.

"I usually don't do things like this," he continued (referring to breaking the law), "but if I got stung way out here miles from a hospital or anything, I would get deathly ill." The officer was just about to believe the man's story and let him go with only a verbal warning when he stopped to look at the dead bee. "This is odd, sir. But it seems that this bee isn't smashed at all. It looks dried out." The man then confessed that it was all a hoax. He kept a dead bee in a small vial in his glove compartment, and he'd pull out the bee and the newspaper props whenever he needed a good excuse to avoid a ticket. He had used this ruse many times in the past. However, it took an observant officer to see through the deception.

This story, presumably a true incident, was reported by an Indiana police officer to friends and was circulated in the media in the late 1980s. It is a humorous story that highlights the extent to which people will go to protect themselves. This chapter focuses on how we defend ourselves, or how we defend a particular public view of ourselves, when we have engaged in actions that others find questionable. When we are accused of doing something wrong (like speeding and driving erratically), we frequently give an explanation for why the behavior occurred. When communicating these explanations we offer an account for our actions. Because the driver didn't want to get any more tickets, he had devised a plan to convince police that he was not a person who routinely exceeded the speed limit (which was not the truth). He wanted the officer to believe that the bee (and the threat of being stung) caused his poor driving and that this single episode of violating the law was a one-time fluke. Police officers are more likely to forgive a victim of circumstances beyond human control. Accounts are commonly used to manage people's perceptions of our behavior and of whether we are responsible for our actions or are victims of external causes.

Chapter 6 focused on individuals' attempts to create and maintain a public image, and Chapter 7 focused on how we reveal ourselves to others. This chapter reviews how we defend ourselves when it appears that things go wrong (or, at least, could go wrong). Many of you may already have read amusing stories on excuses (defined below) that focus on breaking dates, breaking one's diet, failing to pay bills, avoiding jury duty, explaining away school or work mishaps, and more (see the box "Samples of Favorite Excuses Shared On-line"). Some of these may be lies (like our bee-fearing driver in the chapter-opening scenario), but many are truthful explanations for events. Further, while some of these excuses can be amusing, there are some serious

SAMPLES OF FAVORITE EXCUSES SHARED ON-LINE

Excuses focusing on clarity of rules, obligations, prescriptions; "the requirements were unclear," "rules make no sense," "handbook is filled with confusing material, contradictions":

I was unaware of your practice of restricting free speech since you only appear to accept answers that meet some sort of mysterious guidelines that you mask under the guise of "the correct answer." This appears to be a violation of my First Amendment rights.

Excuse me for not doing my homework, it's cause you ASKED me to do it, you didn't TELL me to do it, so I thought it was optional.

I did not know it was "homework" that I was supposed to bring back to school.

I didn't know I couldn't switch lanes in an intersection.

I don't see how sending her flowers can be "Sexual Harassment."

Excuses focusing on personal control; "accidents happen," "unforeseeable outcomes occurred," "unanticipated obstacles interfered with my intentions":

I really spent a lot of time studying for your exam. Even though I felt that I knew every thing, I decided to call LaWanda at the Psychic Friends Network to ask her advice. She determined that because Mars was in Cancer, my performance on the exam would not be favorable on the day of the exam. She also advised me not to leave the house before 11 AM the next day. Now that Jupiter is in Libra, I am ready to REALLY take the exam.

Hello Jennifer I can not meet you tonight and go out like we wanted to. I went surfing today and I like got washed out to sea and you know like it took me all day to get back in so I'm still here and like I won't be home in time for our date.

I'm sorry that I have to break our date, but you see I was out bowling with my friends tonight and I got my hand stuck in the ball, and they had to take me to the E.R. Where they had to saw it off of my hand. My hand is now swollen to extreme measures, and they have me on this really weird medicine . . .

One time when a guy was suppose to go to a dance with me, he broke the date 2 hours before saying he ate dog poop, thinking it was Pate, and was rushed to the hospital!

Excuses focusing on personal obligations; "not my responsibility," "not my job," "conflicts with my true identity as wife, husband, mother, etc.":

You cannot hold me responsible for knowing the material on this test, as I was sleeping during all of your lectures. As you did not wake me up, I assumed that you sympathized with my tiredness and were excusing me from the information being covered. Not needing to know the information, I assumed that I would not have to take a test on it. You might have made some kind of mistake in handing me this test, since I don't have to take it, so I am just writing this to remind you.

When I got my notice of jury duty I was about to give birth, and after my daughter was born I had to stay home to nurse the baby.

I am not on the recruitment committee. I'm not going to more meetings!

Well, it's really sweet of you to ask (for a date), but I have to take my kids to see their father in prison that day.

Source: http://members.tripod.com/Madtbone, http://www.excuses.co.uk, http://ull.chemistry.uakron.edu/excuses, http://www .zipworld.com.au/~verysoft/speeding/index.html, http://www.collectionagency.com/abs/excuses.html

consequences to a person's public image, legal penalties, and more when people fail to offer accounts appropriately. In this chapter we first discuss the various ways in which people offer accounts, and then discuss the communication functions offered by the accounts. Four approaches to account-giving are presented:

1. We use accounts to be polite and coordinate our actions with others during interactions.

2. We use attributions (see Chapter 2) to place blame on external causes (or we accept responsibility for what happened).

3. We use a triangle model of responsibility (discussed later in this chapter) to evaluate the credibility of an account, and to evaluate people as they communicate excuses.

4. We use impression management (see Chapter 6) to promote, or maintain, a particular public image.

WHAT ARE ACCOUNTS?

An **account** is "a linguistic device employed whenever an action is subjected to valuative inquiry" (Scott & Lyman, 1968, p. 171). "Valuative inquiry" is a request for an explanation of either an inappropriate or unexpected behavior ("Why were you flirting with Pat?") or a failure to engage in an appropriate or expected behavior ("Why didn't you pay the phone bill on time?"). Such a request usually comes when

Police officers are familiar with the types of accounts people use when accused of questionable behavior, such as speeding.

Gary S. Weber/Photo Researchers

one individual realizes that some failure event has occurred and wants to hear an explanation for it.

Scott and Lyman proposed the first list of the types of accounts in 1968, when attention focused on accounting for so-called deviant behavior (taking drugs, becoming a juvenile delinquent, etc.). Schönbach (1980), however, argued that the original list of accounts missed a number of important types of accounts, and he offered an expanded list. We will present both lists of accounts.

Types of Accounts

Scott and Lyman (1968) identified the two most common forms of accounts as **excuses** and **justifications** (see Table 8.1). When using an excuse, the communicator admits that the act in question occurred but claims not to be fully responsible for it. The appeal to accident is one of the most common forms of an excuse; it includes such claims as "the dog ate the homework," "the traffic was backed up," and "the tire was flat."

An appeal to biological drives generally deals with an appeal to fate or limits to human endurance. An appeal to biological drives includes claims that men are men, women are women, boys will be boys, and so on. When two friends talk about why a particular boy on the swimming team is "playing around," one might say "Boys don't have any sense of commitment, like girls," thus the boy is excused based on biological

Table 8.1

TYPES OF ACCOUNTS

Accounts	Examples
Excuses	
Appeal to accidents	The tire was flat when I went out to the driveway this morning.
	A truck carrying a load of fruit jackknifed on the freeway this morning, and two lanes were closed for hours.
Biological drives, fatalism	Boys will be boys.
	That's just the way people are.
Appeal to defeasibility	I didn't *intend* to burn rubber like that.
	I knew they were unhappy, but I had no idea that things had become so miserable.
Scapegoating	Satan made me do it.
	The dog ate my science project.
Justifications	
Denial of injury, minimization of harm	Oh, Mom! Nothing happened!
	Yeah, I did it. But it was no big deal.
Denial of victim	Who cares about a Gypsy palm reader?
	So what if he got hurt? Tourists usually cause their own trouble anyway.
Appeal to loyalties	I was speeding because I am late for work.
	I engaged in burglary in order to gain information helpful to my political candidate.
Self-fulfillment	Yes, I went bungee jumping. I wanted to prove to myself I could do it.
	Good LSD is great. You see everything so much clearer afterward.
Condemnation of the condemners	But officer, I was just flowing with traffic. Everyone else was doing seventy.
	Everybody cheats a little on their tax forms.
Sad tale	I am working two part-time jobs and taking two courses. My boyfriend and I just had a fight, and I just can't concentrate on a test right now.
	When you are from the streets like me, you learn to cut corners in order to get ahead.

Source: Adapted from Scott & Lyman, 1968.

210

drives. An appeal to biological drives also includes biological reasons such as fatigue or falling asleep and not being in the best physical condition (an excuse athletes might offer for poor performance).

When employing the appeal to defeasibility, the accounter claims that he or she did not have full knowledge about an action and its consequences and therefore should not be held responsible for what occurred. For instance, a teenage boy teases his sister about her boyfriend, and she begins to cry. When asked why he behaved so cruelly, the boy confesses that he didn't know the two had argued and separated (and hence that he should not be blamed or considered cruel). Cases of scapegoating are fairly common ("But my secretary told me this was the correct form").

When using a justification, the accounter accepts responsibility for the act in question but denies that it was harmful or tries to claim that it actually had positive consequences. A student might tell his or her professor that an assignment is late because the student was involved in an emergency, requiring a call for an ambulance and filing a police report. The student justifies why an assignment is late — saving a human life has more positive consequences than turning in an assignment on time. One of the more popular forms of justifications is using a denial of injury; the accounter admits that an action occurred and that he or she was responsible for it, but because no harm came from it, no penalty should be assessed. High school students can tell their parents, "Yes, we took the car and stayed out last night, but nothing happened. Everybody's okay." When making this claim, they admit the action took place and that they were responsible, but they claim that no negative sanctions or judgment of them should follow because "nothing happened." In a denial of victim, the accounter argues that the person who was hurt isn't worthy of concern: "Who cares? She would have ripped me off if she could have."

When using an appeal to loyalty, the accounter asserts that loyalty to a group or a friend is more important than the rules that were violated. Some drivers do, in fact, claim that being late for a date is the reason why they were speeding, and police usually ticket such drivers. The claim that being on time for a date is a more important loyalty than obeying the speed laws is a poor communication strategy. When using a self-fulfillment message, the accounter accepts responsibility for the act but claims that the act had value — growth, maturity, or self-fulfillment. Some drug users justify the use of LSD as a means to expand the mind, and thrill seekers may want to prove something to themselves by skydiving or driving fast. The condemnation of the condemner justification involves the claim that because others break the same rules, the accounter shouldn't be personally reprimanded: Everyone cheats on tax forms, drives a little over the speed limit, and so on. Finally, in the use of a sad tale, the accounter claims that highlights of a dismal past can be used to explain current behaviors. Criminals sometimes employ the sad tale (unhappy childhood, deprivation, etc.) to justify a life of crime.

An Expanded Typology of Accounts

Schönbach (1980) added two categories to the taxonomy of accounts (see Table 8.2): concessions and refusals. In a **concession,** the accounter simply confesses or admits

Table 8.2

SCHÖNBACH'S EXPANDED TYPOLOGY OF ACCOUNTS

Concessions

1.0	Explicit acknowledgment of own responsibility or guilt
1.1	Full confession of guilt, without reservations
1.2	Partial confession of guilt, with reservations
2.0	Explicit abstention from excuse or justification; concession of inappropriateness of excuses or justification in the present case
3.0	Expression of regret concerning the failure event (commission or omission)
3.1	Expression of regret concerning the consequences of the failure event
4.0	Restitution or compensation
4.1	Appeal to restitutions or compensations already performed
4.2	Offer to restitutions or compensations

Excuses

1.0	Appeal to own human shortcomings
1.1	Appeal to insufficient knowledge or skill
1.2	Appeal to will impairment
2.0	Reasons for the appeal to own shortcomings
2.1	Appeal to biological factors, such as arousal
2.2	Appeal to illness, addiction, drunkenness
2.3	Appeal to one's own negative past
2.4	Appeal to provocations by other persons
2.5	Appeal to duress by powerful agents
2.6	Appeal to loyalties
2.7	Appeal to the specific external circumstances of the situation
3.0	Appeal to own effort and care before and during the failure event
4.0	Appeal to shortcomings or misdeeds of other persons as frame of reference for the evaluation (hence a mild judgment is appropriate)
4.1	Appeal to shortcomings or misdeeds of the accuser as frame of reference for the evaluation of the failure event (hence a mild judgment is appropriate)
5.0	Appeal to participation of other persons in the failure event
5.1	Appeal to participation of the accuser in the failure event

(Continued)

(Table continued from previous page)

Justifications

1.0	Denial of damage
2.0	Minimization of damage
2.1	Minimization of damage in view of the circumstances that provoked the failure event
2.2	Appeal to the positive consequences of the failure event
3.0	Appeal to the role of the victim
3.1	Justification of damage with qualities of the victim
3.2	Justification of damage with acts of the victim
4.0	Appeal to the right of self-fulfillment
4.1	Appeal to the right of self-fulfillment in view of one's own negative past
5.0	Appeal to loyalties
6.0	Appeal to positive intentions
7.0	Appeal to shortcomings or misdeeds of other persons as frame of reference for evaluation of the failure event (account giver's moderation should be acknowledged)
7.1	Appeal to shortcomings of misdeeds or the accuser as frame of reference for evaluation of the failure event (account giver's moderation should be acknowledged)

Refusals

1.0	Claiming that the failure event simply did not occur
2.0	Explicit refusal of a confession of guilt
3.0	Unrestricted attribution of guilt to other persons
3.1	Unrestricted attribution of guilt to the accuser
4.0	Denial of the right of reproach
4.1	Denial of the right of reproach on the basis of own identity or role in relation to the accuser
4.2	Denial of the right of reproach in view of the negative qualities or deeds of the accuser
5.0	Referral to other sources of information
6.0	Evasions or mystifications

Source: Adapted from Schönbach, 1980. Copyright John Wiley & Sons Ltd. Reproduced with permission.

to the act in question. Some concessions are nothing more than admissions of guilt, but other forms of concessions contain any of several elements of apologies. Schön-bach includes some elements of apologies in the higher levels of concessions (see items 3.0 through 4.2 under "Concessions" in Table 8.2). Schlenker (1980) similarly noted five elements of a "full apology": (1) an expression of guilt, remorse, or embar-rassment; (2) clarification that one recognizes what the appropriate conduct should have been and an acknowledgment that negative sanctions apply for having commit-ted the failure event; (3) rejection of the inappropriate conduct and disparagement of the "bad self" that misbehaved; (4) acknowledgment of the appropriate conduct and a promise to behave accordingly in the future; and (5) penance, restitution, or an offer to compensate the victim or victims.

In the **refusal** category, the accounter denies that the questionable act occurred or denies responsibility. Refusals can be divided into several relevant types (see Table 8.2). A person can prove innocence by using logical argument, physical evidence, or other means. Second, a person can refuse to offer an account by challenging the authority of the person asking for one: "We broke up months ago! I don't have to ex-plain to you what I do on weekends!" A third variation on refusals is to reject the def-inition of an offense: The accounter admits that the act took place but claims that it is wrong to label it an "offense": "Yes, I had lunch with my ex, but it was just a lunch. There is nothing wrong with having lunch!"

The Functions Served by Accounts

Each type of account serves a specific function. By definition, an excuse attempts to exonerate the accounter of being held responsible for an offense, whereas a justifi-cation makes the action seem less negative or even positive (see the section "The Tri-angle Model of Responsibility" later in this chapter). When using a concession, the accounter accepts responsibility for the act and its consequences and promises, if ap-propriate forms of an apology are used, not to engage in the act again and/or to make restitution. In a refusal, however, the accounter asserts (or proves) innocence.

Snyder and Higgins (1990) argue that we are appraised on two dimensions: the enhancing processes that reflect our attempts to link ourselves to positive actions and behaviors and the protective processes that reflect our attempts to either make a neg-ative act appear less negative or disassociate ourselves from the act (see Figure 8.1). The first dimension involves the perceived linkage of the accounter to a particular act or outcome (e.g., failing to make a complete stop at a stop sign). The accounter may have no link to the act in question (he may believe that he did, in fact, come to a com-plete stop) and would probably use a refusal. Otherwise, the accounter may be fully or only partially linked to the act in question (he may, in fact, have intended to hurry through the intersection, or his foot may have slipped off the brake pedal); in this case, an excuse serves the function of reducing the link or association between the ac-counter and the questionable act.

The second dimension is a valence dimension. We normally do not want to be associated with negative acts, so we attempt to make questionable acts appear to be less negative (or even positive). To do this, we use justifications. Further, we use apologies to imply that we were bad only temporarily.

In sum, excuses operate directly on the linkage dimension by making it appear that we are less directly or intentionally related to negative acts. A refusal operates to eliminate any link between the act and us. A justification attempts to reduce the negativity of the act, and concession (coupled with forms of an apology) places us temporarily in the role of the "bad self."

Goals Achieved through the Communication of Accounts

Accounts are used to achieve the general goal of defending the self. Accounts also are communicated to satisfy particular goals: to create or maintain a positive public image, repair relationships, cope with embarrassment, control emotions, manage or avoid conflict, and avoid punishments. The following sections each focus on a different approach to defending the self.

Facework and Politeness Theory

Erving Goffman, described in Chapter 6 as the father of the dramaturgical approach, also discussed how we promote and protect our public face (Goffman, 1967). A good definition of **face** is provided by Ting-Toomey (1994, p. 1):

> Face entails the presentation of a civilized front to another individual within the webs of interconnected relationships in a particular culture. . . . Face is a claimed sense of self-respect in an interactive situation. It has been viewed, alternatively, as a symbolic resource, as a social status, as a projected identity issue, and as a fundamental communication phenomenon. Facework involves the enactment of face strategies, verbal and nonverbal moves, self-presentation acts, and impression management interaction.

Following from the earlier works of Goffman (1967), Brown and Levinson (1978, 1987) advanced "politeness theory," which has received wide attention in interpersonal settings, gender studies, and cross-cultural studies (Cupach & Metts, 1994; Holmes, 1995; Ting-Toomey, 1994). Brown and Levinson's theory presumes two types of "face needs": positive face and negative face. *Positive face needs* refer to the desire to be liked and respected by others. Positive face occurs and is maintained when the people with whom we interact communicate messages that reflect appreciation for us, reinforce a view of ourselves as competent, likable, and sharing common interests (Holtgraves, 1997; Lim & Bowers, 1991). Examples of statements that validate positive face include "Thanks for helping out, I knew you'd come through" [as a reliable, good friend], "Yes [thanks for noticing], I took dance lessons last summer," and,

"I love spending time like this with you." Threats to positive face occur when we are evaluated in ways we find undesirable — which fail to support the positive view of self we had hoped to groom with our self-presentational strategies (Chapter 6). Threats include "You are always late [you are inconsiderate]," "I have never danced with someone so clumsy before," "You always think of yourself first, don't you?"

Negative face needs deal with our desire to be free from constraints and obligations — we are autonomous, independent, and not tied down to anyone. Validating negative face are messages that show respect for our autonomy — "You are a big girl now, you can do what you like," or "You are free to come and go as you wish." Threats to negative face include "Be home by 10 PM," "You girls probably won't like this joke, but I am going to tell it anyway," or "I forbid you to go there tonight! You stay put, young man, and listen to every word I say!"

We develop the ability to manage our own face as well as others' faces during everyday conversations for three reasons. First, we are judged as more competent and have a better chance to fulfill our own goals by attending to the face needs of both ourselves and those with whom we interact: ". . . getting ahead ordinarily entails getting along, which in turn necessitates sensitivity to the face needs of others" (Cupach & Metts, 1994, p. 15). In normal conversations, then, partners implicitly agree to maintain each other's positive face. Second, typically people want to have their identity confirmed. Third, effective facework will garnish mutual respect from one another, and conversations will progress in relatively smooth fashion. On the other hand, partners who pose threats to both positive and negative face produce intensely negative feelings and will eventually be ignored and avoided if threats to face persist.

When are we polite? Although as a general rule we may want to appear polite in every interaction because doing so makes and keeps friends, three context variables predict when we are more likely to be polite: when we are with others who are more powerful and who might control more rewards and resources, when the type of offense or goal at hand is relatively more serious or important, when we are with others who are socially distant — we don't have to be polite to our family members anymore, relative to neighbors or strangers. Holmes (1990), however, noted that we may be most polite when interacting with others who are neither strangers nor intimates, where relational definitions are less certain and less predictable, and where our public image may be bolstered by acting politely.

Performing **facework,** validating positive face and avoiding threats to negative face, is obviously related to how we promote ourselves (Chapter 6) — we compliment others, gain liking by showing liking to others, provide symbols of attainment for our self-presentations, and so forth. We introduce facework and politeness theory in this chapter because they pertain directly to a series of communication moves we engage in when we encounter threats to positive or negative face: disclaimers, preferred accounts, and coping with embarrassment. Facework is also important when we disengage from relationships, gain compliance from others, and cope with conflict (see Chapters 12–15 on instrumental goals).

DISCLAIMERS. If you believe that what you are about to say and do might offend someone in the audience or might result in your identity being called into question, you might preface your statement or action with a disclaimer (Hewitt & Stokes, 1975). By using a disclaimer, the speaker admits that what is to follow may seem odd or unusual (a threat to the audience member's face), and the speaker requests not to be judged negatively on the basis of what he or she says. Disclaimers occur in face-to-face settings, but they may also occur in chat rooms when a person wants to voice an opinion that might run contrary to the opinion of others. If a disclaimer works well, we will not suffer any negative loss of face, and an account may not be needed or requested. Forms of disclaimers include (see Cupach & Metts, 1994; Hewitt & Stokes, 1975):

1. *Hedging.* A hedge indicates uncertainty and receptivity to suggestions ("I may be wrong, but . . ."; "Let me play the devil's advocate, and disagree with you . . .").

2. *Credentialing.* Presenting credentials indicates that there are good reasons and appropriate qualifications for engaging in an action ("I was raised a Catholic and I was an altar boy, so I believe my complaints against the Church are not mere bias, but . . ."; "I pay equal rent, so I am entitled to have my friends over").

3. *Sin license.* The speaker requests permission for a rule violation that should not be taken as a change in public image or as a threat to others' face ("Hey, I know we are on a budget, but let's splurge tonight"; "I know you don't like to hear jokes about _____, but I heard one that was good today. Do you mind if I tell it?").

4. *Cognitive disclaimer.* A prefacing device is used to tell others that what follows is reasonable and that the speaker is in control of his or her faculties, despite appearances ("I know this sounds crazy, but . . .").

5. *Appeal for suspended judgment.* A speaker requests that judgment be withheld until what might at first appear to be an offensive act has been fully explained ("Hear me out before you get upset").

Speakers are considered more sensitive, polite, competent, and appropriate if they use disclaimers when introducing controversial comments and even jokes (Cashion, Cody, & Erickson, 1987; Cupach & Metts, 1994).

PREFERRED ACCOUNTS. Some forms of accounts are more polite relative to others. Concessions in the form of apologies and excuses are more likely to be perceived as polite, preferable, and effective than justifications and refusals. The reasoning is simple. When we ask for an account from someone, we prefer to hear an admission of guilt coupled with some form of apology. An **apology** may be called a *full apology* if it contains all of the elements described earlier (Schlenker, 1980 — including promises of restitution and expressions of remorse), and full apologies are perceived as more polite, they are preferred by listeners, and they are more useful than other accounts in solving disputes.

An excuse is the second most polite response because the accounter communicates a lack of intention to behave in an offensive manner. Justifications come third in politeness, preference, or usefulness. An accounter who justifies an offense is trying to show that there was some good reason for the offense, but often we don't like to hear this. The driver who justifies speeding by citing lateness for work, for example, is offering an account that police officers prefer not to hear. Refusals are the least preferred type of account to receive. We seldom like to be challenged, proved wrong, or contradicted on matters of ethics.

Holtgraves (1989) demonstrated that apologies and excuses are preferable and more helpful than justifications (he did not study refusals). Students read the following scenario:

> James and Paul have known each other for several years and are good friends. They recently made plans to attend a concert together in a nearby city. On the night of the concert, James is supposed to pick up Paul and drive them to the concert. However, James arrives an hour and a half late, too late to go to the concert. When James arrives, Paul confronts him and tells him how upset he is.

They then read one of the following accounts offered by James:

> *Full-blown apology:* (Holtgraves called this *compensation*.): "I apologize for making us miss the concert. It was a terrible thing to do, and I'm very sorry. It won't happen again. Please forgive me. Is there anything I can do to make it up to you?"
>
> *Apology:* "I apologize for making us miss the concert."
>
> *Regret:* "I'm sorry for making us miss the concert."
>
> *Regret plus excuse:* "I'm sorry for making us miss the concert. I got so busy at work I forgot all about the concert."
>
> *Excuse:* "I got so busy at work I forgot all about the concert."
>
> *Regret plus justification:* "I'm sorry for making us miss the concert, but it's not that big a deal; it wasn't going to be that good a concert anyway."
>
> *Justification:* "It's not that big a deal; it wasn't going to be that good a concert anyway."

After reading the scenario and one of the accounts, Holtgraves had the students complete a questionnaire asking them to rate the various accounts in terms of how satisfied the listener would be with the account, how difficult it would be for the speaker to say the account, how helpful the account would be in solving the conflict, and how likely it is that the speaker would use the account.

218

Six-year-old Calvin resorts to scapegoating so that he won't be responsible for his actions.

Here, he struggles with the realization that he should apologize to Susie, but apologizing is a hard thing to do.

Susie at first accepts Calvin's "perfunctory apology" and then realizes that she'd rather hear a "full-blown" one.

Calvin and Hobbes, copyright Bill Watterson. Dist. By Universal Press Syndicate. Reprinted with permission. All rights reserved.

Table 8.3 presents the students' perceptions. Justifications were rated as the least satisfying, followed in order by the regret plus justification and the excuse accounts. The full-blown apology (compensation) was rated highest in hearers' satisfaction. Similarly, the justification, regret plus justification, and excuse were rated low in helping solve the conflict, followed by regret only, which was rated lower in helpfulness than regret plus excuse. The apology and full-blown apology were rated highest in helpfulness. Generally speaking, apologies were rated as more polite, preferred,

Table 8.4

METHODS FOR COPING WITH EMBARRASSMENT

Tactics for Coping with Embarrassment

Tactics	*Definition and Example*
Simple apology	Clichéd statements of regret and requests for pardon: "I'm sorry," "Please excuse me," "Please forgive me."
Excuse	Acknowledgment of a questionable act while claiming minimal or no responsibility: "I've had so much on my mind with exams and papers."
Justification	Acknowledgment of responsibility for an act while claiming minimal, no, or positive consequences: "Mom, this is not what it seems."
Humor	Laughter and joking. After falling down a flight of stairs in full skirt and high heels: "Hi, I just thought I'd drop in."
Remediation	Correcting the problem: Clean up spill, collect dropped packages, clean a stain.
Escape	Physically retreating from the scene.
Avoidance	Ignoring the problem: "Having spilled beer on my pants, I just smiled and acted like it didn't bother me."
Aggression	Physically or verbally attacking another person as retaliation.

Tactics Available to Others When Helping Persons Cope
with Embarrassment

Tactics	*Definition and Example*
Simple apology	Expressions of regret offered by observers who feel responsible for the embarrassment of another: "I'm sorry" offered by a person who bumped a drink tray, causing the respondent's embarrassing incident.
Excuse	Acknowledgment of an untoward act but minimization of the embarrassed person's responsibility for its occurrence. When an embarrassed person fell while sweeping a floor at work, her boss offered: "The broom handle is rotten."
Justification	Acknowledgment of an untoward act but minimization of the offensiveness of the act: When an embarrassed person spilled gum and candy while restocking, a co-worker said: "Don't worry about it — it's just gum, not glassware."

(Continued)

Tactics	Definition and Example
(Table continued from previous page)	
Humor	Laughing along with an embarrassed person or making jokes. When a manager of a fast-food restaurant was sprayed with strawberry milkshake because the embarrassed person did not put a lid on the blender, she said: "Luckily, I look good in pink."
Remediation	Helping clean up messes, spills, dropped packages, and so on.
Avoidance	Acting as though no infraction has occurred. When an embarrassed person tripped in church after receiving communion, her family made room for her in the pew as if nothing had happened.
Empathy	Assuring the embarrassed person that his or her predicament or behavior is not unique and happens to others. When an embarrassed person found that he had been sitting in the wrong class for ten minutes, a classmate said: "The same thing happened to me last semester."
Support	Verbal and nonverbal assurances of continued positive regard for the embarrassed person. When the embarrassed person tripped in church, her mother patted her leg when she returned to her seat.

Source: Adapted from Metts & Cupach, 1989. Copyright by the Speech Communication Association. Reprinted by permission of the publisher and authors.

embarrassment entail sequences of tactics, usually involving apologies and humor. Common sequences include apology, remediation; apology, escape, remediation; humor, apology; humor, excuse; and humor, escape, remediation.

Although accounts (and humor) are critically important in our attempts to avoid a negative evaluation when we engage in embarrassing actions, accounts are not particularly useful in actually reducing our feelings of embarrassment. According to Cupach and Metts (1990), the actions of both the embarrassed person and the other are important for effectively handling embarrassment. Two conclusions can be cited. First, only a few of the tactics used by the embarrassed person were considered effective in reducing embarrassment. Second, many of the tactics used by the other person were effective in helping reduce the embarrassed person's uncomfortable feelings. We depend on our friends to help us overcome the emotional aspects of embarrassment.

Only humor, remediation, and excuses were rated as effective by the embarrassed party for reducing felt embarrassment — and humor was the most effective. Escape from the scene was considered ineffective. By contrast, others can help the embarrassed person reduce feelings of discomfort by using nearly all of the tactics listed in the lower portion of Table 8.4. Remediation (helping) was most effective, followed by empathy, justification, support, avoidance, and humor.

What these studies show is that we can use accounts (and humor) effectively to reduce the likelihood that others will evaluate us negatively. However, our feelings of embarrassment can linger on after we use tactics such as apology plus remediation or humor plus remediation. The other person can help us feel better by using remediation, sympathy, empathy, justification, humor, and avoiding mention of our predicament.

CULTURE AND THE COMMUNICATION OF ACCOUNTS

Culture plays a major role in the use of accounts, and a growing body of literature compares and contrasts the use of accounts between cultures, with considerable attention focused on politeness theory (see discussion earlier in this chapter) and apologies. Itoi, Ohbuchi, and Fukuno (1996), for example, compared Japanese and American students' motives for using accounts and preferences for using accounts.

Effective ways of coping with embarrassment include excuses, apologies, and humor.

Alan Carey/The Image Works

The Japanese students indicated that their primary motivation when communicating an account was for "emotional alleviation" (to reduce guilt, etc.), compared to improving a public impression or to avoid punishment. American participants, however, rated the motivation of "improving their impression" as the most important reason, followed by "emotional alleviation" and "avoidance of punishment." Japanese participants overwhelmingly preferred to use apologies, relative to American participants. American participants also rated apologies as preferred tactics but indicated they would use "direct" tactics like justifications, excuses, and denials as well. Japanese participants also indicated that they would use "no account" (be silent) when involved with strangers, indicating that they would reduce anger and manage their impressions by being apologetic or by avoiding confrontations and denials. Among American participants, relational closeness reduced the likelihood that they would use apologies; among Japanese participants, relational closeness increased the likelihood that they would say something to their partners — they felt obligated to say something to close friends, whereas avoidance or saying nothing is used for relationally distant others.

Takaku, Weiner, and Ohbuchi (2001) also found differences in motivations underlying accounts. Compared to Americans, Japanese students placed significantly more emphasis on maintaining a good relationship with their classmates and on how similar others would react in the situation, emphasizing relational and normative motives. On the other hand, Americans placed greater emphasis on justice and fairness in the situation. Hamilton and Hagiwara (1992) found that Americans and males in particular were likely to be aggressive in their accounts, denying and justifying actions, rather than apologizing (the preference of Japanese, and American females).

A number of papers have focused on the communication of apologies among Japanese and among Americans (Ide, 1998; Sugimoto, 1997, 1998). Sugimoto (1998) found that in Japan there is greater concern with the communication of apologies in private settings (rather than public), with an emphasis placed on apologizing to people within a person's in-group. Americans focus greater concern on communicating apologies for their own individual actions and do so in public (relative to Japanese). Americans also seem to individualize apologies, giving preference to providing an originally phrased, spontaneous apology that appears sincere (using a number of the elements of an effective apology listed earlier). On the other hand, apologies in Japan are more ritualistic, promoting a particular image of the speaker to particular receivers.

The Japanese and American contrasts involve collectivist cultures and individualistic cultures. Tata (2000) compared Mexican Americans, a culture that is both collectivist and high in "power distance," and Anglo Americans, who are individualistic and low in power distance (see Chapter 4 for a discussion of cultural differences). While other research indicates that Japanese are generally more likely than Americans to use mitigating accounts, Tata found that Mexican Americans and Anglo Americans differed significantly only when status of the receiver was important, implying that the power distance cultural dimension was more important than the collectivist versus individualist designation. When communicating with superiors, Mexican Americans placed greater interest on maintaining the superiors' face concerns, and reported preference for, and perceived effectiveness of, mitigating accounts (apologies and excuses). When communicating with subordinates, Anglo Americans expressed a greater desire to maintain the subordinates' face concerns, and rated mitigating accounts as more likely to be used and as more effective (compared to Mexican Americans). Thus, individuals from a high power distance culture expressed greater concern and indicated a preference for polite forms of accounts when communicating with superiors (maintaining a status differential). Individuals from a low power distance culture expressed concern and indicated a preference for polite forms of accounts when communicating with subordinates (reducing the status differential).

Culture also plays an important role in coping with embarrassment. Edelmann (1994) found that apologies were far more common in Japan, the United Kingdom, and Germany, and less often used in (descending order) Portugal, Greece, Spain, and Italy. The use of humor as a means for diffusing embarrassment was virtually nonexistent in Japan.

ATTRIBUTION THEORY AND THE COMMUNICATION OF ACCOUNTS

Attribution theory is an important theory of human cognition that is relevant to many aspects of interpersonal communication. It is important with reference to accounts for two reasons. First, attribution theory deals with our judgments concerning why people behave the way they do, and these judgments influence our evaluation of the accounts that are communicated. Second, excuses themselves suggest causes for questionable behavior, and certain types of excuses are effective in achieving remedial goals and in controlling the emotions of the people with whom we speak.

As we mentioned in Chapter 2, Kelley (1973) argued that there are three features of observing others that influence our judgments: distinctiveness, consistency, and consensus. *Distinctiveness* deals with whether or not a person's behavior is distinctly different in one situation than in other situations. *Consistency* refers to the extent to which the student's behavior is the same over time. *Consensus* deals with the perception of similar others in similar situations (see examples in Chapter 2). Attribution theory deals with the fundamental issue of how we make attributions concerning why people behave the way they do. We are likely to believe that a person's behavior is caused by external factors when distinctiveness is high (receiving good grades in all classes but one), when consistency is high (receiving good grades consistently over time except in this one class), and when consensus is high (all students were performing poorly in this class). In such circumstances, we are likely to believe our friend's excuses for the poor grades. By contrast, if we perceive the friend as making poor grades in all classes, making poor grades consistently over time, and making poor grades when other students are making good grades, we judge the behavior as being caused by internal factors, and we are likely to view any excuse this person communicates as unconvincing.

Attribution theorists have added several other types of causes of behavior. Bernie Weiner (1986, 1992) has added four that are relevant to the communication of accounts:

1. Causes can be *stable* or *unstable*. Stable causes recur consistently and predictably over time. Traffic is congested at 8 AM and at 5 PM and is especially bad on Monday mornings, Friday afternoons, and whenever it snows or rains. Unstable causes are ones that cannot be predicted — freezing rain in April, a truck that jackknifed, an insect bite, and so on. Stable causes are linked to the perception of consistency. The student who received poor grades is likely to be perceived as a poor student if she received poor grades consistently (stably over time).

2. As mentioned elsewhere, causes can be *internal* ("I didn't want to go to the concert because I don't like that group anymore") or *external* ("My car was hit by a hit-and-run driver, and I can't go because I have to wait for the insurance adjuster"). Such causes can also be referred to as *personal* ("I don't like Chinese food," "I've decided to change my major") or *impersonal* ("My parents insist that I major in business," "Because of money problems at home, I have to drop out of school"). In our example of the student who received poor grades, the attribution of internal or external causes was strongly linked to the perception of distinctiveness.

3. Causes can be *controllable* or *uncontrollable*. The claim "I ran out of gas" may be external and unintentional, but it is controllable; the amount of gas in the tank is under the driver's control. An uncontrollable cause is one outside our ability to alter or change: "The baseball game ended early because of the rain, and I unexpectedly got stuck in traffic." In our example of the student who received poor grades, the perception of consensus is relevant to the judgment of whether she can control the behavior: If all students received poor grades, it is likely that the students did not have much control over the grades they received.

4. Causes can be *intentional* ("I was in a hurry to get home because it was dark and I was in a high-crime area") or *unintentional* ("I didn't mean to spin my wheels and burn rubber when I accelerated").

The driver who lied about the bee (in the chapter-opening scenario) communicated an account in such a way as to increase the likelihood that he would not be ticketed. The driver claimed that the bee and its potential sting caused him to speed and to drive erratically. This explanation involves a cause that is unintentional (the bee's presence distracted him from driving), uncontrollable (the driver can control neither the bee nor his driving behavior when he tried to avoid the bee), unstable (he rarely has to confront a problem like this one), and external (the bee is an environmental feature that caused the driver's behavior). Thus the communicated excuse involved a cause that was uncontrollable, unintentional, unstable, and external. The true, or withheld, reason, however, is best characterized as controllable, intentional, stable, and internal — the driver controls his speed, intends to speed, speeds often, and is personally causing the speeding.

Credibility of Excuses

The central proposition concerning attributions and the credibility of excuses is that communicated excuses that cite causes that are unintentional, unstable, uncontrollable, and external are more effective in achieving interpersonal goals than excuses

STUDENT AS OBSERVER: ACCOUNTS ON REALITY TV

The communication of accounts takes place frequently in reality TV shows. People voted off *Survivor* explain why they think they were voted off. After winning or losing their cases, people appearing on *The People's Court*, likewise offer an explanation to the television audience. On shows like *The Real World* or *Blind Date*, participants often explain their actions, or their opinions about others' actions, in a separate interview portion.

Watch an episode of a reality TV show that includes an accounts section and answer these questions:

1. Choose an incident involving two people on the show after which each person gives an account of the incident. What happened? Who were the people involved?
2. What was the first person's explanation for what happened? In explaining his or her reactions, does he or she use an apology (even if only perfunctory, "well, I'm sorry, but . . ."), an excuse, a justification, or a refusal (see text)?
3. What was the second person's explanation for what happened? In explaining his or her reactions, does he or she use an apology (even if only perfunctory, "well, I'm sorry, but . . ."), an excuse, a justification, or a refusal? (See text.)
4. What were the perceived underlying causes of the event? Intentional? Controllable? Internal? Stable?
5. Who is responsible (or to blame) for what happened? Is one person solely responsible? Or, do they share responsibility?
6. What were the disengagement strategies used (if any are portrayed on the show)?
7. Are the two people being polite to each other? (See text for discussion of politeness theory and facework.)
8. Is either of them, or both, embarrassed, and if so, how did they cope with their embarrassment?

that are intentional, stable, controllable, and internal. A very simple study by Weiner, Amirkhan, Folkes, and Verette (1987) demonstrated this clearly.

Weiner and his colleagues had pairs of students show up for a study purportedly on first impressions, and one student in each pair of students was asked to wait for the partner to show up so that the study could begin. The other student, however, was asked to do a bit of acting by pretending that he or she was late and to give an excuse to the waiting student, one of four kinds of excuses. One group was told to communicate whatever they thought would be a bad excuse, one that would evoke anger. Another group was told to communicate whatever they thought would be a good excuse, and a third group was told to communicate any excuse they wanted to communicate. The fourth group of students were told not to communicate any reason for being late.

Weiner and his colleagues found that the excuses that the students believed to be good excuses involved causes that were uncontrollable, external, unintentional, and unstable; 83% of the good excuses involved claims that the student had a sudden, unexpected obligation ("I had to take my mother to the hospital"), a problem in transportation or arrival ("I could not find the room"), or a school demand that kept them from being prompt ("My midterm took longer than expected"). Students instructed to communicate any excuse communicated ones that were similar to the good ones. This suggests that people normally try to communicate good excuses. However, students who constructed bad excuses used reasons that were internal, intentional, or controllable: "I ran into some friends and stayed to talk with them for a while," "I forgot," and the like. The students rated each other in terms of emotions (angry, warm, irritated, etc.), interpersonal traits (dependable, sensitive, friendly, etc.), and social behavior (whether they liked the partner). Students who communicated good excuses were perceived as having a more favorable personality, being more likable, and having more positive feelings than students who communicated bad excuses or who failed to communicate any reason for being tardy (also see Weiner, 1992).

Control of Emotions

We do not usually want to hurt other people's feelings, and excuses are used strategically so that we do not make others feel rejected. Folkes (1982) demonstrated this in a study in which students were asked to report how they turned down offers for dates. Students were asked to recall encounters in which they asked others for dates but were rejected. They were asked to write what was said to them when the rejecting party declined the date offer. They were also asked to recall encounters in which they were asked for dates and rejected others. The students were also asked to write out two sets of reasons: reasons privately held for rejecting the date offer and the publicly communicated reasons for rejecting the date offer. The central idea is that we have personal reasons for rejecting date offers but publicly communicate impersonal, uncontrollable, and unstable causes to others so that they will not feel personally rejected.

Folkes coded all the reasons written on three of the parameters of causes we discussed earlier: personal versus impersonal (internal versus external), controllable versus uncontrollable, and stable versus unstable. The results are presented in Table 8.5.

Table 8.5
REASONS FOR REJECTION OF DATE OFFERS

Type of Reason	Public Reason Reported by Rejected Persons (%)	Reasons Reported by Rejectors	
		Public (%)	*Private (%)*
Impersonal, uncontrollable, unstable (rejector had to study for finals)	59	64	30
Impersonal, uncontrollable, stable (rejector was seriously involved with someone)	9	8	7
Impersonal, controllable, unstable (rejector would rather go to a dance than to the movies)	22	15	12
Impersonal, controllable, stable (rejector did not want to jeopardize a relationship with someone they were currently dating)	1	3	4
Personal, uncontrollable, unstable (rejector was in a bad mood)	3	0	5
Personal, uncontrollable, stable (rejected person was too old)	1	8	26
Personal, controllable, unstable (rejected person had a lot of nerve asking the rejector out only hours in advance)	3	1	2
Personal, controllable, stable (rejector did not agree with the rejected person's religious beliefs)	1	1	14
Total number of reasons listed:	68	96	207

Source: Adapted from Folkes, 1982, tab. 242. Reprinted with permission of Academic Press.

Most reasons were privately held, and usually only one reason was communicated to the rejected person. Most reasons communicated to rejected parties involved impersonal causes for the rejection. When students recalled being rejected, the vast majority of reasons communicated to them were impersonal — the rejector had to study for finals, was seriously involved with someone else, or preferred an activity different from the one offered in the date.

A similar conclusion is reached when we look at the publicly communicated reasons for why we reject dates. The most frequently used reasons are impersonal, uncontrollable, and unstable ones (64% of all publicly communicated reasons for rejection). When we tell others that we can't see them because we have to take a test, drive a friend to the airport, or visit a friend in the hospital, we try to avoid making the others feel personally rejected. In reality, our true, privately held reasons for rejecting date offers are more often personal, uncontrollable, and stable ("The guy was too old"), or personal, controllable, and stable ("We're of different religions. It just wouldn't work out").

Folkes demonstrated that we use excuses strategically to avoid hurting the feelings of rejected parties. It is easier, gentler, and less hurtful when we say that we have to spend the weekend visiting our grandparents than to tell a person that he or she is old, weird, or inadequate.

Attribution theory seeks to explain the judgments that people make about the causes of behavior. Communicators withhold certain reasons for behaving and publicly communicate reasons in such a way as to maintain positive relationships with others and to reduce feelings of anger and rejection.

Other than dating, there are many situations involving the communication of bad news that prompts communicators to use excuses that locate the presumed cause of the bad news to external, uncontrollable, unstable, or unintentional reasons. These events include rejection letters from potential employees, cutbacks in work hours, and failing to get a promotion (see Bies & Sitkin, 1992). Although some employers locate the blame directly on the shoulders of the worker ("Your performance does not merit a promotion or an increase in pay"), other managers and supervisors communicate excuses that control the emotions of the recipients of bad news.

THE TRIANGLE MODEL OF RESPONSIBILITY

An *excuse* is defined as a tactic used by a communicator who admits a questionable action has taken (is taking) place, but denies to be fully responsible for it. There are thousands of excuses individuals can give, and one way to view types of excuses is to see how they operate to reduce our responsibility. Schlenker and his colleagues (Schlenker & Pontari, 2000; Schlenker, Pontari, & Christopher, 2001) argue that there are three components underlying the perception that someone is responsible. Excuses operate to reduce the association between our self and one or all of these three components. Based on this triangle model of responsibility (see Figure 8.1) we are perceived to be responsible for our actions due to prescription clarity, personal obligation, and personal control.

PRESCRIPTION CLARITY.   For many events, clear prescriptions or knowledge for how we should act exist in particular settings and in particular activities. We all should know how to behave while driving, when in a place of worship, on a blind date, at work, in class, and so on. *Prescription clarity* is a component of responsibility

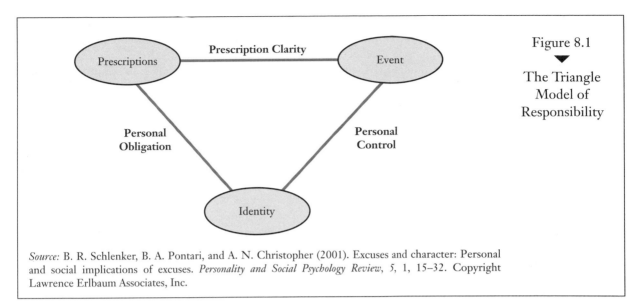

Figure 8.1
▼
The Triangle
Model of
Responsibility

Source: B. R. Schlenker, B. A. Pontari, and A. N. Christopher (2001). Excuses and character: Personal and social implications of excuses. *Personality and Social Psychology Review*, 5, 1, 15–32. Copyright Lawrence Erlbaum Associates, Inc.

that focuses on our ability to state clearly what our goals are and that we can describe accurately the procedures to achieve them. Thus, if a person wanted to have a successful blind date, he or she would possess the knowledge about being punctual, would know how to be appropriately dressed, would know what to say, not say, and what constitutes being amusing and funny, and so forth. Many blind dates don't work out well because one of the parties said, did, or wore something inappropriate. In working on group projects, successful groups, in our experience, spend time discussing how group members will work together so that each person's duties and due dates are clearly understood by all group members. Failure to do so means that a number of excuses can be offered about why individuals in the group are not responsible for performing duties, performing duties on time, or failing to coordinate with others. Similarly, professors who fail to make their work assignments clear and precise open the door to any number of excuses and delays.

Communicators can express a strong sense of responsibility by articulating a clear purpose and clear procedures for achieving the goals and expressing confidence in both the knowledge of prescriptions and ability to perform them adequately. On the other hand, an excuse maker can claim low levels of responsibility by claiming "The requirements were unclear," "The rules make no sense," "These instructions are confusing," and so forth. In our earlier examples (top panel in the box "Samples of Favorite Excuses Shared On-line"), excuse makers claim that they believed homework was optional, and did not know it was illegal to switch lanes in an intersection or to make a U-turn in a business district. In research on the definitions of sexual harassment, the authors found that many individuals point out they did not know the rules or prescriptions for what is or is not sexual harassment. (Today, however, nearly every organization includes a specific definition of sexual harassment in published handbooks,

232

and circulating a clear definition of harassment reduces the frequency of using the "I didn't know" type of excuse, as well as its credibility in organizations.) Excuses based on a lack of prescription clarity may have some credibility if there is collaborative evidence from others or documentation of ambiguity. Without collaboration that rules were unclear or ambiguous, the excuse maker who reduces responsibility based on the prescription clarity is likely to be perceived as confused, unknowledgeable, and oblivious as to how to behave and accomplish goals (Schlenker et al., 2001).

PERSONAL CONTROL.   An individual seeking to be perceived as responsible for an outcome (obtains a job, a good grade, a successful, satisfying date or relationship) is likely to communicate that she or he exerted personal control over events to cause or to help cause the event to occur. That is, the individual had the resources to achieve the desired goal and acted in ways to produce the desired outcome intentionally. When a person is successful in achieving a goal and is perceived as responsible for the achievement, we are likely to perceive the person as motivated and high in self-efficacy and persistence. On the other hand, excuses that lower perceptions of control (and lower perceptions of responsibility) claim that the individual lacked personal control because accidents happened, unforeseeable outcomes occurred, or unanticipated obstacles interfered with achieving the intended outcomes. In the authors' work in accounts, the lack of personal control represents one of the most common forms of excuses communicated by students and organizational workers.

Because an accident can, by its very nature, befall anyone, there is some chance that this excuse has credibility when used rarely. However, the excuse maker that uses this form of excuse runs the risk of being perceived as incompetent, unworthy, and possessing little or no self-efficacy.

PERSONAL OBLIGATION.   A person seeking to be perceived as responsible will claim that he or she knew the prescriptions (what to do) and claim that he or she personally and intentionally engaged in the necessary steps to bring about the desired outcome. An excuse maker who wants to claim that he or she is not obligated, and thus responsible, for an outcome will claim that "it wasn't my job," or "it was someone else's job." It is the instructor's responsibility, for example, to wake up the student sleeping in class if the professor is going to say something important (see the box "Samples of Favorite Excuses Shared On-line"). We laugh when Homer Simpson uses these excuses, but in reality people who use these excuses seem confused, purposeless, alienated, unreliable, lacking in initiative — a worker who needs to be monitored all of the time (Schlenker et al., 2001).

IMPRESSION MANAGEMENT

So far we have made a strong case for apologies and for excuses. Apologies — especially full ones, containing remorse, promises of restitution, and so forth — are useful in many contexts, no matter how blameworthy we are judged (Gonzales, Manning, & Haugen, 1992). Apologies are popular when we are engaged in accidents, intentional actions that turned out poorly, and especially for negligent actions (Gonzales et al., 1992). The beauty of apologies is that we accept responsibility for our actions and promise restitution or to do better next time. Angry feelings are reduced, and friendships maintained. The problem is that full apologies are more difficult for many individuals to communicate. Excuses are easier to communicate and can be credible if used rarely or in moderation and when receivers acknowledge that either our behavior may have been unintentional or events otherwise got out of control.

Justifications can also be credible and can provide benefits to the individual if delivered to the right target audience. In a justification, the speaker accepts responsibility for an action and communicates the message that the action in question should not be viewed as negative (and it may even be viewed as positive). Unfortunately, justifications are not as thoroughly studied as apologies or excuses. They are, clearly, assertive tactics used to communicate that the speaker behaves as an individual and accepts responsibility — that he or she knows the rules (prescriptions), can perform behaviors intentionally and purposefully, and is in sufficient control to bring about intended outcomes. Our research indicates that, in interpersonal communication, people use justifications when they change roles or relationships. For example, if a couple breaks up after dating for years, one of the pair may justify the action and try to convince others that the breakup was a good move, and that he or she has regained his or her identity, freedom, and so forth (see Chapter 11).

Impression management theorists (Schlenker, 1980; Schlenker & Weigold, 1992) emphasize that we need to take the values and beliefs of the audience into consideration when we offer accounts. Hale (1987) compared excuses ("I need an extension on the due date for the paper because I got behind in my work because of my busy schedule") with a "higher loyalty" form of a justification ("I need an extension because I got behind in my work when I was involved with job interviewing for the job I hope to get on graduation"). We like the student more when he or she is working toward a career, which is one of the reasons why students are enrolled in college in the first place. We may have sympathy for the excuse-giving student, but we don't think of him or her as dedicated, competent, or likable. However, the appeal to a higher loyalty is an academic/career-oriented one. We would think differently of the student who needed an extension because he or she was rehearsing with a rock and roll band, for example — the message being communicated would be that practicing music was more important than studies.

Braaten, Cody, and Bell-DeTiene (1993) also found that a higher loyalty justification promoted a person's public image at work if the higher loyalty incorporated the values and interests at work: "I am late in completing my daily work because I was busy helping one of our clients solve an emergency all morning." Such a justification is credible to other workers and promotes an image of the individual as competent, dedicated, and likable (although he or she did not complete his or her daily work). Note that a rival higher loyalty would not be as effective. The statement "I am late in completing my daily work because my child was sick and I had to take care of him this morning" may derive some sympathy, but it would not elicit the same strong image at work. The point is that justifications can also be useful for communicators, but the justification communicated has to resonate with the values and beliefs of the members of the audience.

Public Images

An A student with perfect attendance who wrote a wonderful paper, topped the grading curve on the midterm, and holds a major scholarship enters the professor's office and says: "You won't believe it, but when I cleaned off my desk last weekend, I accidentally threw away my list of references and notes concerning my second paper. The paper won't be ready on time."

A C student with a shoddy attendance record who turned in a poorly written paper (late), blaming a computer breakdown, and who had to make up a midterm because his car broke down on the day the test was scheduled enters the professor's office and says: "Sir, you won't believe it, but when I cleaned off my desk last weekend, I accidentally threw away my list of references and notes concerning my second paper. The paper won't be ready on time."

What is your impression of these two students? Who is more competent? Dedicated? Likable? Who is pathetic and helpless? Would you, as the professor, forgive each student equally? Would you lecture both of them on being more responsible? Would you penalize both papers for being late?

Two interrelated issues are important when we consider the relationship between accounts and impressions. The account a person uses has an impact on our impression of that person, and our impression of an accounter has an impact on the credibility of an account the next time that person communicates one. The most obvious illustration of this is when a series of mistakes befalls a person who always uses an excuse to deny personal responsibility: "I am late because my alarm didn't go off," "My car wouldn't start," "I can't stay because I misplaced my wallet and have to go find it or go to the lost and found," and so on. As noted earlier, an excuse that appeals to an accident or to low personal control may be accepted once or occasionally by others, because an appeal to accident can happen to anyone. However, it is unusual and suspicious if a series of mistakes and errors occurs over time and the person involved persists in blaming fate, accidents, or others. Ultimately we tell such communicators to take responsibility for their lives, to plan ahead and budget their time: Buy a new alarm clock, leave for work earlier, don't wait until the last minute to cram for the test, and so forth. Though some events occur without warning and cannot be controlled by anyone, hundreds of questionable acts occur every day that could have been prevented or avoided by planning ahead.

Communicators who rely too heavily on excuses will ultimately be perceived as incompetent, helpless, and irresponsible. Indeed, we coined the expression "the **accounter's dilemma**" to apply to the choice — using excuses means we can go through life denying personal responsibility for mistakes, but doing so means that we admit that we have little to no control over our immediate social and physical world.

On one hand, we can be forgiven by others because we were not responsible; but we pay the price by being perceived as incompetent, ineffective, and unreliable.

By contrast, justifiers are perceived as more competent than excuse-givers. When we use a justification, we are admitting responsibility for an action but claiming that the action wasn't actually negative (or that the consequences were positive). As justifiers, then, we argue that we know what we are doing; that we are responsible, not helpless; and that we are competently working on certain goals. Although it is true that our goals may be different from those of the person asking for an account and that we may have a conflict over goals, as justifiers we are nonetheless still responsible and competent at pursuing our particular goals (even if they involve questionable behaviors).

One study that examined the impressions we make of different types of accounters had students read a scenario in which a new employee fails to do a computer check on financial records at the close of the workday. The former supervisor, who had been training the new employee, notices this error and asks why the "standard error detection" runs have not been done. The students then read one of nine versions of accounts:

Apologies

Full-blown apology: "Yes, I know I made an error. I'm terribly sorry about this. I'm solving it right now before I go home. I'll be more careful in the future!"

Perfunctory apology: "Yes, I know I made an error. I'm sorry."

Excuses

Appeal to accident: "The computer was down nearly all day. I couldn't finish the work today."

Denial of intent: "I didn't intend to be sloppy. I have been suffer- with this stomach flu that has been going around. It is slowing me down and making me groggy."

Justifications

Minimizing harm: "Yes, there was an error. I was using some new software that presumably will do a faster job than our old software. It was faster, but obviously made at least one error."

Higher loyalty or involvement: "One of our major clients called in today with a crisis, and I spent well over an hour trying to trace down the paper trail to resolve it. Given my limited time, I decided it was more important to handle the emergency than to run the standard tests on schedule."

Refusals

Denial of offense:	"No, you must have some other day-end statement, or perhaps you are reading it wrong. There is no error in my accounts for today."
Challenge to authority:	"You are no longer my supervisor and no longer associated with this unit. I do not have to explain myself to you. I handle things here now."
Logical proof:	"Yes, I saw that statement. I ran the checks. As you can tell from these printouts, the error does not originate from this office."

Students then rated their impressions of the accounter along the lines of the five self-presentational styles discussed in Chapter 6.

A person who communicated a full-blown apology was rated as likable, dedicated, competent, and low on intimidation. The accounter who relied on a mere perfunctory apology, however, was rated as incompetent, helpless, weak (lowest in intimidation), but still likable. Accounters who relied on excuses were perceived as helpless and incompetent and were generally undistinguished on other perceptions. Accounters who relied on justifications were perceived as highly dedicated and competent and were rated low in intimidation and supplication — they were seen as neither ruthless nor helpless. Further, the higher loyalty message was especially effective; accounters who used it were perceived as highly likable, as well as highly dedicated and competent.

Accounters who challenged the authority of others were perceived as intimidating, unlikable, and lacking in dedication, as were accounters who denied their offense. Although most people might view such tactics negatively, we should recognize that intimidators are probably not interested in resolving conflicts or in repairing relationships. Intimidators use these tactics to take control of their work area and to show off to others who possess authority and power. Logical proofs, however, operated much differently: People who proved their innocence by displaying physical evidence were perceived as dedicated and competent.

Earlier we had concluded that apologies and excuses were effective in repairing relationships when people communicated accounts for a single act (failing to pick up a friend for a concert). An accounter who focused on creating a public image of dedication and competence, however, should not rely on excuses. Rather, the perceptions of dedication and competence are best created and maintained when accounters employ full-blown apologies, justifications, and logical proofs.

Research has also examined accounts that people communicate when accused of harassing others (of being too friendly, unwanted flirting, asking a person out on a date, etc.) (Dunn & Cody, 2000). If these behaviors create a hostile work environment, the repercussions can be serious. For such offenses, men who used excuses ("Boys will be boys," "I did not intend for that to happen") were rated low in likability, competence, and dedication; and observers had a lot of sympathy for the victim. People who accepted responsibility for their actions, promised to change, apologized, and claimed they had misread the situation ("I thought she liked me and was flirting. Since I misread the cues, I accept responsibility and I'll correct the mistake") were rated as dedicated, competent, and more likable than other males. Finally, if the male denied the accusation and claimed the woman was lying and filing a false report, the public image of both the accuser and defender is tarnished (low in liking, dedication, and competence) because observers must now seek out more information and investigate blame and responsibility. What you should remember from this section of the chapter is that in many situations involving serious outcomes, accepting responsibility (justifications) results in more positive outcomes than offering excuses. Justifications are credible when a speaker communicates intentions and behaviors that are valued by audience members — such as solving the problem, performing well on the job, and so forth.

A CASE STUDY: TRAFFIC COURT

We often have to communicate accounts to bureaucrats, and apologies and excuses may not be the most effective tactics in these more formal contexts. A study conducted in traffic court demonstrated this nicely. Cody and McLaughlin (1988) studied the accounts that 375 drivers communicated in traffic court. Seventy-four of the drivers appeared in court and used concessions — admissions of guilt with or without apologies. In this particular setting, using an apology for engaging in a moving violation (speeding, running a red light) carried no weight. A full 97% of the drivers who used concessions or apologies were simply penalized and asked to pay the whole fine. Did any drivers find this type of account helpful? Yes. Of the 74 drivers who used concessions, 19 asked for an alternative and cost-free punishment, attendance at traffic school. They were allowed to attend traffic school if they were apologetic, were guilty of relatively minor offenses, and had good driving records.

Excuses were the most popular type of argument made in traffic court — over a third of the drivers used one. However, only 25% of the excuse-givers were actually effective in avoiding penalties or in getting penalties reduced. Why? Because the judge reduces the fine and may do so only in certain circumstances. Different types of excuses varied widely in their effectiveness.

The least effective form of an excuse was scapegoating: "I had to drive on the shoulder of the freeway because other drivers wouldn't let me merge in." More than 80% of the drivers who tried to make "other drivers" the scapegoat for their offense were fully penalized. A second ineffective form of excuse was a lack of knowledge: "I didn't know that it was illegal to make a U-turn in *any* business district in town. I thought 'No U-Turn' signs had to be posted." Approximately 80% of the lack-of-knowledge drivers also were penalized fully. A third ineffective excuse was the impairment or illness claim that the driver's vision was impaired, the driver became ill, the road condition or lack of lighting impaired vision, or the like. Ultimately 70% of these drivers were penalized in full.

Only one type of excuse was helpful, a hybrid of apology plus denial of intent:

Your Honor, I'm really sorry that this had to occur. I didn't intend to do anything wrong. I picked up the kids from school and left through the back alley. The kids were screaming and singing because we

(Continued)

(Box continued from previous page)

were going Christmas shopping. I sped up and then the officer pulled me over even before I saw the flashing lights [at the school zone, indicating a reduction in speed when children are getting out of school]. I drive on this street every day, and usually there is no reduction in speed at noon, but this day was different because school was being let out early.

Only 30% of the drivers using such a combined argument were asked to pay the full penalty, but few relied on this approach.

Justifications were rarely used in traffic court (only 45 of the 375 drivers resorted to them). Why? It simply is not a good tactic to argue that the driver has "good reason" to violate the law:

Your Honor, it is true that I went through the light when it was yellow and it turned red. But there was good reason. It was raining, the streets were wet, and the driver behind me was tailgating me. I thought that if I slammed on my brakes, I would have been rear-ended. I thought it was safer simply to go through the intersection.

That is not an effective argument. Nor is this one: "I left my curling iron on and was hurrying home so that the house wouldn't burn down." Over 90% of the drivers who relied on justifications were penalized fully for their offenses.

There were three types of refusals or denials. Some drivers challenged the authority of the officer by questioning competence or integrity: "I am a good taxpaying citizen, and I should not be getting a ticket in this *speed trap!*" "I might have been going sixty, but I was not going anything like seventy. I think the officer added those extra miles on just to make me more upset." Over 90% of the drivers who used this type of account were penalized in full.

A second type of refusal or denial was denying the offense. Drivers usually recounted their story about what happened and accepted responsibility for what happened but claimed that what actually took place was not really an offense. For example, they might claim that the light had not yet turned red when they went through it or that they had, in their opinion, come to a complete stop. Over 80% of these drivers were penalized fully.

The only form of refusal or denial that was effective was logical proof. Drivers provided photographs of the scene to support the claim that the view of the stop sign was blocked, work orders from the city office to indicate that a curb had not been painted in years, or a sheaf of complaints about the site filed by other people. Certain drivers presented convincing logical arguments; for example, one driver had been ticketed for speeding in a residential area, but he was not ticketed for failing to stop at the stop signs on each corner. He claimed that he could not have accelerated to 45 miles per hour in his Volkswagen minivan in one city block and yet have come to a complete stop. Only 25% of the drivers who attempted the logical proof claim were fined. However, not many drivers relied on this strategy.

Logical proof arguments were effective because they successfully raised a question of reasonable doubt about the driver's guilt. Apology plus denial of intent arguments were effective because the driver displayed remorse and made a credible claim concerning unintentional causes for the violation. However, simple apologies, most excuses, most refusals or denials, and all justifications were ineffective.

A NOTE ON FORGIVENESS

We emphasize in this chapter ways in which communicators defend the self. In many of these situations, communicators offer excuses and apologies in the hopes that their image and the relationship will continue on without interruption. For serious offenses and perceived persistent injustice, however, an effective account has to increase empathy from others (Davidson & Friedman, 1998; Kelley, 1998; McCullough et al., 1998; McCullough, Worthington, & Rachal, 1997). In work on interpersonal forgiveness, for example, McCullough and his colleagues found that actually forgiving others in interpersonal relationships involved two parallel processes. The first sequence involved the level of intimacy in the relationship, the communication of a full apology, empathy, avoidance, and revenge. High levels of intimacy increased the likelihood that a full apology would be communicated, and both intimacy and the communication of an apology increased the chance that the relational partner would have empathy (emotional identification, compassion, understanding) for the one communicating the apology. Empathizing with the partner was highly and negatively correlated with revenge and avoidance. This is extremely important, because there is a natural tendency to seek revenge on and to avoid a person who hurt our feelings. Empathy for the relational partner and continuing to see him or her (that is, not purposefully avoiding them) is related to maintaining closeness (i.e., forgiving them). The second sequence involved closeness, rumination, revenge, and avoidance. When a close intimate friend hurts our feelings, there is an increased chance of ruminating (thinking about, imagining, having thoughts about them intrude on our consciousness), which is related to increased thoughts of seeking revenge. Increased thoughts of seeking revenge increase the chance that a person will actively avoid the partner, which results in a decrease in returning to intimacy. Although there are variations on the process of forgiveness (see Kelley, 1998), what is important is that an apology initiates a sequence of actions (empathy, avoidance of revenge, avoidance of purposefully avoiding others) that increase the chance that we will be forgiven.

CHAPTER SUMMARY

Verbal messages, called accounts, can be used to repair interpersonal relationships, cope with embarrassment, create public impressions, and assuage bureaucrats. We are often motivated to behave in a polite manner and protect ourselves and others from threats to positive and negative face. We also rely on attribution theory to control emotions and the potential hurt feelings of others. Finally, our public image is influenced by the type of account we communicate.

Generally speaking, a full-blown apology produces more overall positive consequences, resolves interpersonal disputes as well as problems in embarrassing situations (along with humor), and creates an image of competence, dedication, and likability. Excuses are also effective in repairing relationships but are linked to lower ratings of competence. Justifications are not as effective as apologies and excuses in improving interpersonal situations, but they are effective in promoting an image of competence, dedication, and, to a lesser degree, likability (much as logical proof accounts do). At the other extreme are refusals that deny the offense or challenge authority. These do not help mend interpersonal relationships or interactions, but they do give rise to perceptions of strength and power (the intimidation style of self-presentation). Apologies can initiate forgiveness in interpersonal relationships by eliciting empathy from others.

KEY TERMS

account, p. 207
accounter's dilemma, p. 234
apology, p. 216
attribution theory, p. 225
concession, p. 210
excuse, p. 208

face, p. 214
facework, p. 215
impression management, p. 233
justification, p. 208
refusal, p. 213

EXERCISES FOR FURTHER DISCUSSION

1. Think about a situation in which the excuse you gave for some action or behavior may have been less than honest. Write a short paragraph explaining why you gave the excuse that you did.
   a. What ethical principles do you think guided your choice about whether or not to tell the complete truth?
   b. Do you think that it is acceptable to use excuses that are somewhat dishonest with a parent? With a boyfriend or girlfriend? With a manager or employer? With someone you are trying to avoid?
   c. If you see a difference between these situations, what principles would you say guide your behavior?
2. Analyze your success or failure at providing accounts to your teachers or to an authority figure at work. Think of some situations in which you were successful and some in which you were not.
   a. In the situations in which you were successful, why were you successful?
   b. In the situations in which you were unsuccessful, what do you think you could have done differently?

   c. How important is it to you that authority figures (teachers or managers) have a good impression of you?

   d. Do you think that your authority figures react better to excuses or to justifications?

3. Almost every day in the newspaper, we see some types of accounts. For example, coaches and players use accounts to explain why they lost a game, and politicians use accounts to explain why crime, inflation, or unemployment is increasing. Go through a newspaper and write down as many accounts as you can find, identifying each according to the types presented in this chapter.

   a. How many of each type of account did you find?

   b. Which accounts did you find most convincing or believable?

   c. Which accounts did you find least convincing or believable?

4. The following list asks you to think about a variety of situations in which you and a friend would need to offer accounts. Working with a good friend or classmate, read each item, and write down the account you would use. When you are done, answer the questions that follow.

   a. You and a friend want to skip a wedding and wedding reception to do something that you would both find more enjoyable. You need to offer an account to the groom, who is an acquaintance from work.

   b. You and a friend want to skip a dinner dance hosted by an organization you belong to (for example, your fraternity or sorority) in order to do something that you would find more enjoyable. You need to offer an account to the chairperson of the Social Committee.

   c. You want to cancel a trip home that you planned for the end of the month. You had planned to take a new friend home to be introduced to your parents, but that person would rather put the meeting off for a while. You need to offer an account to your parents.

   d. You have made plans to spend the holidays skiing with a friend, but members of your family have called to ask when they can expect you to come home. You need to offer an account for why you are not coming home.

   e. You and a friend are asked to dinner by a friend whom you like but who is notoriously opinionated and overbearing. You need to provide an account for why the two of you are not able to come to dinner.

     1. Did the two of you give similar accounts?

     2. If there were differences in the types of accounts you gave, discuss your reasons for giving the different types of accounts, and try to decide which account would be more successful.

     3. What problems could you envision if you each provided different accounts to the same people?

     4. How important do you think it is that people who do things together have a common understanding of the types of accounts to use in different situations?

SUGGESTED READING

▼

ACCOUNTS

McLaughlin, M. L., Cody, M. J., & Read, S. J. (Eds.). (1992). *Explaining the self to others: Reason-giving in a social context.* Hillsdale, NJ: Erlbaum. This volume contains chapters devoted to how accounts, or, more generally, explanations, are used to pursue specific communicative functions. Special attention is given to (a) the psychological underpinnings of creating and communicating social explanations to various audience members and (b) the role of accounts in managing, or escalating, conflict in interpersonal, legal, and managerial settings.

Schönbach, P. (1990). *Account episodes.* Cambridge, England: Cambridge University Press. This book devotes considerable attention to an extensive typology of accounts and emphasizes the importance of reproaches in the communication of accounts and their evaluations. Reproaches are used by individuals when they ask for an account (e.g., "Son, why did you leave the car lights on all night?"), and Schönbach demonstrates that severely or harshly phrased accounts cause account-makers to behave defensively — communicating fewer apologies and excuses and communicating more justifications and refusals.

Snyder, C. R., Higgins, R. L., & Stucky, R. J. (1983). *Excuses: Masquerades in search of grace.* New York: Wiley/Interscience. This volume focuses attention on how the excuse operates to protect the self from being viewed negatively.

ACCOUNTS IN MANAGER-WORKER RELATIONSHIPS

Bies, R. J., & Sitkin, S. B. (1992). Explanation as legitimization: Excuse-making in organizations. In M. L. McLaughlin, M. J. Cody, & S. J. Read, *Explaining the self to others: Reason-giving in a social context* (pp. 183–198). Hillsdale, NJ: Erlbaum. Bies and Sitkin offer an extensive overview of how corporations and managers use accounts to resolve disputes and/or differences in perceptions. Of particular interest is how managers communicate accounts when communicating negative information to employees, concerning a decline to hire or promote, a decision to freeze budgets, and the like.

Braaten, D. O., Cody, M. J., and Bell-DeTiene, K. (1993). Account episodes in organizations: Remedial work and impression management. *Management Communication Quarterly, 6,* 219–250. Two studies are reviewed: one demonstrating the importance of using apologies and excuses in smoothing over interpersonal disputes on the job, the second assessing how hearers perceive communicators who employ different types of accounts.

ACCOUNTS AND EMBARRASSMENT

Cupach, W. R., & Metts, S. (1990). Remedial processes in embarrassing predicaments. In J. A. Anderson (Ed.), *Communication yearbook 13* (pp. 323–352). Newbury

Park, CA: Sage. Cupach and Metts thoroughly review the research on embarrassment, including what communicators say and do when they are embarrassed and what tactics are best for coping effectively with embarrassment.

REFERENCE LIST

▼

Bennett, M., & Earwaker, D. (1994). Victims' responses to apologies: The effects of offender responsibility and offense severity. *Journal of Social Psychology, 134,* 457–464.

Bies, R. J., & Sitkin, S. B. (1992). Explanation as legitimization: Excuse-making in organizations. In M. L. McLaughlin, M. J. Cody, & S. J. Read (Eds.), *Explaining the self to others: Reason-giving in a social context* (pp. 183–198). Hillsdale, NJ: Erlbaum.

Braaten, D. O., Cody, M. J., & Bell-DeTiene, K. (1993). Account episodes in organizations: Remedial work and impression management. *Management Communication Quarterly, 6,* 219–250.

Brown, P., & Levinson, S. C. (1978). Universals in language usage: Politeness phenomena. In E. N. Goody (Ed.), *Questions and politeness: Strategies in social interaction* (pp. 118–119). Cambridge, England: Cambridge University Press.

Brown, P., & Levinson, S. C. (1987). *Politeness: Some universals in language use.* Cambridge, England: Cambridge University Press.

Cashion, J. L., Cody, M. J., & Erickson, K. V. (1987). "You'll love this one . . ." An exploration into joke-prefacing devices. *Journal of Language and Social Psychology, 5,* 303–312.

Cody, M. J., & McLaughlin, M. L. (1988). Accounts on trial: Oral arguments in traffic court. In C. Antaki (Ed.), *Analyzing everyday explanation: A casebook of methods* (pp. 113–126). London: Sage.

Cody, M. J., & McLaughlin, M. L. (1990). Interpersonal accounting. In H. Giles & P. Robinson (Eds.), *Handbook of language and social psychology* (pp. 227–255). London: Wiley.

Cupach, W. R., & Metts, S. (1990). Remedial processes in embarrassing predicaments. In J. A. Anderson (Ed.), *Communication yearbook 13* (pp. 323–352). Newbury Park, CA: Sage.

Cupach, W. R., & Metts, S. (1994). *Facework.* Newbury Park, CA: Sage.

Darby, B. W., & Schlenker, B. R. (1982). Children's reactions to apologies. *Journal of Personality and Social Psychology, 43,* 742–753.

Davidson, M., & Friedman, R. A. (1998). When excuses don't work: The persistent injustice effect among Black managers. *Administrative Science Quarterly, 43,* 154–183.

Dunn, D., & Cody, M. J. (2000). Account credibility and public image: Excuses, justifications, denials, and sexual harassment. *Communication Monographs, 67,* 372–391.

Edelmann, R. J. (1994). Embarrassment and blushing: Factors influencing face-saving strategies. In S. Ting-Toomey (Ed.), *The challenge of facework* (pp. 231–268). Albany: State University of New York Press.

Folkes, V. S. (1982). Communicating the causes of social rejection. *Journal of Experimental Social Psychology, 18,* 235–252.

Goffman, E. (1967). *Interaction ritual: Essays on face-to-face behavior.* New York: Pantheon.

Gonzales, M. H., Manning, D. J., & Haugen, J. A. (1992). Explaining our sins: Factors influencing offender accounts and anticipated victim responses. *Journal of Personality and Social Psychology, 62*, 958–971.

Hale, C. (1987). A comparison of accounts: When is failure not a failure? *Journal of Language and Social Psychology, 6*, 117–132.

Hamilton, V. L., & Hagiwara, S. (1992). Roles, responsibility, and accounts across cultures. *International Journal of Psychology, 27*, 157–179.

Hewitt, J. P., & Stokes, R. (1975). Disclaimers. *American Sociological Review, 40*, 1–11.

Holmes, J. (1990). Apologies in New Zealand English. *Language in Society, 19*, 155–199.

Holmes, J. (1995). *Women, men and politeness*. London: Longman.

Holtgraves, T. (1989). The form and function of remedial moves: Reported use, psychological reality, and perceived effectiveness. *Journal of Language and Social Psychology, 8*, 1–16.

Holtgraves, T. (1997). Yes, but . . . Positive politeness in conversation arguments. *Journal of Language and Social Psychology, 16*, 222–239.

Ide, R. (1998). 'Sorry for your kindness': Japanese interactional ritual in public discourse. *Journal of Pragmatics, 29*, 509–529.

Itoi, R., Ohbuchi, K. I., & Fukuno, M. (1996). A cross-cultural study of preference of accounts: Relationship closeness, harm severity, and motives of account making. *Journal of Applied Social Psychology, 26*, 913–934.

Kelley, D. (1998). The communication of forgiveness. *Communication Studies, 49*, 255–271.

Kelley, H. (1973). The processes of causal attribution. *American Psychologist, 28*, 107–128.

Lim, T., & Bowers, J. W. (1991). Facework: Solidarity, approbation, and tact. *Human Communication Research, 17*, 415–450.

Manusov, V., Cody, M. J., Donohue, W., & Zappa, J. (1994). Accounts in child custody mediation sessions. *Journal of Applied Communication, 22*, 1–15.

McCullough, M. E., Rachal, K. C., Sandage, S. J., Worthington, E. L., Brown, S. W., & Hight, T. L. (1998). Interpersonal forgiving in close relationships: II. Theoretical elaboration and measurement. *Journal of Personality and Social Psychology, 75*, 1586–1603.

McCullough, M. E., Worthington, E. L., & Rachal, K. C. (1997). Interpersonal forgiving in close relationships. *Journal of Personality and Social Psychology, 73*, 321–336.

Metts, S., & Cupach, W. R. (1989). Situational influence on the use of remedial strategies in embarrassing predicaments. *Communication Monographs, 56*, 151–162.

Mongeau, P. A., Hale, J. L., & Alles, M. (1994). An experimental investigation of accounts and attributions following sexual infidelity. *Communication Monographs, 61*, 326–344.

Ohbuchi, K., & Sato, K. (1994). Children's reactions to mitigating accounts: Apologies, excuses, and intentionality of harm. *Journal of Social Psychology, 134*, 5–17.

Schlenker, B. R. (1980). *Impression management*. Pacific Grove, CA: Brooks/Cole.

Schlenker, B. R., & Darby, B. W. (1981). The use of apologies in social predicaments. *Social Psychology Quarterly, 44*, 271–278.

Schlenker, B. R., & Pontari, B. A. (2000). The strategic control of information: Impression management and self-presentation in daily life. In A. Tesser, R. Felson, & J. Suls (Eds.), *Perspectives on self and identity* (pp. 199–232). Washington, DC: American Psychological Association.

Schlenker, B. R., Pontari, B. A., & Christopher, A. N. (2001). Excuses and character: Personal and social implications of excuses. *Personality and Social Psychology Review, 5*, 15–32.

Schlenker, B. R., & Weigold, M. F. (1992). Interpersonal processes involving impression regulation and management. *Annual Review of Psychology, 43*, 133–168.

Schönbach, P. (1980). A category system for account phases. *European Journal of Social Psychology, 10*, 195–200.

Schönbach, P. (1990). *Account episodes.* Cambridge, England: Cambridge University Press.

Scott, M. B., & Lyman, S. M. (1968). Accounts. *American Sociological Review, 33*, 46–62.

Snyder, C. R., & Higgins, R. L. (1990). Reality negotiation and excuse-making: President Reagan's March 4, 1987, Iran arms speech and other literature. In M. J. Cody & M. L. McLaughlin (Eds.), *The psychology of tactical communication* (pp. 207–228). Clevedon, England: Multilingual Matters.

Sugimoto, N. (1997). A Japan-U.S. comparison of apology styles. *Communication Research, 24*, 349–369.

Sugimoto, N. (1998). Norms of apology depicted in U.S. American and Japanese literature on manners and etiquette. *International Journal of Intercultural Relations, 22*, 251–276.

Takaku, S., Weiner, B., & Ohbuchi, K. I. (2001). A cross-cultural examination of the effects of apology and perspective taking on forgiveness. *Journal of Language and Social Psychology, 20*, 144–166.

Tata, J. (2000). Implicit theories of account-giving: Influence of culture and gender. *International Journal of Intercultural Relations, 24*, 437–454.

Ting-Toomey, S. (Ed.). (1994). *The challenge of facework.* Albany: State University of New York Press.

Weiner, B. (1986). *An attribution theory of motivation and emotion.* New York: Springer-Verlag.

Weiner, B. (1992). Excuses in everyday interaction. In M. L. McLaughlin, M. J. Cody, & S. J. Read (Eds.), *Explaining one's self to others: Reason-giving in a social context* (pp. 131–146). Hillsdale, NJ: Erlbaum.

Weiner, B., Amirkhan, J., Folkes, V. S., & Verette, J. A. (1987). An attributional analysis of excuse giving: Studies of a naive theory of emotion. *Journal of Personality and Social Psychology, 52*, 316–324.

P A R T I I I

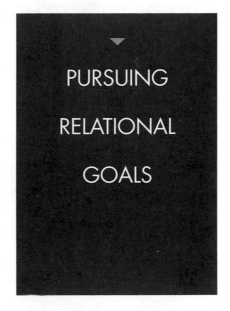

PURSUING RELATIONAL GOALS

In Part III, we take a closer look at relational goals, specifically how people escalate, maintain, and de-escalate their personal relationships. Chapter 9 discusses relational escalation: the advantages and disadvantages of involvement, the emotional processes of attraction and intimacy, and some current research on relational escalation — including a word about love. Chapter 10 centers on relational maintenance: the reasons why people choose to maintain relationships, the strategies they use, and the different forms that long-term relationships can take. Chapter 11 discusses why and how relationships end or de-escalate. We look at the four phases of disengagement, the communicative methods people use to break up, and the emotional consequences of ending a relationship.

C H A P T E R   9

ESCALATING

RELATIONSHIPS

FEATURES OF RELATIONAL ESCALATION

Advantages of Escalating Relationships

Disadvantages of Escalating Relationships

INTERPERSONAL ATTRACTION:
THE CATALYST OF ESCALATION

Anthropological Class: Physical Beauty

Reinforcement Class: Supportiveness

Cognitive Class: Attitude Similarity

Structural Class: Communication Behaviors

INCREASING INTIMACY DURING
INTERACTION

Behaviors That Communicate Liking and
   Intimacy

Courtship and Quasi-Courtship Behaviors

Cognitive Valence Theory

RELATIONAL DEVELOPMENT PROCESSES

Social Penetration Revisited

Developing Relationships On-Line

Stages of Relational Escalation

Research on Relational Escalation

Turning Points

CHAPTER SUMMARY

Tracy worked part time at a video store, supporting herself while she finished her B.A. It was ironic that she worked in a video store because she was an English literature major who did not spend much time watching videos at home. Occasionally she would recognize people from school — fellow students, teachers, and others — and they would recognize her. Tracy took good care of herself, was very helpful to customers, and had a very pleasant voice. Men were attracted to her.

One was Brad, a graduate student. Although he never went out of his way to talk with Tracy, Brad showed interest. He would compliment her on her appearance, ask how her day had gone, and be attentive to her responses. Tracy was also attracted to Brad, so she smiled and asked him about his interests. When she discovered that Brad didn't have a girlfriend, Tracy hinted that she was available for a date.

FEATURES OF RELATIONAL ESCALATION

What does it mean to escalate a relationship? Most people would point to increases in intimacy. Perlman and Fehr (1987) summarized seven qualities of intimate relationships:

1. Interaction increases in terms of frequency, duration, and number of social contacts.

2. Partners gain knowledge of one another's innermost levels of being. Topics for discussion and level of personalness of topics increase, and partners develop personal communication modes (or idiosyncratic messages).

3. Partners become more skilled at tracing and predicting each other's behavior.

4. Partners increase their own investments (time, money, emotional energies, etc.) in the relationship.

5. Interdependence and a sense of "we-ness" increase.

6. Partners feel that their separate interests are linked to the well-being of the relationship.

7. Positive affect (warmth, liking, loving, etc.) and sense of caring, commitment, and trust increase.

From this list and other research (e.g., Burgoon & Hale, 1984; Kelley, 1979; Morton, Alexander, & Altman, 1976; Prager, 1995), we can make four general observations. First, escalation of relationships means the successful "negotiation" of both intimacy and control. Not only do partners learn more about each other cognitively and emotionally, but they must also learn how to respond to each other behaviorally by coordinating actions and activities. Second, relational escalation moves partners from social relationships to personal involvements. Broadly speaking, social relationships are role relationships in which participants can be replaced by other people; personal relationships are unique insofar as you cannot replace the other person yet have the relationship continue (Duck et al., 1984). Third, cross-cultural comparisons regarding escalating relationships and the value of intimacy indicate, for example, that North Americans might emphasize companionship needs when seeking out friends and lovers, whereas Japanese might emphasize the instrumental resources of the other person (e.g., Kamo, 1993). So, the findings we present are largely informed by relationships surveyed in the United States and may only be applied to other cultures with great care. Finally, it is impossible to discuss relational initiation and escalation without discussing communication behavior. Communication is the primary instrument used for relational initiation and escalation.

Advantages of Escalating Relationships

Five advantages of escalating relationships can be located in the research. One advantage is that intimacy positively affects an individual's personal welfare (Prager & Buhrmester, 1998). Psychologists have identified two areas of personal welfare: communal and agentic. Communal welfare needs concern sexual satisfaction, affection, feeling part of another person, nurturance, and companionship. Agentic welfare needs include self-esteem, positive identity, self-actualization, purpose in life, and so forth (Prager & Buhrmester, 1998). Prager and Buhrmester specifically tested the extent to which relational intimacy associates with communal and agentic welfare and found that intimacy was positively related to the communal needs of both men and women, and to the agentic needs of women.

A second advantage of escalating a relationship is that an individual becomes more interdependent with the other person as the relationship matures, and this helps the individual achieve desired personal outcomes (Kelley, 1979). That is, the closer you become to someone, the more you affect each other's goals. Making dinner while your friend helps you type a paper, pooling money for a long road trip, and borrowing each other's clothes are examples of achieving personal goals together.

A third advantage is the satisfaction of particular interpersonal needs. Schutz (1966) identifies three fundamental interpersonal needs: *inclusion*, *control*, and *affection*. According to Schutz, you need to include others as part of your world or to be included. Once the inclusion need is met, you may have a need to direct others or to be directed. Finally, you may have a need to express or receive affection. Relational escalation involves meeting these particular needs. This translates into greater efforts to share such interests as art, seasonal activities, and music (inclusion); to coordinate such issues as how to get to school, where to look for a job, and how much money to save (control); and to extend such personal expressions as hugs, birthday cards, and compliments (affection).

A fourth advantage to escalating relationships is achieving an understanding of your partner, whether that person is a friend, relative, or lover. Miller and Steinberg (1975) argue that a truly interpersonal relationship is based on unique knowledge of the other person. Andersen (1989) observes that "interpersonal relationships are characterized by relational uniqueness and a psychological understanding of one's relational partner rather than stereotyping and purely functional orientation toward the other" (p. 5). In short, knowing another person is an important outcome of relational escalation, one that most people view as positive.

The last advantage is that relational escalation helps reduce uncertainty about the other person (Berger & Calabrese, 1975). Berger and Calabrese posit that uncertainty is generally an anxious experience and that information about another person helps reduce uncertainty. Such information is obtained by interacting with the individual as well as by observing the other person in various social settings. Over time, this store of information helps reduce uncertainty about the person and the relationship (Miell & Duck, 1986).

Disadvantages of Escalating Relationships

Five disadvantages of pursuing closer involvements with others have been presented by Hatfield (1984). First, you may be personally exposed. Your private feelings and dreams might be revealed, and many of these may be very personal or painful, which makes you vulnerable. Second, you may be abandoned. Many of us have experienced the heartache of losing someone we loved and trusted. For many people, the fear of abandonment is reason enough for not seeking new relationships. Third, you may fear angry attacks by your partner. In close relationships, people can be more malicious and hurtful than in social relationships. Knowing another intimately also means knowing how to hurt that person. Fourth, you may lose control over the situation. It is often easier to control your life alone. It is especially easier to control yourself when emotions are not rampaging through your thoughts. Finally, you may fear your own destructive impulses. Some people believe that they cannot make a commitment to someone, so they hold people at a safe distance to protect them. Others know that they have a quick temper, a jealous mind, or abusive tendencies. Because these destructive impulses could harm others, people may choose to keep others at a distance.

In addition to the general disadvantages, it is clear that not all people want to escalate relationships. For instance, people with fearful or dismissing attachment styles who have a negative expectation of relationships do not seek to develop relationships as readily as people with secure or preoccupied attachment styles (Bartholomew, 1993; Guerrero, 1996). More will be said about attachment styles when we discuss individual differences and personality factors in Chapter 15. Also, gay and lesbian (versus heterosexual) individuals appear to suffer more from loneliness as a result of fearing intimacy, in part because lesbians and gay males find more satisfaction of their intimacy needs with romantic partners and friends than with relatives (versus heterosexuals who can more readily rely on parents and siblings for relational closeness; see Greenfield & Thelen, 1997).

Still, people often are willing to take the risks involved in escalating relationships with acquaintances, friendships, co-workers, and romantic partners due to the potential rewards these involvements offer. Accordingly, this chapter explores the paths of relational escalation, from the early stages of attraction to later stages involving commitment and intimacy.

INTERPERSONAL ATTRACTION: THE CATALYST OF ESCALATION

Interpersonal attraction refers to the various forces that draw people together. As Huston (1974) notes, attraction involves emotional responses toward another person, as well as beliefs, evaluations, and behaviors regarding that person. In other words, a variety of forces draw people together, and attraction evokes different responses.

Research has uncovered various dimensions of interpersonal attraction. Mc-Croskey and McCain (1974) report three dimensions: *social, task,* and *physical.* A person can be socially adept, good at doing a particular job, and/or physically beautiful. Berger, Weber, Munley, and Dixon (1977) offer a different set of dimensions: *supportiveness, character,* and *sociability.* Supportiveness is reflected in the extent to which someone understands you, likes you, and is interested in your welfare; character refers to how sincere, dependable, and ethical that person is; and sociability concerns how outgoing, popular, and pleasant that person is. Berger and colleagues found that these dimensions changed in importance across relationships. For example, close friends and lovers rated supportiveness as more important than acquaintances did. The Berger study reveals that the bases for attraction vary across relationships and that these bases may actually shift in importance as a particular relationship develops.

Clatterbuck (1980) provides an effective scheme for organizing the research on interpersonal attraction. He separates the attraction research into four classes: *anthropological, reinforcement, cognitive,* and *structural.* The anthropological class includes studies that have examined attraction on a social level, for example, the relationship between physical beauty and liking. The reinforcement class refers to studies of interpersonal attraction as a learned response to reinforcements (see Byrne, 1971). The cognitive class concerns how people's similarities in cognitions lead to liking. The structural class refers to how people structure their communication in order to be seen as attractive. Although it is impossible to review all of the research regarding interpersonal attraction, let us look at some of the most important findings in each of the four classes referenced by Clatterbuck.

Anthropological Class: Physical Beauty

When we hear the term *attractive*, most of us think of physical beauty. And research reveals that a person's physical appearance can dramatically affect our response to that person. Bull and Rumsey (1988) document several correlates of physical beauty. These include favorable attributions about the person, such as kindness, warmth, intelligence, and honesty; sexual experiences, where more physically appealing people experience more opportunities; earlier romantic involvements and marriage; and perceived similarity (in beliefs and values). In addition, Bull and Rumsey review several studies indicating that people who are unusual looking may be stigmatized. For example, people with cleft palates have difficulty meeting new people, and they marry less frequently and have fewer children than those without cleft palates. Hatfield and Sprecher (1986) offer a similar view when they conclude, "These studies actually demonstrated that 'what is beautiful is good; what is ugly is bad'" (p. 356).

Clearly people are drawn to others that they find physically attractive. Two observations about the effects of physical beauty should be made. First, physical beauty is often defined by cultural standards. For example, Hatfield and Sprecher (1986) note that "in some societies (like our own), a slim woman is the ideal. The opposite, however, is true in most other societies — the fatter the better" (p. 7). Second, the manner in which a person communicates affects whether that person is seen as beautiful. Levinger (1974) notes the possibility of how "initial impressions of a 'beautiful person' are outweighed by subsequent interaction with him or her; or how an 'ugly' person may gradually or suddenly become attractive for reasons other than a change in physical appearance" (p. 105).

Although beauty is preferred and certainly offers advantages, a considerable amount of literature indicates that people date and become involved in long-term relationships when the two are matched in beauty (Bull & Rumsey, 1988). If one partner is vastly more attractive than the other, the attractive party may have more power in the relationship, and the other may have to work harder to make the relationship an equitable one (see the section on relational maintenance and equity in Chapter 10). Indeed, people in stable, long-term relationships tend to be matched in level of attractiveness, as Figure 9.1 illustrates.

Reinforcement Class: Supportiveness

The reinforcement class of studies regards interpersonal attraction as a learned response (Byrne, 1997). Byrne and Krivonos (1976) explain that communication and other social activities can be classified as either rewarding or punishing. The rewarding messages and activities lead to positive feelings, which are linked to the source of those messages and activities. Hence "we like others who reward us because they elicit our good feelings" (p. 1).

How do we reward others and thereby increase our own attractiveness? Four ways are most salient. First, showing that we have similar attitudes and values increases

Figure 9.1

▼

Amount of Liking
Predicted for
Dates of Various
Levels of
Attractiveness by
"Ugly," "Average
Looking," and
"Attractive"
Participants

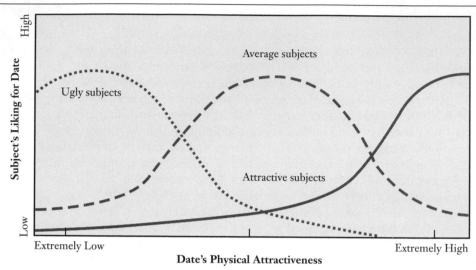

Source: From Hatfield, Berscheid, & Walster, 1976, fig. 1. Used with permission of the authors.

attraction because this indicates to the other person that his or her way of thinking about the world is correct (Byrne & Clore, 1970). Second, we reward others by being supportive of their goals and interests, as Byrne (1997) indicated: "any stimulus that elicits an affective response or is associated with an affective response is evaluated on the basis of the relative number and the relative strength of positive and negative units of affect" (p. 426). Third, as mentioned in Chapter 4, we can confirm others by responding in direct and affirmative ways. Finally, complimenting can be highly reinforcing (but see the section on ingratiation in Chapter 6).

Cognitive Class: Attitude Similarity

According to the cognitive approach, attitude similarity increases interpersonal attraction because people like to remain consistent in their beliefs, values, and behaviors. And, because it is easier to retain consistency in a relationship with someone who agrees (rather than disagrees) with us, we are drawn to others who have beliefs, values, and behaviors similar to our own. This tendency to be attracted to others who have similar cognitions is called **homogamy** (Kerckhoff, 1974), the principle behind the saying "birds of a feather flock together."

If you are tempted to counter with the adage "opposites attract," you would be right to do so; in a fundamental way, both truisms are correct. According to Schutz's (1966) "postulate of compatibility," one person's interpersonal needs for inclusion, control, and affection must be "balanced" by his or her partner's needs. So, for example, if one person has a high need to receive affection, the partner should have a high need to give affection in order for the couple to be compatible. Likewise, if one person needs to control others, the partner must want to be controlled in order to have a satisfying relationship. Finding support for this postulate, Kerckhoff and Davis (1962) found that couples in long-term romantic relationships had higher need compatibility than couples in short-term relationships. In addition, the long-term couples had higher similarity of values. Given this study and many others on attitude similarity and attraction, we conclude that "birds of a feather flock together" is true regarding attitudes, beliefs, and values, whereas "opposites attract" holds true when discussing interpersonal needs.

Sunnafrank (1991; see also Sunnafrank & Miller, 1981) points out that the link between attitude similarity and attraction can be understood only as a function of partners communicating their similarities. The lion's share of the research regarding attitude similarity and attraction ignores communicative influences, although other studies show that how people communicate with one another filters the effects of attitude similarity on attraction (e.g., Sunnafrank & Miller, 1981). Likewise, Duck and Miell (1984; see also Duck, 1976) note that during the development of relationships, people obtain different kinds of information through communication. At the acquaintance stage, global assessments of attitudes and personality are obtained and act as filters for further acquaintance. More precise information about the partner's personality and world view become important as the relationship progresses.

Structural Class: Communication Behaviors

Clatterbuck (1980) laments that relatively few studies have examined the manner in which interpersonal communication functions as a basis of attraction. Cappella (1984) further argues that attraction should be understood as the meshing of interaction styles.

Wallace (1992) examined the research in order to discover specific interaction behaviors tied to interpersonal attraction. She uncovered 85 behaviors and identified four

The initial phases of a relationship are often charged with energy.

underlying factors: *sensitivity, confidence, talkativeness,* and *flirtatiousness,* or *immediacy.* Sensitivity refers to conveying a feeling of trust, of a sensitive attitude toward others, and seeking other people's opinions. Confidence entails expressing oneself well verbally, being committed to one's beliefs, and appearing motivated to achieve. Talkativeness, the only factor that reflected an unattractive person, comprised drawing attention to oneself, dominating a conversation, and speaking loudly. Finally, flirtatious, or immediate, behaviors included standing close to others, maintaining eye contact, and hugging others. Wallace found that communicator use of sensitivity and confidence behaviors were positively associated with perceptions of communicator attraction, regardless of communicators' physical beauty, but flirtatious behavior varied with physical attractiveness and type of relationship. Of course, throughout this book we indicate communication behaviors that bring about liking, including self-presentation strategies (Chapter 6), supportive interactions (Chapter 10), and even conflict behaviors (Chapter 13).

In sum, four factors of interpersonal attraction are physical beauty, reinforcement, attitude similarity, and communication. One prevailing notion is that these attraction factors are partly or entirely dependent on interaction behaviors. The next section elaborates on the kinds of behaviors that individuals use when they communicate that they like another person and want to be seen as attractive in some way.

INCREASING INTIMACY DURING INTERACTION

This section discusses how communicators convey their desire for relational escalation. The following material reflects the lion's share of research on the topic, which emphasizes heterosexual romantic involvements.

Behaviors That Communicate Liking and Intimacy

According to Burgoon, Buller, and Woodall (1989), the nonverbal expression of intimacy involves communicating several different, yet related, themes that jointly characterize the total degree of intimacy in a relationship. We highlight the three most important areas in intimacy and liking:

1. *Involvement and immediacy.* *Involvement* means signaling interest in a particular interaction; *immediacy* refers to psychological closeness. We communicate interest and closeness when we maintain a close conversational distance; maintain a direct body orientation; lean forward; increase direct eye gaze; nod, smile, or display other pleasant facial expressions; maintain an open sitting position; increase gesturing; and, sometimes, touch more frequently. In the vocal channel, people communicate increased levels of involvement by speaking louder and faster, lowering and varying pitch, using fewer silences and briefer latencies, and using more coordinated speech and a warmer tone of voice.

The behaviors associated with close romantic involvement can be obvious, such as touching. Increases in intimacy are also associated with verbal behaviors, such as use of inclusive language, nicknames, and metarelational talk.

© Joel Gordon

2. *Depth and similarity.*   Friends gaze more, smile more, show more positive facial affect, sit closer, and touch more while decreasing such signs of anxiety or discomfort as self-touching, crossed arms, and closed postures. Friends show depth and similarity by adopting similar dress, vocal patterns, hand movements, and posture while mimicking ways of walking, use of language, and facial expressions; their speech styles converge mutually.

3. *Affection, attraction, liking, and love.*   People in love spend more time gazing into each other's eyes (mutual gaze) and at close range. Arousal is also indicated by pupil dilation, and dilated pupils are associated with attraction. Besides smiling and positive facial affect, good friends and potential intimates engage in **postural mirroring** (standing or sitting in exactly the same manner). Touching, holding, and caressing increase and are perceived as warm, friendly, loving, and intimate. Vocally, people express their love using "oversoft, slurred, drawling, resonant, high-pitched voices" (Burgoon et al., 1989, p. 321).

Courtship and Quasi-Courtship Behaviors

Very few studies have examined behaviors that parallel the process of actual courtship (see Burgoon et al., 1989). The term *quasi-courtship* has been used to refer to situations in which people (such as patients and doctors) engage in courtship behaviors, but the flirting may or may not be serious and may never lead to any intimate act beyond merely showing liking. Indeed, Afifi and Johnson (1999) found that cross-sex friends engaged in many of the same touching behavior in public as did dating partners (e.g., hand-holding, embracing). Scheflen (1965), credited for laying down the basic research in this area, identified five stages of courtship, quasi-courtship, and flirting:

1. *Attention.* Interested parties engage in signals and gain the attention of others. Catching a person's eye, a smile, handshakes, excited greetings, nervous laughter, or even childish expressions may be used to gain attention or elicit affectionate responses from a particular other.

2. *Recognition.* If the particular other ignores the attention-getting actions, the interaction is over (at least temporarily). However, the individual may signal recognition by raised eyebrows, improved posture, heightened alertness, a rosier complexion (due to blood flooding the capillaries of the face), or increased grooming or preening (smoothing hair, straightening clothing, tugging on socks, checking makeup). There is some anxiety in courtship behaviors. People may not be certain that they are the target of a person's attentions, and some people do not want to be obvious in sending signals; therefore, some ambiguity may be witnessed at this stage. Individuals may raise eyebrows and groom but then yawn or stretch. Also, communicators may exhibit submissive behaviors at this stage to show that they are not dominating or threatening and that they are likely to accept the approaches of the other. Givens (1978) describes the shoulder shrug composite, which combines a shrug, raised eyebrows, a head tilt, and an open mouth or a pout.

3. *Positioning.* People who are attracted to one another next engage in close face-to-face positions that make personal conversation possible while also possibly excluding others from interrupting.

4. *Invitations and sexual arousal.* Provocative gestures include the grooming of the partner, carrying or holding activities, and explicit sexual actions such as rolling or protruding the pelvis; protruding the chest (chest thrust); cocking the head; exposing the thigh when crossing the legs; stroking a wrist, arm, or thigh; unbuttoning clothes.

5. *Resolution.* Either an approach is made, or the interactants decide to terminate the contact.

Unresolved is the issue of whether a person engaging in flirting is in fact serious about making an intimate commitment. Frequent mistakes occur in flirting. Is a person being merely friendly, showing liking, or being seductive?

Abbey and her colleagues (Abbey, 1982, 1987; Abbey, Cozzarelli, McLaughlin, & Harnish, 1987) found that males very often perceive a higher level of sexual intent than do females. Shotland and Craig (1988), however, argue that males can distinguish between friendliness and seductive behaviors, or "showing sexual interest." Seductive encounters include long eye contact, many short smiles, moving around, forward and backward leans, frequent asking of questions, offers of help or assistance, and so forth; in contrast, friendly encounters include brief eye contact, being distracted by other activities (e.g., eating, showing less undivided attention to the other by playing with inanimate objects, and the like). Moreover, Afifi and Johnson (1999) found that men are more likely than women to interpret touching as an indication of sexual interest in cross-sex friendships but not in dating relationships. So, it appears that the general tendency for males to view displays of affection as sexual depends on types of behavior examined as well as the type of relationship under discussion.

Research is still unraveling the problem of the individual's competence at distinguishing friendliness from flirtation from seductiveness. We all need to keep in mind that males, in general, have a greater sexual appetite and project this higher level of sexual interest onto others they encounter. Males who want to avoid making mistakes in flirting should continually remind themselves to look for multiple and repeated cues from more than one channel (face, body, tone of voice, words spoken) before taking action. Further, certain behaviors that females engage in that clearly denote more than friendliness should be used judiciously in order to reduce the chances of misinterpretation.

Moreover, verbal requests for dates can vary from being very implicit (e.g., "I hear that the new theater is opening") to quite explicit (e.g., "You have to take me out tonight!"). In examining college students' implicit versus explicit date requests, Solomon (1997) found that when affection for the target was high, but the couple were not close (i.e., intimate), date requests were more implicit. Sex differences revealed that men were more explicit than women in their date requests, as a rule. However, the more the man liked the woman, the more implicit the date request was; but the more the woman liked the man, the more explicit the woman was in requesting a date. That is, women actually were more explicit than men when it came to asking someone out if she liked the person enough. Thus it appears that the simple act of asking someone out is moderated by the degree to which you are attracted to the person, your sex, and how close you feel to that person to begin with.

Cognitive Valence Theory

Imagine that you have a friend who enacts a few of the behaviors just enumerated to show that he or she wants to escalate the relationship. What would you do? How you respond during interaction depends on several factors, such as where you are at that moment, rules the two of you have established, and how you feel physically. Cognitive valence theory accounts for such factors.

As we discussed in Chapter 5, Andersen (1985, 1989; see also Andersen & Andersen, 1984) developed **cognitive valence theory** to explain how people respond to messages that signal increased intimacy. This theory "begins when the behavioral intimacy of a relational partner increases above the typical level that has been manifested previously in the relationship" (Andersen, 1989, p. 5).

SHALL WE DANCE?

We conducted our own study on flirting in singles bars. Working in pairs and in small groups, our students would enter an establishment relatively early (before the dance music was turned up or the band played) and randomly select females to observe (males walk around these establishments so much that it is hard to follow them). The women's communication styles were observed in two phases: before the music was supplied (or turned loud) and while the dance music was being played. The question we sought to answer was "Which females would get dance offers in the first hour that dance music was played (or when the band played its first musical set)?" The following table summarizes the results from observing 287 women.

Women who appeared more outgoing and expressive before the dance music was supplied got more dance offers later in the evening. They engaged in more illustrating, more smiling, and more open sitting positions and were judged the "most talkative" in their group. They also engaged in a "jewelry flash," a "lip-moistening" action, and a "chest thrust" (types of courtship cues) more than women who did not get dance offers. Later, when music was supplied, women who displayed some of the courtship behaviors were quick to get dance offers. Dancing while seated, hair grooming, head or hair tosses, leg and foot movements, lip moistening, and chest thrusts helped attract dance offers.

Men do not want to be rejected or embarrassed when they ask someone to dance. So cues that indicate that a woman wants to dance, coupled with cues that indicate openness, an outgoing nature, and friendliness, help secure dance offers. Note, however, that we did not assess eye behavior because it was impossible to do so reliably under the circumstances. Another study of this nature found that males approached females 60 percent of the time when the female repeated eye contact and also engaged in smiling (Walsh & Hewitt, 1985). These authors concluded that males need a certain amount of encouragement before approaching a female and that this encouragement is most likely given when several behaviors are repeated in several channels.

BEHAVIORS OF WOMEN WHO DID AND DID NOT RECEIVE DANCE OFFERS

Variable	Females Receiving Dance Offers	Females Not Receiving Dance Offers	Was Difference Significant?
Predance Observations			
Group size (mean)	2.82	2.86	No
Illustrators (mean)	2.87	2.49	Yes
Smiling (mean)	3.34	2.84	Yes
Open sitting position (mean)	2.40	1.70	Yes

Time in talk	73%	49%	Yes
Eye contact	61%	51%	No
Hair grooming	56%	40%	No
Clothing adjustments	36%	35%	No
Glasses	10%	11%	No
Jewelry	39%	8%	Yes
Lip moistening	31%	16%	Yes
Body adapters	28%	30%	No
Chest thrust	22%	8%	Yes
Head toss	34%	35%	No
Thigh exposure	27%	22%	No
Leg or foot movement	61%	57%	No
Dance Music Observations			
Postural shifts (mean)	3.17	2.73	No
Dancing in seat	67%	30%	Yes
Hair grooming	63%	40%	Yes
Clothing adjustments	41%	32%	No
Jewelry	35%	22%	No
Lip moistening	42%	16%	Yes
Body adapters	41%	46%	No
Chest thrusts	23%	8%	Yes
Head toss	48%	32%	Yes
Thigh exposure	22%	10%	No
Leg or foot movement	69%	49%	Yes

Source: Supplied by Michael J. Cody, University of Southern California.

To illustrate this theory, we refer to the character in the story at the beginning of this chapter. According to cognitive valence theory, if Brad attempts to increase intimacy during interaction and Tracy perceives those attempts, several factors are considered. As Figure 9.2 indicates, if Tracy experiences low arousal as a result of Brad's intimacy gestures, she will not respond to Brad's change in intimacy. If Tracy experiences high arousal (increase in heart rate or fear), she will compensate for Brad's attempt to increase intimacy. Such compensation could include many behaviors: averting a gaze, increasing distance, not talking, or perhaps demanding that he leave her alone. It is at the moderate levels of arousal (heightened interest without fear) that cognitive valence theory predicts interesting variations (Figure 9.2).

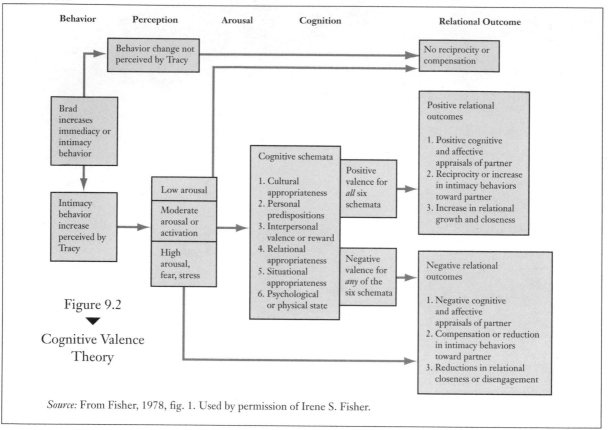

Figure 9.2

▼

Cognitive Valence Theory

Source: From Fisher, 1978, fig. 1. Used by permission of Irene S. Fisher.

If Tracy experiences moderate arousal (heightened interest without fear), she would cognitively assess Brad's attempt at intimacy according to six cognitive schemata.

1. Cultural appropriateness asks whether Brad's behavior conforms to expected behaviors given the culture's rules and norms.

2. Personal predispositions are Tracy's tendencies to affiliate with other people. If she is affiliative generally, she is more likely to reciprocate Brad's intimacy behaviors.

3. Interpersonal valence, or reward, concerns Brad's reward value — is he rewarding?

4. Relational appropriateness asks whether Brad's behavior is understandable given the nature and expectations developed between him and Tracy.

5. Situational appropriateness refers to whether or not this kind of behavior is appropriate to the context (e.g., flirting at work is often inappropriate).

6. Psychological or physical state refers to internal feelings. If Tracy has the flu, for example, she may not feel up to reciprocating Brad's interactional intimacy.

According to Andersen's cognitive valence theory, if all six of the schemata are positive, positive relational outcomes will occur. In this case, Brad will be viewed in a favorable light, Tracy will reciprocate his communication, and intimacy will increase. If, however, any of the six schemata is negative, negative relational outcomes are predicted. Brad will be seen less favorably, Tracy will compensate for Brad's gestures of intimacy, and the relationship may de-escalate. Andersen (1989) notes that "this model has suggested that movement toward intimacy is a fragile, perilous process. Behavioral intimacy increases must undergo positive schematic analysis across at least six relational schemata" (p. 41).

RELATIONAL DEVELOPMENT PROCESSES

In discussing the general progression of relationship intimacy, we examine properties of communication that change, stages of relational escalation, research on escalation, and developmental turning points. Overall, this material emphasizes that relationships develop in different ways.

Social Penetration Revisited

We turn again to social penetration theory to examine relational escalation processes because it has guided much theory and research on relational escalation. Recall from Chapter 7 that social penetration theory concerns how individuals reveal information about themselves according to the dimensions of breadth (number of topics) and depth (how personal the disclosure is). Moreover, relational rewards are compared against costs: If the relationship is rewarding, it is pursued; if the relationship is more costly than rewarding, it is not pursued. Such bookkeeping takes into account the present status of the relationship as well as forecasts for the future (e.g., "Once she moves back home, this relationship won't be so frustrating"). According to Taylor and Altman (1987), "social penetration processes proceed in a gradual and orderly fashion from superficial to intimate levels of exchange as a function of both immediate and forecast outcomes" (p. 259).

Altman and Taylor (1973) identify eight dimensions of communication that they believe increase as the relationship escalates:

1. Richness, or breadth of interaction along various topics
2. Uniqueness of interaction, where the couple exchange verbal and nonverbal messages known only to them

3. Efficiency of exchange, or the accuracy and sensitivity of message exchange that does not require elaboration

4. Substitutability and equivalency, which means that "more ways become available to communicate the same feeling in a substitutable and equivalent fashion" (p. 132)

5. Synchronization and pacing, or the spontaneous coordinating and interweaving of behaviors (e.g., washing dishes together, agreeing quickly, sharing the bathroom without conflict)

6. Permeability and openness, or verbal and nonverbal exchanges of intimacy, including sexual closeness

7. Voluntariness and spontaneity of change, or the couple's ability to be creative and spontaneous in their communication with each other

8. Evaluation, or the increased tendency to point out the negative and positive aspects of the other

Research offers mixed support for the claim that these dimensions increase as the relationship matures. Knapp, Ellis, and Williams (1980) found that personalized messages (e.g., sharing secrets, using greater numbers of channels, using messages only the dyad understands) were perceived more in relationships having greater intimacy. The researchers also found that synchronized messages (messages that are smooth-flowing and spontaneous) were also perceived more in intimate relationships. However, contrary to social penetration theory, difficulty (awkwardness, inability to understand) of communication did not differ among relationships that varied in intimacy. These findings indicate that communication generally becomes more personal and spontaneous, but not less difficult, as the relationship progresses. Using student diaries, Baxter and Wilmot (1983) also found that communicating high levels of personalness increased as social penetration theory predicts. But, Baxter and Wilmot also reported that frequency of contact and breadth of topics discussed did not increase over time. Finally, Hammer (1986) studied European Americans and African Americans and found that attitude similarity, but not ethnic similarity, predicted depth of social penetration (i.e., intent to get to know others better).

Developing Relationships On-Line

Relationships sometimes develop and escalate over the Internet. Parks and colleagues (Parks & Floyd, 1996; Parks & Roberts, 1998) have studied the frequency with which personal relationships develop on-line, and how they progress. They found that, among people who met in Usenet newsgroups (where people from across the world who are originally strangers to one another discuss topics of mutual interest), 61% formed a personal relationship on-line. Most of the relationships initiated on-line were friendships, although 10% of them were romantic. All of these relationships lasted from one month to over six years, and 64% of the respondents indicated their relationships were intimate. In a similar assessment of MOO-users (users of real-time multi-user chat spaces that have textual depictions of rooms and objects), 94% of participants reported forming personal relationships on-line, among which 67% were friendships and 26% were romantic. About a third of these relationships migrated to at least one face-to-face meeting, after moving through other channels (i.e., e-mail, letters, and phone calls). However, Parks and colleagues could not indicate why some people form relationships on-line, and others do not.

In another study, Utz (2000) examined how people form relationships in Multi-User Domains (MUDS) — on-line interaction spaces for role-playing games. Utz found that the degree to which people formed friendships on-line had to do with two factors: first, whether or not users were optimistic that computer-mediated communication was capable of expressing emotional and personal feelings; second, the degree to which users took advantage of emoticons (discussed in Chapter 5) and other computer-based scripts within the MUD that triggered the system to display text portraying affectionate or jocular behavior (e.g., invoking text that all in a chat room can see, suggesting that someone is waving, teasing, etc.). It is unclear from Utz's research whether people interpret these latter behaviors as friendly or whether people who invoke them are also engaging in other friendship-initiating messages. In general, however, the research suggests that relationships that begin on-line are similar to those that begin face-to-face.

Stages of Relational Escalation

Knapp and Vangelisti (1992) offer an account of how communication is associated with relational escalation. **Initiating** is the first stage, and it refers to the processes and behaviors involved in coming into contact with someone. People ask themselves questions such as "How do I meet this person?" and "Is this person open to meeting me?" According to Wilmot (1987), initiating actually begins when you become aware of someone who is aware of you. Many relationships never escalate past the initiating stage. Although we may meet many people in a given day, nothing more than recognition or greetings is usually exchanged.

Knapp and Vangelisti's next stage is **experimenting.** In this stage, "name, rank, and serial number" are offered ("So, what's your middle name?" "I am the firstborn," "My astrological sign is Leo — what's yours?"). In other words, during the experimenting stage, people engage in small talk. The objective in this stage is to present oneself as socially competent and to experiment with possible avenues for future interaction ("Do you like to ski?" "Does your son like preschool?" "Do you play chess?"). People can become frustrated at making small talk, especially if none of their relationships seem to progress beyond that stage. Nevertheless, as Knapp and Vangelisti point out, small talk functions to maintain most of our relationships and to serve as a springboard for escalating others.

Intensifying occurs when people move beyond superficial knowledge of one another to explore more intimate aspects. Knapp and Vangelisti offer several communication behaviors that accompany intensifying. These include increases in personal self-disclosure, informal forms of address ("Bro," "Darlink"), use of the first person plural ("Let's go to a movie," "Where are we having Thanksgiving?"), direct expressions of affection that may be reciprocated ("I think you're great," "Well, you're fantastic"), verbal shortcuts that both people understand to replace full sentences ("Seatbelt" instead of "Please fasten your seatbelt"), and a clearer understanding of nonverbal messages (e.g., a sigh does not necessarily mean frustration).

Next, the **integrating** stage occurs when the two unique personalities begin to merge into a more singular identity (Knapp & Vangelisti, 1992). Specific communication behaviors accompany this stage: intimacy "trophies" (such as rings and pictures) are exchanged; social networks merge, or one person's friends are adopted; particular attitudes, beliefs, and activities are developed together (e.g., going to church together, taking classes together, changing political positions); nonverbally, the dyad becomes synchronized so that the two act in unison; the couple identify with particular events or places (our song, our favorite Italian restaurant, the day we met, etc.); and similarities in dress, speech, and mannerisms occur (e.g., matching outfits, adjusting speaking speed to accommodate the partner).

STUDENT AS OBSERVER: A RELATIONSHIP'S PROGRESS

Do relationships progress in a linear manner, as Knapp and Vangelisti state in their 1992 book? The stages of relational escalation offered by Knapp and Vangelisti have yet to be confirmed through research. The following piece of research might help determine whether the model of development they present can be generalized to various romantic relationships.

1. Write a short 1–2 page essay regarding how an intimate romantic relationship developed. Please refer to one you have experienced or one you have observed — such as a friend's or relative's. Begin at the very start of the relationship, discussing how the two people noticed each other. Proceed through the history of the relationship to the point where the couple wanted to make their joint identity known to other people.
2. On a separate sheet of paper write the five stages (and brief descriptions) in order: initiating, experimenting, intensifying, integrating, and bonding.
3. Now code your essay using the five stages. Specifically, you should write down the name of the stage that best describes each event in your essay.
4. Determine how the development of your relationship corresponds to the sequence provided by Knapp and Vangelisti.
5. Also note variations from the sequence of stages. In what ways does your experience add to, or even change the sequences of stages?
6. Compare your findings with other students in the class. Do they confirm or disconfirm the stages proposed by Knapp and Vangelisti?

Cynthia Benjamins/Black Star

Research indicates that relational escalation is marked by ebbs and flows of messages that signal increased involvement. A couple's interpersonal communication will tend toward a level of intimacy that can be sustained over time.

Knapp and Vangelisti's final stage of relational escalation is **bonding** — a public announcement of sorts that the relationship is indeed unique and should be respected. Adolescents becoming "blood brothers," weddings, and other proclamations of commitment reflect bonding. Bonding communicates clearly that the two parties treasure a particular relationship, which is often (though not consistently) sanctioned legally. Few bonding rituals have been institutionalized by society for nonromantic relationships.

The discussion regarding stages focuses our attention on several ways in which communication behavior is theoretically tied to the development of personal relationships. This discussion might also imply that all relationships develop in a single, simple, and linear manner, graduating to higher levels of intimacy, and that each stage must include the behaviors described. But this is not the case. The process for many is not simple or linear. Instead, relational escalation involves alternate cycles of growing together as well as periods of stability and stagnation, as research suggests.

Research on Relational Escalation

Research indicates that relationships do not usually progress in a linear manner. That is, as the relationship grows, partners reveal more about each other, display more immediate nonverbal cues, and become more efficient in their use of messages, to a point. But such disclosures, displays of affection, and efficiency are not continual. After a period of time, they subside. In addition, the communication behaviors that signal increased intimacy alternate with talk about routine and mundane topics and with periods of lack of affection, conflict, and awkward or inefficient communication.

Research suggests that relationships grow in intimacy to a point, then subside as the relationship becomes stable. Van Lear (1987) found that as relationships progress, private and personal disclosures increase until they reach a peak in personalness, after which the number of such messages declines. Likewise, Hays (1984) studied the development of friendships and found that intimate communication is highest in the six- to nine-week range, and intimate messages decrease at twelve weeks. However, participants who were not close experienced a steady decline in intimacy of communication almost from the outset of the study. Guerrero and Andersen (1991) found that seriously dating and marriage-bound participants touch each other more than married people, casual daters, or couples just beginning to date. Guerrero and Andersen noted that once the feelings of attachment have been secured, the need for personal disclosures and displays of affection diminishes. Van Lear (1992) found that during a given conversation or between conversations, acquaintances cycle back and forth between personal and superficial issues. But overall the discussions become more intimate to a point, whereupon the intimacy declines.

Huston, McHale, and Crouter (1986) interviewed married couples at the beginning of the marriage and then a year later. In general, they found that couples became less satisfied with their relationship and with the quantity of various kinds of communication during their first year of marriage. Behaviors that were less frequent after one year of marriage were approving or complimenting the spouse, making the partner laugh, expressions of love, initiating sex, doing something nice for the partner, sharing physical affection (besides sex), and sharing emotions, feelings, or problems. The most harmful communication behavior was being negative (criticism, sarcasm, etc.). This study provides further evidence that intimate messages tend to subside toward the end of the relational escalation process.

Research indicates that relational escalation is marked by ebbs and flows of increased involvement. After a period of time, communication decreases to a level of intimacy fluctuation that can be sustained over time. Figure 9.3 contrasts how some people think relationships should escalate in a straight line over time with how the research suggests relationships actually do progress in cycles to a high point of intimate exchange and then down to a point of stable exchange.

Do couples escalate their relationships at the same rate? Associated with this question is the issue of what events, if any, mark the escalation of relationships. An examination of romantic couples' turning points addresses both of these issues.

Turning Points

Baxter and Bullis (1986) define the **turning point** as "any event or occurrence that is associated with change in a relationship" (p. 470). When you recall a friendship or a

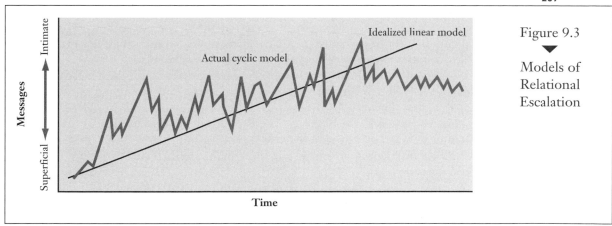

Figure 9.3
▼
Models of
Relational
Escalation

romantic involvement, can you pinpoint particular events where the relationship changed? Such events as deciding to be committed to each other, a death in the family, or making up after a separation can significantly affect the escalation of the relationship.

One method of demarcating turning points is the Retrospective Interview Technique (RIT) (Huston, Surra, Fitzgerald, & Cate, 1981). Using RIT, researchers can locate turning points of relationships on a grid. The points can be plotted by using the x axis to represent time and the y axis to represent degree of commitment (from no commitment to 100%). Figure 9.4 illustrates the escalation of a hypothetical relationship using this method.

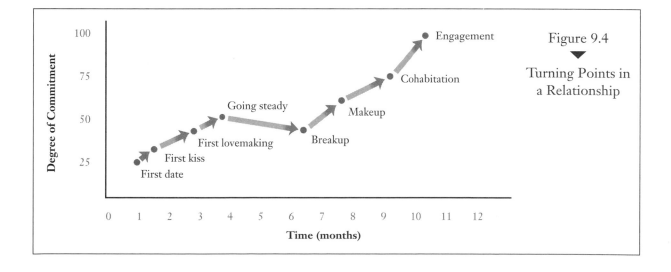

Figure 9.4
▼
Turning Points in
a Relationship

Using RIT, Huston and colleagues (1981) reported on two studies on courtship that revealed three couple types that vary in their escalation toward commitment (marriage). According to Huston and co-workers, accelerated courtship escalates rapidly to commitment. These couples marry quickly, have relatively low levels of conflict, and require minimal efforts to maintain their relationships. The intermediate courtship type involves high levels of love and a relatively rapid progression to commitment. The third type is prolonged. These couples escalate the relationship in a "gradual and uncertain fashion" (p. 72). Prolonged couples have just as much love as intermediates, and more than accelerated couples, but their relationships are marked by conflict and slow movement toward commitment. Figure 9.5 illustrates these three courtship types.

As these analyses indicate, not all courtships escalate at the same rates (see also Surra & Hughes, 1997). These couples vary in their experience of the escalation stages reviewed earlier. According to Huston and colleagues, accelerated courtships moved from 25% commitment to 75% commitment in about three months; intermediate couples moved from 25% commitment to 75% commitment from six to nine months; prolonged courtships required between 17 and 28 months to move from 25% commitment to 75% commitment. In addition, these couples differed in the number of turning points they experienced. As would be expected, the prolonged couples experienced more turning points (an average of 11.4) than either the accelerated (5.4) or intermediate courtship types (5.3).

Baxter and Bullis (1986) wanted to uncover the specific content of turning points, to explore precisely what was altering the trajectory of romantic relationships. They

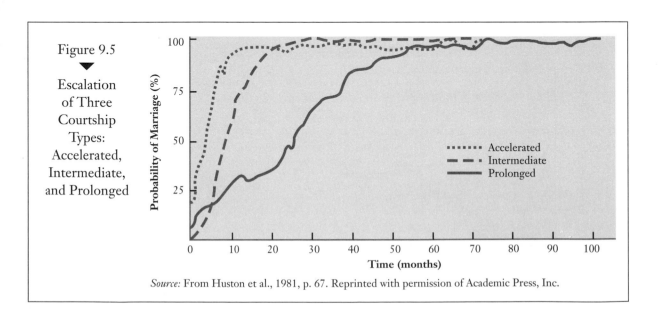

Figure 9.5

▼

Escalation of Three Courtship Types: Accelerated, Intermediate, and Prolonged

Source: From Huston et al., 1981, p. 67. Reprinted with permission of Academic Press, Inc.

uncovered 25 different types of turning points, which were collapsed into 13 categories. Table 9.1 presents the 13 turning point types and the percentage change in commitment associated with each type. As Table 9.1 shows, most turning points helped the couple escalate toward commitment. As might be expected, a few of the turning points — external competition, disengagement, and negative psychic change — impeded movement toward commitment. The researchers also found that many of

	Table 9.1		
	TURNING POINT TYPES AND COMMITMENT SCORES		
Turning Point Type	Description	Example	Commitment Score* (%)
"Getting to know you" time	Events that help the parties get to know each other	Studying together	21.13
Quality time	Time spent enjoying each other's company for its own sake	Getting away together	15.18
Physical separation	Time spent apart, but not breakups	School break, vacation	−.30
External competition	Another person or demand competing with the relationship	Return of an old flame	−13.44
Reunion	Reunion after a physical separation	First night together after six weeks apart	10.72
Passion	Physical or emotional affection acutely experienced	Love at first sight, first kiss	20.35
Disengagement	Breakup initiated by one or both parties	Trial separation	−23.28
Positive psychic change	Change of attitude to feel more positive about the relationship	Realization of intensity of partner's feelings	18.98
Exclusivity	Agreement not to date others	Going steady, avoiding former romantic partners	19.21

(Continued)

(Table continued from previous page)

Turning Point Type	Description	Example	Commitment Score* (%)
Negative psychic change	Change of attitude to feel less positive about the relationship	Realization that both parties are unhappy	–9.00
Making up	Repair of the relationship after a breakup or fight	Agreeing to give the relationship one more try	21.60
Serious commitment	Event committing the partners for the future	Moving in together, engagement	23.26
Sacrifice	One person's giving of self on the partner's behalf	Help in a time of crisis, giving a gift	17.61

*The percentage change in commitment following the turning point.
Source: Adapted from Baxter & Bullis, 1986.

the turning points involved relational talk, or messages about the nature of the relationship. In a study that examined how couples jointly reconstruct their turning points, Baxter and Pittman (2001) found that quality time, passion, get-to-know-you time, and exclusivity were most prominent in couples' recollections. That is, these four turning points were the most common types and emerged in couples' reminiscing, telling stories, mementos, and other traditions.

CHAPTER SUMMARY

Much has been said about the ways in which relationships escalate. A majority of the research has focused on the relational property of intimacy and how couples achieve intimacy. Our review reflects this research bias. At the same time, we have noted that relationships are not comprised only of intimacy. Other important relational features must be considered — the accomplishment of trust, for example. Also, more needs to be done to research how friends escalate their relationships. For example, how do friends become friends? What separates best friends from other friends? Does the development of friendship change as people get older?

Bases of attraction, such as attitude similarity and reinforcement, cannot be brought about without communication. In other words, people rely on communication to make their attitudes and values known, to reveal their personalities, to compliment acquaintances, and to achieve other goals. As scholars have long noted, interpersonal communication is the conduit for establishing and escalating relationships (see, for example, Duck, 1976).

People also rely on communication to increase intimacy. Cognitive valence theory highlights issues that influence how people respond to increases in intimacy behaviors. The six schemata presented by Andersen (1989) appear quite reasonable as those that most people would use in a relatively brief period.

Concerning relational development processes, social penetration theory provides the background for much of the thinking and research on the topic, as reflected in the general cyclic model appearing in Figure 9.3. Relationships escalate in cycles, and communication becomes less personal at particular points of escalation, with the most stable relationships reporting less intimacy over time. Relational turning points are excellent benchmarks for noting how a relationship escalates. Research on the topic reveals that about a dozen turning points exist and that accelerated, intermediate, and prolonged courtships vary in length and in the number of turning points. In short, in terms of intimacy, relationships begin and develop in various ways. Reading about these differences and noting the role of communication in various patterns of relational escalation should enable us to understand better how people achieve their relational escalation goals.

KEY TERMS

▼

bonding, p. 267
cognitive valence theory, p. 259
experimenting, p. 265
homogamy, p. 254
initiating, p. 265

integrating, p. 266
intensifying, p. 265
interpersonal attraction, p. 252
postural mirroring, p. 257
turning point, p. 268

EXERCISES FOR FURTHER DISCUSSION

▼

1. Review the factors contributing to interpersonal attraction: physical beauty, supportiveness, attitude similarity, and communication. Now consider how these factors have affected your own interpersonal relationships.
   a. Which of these factors do you find most important in your relationships?
   b. Are some of these factors more important in one kind of relationship than in others? Which ones are most important in which relationships?
   c. Are some factors more important in earlier stages of a relationship and others more important in later stages?
2. Write a short paragraph in which you describe a situation in which someone tried to increase intimacy through interaction behaviors.
   a. What did you do at the time?
   b. Did your reactions correspond to what cognitive valence theory predicts?
3. Interview someone you know who is married or engaged. Ask this person to relate the story of his or her relationship, beginning when they first met. Try to get the person to be as specific as possible about any critical events that affected the relationship. Then try to construct a graph similar to the one in Figure 9.3, noting where the critical events took place. Discuss with the person whether or not the graph provides an accurate reflection of that person's relational escalation. If it does not, what would that person include or exclude?

SUGGESTED READING

▼

INTERPERSONAL ATTRACTION

Clatterbuck, G. W. (1980). A metatheoretical perspective on interpersonal attraction: The role of communication constructs. In B. W. Morse & L. A. Phelps (Eds.), *Interpersonal communication: A relational perspective* (pp. 119–131). Minneapolis: Burgess. This review of the attraction literature analyzes four major approaches. Clatterbuck emphasizes the need to study the communication foundations of interpersonal attraction.

Hatfield, E., & Sprecher, S. (1986). *Mirror, mirror. . . : The importance of looks in everyday life*. Albany: State University of New York Press. A very readable book and an excellent review of research on physical beauty. Individual and cultural standards for attractiveness are discussed.

ESCALATION PROCESSES

Altman, I., & Taylor, D. A. (1973). *Social penetration: The development of interpersonal relationships*. Austin, TX: Holt, Rinehart and Winston. This book discusses dimensions of intimate relationships and stages of intimacy.

Knapp, M. L., & Vangelisti, A. (1992). *Interpersonal communication and human relationships* (2nd ed.). Needham Heights, MA: Allyn & Bacon. This book analyzes different stages of relational growth and decay. The discussion of how communication is linked to these various stages is one of the major strengths of this text.

TURNING POINTS

Baxter, L. A., & Bullis, C. (1986). Turning points in developing romantic relationships. *Human Communication Research, 12*, 469–493. This study examines the various turning points in romantic relationships. Both positive and negative turning points are associated with relational satisfaction.

LOVE

Hendrick, C., & Hendrick, S. (1991). *Romantic love*. Newbury Park, CA: Sage. The Hendricks provide an excellent summary of research on love. Various types of romantic love are explored.

REFERENCE LIST

▼

Abbey, A. (1982). Sex differences in attributions for friendly behavior: Do males misperceive females' friendliness? *Journal of Personality and Social Psychology, 42*, 830–838.

Abbey, A. (1987). Misperceptions of friendly behavior as sexual interest: A survey of naturally occurring incidents. *Psychology of Women Quarterly, 11*, 173–194.

Abbey, A., Cozzarelli, C., McLaughlin, K., & Harnish, R. J. (1987). The effects of clothing and dyad sex compositions on perceptions of sexual intent: Do women and men evaluate these cues differently? *Journal of Applied Social Psychology, 17*, 108–126.

Afifi, W. A., & Johnson, M. L. (1999). The use and interpretation of tie signs in a public setting: Relationships and sex differences. *Journal of Social and Personal Relationships, 16*, 9–38.

Altman, I., & Taylor, D. A. (1973). *Social penetration: The development of interpersonal relationships*. Austin, TX: Holt, Rinehart and Winston.

Andersen, P. A. (1985). Nonverbal immediacy in interpersonal communication. In A. W. Siegman & S. Feldstein (Eds.), *Multichannel integrations of nonverbal behavior* (pp. 1–36). Hillsdale, NJ: Erlbaum.

Andersen, P. A. (1989). *A cognitive valence theory of intimate communication*. Paper presented at the conference of the International Network on Personal Relationships, Iowa City, Iowa.

Andersen, P. A., & Andersen, J. F. (1984). The exchange of nonverbal intimacy: A critical review of dyadic models. *Journal of Nonverbal Behavior, 8*, 327–349.

Bartholomew, K. (1993). From childhood to adult relationships: Attachment theory and research. In S. Duck (Ed.), *Learning about relationships* (pp. 30–62). Newbury Park, CA: Sage.

Baxter, L. A., & Bullis, C. (1986). Turning points in developing romantic relationships. *Human Communication Research, 12*, 469–493.

Baxter, L. A., & Pittman, G. (2001). Communicatively remembering turning points of relational development in heterosexual romantic relationships. *Communication Reports, 14*, 1–18.

Baxter, L. A., & Wilmot, W. W. (1983). Communication characteristics of relationships with differential growth rates. *Communication Monographs, 50*, 264–272.

Berger, C. R., & Calabrese, R. J. (1975). Some explorations in initial interaction and beyond: Toward a developmental theory of interpersonal communication. *Human Communication Theory, 1*, 99–112.

Berger, C. R., Weber, M. D., Munley, M. E., & Dixon, J. T. (1977). Interpersonal relationship levels and interpersonal attraction. In B. D. Ruben (Ed.), *Communication yearbook 1* (pp. 245–262). New Brunswick, NJ: Transaction Books.

Bull, R., & Rumsey, N. (1988). *The social psychology of facial appearance*. New York: Springer-Verlag.

Burgoon, J. K., Buller, D. B., & Woodall, W. G. (1989). *Nonverbal communication: The unspoken dialogue*. New York: HarperCollins.

Burgoon, J. K., & Hale, J. L. (1984). The fundamental topoi of relational communication. *Communication Monographs, 51*, 193–214.

Byrne, D. (1971). *The attraction paradigm*. Orlando, FL: Academic.

Byrne, D. (1997). An overview (and underview) of research and theory within the attraction paradigm. *Journal of Social and Personal Relationships, 14*, 417–431.

Byrne, D., & Clore, G. L. (1970). A reinforcement model of evaluative responses. *Personality, 1*, 103–127.

Byrne, D., & Krivonos, P. D. (1976). *A reinforcement-affect theory of interpersonal communication*. Paper presented at the Speech Communication Association convention, San Francisco.

Cappella, J. N. (1984). The relevance of microstructure interaction to relationship change. *Journal of Social and Personal Relationships, 2*, 239–264.

Clatterbuck, G. W. (1980). A metatheoretical perspective on interpersonal attraction: The role of communication constructs. In B. W. Morse & L. A. Phelps (Eds.), *Interpersonal communication: A relational perspective* (pp. 119–131). Minneapolis: Burgess.

Duck, S. W. (1976). Interpersonal communication in the acquaintance process. In G. R. Miller (Ed.), *Explorations in interpersonal communication* (pp. 127–149). Newbury Park, CA: Sage.

Duck, S., Lock, A., McCall, G., Fitzpatrick, M. A., & Cayne, J. C. (1984). Social and personal relationships. *Journal of Social and Personal Relationships, 1*, 1–10.

Duck, S. W., & Miell, D. (1984). Towards a comprehension of friendship development and breakdown. In H. Tajfel, C. Fraser, & C. Jaspers (Eds.), *The social dimension: European perspectives on social psychology* (pp. 228–248). Cambridge, England: Cambridge University Press.

Givens, D. B. (1978). The nonverbal basis of attraction: Flirtation, courtship, and seduction. *Psychiatry, 41,* 346–359.

Greenfield, S., & Thelen, M. (1997). Validation of the fear of intimacy scale with a lesbian and gay male population. *Journal of Social and Personal Relationships, 14,* 707–716.

Guerrero, L. K. (1996). Attachment style differences in intimacy and involvement: A test of the four-category model. *Communication Monographs, 63,* 269–292.

Guerrero, L. K., & Andersen, P. A. (1991). The waxing and waning of relational intimacy: Touch as a function of relational stage, gender, and touch avoidance. *Journal of Social and Personal Relationships, 8,* 147–165.

Hammer, M. R. (1986). The influence of ethnic and attitude similarity on initial social penetration. In Y. Y. Kim (Ed.), *Interethnic communication: Current research* (pp. 225–237). Newbury Park, CA: Sage.

Hatfield, E. (1984). Epilogue: The dangers of intimacy. In V. J. Derlega (Ed.), *Communication, intimacy, and close relationships* (pp. 207–220). Austin, TX: Academic.

Hatfield, E., Berscheid, E., & Walster, G. W. (1976). New directions in equity research. In L. Berkowitz & E. Hatfield (Eds.), *Equity theory: Toward a general theory of social interaction* (pp. 1–42). Orlando, FL: Academic.

Hatfield, E., & Sprecher, S. (1986). *Mirror, mirror . . . : The importance of looks in everyday life.* Albany: State University of New York Press.

Hays, R. (1984). The development and maintenance of friendship. *Journal of Social and Personal Relationships, 1,* 75–98.

Huston, T. L. (1974). A perspective on interpersonal attraction. In T. L. Huston (Ed.), *Foundations of interpersonal attraction* (pp. 3–28). Orlando, FL: Academic.

Huston, T. L., McHale, S. M., & Crouter, A. C. (1986). When the honeymoon's over: Changes in the marriage relationship over the first year. In R. Gilmour & S. W. Duck (Eds.), *The emerging field of personal relationships* (pp. 109–132). Hillsdale, NJ: Erlbaum.

Huston, T. L., Surra, C., Fitzgerald, N. M., & Cate, R. (1981). From courtship to marriage: Mate selection as an interpersonal process. In S. W. Duck & R. Gilmour (Eds.), *Personal relationships 2: Developing personal relationships* (pp. 53–88). Orlando, FL: Academic.

Kamo, Y. (1993). Determinants of marital satisfaction: A comparison of the United States and Japan. *Journal of Social and Personal Relationships, 10,* 551–568.

Kelley, H. H. (1979). *Personal relationships: Their structure and processes.* Hillsdale, NJ: Erlbaum.

Kerckhoff, A. C. (1974). The social context of interpersonal attraction. In T. L. Huston (Ed.), *Foundations of interpersonal attraction* (pp. 61–78). Orlando, FL: Academic.

Kerckhoff, A. C., & Davis, K. E. (1962). Value consensus and need complementarity in mate selection. *American Sociological Review, 27,* 295–303.

Knapp, M. L., Ellis, D. G., & Williams, B. A. (1980). Perceptions of communication behavior associated with relationship terms. *Communication Monographs, 47,* 262–278.

Knapp, M. L., & Vangelisti, A. (1992). *Interpersonal communication and human relationships* (2nd ed.). Newton, MA: Allyn & Bacon.

Levinger, G. (1974). A three-level approach to attraction: Toward an understanding of pair relatedness. In T. L. Huston (Ed.), *Foundations of interpersonal attraction* (pp. 99–120). Orlando, FL: Academic.

278

McCroskey, J. C., & McCain, T. A. (1974). The measurement of interpersonal attraction. *Speech Monographs, 41,* 261–266.

Miell, D., & Duck, S. W. (1986). Strategies in developing friendships. In V. J. Derlega & B. A. Winstead (Eds.), *Friendships and social interaction* (pp. 129–143). New York: Springer-Verlag.

Miller, G. R., & Steinberg, M. (1975). *Between people.* Chicago: Science Research.

Morton, T. L., Alexander, J. F., & Altman, I. (1976). Communication and relationship definition. In G. R. Miller (Ed.), *Explorations in interpersonal communication* (pp. 105–125). Newbury Park, CA: Sage.

Parks, M. R., & Floyd, K. (1996). Making friends in cyberspace. *Journal of Communication, 46,* 80–97.

Parks, M. R., & Roberts, L. D. (1998). "Making MOOsic." The development of personal relationships online and a comparison to their off-line counterparts. *Journal of Social and Personal Relationships, 15,* 517–537.

Perlman, D., & Fehr, B. (1987). The development of intimate relationships. In D. Perlman & S. W. Duck (Eds.), *Intimate relationships* (pp. 13–42). Newbury Park, CA: Sage.

Prager, K. (1995). *The psychology of intimacy.* New York: Guilford.

Prager, K., & Buhrmester, D. (1998). Intimacy and need fulfillment in couple relationships. *Journal of Social and Personal Relationships, 15,* 435–469.

Scheflen, A. E. (1965). Quasi-courtship behavior in psychotherapy. *Psychiatry, 28,* 245–257.

Schutz, W. C. (1966). *The interpersonal underworld* (reprint ed.). Palo Alto, CA: Science and Behavior Books.

Shotland, R. L., & Craig, J. M. (1988). Can men and women differentiate between friendly and sexually interested behavior? *Social Psychology Quarterly, 51,* 66–73.

Solomon, D. H. (1997). A developmental model of intimacy and date request explicitness. *Communication Monographs, 64,* 99–118.

Sunnafrank, M. (1991). Interpersonal attraction and attitude similarity: A communication-based assessment. In J. A. Andersen (Ed.), *Communication yearbook 14* (pp. 451–483). Newbury Park, CA: Sage.

Sunnafrank, M., & Miller, G. R. (1981). The role of initial conversations in determining attraction to similar and dissimilar strangers. *Human Communication Research, 8,* 16–25.

Surra, C., & Hughes, D. (1997). Commitment processes in accounts of the development of pre-marital relationships. *Journal of Marriage and the Family, 59,* 5–21.

Taylor, D. A., & Altman, I. (1987). Communication in interpersonal relationships: Social penetration processes. In M. E. Roloff & G. R. Miller (Eds.). *Interpersonal processes: New directions in communication research* (pp. 257–277). Newbury Park, CA: Sage.

Utz, S. (2000). Social information processing in MUDs: The development of friendships in virtual worlds. *Journal of Online Behavior, 1* (1) [On-line]. Available: http://www.behavior.net/JOB/v1n1/utz.html

Van Lear, C. A. (1987). The formation of social relationships: A longitudinal study. *Human Communication Research, 13,* 279–322.

Van Lear, C. A. (1992). Testing a cyclical model of relational development: Two longitudinal studies. *Communication Monographs, 58,* 337–361.

Wallace, L. A. (1992). *Interpersonal attraction and communication: Development of the communication based measure of attraction*. M.A. thesis, Ohio University, Athens.

Walsh, D. G., & Hewitt, J. (1985). Giving men the come-on: Effects of eye contact and smiling in a bar environment. *Perceptual and Motor Skills, 61*, 873–874.

Wilmot, W. W. (1987). *Dyadic communication* (3rd ed.). New York: Random House.

C H A P T E R   1 0

MAINTAINING

RELATIONSHIPS

RELATIONAL MAINTENANCE
AND EQUITY

RELATIONAL MAINTENANCE STRATEGIES

Positivity

Openness

Assurances

Social Networks

Sharing Tasks

RELATIONAL DIALECTICS

Dialectical Tensions

Responding to Dialectical Tensions

MAINTAINING PLATONIC FRIENDSHIPS

MAINTAINING DIFFERENT TYPES OF
ROMANTIC RELATIONSHIPS

Love Styles and Love Ways

Fitzpatrick's Marital Typology

Differences in Communication among
   Marital Types

CHAPTER SUMMARY

"There was one ritual we developed when we were very small that we revealed to not another living soul. Whenever we were hurting or damaged or sad, whenever our parents had punished or beaten us, the three of us would go to the end of the floating dock, dive into the sun-sweet water, then swim out ten yards into the channel and form a circle together by holding hands. We floated together, our hands clasped in a perfect unbreakable circle. I held Savannah's hand and I held Luke's. All of us touched, bound in a ring of flesh and blood and water. Luke would give a signal and all of us would inhale and sink to the bottom of the river, our hands still tightly joined. We would remain on the bottom of the river until one of us squeezed the hands of the others and we would rise together and break the surface in an explosion of sunlight and breath."

— Pat Conroy, *The Prince of Tides*, pp. 442–443

In *The Prince of Tides*, novelist Pat Conroy relates how three children — Luke, Savannah, and Tom — survive the cruel lessons of an abusive father and a manipulative mother. We see how the children bond together, protect one another, and engage in activities that mark their special relationships. Their childhood ritual of holding hands and sinking to the bottom of the river symbolizes their connection and support for one another. As the children mature, they develop their own lives. And although their communication is sporadic, it is clear that Luke, Savannah, and Tom maintain their deep affection and unfaltering support for one another in adulthood.

Friendships fade, romances die, and family ties wither unless we make efforts to ensure their continuance. What factors influence the choice of maintenance behaviors? What communication strategies do people use to maintain their relationships? Are there tensions that reflect being in relationships? This chapter addresses these questions in examining how people attempt to maintain their relationships.

Dindia and Canary (1993) provided four definitions of *relational maintenance*. The first is to keep the relationship in existence — or stability. This is the most fundamental aspect of maintenance (Dindia, 2000). The second definition is to keep a relationship in a specified state or condition, for example, to keep the relationship from becoming more (or less) intimate (Duck, 1988). The third definition is to sustain a satisfactory relationship. The fourth definition is to repair a relationship that has undergone some sort of challenge. Montgomery (1993) suggested that maintenance involves *sustaining* a relationship that experiences various inevitable changes that arise from dialectical forces (discussed later in this chapter). From experience, most of us can relate to these types of situations. Moreover, we recognize in these definitions that the goal of maintaining relationships is not an easy task.

Why people even try to maintain their close relationships can be a tricky question. According to Wilmot (1987), people maintain their close relationships for three reasons: because the relationship serves its functions well (e.g., your romantic partner is affectionate), because it provides security and support in a changing world and during crises (e.g., you move back home after a divorce), and because the relationship offers a sense of pride in being in it (e.g., you are proud to hang with your friends because they are so fun). Rusbult (1987) adds other reasons more specific to romantic relationships. She holds that people become committed to their relationships due to the amount of satisfaction, investment (for example, time, money, and emotional energy), and lack of potential alternative relationships or activities. And committed people are much more likely to maintain their relationships.

RELATIONAL MAINTENANCE AND EQUITY

Steve and Jennifer began dating when Jennifer was in law school, and they married just before her bar exam. Steve is a real estate agent and earns decent money, though he will never be wealthy. He is also responsible and faithful. Jennifer is intelligent and exciting, and she introduces Steve to different ideas and new, cultural things to do. Jennifer knows that Steve isn't deeply committed to his career, but she appreciates his responsibility and how he supported her during law school.

Jennifer passes her bar exam and accepts a position in a respected law firm. Within a year, Jennifer earns twice as much money as Steve does, and she has much potential for career advancement. Typically the junior members of the firm go out for drinks after work. But Steve disapproves of Jennifer socializing with her associates after work hours, and he wants her to spend more time at home, as she did before.

Jennifer has become tired of being constrained and being the one who plans for special activities. She feels that the fun has disappeared from the marriage. Jennifer also believes that she needs someone smarter to share her ideas with. In short, Jennifer resents that she now pays most of their bills and feels that Steve restricts her activities. Steve feels a bit guilty for not pulling his weight, but he recalls how he helped put Jennifer through school. Still, he thinks that it's only fair that she stick it out. Mostly, Steve is anxious that Jennifer will leave him because she has so much else going for her.

As this story illustrates, people stay in relationships to the extent that they are rewarding and equitable. Research by Hatfield, Traupmann, Sprecher, Utne, and Hay (1985; also Sprecher & Schwartz, 1994; Utne, Hatfield, Traupmann, & Greenberger, 1984) reports that maintaining relationships is strongly linked to the amount of rewards and equity in the relationship. The most satisfying relationships are those that are rewarding and fair. Hatfield and associates (1985; Hatfield, Walster, & Berscheid, 1978) specify the main propositions of equity theory:

Proposition 1: Individuals try to increase their rewards and minimize their punishments.

Proposition 2a: Groups, including relationships, can maximize their rewards by developing systems of equity and influencing others to adopt those systems of equity.

Proposition 2b: Groups usually reward persons who treat others equitably and punish those who do not treat others equitably.

Proposition 3: People become distressed when they see their relationships as inequitable. The more inequitable the relationship, the greater the distress.

Proposition 4: People who perceive inequity try to restore equity. The greater the inequity, and the accompanying distress, the harder people try to restore equity.

Equity specifically refers to the principle of fairness that is based on a comparison of what two people put in (inputs) and obtain (outputs) from each other. If the input-outcome ratios are equal, the relationship is equitable. Of course, some relationships suffer from inequity. People who receive fewer rewards relative to their partners are *underbenefited*. Those who receive greater rewards relative to their partners are *overbenefited*. Research shows that underbenefited partners are less satisfied because they are in inequitable arrangements and derive relatively few rewards; overbenefited people still obtain more rewards than their partners (e.g., Buunk & Mutsaers, 1999). Sprecher (1986) found that underbenefitedness was strongly associated with negative emotional responses to the partner (such as anger, resentment, and depression). These negative emotional reactions to underbenefitedness may contribute to a lack of effort to maintain the relationship. For example, Canary and Stafford (1992, 2001) found that underbenefited people do not expend as much effort as equitably treated people to maintain their marriages.

Research has shown that underbenefited persons are less content in their relationships and are angry at their partner, whereas highly overbenefited persons feel guilty (Hatfield et al., 1985). Researchers have found that people who feel underbenefited more readily seek extramarital affairs than those who feel equitably treated (Hatfield et al., 1985; Prins, Buunk, & Van Yperen, 1993). The most satisfying relationships are those in which both partners feel rewarded on an equal basis. Figure 10.1 illustrates the connection between relational contentment and equity.

Equity also operates in people's attributions of how much the other tries to maintain the relationship. For example, in a study of how dating partners maintain their relationships, Fletcher, Fincham, Cramer, and Heron (1987) found that relational commitment, happiness, and love were highest when efforts to maintain the relationship were seen as equal. But people reporting much greater or lesser degrees of effort

Figure 10.1

The Relationship
between Equity
and Contentment

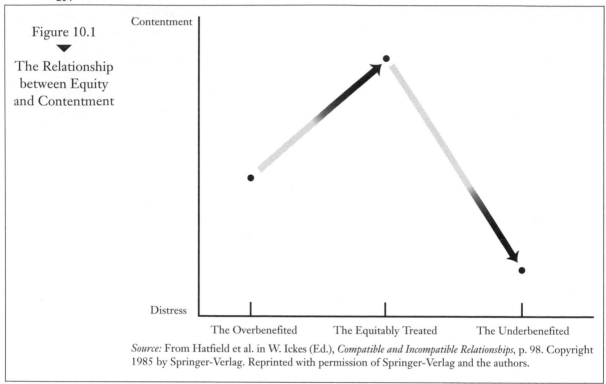

Source: From Hatfield et al. in W. Ickes (Ed.), *Compatible and Incompatible Relationships*, p. 98. Copyright 1985 by Springer-Verlag. Reprinted with permission of Springer-Verlag and the authors.

at maintaining the relationship, relative to perceptions of the partner's efforts, were dissatisfied with their relationships. Imagine if your attempts to keep a relationship going are not reciprocated (you write letters and cards, but your friend does not; you try to be upbeat, but your partner only complains about your behavior; your roommate doesn't help you at all with the household chores).

Equity also relates to other predictors of stability, such as satisfaction and intimacy. For example, Sprecher (2001), who studied a small group of couples over years, found that people were most likely to stay in a relationship if they found it rewarding to do so, and rewarding relationships are satisfying ones. Women who felt committed to the partner and relationship, and both men and women who felt satisfied in a rewarding relationship, and who did not experience the feeling of being underbenefited were more likely to stay in a relationship. In a study of married couples, Willigen and Drentea (2001) found that perceptions of equitable, fair treatment in household labor were associated with high levels of perceived social support, which is related to psychological well-being and a number of positive psychological outcomes. Mackey, Diemer, and O'Brien (2000) conducted in-depth interviews to explore long-term romances and friendships (lasting thirty years on average), focusing on why some people achieve high levels of psychological intimacy (defined as a sense that one could be open and honest in talking with a partner about personal thoughts and feelings not often experienced in other relationships). A sense of equity in the relationship, the absence of a major conflict, expression of attraction, and a confrontive conflict management style (they had direct, face-to-face discussions of differences) were related to higher levels of psychological intimacy, which is rewarding in and of itself.

In sum, perceptions of equity and inequity combine with other factors to affect people's motivation to maintain their relationships. People who feel underbenefited or overbenefited are less likely to expend effort to maintain their relationships, versus people who find their relationships both rewarding and equitable.

RELATIONAL MAINTENANCE STRATEGIES

Before we present the five maintenance strategies that we develop in this chapter, a comment is in order concerning relational factors that affect the manner in which relationships are maintained. For example, Attridge (1994) notes several barriers to breaking up, including the degree to which a person's identity is wrapped up in his or her relational partner, joint possessions, religion, children, and other concerns. Rusbult, Drigotas, and Verette (1994; Van Lange et al., 1997) show how people maintain their marriages psychologically by derogating alternative relational partners, by sacrificing personal rewards for the sake of the relationship, and by believing in the perceived superiority of the marriage over other marriages.

At the sociological level, culture and race also affect how relationships fare. For example, Yum and Canary (in press) reported that South Korean (versus U.S.) partners rely more on their cultural context and shared sense of fate to maintain their relationships, and they rely less on maintenance strategies to sustain their romantic involvements than do their American counterparts. Yum and Canary argued that relational stability depends on cultural principles, such as *uye-ri* (i.e., moral obligation to remain) in South Korea and other cultures. Regarding interethnic, or mixed-race, dyads, the literature indicates that interethnic marriages, for example, are very difficult to maintain. Approximately 67% of interethnic marriages end in divorce (compared to the 50% rate for all marriages; see Gaines & Agnew, in press, for a review). One reason that interethnic relationships often fall apart concerns how they are not valued in the United States. For example, Garcia and Rivera (1999) assessed perceptions held by racially similar (same-race) and dissimilar (mixed-race) dyads (friends and couples). Participants reported that (1) same-race dyads were more positive about themselves and their relationship quality than were mixed-race pairs; (2) mixed-race friends reported more positive perceptions held about them by others than did mixed-race couples; however (3) all relationships were seen relatively positively. The authors concluded that the level of intimacy in people's mixed-race relationships influences people's perceptions about them (i.e., people are more positive if the pair members are only friends). These findings regarding differing perceptions, in addition to other research findings, indicate that interethnic romances are not as positively sanctioned as are relationships between people with the same ethnic background (Gaines & Agnew, in press). Of course, such discrimination represents an unfortunate hurdle for mixed-race couples.

Given the contexts of external barriers and of alternative cultures, people still must engage in activities to maintain their relationships. In other words, people have goals for their long-term involvements, and they use communication behaviors to pursue those objectives. In this chapter, we discuss various interactive strategies that people use to maintain their relationships.

The various maintenance strategies reported here have been shown to positively affect important relational characteristics, such as commitment, trust, and relational quality (e.g., Canary & Stafford, 1992; Weigel & Ballard-Reisch, 1999a, 1999b). The list of strategies is adapted from research on relational maintenance by Stafford and Canary (1991), a widely used typology in the field of communication (for others, see Canary & Zelley, 1999; Dindia, 2000; Haas & Stafford, 1998). Stafford and Canary examined the literature (e.g., Dindia & Baxter, 1987), asked open-ended questions about how romantic partners maintained their relationships, and statistically revealed five strategies: positivity, openness, assurances, social networks, and sharing tasks. These strategies have also been shown to be effective in friendship (Messman, Canary, & Hause, 2000), sibling (Myers, 2001), and parent-child relationships (Vogl-Bauer, Kalbfleisch, & Beatty, 1999).

Positivity

Positivity involves such behaviors as acting cheerful, being courteous, and refraining from criticism. Positivity can be an effective means of maintaining a relationship because being positive can increase the reward level of the partner. We all know people who are genuinely positive and rewarding to be with; they smile when they see us, tell us how appreciative of us they are, and never complain about the relationship. Sampling romantic relationships, Canary and Stafford (1992) and Stafford and Canary (1991) found that positivity was strongly associated with liking the partner. Another way of being positive in romantic relationships is to use what Dindia (1989) calls romantic tactics — showing affection, being fun and spontaneous, and so on.

Positivity is similar to Bell, Daly, and Gonzalez's (1987) idea that relational maintenance is achieved through affinity-seeking behaviors. *Affinity seeking* refers to a person's attempt to get another to like him or her. Bell and co-workers found that wives reported that their husbands' most effective affinity-maintenance tactics were honesty, physical affection, self-inclusion (husbands including themselves in the wives' activities), sensitivity, and shared spirituality.

Perhaps the opposite of positivity is using **antisocial tactics** (Dindia, 1989). Antisocial tactics "represent people's attempts to obtain relational rewards by imposing their position on another through force or deception" (Roloff, 1976, p. 181). Dindia (1989) found that husbands' use of antisocial tactics was negatively associated with wives' satisfaction. People may use antisocial strategies to limit a relationship's intimacy or to assert control over the partner. Sometimes people act rude to discourage their partners from escalating the relationship (not returning phone messages, lying about plans for the weekend, threatening or intimidating the partner, etc.).

Openness

The strategy of **openness** reflects the extent to which partners explicitly discuss the nature of their relationship. (This strategy has also been called *directness* by Ayres [1983].) Using openness, people attempt to maintain their relationships by disclosing

It is sometimes difficult to maintain your relationships unless you are open about what you want from them.

Cathy copyright Cathy Guisewite. Reprinted with permission of Universal Press Syndicate. All rights reserved.

their feelings about the relationship, asking how their partner feels about the relationship, discussing relational goals, and having periodic talks about the relationship.

Openness helps maintain the relationship insofar as partners discuss topics salient to the relationship (such as the agreement to have an exclusive sexual relationship). For instance, being open about successes and confiding in each other constitute two important ways in which friendships are maintained (Argyle & Henderson, 1984). It is often difficult to maintain a relationship at a satisfactory level without being open about what you want.

Though openness can be effective, research indicates that being too open (and especially being negative) may harm the relationship (see, for example, Hecht, Shepard, & Hall, 1979; see also Chapter 7). In addition, Ayres (1983) found that openness was not a preferred strategy if the communicator thought the partner wanted to change the level of intimacy in the relationship, but the communicator did not. Instead, actors preferred avoidance (ignoring the person) when the partner wanted to increase the level of intimacy and balance (keeping emotions constant) if they wanted to maintain their relationship when the other person wanted to de-escalate the relationship.

Baxter and Wilmot (1985) report that couples shy away from discussing taboo topics, or topics seen by either or both partners as off limits. Sampling opposite-sex friendships and romantic involvements, Baxter and Wilmot found the following common taboo topics: state of the relationship, extrarelationship activity (such as other romantic parties), relationship norms (discussion of the relational rules), prior relationships, conflict-inducing topics, and negatively valenced disclosure. These researchers also examined the motives for various taboo topics. For example, discussing the state of the relationship could possibly destroy the relationship if commitment levels differed greatly.

Assurances

A third approach to maintaining relationships is to use **assurances.** Using this strategy, communicators show that they are faithful, stress their commitment to the relationship, and clearly imply that the relationship has a future (Stafford & Canary, 1991). Friends engage in assurances by demonstrating emotional support, trusting one another, and offering to help in time of need (Argyle & Henderson, 1984). Likewise, Guerrero (1997) found that friends showed more nonverbal involvement in their conversations when they felt close to their partner. In other words, friends demonstrated conversational support using such nonverbal behaviors as direct body orientation, smiling, vocal interest, animated gestures, and so forth. In short, assurances show that you are committed to the relationship in both word and deed.

Assuring the partner through various actions maintains the relationship by reinforcing the assumption that the other will be there indefinitely. If the partner feels insecure about the future of the relationship, the communicator can maintain the relationship by seeking or offering assurances. Or, on the contrary, to maintain a low commitment level, the communicator could avoid offering assurances about the future.

Related to the strategy of assurances is the communication activity of comforting your partner. Comforting a friend requires sensitivity and skill, partially because the communicator must take into account the identity needs of the person to be comforted: People who require assistance also want to keep their integrity (Burleson & Goldsmith, 1998; Goldsmith, 1992). Burleson and Samter (1985; Samter & Burleson, 1984) have shown that the more effective comforting tactics are those that focus on and offer information about the other person's needs (they take the perspective of the other person; see Chapter 15). A sampling of effective comforting messages is presented in Table 10.1.

Table 10.1

COMFORTING BEHAVIORS

Behavior Type	Description	Example[a]
Responsive acknowledgment	Utterances that offer emotional support	"Really? I'm sorry to hear that."
Psychological information	Questions about state of mind	"Do you still like him?"
Applied disclosure	Topical responses with relevant references	"The same thing happened to me a couple of years ago."
Emotional advice	Utterances that suggest methods of emotional coping	"Give yourself some time to think about things."
Explicit recognition	Utterances that show clear understanding of the suffering	"I know that this is a very difficult time for you."
Elaborated acknowledgment	Statements of recognition, explanation, and understanding	"I know that it hurts a lot now, but after a while the pain subsides, and soon you won't even remember his name."
Perspective	Statements offering a perspective on the problem	"You're young and have many opportunities. That may not be what you want to hear right now, but it's true. There are lots of other fish in the sea."

[a]Responses to the statement "My boyfriend broke up with me last night, and I don't know what to do. I feel so hurt!"
Source: Adapted from Samter & Burleson, 1984, pp. 244–246. Reprinted by permission of Oxford University Press, UK.

Social Networks

A fourth strategy that people use to maintain their relationships is to rely on their **social networks,** their friends and family. Milardo (1986) has argued that friends in particular are bound together in sharing their networks. Furthermore, Stafford and Canary (1991) found that married couples made more use of social networks than did dating couples. This may be because marriage involves increased shared activities and common social circles (e.g., having dinner at the in-laws every Sunday, having parties with other couples), whereas dating may be a time of redefining friendship ties. People who have established common social networks are more likely to use them to maintain their relationships than people who do not share social networks. In a study of gay male and lesbian relationships, Haas and Stafford (1998) likewise found that partners relied on supportive social environments to maintain their relationships (e.g., participating in gay/lesbian events, visiting a gay guest house).

Relationships with social support appear to be more stable than those without such support. Parks and Adelman (1983) found that social networks help us reduce uncertainty about the partner. Also, Milardo (1986) has argued that relationship stability increases when the social networks of friends are close and interconnected. How many times have we relied on "a friend of a friend" to help us understand a relationship or had a party to reinforce the relationship? Indeed, lack of social support (among other reasons) may actually speed up the termination of the relationship (see Chapter 11).

Sharing Tasks

The fifth maintenance strategy Stafford and Canary (1991) found was **sharing tasks,** performing one's "fair share" of the work in the relationship. For example, one person may prepare dinner while the other cleans the kitchen, or one person may wash the dishes if the partner folds the laundry. On another level, sharing tasks may refer to one person's working overtime to relieve the burden of certain personal expenses on the partner (e.g., working extra hours to afford the vacation you both want to take).

Showing your partner that you shoulder your responsibilities illustrates equity in operation. Clearly, one way to maintain relational harmony and demonstrate an equitable relationship is to perform specific jobs and expectations. In other words, sharing tasks can be symbolic. For example, cleaning the house when your partner is very tired demonstrates your care for that person and your willingness to be interdependent. In addition, two people sharing tasks implies that they are equal in each other's eyes — neither is too good to do a particular chore (Haas & Stafford, 1998).

Conversely, not helping your roommate, friend, parent, or partner can convey an attitude of entitlement — that you do not need to do any of the work that must be done. Such people often distort their contributions by comparing themselves to other people and not the partner (e.g., comparing yourself to the neighbor who never cleans as opposed to your partner who most often cooks and cleans). However, people who strive for equity perform their share of tasks, and they compare their contributions directly to their partners' inputs (Coltrane, 1989, 1996).

People who strive for equity in their relationships perform their share of tasks and compare their contributions to those of their partner.

© Susie Fitzhugh

RELATIONAL DIALECTICS

So far we have based our discussion of relational maintenance on research related to how individuals maintain their relationships to restore rewards and equity. Now we take a different approach, based on different assumptions about relationships and how people maintain them. The first assumption is that people in relationships experience tensions that reflect the presence of polar opposites that coexist in any relationship.

The second assumption is that one such polar experience becomes meaningful only if its opposite is present. In other words, both conditions must occur if either is to have meaning. The interplay between polar opposites is called **relational dialectics** (Baxter, 1994; Baxter & Dindia, 1990; Baxter & Montgomery, 1996; Montgomery, 1993; Rawlins, 1992; Wilmot, 1987). Third, as Montgomery notes, "The presence of inherent, oppositional forces in a relationship results in constant change" (p. 208). Accordingly, relational dialectics are tensions that are natural by-products of being in a relationship that constantly changes. In this section, we first discuss types of dialectics, then we discuss how people respond to them communicatively.

Dialectical Tensions

Research reveals that at least four dialectical tensions exist between lovers and friends (Baxter & Montgomery, 1996; Conville, 1998; Cupach & Metts, 1988). The first dialectic is **interdependence-autonomy.** You experience the pull of wanting to be connected with someone and share activities with someone, but you also want to assert your own individuality and separateness. The second dialectic is **openness-closedness.** You want to open yourself to your partner to disclose who you are, but you also need to protect yourself and your partner by being closed (Rawlins, 1983). The third dialectic is **predictability-novelty.** You may want to be able to predict your partner and know how to respond with that person, but you may also want new experiences. The fourth dialectic is **passion-stability.** Passion is emotional heat in the relationship, but it must be balanced with stability to prevent the relationship from burning out.

At issue, then, are not problems in the conventional sense. Relational dialectics are an aspect of relationship life itself. Relational partners must learn how to respond to these dialectical tensions in order to maintain their relationships. Cupach and Metts (1988) indicate that when people have trouble managing their relational dialectics, they experience relational conflict and personal anxiety.

Responding to Dialectical Tensions

Recently researchers have uncovered ways in which people respond to dialectical tensions. The first response is called *selection*. The couple might select one dialectical tension over the other. For example, some people decide to avoid the partner when their needs for privacy outweigh their needs to be with the partner. A second response is *separation*. Couples deny the presence of the dialectic by somehow separating the opposite tensions from one another. For example, you might have a "women's night out" in order to secure some time away from your partner every week. The response of *neutralization* refers to compromising the opposite tensions. One way to do this is to avoid the issue or handle the topics ambiguously (e.g., "We don't have to have affection to show affection"). The alternative approach to neutralization is *discussion*, where partners talk openly about the tension. *Revitalization* refers to a proactive but indirect response to the dialectics. For example, to revitalize passion, you might arrange to meet your partner in a new, romantic place (such as a restaurant at the top of a skyscraper).

Perhaps the most difficult response is *reframing* (see also Baxter, 1990). Reframing involves placing your dialectical tensions in a different light so that the experience of both tensions is no longer contradictory. If you can accept that dialectics are a natural aspect of relationships, you may rise above the tension you feel. For example, you may feel smothered by your child; but you realize that this is a common phenomenon between parents and their children, so you redefine the issue ("My child isn't really smothering me, it's just that I need some time alone and can't get away right now").

Some people give in to a particular dialectical pole. *Acquiescence* refers to giving in to a relational feature, not wishing to solve the dialectical problem. For example, you might accept that being married involves a higher degree of stability and less passion than you want. So you give in to the dialectic of stability saying, "No marriage has unbridled passion because people just cannot sustain that kind of emotion over the long haul." As you might imagine, the effectiveness of these responses varies according to the dialectical tensions. For example, when used as a response to the dialectical tensions of interdependence-autonomy or predictability-novelty, reframing was positively correlated with relational satisfaction (Baxter, 1990). Although reframing is a sophisticated strategy, it appears to help couples resolve issues concerning togetherness and predictability. But when faced with the tension of openness-closedness, use of neutralization (by being ambiguous) was negatively associated with relational satisfaction (Baxter, 1990). It appears that being unclear about the issue does not help a couple manage the need to balance openness and closedness.

In sum, relational dialectics are tensions that dyads experience when they feel the pull of opposite, but unavoidable, elements of relational life. Effective responses for dealing with dialectics function to maintain the relationship.

MAINTAINING PLATONIC FRIENDSHIPS

Whether the friendship exists between two opposite-sex heterosexuals or between two same-sex gay male or lesbian friends, these friends must engage in strategies to retain the platonic (i.e., nonsexual) nature of their friendship. **Platonic relationships** refer to friendships that lack sexual involvement, despite possibilities for such involvement. Research suggests that about 70% of people in cross-sex friendships keep them defined as platonic relationships, whereas approximately 30% engage in some form of sex (e.g., Werking, 1997). Of course, some opposite-sex or same-sex gay friends reframe the definition of their friendship (e.g., "friends with benefits"), or they might deny the significance of a sexual encounter ("that happened only once or twice"). However, it appears that most of us derive rewards that are intrinsic to opposite-sex friendships and maintain those friendships as platonic. (For one view of the challenges of maintaining an interracial friendship, see the box "Maintaining a Friendship in *Driving Miss Daisy*.")

MAINTAINING A FRIENDSHIP IN *DRIVING MISS DAISY*

Driving Miss Daisy is a film about maintaining a friendship over many years as well as overcoming prejudice. Miss Daisy (Jessica Tandy) is an elderly Jewish woman who can no longer drive herself. Her son (Dan Aykroyd) hires an older black man, whose name is Houk (Morgan Freeman), to drive her car. Although Miss Daisy claims she holds no prejudices against black people, she actually does. Miss Daisy complains to her son about "those people," about how they like to meddle in her affairs, and about how they cannot be "trusted."

Houk finally wins the trust of Miss Daisy, and he drives her wherever she needs to go. And Miss Daisy, a retired teacher, teaches Houk to read and write. On one extraordinary long trip, they travel to Mobile, Alabama, from Atlanta, Georgia. We see how dependent she has become on Houk at this point: When he leaves the car for a few minutes, she cries out for him, apparently frightened to be alone. And at first she is very picky about his behaviors. He is not allowed to drive at the speed limit, he is not to park close to the front door of the synagogue, and he can't use the air conditioner. But later she stops criticizing him.

Houk manages to find a balance between being an employee and being a friend. One morning there is an ice storm, and Houk brings Miss Daisy some coffee. The following dialogue illustrates their friendship:

Houk:	I figured your stove was out, so I stopped by the Krispy Kreme — I know how you got to have your coffee in the morning.
Miss Daisy:	How sweet of you, Houk.
Houk:	Yes'm. Shoot, we ain't had no good coffee since Idella passed away.
Miss Daisy:	I can fix her biscuits and we both know how to make her fried chicken, but nobody can make Idella's coffee.
Houk:	Ain't that the truth.
Miss Daisy:	Idella was lucky.
Houk:	Yes'm, I expect she was. Well . . . (*he picks his things up*).
Miss Daisy:	Where you going?
Houk:	Just goin' to go out here, take these things.
Miss Daisy:	I don't know what you can do here today except keep me company.
Houk:	I might see if I can make us some fire.

But things are still not entirely smooth. When Martin Luther King Jr. comes to Atlanta, Miss Daisy obtains tickets for a dinner where King will speak. She doesn't feel comfortable inviting Houk, although her son suggested it. Finally, on the way to the dinner, Miss Daisy indirectly asks Houk if he is interested in attending the dinner.

Houk:	Now, what do you think I am, Miss Daisy?
Miss Daisy:	What do you mean?

Houk:	This invitation to this here dinner come a month ago. Now, it be you want me to go with you, how come you wait 'til we're in the car and on the way before you ask me?
Miss Daisy:	What? All I said is [my son] said you wanted to go.
Houk:	Well, next time you want me to go somewhere, you ask me regular.
Miss Daisy:	You don't have to carry on so much.
Houk:	Well, now let's just leave it alone.
Miss Daisy:	Honestly.
Houk:	*(to himself)* Talk about things changing — ain't changin' all that much.

But by the end of the film, we see that most of the prejudice has been replaced by genuine friendship. The two confide in each other, depend on each other, and look forward to seeing each other. Miss Daisy shows her affection for Houk in the following scene:

Miss Daisy:	You ought not to be driving anything, the way you can see.
Houk:	How'd you know how I can see, 'less'n you can look out my eyes, hmm?
Miss Daisy:	Houk, you are my best friend.
Houk:	No, Miss Daisy.
Miss Daisy:	*(she reaches for and holds his hand)* You are. You are.
Houk:	Yes'm.

Soon after that, Miss Daisy must receive care at a nursing home. Houk continues the effort to maintain their relationship. Although he has stopped driving due to his failing vision, he still visits her by taking a taxi or having his daughter drive him. The final scene symbolizes their friendship: Houk feeds Miss Daisy bites of her Thanksgiving pie, which she eats joyfully.

Driving Miss Daisy shows that relationships require effort, or else they deteriorate. Houk works hard at establishing a good working relationship and then a friendship with Miss Daisy. Houk continues to work at the relationship by being positive and complimentary and by doing favors for Miss Daisy. *Driving Miss Daisy* is an excellent film for the analysis of how friendships are maintained as well as how prejudice can be overcome.

Excerpts from *Driving Miss Daisy* by Alfred Uhry. By permission of The Zanuck Company.

Opposite-sex friendships are now widely accepted and most appear to offer rewards not found in other associations. Buhrke and Fuqua (1987) reported that, on the average, men and women in their sample reported over three close opposite-sex friends. Werking (1997) indicated that platonic friendships (vs. romantic involvements) are characterized by: (1) "attraction of the spirit," not physical attraction; (2) an end in themselves, not a way to reach marriage; (3) more equality; and (4) lack of exclusivity. Also, research indicates that the maintenance of cross-sex friendships entails relational dimensions of liking and equity, while such friends successfully downgrade sexual tensions that might exist (e.g., Monsour, Harris, & Kurzweil, 1994). How do friends with potential to become romantic partners maintain the platonic nature of their relationship?

Messman, Canary, and Hause (2000) examined the maintenance strategies that opposite-sex platonic friends use. Table 10.2 reports the maintenance strategies that these researchers found. The most commonly used maintenance strategies for opposite-sex friends included give/seek advice, assurances, positivity, cards/letters/calls, share activity, and then openness. Interestingly, the least likely strategies that

---

Table 10.2

PLATONIC FRIENDS' MAINTENANCE STRATEGIES AND EXAMPLE ITEMS

In order to maintain my opposite-sex friendship, I . . .

Share Activity

- Help him/her with his/her tasks (e.g., classes, homework, laundry).
- Share time with him/her (e.g., dinner, movies, play cards).
- Share specific routine activities with him/her (e.g., hang out at a particular place).

Cards, Letters, and Calls

- Visit him/her (e.g., visit each other's school or go out during breaks from school).
- Call him/her and make future plans with him/her (e.g., activities for breaks from school, trips).

Assurances

- Show that I recognize significant events in his/her life (e.g., birthdays, holidays).
- Comfort him/her in time of need.
- Try to satisfy his/her need for companionship.

Advice

- Disclose personal information to him/her (e.g., talk about feelings, dates).
- Discuss experiences that we have shared in the past.
- Give/seek advice (e.g., about love, school, plans).

Avoidance

- Avoid discussing certain topics with him/her.
- Avoid him/her (e.g., don't return phone calls).
- Am not completely honest with him/her (e.g., do not mention things).

Openness

- Talk about my feelings about our relationship.
- Am direct about my feelings when we have conflicts.
- Seek to discuss the quality and/or nature of our friendship.

No Flirting

- Avoid flirting with him/her.
- Do not encourage overly familiar behaviors (e.g., flirting, eye gaze, touching).

Positivity

- Attempt to make our interactions enjoyable.
- Am positive and cheerful with my friend.
- Avoid criticizing my friend.

Source: Adapted from Messman, Canary, & Hause, 2000.

people used were avoidance and not flirting (i.e., opposite-sex friends tended to flirt with each other in teasing, but nonseductive, ways). Messman et al. argued that these findings suggest that opposite-sex friends are maintained primarily through messages that convey a person's fundamental support for the friend.

In addition to maintenance strategies, Messman and colleagues also investigated the role of equity and various *motives*, or reasons that people offered for keeping their potentially romantic involvements platonic. They found that equity was more important to romantic partners than friends. Apparently people are more "exchange-minded" when in dating relationships than with friends. Still, being taken advantage of (feeling underbenefited) negatively affected the use of most maintenance strategies. These authors also found that the motive to "safeguard the relationship" was the most powerful predictor of maintenance strategies in comparison to other motives — having concerns about third parties (such as the friend's romantic partner), not finding the friend attractive, being uncertain of the friend's intentions. In brief, it appears that opposite-sex friends enjoy the benefits of those relationships, and most people attempt to keep their friendships platonic by keeping in touch, being positive and open, and offering supportive messages.

MAINTAINING DIFFERENT TYPES OF ROMANTIC RELATIONSHIPS

Whereas platonic relationships refer to nonsexual involvements, a great deal of literature has revealed that not all romantic relationships — dating, engagements, and marital relationships — are alike. Love relationships differ, marriage types vary, and those differences have implications for relational maintenance behaviors.

Love Styles and Love Ways

What does it mean to you when you say or hear the words "I love you"? Does it mean commitment? Passion? Devotion? Intimacy? Being "one" with someone — two people doing things together, helping each other, sacrificing for each person's benefit? Being with someone who is physically ideal, sexually pleasing?

The role that love plays in maintaining relationships is complex, for several reasons. First, people have different meanings for the term. In addition, love is difficult to measure because it involves intense feelings (anxiousness, jealousy, passion, thrills, happiness, serenity, and other feelings) and because it involves many thoughts or cognitions about the loved partner. Also, being in love and staying in love is best viewed as a process that changes over time — the quality and experience of love changes as partners get to know each other, adjust to each other, and so forth (Barnes & Sternberg, 1997). Thus to study *love* and how partners maintain their love relationships requires that we look at different meanings of love. Two complementary approaches to examining love provide insight into the way in which people might maintain love: **love styles,** which focus more on individual tendencies and relationship outcomes, and **love ways,** which emphasize how love experiences are expressed in communicative behaviors.

LOVE STYLES. Early research on love styles, or types of loving relationships, identified six types, and scholars provided them with Greek names (Lee, 1973): *eros, ludus, storge, pragma, mania,* and *agape.* Hendrick and Hendrick have done the most research on love styles (e.g., Hendrick & Hendrick, 1986, 1997; Hendrick, Hendrick, & Dicke, 1998; Traban, Hendrick, & Hendrick, 1998). Examples of how these styles are measured appear in Table 10.3.

Hendrick and Hendrick (1997) summarize the styles as follows:

1. *Eros* love is passionate love characterized by intensity and commitment, idealism in sexuality, self-disclosure, the ability to elicit self-disclosure from a partner, and higher levels of self-esteem. Although eros is unrelated to sensation-seeking motives, it is characterized by passion in one's love relationship.

2. *Ludus* love is game-playing love associated with sensation-seeking fun, casual and sometimes manipulative love, greater extraversion, aggressiveness, dating variety, and playfulness. There is less self-disclosure.

<table>
<tr><td colspan="1">

▼
Table 10.3

SAMPLE ITEMS FROM THE HENDRICK, HENDRICK, & DICKE MEASURE OF LOVE ATTITUDES

</td></tr>
</table>

Eros

1. My partner and I have the right physical "chemistry" between us.
2. My partner fits my ideal standards of physical beauty/handsomeness.

Ludus

1. I believe that what my partner doesn't know about me won't hurt him/her.
2. My partner would get upset if he/she knew of some of the things I've done with other people.

Storge

1. Our love is the best kind because it grew out of a long friendship.
2. Our friendship merged gradually into love over time.

Pragma

1. A main consideration in choosing my partner was how he/she would reflect on my family.
2. An important factor in choosing my partner was whether or not he/she would be a good parent.

Mania

1. When my partner doesn't pay attention to me, I feel sick all over.
2. If my partner ignores me for a while, I sometimes do stupid things to try to get his/her attention back.

Agape

1. I would rather suffer myself than let my partner suffer.
2. I am usually willing to sacrifice my own wishes to let my partner achieve his/hers.

Source: From Hendrick et al., 1998, p. 151.

3. *Storge* love is friendship-oriented love. In some projects, about 50% of participants indicated that their loved partner was also their best friend. This love is stable, steady, and somewhat related to idealism about sexuality; it is linked to self-disclosure.

4. *Pragma* love is marked by practicality and rationality. This love is associated with selecting and/or rejecting partners on the basis of image concerns for career, family life, etc. Seemingly detached from passion, this love is low on sensation seeking.

5. *Mania* love is related to possessive, dependent types of relationships and is characterized by mood swings, some amount of sexual idealism, and lower self-esteem; frequent attention and recognition is demanded or needed.

6. *Agape* love is associated with altruism, idealism about love, disclosure to partner, and good listening skills. It is not related to casual sexuality or to sensation seeking.

Hendrick and Hendrick (1997) found that both men and women experiencing eros love reported greater relational satisfaction, whereas ludus love was related to lower levels of relational satisfaction. In fact, eros love has been consistently linked to relational satisfaction for a number of studies, including both Anglos and Mexican-American couples. After eros, the forms of love that are associated with some degree of relational satisfaction are storge and agape; mania love is also sometimes linked to reduced relational satisfaction. We conclude that love that involves passion, friendship, togetherness, and a willingness to place the partner's happiness over one's own happiness (Eros, Storge, Agape) tends to be associated with relational satisfaction and staying friends; ludus and mania are related to less satisfaction and to terminating relationships (Hendrick & Hendrick, 1997).

LOVE WAYS.   Hecht, Marston, and colleagues (Hecht, Marston, & Larkey, 1994; Marston, Hecht, & Robers, 1987) conceptualized love as an experience of "polyvalent" and interdependent thoughts, feelings, and behaviors. Love "involves the individual in all aspects of his or her being: Thought, . . . action, . . . and feelings" (Marston et al., 1987, p. 391). These authors have found five types of love ways:

1. *Companionate love* is active love characterized by shared experiences and feelings. It is communicated in talks about one's feelings and doing things together.

2. *Secure love* is defined by the feelings of security it offers the couple. It is communicated when the partners discuss personal, intimate topics and when one partner does favors for the other.

3. *Intuitive love* is evident in the couple in which partners do not have to say anything because their love is communicated primarily through nonverbal means (by a certain look or tone of voice). Intuitive love involves feelings of warmth, nervousness, and loss of appetite.

4. *Committed love* is defined as togetherness. It is communicated in explicit messages about being committed to each other and making plans for the future.

5. *Traditional romantic love* is experienced with feelings of warmth and of being beautiful and confident. These lovers express their emotional reactions to each other.

Marston et al. found that most of the participants in their project reported more than one love way for the same relationship (typically, two love ways). For example, some individuals can experience love in intuitive and secure ways, whereas the partner may experience love in traditional and committed ways.

As to relational quality and satisfaction, Hecht, Marston, and Larkey (1994) found that individuals experiencing committed love have higher quality relationships, followed by couples who jointly experienced high levels of companionate love (collaborative and active forms of love; expressing love and sharing experiences). Couples experiencing similar levels of secure love and/or companionate love had higher quality relationships than couples who did not share similar views. Hendrick and Hendrick (1997) noted similar findings in difficult cultures, highlighting that sharing tasks, friends, and experiences is important to creating and maintaining love.

If you conclude from the preceding material that not all people have the same love way or love style you would be correct. Marston and Hecht (1994) point out that one problem that partners face concerns how each one might have a love way or love style that frustrates the other. Our love styles and love ways also depend on the implicit

STUDENT AS OBSERVER: LOOKING AT MAINTENANCE STRATEGIES

This exercise is designed to have you observe a relationship's maintenance strategies. This assignment will require some familiarity of a couple and, perhaps, some observation.

1. Select a couple you know. You can choose a relationship you are in yourself.
2. Observe the extent to which both partners use each of the five maintenance strategies identified by Stafford and Canary (1991): positivity, openness, assurances, social networks, and sharing tasks.
3. Does the amount of these behaviors reflect on the couple's level of satisfaction? In other words, do you notice that strategy use is linked to increased satisfaction?
4. Are there any sex differences in terms of who uses which strategy? What can explain these differences, if there are any?
5. Which strategy do think is most effective?

models we hold for relationships, a point we discuss in the following section (see also the section on attachment styles in Chapter 14).

Fitzpatrick's Marital Typology

Fitzpatrick (1988) has presented research on the question, "What does marriage look like in the latter half of the twentieth century?" Her answer reveals that people have different models and types of marriages and that these marriage types differ in their communication behavior. This research has important implications for people who seek to maintain their marriages. The most obvious implication is that people should know what type of relationship they are in so that they can better understand their communication behaviors.

Fitzpatrick (1988) identifies three primary types of marriages (which have been independently confirmed in other research; for example, Gottman, 1994). **Traditional couples** adopt an "ideology of traditionalism." Traditionals believe that people should have faith in its social institutions, that the woman should take the man's last name when they are married, and so on. Traditionals also are interdependent (they share in activities) and have conflict over major issues. **Separate couples** are similar to Traditionals in their ideology of traditionalism, but Separates are autonomous and avoid conflict of all kinds. **Independent couples** do not have traditional beliefs about the relationship, so they must negotiate many issues. Independents must negotiate answers to questions already decided by traditional norms, such as "Should we attend church?" "Who cooks tonight?" and "Which days are you getting the children?" Independents also tend to be interdependent and have conflict over anything. Finally, Fitzpatrick reports that about half of the marriages she has studied consist of **mixed couples,** in which the husband and the wife have different definitions for their marriage. The most common mixed type is the traditional wife and the separate husband.

Fitzpatrick (1988) argues that people enter and maintain their marriages through reliance on **marital schemata,** which she defines as "knowledge structures that represent the external world of marriage and provide guidelines about how to interpret incoming data" (p. 255). Accordingly, Traditionals view marriage in terms of traditional role behaviors. Knowing how to enact such behaviors, Traditionals experience routine interactions and little discord. Separates, who essentially want little involvement with each other, have few interactions. Independents see marriage as the coordination of two individuals' goals. Accordingly, Independents view interruptions of their individual goals more intensely than do Traditionals or Separates.

Differences in Communication among Marital Types

How do these couples communicate? Traditionals tend to be attuned to each other's needs. For example, traditional wives are the most accurate in perceiving their husbands' signs of affection and sexual interest. Traditionals appeal to the nature of their relationship and are honest when trying to persuade each other (Witteman & Fitzpatrick, 1986).

As Fitzpatrick and Best (1979) put it, Separates are "emotionally divorced" from each other. Separates are the least accurate in gauging each other's feelings, and they maintain their distance by vigilantly keeping information and emotions from surfacing in their conversations. In one study on conflict, Separates used blatant forms of avoiding the issues, such as explicitly denying to each other that there was a problem, even after having told the researchers that a problem did indeed exist (Sillars, Pike, Jones, & Redmon, 1983). Likewise, Witteman and Fitzpatrick (1986) found that Separates constrained the other person's behaviors and did not seek information from the other person, but appealed to their partner's sense of values.

Unlike Separates, Independents tend to share information and become emotionally involved in their conversations. Independents are likely to engage in refutation, to discount the other person's arguments, and to seek information more than do other types (Witteman & Fitzpatrick, 1986). Also, Independents counter dominant actions of the spouse with dominant actions of their own (Williamson & Fitzpatrick, 1985). Interestingly, Sillars and colleagues (1983) found that Independents' relational satisfaction scores are positively associated with negative emotional displays (e.g., raising the voice), but their satisfaction scores are inversely correlated with neutral emotional signals. Independents are also relatively accurate in assessing their partners' nonverbal cues of pleasure and affection (Fitzpatrick, 1988).

One study in particular examined how couple types differ in their relational maintenance strategies. Weigel and Ballard-Reisch (1999a) surveyed married couples and found that overall Traditional partners and then Independent partners tend to engage in more relational maintenance behaviors than do Separate partners. In particular, Traditional and Independent couple types both used more assurances and openness than did Separate couple types. Moreover, Traditional marriages involved more task sharing than did either Independent and Separate marriages. These findings make intuitive sense, insofar as people in Separate marriages want to limit the amount of information they exchange, whether it be in terms of underscoring their commitment to each other or simply discussing what they want out of the relationship. Interestingly, however, only partners in Independent marriages tended to reciprocate the extent to which each person engages in maintenance activities. In other words, Independent partners would tend to engage in maintenance strategies to the extent their partners do. However, people in Traditional and Separate marriages tended to engage in various maintenance strategies, whether or not their partner did. These latter findings suggest that Independent couples are very mindful of the efforts that their partners are offering, whereas Traditional and Separate couples focus more on conventional roles to determine the extent to which they work to maintain the relationship. Finally, this study extended others in showing that these relational maintenance strategies are powerfully linked to important relational features, such as commitment, satisfaction, and love.

304

David Burnett/Contact Press Images

People have different types of marriages, and the manner in which they communicate with each other varies according to these types. That there are different marital types is exemplified in the marriages of the Clintons and the Bushes.

© Tannen Maury/The Image Works

CHAPTER SUMMARY

This chapter reviewed why and how people maintain their relationships. People are motivated to maintain relationships to the extent that the relationships are rewarding and equitable. Accordingly, the various strategies for maintaining a relationship affect relationships differently. The five maintenance strategies tend to help most relationships stay on an even keel. These strategies have also been extended to apply to other relational types, such as opposite-sex friends.

In addition, we noted that dialectical contradictions frequently occur in close involvements. Such contradictions require responses, such as segmenting the contradiction. The point is that people in relationships do not experience flat-line stability. Instead, people experience fluctuations that are represented by dialectical contradictions. How people respond to these contradictions communicatively probably impacts the overall quality of their relationships, nonetheless.

Finally, we discussed how marriages vary according to type. Our view is that one type is not superior to any other. Nor are the communication behaviors that are used to maintain a particular type of relationship superior in quality to those used to manage others. The critical issue for us concerns whether your communication functions so that you and your friends, relatives, and lovers can achieve the goal of maintaining your relationships as you both want them.

KEY TERMS

▼

antisocial tactics, p. 286
assurances, p. 288
equity, p. 283
independent couples, p. 302
interdependence-autonomy, p. 292
love styles, p. 298
love ways, p. 298
marital schemata, p. 302
mixed couples, p. 302
openness, p. 287

openness-closedness, p. 292
passion-stability, p. 292
platonic relationship, p. 293
positivity, p. 286
predictability-novelty, p. 292
relational dialectics, p. 292
separate couples, p. 302
sharing tasks, p. 290
social networks, p. 290
traditional couples, p. 302

EXERCISES FOR FURTHER DISCUSSION

▼

1. Duck (1988) offered three situations involving relational maintenance activities: to sustain the existence of a relationship, to keep the relationship from becoming more intimate, and to stabilize an unstable relationship. Think of an example from your own life for each of these situations.
   a. What was the situation? Describe it as precisely as possible.
   b. Which person in the relationship was more active in maintaining it at the same level?
   c. What types of communication behaviors were used to maintain the relationship?

2. List five of the most important relationships in your life. Think of situations in which you share tasks with the people you listed.
   a. What types of tasks do you share with people?
   b. Are there some tasks that you do with some people and other tasks that you do with other people?
   c. What do you think is the symbolic significance of the tasks you share with other people?
   d. Can you think of a situation in which someone expressed unhappiness in a relationship by not sharing in a task?

3. List three dialectical tensions that you think cause problems in your relationships.
   a. In what types of relationships do you experience these tensions?
   b. In what ways do you handle these tensions?
   c. Can you think of some new ways to handle these tensions, based on the ideas presented in this chapter?

4. Consider your cross-sex, platonic friendships.
   a. What are the advantages to having cross-sex friendships?
   b. What are the disadvantages to having cross-sex friendships?
   c. How do you maintain your cross-sex friendships as platonic relationships?
   d. What are some of the challenges in maintaining cross-sex friendships?

5. Two complementary bodies of love research were presented.
   a. Of the love styles, which comes the closest to your idea of *love?*
   b. Do you have more than one love style or love way?
   c. Have you ever been in a relationship where your love style or love way was not the same as your partner's?
   d. Do you think people are aware that they have different love styles and love ways?
   e. How can knowing the research on love styles and love ways help people maintain their love relationships?

6. Reflect on Fitzpatrick's three types of married couples: traditional, independent, and separate.
    a. What type of marriage do you think your parents have?
    b. What type of marriage do you think you are in or would choose?
    c. In what ways does the type of marriage your parents have influence your own relationships?
    d. How might sex differences in behavior vary in different marital types?

SUGGESTED READING

▼

APPROACHES TO RELATIONAL MAINTENANCE

Canary, D. J., & Dainton, M. (in press). *Maintaining relationships through communication: Relational, contextual, and cultural variations*. Mahwah, NJ: Erlbaum. This book discusses how communication scholars investigate the ways in which various types of relationships (e.g., family, friendships, romantic [heterosexual as well as gay and lesbian]) are maintained in various contexts and cultures.

Canary, D. J., & Stafford, L. (1994). *Communication and relational maintenance*. New York: Academic. This book examines how relationships are maintained. Noted scholars from communication and psychology emphasize different aspects of maintaining relationships.

Harvey, J. H., & Wenzel, A. (2001). *Close romantic relationships: Maintenance and enhancement*. Mahwah, NJ: Erlbaum. This anthology features psychological views on how to maintain and enhance relationships.

EQUITY

Hatfield, E., Traupmann, J., Sprecher, S., Utne, M., & Hay, J. (1985). Equity and intimate relationships: Recent research. In W. Ickes (Ed.), *Compatible and incompatible relationships* (pp. 91–117). New York: Springer-Verlag. Theoretical propositions, supporting research, and future extensions are covered in this review of equity theory.

RELATIONAL DIALECTICS

Baxter, L. A., & Montgomery, B. M. (1998). *Relating: Dialogues and dialectics*. New York: Guilford. An excellent review and synthesis of theory and research on relational dialectics.

Montgomery, B. M. (1993). Relationship maintenance versus relationship change: A dialectical dilemma. *Journal of Social and Personal Relationships, 10*, 205–224. Montgomery argues that change is fundamental to stable relationships. Implications for the study of relational maintenance are examined.

LOVE

Traban, C. B., Hendrick, S. S., & Hendrick, C. (1998). Loving and liking. In P. A. Andersen & L. K. Guerrero (Eds.), *Handbook of communication and emotion* (pp. 331–351). San Diego: Academic. This is an excellent summary paper on the emotion of love.

MARITAL TYPES

Fitzpatrick, M. A. (1988). *Between husbands and wives: Communication in marriage.* Newbury Park, CA: Sage. Fitzpatrick presents an interesting review of her research on different types of marriage, including a first-rate discussion of couple types.

REFERENCE LIST

▼

Argyle, M., & Henderson, M. (1984). The rules of friendship. *Journal of Social and Personal Relationships, 1,* 211–237.

Attridge, M. (1994). Barriers to dissolution of romantic relationships. In D. J. Canary & L. Stafford (Eds.), *Communication and relational maintenance* (pp. 141–164). San Diego: Academic.

Ayres, J. (1983). Strategies to maintain relationships: Their identification and perceived usage. *Communication Quarterly, 31,* 62–67.

Barnes, M. L., & Sternberg, R. J. (1997). A hierarchical model of love and its prediction of satisfaction in close relationships. In R. J. Sternberg & M. Hojjat (Eds.), *Satisfaction in close relationships* (pp. 79–101). New York: Guilford.

Baxter, L. A. (1990). Dialectical contradictions in relationship development. *Journal of Social and Personal Relationships, 7,* 69–88.

Baxter, L. A. (1994). A dialogic approach to relationship maintenance. In D. J. Canary & L. Stafford (Eds.), *Communication and relational maintenance.* Orlando, FL: Academic.

Baxter, L. A., & Dindia, K. (1990). Marital partners' perceptions of marital maintenance strategies. *Journal of Social and Personal Relationships, 7,* 187–208.

Baxter, L. A., & Montgomery, B. M. (1996). *Relating: Dialogues and dialectics.* New York: Guilford.

Baxter, L. A., & Wilmot, W. W. (1985). Taboo topics in close relationships. *Journal of Social and Personal Relationships, 2,* 253–269.

Bell, R. A., Daly, J. A., & Gonzalez, C. (1987). Affinity maintenance in marriage and its relationship to women's marital satisfaction. *Journal of Marriage and the Family, 49,* 445–454.

Buhrke, R. A., & Fuqua, D. (1987). Sex differences in same- and cross-sex supportive relationships. *Sex Roles, 17,* 339–352.

Burleson, B. R., & Goldsmith, D. (1998). How the comforting process works: Alleviating emotional distress through conversationally induced reappraisals. In P. A. Andersen & L. K. Guerrero (Eds.), *The handbook of communication and emotion: Research, theory, applications, and contexts* (pp. 245–280). San Diego: Academic.

Burleson, B. R., & Samter, W. (1985). Consistencies in theoretical and naive evaluations of comforting messages. *Communication Monographs, 52,* 103–123.

Buunk, B., & Mutsaers, W. (1999). Equity perceptions and marital satisfaction in former and current marriage: A study among the remarried. *Journal of Social and Personal Relationships, 16,* 123–132.

Canary, D. J., & Stafford, L. (1992). Relational maintenance strategies and equity in marriage. *Communication Monographs, 59,* 243–268.

Canary, D. J., & Stafford, L. (2001). Equity in the preservation of personal relationships. In J. H. Harvey & A. Wenzel (Eds.), *Close romantic relationships: Maintenance and enhancement* (pp. 133–151). Mahwah, NJ: Erlbaum.

Canary, D. J., & Zelley, E. (1999). Current research programs on relational maintenance behaviors. In M. E. Roloff (Ed.), *Communication yearbook 23.* Thousand Oaks, CA: Sage.

Coltrane, S. (1989). Household labor and the routine production of gender. *Social Problems, 36,* 473–490.

Coltrane, S. (1996). *Family man.* New York: Oxford University Press.

Conroy, P. (1987). *The prince of tides.* New York: Bantam.

Conville, R. L. (1998). Telling stories: Dialectics of relational transition. In B. M. Montgomery & L. A. Baxter (Eds.), *Dialectical approaches to studying personal relationships* (pp. 17–40). Mahwah, NJ: Erlbaum.

Cupach, W. R., & Metts, S. (1988). *Perceptions of the occurrence and management of dialectics in romantic relationships.* Paper presented at the Fourth International Conference on Personal Relationships, Vancouver, Canada.

Dindia, K. (1989). *Toward the development of a measure of marital maintenance strategies.* Paper presented at the International Communication Association Conference, San Francisco.

Dindia, K. (2000). Relational maintenance. In C. Hendrick & S. Hendrick (Eds.), *Sourcebook on personal relationships.* Thousand Oaks, CA: Sage.

Dindia, K., & Baxter, L. A. (1987). Strategies for maintaining and repairing marital relationships. *Journal of Social and Personal Relationships, 4,* 143–158.

Dindia, K., & Canary, D. J. (1993). Definitions and theoretical perspectives on maintaining relationships. *Journal of Social and Personal Relationships, 10,* 163–173.

Duck, S. W. (1988). *Relating to others.* Milton Keynes, England: Open University Press.

Fitzpatrick, M. A. (1988). *Between husbands and wives: Communication in marriage.* Newbury Park, CA: Sage.

Fitzpatrick, M. A., & Best, P. (1979). Dyadic adjustment in relational types: Consensus, cohesion, affectional expression, and satisfaction in enduring relationships. *Communication Monographs, 46,* 165–178.

Fletcher, G. J. O., Fincham, F. D., Cramer, L., & Heron, N. (1987). The role of attributions in the development of dating relationships. *Journal of Personality and Social Psychology, 53,* 510–517.

Gaines, S. O., Jr., & Agnew, C. R. (in press). Relationship maintenance in intercultural couples: An interdependence analysis. In D. J. Canary & M. Dainton (Eds.), *Maintaining relationships through communication: Relational, contextual, and cultural variations.* Mahwah, NJ: Erlbaum.

Garcia, S. D., & Rivera, S. M. (1999). Perceptions of Hispanic and African-American couples at the friendship or engagement stage of a relationship. *Journal of Social and Personal Relationships, 16,* 65–86.

Goldsmith, D. (1992). Managing conflicting goals in supportive interaction: An integrative theoretical framework. *Communication Research, 19,* 264–286.

Gottman, J. M. (1994). *What predicts divorce?* Hillsdale, NJ: Erlbaum.

Guerrero, L. K. (1997). Nonverbal involvement across interactions with same-sex friends, opposite-sex friends, and romantic partners: Consistency or change? *Journal of Social and Personal Relationships, 14,* 31–58.

Haas, S. M., & Stafford, L. (1998). An initial examination of maintenance behaviors in gay and lesbian relationships. *Journal of Social and Personal Relationships, 15,* 846–855.

Hatfield, E., Traupmann, J., Sprecher, S., Utne, M. K., & Hay, J. (1985). Equity and intimate relationships: Recent research. In W. Ickes (Ed.), *Compatible and incompatible relationships* (pp. 91–117). New York: Springer-Verlag.

Hatfield, E., Walster, G. W., & Berscheid, E. (1978). *Equity: Theory and research.* Needham Heights, MA: Allyn & Bacon.

Hecht, M. L., Marston, P. J., & Larkey, L. K. (1994). Love ways and relationship quality. *Journal of Social and Personal Relationships, 11,* 25–43.

Hecht, M. L., Shepard, T., & Hall, T. J. (1979). Multivariate indices of the effects of self-disclosure. *Western Journal of Speech Communication, 43,* 235–245.

Hendrick, C., & Hendrick, S. S. (1986). A theory and method of love. *Journal of Personality and Social Psychology, 50,* 392–402.

Hendrick, C., & Hendrick, S. S. (1997). Love and satisfaction. In R. J. Sternberg & M. Hojjat (Eds.), *Satisfaction in close relationships* (pp. 56–78). New York: Guilford.

Hendrick, C., Hendrick, S. S., & Dicke, A. (1998). The love attitudes scale: Short form. *Journal of Social and Personal Relationships, 15,* 147–159.

Lee, J. A. (1973). *The colors of love: An exploration of the ways of loving.* Don Mills, Ontario: New Press.

Mackey, R. A., Diemer, M. A., & O'Brien, B. A. (2000). Psychological intimacy in the lasting relationships of heterosexual and same-gender couples. *Sex Roles, 43,* 201–227.

Marston, P. J., & Hecht, M. L. (1994). Love ways: An elaboration and application to relational maintenance. In D. J. Canary & L. Stafford (Eds.), *Communication and relational maintenance* (pp. 187–202). San Diego: Academic.

Marston, P. J., Hecht, M. L., & Robers, T. (1987). "True love ways": The subjective experience and communication of romantic love. *Journal of Social and Personal Relationships, 4,* 387–404.

Messman, S. J., Canary, D. J., & Hause, K. S. (2000). Motives to remain platonic, equity, and the use of maintenance strategies in opposite-sex friendships. *Journal of Social and Personal Relationships, 17,* 67–94.

Myers, S. A. (2001). Relational maintenance behaviors in the sibling relationship. *Communication Quarterly, 49,* 19–34.

Milardo, R. M. (1986). Personal choice and social constraint in close relationships: Application of network analysis. In V. J. Derlega & B. A. Winstead (Eds.), *Friendship and social interaction* (pp. 145–166). New York: Springer-Verlag.

Monsour, M., Harris, B., & Kurzweil, N. (1994). Challenges confronting cross-sex friendships: "Much ado about nothing?" *Sex Roles, 31,* 55–77.

Montgomery, B. M. (1993). Relationship maintenance versus relationship change: A dialectical dilemma. *Journal of Social and Personal Relationships, 10,* 205–224.

Parks, M. R., & Adelman, M. B. (1983). Communication networks and the development of romantic relationships: An expansion of uncertainty reduction theory. *Human Communication Research, 10,* 55–79.

Prins, K. S., Buunk, B. P., & Van Yperen, N. W. (1993). Equity, normative disapproval, and extramarital relationships. *Journal of Social and Personal Relationships, 10,* 39–53.

Rawlins, W. K. (1983). Openness as problematic in ongoing friendships: Two conversational dilemmas. *Communication Monographs, 50,* 1–13.

Rawlins, W. K. (1992). *Friendship matters: Communication, dialectics, and the life course.* Hawthorne, NY: Aldine.

Roloff, M. E. (1976). Communication strategies, relationships, and relational change. In G. R. Miller (Ed.), *Explorations in interpersonal communication* (pp. 173–196). Newbury Park, CA: Sage.

Rusbult, C. E. (1987). Responses to dissatisfaction in close relationships: The "exit-voice-loyalty-neglect" model. In D. Perlman & S. W. Duck (Eds.), *Intimate relationships: Development, dynamics, and deterioration* (pp. 209–237). Newbury Park, CA.: Sage.

Rusbult, C. E., Drigotas, S. M., & Verette, J. A. (1994). The investment model: An interdependence analysis of commitment processes and relationship maintenance phenomena. In D. J. Canary & L. Stafford (Eds.), *Communication and relational maintenance.* Orlando, FL: Academic.

Samter, W., & Burleson, B. R. (1984). Cognitive and motivational influences on spontaneous comforting behavior. *Human Communication Research, 11,* 231–260.

Sillars, A. L., Pike, G. R., Jones, T. S., & Redmon, K. (1983). Communication and conflict in marriage. In R. N. Bostrom (Ed.), *Communication yearbook 7* (pp. 414–429). Newbury Park, CA: Sage.

Sprecher, S. (1986). The relation between inequity and emotions in close relationships. *Social Psychology Quarterly, 49,* 309–321.

Sprecher, S. (2001). Equity and social exchange theory in dating couples: Associations with satisfaction, commitment, and stability. *Journal of Marriage and Family, 63,* 599–613.

Sprecher, S., & Schwartz, P. (1994). Equity and balance in the exchange of contributions in close relationships. In M. J. Lerner & G. Mikula (Eds.), *Entitlement and the affectional bond. Justice in close relationships* (pp. 11–42). New York: Plenum.

Stafford, L., & Canary, D. J. (1991). Maintenance strategies and romantic relationship type, gender, and relational characteristics. *Journal of Social and Personal Relationships, 8,* 217–242.

Traban, C. B., Hendrick, S. S., & Hendrick, C. (1998). Loving and liking. In P. A. Andersen & L. K. Guerrero (Eds.), *Handbook of communication and emotion* (pp. 331–351). San Diego: Academic.

Utne, M. K., Hatfield, E., Traupmann, J., & Greenberger, D. (1984). Equity, marital satisfaction, and stability. *Journal of Social and Personal Relationships, 1,* 323–332.

Van Lange, P. A. M., Rusbult, C. E., Drigotas, S. M., Arriaga, X. B., Witcher, B. S., & Cox, C. L. (1997). Willingness to sacrifice in close relationships. *Journal of Personality and Social Psychology, 72,* 1373–1395.

Vogl-Bauer, S., Kalbfleisch, P. J., & Beatty, M. J. (1999). Perceived equity, satisfaction, and relational maintenance strategies in parent-adolescent dyads. *Journal of Youth and Adolescence, 28,* 27–49.

Weigel, D. J., & Ballard-Reisch, D. S. (1999a). All marriages are not maintained equally: Marital type, marital quality, and the use of maintenance behaviors. *Personal Relationships, 6,* 291–303.

Weigel, D. J., & Ballard-Reisch, D. S. (1999b). Using paried data to test models of relational maintenance and marital quality. *Journal of Social and Personal Relationships, 16,* 175–191.

Werking, K. J. (1997). *We're just good friends: Women and men in nonromantic relationships.* New York: Guilford.

Williamson, R. N., & Fitzpatrick, M. A. (1985). Two approaches to marital interaction: Relational control patterns in marital types. *Communication Monographs, 52,* 236–252.

Willigen, M. V., & Drentea, P. (2001). Benefits of equitable relationships: The impact of sense of fairness, household division of labor, and decision-making power on perceived social support. *Sex Roles, 44,* 571–597.

Wilmot, W. W. (1987). *Dyadic communication* (3rd ed.). New York: Random House.

Witteman, H., & Fitzpatrick, M. A. (1986). Compliance-gaining in marital interaction: Power bases, processes, and outcomes. *Communication Monographs, 53,* 130–143.

Yum, Y-O., & Canary, D. J. (in press). Maintaining relationships in Korea and the United States: Features of Korean culture that affect relational maintenance beliefs and behaviors, In D. J. Canary & M. Dainton (Eds.), *Maintaining relationships through communication: Relational, contextual, and cultural variations.* Mahwah, NJ: Erlbaum.

C H A P T E R   1 1

DE-ESCALATING

RELATIONSHIPS

WHY BREAK UP?

CONFRONTING RELATIONAL
UNHAPPINESS: THE FOUR PHASES
OF DISENGAGEMENT

The Importance of Equity, Commitment,
and Rewards

Reasons for Disengagement and
Termination

Attribution Theory

The Valence and Frequency of Problems

The Dark Side of Relationships: Power,
Control, and Infidelity

The Cascade Model of Dissolution

METHODS USED IN RELATIONAL
DISENGAGEMENT

Tactics Used in Relational Disengagement

Facework and Politeness Theory

THE CONSEQUENCES OF RELATIONAL
DISENGAGEMENT

Emotional Consequences

Staying Friends

Grave Dressing and Adjustment

CHAPTER SUMMARY

Ilsa: You're saying this only to make me go.

Rick: I'm saying it because it's true. Inside us we both know you belong with Victor. You're part of his work — the thing that keeps him going. If that plane leaves the ground and you're not with him, you will regret it. Maybe not today. Maybe not tomorrow. But soon, and for the rest of your life.

Ilsa: But what about us?

Rick: We'll always have Paris. We didn't have. . . . We, we lost it until you came to Casablanca. We got it back last night.

Ilsa: And I said I'd never leave you.

Rick: And you never will. But I have a job to do too, and where I'm going you can't follow. What I've got to do, you can't be any part of. Ilsa, I'm not good at being noble. But it doesn't take much to see that the problems of three little people don't amount to a hill of beans in this crazy world. Someday you'll understand that. . . . Now, now. . . . Here's looking at you, kid.

From *Casablanca*, American film, 1950s

Udall: "What's wrong?"

Carol: "I don't think I want to know you anymore. All you do is make me feel bad about myself."

           Carol walks away.

From *As Good As It Gets*, American film, 1998

This chapter focuses on the process by which people reduce the level of intimacy or commitment in a relationship. As people self-disclose and escalate relationships, they often learn that the person they are seeing and spending time with has shortcomings and liabilities, or simply is incompatible in some way. People often withdraw emotionally from the relationship when this happens. Sometimes they openly discuss the relationship and advocate "seeing less of each other" (called *de-escalation*). Sometimes they propose "not seeing each other anymore" (called *termination*). Managing a relational breakup is an important skill to have, and understanding the process is important. Further, coping with relational problems and changes is one of the more emotionally arousing and involving interpersonal goals pursued. For instance, data from the National Longitudinal Study of Adolescent Health indicate that adolescent romances are one of the most important determinants of depression, especially among females and people who recently broke up (Joyner & Udry, 2000). In this chapter, we discuss why people decide to de-escalate or terminate relationships, and we talk about the strategies used to redefine relationships and discuss why different strategies are used. We then discuss how people cope with relational loss.

WHY BREAK UP?

The first major study of disengagement was published by Hill, Rubin, and Peplau in 1976, who found that nearly half of 231 couples studied (43%) broke up over a two-year period. The study was significant because it tracked the same people over a two-year period, and the researchers managed to keep records of both partners in each relationship. Summary results are reported in Table 11.1. Several more recent studies also tracked romantic partners over time providing more information on how young couples succeed or fail to build satisfying relationships together, or break up (Orbuch, Veroff, & Holmberg, 1993; Ruvolo, 1998; Ruvolo & Brennan, 1997; Ruvolo & Ruvolo, 2000; Ruvolo & Veroff, 1997; Sprecher, 2001; Sprecher & Metts, 1999). The following list provides some of the factors related to quality relationships as well as those related to less satisfying relationships that eventually result in breakups.

1. *The more "in love" you are, the more likely you are to stay together.* Hill and colleagues (1976) looked at a number of measures of intimacy and found that couples were more likely to stay together when both partners were "in love," had thought of marriage, rated the relationship high in closeness, dated each other exclusively, and had dated for a longer period of time (about a year). More recently, Sprecher (2001) found that the woman's commitment was the strongest predictor of relationship stability, along with perceptions of the woman's rewards, and levels of relational satisfaction reported by both men and women. Lack of commitment, fewer rewards, and low levels of satisfaction prompted more couples to break up. One recent study found that dating couples who experienced a sense of "weness" (doing and sharing together) versus a sense of separateness were relationally more satisfying; they also "glorified" overcoming past struggles and stresses to their relationships together (Flora & Segrin, 2000). Ruvolo and Brennan (1997) examined the relationships between love, perceptions of supportive assistance, how much each person became closer to their "ideal selves" and how much closer their partners became to their partner's "ideal selves." They found that over a five-month period both the partner's love and the individual's perceptions of assistance helped each person in the relationship "grow" toward their "ideal selves." Being in love, and perceiving and receiving supportive assistance, facilitates growth and helps each person move toward a preferred sense of self. Another study found that the greater the discrepancy between ratings of partner and one's "ideal" partner, the lower the ratings of marital well-being (Ruvolo & Verloff, 1997), which increases general unhappiness over time (Ruvolo, 1998).

Table 11.1
FACTORS CONTRIBUTING TO THE ENDING OF A RELATIONSHIP

	Women's Reports (%)	Men's Reports (%)	Agreement That Cause Contributed to Breakup
Dyadic Factors			
Bored with relationship	76.7	76.7	Yes
Differences in interests	72.8	61.1	No
Differences in backgrounds	44.2	46.8	No
Differences in intelligence	19.5	10.4	No
Conflicting sexual attitudes	48.1	42.9	Yes
Conflicting marriage ideas	43.4	28.9	Yes
Nondyadic Factors			
Woman's independence	73.7	50.0	Yes
Man's independence	46.8	61.1	Yes
Woman's interest in another man	40.3	31.2	Yes
Man's interest in another woman	18.2	28.6	Yes
Living too far apart	28.2	41.0	Yes
Pressure from woman's parents	18.2	13.0	Yes
Pressure from man's parents	10.4	9.1	Yes

Source: Adapted from Hill, Rubin, & Peplau, 1976. Used with permission of the authors and the Society for the Psychological Study of Social Issues.

2. *Couples who were equally involved in the relationship were more likely to stay together than couples who were in inequitable relationships.* Of partners who indicated that they were equally involved, only 23% broke up. However, 54% of the couples involved in inequitable relationships broke up. Sprecher (2001) found that women who perceived they were underbenefited were more likely to break up their relationships, and both men and women who had more rewarding alternatives to date were more likely to leave their partners (compared to men and women who did not have alternatives to date who were more rewarding than the ones they were currently dating). More recent studies have investigated how couples (cohabiting and married ones) coordinate time constraints and work in order to balance work and relational obligations, form shared meanings for their relationships, and manage dialectical tensions between

autonomy, openness, and the like (also see Chapter 10) (Chadiha, Veroff, & Leber, 1998; Golden, 2002; Hoppe-Nagao & Ting-Toomey, 2002; Kalmijn & Bernasco, 2001; Van Willigen & Drentea, 2001).

3. *Couples with similar characteristics and attitudes were more likely to stay together than dissimilar couples.* All couples in the study were matched in height, religion, and attitudes toward women's rights, religiosity, and number of children desired. The typical couple had been dating for eight months when the study began, so it is possible that pairs work out such matters fairly early on. What predicted staying together over the next two years? People who stayed together were also matched in SAT scores, educational aspirations, beauty, and age. Recent studies also indicate that couple members project similarities onto their partners, perceiving that the two are similar in attachment characteristics (Ruvolo & Fabin, 1999).

4. *In the 1976 Hill, Rubin, and Peplau study people took advantage of vacations to separate from their partners and "get away from it all."* Fully 71.1% of breakups occur during the summer months (April to September), and those who were the least involved emotionally in the relationship were likely to take advantage of vacations (to start over, date others). Because it is sometimes difficult to say precisely when any relationship begins to decay and fall apart, these results imply that the less involved person may have given up much earlier than the more involved partner, who often indicated that the relationship fell apart at a later date. Also, as discussed later in this chapter, some partners (those with low self-esteem) may psychologically distance themselves from a partner and prepare for a breakup when problems emerge, compared to a partner with high self-esteem.

5. *Both people claim credit for initiating the breakup.* Women indicated that they initiated the breakup 51.3% of the time, that the man did so in 35.5% of the relationships, and that it was mutual in 13% of the cases. Among men, 46.1% indicated that they had initiated the breakup, 39.5% reported that the woman had done so, and 15% said the decision was mutual.

6. *Women list more relational problems than do men.* Table 11.1 provides a list of factors that contributed to the decision to break up. The most frequently cited reasons included boredom, differences in interests and backgrounds, desire to be independent, and conflicting attitudes on sex and marriage. Women provided more reasons for breaking off relationships than did men, citing differences in interests, differences in intelligence, conflicting ideas about marriage, independence, and interest in seeing someone else. Women were more sensitive to problem areas in the relationship and compared it with alternatives that appeared to be more promising. Also, it is the women's sense of commitment to the partner that predicts stability (Sprecher, 2001).

7. *Successful couples listen and share; unsuccessful couples tend not to listen.* Ruvolo and Ruvolo (2000) completed interviews with newlywed couples over three years.

They found that individuals who listen and try to understand their partner's feelings during conflict episodes or when people expressed negative feelings about the functioning of the relationship changed more than those who did not listen or try to understand their partner's feelings.

8. *Relationships are more likely to survive over time if participants perceive that important people in their social networks approve of the relationship* (Felmlee, 2001). Relationships are likely to continue if a person perceives that both friends and family members approve of the relationship. In fact, perceived approval and support were more predictive of staying together than actual approval and support. When individuals decided to break up their relationships, it was usually the friends who encouraged the breakup rather than family members (Felmlee, 2001).

In sum, people are more likely to stay together when they are in equitable relationships, are committed to each other, have many similarities and matching interests, find the relationship to be rewarding, develop a sense of "we-ness" or bonding, develop a life together as a couple, facilitate growth toward the "ideal self," benefit from listening, and bask in the approval of friends and family members. This latter issue is a fairly frequent theme in American television programs like "Sex and the City," "Friends," and "Seinfeld," where characters seek approval from their friends for whom they date, and there is a relationship between length of dating and friends' lack of approval.

CONFRONTING RELATIONAL UNHAPPINESS: THE FOUR PHASES OF DISENGAGEMENT

Every relationship will have problems. Why are people able to cope with certain problems but not with others? According to Duck (1982), a person can proceed through four phases when deciding what to do about a relationship (see Figure 11.1): the **intrapsychic phase,** the **dyadic phase,** the **social phase,** and the **grave-dressing phase.** The grave-dressing phase deals with the final phase of disengagement, explaining why a relationship decayed and ended. It is called *grave dressing* because after a relationship is "dead," each participant is likely to "dress up" the grave by promoting a positive image of his or her role in the relationship. Grave dressing is discussed later in the chapter when we look at the consequences of relational disengagement; here we emphasize the earlier phases of disengagement. Duck (1984) later raised the issue of how a person might try to repair a relationship if motivated to do so. Table 11.2 outlines some repair strategies that can be made at each phase of the disengagement process.

During the intrapsychic phase a person reflects on the quality of the relationship, possibly comparing the relationship to others, and comparing the relational partners to potential partners. Intrapsychic conflict takes place when the individual weighs

Figure 11.1

▼

Steps and
Decisions in
Relationship
Development
and Decline

Breakdown: Dissatisfaction with relationship

| **Threshold: I can't stand this anymore.** |

Intrapsychic Phase
- Focus on partner's behavior
- Assess adequacy of partner's role performances
- Depict and evaluate negative aspects of being
  in the relationship
- Consider costs of withdrawal
- Assess positive aspects of alternative relationships
- Face the dilemma of expressing or repressing feelings

| **Threshold: I'd be justified in withdrawing.** |

Dyadic Phase
- Face the dilemma of choosing between confrontation
  and avoidance
- Confront partner
- Negotiate in relationship talks
- Attempt repair and reconciliation
- Assess joint costs of withdrawal or reduced intimacy

| **Threshold: I mean it.** |

Social Phase
- Negotiate post-dissolution state with partner
- Initiate gossip or discussion in social network
- Create publicly negotiable face-saving and blame-placing
  stories and accounts
- Consider and face up to implied social network effects, if any
- Call in intervention teams

| **Threshold: It's now inevitable.** |

Grave-Dressing Phase
- Heal wounded emotions
- Reformulate postmortems
- Circulate own version of breakup

Source: Adapted from Duck, 1982. Reprinted with permission of
Academic Press, Inc., and the author.

Table 11.2

GENERAL METHODS EMPLOYED TO REPAIR RELATIONSHIPS

The Breakdown Phase: Dissatisfaction with the Relationship

Major repair concerns:
- To reduce turbulence in interactions
- To improve communication
- To focus on attractions in the relationship
- To increase relational intimacy

The Intrapsychic and Dyadic Phases (see Figure 11.1)

Major repair concerns:
- To bring out partner's positive side
- To focus on the positive aspects of relationship
- To reinterpret partner and partner's behavior as positive and well intentioned
- To reduce negativity toward partner and strike a more balanced view
- To reevaluate difficulties in leaving
- To reevaluate attractiveness of alternative relationships and partners

Social Phase and Beyond (see Figure 11.1)

Major repair concerns:
- To enlist the support of others to hold relationship together
- To obtain help to rectify matters or end the relationship
- To obtain help in understanding the breakup
- To obtain support and help during separation and after breakup
- To create acceptable public and private accounts of breakup
- To save face and justify breakup to self
- To circulate own version of breakup

Source: Adapted from Duck, 1984.

many issues in an internal struggle. There are six major concerns: to size up the partner's behavior, to assess the internal dynamics of the relationship, to express discomfort (but not directly to the partner), to question one's relationship judgments, to find ways to modify the partner's behavior and change relationship outcomes, and to convince oneself that leaving could be better than staying. During this phase, the person who scrutinizes the relationship identifies the reasons or the causes of dissatisfaction and decides whether the problems can be solved and whether he or she is sufficiently motivated to continue to work in the relationship.

We now know that the process of scrutiny is done quite differently by different people. Murray and Holmes (2000) provide evidence that we view our relational partners through a lens of "self-appraisal" and that we typically view our partners in generous, idealized ways, called "positive reflected appraisals" (Murray & Holmes, 2000, p. 174). Little things that might be considered annoyances by others are considered cute, the positive is accentuated, and problems might be trivialized or considered issues to address later. However, when individuals confront a problem, especially a threat to one's sense of self, low self-esteem individuals behave much differently than high self-esteem individuals. Low self-esteem individuals possess a more tentative, insecure, less positive, less certain, and more conflicted sense of self, compared to high self-esteem individuals (see Murray & Holmes, 2000). One would think that a low self-esteem individual might become more dependent on a partner who likes, loves, and holds the partner in positive regard, and that their relational partner would operate as a rock of support for the low self-esteem individual. Actually, when a low self-esteem individual confronts a serious problem, they experience a different element in the intrapsychic phase. On one hand, they can become closer to their relational partner, trust that partner, rely on him or her and help solve a problem together, which would boost the individual's self-concept or esteem. On the other hand, becoming closer is terrifying because of the low self-esteem individual's perceptions that others don't and won't support him or her and that others are critical and rejecting.

Research indicates that when a serious problem emerges, the low self-esteem individual reacts by leaning toward avoidance, and by projecting his or her felt low self-regard on their partners, thinking that their partners have already lowered their positive appraisals, anticipating criticism. Low self-esteem individuals jump the gun by devaluing the relationship earlier than high self-esteem individuals, preparing for the demise of the relationship. Considerable research indicates that low self-esteem individuals are involved in less satisfying and less stable dating relationships and that those with low self-esteem have a less generous view of their partners, which grows less generous over time (compared to high self-esteem individuals). On the other hand, high self-esteem individuals, when confronting a problem, confidently rely on the support of their loving partner, and are more confident of solving external threats to the self and relationship (as Duck proposes in Figure 11.1).

With regard to repairing relationships, Duck (1984) argues that when we first see signs of distress in a relationship, we may attempt to reestablish liking and attraction in the relationship by focusing on several communication-related activities (see Table 11.2). First, to reduce turbulence in interactions, the partner (or both partners) can attend workshops on social skills training and on specific skill acquisitions. Communicators have to eliminate or reduce the cause of the unhappiness in the relationship, and the unhappiness may stem from inappropriately communicated anger, frustrations from one's job that affect the relationship, difficulty in confiding one's emotions and feelings to the partner, and so on. Some of the changes partners have to make involve basic communication skills. Some communication skills programs, however, only teach participants how to identify the problems they have in the relationship and how to avoid turbulence.

However, improved communication must occur in reality — actually engaging in improved listening skills and increased time allocated to metacommunicating — and must occur on a regular basis. Another element of repair is to focus on rekindling the attractions that were once prominent in the relationship, perhaps returning to the activities the partners shared at one time. An additional repair strategy includes reintroducing intimacy into the relationship. Increased self-disclosure, engaging in trust-building exercises and couple enrichment programs, and increasing quality time together in new activities are some important ways to increase intimacy.

The dyadic phase involves confronting the partner with the dissatisfaction (Figure 11.1). There are nine major concerns at this phase: to confront the partner with one's dissatisfaction; to present our view of the relationship; to express discomfort directly to the partner; to assess the costs of being in the relationship and how to deal with the dissatisfaction; to evaluate the partner's views of the relationship; to cope with the partner's rejoinders, excuses, or apologies; to size up the relationship together; to consider alternatives; and to choose to repair or dissolve the relationship.

In the social phase, the individual goes public with his or her unhappiness with the relationship, seeking advice and support from others, perhaps asking for intervention from others. Concerns include creating an agreed-on post-dissolution state of the relationship (for example, agreements might be reached concerning how much emotional and physical withdrawal will take place, as well as a statement concerning possible reconciliation), creating acceptable definitions for the partners (friends, acquaintances, etc.), considering implied status changes in terms of roles (for example, will both partners stay in the church choir?), evaluating the consequences of dissolution (who stays friends with the couple's friends?), placing blame, saving face, and obtaining acceptance of the dissolution from others (friends say, "You deserve someone better").

It is during the dyadic and social phases that others notice that something is different. The nonverbal bonding behaviors outlined in relational escalation phases are no longer exhibited in public, and others notice their absence. Communication is problematic: Channel discrepancy is noted in sarcastic comments (smiling face, negative tone of voice), or the couple uses a tone of voice that lacks warmth and friendliness. Channel discrepancy may make it more difficult for distressed couples to talk openly with each other because mixed messages are more difficult to respond to and are basically unpleasant to view (see Leathers, 1992). Nonetheless, distressed couples sit farther apart, refrain from touching, look less often at each other, lean away from each other, and fail to communicate many of the behaviors that indicate affiliation, liking, and intimacy.

Several repair tactics are available during both these phases (see Table 11.2). Repair-makers want to reestablish the partner's attraction to each other and their liking for each other as persons (but no longer as a couple, which was a motive at the breakdown phase). Four possible tactics are accentuating the partner's positive qualities while downplaying the negative, accentuating the positive outcomes from the relationship, reinterpreting the causes of the partner's unacceptable or annoying behaviors

324

Nonverbal behaviors of people in troubled and de-escalating relationships can be obvious even to strangers.

Nat Antman/The Image Works

in positive ways, and finding fewer faults that can be blamed solely on the partner. The first two tactics generally deal with the attempt to perceive that one is in fact in an equitable relationship. The reestablishment of equity as a repair strategy is discussed in the next section of this chapter.

The third and fourth tactics deal with the attributions the repair-maker makes concerning the causes of the relational problems. We outlined attribution theory in several previous chapters, and we have more to say about it shortly. Basically, whether repairing relationships is judged as easy or difficult reflects the partner's assessment of the underlying causes. If the causes of the unhappiness are perceived to be stable, internal, intentional, and controllable (e.g., the partner has become extremely possessive), the partner is likely to believe that repair is difficult or even impossible to achieve and is likely to exit the relationship.

Repair tactics available during the final stages of the disengagement process are listed at the bottom of Table 11.2. First, a person might try to enlist the assistance of friends in holding the relationship together or removing obstacles that block relational growth (e.g., to stop in-laws from interfering in the relationship). Second, a person may seek social support from friends during the breakup period. Third, if the two continue toward breakup and dissolve the relationship, both are motivated to portray themselves in a positive light and to protect a threatened self-esteem. Both then begin to circulate stories or narratives (accounts) concerning what happened, who was to blame, and so on.

Although Duck (1984) summarizes the disengagement process as four stages, Battaglia, Richard, Datteri, and Lord (1998) identified the same pattern of dissolving relationships by progressing through many steps. First, people use indirect/withdrawal strategies and behave cautiously, as if they are indecisive about breaking up. This is followed by assessing the situation, assessing one's options, communicating feelings, and ultimately breaking up. Battaglia and colleagues emphasized the considerable "vacillation" between staying and resolving differences, and leaving.

The Importance of Equity, Commitment, and Rewards

In the previous chapter, we presented the primary propositions for equity theory. Recent evidence suggests that equity, in combination with other relational properties, affects the stability of close involvements. For instance, Sprecher (2001) concluded that while rewards are more strongly associated with stability, the role of perceived equity in a relationship may be more salient at the beginning of a relationship and at the end of a relationship. It is important at the beginning of the relationship because participants are likely to monitor how they are treated and are unlikely to initiate a relationship with someone who does not treat them fairly (although they might be tempted to date someone for a while who is highly rewarding and attractive). Once a pair of individuals commits to a long-term relationship, a sense of commitment, positive appraisal, rewards, and liking are more salient, and perceived inequity may not be perceived as harmful. If things go well for this relationship, a couple will probably experience a sense of "we-ness" (not separateness) and will not verbally express relational disappointment — and both "we-ness" and not voicing complaints are related to satisfaction (Flora & Segrin, 2000). Quality relationships involve a number of important factors (as mentioned in Chapter 10): satisfaction, commitment, intimacy, trust, passion, and love (Fletcher, Simpson, & Thomas, 2000). However, if sufficient stresses occur in the relationship (external pressure from parents, infidelity, a decrease in rewards), optimism for the future wanes, more of a sense of separateness is experienced, and perceived inequity becomes a salient. The implication from these studies is that relationships can be maintained (see Chapter 10 as well) and repaired by increasing rewards for one's partner and returning the relationship to an equitable status.

Equity theory outlines several tactics that individuals can use to restore equity. Tactics used to restore **psychological equity** create a perception of equity when, in fact, the relationship is not equitable. Other tactics can be used to restore **actual equity** — one person in the relationship takes a specific action to make sure that resources (inputs and outcomes) are distributed fairly between the partners. Both the underbenefited and the overbenefited partner may use several tactics to restore actual or psychological equity. However, we focus on the options available to the underbenefited partner.

Underbenefited partners may engage in certain actions to restore perceived psychological equity: distort inputs and outcomes, hope that the future will be better, compare the relationship to ones that are even less equitable, resign themselves to a higher order of justice, and devalue themselves. A popular theme in television shows (comedies, talk shows, and soap operas) is fair treatment of others in relationships, including such popular shows as "Friends," "Seinfeld," and others. The character George, on "Seinfeld," was ever-vigilant that he never emerge as underbenefited in any of his dating, business, or social relationships — preferring to be the overbenefited partner (who easily coped with guilt) but who never formed any close relationships, of any duration, with women. Movies like *Nurse Betty* and *Thelma and Louise* contain scenes (early in the movies) highlighting some extreme examples of inequitable relationships.

Sometimes victims admit to themselves that they are in inequitable relationships, but they might believe that they cannot really do anything about it (for example, they are against divorce) or that they do not have the power to change the situation. One way to cope with inequity is to compare one's level of inequity with other relationships that are even more inequitable, a consoling strategy that makes the victims feel better.

Another tactic is to convince oneself that a higher sense of justice will prevail; for example, victims may believe that they have worked hard in their relationship but have nothing to show for it. Victims may come to believe that God, the IRS, or some other higher authority will intervene at some time ("People get what they deserve").

Finally, victims may come to devalue themselves. They may admit that they are in an inequitable relationship and recall that they have been in similar relationships in the past. A history of getting into inequitable relationships may result in the victims' coming to believe that it is their fate to be in such relationships and that they can expect no better. Having low expectations in relationships can help victims cope with inequity, at least temporarily.

How can the underbenefited partner restore actual equity? Three alternatives are to seek compensation (or restitution), retaliate, or withdraw. First, the underbenefited person may confront (or have a third party confront) the overbenefited partner with the inequity. By talking over the issue of involvements, the future of the relationship, and both partners' perceptions of the relationship, the person may elicit a change in inputs and a promise to maintain equity in the future.

People may not like to confront partners openly, and so they may act in indirect ways to prompt others to increase inputs into the relationship. For example, White (1980) identified five motivations college students claimed for causing intentional jealousy. These included to get the partner to increase rewards or inputs into the relationship, to test the relationship, to seek revenge on the partner, to bolster self-esteem, and to punish the partner. Women who believed that they were the more involved partner were much more likely to try to make their partners jealous with the intent of getting their partners to increase inputs into the relationship. That is, underbenefited women would flirt, seek a date, or actually date another, so that their partners would increase attention toward them and increase their inputs in the relationship.

Another indirect way to establish actual equity seems, at first glance, to be counterproductive. Some victims may temporarily increase their inputs even more in the hope that partners will notice the extra attention and increase their inputs as well. Once partners have increased their contributions, they can reduce some of the new special favors, and with luck, the partners will continue to provide the new inputs, thus leaving the relationship more equitable than it had been in the past.

Another way to restore actual equity is to retaliate against the overbenefited partner. The underbenefited partner can increase costs for the harm-doer (and derive some personal satisfaction), thereby making the relationship more equitable. What people do to retaliate may depend on the relationship and on the likes and dislikes of the partner. One form of revenge that hurts a partner or former partner is to cheat on the partner and spread the news through a circle of friends, so that the partner is the last to know (see material on infidelity later in the chapter).

Finally, partners can withdraw some or all inputs. If the underbenefited partner had done most of the work, he or she can pull out some of the involvement so as to make the contributions to the relationship more equal. Later, the underbenefited partner may withdraw all inputs, and no relationship will exist.

Reasons for Disengagement and Termination

People give many specific reasons for disengagement besides (or in addition to) the importance of equity. Knapp and Vangelisti (1992) cite Safran (1979) as identifying ten common trouble areas: (1) a breakdown in communication, (2) the loss of shared goals or interests, (3) sexual incompatibility, (4) infidelity, (5) diminution of excitement or fun, (6) money, (7) conflicts about children, (8) alcohol or drug abuse, (9) women's equality issues, and (10) in-laws. Similar reasons are given by gay and lesbian couples: (1) frequent absence, (2) sexual incompatibility; (3) mental cruelty, (4) lack of love, (5) infidelity, (6) job/school commitments, (7) excessive demands, and (8) financial problems (Kurdek, 1991). Felmlee (1995) also reports that certain qualities associated with attraction to a partner (i.e., being successful) were later recast as problems (i.e., being a workaholic and not sharing time together), which contributed to dissatisfaction. Infidelity, listed in the surveys above as the fourth and fifth problems in breaking up relationships in both straight and gay relationships, is a topic of considerable research today, which we summarize later in the chapter.

Certain problems are unique to individuals involved in intercultural dating and marriage situations. Morris, Moeai, and Shimizu (1985) found that during the early stages of dating, intercultural couples were susceptible to a Romeo and Juliet effect;

they were more "in love" and committed to each other in the face of pressures by others (like parents) not to date and marry. Over time, however, such couples face increased levels of parental interference, more criticism, and decreased trust. Intercultural couples faced more negative comments from others than did same-culture couples; many wives had difficulty accepting their husband's culture; and differences in conflict resolution styles and in attitudes toward children and child-rearing took a toll on the quality of life among intercultural couples.

A number of scholars investigated the types of messages disengagers use when terminating relationships (e.g., Baxter, 1983, 1985; Cody, 1982). Cody (1982) had students rate the importance of twenty-four potential reasons for disengagement and found that the reasons can be grouped into three general types: faults, refusals to compromise, and constraints (see Table 11.3). By faults, we mean that the initiator believed that some aspect of the partner's personality was at fault and clearly placed the blame for the disengagement on the partner. Refusals to compromise reflect the belief that the partner was unwilling to compromise for the good of the relationship, took the partner for granted, stopped being romantic, and so forth. The third category of reasons, constraints, reflects the belief that the partner wanted a far more intimate relationship than the disengager wanted. Both refusals to compromise and constraints tap into a person's level of commitment to a relationship. When you conclude that your partner refuses to compromise, you believe that you are putting more work into the relationship; you are more committed and involved. By contrast, when you feel that your partner constrains you, you believe that too much is expected of you; the partner is more involved in the relationship than you want to be. Unequal commitments and investments are strongly related to disengagement, and all three categories of problems (faults, refusals to compromise, and constraints) affect communication during disengagement.

| **Table 11.3** | |
REASONS CITED AS PRECIPITATING RELATIONAL DISENGAGEMENT	
Type of Reason	Examples
Faults	My partner had too many faults.
	My partner's personality was incompatible with mine.
	My partner was too demanding.
	My partner behaved in ways that embarrassed me.
	My partner's behavior or personality was more to blame for the breakup than anything else.

Refusals to compromise	My partner was unwilling to contribute enough to the relationship.
	My partner no longer behaved as romantically toward me as before.
	My partner took me for granted.
	My partner wasn't willing to compromise for the good of the relationship.
Constraints	The relationship was beginning to constrain me; I felt a lack of freedom.
	Although I still cared for my partner, I wanted to start dating others.
	Although the relationship was a good one, I was getting bored with it.
	My partner contributed too much, and I started to feel suffocated.
	My partner was becoming too possessive of me.
Miscellaneous	Although I still liked my partner, the romance had gone out of the relationship.
	I was primarily interested in having a good time, not committing to a relationship.
	My partner was too dependent on me.
	The two of us developed different interests and had less in common.
	I couldn't trust my partner.
	One of us moved away, and we couldn't see each other very much anymore.
	Most of my friends didn't like my partner (or most of my partner's friends didn't like me), causing problems that detracted from the relationship.
	The relationship itself didn't seem right, and its failings can't be blamed on one person or the other.
	My parents didn't approve of my partner (or my partner's parents didn't approve of me).
	My partner showed too much physical affection (or was too aggressive).

Source: Adapted from Cody, 1982.

Metts and Cupach (1986) identified ten themes that characterize disengagements (see Table 11.4). For women, the three most common reasons given for opposite-sex relationship decay were drifting apart, rule violation, and third-party involvement; for men, they were drifting apart, rule violation, and a critical event.

Listing problems, however, provides only limited information concerning why or how people break up. Several theories address why certain problems result in decay. One of these, discussed in Chapter 9, focuses on the increases in uncertainty that certain problems cause, and because we neither like nor tolerate high levels of uncertainty, we dissociate ourselves from those who cause it. Here we outline three

---

Table 11.4
DISENGAGEMENT THEMES

Theme	Description
Drifting apart	The relationship erodes naturally over time, due primarily to increased interaction distance, decreased quantity and quality of communication, changing interests and values, or mutual diminished efforts to maintain the relationship.
Critical event	A single event, fight, argument, or confrontation alters the relationship permanently.
Rule violation	One partner engages in behavior deemed inappropriate to the relationship.
Third-party involvement	One or both relational partners put considerable time and effort into a new relationship, at the expense of their own.
Network involvement	One or both relational partners develop a new network of friends that displaces their own friendship or causes friction.
General incompatibility	Problematic personality differences or a basic lack of commonality.
Value difference	One person expresses values extremely different from those of the partner.
Overconsumption	Individuals spend too much time together, leading them to get tired of each other.
Relational or role definition	The partners clash over their roles in the relationship and their definition of intimacy.
Nonmutuality of effort	One partner puts in more work than the other.

Source: Adapted from Metts & Cupach, 1986. Used by permission of the authors.

other approaches to disengagement: attribution theory, valence of relational problems, and the cascade model.

Attribution Theory

Attribution theory, already described in earlier chapters, is widely used in many areas of interpersonal communication, including relational disengagement. Cody, Kersten, Braaten, and Dickson (1992), for example, demonstrated how strongly attributed causes are related to the disengagement process. Six common problems were examined: lack of confiding (the partner failed to confide feelings and thoughts to a dating partner), lack of shared time (the partner failed to share quality time and to make time with the partner), rudeness (the partner was rude in public and embarrassed the dating partner), presentability (the partner failed to be presentable and well groomed in public), possessiveness, and jealousy. Participants in the study indicated that public rudeness and possessiveness are caused both intentionally and by internal causes. Further, these two relational problems were rated as more stable than problems like lack of confiding and lack of shared time. Jealousy was also perceived as an internally caused problem. Of these three problems, possessiveness and jealousy were rated as difficult to control, whereas it was thought that partners should be able to exert some control over rudeness.

By contrast, problems of presentability were rated as easily controllable, as were the problems of lack of shared time and, to a lesser degree, lack of confiding. These three problems were also rated as unintentional (especially lack of confiding and problems of presentability). Both problems of presentability and lack of shared time were rated as problems that were caused externally, and lack of confiding received average ratings on internality-externality, suggesting, perhaps, that some people believe this problem to be caused internally by the person's shyness and reticence or by a lack of trust in the partner.

The underlying attributional causes were related to the decision to break up in three ways. First, the students indicated that they were likely to withdraw from the relationship and were less likely to work on salvaging the relationship when the relational problems were caused by intentional, internal, and stable causes. The problems of possessiveness and rudeness are the result of a person who is internally motivated by personality (or by a need to dominate) to act intentionally and to do so consistently over time. Such a relational problem significantly reduced the attractiveness of the relationship, as well as the motivation to work hard to change the partner.

Second, the researchers had participants rate the extent to which problems were easy to solve. Problems that were easy to control and occurred unintentionally (problems of presentability and lack of shared time) were perceived as easier to solve than problems that are less controllable and occur intentionally (possessiveness, jealousy). Third, Cody and associates (1992) asked participants to indicate the extent to which they would accept a full-blown apology as a believable remedial tactic and wait to give the partner the chance to change his or her behavior, eliminate the problem, and salvage the relationship. Participants indicated that only when the problem was not caused intentionally by the partner, under the partner's control, and solvable would a full-blown apology effectively help patch up the differences and prompt the granting of a second chance. That is, apologies were considered effective for problems of presentability and lack of shared time but ineffective for the problems of possessiveness and jealousy.

Although this project looked at only six relational problems, it is easy to see that these underlying factors apply to other problems you might experience. Are you and your partner fighting and arguing? What are the underlying causes? If the partner is trying to control you, the pressure placed on you is undeniably intentional and internal and may (as you date over months) become a stable, recurring problem. You may seriously question if you want to continue such a relationship. Alternatively, if the fighting and arguing are caused by your partner's being under a lot of pressure because of taking the Law School Admissions Test, you might perceive the causes as external, unstable, and unintentional (the person didn't intend to be bossy). You might stay in the relationship, work on a solution, and perceive a full-blown apology as a believable remedial tactic.

The Valence and Frequency of Problems

Vangelisti (1992) offered a somewhat different view of the link between relational problems and relational dissatisfaction. She argued that for a behavior to be judged as problematic, at least two of the following criteria must be fulfilled: The behavior must be negatively valenced (judged to be very negative in its impact on the relationship) and it must occur with some degree of frequency. If it does not occur with some degree of frequency, it must be salient enough for one or both partners to remember it and identify it as a continuing source of displeasure or difficulty. Vangelisti interviewed couples who had been dating for an average of six years, and found that the most frequently cited communicative problem was withholding expression of negative feelings (listed three times more frequently than any other problem), followed by not taking the other person's perspective when listening, withholding expression of any type of feelings, and needing more time together to communicate.

Vangelisti also found that relational problems occur fairly frequently: 16% of her respondents said that they occur more than once a week, 21% said they occur once a week, 19% said they occur every two weeks, and 16% said they occur every two months. Also, individuals rated their satisfaction lower when their partner was believed to have caused several communicative problems; for example, dissatisfaction stemmed from three or four of the problems occurring over a few weeks' time or one problem recurring over the course of months. The greater the number of problems a partner causes, the greater the dissatisfaction. Finally, Vangelisti found that attributions were important. Of the serious problems listed by her interviewees, 44% of the problems were judged to be internally caused, and 63% were judged to be stable.

Vangelisti and Young (2000) also applied attribution theory to the area of communicating hurtful messages. When people receive hurtful messages, it has a chilling effect on a relationship, and Vangelisti and Young found that those who perceived a message as intentionally hurtful were more likely to distance themselves from the communicator; a person who uses words to hurt others intentionally and frequently will drive others away, to avoid the hurtful person and withdraw from the relationship.

The Dark Side of Relationships: Power, Control, and Infidelity

As noted earlier, failed romances among adolescents are a leading cause of depression, and it is also related to a deterioration in relationships with parents, delinquency, alcohol consumption, and similar social and emotional problems (Joyner & Udry, 2000). Some states and some universities, having recognized a serious social problem, offer advice and counseling for people who may be headed toward unhealthy or abusive relationships. Table 11.5, for example, lists characteristics of a healthy relationship and an unhealthy one. The unhealthy relationship is often characterized by too much dependence by one partner on another, control of one partner, poor communication, inability to communicate boundaries, and lack of acceptance of the other person as he or she is. Table 11.6 is part of the publication "Trust Betrayed" that is published by the State of West Virginia. It lists warning signs concerning how one partner tries to gain power and control over another. Gaining control over another includes trying to isolate that person from others, and reducing the person's self-esteem by engaging in emotional and sexual abuse. The partner then engages in actions that make the individual fearful and compliant by using threats, being bossy, or intimidating the individual. By stalking, the intimidator communicates the message that he or she is monitoring the individual's behavior when they are not technically together; hence, the victim has no free time for himself or herself. The isolation, reduced self-esteem, lack of freedom, and fear combine to change a person (the victim) to be a dependent, compliant follower, rather than an individual with any sense of self-worth. Most universities recommend people engaged in such relationships to seek counseling.

Infidelity is a common reason for breaking up one's relationships (www.infidelity.com provides information and social support if you have had a person cheat on you). Some scholars make a distinction between sexual infidelity and emotional infidelity, with women indicating greater betrayal than men by emotional infidelity; other studies find no sex differences and found that the greatest threat to a relationship stems from both emotional and sexual infidelity (see Knox, Zusman, & Kaluzny, 2000). Surveys of individuals engaged in college dating relationships indicate that 38% of individuals have been unfaithful in their most serious dating relationships, but that statistics for any type of extradyadic dating or sexual activity indicate that as many as 75% of men or 68% of women might be unfaithful (see Afifi, Falato, & Weiner, 2001). Reactions to infidelity vary widely. Roscoe, Cavanaugh, and Kennedy (1988) found that 44% of those surveyed would terminate the relationship immediately upon discovery of the infidelity. A more recent study (Knox et al., 2000) found that 69.4% of college sophomores and freshmen would end the (hypothetical) relationship with a person who was unfaithful; in fact, 45% claimed to have already done so in the past. Infidelity with homosexual implications may be even more difficult to tolerate for many reasons, but especially for women since bisexuality among men is more stigmatizing (Wiederman & LaMar, 1998).

Table 11.5
HEALTHY OR UNHEALTHY RELATIONSHIP?

Healthy Relationships	Unhealthy Relationships
Each person feels like an individual.	One or both partners feel incomplete without the other.
Each person feels responsible for his/her happiness.	One or both partners rely on the other partner for their own happiness.
Each person is responsible for his/her self-esteem.	One or both partners rely on the other for their self-esteem.
Togetherness and separateness are balanced.	Levels of togetherness are out of balance.
Relationships are established and maintained outside the partnership.	There is an inability to establish and maintain relationships with others.
Each person communicates effectively: open, honest, assertive, clear, willingness to listen.	One or both partners practice ineffective communication: game playing, passive/aggressive, beating around the bush, unwillingness to listen.
The opportunity exists for support and growth — for each person and for the couple.	Lack of opportunity for individual and/or relationship growth.
Finds commitment acceptable.	Attachment, addiction, or lack of commitment.
Accepting of each other.	Trying to change partner.
Each person has established healthy, comfortable limits or boundaries.	Limits or boundaries are poorly established or defined.
A willingness to recognize when the relationship is changing.	The illusion that the relationship (should) always be the same is maintained.
Brings out the best qualities in both people.	Brings out the worst qualities in both people.
Each person feels the freedom to honestly ask for what is wanted.	One or both partners feel unable to express needs or desires.
Accepts endings.	Unable to let go.
Achieves intimacy without the use of alcohol or other drugs.	Uses alcohol/other drugs to reduce inhibitions and create a false sense of intimacy.

Source: From the Student Health pages, University of Iowa. [On-line]. Available: www.uiowa.edu/~shs/sex2.htm

While infidelity is a good reason to terminate a relationship, it may take more than infidelity to prompt a person to terminate. Knox and his colleagues (2000) found that 67% of individuals who had been emotionally abused in their relationships terminated when their partner also was unfaithful, while only 46% of those who had not been emotionally abused said they ended the relationship with a cheating partner.

Table 11.6

EXAMPLES OF HOW A PARTNER TRIES TO GAIN POWER AND
CONTROL IN A DATING RELATIONSHIP

Isolation

forbids you to talk to your friends
accuses you of cheating
decides the social and school activities in
    which you will participate
controls what clothes you wear
discredits your parents' advice
encourages you to turn against your parents

Emotional Abuse

puts you down or makes you feel bad about
    yourself
breaks dates or cancels plans without any
    reason
embarrasses you in front of family and friends
uses words or tells jokes that humiliate you
uses drugs and alcohol to excuse abusive
    behavior
changes moods abruptly

Sexual Abuse

pressures you to engage in sexual activity
spreads rumors about your sexual behavior
puts down or makes fun of your sexual
    behavior

Threats

threatens to hurt you if you decide to break up
threatens to commit suicide when you talk of
    breaking up
threatens to hurt others who talk to you
threatens your family and friends

Bossy

makes all the decisions in the relationship
uses phrases like, "I just showed who's boss" or
    "I just made it clear who runs the show" to
    justify abusive behavior

Intimidation

destroys your personal belongings
speeds or drives recklessly to scare you
uses a loud or intimidating tone of voice
calls repeatedly to check up on you or to
    harass you

Stalking

frequently follows you
makes persistent and unwanted contacts
leaves messages intended to show that you are
    being watched

Source: From the publication "Trust Betrayed," supported in part by a grant from the 93.991 Preventive Health Services Block Grant, Center for Disease Control and Prevention, Public Health Service, Department of Health and Human Services, West Virginia. [On-line]. Available: www.wvdhhr.org/bph/trust/respect.htm.

Similarly, 70% of individuals who had been physically abused terminated the relationship when the partner also cheated, compared to 52% who had not been physically abused who said they ended the relationship with a cheating partner. The argument here is that discovery of a partner's cheating adds another serious problem to a growing list of problems, surpassing an individual's limits or tolerance.

How one comes to learn about the infidelity has a significant impact on a person's feelings and reactions. Afifi and colleagues (2001) found four ways in which a person can discover the infidelity. The first is "unsolicited third party discovery," including instances in which a person directly tells the individual (including the other man or woman involved in the indiscretion), overheard communication about the indiscretion, or having someone hint about the affair. The second approach, "unsolicited partner discovery," involves the partner confessing or implying that he or she had not been faithful. The third approach, "solicited discovery," includes the individual asking the partner, seeking information and obtaining confirmation prior to asking. The fourth was a "'red handed' discovery," or catching the partner in the act. Of these discovery methods, the "'red handed' discovery" and the "unsolicited third party discovery" methods of discovery were most damaging to the relationship, while the "unsolicited partner" confession was the least damaging. A person is much less likely to forgive a partner if the discovery method was "red handed" or "unsolicited third party," compared to "solicited information" or "unsolicited partner" confessions. Why? In part, the "red handed" and "unsolicited third party" methods of discovery are tremendously face threatening, embarrassing, and emotionally upsetting and are a blow to one's public image and pride. On the other hand, the "unsolicited partner" confession is relatively less face threatening, allows the guilty party to accept responsibility and communicate a full apology (or portions of a full apology) that may be credible, relative to other discovery methods.

The Cascade Model of Dissolution

The **cascade model** of marital dissolution describes a sequence of behaviors people employ when dissolving a relationship (Battaglia et al., 1998; Gottman, 1994; Gottman & Levenson, 1992). One partner in a relationship begins to criticize and complain about the other partner. Feelings of love, liking, and attraction are replaced by feelings of contempt, and as the feelings of contempt escalate, the partner being attacked becomes defensive. Both partners are critical of one another, and both act defensively. At some point, one individual (usually the male) begins to avoid interacting with the partner. This action is labeled stonewalling, as silence and emotional withdrawal are easier to cope with than negative interactions. The four horsemen of marital apocalypse are as follows: (1) complain/criticize, (2) contempt, (3) defensiveness, and (4) stonewalling. Any number of important relational problems can precipitate a cascade effect, and the problems and disputes that one could cope with when one was "in love" are now intolerable.

In sum, relationships fail in part because relational partners decide to withdraw from relationships when there are fewer and fewer rewards, when relationships are inequitable, and when serious, multiple problems are judged to be stable, internally caused, and intentionally caused. Partners are likely to withdraw from the relationship if they perceive that the problems are not easy to solve. Further, once a partner (or both partners) starts to criticize and complain openly, a cascade of negativity can engulf and eventually ruin a relationship.

METHODS USED IN RELATIONAL DISENGAGEMENT

Tactics Used in Relational Disengagement

Once the decision has been made to disengage, some message is usually used to communicate the initiator's intent. Baxter (1982) and Cody (1982) identify some of the tactics people report using when disengaging (see Table 11.7). These studies focus on what people recall having said or heard during their recent breakups and should be viewed as one of possibly several messages communicated during a time when former romantic partners uncoupled. Battaglia and colleagues (1998), as noted earlier, discussed that many individuals vacillate between staying and resolving differences, or leaving. Also, Sanders and Fitch (2001) recently demonstrated that social influence processes, like relational disengagement, occur interactionally and incrementally, as both people come to understand that the relationship will be altered and both share some role in redefining a new relationship, which includes deciding if they are to see each other in public and redefining their public images and feelings. One of our stories at the start of the chapter involved a waitress named Carol telling a hurtful man named Udall, "I don't think I want to know you anymore. All you do is make me feel bad about myself." In saying this, she clearly states a desire not to see him anymore (to terminate the would-be relationship). However, she later is seen wondering if she said or did the correct thing, and Udall comes to her home to apologize and talk; she is willing to give him another chance at "being a better man." Thus, some disengagements require both individuals to cooperate on changing definitions of a relationship. Our assumption is that disengagers will begin the process by withdrawing emotionally from the relationship, and that they start disengaging from their partner using relatively positive and rational arguments about growing up, learning about oneself, and so on. Stronger and more forceful messages are used later, or when a person is sufficiently hurt by emotional and/or physical abuse and infidelity, they are highly motivated to exit the relationships quickly.

The first type of disengagement message involves **positive-tone messages,** which have two important characteristics. First, positive-tone messages are very emotional; they try to make the rejected partner not feel rejected and hurt and also release tension that the disengager experiences during disengagement. Second, the messages state or imply a desire to de-escalate (see less of each other) but not terminate the relationship. Some variations on this general tactic are labeled *fairness, compromise,* and *fatalism.*

A second popular tactic uses **de-escalation messages,** which also have two characteristics. First, as with positive-tone messages, the initiator explicitly proposes that the two "see less of each other"; however, de-escalation messages are not quite as emotional as positive-tone ones. Second, a reason is given for why the two should see less of each other. Reasons can involve spending too much time together, being too young, and needing to experience other people before getting serious.

Table 11.7
MESSAGES USED IN RELATIONAL DISENGAGEMENT

Type	Example
Positive Tone	
Fairness	"I would say: 'It is unfair on my part and would be unfair to you to continue our relationship if one of us had to fake it. I care a great deal about you, but I don't feel as strongly toward you as you do toward me. It would be cheating you if I were to pretend I felt this way and would cause more heart-ache if I continue to do so. I think it would be wise if we stopped seeing so much of each other.'"
Compromise	"I would be very scared, I think. First, I would explain why I was dissatisfied with the relationship. Then I would say: 'I care about you and I want to be friends and there is no reason not to see each other.' We'd then talk and I would try to work out a compromise."
Fatalism	"In the kindest way possible I would say: 'My feelings have changed and I have really spent a lot of time praying about it and seeking God's guidance in this situation. I feel that it's not God's will for us to continue at this time.'"
De-escalation	
Promised friendship	"I would say: 'I think we need to stop seeing quite so much of each other. I am not ready to settle down yet. We can still see each other and remain great friends.'"
Implied possible	"I would say: 'I'm sorry, but for a close relationship reconciliation to work there must be mutual love, understanding, and close feelings, and at the moment I don't feel as close as I should. I think that it would be best to lay off for a while. If this relationship was meant to work, it will. If not, then it was never meant to be.'"
Relationship fault	"I would say: 'I think we are becoming too dependent on each other, so we have nothing individual to bring to the relationship at this point. If we take a period of time to do things on our own and make discoveries about ourselves and others, we will be capable of continuing or beginning a new relationship.'"
Appeal to independence	"I would say: 'Now is not the time for us to be tied down. Maybe in the future we could pick it up again.'"
Test of relationship	"I would say: 'I think that maybe we have been seeing too much of each other. I think we should see other people, meet other people, to see if we really want to be together.'"

Type	Example
Withdrawal or Avoidance Tactics	
	"I wouldn't say anything. I would just avoid the person as much as possible."
	"Without explaining my intentions to break it off, I would avoid scheduling future meetings with the person."
	"I wouldn't bring up the topic of breaking up, I would just never call the person again and never return any phone calls."
Justification	
Positive consequences of disengaging/target responsibility	"I would say: 'A good relationship meets the needs of both people and ours isn't meeting my needs. I don't want to change you and I would have to if you are going to meet my needs. So, I don't think we should see each other anymore.'"
Positive consequences of disengaging/disengager responsibility	"I would say: 'I'm really changing inside and I don't feel good about our relationship anymore. I think we'd better stop seeing each other.'"
Negative consequences of non-disengaging	"I would say: 'Continuing to see each other wouldn't work because we'd begin to hate each other and the relationship would really start to deteriorate.'"
Negative Identity Management or Manipulation	
Enjoyment of life	"I would say: 'Life is too short and we should enjoy other people and I myself would like to date other people, to see if we really want to be together.'"
Thought manipulation	"I'd beat around the bush for a while, then ask: 'You're not very happy are you? What's wrong (hoping to create anger)? Well, I think we need to talk about us, like, why don't we date other people for a while? If you don't want to, at least let me so I can figure out if I still feel the same way about us as I need to.'"
Nonnegotiation	"I would say: 'I think we should date around' (and then just date other people)."
Implicit expertise	"I would say: 'It would be better for the both of us, that we need more time to date others and be sure to find the right person to marry.'"

Source: Adapted from Cody, 1982. Also see Baxter (1982), Baxter (1987), Metts (1992).

A very different approach uses **withdrawal or avoidance tactics.** Sometimes disengagers say nothing to their partners concerning their intentions to change. Sometimes disengagers avoid the partner, refuse to answer phone messages, decline to return calls, and keep encounters brief.

A fourth disengagement tactic uses **justification messages,** which have three important features. First, they communicate that the partners should terminate the relationship and "stop seeing each other." Second, a reason is given to support the decision, usually that there is a cause for dissatisfaction, that the relationship is not a good one, or that the relationship isn't meeting the needs of the disengager. Justification tactics may also state or imply that the disengager believes that the problem cannot be solved or remedied, even claiming (in the variation called *negative consequences of not disengaging*) that things will become worse if the two don't stop seeing each other.

Finally, the tactics of **negative identity management** (or **manipulation**) are in contrast to the positive-tone tactics. Instead of making an effort to help keep the disengager from feeling rejected, the very nature of negative identity management tactics is to arouse emotions in such a way as to quicken disengagement, with low regard for the partner's feelings of rejection. Several of the variations are insulting to the dating partner. For example, in the *enjoyment of life* version, the disengager says that he or she does not enjoy life with the partner, which is insulting to a person whom one has been dating for weeks or months. In the *implicit expertise* version, the disengager first claims to know what is "better for both of us" and then claims that one should find the "right person to marry" (which apparently is not the person he or she is currently dating). The *nonnegotiation* version flatly informs the partner what will happen ("we should date around") and implies that there is no room for discussion or compromise. The *thought manipulation* version is one of the cruelest: make the partner angry, and then propose that because the relationship isn't working out, it should end.

The negative identity management tactics sound very coldhearted, and the messages create the impression of an unlikable person. However, remember that some partners are highly resistant to the idea of a breakup. Some people do not take "no"

Some messages used to communicate disengagement are, in fact, "classic."

for an answer, some people are possessive, and some people believe that they can win back the disengager's love. If a person doesn't first agree with positive-tone or other tactics, what would you do, especially if you were certain that you wanted out of a relationship? You would probably use a stronger message. Negative identity tactics are usually not the first messages that disengagers employ when breaking up (unless they desperately need to get away from a very undesirable person).

Both Baxter (1982) and Cody (1982) analyzed what people say to disengage and what people said to others during some segment of the relational disengagement process. In reality, disengagers can alter their relationships in several different ways simultaneously using indirect or direct methods, and the disengagement can be unilateral or bilateral (both partners acknowledge that the relationship is over). Baxter (1987) further elaborated on the tactics of disengagement by proposing six ways in which individuals, unilaterally or bilaterally, de-escalate or terminate relationships (also see Metts, 1992):

1. **Indirect-unilateral.** Includes three general, but indirect, ways in which a disengager can attempt to de-escalate a relationship: withdrawal (reducing the amount of contact, lessening of intimacy), pseudo–de-escalation (declaring that one wants to retain some type of relationship when one in fact does not and has no intention of doing so), and cost escalation (increasing the costs of being in the relationship for the partner by being rude, inconsiderate, and so forth).

2. **Indirect-bilateral.** Includes two indirect ways in which both partners may implicitly acknowledge relational de-escalation: mutual pseudo–de-escalation (both partners share the deception that some level of commitment will be retained) and fading away (implicitly knowing that the relationship is over, no more ruminations, thinking about partner).

3. **Direct-unilateral.** Includes two direct ways in which one partner can attempt a disengagement: fait accompli (one partner uses a simple statement to report that the relationship is over, but with no discussion or account) and state-of-the-relationship talk (one partner explicitly states the nature of the dissatisfaction and communicates the desire to exit in the context of a bilateral discussion of the relationship's problems).

4. **Direct-bilateral.** Includes two direct ways in which both partners openly discuss exiting or de-escalating: attributional conflict (conflict not over whether or not to exit, but why the exit is necessary; assigning blame) and negotiated farewell (explicit two-way discussion of the relationship and its decay, reasons for termination, sense-making session without blame).

5. **Self-orientation.** Includes four ways in which the individual disengager protects self, defends self, and increases pressure on the disengagee to de-escalate or terminate: costs escalation (increase the costs of being in the relationship for the partner

by being rude, and so forth), fait accompli (one partner uses a simple statement to report that the relationship is over), withdrawal, and attributional conflict (reason giving with blame placing).

6. **Other-orientation.** Includes five ways that are generally polite (or at least avoid placing blame) to address the face concerns of the partners involved: state-of-the-relationship talk, pseudo–de-escalation, bilateral pseudo–de-escalation, fading away, and negotiated farewell. Some of these approaches are obviously polite and satisfy the face needs of one or both partners, even though the message may be deceptive. That is, bilateral pseudo–de-escalation involves both partners entering into a state of collusion in which both save face, control feelings of rejection, and control emotions. Other approaches obviously are less polite and more aggressive — such as cost escalation and attributional conflict approaches.

A few studies have examined the use of messages designed to de-escalate or terminate relationships (Banks, Altendorf, Greene, & Cody, 1987; Baxter, 1982; Cody, 1982), and the results support three simple propositions. First, the more intimate the relationship, the more likely it is that the disengager will use some form of verbal message to communicate an intention to alter the relationship. Obviously a disengager is obligated to say something to an intimate, and it is hardly effective or normative simply to disappear after having been involved in an intimate long-term relationship. By contrast, withdrawal or avoidance tactics are used more often when the relationship is less intimate (after one or a few dates). Baxter (1982) also studied the impact of external versus internal causes and found that disengagers simply let a relationship die (they used more withdrawal tactics) when the cause was external (partner moved to a new city), compared to when the cause was internal (the two disagreed about life goals). In the former, both partners can use indirect bilateral strategies because they both know that the relationship is over. In the latter case, friends and intimates are more likely to feel some obligation to explain the loss in intimacy or decline in relational closeness.

Second, when we want to stay friends with our ex-partners, we use either positive-tone or de-escalation tactics, and when we want out of the relationship completely, we use justification, withdrawal, or negative identity management tactics. A disengager would use positive-tone tactics to maximize the chance that the two partners would stay friends after the breakup. Third, in most normal circumstances, disengagers monitor the face concerns of both interactional partners. Typically we would like to leave a relationship believing that neither our public image nor the image of our ex-partner is tarnished. Because we may want to leave a relationship gracefully and with a positive self-image intact, we employ facework to ensure that there are no hurt feelings and that emotions and attributions of blame or causality are monitored.

Facework and Politeness Theory

Members of all societies engage in facework activities, and we are motivated to be polite when we are interacting with more powerful others, with strangers, and when the offense at hand is severe. Relational disengagement is a unique circumstance, however, in that we intend to be polite toward individuals with whom we were once close (but who will now be less intimate, maybe even strangers), and although they do not have greater status, they do have power in the sense that they have had access to personal information about us.

The "severity of offense" was discussed fully by Metts (1992, 1997), who argued that a general sense of the level of offense is the amount of loss experienced, and loss is a "function of several factors, including, for example, how long a couple has been dating or married, the amount of network overlap, how enmeshed they have become (children, home, property), and how strongly the dissolution is desired by one partner relative to the other" (pp. 119–120). Thus "high severity" occurs when people have been dating for a relatively long period; they share many friends; they have invested or "enmeshed" much of their lives, time, money, and so on; and one partner wants to leave the relationship but the other does not. Much less severity occurs among those who dated briefly, without involving friends or a big investment, and when both knew that the relationship had a limited, if any, future.

Metts (1992) offered a model of the types of messages individuals communicate as low to high levels of politeness and levels of severity of the offense, from the point of view of the disengager (Figure 11.2). When the severity of the offense is low, some or most disengagers would employ "off the record," indirect ways to disengage, including fading away, avoidance, behavioral de-escalation, manipulation, and cost escalation (all of these tactics were described earlier). These are low in politeness because they fail to demonstrate a motivation to support, or show respect for, the hearer's positive face; in fact, manipulation and cost escalation are likely to involve a threat to negative face (telling or communicating messages that are an assault to the hearer's sense of autonomy and freedom). Individuals who rely on withdrawal tactics like avoidance and behavioral de-escalation are rated negatively (low in favorableness) by others and express regrets over having selected the strategy (Metts, 1992; Wilmot, Carbaugh, & Baxter, 1985). Truly poor management of conflict and public image results, however, from the use of manipulation (or cost escalation) (Baxter, 1987; Metts, 1992). Cost escalation poses a threat to both the positive face of the hearer (lack of support), and negative face (threat to autonomy), and coerces the hearer into the role of a hurt, angered, or shamed individual who has to engage, reactively, in the disengagement act. Users of cost escalation are shameless and heartless.

The four categories of disengagement we describe in the remainder of this section (bald on record, attributional conflict, relationship talk, and unilateral facework) vary in levels of politeness. All bald on record disengagement strategies communicate a message to the hearer that, at a minimum, shows others that the disengager is concerned with face obligations and the expectations that accompany close relationships (Baxter, 1987; Metts, 1992). **Bald on record tactics** include three variations of "efficient and unambiguous" messages: *fait accompli, negative identity management,* and *justification/reason giving* (the types of justifications listed by Cody, 1982). These tactics are minimally polite and are probably used sparingly. They are considered low in politeness because they do not redress the hearer's positive face through the use of apologies

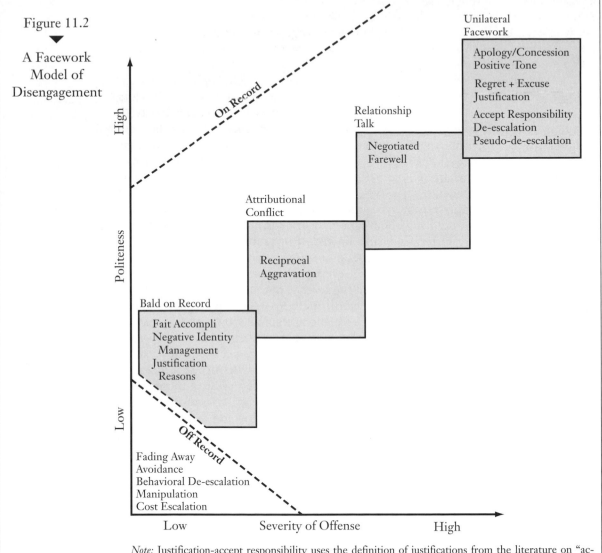

Figure 11.2

▼

A Facework
Model of
Disengagement

Note: Justification-accept responsibility uses the definition of justifications from the literature on "accounts." Justification-reasons uses the definition used by Cody, 1982, dealing with reasons for terminating the relationship.
Source: Adapted from S. Metts, 1992. Reprinted by permission of the author and Springer-Verlag, NY.

or elaborate explanations or accounts. These tactics are probably used when the disengager believes that the relationship is substantial enough to merit a message regarding his or her exiting from it and its dissolution but that there is insufficient emotional commitment, involvement, or an enmeshment of networks or resources to require more elaborate messages. The tactics are probably perceived as relatively appropriate if the hearer or others agree that a minimal relationship was in place. The tactics may be inappropriate if the hearer has been led to believe that the relational definition is more definite, that there was a future to the relationship, or that there was a greater enmeshing of their lives. Such a hearer would expect a higher level of politeness.

The third least polite form of disengagement is **attributional conflict,** which is reflected by *reciprocal aggravation*. What this term means is that both parties agree to change the current definition of the relationship, but they disagree on the reasons why. One person may claim that the partner was inconsiderate and "never there for me," but the partner claims that the disengager was too controlling. Or, one may claim that pressures from in-laws caused arguments, and the other points to a lack of agreement on how to spend money in a joint budget. Why is this category, so directly linked to conflict, rated as relatively polite? Open discussions of reasons redress both participants' negative face; that is, by being able to talk it out both partners are able to save their sense of autonomy and freedom (compared to cost escalation, manipulation, fait accompli, or negative identity management). Also, both participants have agreed that the dissolution is desirable, and the loss of positive face to one another is less threatening than when unilateral withdrawal is involved (Metts, 1992, p. 123).

The second most polite category of approaches is **relationship talk,** which includes *negotiated farewell* and *state-of-relationship talk*. These approaches are relatively more polite than attributional conflict because relationship talk includes bilateral conversations of relational disengagement and termination, allowing both partners to air their feelings and thoughts and to say their farewells.

Unilateral facework is the most polite category, and it includes *positive tone*, *apologies/concessions*, complex accounts of a *regret + excuse + justification* (accepting responsibility) nature (see Chapter 8), *de-escalation*, and *pseudo–de-escalation*. According to the Metts model, these forms of de-escalation are used when severity is high: when people have dated for a long time, one partner may want the relationship to continue, the partners' lives are enmeshed, and the two share friends. Research supports some of these hypotheses, and some of the more polite tactics are in fact related to staying friends after the disengagement.

THE CONSEQUENCES OF RELATIONAL DISENGAGEMENT

Depending on the amount of time spent together, commitment, trust placed in others, feelings of love, and more, people have widely different reactions and feelings when they break up their relationships. Some are relieved and feel free, others are depressed and question their self-worth. Others cope by denying their feelings and reactions, claiming that "everything is fine." Not surprisingly, some universities and others post advice on-line and offer assistance to those having a difficult time with a breakup. One such list of advice is reproduced in Table 11.8. Below we review the few empirical studies focusing on the aftermath of relational breakups.

Table 11.8

COPING WITH A BREAKUP

Ending a relationship is one of the most avoided and feared human experiences. As a culture, we have no clear-cut rituals for ending relationships or saying good bye to valued others. We are often unprepared for the variety of feelings we experience in the process. Some common reactions are as follows:

Denial — We can't believe that this is happening to us and that the relationship is over.

Anger — We are angry and often enraged at our partner or lover for shaking our world to its core.

Fear — We are frightened by the intensity of our feelings. We are frightened that we may never love or be loved again. We are frightened that we may not survive our loss, but we will do so.

Self-blame — We blame ourselves for what went wrong. We replay our relationship over and over, saying to ourselves, "If only I had done this. If only I had done that."

Sadness — We cry, sometimes for what seems an eternity, for we have suffered a great loss.

Guilt — We feel guilty, particularly if we choose to end a relationship. We don't want to hurt our partner, yet we don't want to stay in a lifeless relationship.

Disorientation and confusion — We don't know who or where we are anymore. Our familiar world has been shattered. We've lost our bearings.

Hope — Initially we may fantasize that there will be a reconciliation, that the parting is only temporary, that our partner will come back to us. As we heal and accept the reality of the ending, we may dare to hope for a newer and better world for ourselves.

Bargaining — We plead with our partner to give us a chance. "Don't go," we say. "I'll change this and I'll change that if only you'll stay."

Relief — We can be relieved that there is an ending to the pain, the fighting, the torment, and the lifelessness of the relationship.

While some of these feelings may seem overwhelming, they are all "normal" reactions. They are necessary to the process of healing, so that we can eventually move on and engage in other relationships. Be patient with yourself.

Here are some guidelines many people find helpful:

Allow yourself to feel the sadness, anger, fear, and pain associated with an ending. Denying those feelings or keeping them inside will only prolong them.

Recognize that guilt, self-blame, and bargaining are our defenses against feeling out of control and unable to stop the other person from leaving us. But there

> are some endings we can't control, because we can't control another person's behavior.
>
> Give yourself time to heal, and be kind to yourself for the duration: Pamper yourself, ask for support from others, and allow yourself new experiences and friends.
>
> Talk it over with someone. This can often give us perspective. If you feel stuck in a pattern and unable to change it, talking to a professional counselor may help.
>
> ▲
>
> *Source:* From the Student Counseling Center, University of Texas at Dallas, with links to similar sites at other universities (Melbourne, Buffalo). [On-line]. Available: www.utdallas.edu/student/slife/counseling/coping.html

Emotional Consequences

Banks and colleagues (1987) assessed emotional consequences of relational disengagement. Disengagers felt a greater sense of freedom from their partners when the partners constrained them and the partners were rated low on desirability (a general index of beauty and popularity). To free themselves from their partners, disengagers employed negative identity management tactics and avoided positive-tone tactics. Disengagers indicated that they were depressed when they were involved in intimate relationships with nonconstraining partners who failed to compromise; that is, disengagers reported being depressed if they wanted more out of the relationship than their partners did and the partners took them for granted. Depressed individuals also indicated that they had used more positive-tone and de-escalation tactics but had avoided justification tactics. The results suggest that the people who were most likely to become depressed were those who had been at a disadvantage in the relationship, or who were more committed to it, or who had struggled to keep it going.

Similar findings have been uncovered by researchers studying feelings of distress (feeling upset and unhappy) (Feeney & Noller, 1992; Fine & Sacher, 1997; Fraizer & Cook, 1993; Simpson, 1987; Sprecher, 1994; Sprecher, Felmlee, Metts, Fehr, & Vanni, 1998). People experience greater distress when they have placed greater effort in initiating a relationship. They were more committed to it, they had found it satisfying at some time, it had been maintained for some time, they felt left behind (their partner left them for another), and they were prone to higher levels of anxiety (see Chapter 14 regarding fearful attachment style). Similar results have been obtained for depression: Postbreakup depression might be caused by how much the individual wanted to end the relationship, the duration of the relationship, how much the partner wanted to end it, and the intensity of love and other feelings for the partner (Hindy, Schwarz, & Brodsky, 1989; Mearns, 1991). Ruvolo, Fabin and Ruvolo (2001) found that women became less secure after a breakup, while women who stayed in their relationships became more secure over time.

Staying Friends

Banks and colleagues (1987) found that people claimed to stay friends if the disengager had used de-escalation tactics and perceived the partner to be desirable (attractive, likable, competent, etc.). The use of justification tactics and withdrawal or avoidance was related to terminating relationships in such a way that the two did not stay friends afterwards. In this study, however, the use of positive-tone or negative identity management tactics was unrelated to staying friends — sometimes people stayed friends, and sometimes they didn't.

Metts, Cupach, and Bejlovec (1989), however, examined the responses of both disengagers and disengagees. Disengagees claimed that they stayed friends if the two had been friends prior to becoming romantically involved and were likely to stay friends if the disengager had used positive tone and had avoided using any negative identity (or other manipulative) tactic during the breakup. Likewise, disengagers claimed that the two stayed friends if they had been friends prior to becoming romantically involved. However, disengagers claimed that different tactics affected the choice of staying friends: Disengagers were less likely to stay friends after the breakup if they had been the underbenefited partner and if they had used withdrawal or avoidance tactics.

Very few studies have examined the question of staying friends after a relational disengagement. It would seem wise to recommend, if you want to stay friends, using positive-tone or de-escalation tactics; avoiding justification, manipulation, or withdrawal tactics; treating the partner equitably; and dating a partner who is desirable and was a friend prior to the romantic involvement. Also, people may stay friends if the agreement to break up is mutual.

Grave Dressing and Adjustment

Breaking off a serious relationship can be traumatic and stressful. Several important works have addressed issues dealing with the process whereby individuals try to cope, resolve, and account for what occurred prior to and during the relational decay phases (Baxter, 1984; Conville, 1991; Lee, 1984; Vaughan, 1987; Weiss, 1975). One recent program of research focusing on this matter has been conducted by Harvey, Orbuch, and Weber (Harvey, Agostinelli, & Weber 1989; Harvey, Orbuch, & Weber, 1990; Harvey, Orbuch, Weber, Merbach, & Alt, 1992; Harvey, Weber, Galvin, Huszti, & Garnick, 1986; Harvey, Weber, & Orbuch, 1990). Their model is critically important because it focuses on psychological needs, communication, and mental health.

In Chapter 8, we talked about accounts as short-term tactics that we communicate to others when we defend ourselves from the accusation that we have been bad or that we are responsible for questionable actions. Harvey and colleagues argue that after a traumatic experience, such as the disruption of a loving relationship, we naturally experience a need to explain fully what happened to us. The accounting process in this particular context may require months or even years to develop fully because it involves so much information, so many details, so much potential for second guessing (Did I try hard enough to repair it? What if I had given my partner one more chance? Did I make the right decision? What if I had changed?), so much intimate knowledge, and often so many other people in the couple's social networks. The accounting process involves the construction of a detailed, coherent story or narrative about the relationship, what happened, when, why, and with what consequences.

Figure 11.3 presents a model of account making (Harvey et al., 1992), and the box "Student as Observer: Case Study on Relational Dissolution Processes" provides an anecdotal view. The sequence is initiated with the **traumatic event** — the breakup itself or certain knowledge of the partner that prompted an immediate need to terminate the relationship. Shock, numbness, and the feeling of being overwhelmed occurs naturally at this point. The second phase is **outcry,** in which the individual may experience several negative emotions — panic, despair, hopelessness, and exhaustion. This stage deals largely with the release of emotional tensions that inevitably follow a traumatic experience.

The third stage is **denial,** in which the individual cuts off from others to be alone — staying at home, avoiding people at church or work, and so on. At this stage,

At the beginning of the accounting process, individuals might experience panic, despair, and hopelessness.

Joel Gordon

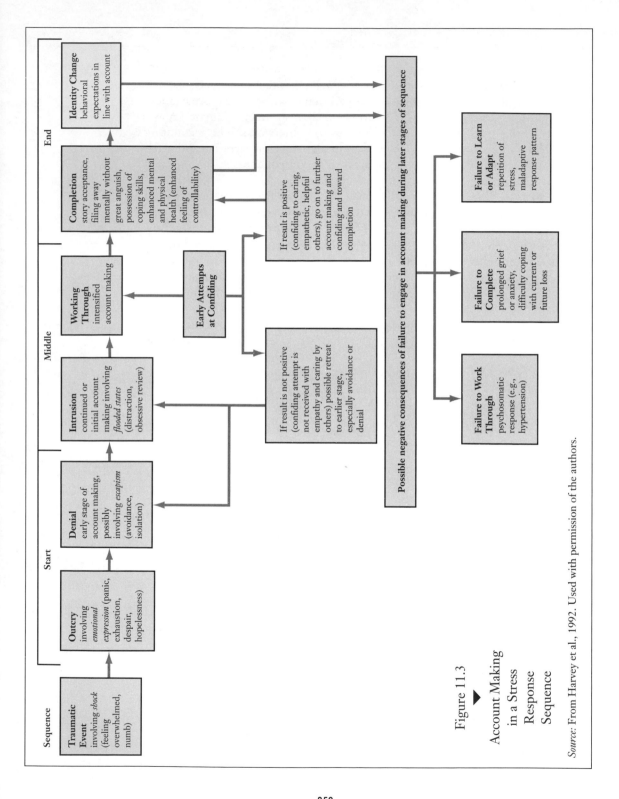

Figure 11.3

▶ Account Making
in a Stress
Response
Sequence

Source: From Harvey et al., 1992. Used with permission of the authors.

the individual begins to think about the many reasons why the loving relationship soured. The interruption of daily routines facilitates thinking about why the relationship failed. Also, the depression the individual experiences at this stage facilitates a drive to come to closure, or complete an explanation, so that the individual can close the door on the past and move on to new experiences and relationships. Alternatively the maintenance of escapism and avoidance, without expressing grief openly or without talking with others about why events happened, may result in a number of psychological problems.

In the middle stages, the individual first experiences **intrusion,** including occasional flooded states in which he or she cannot think about anything but the relational disengagement. For example, although back at work and back to "normal," the person might wake up one night trying to reconcile the breakup with the wonderful, romantic vacation the couple took only months before the breakup; or an old song or movie is unexpectedly overwhelming and the person has to reconcile certain feelings.

STUDENT AS OBSERVER: CASE STUDY ON RELATIONAL DISSOLUTION PROCESSES

A number of movies feature what people do when they cope with the dissolution of intimate relationships, and these movies provide a way of discussing examples of the causes of breaking up, reasons and attributions, the use of disengagement strategies, and coping afterwards.

Watch either *First Wives Club* or *Living Out Loud.* Take notes on the following elements and write a summary of the process of disengagement and the accounting process that followed.

1. What information is provided about the reasons for the breakup for each of the marriages? Power, control, infidelity, frequency of problems, valence of problems?
2. What were the perceived underlying causes of problems that led to the breakups? Intentional? Controllable? Internal? Stable?
3. Who is to blame for the breakup? Is the male solely responsible, the woman solely responsible? Or, do they share responsibility?
4. What were the disengagement strategies used (if any are portrayed in the film)?
5. What were the emotional consequences, sense of freedom, guilt, anger, etc.
6. Discuss how, for each relationship, the sequence of steps in the accounting process, of traumatic event, outcry, denial, and so forth.
7. How important was each person's interpersonal communication with friends in terms of (a) a reality check on marriage, causes of and coping with loss, and (b) social support and the reconstruction of a person's sense of identity?

352

In the **working-through stage,** the individual provides explanations that are complete stories for various aspects on the relationship — the good and positive aspects, what went wrong, when things went wrong, when the realization dawned that things had gone wrong, denials and acceptances for blame and responsibility, and so on. It is critically important for the disengager to confide these stories to others at this time, for several reasons. Telling the stories to others and getting feedback from them provides a reality check on the account process; alternatively, an individual can create any

RELATIONAL WOES: SHALL I STAY OR SHALL I GO?

There are a number of relationships between men and women in movies and on television that reflect the relational disengagement process, from movies like *Singles*, to relationships portrayed on "Sex and the City," "Ally McBeal," and "Friends." As a case study, consider "Sex and the City." Carrie Bradshaw, played by Sarah Jessica Parker, has been involved in several relationships featuring relational dissolution, attempts at repair, breaking up, and getting back together again. Her relationships, and her thoughts communicated to the viewers, reflect both Duck's notions of phases of disengagement as well as the Battaglia, Richard, Datteri, and Lord (1998) phases of disengagement (see text). For example, for quite some time, Carrie dated Big, who was a man who mystified her and exerted control over her. They had a bumpy relationship and separated. Because Big could not say the words "I love you," they broke up. Carrie suffered from depression, but her friends provided her with social support. She engaged, later, in grave dressing, by putting the breakup in a positive light. However, Carrie still harbored feelings for Big, even when dating Aidan, the down-to-earth hunk she started seeing (reluctantly at first). Big returned to the picture married to a model. Carrie mentally compared the two men, and, in comparing her options, had a difficult time deciding what to do. Ultimately, her feelings for Big resulted in her having an affair with him, which then led to his divorce from the model. She confided in Aidan about her affair. He dumped her. She was then desperate to win him back. Aidan slowly learned to trust her and he ultimately proposed. As they plan to move in together, they experience stress, but manage to cope and decide they need to work on their relationship.

What examples like these reveal about relationships (on television and elsewhere) is that relational breakups are part of a process through which partners proceed through several states, and often vacillate between staying or leaving. Disengagers often form relationships, evaluate those relationships, assess the situation they are in, withdraw from the partner, or otherwise break off the relationship, mentally compare the next relationship with various options, decide to return to the old relationship, realize this is wrong, realize whom they actually love, communicate feelings and break up with the one and work to keep the relationship alive with the other. However, this story has no ending. Relationships are always changing.

number of scenarios that might be false, portraying the individual as too much of a hopeless victim or as too innocent, and so forth. In reality, no one is totally charming or perfect. Another critical role played by communicating these accounts is hearing one's friends verify and agree with the explanations concerning various aspects of the former relationship. Self-esteem is bolstered and tension is released as a person communicates accounts and gets beyond persistent and bewildering thoughts and doubts.

During this process, the individual puts together a fairly coherent, complete, detailed story concerning the dissolution and nearly all aspects of former relational life that has been reality-tested, verified, and accepted by friends and family members. The ability to create a complete story has been linked with the teller's well-being (Koenig & Manusov, in press). During the **completion** and **identity change stages,** the individual not only possesses stories and explanations about the breakup but has also developed coping skills and has perhaps altered his or her behavior in view of having learned from the account-making process. Coping skills may deal with certain behaviors revealed to be ineffective or even harmful in the previous relationship (placing work above family, drinking too much, being too quick to judge others, being too quick to anger, etc.) and changing personal habits, routines, and skills. Behavioral changes relate to how the individual pursues relational goals. For example, if a person has concluded that the last relationship ended because he or she moved too fast toward intimacy or had expectations that were too high, the individual might escalate the next relationship more slowly or adopt more realistic expectations.

As indicated in Figure 11.3, failing to engage in account-making has three possible negative consequences: persistence of negative emotions (the flooded states characteristic of intrusion persist as hypertension, insomnia, etc.), prolonged grief and anxiety, and failure to learn and adopt more realistic standards of relational life, romance, and dating. Regarding this last consequence, if individuals place all the blame on the relational partner, fail to proceed through the account-making phase, and quickly return to dating, there is a good chance that they have not learned anything about themselves or about dating. Such individuals will tend to date people who are quite similar to the partners they just left and may end up in the same type of relationship from which they just exited.

CHAPTER SUMMARY

This chapter began with a discussion of why some partners stay together and why others disengage from their relationships. A few of the factors contributing to relational longevity were being in love, maintaining equitable relationships, dating someone similar to oneself, and being equally involved and committed to the relationship. A few of the factors contributing to disengagement were boredom, differences in interests and backgrounds, conflicting ideas about marriage and sex, and the need to be independent.

354

We also discussed several disengagement tactics. Harsher tactics are more likely to be used when a disengager strongly desires to quickly terminate a relationship. Partners are more likely to stay friends after the breakup when the disengager uses a positive-tone or de-escalation tactic and avoids justification, manipulation, or withdrawal tactics, and when the relationship is marked by equity, the partner was considered desirable, the decision to break up was mutual, and the partners were friends prior to the disengagement.

Disengagement is a process that progresses through four stages: intrapsychic, dyadic, social, and grave dressing. We emphasized grave dressing and other matters of adjustment in the last half of this chapter. Progressing through these stages helps an individual work through the process, bringing not only a resolution of grieving, but also a new awareness of self.

KEY TERMS

▼

actual equity, p. 326
attribution theory, p. 331
attributional conflict tactics, p. 345
bald on record tactics, p. 343
cascade model, p. 336
completion stage, p. 353
de-escalation messages, p. 337
denial, p. 349
direct-bilateral, p. 341
direct-unilateral, p. 341
dyadic phase, p. 319
grave-dressing phase, p. 319
identity change stage, p. 353
indirect-bilateral, p. 341
indirect-unilateral, p. 341
infidelity, p. 333

intrapsychic phase, p. 319
intrusion, p. 351
justification messages, p. 340
negative identity management (manipulation), p. 340
other-orientation, p. 342
outcry, p. 349
positive-tone messages, p. 337
psychological equity, p. 325
relationship talk tactics, p. 345
self-orientation, p. 341
social phase, p. 319
traumatic event, p. 349
unilateral facework tactics, p. 345
withdrawal or avoidance tactics, p. 340
working-through stage, p. 352

EXERCISES FOR FURTHER DISCUSSION

▼

1. Write a short paragraph in which you discuss a romantic relationship that decayed or resulted in disengagement. Then write a short paragraph in which you discuss a friendship that deteriorated.

a. What caused the relationship to decay?
b. What were the consequences of the decay or disengagement?
c. Was the intensity of emotional consequences greater in one type of relationship?
d. Was staying in touch afterward equally important in both situations?
e. What were the verbal messages used in each type of relationship to disengage? How were they similar or different?
f. In what ways do you think the disengagement process is different for romantic relationships and friendships?

2. Equity can be used as a means of repairing a relationship if the partners succeed in balancing inputs and outcomes. Think of two characters, either from a book you have read recently or from a television series that you watch regularly, who are in a long-term relationship that involves inequities. Now think about some of the ways in which these two characters use equity-restoring tactics.
a. In what ways was the relationship initially inequitable?
b. What sorts of tactics did the characters use to try to restore equity?
c. Were the tactics effective? If so, which ones were the most effective?

3. Think of some situations you have either been in or observed in which one partner tried to use jealousy to increase relational involvement.
a. Was the tactic effective in increasing relational involvement?
b. Were there any negative consequences to this tactic?
c. In your experience, are men or women more likely to use this tactic? If there is a difference, why do you think it exists?

4. Think of a situation you have either been in or observed in which a relationship broke up, but the partners remained friends. Now think of a situation in which a relationship broke up, but the partners did not remain friends.
a. Was there a difference in the tactics used to break up?
b. In your experience, are men or women more likely to want to remain friends after disengaging?
c. If one of the partners experiences depression or despair after a breakup, do you think it is better or worse for them to continue to be friends? What would some advantages be? What would some disadvantages be?

5. Think of a film you have seen recently in which relational decay and disengagement was an important theme.
a. What was the source of the relational decay?
b. Were the causes of the relational decay stable, controllable, intentional, and internal?
c. Were the problems the couple experienced highly valenced (negatively charged)? In what ways?
d. What repairs were attempted?
e. What relational breakup communication tactics were used?
f. What was the process of post-disengagement adjustment?

SUGGESTED READING

▼

Orbuch, T. L. (Ed.). (1992). *Close relationship loss.* New York: Springer-Verlag. This volume contains a number of excellent chapters that focus on how the accounting process is involved in coping with relational decay.

ACCOUNTING FOR RELATIONSHIP DECAY

Harvey, J. H., Orbuch, T. L., & Weber, A. L. (Eds.). (1991). *Attributions, accounts, and close relationships.* New York: Springer-Verlag.

Harvey, J. H., Weber, A. L., & Orbuch, T. L. (1990). *Interpersonal accounts: A social psychological perspective.* Cambridge, MA: Basil Blackwell.

Both of these volumes provide excellent examples of the accounts, or narratives, individuals employ when creating and communicating explanations for why relationships decayed. The 1990 volume is an excellent starting point for understanding accounts as stories or narratives we develop after a traumatic event. Several examples from literature, biographies, and life stories are examined.

POST-DISENGAGEMENT ADJUSTMENT

Harvey, J. H., Orbuch, T. L., & Weber, A. L. (1990). A social psychological model of account making in response to severe stress. *Journal of Language and Social Psychology, 9,* 191–207. This article is a good place to read, in more detail, about the model we presented in this chapter on stages of the accounting process.

Sprecher, S., Felmlee, D., Metts, S., Fehr, B., & Vanni, D. (1998). Factors associated with distress following the breakup of a close relationship. *Journal of Social and Personal Relationships, 15,* 791–809. This article provides a recent summary of research on experiencing distress immediately after a breakup and later in time.

REFERENCE LIST

▼

Afifi, W. A., Falato, W. L., & Weiner, J. L. (2001). Identity concerns following a severe relational transgression: The role of discovery method for the relational outcomes of infidelity. *Journal of Social and Personal Relationships, 18,* 291–308.

Banks, S. P., Altendorf, S. M., Greene, J. O., & Cody, M. J. (1987). An examination of relationship disengagements: Perceptions, breakup strategies, and outcomes. *Western Journal of Speech Communication, 51,* 19–41.

Battaglia, D. M., Richard, F. D., Datteri, D. L., & Lord, C. G. (1998). Breaking up is (relatively) easy to do: A script for the dissolution of close relationships. *Journal of Social and Personal Relationships, 15,* 829–845.

Baxter, L. A. (1982). Strategies for ending relationships: Two studies. *Western Journal of Speech Communication, 46*, 233–242.

Baxter, L. A. (1984). Trajectories of relationship disengagement. *Journal of Social and Personal Relationships, 1*, 29–48.

Baxter, L. A. (1987). Cognition and communication in the relationship process. In R. Burnett, P. McGhee, & D. D. Clarke (Eds.), *Understanding personal relationships* (pp. 192–212). London: Sage.

Chadiha, L. A., Veroff, J., Leber, D. (1998). Newlywed's narrative themes: Meaning in the first year of marriage for African American and white couples. *Journal of Comparative Family Studies, 29*, 115–130.

Cody, M. J. (1982). A typology of disengagement strategies and an examination of the roles intimacy, reactions to inequity, and relational problems play in strategy selection. *Communication Monographs, 49*, 148–170.

Cody, M. J., Kersten, L., Braaten, D. O., & Dickson, R. (1992). Coping with relational dissolutions: Attributions, account credibility, and plans for resolving conflicts. In J. H. Harvey, T. L. Orbuch, & A. L. Weber (Eds.), *Attributions, accounts, and close relationships* (pp. 93–115). New York: Springer-Verlag.

Conville, R. L. (1991). *Relational transitions: The evolution of personal relationships.* New York: Praeger.

Duck, S. W. (1982). A typography of relationship disengagement and dissolution. In S. W. Duck (Ed.), *Personal relationships 4: Dissolving personal relationships* (pp. 1–30). New York: Academic.

Duck, S. W. (1984). A perspective on the repair of personal relationships: Repair of what, when? In S. W. Duck (Ed.), *Personal relationships 5: Repairing interpersonal relationships* (pp. 163–184). New York: Academic.

Feeney, J. A., & Noller, P. (1992). Attachment style and romantic love: Relationship dissolution. *Australian Journal of Psychology, 44*, 69–72.

Felmlee, D. H. (1995). Fatal attractions: Affection and disaffection in intimate relationships. *Journal of Social and Personal Relationships, 12*, 295–311.

Felmlee, D. H. (2001). No couple is an island: A social network perspective on dyadic stability. *Social Forces, 79*, 1259–1287.

Fine, M. A., & Sacher, J. A. (1997). Predictors of distress following relationship termination among dating couples. *Journal of Clinical and Social Psychology, 16*, 381–388.

Fletcher, G. J. O., Simpson, J. A., & Thomas, G. (2000). The measurement of perceived relationship quality components: A confirmatory factor analytic approach. *Personality and Social Psychology Bulletin, 26*, 340–354.

Flora, J., & Segrin, C. (2000). Relationship development in dating couples: Implications for relational satisfaction and loneliness. *Journal of Social and Personal Relationships, 17*, 811–825.

Fraizer, P. A., & Cook, S. W. (1993). Correlates of distress following heterosexual relationship dissolution. *Journal of Social and Personal Relationships, 10*, 55–67.

Golden, A. G. (2002). Speaking of work and family: Spousal collaboration on defining role-identities and developing shared meanings. *Southern Communication Journal, 67*, 122–141.

Gottman, J. M. (1994). *What predicts divorce? The relationship between marital process and marital outcomes.* Hillsdale, NJ: Erlbaum.

Gottman, J. M., & Levenson, R. W. (1992). Marital processes predictive of later dissolution: Behavior, physiology, and health. *Journal of Personality and Social Psychology, 63*, 221–233.

Harvey, J. H., Agostinelli, G., & Weber, A. L. (1989). Account making and the formation of expectations about close relationships. In C. Hendrick (Ed.), *Close relationships* (pp. 39–62). Newbury Park, CA: Sage.

Harvey, J. H., Orbuch, T. L., & Weber, A. L. (1990). A social psychological model of account making in response to severe stress. *Journal of Language and Social Psychology, 9*, 191–207.

Harvey, J. H., Orbuch, T. L., Weber, A. L., Merbach, N., & Alt, R. (1992). House of pain and hope: Accounts of loss. *Death Studies, 16*, 99–124.

Harvey, J. H., Weber, A. L., Galvin, K. S., Huszti, H. C., & Garnick, N. N. (1986). Attribution in the termination of close relationships: A special focus on the account. In R. Gilmour & S. W. Duck (Eds.), *The emerging field of personal relationships* (pp. 189–201). Hillsdale, NJ: Erlbaum.

Harvey, J. H., Weber, A. L., & Orbuch, T. L. (1990). *Interpersonal accounts: A social psychological perspective*. Cambridge, MA: Blackwell.

Hill, C., Rubin, Z., & Peplau, L. A. (1976). Breakups before marriage: The end of 103 affairs. *Journal of Social Issues, 32*, 147–168.

Hindy, C. G., Schwarz, J. C., & Brodsky, A. (1989). *If this is love, why do I feel so insecure?* Boston: Atlantic Monthly Press.

Hoppe-Nagao, A., & Ting-Toomey, S. (2002). Relational dialectics and management strategies in marital couples. *Southern Communication Journal, 67*, 142–159.

Joyner, K., & Udry, J.R. (2000). You don't bring me anything but down: Adolescent romance and depression. *Journal of Health and Social Behavior, 41*, 369–391.

Kalmijn, M., & Bernasco, W. (2001). Joint and separated lifestyles in couple relationships. *Journal of Marriage and the Family, 63*, 639–654.

Knapp, M. L., & Vangelisti, A. L. (1992). *Interpersonal communication and human relationships* (2nd ed.). Newton, MA: Allyn & Bacon.

Knox, D., Zusman, M. E., Kaluzny, M. (2000). Attitudes and behavior of college students toward infidelity. *College Student Journal, 34*, 162–164.

Kurdek, L. (1991). The dissolution of gay and lesbian couples. *Journal of Social and Personal Relationships, 8*, 265–278.

Leathers, D. G. (1992). *Successful nonverbal communication: Principles and applications* (2nd ed.). New York: Macmillan.

Lee, L. (1984). Sequences in separation: A framework for investigating endings of the personal (romantic) relationship. *Journal of Social and Personal Relationships, 1*, 49–73.

Mearns, J. (1991). Coping with breakup: Negative mood regulation expectancies and depression following the end of a romantic relationship. *Journal of Personality and Social Psychology, 60*, 327–334.

Metts, S. (1992). The language of disengagement: A face-management perspective. In T. Orbuch (Ed.), *Close relationship loss: Theoretical approaches* (pp. 111–127). New York: Springer-Verlag.

Metts, S. (1997). Face and facework: Implications for the study of personal relationships. In S. Duck (Ed.), *Handbook of personal relationships: Theory, research and interventions* (2nd ed.) (pp. 373–390). Chichester, England: Wiley.

Metts, S., & Cupach, W. R. (1986). *Disengagement themes in same-sex and opposite-sex friendships.* Paper presented to the Interpersonal Communication Interest Group, Western Speech Communication Association, Tucson, AZ.

Metts, S., Cupach, W. R., & Bejlovec, R. A. (1989). "I love you too much to ever start liking you": Redefining romantic relationships. *Journal of Social and Personal Relationships, 6,* 259–274.

Morris, G., Moeai, J., & Shimizu, L. (1985). Intercultural marriages: An intrareligious perspective. *International Journal of Intercultural Relations, 9,* 427–434.

Murray, S. L., & Holmes, J. G. (2000). Seeing the self through a partner's eyes: Why self-doubts turn into relationship insecurities. In A. Tesser, R. B. Felson, & J. Suls (Eds.), *Psychological perspectives on self and identity* (pp. 173–187). Washington DC: American Psychological Association.

Orbuch, T. L., Veroff, J., & Holmberg, D. (1993). Becoming a married couple: The emergence of meaning in the first years of marriage. *Journal of Marriage and the Family, 55,* 815–826.

Roscoe, B., Cavanaugh, L. E., & Kennedy, D. R. (1988). Dating infidelity: Behaviors, reasons and consequences. *Adolescence, 23,* 35–43.

Ruvolo, A. P. (1998). Marital well-being and general happiness of newlywed couples: Relationships across time. *Journal of Social and Personal Relationships, 15,* 470–489.

Ruvolo, A. P., & Brennan, C. J. (1997). What's love got to do with it? Close relationships and perceived growth. *Personality and Social Psychology Bulletin, 23,* 814–823.

Ruvolo, A. P. & Fabin, L. A. (1999). Two of a kind: perceptions of own and partner's attachment characteristics. *Personal Relationships, 6,* 57–79.

Ruvolo, A. P., Fabin, L. A., & Ruvolo, C. M. (2001). Relationship experiences and change in attachment characteristics of young adults: The role of relationship breakups and conflict avoidance. *Personal Relationships, 8,* 265–281.

Ruvolo, A. P., & Ruvolo, C. M. (2000). Creating Mr. Right and Ms. Right: Interpersonal ideals and personal change in newlyweds. *Personal Relationships, 7,* 341–362.

Ruvolo, A. P., & Veroff, J. (1997). For better or worse: Real-ideal discrepancies and the marital well-being of newlyweds. *Journal of Social and Personal Relationships, 14,* 223–242.

Safran, C. (1979). Troubles that pull couples apart: A Redbook report. *Redbook,* January, pp. 138–141.

Sanders, R. E., & Fitch, K. L. (2001). The actual practice of compliance-seeking. *Communication Theory, 11,* 263–289.

Simpson, J. A. (1987). The dissolution of romantic relationships: Factors involved in relationship stability and emotional distress. *Journal of Personality and Social Psychology, 53,* 683–692.

Sprecher, S. (1994). Two sides of the breakup of dating relationships. *Personal Relationships, 1,* 199–222.

Sprecher, S. (2001). Equity and social exchange theory in dating couples: Associations with satisfaction, commitment, and stability. *Journal of Marriage and Family, 63,* 599–613.

Sprecher, S., Felmlee, D., Metts, S., Fehr, B., & Vanni, D. (1998). Factors associated with distress following the breakup of a close relationship. *Journal of Social and Personal Relationships, 15,* 791–809.

Sprecher, S., & Metts, S. (1999). Romantic beliefs: Their influence on relationships and patterns of change over time. *Journal of Social and Personal Relationships, 16,* 834–851.

Vangelisti, A. L. (1992). Communication problems in committed relationships: An attributional analysis. In J. H. Harvey, T. L. Orbuch, & A. L. Weber (Eds.), *Attributions, accounts, and close relationships* (pp. 144–164). New York: Springer-Verlag.

Vangelisti, A. L., & Young, S. L. (2000). When words hurt: The effects of perceived intentionality on interpersonal relationships. *Journal of Social and Personal Relationships, 17,* 393–424.

Van Willigen, M., & Drenta, P. (2001). Benefits of equitable relationships: The impact of sense of fairness, household division of labor, and decision making power on perceived social support. *Sex Roles, 44,* 571–597.

Vaughan, D. (1987). *Uncoupling: How relationships come apart.* New York: Vintage Books.

Weiss, R. S. (1975). *Marital separation.* New York: Basic Books.

White, G. L. (1980). Inducing jealousy: A power perspective. *Personality and Social Psychology Bulletin, 6,* 222–227.

Wiederman, M. W., & LaMar, L. (1998). 'Not with him you don't': Gender and emotional reactions to sexual infidelity during courtship. *The Journal of Sex Research, 35,* 288–297.

Wilmot, W. W., Carbaugh, D. A., & Baxter, L. A. (1985). Communicative strategies used to terminate romantic relationships. *Western Journal of Speech Communication, 49,* 204–216.

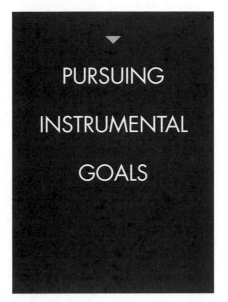

PURSUING

INSTRUMENTAL

GOALS

In Part IV, we focus on instrumental goals, which refer to how we obtain valued resources and favors from others. Four chapters review what we know about interpersonal influence and managing conflict when our influence attempts fail. In Chapter 12, we look at the principles that explain why people comply or refuse other people's influence attempts. We note that people tend to reciprocate behavior, remain committed to causes, want to be liked, and so forth, and that these principles motivate behavior. The chapter also presents some of the compliance-gaining strategies that are used in everyday life. Chapter 13 looks more closely at interpersonal conflict and the communication behaviors people use to manage conflicts. We present a definition of interpersonal conflict, look at some of the different styles and strategies of managing conflict, and then discuss some of the consequences of various types of conflict behaviors. Chapter 14 summarizes the importance of achieving various goals over the life span, from childhood to later decades. The formation, development, and maintenance of interpersonal relationships are important throughout a person's life. Chapter 15 summarizes work on personality differences and their role in interpersonal relationships.

C H A P T E R   1 2

PRINCIPLES OF

INFLUENCE

COMPLIANCE AND COMPLIANCE-GAINING MESSAGES

Why People Agree to Do Things

Anchors and Contrast Effects

Reciprocity

Reciprocal Concessions or Guilt?

Commitment

Liking

Social Proof or Social Validation

Authority

Scarcity

WHAT ARE COMPLIANCE-GAINING MESSAGES?

Marwell and Schmitt's Typology

Falbo's Power Tactics

Bisanz and Rule's Persuasion Schema

WHEN PEOPLE USE TACTICS

Social Power

Politeness Theory and Image Concerns

Attribution Theory Revisited

COMPLIANCE-RESISTING TACTICS

CULTURE AND COMPLIANCE

CHAPTER SUMMARY

Frank, an art dealer, is trying to get someone to care for his client's small dog while the client is in the hospital. Frank first asks an elderly lady, who initially is friendly. After Frank politely asks, she says, "No, no, no, sorry, no!" and shuts the door on Frank and the dog. Frustrated, Frank turns to another, grumpy mean-spirited, neighbor, Mr. Udall.

Frank:	"YOU'RE taking him. Yes! Yes, you are. Get the hell out of the way! You're taking him."

Frank pushes the dog into Udall's apartment: "Listen, you're home working on books . . ."

Mr. Udall (softly interrupting):	"Wait, wait, wait . . ."
Frank (loudly):	"You want to say No to me? You want to say No to me? Huh? (softly, seething in anger). You want to say No to me?"
Mr. Udall (softly):	"I don't want to say nothing to you."
Frank:	"Because I've never felt this crazy as I do right now. I almost, almost want you to say No."

The two silently confront one another in the hall for a few seconds. The elevator opens.

Frank:	"Thanks for looking after him." And tosses the dog's dish to Mr. Udall.
Mr. Udall:	"Hey, where are you going?"
Frank (loudly):	"You don't want to mess with me today!"

Adapted from the movie *As Good As It Gets*

COMPLIANCE AND COMPLIANCE-GAINING MESSAGES

Every day you try to gain compliance from friends, family members, co-workers, and strangers. By *compliance* we mean that you try to change another person's behavior or opinion. You may try to convince your parents to buy you certain things you need, provide help with money, to permit or give approval for a trip with friends, to approve of a friend or date, and more. You may try to convince roommates to clean house more routinely, to do you a favor (pick up something from campus or the store), to have a party, to be quiet, etc. You may also use compliance messages with professors (to get a letter or recommendation, help, or extensions on projects), at work, or to ask for a date. The goal of gaining compliance is a very common, and important, communication activity.

The first half of the chapter focuses on the psychological reasons as to why people say "yes" or "no" when others make requests of them, ask them for favors, or try to gain assistance from them. This section overviews several psychological principles that expert practitioners use to influence others. Cialdini and Trost (1998; see also Cialdini, 1993, 1994) argued that we need only a few fundamental psychological principles to explain compliance. Work in the area of compliance principles focuses on how simple statements and requests are used to make people feel guilty, or comply because they want to fulfill an obligation, be liked by others, or do something that is popular or "correct."

The second part of this chapter deals with a larger category of **compliance-gaining messages,** in which people use a wide range of tactics in order to get others to go along with their requests. People whine, beg, force, lie, cry, argue, and/or advance reasons and evidence to try to gain compliance from others. Also, people resist compliance. For example, in the introductory story, an art dealer, Frank, first politely asked one neighbor to help, and she successfully resisted his request (she politely said "no," then emphatically said "no," and shut the door). The second neighbor, Mr. Udall, who already feared Frank, was nearly speechless when he was confronted with Frank's intense emotional outbursts. He was not able to resist very effectively. Frank used greater force in ordering Mr. Udall to watch the dog, and threatened to escalate conflict if Mr. Udall failed to comply.

Why People Agree to Do Things

People try to influence one another in a wide range of situations, from face-to-face sales encounters, commercials, televised auctions, requests to donate to charity to help refugees, children, hunger, and much more (Cialdini, 1993, 1994; Cody, Seiter, & Montagne-Miller, 1995; Wosinska, Cialdini, Reykowski, & Barrett, 1999). We ignore most of these, but we are influenced by many — we give to certain charities, help friends, buy certain clothes that complement other clothes we buy, and so forth. Some years ago Robert Cialdini (1993, 1994) asked the question, "Why do people agree to do things?" He concluded that many of these compliance encounters shared common elements and that there were not hundreds of reasons why people say "yes." Rather, he concluded that successful compliance is often due to the fact that the person seeking compliance was able to tap into one of seven psychological principles of compliance: anchoring and contrast effects, reciprocity, commitment, liking, social proof, authority, and scarcity.

Anchors and Contrast Effects

Every request we make of others involves a certain amount of costs; that is, requests vary in terms of size. An acquaintance may ask you, "This Saturday is the Beach Clean-Up Day — Can you come and help? Meet us at 8 AM and help clean trash off the beach." Or "The first weekend next month is the 10-K Run for Breast Cancer Research, and we are looking for people to help at the check-points on the route. Can you volunteer?" Only a few of the readers of this book would agree to spend a day cleaning a beach or working on a marathon. Requests like these may seem rather large to you — you have to give up a whole day to a good cause, and make up for your own activities that you usually do on a Saturday. Requests could be made that are smaller, for example, the acquaintances could have asked, "Can you show up for two hours to help clean the beach?" or "Can you sponsor a runner at 20 cents a kilometer?"

One interesting aspect of compliance requests is that the perceived size of the requests is relative. To many people, requests like "Can you show up for two hours to help clean the beach?" and "Can you sponsor a runner (for money)?" would appear to be relatively large requests. However, if these same people were first asked to donate a whole day to a cause, and we then asked them to donate two hours or a few dollars, they would tend to think of the second request as relatively smaller, given that they first thought about a larger request.

This phenomena is called **perceptual contrast** or simply **contrast** and involves first **anchoring** a person at one level of a request — usually a high level — and then making a noticeably smaller request. In contrast to the larger request, a noticeably smaller request may appear even smaller (than when no large request is made), appropriate, and fair. In a series of studies, Burger (1986) demonstrated the value of perceptual contrasts. Students were told that a club on campus was planning to sell cupcakes in order to make money, and he asked them: "What is a fair price for a cupcake sold for charity?" The students said, on average, 53 cents. To another group, he announced that they were thinking of charging 75 cents per cupcake, and they were then asked what they thought was a "fair price?" A third group was told that they were thinking of charging $1 a cupcake and were then asked what was a "fair price?" This group said 74 cents was a fair price. Perceptions of a "fair price" varied significantly as a function of the anchor, 53 cents when no anchor was provided, 67 cents when a 75-cent anchor was used, 74 cents when a $1 anchor was used. Burger (1986) conducted a series of studies selling objects for charity purposes, first announcing a relatively high price (a dollar per cupcake, $2 per candle) and then dropping the price (to 75 cents a cupcake or $1 a candle) or sweetening the deal (cupcake + two cookies for a dollar). He obtained more compliance (more sales) when starting with a higher price that was dropped compared to when a control group was simply offered $1 candles or a cupcake and two cookies for a dollar.

Contrast effects are important in compliance settings in several ways. First, a person's generosity can be manipulated by making it appear that others are contributing a certain amount of money to a cause. Second, sales clerks can affect the sales process by showing customers the most expensive items first, so that other items do not seem quite as expensive. Consider a simple situation: A secretary is quitting, and the staff votes to take up a collection to buy a gift. A sign-up sheet is made, and people are asked to give money. When Blake, Rosenbaum, and Duryea (1955) did a study on such a situation, one-half of the people who were asked to make a contribution gave 50 cents, and the other half gave a dollar. The average contribution was 75 cents. We can imagine that 75 cents was the amount that people believed to be typical of what the average person would give. However, Blake and colleagues also constructed several bogus lists of contributions. On one list, it appeared that people were giving an average of 25 cents each; on another list, it appeared that contributors were giving 75 cents each. What happened? When people thought that others were giving only 25 cents, they contributed only 32 cents on the average. When people thought that others were giving 75 cents each, they gave 63 cents on the average. People adapted to the standard of what they believed others were contributing.

This study is a good example of contrast effects and compliance because it demonstrates the two necessary conditions of the contrast effect. First, a standard is created — people thought that others were giving either 25 cents or 75 cents. Second, the amount that a person actually would give (75 cents) is viewed as large when compared (or contrasted) with the standard of what others are donating. People decline to give the large contribution, and they tend to give what others are contributing.

Although this study used the contrast effect to get people to give less money, the effect can be used (and often is used) as a method for increasing contributions, sales, and tips by anchoring people at the high or expensive levels (see Cialdini, 1993). Customers who are exposed to most expensive pool tables, suites, dresses, cars, homes, etc., often become anchored or accustomed to these items, and then the mid-ranged items seem to be more reasonably priced and fairer in value.

Reciprocity

Reciprocity is fundamentally important in interpersonal relationships. When we were children, adults attempted to instill in us a basic belief in sharing, cooperating, and "doing unto others as they do unto us." If a friend invited us for a sleepover, to camp in the backyard, to play, and so forth, our parents would tell us, "It's your turn to have them over next time." When a friend does us a favor, we feel obligated to do a favor in return. When friends invite us to their homes, we reciprocate in kind. If we fail to reciprocate, we often experience guilt, and we may be labeled a "moocher." We will lose friends.

The **reciprocity principle** can be worded as follows: One should be more willing to comply with a request from someone who has previously provided a favor or con-

The art of bargaining often requires the careful use of reciprocal concessions.

Dan Chidester/The Image Works

cession (Cialdini, 1994). The reciprocity principle is used to gain compliance from others in several ways. First, and most obviously, reciprocity is used to gain compliance through creating a feeling of obligation on the part of others by doing them favors or giving them objects or services. Religious group members sometimes go to airports and malls and give out "free" bookmarks, key chains, car stickers, and other objects. After having accepted these "free" gifts and spent a few moments in conversation, people are asked to make a donation. These group members are trying to trigger a reciprocity-based obligation.

Businesses also use the reciprocity rule. Amway, for example, has its sales representatives leave a collection of product samples for potential customers to try "without obligation to buy." However, there is some felt obligation to buy something: The sales representative left a wide array of nice products for the customer's pleasure, and the least the customer can do is buy something. Other companies offer samples of food items in the stores to activate the reciprocity principle.

Another way in which reciprocity is used in compliance has to do with the nature of **reciprocal concessions.** We feel obligated to comply with a request if the asker has made a concession to us. This compliance tactic is called **door-in-the-face** and is described as any compliance situation in which one person makes a large request, which is rejected, and follows this rejection with a noticeably smaller second request. For example, Cialdini and Ascani (1976) asked people to make a series of blood donations at a local blood bank over two years. When individuals said "no" to this large request, they were then asked "Can you give one pint of blood tomorrow, here on campus?" Significantly more people agreed to donate blood (and gave blood the next day) than those in the control group (who were only asked to donate blood the next day on campus). Cialdini and Ascani argued that the increased compliance was caused by a felt obligation to match concessions with the requester. That is, she asked us to donate several pints of blood over two years, and we said "no." When the requester concedes and drops the request to one pint at one point in time, we feel an obligation to concede from zero pints of blood to one pint.

We don't have to look far to see many examples of the door-in-the-face tactic. A political party may phone to ask if we would "buy" a table for eight at the governor's inaugural celebration for $10,000. When that is rejected, the phone solicitor de-escalates the request to, say, dinner tickets for two or a cash gift of $100. Obviously the solicitor is relying on the reciprocity principle (and perhaps feelings of guilt) because most people don't have a spare $10,000 or the time to go to the state capitol with seven friends for such an event. Virtually everyone says no to the first request, but the well-trained phone solicitor has a prepared backup list of requests ready so that we typically agree to some smaller request. Many alumni associations, environmental groups, and charity organizations conduct their fundraising in much the same way.

Reciprocal Concessions or Guilt?

Scholars have recently challenged the "felt obligation" explanation of reciprocity, claiming that a "felt obligation" to match concessions by others may not be a sufficient reason to agree to a request to give blood or money. An alternative explanation is that saying "no" makes people (or at least some people) feel guilty, especially when the request is a prosocial cause such as donating to blood banks, fighting hunger, helping refugees, and so forth. O'Keefe and Figge (1997, 1999) and Hale and Laliker (1999) argued that feelings of guilt experienced by saying "no" motivate people to comply to the second request. Because they felt guilty about not being able or willing to help with the larger request (giving several pints of blood over two years or spending the whole day cleaning a beach), they would help with the smaller request and reduce guilt feelings. Feeling guilty and being motivated to reduce feelings of guilt is a more important motivator than feeling obligated by reciprocal concessions.

Other scholars agree that a sense of indebtedness operates in all situations involving the norm of reciprocity. In a series of studies, Robert Bell and his colleagues (Abrahams & Bell, 1994; Bell, Abrahams, Clark, & Schlatter, 1996; Bell, Cholerton, Davison, Fraczek, & Lauter, 1996; Bell, Cholerton, Fraczek, Rohlfs, & Smith, 1994) studied the impact of three theories underlying the norm of reciprocity: indebtedness theory, perceptual contrast theory, and self-perception theory. **Indebtedness** theory (Greenberg, 1980; Greenberg & Westcott, 1983) is based on the idea that we come to feel indebted to another person when that individual has extended us a benefit. This sense of indebtedness leads to physiological arousal, and the potential psychological discomfort due to inequity motivates us to take action to restore equity. In this model, the size of a gift or offer of a concession (in the use of reciprocity) directly affects the size of the inequity and the need to repay or comply. Indebtedness theory's predictions and explanations for why we comply in order to restore equity have much support in the world of gaining donations from various organizations (Bell et al., 1996) and have been used in intercultural settings (Aikawa, 1988, 1990; also see Wosinska et al., 1999). After giving to some charitable organizations, you should expect to periodically receive free gifts (a brass-plated bookmarker from the L.A. Philharmonic or coupons for a free dessert at a nice downtown restaurant, for example) to keep a sense of indebtedness active.

Perceptual contrast theory is based on the anchoring and contrast principles discussed earlier. When individuals hear how large a first request is, they become anchored at that level or size of costs involving time and money. When they hear a second smaller request, the second request seems to be relatively small in contrast to the large first request.

Self-presentation theory claims that when asked to give a helping hand to others, we monitor the image or impression that others will have of us. If a solicitor is using the door-in-the-face tactic, we may feel bad about not helping out with the first large request (i.e., to donate blood over time). Hence, we are motivated to agree to the second request in order to avoid being judged negatively and to redeem ourselves in the eyes of the solicitor. Compliance in public often helps show the world that we are committed to a cause and engaged in the right behavior of reciprocating favors, compared to complying to requests in private (Whatley, Webster, Smith, & Rhodes, 1999). Based on these theories, it would appear that people comply with requests because they perceive themselves to be indebted, they perceive the size of the request or the cost of the involvement to be relatively small, and they want to promote a positive image of self.

Commitment

Many people wear pins, publicly announcing their commitment to a sorority, fraternity, church, political party, or social or environmental cause. Some people are only privately committed to causes — they send in money and buy calendars. Others wear pins, attend all the dances and mixers, and run for elected office. Later they attend the national conference and run for national office. People usually feel greater commitment to a cause if they are publicly committed to it.

The **commitment principle** simply means that the more committed a person is to a group, organization, or cause, the more likely the person is to comply with requests to aid or assist that group, organization, or cause. Cialdini (1994) puts it this way: After committing oneself to a position, one should be more willing to comply with requests for behaviors that are consistent with that position. Research on the commitment principle has focused on two procedures: the foot-in-the-door tactic and the lowball procedure.

THE FOOT-IN-THE-DOOR TACTIC. The **foot-in-the-door** tactic is so commonly used that examples are practically limitless. A person, for example, belongs to a church and attends services on a fairly consistent basis. The minister or priest approaches the person after services and asks him or her to help out next Sunday because one of the Sunday school teachers had to visit an ailing relative out of town. The person agrees and helps in the Sunday school. Afterward, the person is thanked and praised for doing a wonderful job. Some weeks later, the person is asked to help in Sunday school for a month and agrees. Agreement to a small initial request can blossom into an agreement to a large second (or third) request. The term *foot-in-the-door* is used because the solicitor makes a small request to crack the door open so as to get it open all the way eventually.

THE LOWBALL TACTIC. Cialdini, Cacioppo, Bassett, and Miller (1978) note that a common sales tactic, especially prevalent among new-car dealers, is *throwing a lowball* or *lowballing*. **Lowball** tactics have two ingredients. First, someone makes an offer or a request that is low or small, and you actively and freely agree to it. Second, after you are committed to the deal or to helping the solicitor, you find out that the deal was not as good as you first thought. In new-car sales situations, a dealer might agree with you on a price, and yet once you sit in the dealer's office, you find out that the price you agreed on earlier didn't include the special wheels and tinted glass you want; these will cost you extra. You were lowballed; this is a commitment-then-cost procedure. Many people are reluctant to retreat from an earlier agreement, so they don't walk out of the office and shop elsewhere.

The lowball procedure is used outside of sales situations, of course. In one simple experiment, Cialdini and colleagues (1978) called students to participate in an experiment (for which they'd get credit in their introductory psychology classes). Half of the people were simply asked, "Can you participate in a project on Wednesday or Friday morning at 7 am?" The other half of the students were lowballed — they were first asked to participate in a study on Wednesday or Friday, but were not told beforehand that the experiment required them to be present by 7 am. Only 31% of the students in the control group verbally agreed to show up at 7 am. However, 56% of the students verbally agreed to come to the study when the 7 am time was not revealed to them. However, only 24% of the students in the control group actually showed up at 7 am for the appointment, whereas 53% of the lowballed students showed up on time. Why? According to the researchers, people who are lowballed and who choose freely to agree with the initial request feel a greater amount of commitment and responsibility to their obligation.

Students tell of being lowballed frequently. One group of students, in Texas, told a story in which a sorority sister asked for volunteers for a baton-twirling contest on Saturday. A group of volunteers quickly signed up. Later they were told that they had to be in a town an hour away at 8 am on Saturday. They were lowballed, but they all went to the event because they felt committed and responsible. Another student related being asked to have lunch at the fraternity house with a transfer prospect from another university. Once there, he was asked to give a tour first of the house and then of the campus. He spent four hours with the transfer student and the student's family.

One of the explanations for why commitment works the way it does deals with **self-perception** theory, which argues that we make judgements about ourselves, what we like and don't like, from our behavior. When people give money to a charity, for example, suppose they ask themselves (or their friends ask) "Why did you give money to a person collecting for the Heart Fund?" If the answer is, "Well, I am generous and generous people give to worthwhile causes," or "I support the Heart Fund," then they are providing an explanation of a real commitment of a personal nature that will probably be linked to increases in compliance over time. However, if the perceived reasons for complying involved "I gave that person money to get rid of them," or "She(He) was cute," then the person probably does not perceive his or her sense of self as committed to the particular cause of fighting heart disease, or committed to an image of being generous. Some projects (e.g., Kraut, 1973) actually labeled people who donated to one charity as "generous" and "charitable," and found that they proved their generosity again later to a second person asking for donations for a separate charity. Recent research also indicates that certain people are more consistent in their public behaviors (called *high preference for consistency*) and these people often show a consistent foot-in-the-door effect (they usually increase compliance to a second request following a commitment to a smaller request) (see Guadagno, Asher, Demaine, & Cialdini, 2001).

Liking

We have already talked about the importance of being liked — ingratiation tactics like rendering favors, praising others, and conforming opinions to others are used to increase liking. We also like people who are physically attractive. The liking principle is simply this: One should be more willing to comply to requests from likable, good-looking people than from people who are unlikable and unattractive.

One classic study conducted by Chaiken (1979) quickly shows the power of beauty and liking. Chaiken had 110 students in a class act as solicitors and approach other students on campus, asking them to complete a questionnaire and to sign a petition demanding that the university "stop serving meat at breakfast and lunch at all dining commons." Did students sign the petition simply because the solicitor was good looking? Some did. When approached by an attractive person, more people signed the petition than when approached by a less attractive person. This was especially true for females: 53% of the females signed the petition when approached by an attractive male, 47% when approached by an attractive female. Only a few men agreed to sign the petition if approached by an attractive male (29%) or if approached by an attractive female (35%). When the solicitor was judged as less attractive, only 24 to 38% of the students signed it. Chaiken also found that women were more likely to sign the petition than were men, who may be more committed to a meat diet than women. There are many examples of people complying with requests made by others who are beautiful, socially desirable, and likable.

Social Proof or Social Validation

Sometimes we just don't know how to behave — what the appropriate action should be or what etiquette requires. Some of us don't really know whether the band playing on stage is average, good, great, or fabulous. Some of us don't know the appropriate dress to wear to a particular social function, and some of us don't know the latest fashion trends. When we do not know what to do or have no guidelines, prior experience, evidence, or research, we are uncertain as to how we should behave, and we can be influenced by what is called the **social proof principle:** We act the way others around us behave. Cialdini (1994) also uses the term *social validation:* One should be more willing to comply with a request for behavior if it is consistent with what similar others are thinking or doing. When in doubt, or uncertain about how to behave, we are likely to conform or obey norms as guidelines to our own behavior. Our proof of how to behave is based not on evidence, statistics, facts, logic, insight, individual preference, experience, or research, but on the people in our immediate surroundings.

Social proof can influence us both directly and indirectly. The direct, explicit way is when people tell us, "This is what is currently popular," "This is what everybody is buying this year," "Four out of five people aged eighteen to twenty-four are voting in favor of Proposition A," and so on. The claim is that what is popular is good. In one study, certain shoppers in major clothing stores were told that a product (pants, shorts, etc.) was popular. The claim of popularity influenced the women shoppers — those who heard the claim spent more money ($110.53 each, compared to $56.98 spent by women who did not receive the appeal; see Cody, Seiter, & Montagne-Miller [1995]).

But social proof can influence us in subtle, more indirect ways. We can be influenced by both the verbal and nonverbal reactions of people who sit and stand around us. The fact that others are laughing at a stand-up comic tells us that the comedian's routine has some merit, and we may even think that the comedian is funnier when we hear other people laughing even more. Similarly, when we listen to a band play at a local establishment and see that some people in the audience scream and idolize the band, we conclude that the band must be good.

Research by communication scholars confirms that social proof can be used to influence our behavior and attitudes. Here are two examples. First, most people say that they do not like "canned laughter," the laugh track we hear on TV situation comedies. However, chances are that we hate the laugh track only when we are aware of its presence. We can all be influenced by canned laughter when we are unaware of it, and some people believe that humorous material is funnier if they hear others laughing at it (Cupchik & Leventhal, 1974; Leventhal & Cupchik, 1975, 1976; Leventhal & Mace, 1970).

Social proof can also influence the extent to which we evaluate live performances. One down-to-earth and excellent example was a project completed by Hocking, Margreiter, and Hylton (1977). Hocking had thirty students infiltrate a local campus bar featuring live entertainment on Thursday nights. On certain evenings the students provided positive feedback to the band. They screamed and yelled enthusiastically. On certain other evenings, the students provided negative feedback — they sat quietly or acted bored. Members of the band had given permission for the study and played the same songs on the nights the experiment was being conducted.

While one group of students went to the bar to either give positive or negative feedback, another group of students worked on an assignment to observe the non-verbal behavior of couples in public places. The instructor of this course required the students to attend the bar on certain Thursday nights (some went on positive-feedback nights, others on negative-feedback nights). This second group of students made their observations at the bar, and when they turned in their code sheets the next day, they were asked several questions, including how long they stayed at the bar, whether the band was good, and whether they would like to see the band again. When other audience members yelled and screamed, providing the positive feedback, observers stayed longer (over two and a half hours), rated the band as better, and were also slightly more likely to see the band again.

Social proof is a common reason why we comply with requests. When we are uncertain of how to behave, we are likely to depend on how others behave, even if we are unaware of doing so. Not surprisingly, when we buy gifts — graduation, wedding, etc. — for someone else, we are susceptible to what the sales clerk tells us is popular (see Cody et al., 1995).

Authority

The **authority principle** is quite common and can be worded as follows: One should be more willing to follow the suggestions of someone who is a legitimate authority (Cialdini, 1994). We are taught to be obedient to people in positions of authority. Three types of authority derive from titles, clothes, and trappings. Titles are obviously important in seeking a position of authority over others. People labeled "doctor," "judge," "professor," "officer," or "commissioner" are more likely to gain compliance from others than people labeled "student," "worker," and so on. We are so strongly influenced by titles that pedestrians routinely follow the directions of any person in a uniform who holds a title, and nurses in a hospital comply quickly to requests made by "doctors," even ones who call in prescriptions and are never actually seen (Cialdini, 1993).

Clothing is one of the most easily fakable signs of authority. Well-dressed people are helped more quickly and more readily when they shop, obtain better service, are seated at more desirable tables in restaurants, and are helped more quickly in emergencies. We frequently comply or follow the well-dressed person — for example, if we see a well-dressed businessperson jaywalk, we might be more inclined to do the same.

The trappings of status include jewelry, cars, briefcases, expensive pens, and all other objects that can be used to mark status, prestige, or social class. We are less likely to honk at the drivers of Jaguars or BMWs than we are at the drivers of Fords, and we are more likely to stop and give assistance to a driver of a disabled luxury car than to a driver of an average car or a car of low status. We are also more likely to comply with the requests of drivers who possess high-status trappings.

Another way to tap into the authority principle is through the use of expertise. Some of us go to specialty shops that feature gourmet coffees, imported chocolates, imported shoes, designer clothes, and so on. In such settings, an expert tells us information about how the products are made, materials that were used, the history of the company or family that makes the Scottish knits, and so forth. We often buy products on the basis of information supplied by purported experts.

Scarcity

We love our freedom. We want to be able to go out and stay out as late as we want. We want to date whomever we please, without interference. We want to go to a store and buy an item we want without being told that the store ran out or that the store no longer stocks the item in the color or size or style we want. We want to chew gum without our teachers trying to restrict our freedom.

The **scarcity principle** is simply that opportunities to engage in some activity or to own some object seem more valuable when the opportunity is limited or restricted in some way. Cialdini (1994) puts it this way: One should try to secure those opportunities that are scarce or dwindling. Our daily behavior is shaped by the scarcity principle in three ways: in the desirability of scarce objects, planned scarcity, and restricted freedom. First of all, people are willing to spend more money on one-of-a-kind objects that they will own and no one else will own. Collectors spend considerable amounts of money to purchase such items as baseball cards, first-edition books, and coins or stamps printed with errors. People are also willing to spend more money and effort in order to participate in a unique, opportunity-of-a-life-time event, such as being in Amsterdam for the royal wedding, or being in a prime location for a solar eclipse. Second, given that scarce objects will fetch higher prices, marketers actually plan shortages of certain desirable products so shoppers will pay more. Many gift items advertised heavily at Christmas-time are deliberately held in short supply to keep prices high.

Another example related to these two aspects of scarcity occurs when an individual sells a used car by placing an ad in the newspaper. When you arrive at 12:30 to look over the car, the seller may tell you that someone else is coming to see it at 1:00. Sure enough, someone does come to look at the car and engages in a lot of talking with the seller. If you liked the car when you first saw it, you would probably find it even more desirable when there appears to be competition for it. So you buy the car after only a little bargaining. Note that this could have been a stratagem — the guy selling the car could have had his cousin show up and act like an interested buyer just to motivate you to make a quick decision to buy it. You may have been manipulated without ever realizing it.

The third application of the scarcity principle involves restricted freedom. We have very strong reactions when a freedom we have enjoyed for a long time is restricted. The term **psychological reactance** is used to describe a situation in which our freedoms are restricted and we rebel against the restrictions: We value the restricted behaviors more and we are willing to pay more money to engage in them and to criticize and defy authorities who impose the restrictions. Restricted behaviors like smoking cigarettes in public, buying guns, buying firecrackers, limiting or restricting lyrics on CDs, and the like, become more desirable after restrictions are imposed than before. The potential loss of freedom can also affect our feelings of being "in love." A study of dating students (Driscoll, Davies, & Lipetz, 1972) found that the frequency with which parents attempted to interfere with their children's romantic partners caused the students to become more "in love" over a year's time. The researchers dubbed this the Romeo and Juliet effect.

A song by Mickey Gilley claimed that people become "prettier at closing time." Although the song dealt with loneliness and alcohol, some sobering truth, in fact, underlies our tendency to rate scarce resources (those still available at midnight) as attractive. Why? Earlier in the evening, we have the freedom to meet and get to know many people at a bar, spa, club, or other establishment, and when many people are available, we may perceive the typical person as fairly average. However, as closing time approaches, our options become more limited, and as our freedom to meet someone diminishes, the available people look more attractive.

Pennebaker and colleagues (1979) went to three drinking establishments and asked people to rate others on beauty. Posing as a dating pair, two people approached others in the bars and asked them to participate in an experiment. All agreed to help. They were then asked, "On a scale from 1 to 10, where 1 indicates 'not attractive,' 5 indicates 'average,' and 10 indicates 'extremely attractive,' how would you rate the opposite-sex individuals here tonight?" Next, they were asked: "If you were a member of the opposite sex, how would you rate members of your own sex here tonight, using the same scale as before?" The participants were asked to make a global judgment about the people who were available. Pennebaker and colleagues asked people the judgments at 9:00 pm, 10:30 pm, and midnight. Considering that the bars in this location closed at 12:30, the scarcity effect should have been strong by midnight.

Figure 12.1 presents the results. Look first at the line indicating the evaluation of same-sex people at the bar. There is little change in this judgment over the course of the evening, and people rated members of their own sex as fairly average (between 4.5 and 5.5). However, people judged members of the opposite sex as average (about 5.0) at both 9:00 and 10:30, but significantly and substantially more attractive at midnight (about 6.0). A more complex and involved study by Gladue and Delaney (1990) also investigated attractiveness in bar settings. They too found that men and women rated opposite-sex bar patrons as better looking as the evening wore on. They found

376

Figure 12.1

▼

Perceived
Attractiveness of
Others in a Bar as
Closing Time
Approaches

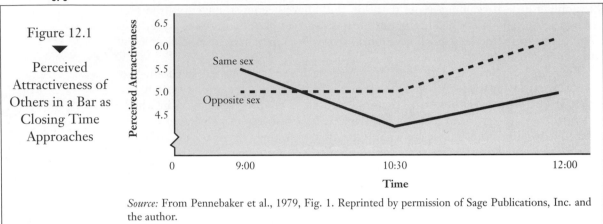

Source: From Pennebaker et al., 1979, Fig. 1. Reprinted by permission of Sage Publications, Inc. and the author.

that men even rated photographs of women to be even more attractive as midnight approached. The conclusion: Scarcity increases desirability.

WHAT ARE COMPLIANCE-GAINING MESSAGES?

If you were to watch the people around you, including those on television and in movies, you would readily see that people use hundreds of ways to gain influence over others — lying, yelling, shoving, forcing, hinting, manipulating feelings, and using reasons, facts, and evidence. Scholars have examined all of these ways of gaining compliance and separated them into certain *typologies* or ways of organizing them (e.g., Bisanz & Rule, 1990; Clark, 1979; Falbo, 1977; Marwell & Schmitt, 1967; Wheeless, Barraclough, & Stewart, 1983; Wiseman & Schenck-Hamlin, 1981). In the next three sections we will look at three of these typologies. Later in this chapter we will look at why people use the messages the way they do in achieving interpersonal goals.

Marwell and Schmitt's Typology

French and Raven (1959) originally presented five bases of social power: reward, coercive, referent, legitimate, and expert. Marwell and Schmitt (1967) later wrote specific messages that can be used in interpersonal settings based on French and Raven's work on social power. The Marwell and Schmitt compliance-gaining messages are listed in Table 12.1.

Table 12.1
MARWELL AND SCHMITT'S TYPOLOGY

---

1. Promise   (If you comply, I will reward you)
   "You offer to increase Dick's allowance if he increases his studying."

2. Threat   (If you do not comply, I will punish you)
   "You threaten to forbid Dick the use of the car if he does not increase his studying."

3. Expertise (Positive)   (If you comply, you will be rewarded because of "the nature of things")
   "You point out to Dick that if he gets good grades he will be able to get into a good college and get a good job."

4. Expertise (Negative)   (If you do not comply, you will be punished because of "the nature of things")
   "You point out to Dick that if he does not get good grades he will not be able to get into a good college or get a good job."

5. Liking   (Actor is friendly and helpful to get target in "good frame of mind" so that he will comply with request)
   "You try to be as friendly and pleasant as possible to get Dick in the 'right frame of mind' before asking him to study."

6. Pre-Giving   (Actor rewards target before requesting compliance)
   "You raise Dick's allowance and tell him you now expect him to study."

7. Aversive Stimulation   (Actor continuously punishes target making cessation contingent on compliance)
   "You forbid Dick the use of the car and tell him he will not be allowed to drive until he studies more."

8. Debt   (You owe me compliance because of past favors)
   "You point out that you have sacrificed and saved to pay for Dick's education and that he owes it to you to get good enough grades to get into a good college."

9. Moral Appeal   (You are immoral if you do not comply)
   "You tell Dick that it is morally wrong for anyone not to get as good grades as he can and that he should study more."

10. Self-Feeling (Positive)   (You will feel better about yourself if you comply)
    "You tell Dick he will feel proud if he gets himself to study more."

11. Self-Feeling (Negative)   (You will feel worse about yourself if you do not comply)
    "You tell Dick he will feel ashamed of himself if he gets bad grades."

12. Altercasting (Positive)   (A person with "good" qualities would comply)
    "You tell Dick that since he is a mature and intelligent boy he naturally will want to study more and get good grades."

13. Altercasting (Negative)   (Only a person with "bad" qualities would not comply)
    "You tell Dick that only someone very childish does not study as he should."

(Continued)

(Table continued from previous page)

14.	Altruism	(I need your compliance very badly, so do it for me) "You tell Dick that you really want very badly for him to get into a good college and that you wish he would study more as a personal favor to you."
15.	Esteem (Positive)	(People you value will think better of you if you comply) "You tell Dick that the whole family will be very proud of him if he gets good grades."
16.	Esteem (Negative)	(People you value will think worse of you if you do not comply) "You tell Dick that the whole family will be very disappointed in him if he fails to get good grades."

Source: From Marwell & Schmitt, 1967. Reprinted by permission of the American Sociological Society.

Reward power operates when a person B (the one to be influenced) perceives that person A (the compliance gainer) can provide rewards to person B if person B complies. Parents provide rewards to their children for earning good grades or for earning achievements, and parents provide rewards when children comply with specific requests. Similarly, students and workers can earn rewards by complying with requests of the instructors and bosses. Marwell and Schmitt concluded that tactics like Pre-Giving, Liking, and Promise represent compliance messages that were found to measure a sense of **rewarding activity.** For example, parents might offer their son rewards or positive feelings (liking) if the son increased studying, tapping into a sense of indebtedness using pre-giving and promising rewards.

French and Raven's notion of *coercive* power operates when person B perceives that failing to comply will result in **punishments** — being grounded by parents, losing benefits, being fired, and so forth. Coercive power is represented by two of the Marwell and Schmitt tactics (see Table 12.1): Threat and Aversive Stimulation, which dealt with punishing the son until such time as the son's grades improved. Often, people try to avoid the use of threats or aversive stimulation because their use has a negative impact on relationships, and harsh tactics like these are often reserved as a tactic of last resort, to be used after the failure to gain compliance through more polite requests. In our earlier example of Frank and Mr. Udall, Frank urgently needed someone to look after the dog, and he did not hesitate to use force and threats because there was no positive relationship at risk; in fact, the two individuals did not like one another.

French and Raven's notion of *referent* power operates when person B identifies with and perceives himself or herself to be similar to person A. In some research, *referent* is the same as *liking* as discussed earlier. Person B complies because he or she sees himself or herself to be just like person A, they have a bond or a "oneness," and/or person B wants to be liked by person A. Hence, if person B perceives that he or she is similar to and wants to be just like his or her idol (Britney Spears, etc.), person B will comply with requests to eat a particular cereal, practice, and generally follow the advice of the person with whom he or she seeks "oneness." Marwell and Schmitt believed that four of the messages in Table 12.1 reflect referent power: Debt, Altruism, Negative Esteem, and Negative Altercasting. If the son liked and identified with his father, he should want to comply and perform better on grades. An appeal to family, love, being a good son or daughter, and being a good reflection on the family are implicit in these tactics. Marwell and Schmitt called these tactics (Debt, Altruism, Negative Esteem, and Negative Altercasting) "activation of personal commitments."

Expert power operates when person B believes that person A has special knowledge in the particular area of the compliance request — what is fashionable, good stocks to buy, what car is safer, what insurance is a good buy. Experts usually have been trained or have studied a particular matter. Because we perceive them to be credible, we comply to the requests (advice, recommendations) of experts. An expertise group of tactics included both the Positive Expertise statement ("If you comply, you will be rewarded by the 'nature of things'") and Negative Expertise statement ("If you do not comply, you will be punished by the 'nature of things'"). The influence agent or compliance gainer is not providing the rewards or benefits (which would categorize these tactics as reward or coercive power) but is claiming to be more expert in knowing how the world operates.

French and Raven's notion of legitimate power is based on the perception that person A has a legitimate right to make a request to which person B is obligated to comply. A police officer, prison guard, security guard, manager, professor, or parent

Tim Wright/Peter Arnold

Expert power operates when person B believes that person A has special knowledge in the particular area of the compliance request. We comply with experts' requests because we perceive them as credible.

can make certain legitimate requests of others to be quiet, exit a building, or stop engaging in certain actions, and others are obligated to comply. Legitimate power is effective only to the extent to which both parties agree in their perceptions of what is and is not legitimate. Marwell and Schmitt believed that legitimate influence was captured in using tactics like Moral Appeals, Positive and Negative Self-Feelings, Positive and Negative Altercasting, and Positive and Negative Esteem. The underlying theme is that parents have a right to request that their college-bound son study hard and be motivated to get into a good college and that the son is obligated to try his best. Failing to put effort into the studying means that the son is failing in a moral obligation (see moral appeal tactic, Table 12.1), so emotional manipulations are employed to shape the son's behavior.

The Marwell and Schmitt set of tactics has been used in many studies about who uses various tactics. Some studies examine five types of messages (as reviewed here), and some studies more generally refer to "socially acceptable" tactics (rewarding, expertise, **activation of impersonal commitments**) and "socially unacceptable" tactics (punishing and **activation of personal commitments**) (Marwell & Schmitt, 1967, p. 362). Other studies rank order the tactics on a continuum from socially acceptable to socially unacceptable (Boster, 1995; Boster, Levine, & Kazoleas, 1993; Boster & Stiff, 1984; Hunter & Boster, 1987; Miller, Boster, Roloff, & Seibold, 1977; Seibold, Cantrill, & Meyers, 1994).

Falbo's Power Tactics

Falbo (1977) asked students to write essays on "How I get my way," and categorized the messages into sixteen forms. Most were similar to Marwell and Schmitt's, but with a few differences. For example, Falbo found that people also hinted, evaded, used deception, used reasoning, and manipulated others' thoughts (see Table 12.2). She had individuals compare and contrast the similarity between the messages, and she associated messages with several personalities and peer ratings. Figure 12.2 shows that the messages fall within two dimensions: direct versus indirect and rational versus nonrational.

Direct message tactics are Assertion, Persistence, and Simple Statement. Fait Accompli and Threat are also direct, but Threat tends toward the nonrational quadrant. Indirect tactics include Hinting, Thought Manipulation, and Emotion-Target (manipulating the emotions of the target of the compliance attempt). Deceit and Emotion-Agent (manipulating the emotions of the agent, or the compliance gainer) are both indirect and tend toward the nonrational quadrant. Rational tactics include Reason, Expertise, Compromise, Bargaining, and Persuasion. Only one tactic was clearly nonrational — Evasion, or doing what one wants by avoiding the person who would disapprove. These dimensions are similar to some of the relational disengagement tactics discussed in Chapter 11.

The lines (or vectors) in Figure 12.2 for peer ratings are labeled PR1 (a considerate person uses these), PR2 (a friendly person uses these), PR3 (an expressive person uses these), PR4 (an honest person uses these), PR5 (this person would be enjoyable

Table 12.2

SIXTEEN STRATEGIES EXAMINED IN FALBO (1977)

Strategy	Definition	Example
Assertion	Forcefully asserting one's way	I voice my wishes loudly.
Bargaining	Explicit statement about reciprocating favors and making other two-way exchanges	I tell her that I'll do something for her if she'll do something for me.
Compromise	Both agent and target give up part of their desired goals in order to obtain some of them	More often than not we come to some sort of compromise if there is a disagreement.
Deceit	Attempts to fool the target into agreeing by the use of flattery or lies	I get my way by doing a good amount of fast talking and sometimes by some white lies.
Emotion-agent	Agent alters own facial expression	I put on a sweet face. I try to look sincere.
Emotion-target	Agent attempts to alter emotions of target	I try to put him in a good mood.
Evasion	Doing what one wants by avoiding the person who would disapprove	I got to read novels at work as long as the boss never saw me doing it.
Expertise	Claiming to have superior knowledge or skill	I tell them I have a lot of experience with such matters.
Fait accompli	Openly doing what one wants without avoiding the target	I do what I want anyway.
Hinting	Not openly stating what one wants; indirect attempts at influencing others	I drop hints. I subtly bring up a point.
Persistence	Continuing in one's influence attempts or repeating one's point	I reiterate my point. I keep going despite all obstacles.
Persuasion	Simple statements about using persuasion, convincing, or coaxing	I get my way by convincing others that my way is best.
Reason	Any statement about using reason or rational argument to influence others	I argue logically. I tell all the reasons why my plan is best.
Simple statement	Without supporting evidence or threats, a matter-of-fact statement of one's desires	I simply tell him what I want.
Thought manipulation	Making the target think that the agent's way is the target's own idea	I usually try to get my way by making the other person feel that it is his idea.
Threat	Stating that negative consequences will occur if the agent's plan is not accepted	I'll tell him I will never speak to him again if he doesn't do what I want.

Source: Falbo, 1977, p. 540. Used with permission of the American Psychological Association.

382

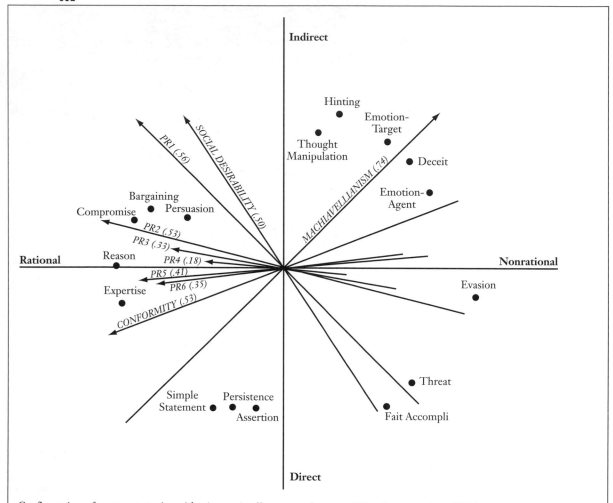

Configuration of power strategies with nine optimally regressed vectors. The six peer ratings (PRs) are coded as follows:

PR1 = How considerate is this person?
PR2 = How friendly is this person?
PR3 = How well does this person express himself (herself)?
PR4 = How honest do you think this person is?
PR5 = How much would you like to participate in another discussion group with this person?
PR6 = How much do you like this person?

Source: Falbo, 1977, p. 542. Used with permission of the American Psychological Association.

Figure 12.2

▼

Dimensions of Compliance-Gaining Tactics

in a group discussion), and PR6 (this person is likable). People rated by others as being considerate by their peers reported using Hinting, Persuasion, and Bargaining; they avoided using Threat and Fait Accompli. All of the other vectors for peer ratings clearly indicate that we like people and rate them as honest and enjoyable when they use Reason, Expertise, and Compromise.

The Machiavellian personality type (see Chapter 15) was associated with Deceit and with the manipulation of emotions. A highly conformist individual preferred using Reason and Expertise, as well as Simple Statement and Persistence. Also, a conformist often avoids evasion. A person who scores high on social desirability is one who wants to give the socially acceptable answers and wants acceptance by others. This type of individual reported using Hinting, Thought Manipulation, and Bargaining. They avoid using Fait Accompli and Threat. The value of the Falbo study is that it investigated essays students wrote about how they influence others, identified two dimensions, and linked tactics to peer ratings and to personality differences.

Bisanz and Rule's Persuasion Schema

Bisanz and Rule (1989, 1990; Rule & Bisanz, 1987; Rule, Bisanz, & Kohn, 1985) focused their interest on understanding the knowledge systems individuals have developed for understanding, recalling, and possibly planning actions. A schema, or a script, is a mental representation we have for an event, situation, or phenomenon (see Chapter 2). We have a mental idea or image of a trip to our grocery store, or an evening at a restaurant, or a first date. We have an idea of entering the situation, what happens first, and what happens in a sequence afterwards. We announce ourselves to the host or hostess, we are led to our table, and so forth.

Bisanz and Rule claim that we learn a **persuasion schema** similar in content and form to the mental images we have of shopping, eating out, and so forth. We learn to expect that certain tactics are used first, or early, in a sequence and that the act of gaining compliance or persuasion follows an ordered list in which we might try different arguments, even force, as we try to gain compliance from others. The tactics of this persuasion schema are presented in Table 12.3.

The Ask tactic is the first and most obvious way to request compliance from others. We may expect a simple request to be the first request, although many adults may skip over this request and move directly to other tactics if they know already that a person isn't going to comply to a simple request. That is, if you know the situation and the target sufficiently, you are likely to move directly to the tactic that was effective in the past or that you perceive to be successful today.

The second category of messages, Self-Oriented tactics, includes claims about how compliance would provide a benefit to the agent or compliance-gainer (usually), or the target. Note that when you use an Ask tactic, you often believe others already know why you are asking for compliance and no mention of a benefit is needed. Hence, to be effective, an Ask statement like "Please pass the salt" usually does not need a reason — the reason or benefit should be implicitly understood. If you ask for

Table 12.3

CONTENTS OF A PERSUASION SCHEMA

Name	Description
Ask	Simply ask the friend to try to get cooperation. No particular reason is given.
Self-Oriented	
Present Information (Invoke personal expertise)	The individual presents facts or evidence to try to get cooperation.
Mention Personal Benefits (Inform personal reason)	In asking, the individual mentions how he or she personally would benefit to try to get cooperation; or the individual mentions how the friend personally would benefit from cooperating.
Dyad-Oriented	
Mention Relationship (Invoke role relationship)[a]	In asking, the individual mentions an existing relationship to try to get cooperation. For example: "A good friend would do this."
Bargain/favor	The individual offers to do a favor in exchange for cooperation.
Social Principles	
Mention Similar Behavior of Others (Invoke norm)	In asking, the individual tells the friend about others who would do the same thing to try to get cooperation.
Mention Benefit to Others (Invoke altruism)	In asking, the individual mentions how the friend's cooperation will benefit others.
Make Moral Appeal (Invoke moral principle)	In asking, the individual makes an appeal to a moral value (e.g., it's the right thing to do) to try to get cooperation.
Negative Tactics	
Butter-up	The individual attempts to make the friend feel wonderful or important to try to get cooperation.
Bargain (object)	The individual offers a highly desired physical object (could be money) in exchange for cooperation.
Emotional Appeal	The individual cries, begs, throws a tantrum, sulks, or uses some other emotional display to try to get cooperation.
Criticize	The individual attacks the friend on a personal level, trying to make him or her feel personally inadequate for not cooperating.
Deceive	The individual misleads the friend to try to get cooperation.
Threaten	The individual informs the friend of negative things that will result from not cooperating.
Force	The individual physically assaults the friend or uses some other means of force to try to get cooperation.

[a]The names in parentheses after the labels provided for participants are the more technical labels used in the taxonomy developed by Rule, Bisanz, & Kohn, 1985.
Source: Adapted from Bisanz & Rule, 1990, pp. 53–54. Used with permission of the authors.

salt and no one passes it to you because the dinner guests are talking, you may move to "My monkfish is really bland tonight, so give me the salt," which might expedite the arrival of salt. The other guests understand that you want to season your fish and eat it before it gets cold, and they would expect the same consideration from others.

Similarly, a child may say, "I need contact cement and pipe cleaners." If the parents appear reluctant to drive to the store to buy these items, the child may move to a Self-Oriented message: "Mom, Dad, I really want to do a good job on my model of the battlefield of Waterloo, and I need contact cement and pipe cleaners to make it." Additional claims can bolster the message by including a benefit to the target (parents) such as "We can pick up dinner while we are out" (or return the videos to the video store, etc.). The idea is that if using an Ask tactic does not seem to work at first, move down the ordered list and provide a reason that benefits the self, or one that benefits the target (or both). (Bisanz and Rule originally proposed that Butter Up be placed in a Negative tactics category, but after several studies, they decided to move it to the Self-Oriented category because people use buttering up, or ingratiation, tactics to derive a personal benefit to self.)

Dyad-Oriented tactics, which include Mention Relationship and Bargain/Favor, rely on an activation of personal commitments — reciprocity and beliefs about how

Calvin relies on *Ask* tactics and then realizes he might need to use other tactics.

Finding that *Ask* tactics don't work, Calvin resorts to a *Negative* tactic.

friends or individuals in a relationship behave toward one another. The child, in our example, can be more explicit about how family members might all work together so that each person's needs are met; hence, dad gets pizza, mom gets ice cream, the child gets glue and pipe cleaners, and we all eat and make the model together. We want to draw attention to the Bargain/Favor tactic in the schema because it is one of the most common approaches used among college students' roommates and among friends (Cody, Canary, & Smith, 1994). One roommate buys blue books while on campus, the other drives the first to the car repair shop. Usually the reciprocity or exchange arrangement is implicit — until one of the roommates fails to uphold the exchange, in which case the issue of fairness is made explicit. If inequity increases, the relationship might decay, and more Negative tactics might be used.

Social Principles tactics focus on social norms or rules; the tactics listed here are similar to the altruism, moral appeals, and appeal to normative behaviors listed in the Marwell and Schmitt and Falbo analyses. Finally, the Negative tactics include many of the approaches that Falbo labeled as nonrational. These tactics may be effective in certain circumstances, but they also are likely to invoke certain costs. The child in our example can criticize parents on the basis of being unfair ("You help out Cecily [sister] when she needs help, but you don't help me"), being inadequate in comparison to other parents ("Rob's parents would take him"), or being inadequate in maintaining family obligations ("Can we call Aunt Sally? She'd take me").

The obvious problem with Negative tactics is that negative feelings may linger, and conflict can escalate. Also, once tactics like Evasion or Deceit are detected, negative relational consequences follow (O'Hair & Cody, 1994). On the other hand, if a relationship is already strained, and you don't expect any improvements, you may have license to use any number of Negative tactics. For example, in our starting story, Frank took the little dog directly to the "nice" neighbor and asked politely if she'd watch the dog. She politely and firmly said "no." Frustrated, Frank turned to the neighbor with whom he (a) already had established a negative relationship and (b) already told him that he "owed" his client and needed to "repay" his client for a previous transgression (Mr. Udall had put the dog in the garbage). Frank had little to lose by using a threatening message.

Bisanz and Rule found that as we mature from the third grade to adulthood we move from relying heavily on Ask and Negative tactics to using a wider range of tactics. Tactics such as Ask and Self-Oriented are rated highest in approval (just as they corresponded to being considerate in Falbo's analysis), and Negative tactics were rated lowest in approval. The Dyad-Oriented and Social Principles tactics were rated midlevel in approval.

The persuasion schema is of interest to us because it offers a different view of compliance-gaining tactics. The first approach (Marwell and Schmitt) took specific statements and grouped them on the basis of similar "likelihood of use ratings." The second approach (Falbo) assessed specific statements on the basis of overall similarity and identified the dimensions or main features that distinguish between the tactics. The persuasion schema perspective includes a rank ordering of tactics from Ask and Self-Oriented as top ranked and are expected as the first tactics to be used, whereas

Negative tactics are ranked at the bottom. This persuasion schema is a general model or image of how strategies develop in real time. We may think that this sequence will be implemented, but we often jump down the ordered list to a more effective tactic if we have more knowledge about the target, situation, or goal.

WHEN PEOPLE USE TACTICS

Much of the work in compliance-gaining messages can be phrased as two key hypotheses (Kellermann & Shea, 1996). First, the **resistance hypothesis** claims that people initiate compliance-gaining attempts with positive and less direct tactics, but when faced with resistance and possible goal failure, they replace these tactics with less polite and more direct ones. That is, people prefer to use tactics listed at the top of the persuasion schema just discussed, and when they are not successful, they move down the list to more direct, less polite, and more forceful tactics. Several research projects indicate that people resort to coercion and other negative tactics if the target failed to comply, especially if the agent is a male who is trying to influence another male (deTurck, 1985, 1987). A parallel view is offered by Sanders and Fitch (2001), who argue that much of our daily compliance-gaining activity involves two people engaging in a conversation marked by incremental changes and where a resolution is mutually agreed upon. In their work, Sanders and Fitch examined conversations between people of equal power, usually in long-term relationships, and found that both individuals contribute equally to an agreement. Two sisters who have to share a car for transportation, for example, often engage in conversations detailing who uses it when, gas money, keeping it clean, and so forth. When one wants to have the car for a special event on a weekend, she might engage in hinting or indirect tactics to see how resistant her sister would be, and both may agree to a compromise where one gets the car a particular weekend, washed and waxed, and the other gets the car during the first half of spring break.

Consider an example where a husband has reconsidered going to the opera on a Friday night with his wife, given that his favorite sports team made it to the playoffs for the first time in years. To find out just how resistant she would be to changing their plans, he may first hint to find out how strongly she feels about going out to the show. As a conversation unfolds, he may come to realize that she expects this to be a special evening out, she has purchased new clothes and shoes, and she expects a special dinner (about which she heavily hints). By hinting and conversing, the man knows that she has high expectations and has invested in the event — she will be resistant to changing her plans. Realizing the resistance, he could escalate and argue more directly with her, but there are emotional consequences to arguing. He could propose alternatives, such as moving their special date to another evening, Saturday, getting better seats, reserving a table at the best restaurant in town, etc., and during this conversation both the wife and husband make concessions and counterproposals. To gain compliance the man moves from hint to ask to bargain categories in the persuasion schema. A more manipulative man (see Chapter 15) might change the date of their special evening and make dinner reservations unilaterally (without telling his wife). He could then spring the new tickets and arrangements on her and lie ("I'm sorry, your favorite restaurant was booked on Friday so I made them for Saturday night."). In this latter example, the husband moved from hint to deceive. Obviously, if the wife voiced little resistance to changing the date to go to the opera, then the conversation on their weekend plans would be dramatically different than these two examples.

The second hypothesis is called the **urgency hypothesis:** When time is of the essence, people shift from their default of using positive and less direct compliance-gaining tactics to using more negative, direct, and explicit tactics (see Kellermann and Shea, 1996). Our example of Frank and Mr. Udall is an example of this — Frank asked a friendly neighbor politely. When this failed and he was in a hurry to find a dog-watcher, he jumped immediately to force and threats. However, the urgency hypothesis not only applies to the selection of compliance-gaining messages, it also applies to the selection of compliance-resistance messages. When involved with sexual encounters, women are more likely to escalate to face-threatening resistance tactics, and do so more quickly than males (Afifi & Lee, 2000). At first, people engage in token or indirect resistance strategies, followed by rejection messages targeted to protect the face threat of the target. Face-protecting strategies include "I'm not sure that we're ready for this," "Are you sure you want to do this?" "We can do other things, but not that," "I can't unless you're committed to me," or "I'd rather not do that." Stronger, more direct resistance tactics include face-threatening strategies: "I don't want to," "It's getting late," "No," "Stop it." Women were more likely than males to more quickly move to face-threatening strategies, especially when their partner was direct in asking for sex; women exhibit a greater urgency to resist.

How polite or aggressive communicators become in their compliance-gaining attempts is influenced by several factors, explained by the following: social power, politeness theory, attribution theory, and culture. Individual differences in the use of compliance-gaining messages will be discussed in Chapter 15.

Social Power

The amount of power a person has over another in a relationship dramatically influences the use of compliance-gaining messages, the credibility and effectiveness of messages, and success in influencing others. We first noted the importance of power in Chapter 6 where we discussed impression management tactics. The individuals most likely to use bullying and strong tactics are those with greater resources (income, property, etc.) who are less dependent on their dating/romantic partners (Howard, Blumstein, & Schwartz, 1986), and uses of such intimidation is also related to more frequent expressions of negative emotions. Howard et al. (1986) indicate that the more dependent individual in a dating couple is likely to use supplication or manipulation (hinting, seduction, altering emotions). A number of projects on compliance gaining have relied on earlier work on power (i.e., Bacharach & Lawler, 1981a,

1981b; Boster, Kazoleas, Levine, Rogan, & Kang, 1995; French & Raven, 1959; Levine & Boster, 2001; Wheeless et al., 1983).

Although there are different definitions of power, many of the definitions share commonalities. Thibaut and Kelly (1959, p. 110), writing on the general nature of power in groups, argued that one person, Albert, is perceived to have power over another, Barbara, to the extent that he has the ability to "affect the quality of outcomes obtained by" Barbara, where the "quality of outcomes" involves the relative amount of rewards versus punishments. Albert has relatively more power over Barbara to the extent that he controls more of her rewards and punishments, increasing or decreasing either. In a parallel view of power, "power-dependency" theory holds that person A's power over B is determined by B's dependence upon A (Bacharach & Lawler, 1981a, 1981b; see Levine & Boster, 2001). In some relationships one person is highly dependent on another for income and resources and has little power (see early portions of the movie *Nurse Betty*). Other relationships are highly interdependent, and one partner does not depend on the other for particular resources or rewards. For example, two sisters sharing a car who live together and are probably similar in looks and employment capabilities are probably in an equal-power highly interdependent relationship. A married couple that carpool to work together and have equal status jobs and income are similarly in an equal power, interdependent relationship.

Levine and Boster (2001) recently reviewed research on power and compliance and reported on a research project in which people engaged in a bargaining exercise in which car sellers and buyers had relatively high levels of power (because they had attractive counter-bids for the cars being sold) or relatively low power (they had only unattractive counter-bids on the cars). Levine and Boster's summary of research and results provides evidence that the relative amount of power a person has in a relationship can influence compliance-gaining behaviors and outcomes in three important ways. First, when a person has relatively more power than another person in the relationship, the more powerful partner is more likely to be successful in influencing others (see Levine & Boster, 2001). The less power a person has, relative to his or her

The less powerful person in a relationship controls fewer resources and may resort to threats and irrational arguments in attempts to control the other person.

Calvin and Hobbes, copyright Bill Watterson. Dist. by Universal Press Syndicate. Reprinted with permission. All rights reserved.

partner, the more they are disadvantaged. There are many reasons for this. Regardless of what compliance-gaining messages a person uses, we tend to comply with requests of those in a power position (whether they are higher in authority, status, beauty, etc.; see principles of compliance discussed previously in the "Why People Agree to Do Things" section). Also, it is likely that their position of power means that their compliance-gaining messages are more credible and effective. By definition a more powerful person can control both punishments and rewards and hence has the ability to punish (use threats or implied threats) the less powerful and to offer credible concessions during negotiations. On the other hand, a less powerful person, controlling few resources, would find it difficult to use threats as long as the relationship continued (see Chapter 11) or offer concessions regarding resources not already controlled by the more powerful partner.

Second, Levine and Boster note that power levels were related to the types of compliance-gaining messages, as well as to the credibility of messages. People relatively low in power attempted more compromises/negotiation strategies, while people relatively high in power used more direct requests and threats (though threats were not commonly employed). Further, proposed compromise/negotiation strategies proposed by low power partners were less effective than compromises/negotiation strategies by more powerful partners.

Third, people were more persistent and used a wider range of compliance-gaining messages when one partner had higher power than another, compared to when both had equal but low levels of power or when both had equal but high levels of power (Levine & Boster, 2001). In fact, when both partners had power and were interdependent, there was very little persistence and little diversity — they would merely make a direct request and propose a compromise/negotiation.

Generally speaking, people with relatively high levels of power are more successful, use more direct and sometimes even forceful tactics, while those low in power are less successful, have fewer credible tactics at their disposal, and use, according to Howard et al. (1986), more emotional appeals than high power partners.

Politeness Theory and Image Concerns

In earlier chapters, we noted that politeness theory claims that we are more likely to be polite when communicating with more powerful others (vs. those of less power), when communicating with strangers (vs. intimates), and when an offense or problem is more severe. Baxter (1984) found that people in high power positions used less politeness than those in low power positions (also see Craig, Tracy, & Spisak, 1986; Lim & Bowers, 1991; Tracy & Baratz, 1994; Wilson, 1992; Wilson & Kang, 1991).

Two new views on politeness theory indicate that tactics (Hints, Threats, Direct Requests, Suggestions, and Promises) vary in perceived politeness and that tactics within each category also vary in politeness — there are polite to impolite ways of phrasing Hints, Promises, Suggestions, and so forth (Kellermann & Shea, 1996). Kellermann and Shea found, for example, that Direct Requests were perceived as very efficient tactics, and that they are not rated as impolite (by Americans). Threats were rated as impolite, as expected, but they were not rated as very efficient — a finding that parallels the use of threats and coercive influence in organizational settings; managers believe that Threats are used as the tactic of last resort and are not effective in changing behavior. Promises were rated moderately polite and were rated equally efficient to threats. Hints were rated as inefficient, as expected, but were not rated as very polite — at least some forms of hinting can be a threat to the hearer's face. The implications of this study include that if you want to be efficient and polite (in America), simply use a direct request!

Wilson, Aleman, and Leatham (1998), Cai and Wilson (2000), and Wilson and Kunkel (2000) argue that goals strongly influence politeness constraints. For example, when giving advice to others, people anticipated threats both to the face of their friend and their own positive face. People displayed strong concern about maintaining both parties' positive face when giving advice and were more likely to provide reasons to justify their requests when giving advice than when pursuing other goals. When asking for favors (e.g., getting a ride to the airport), people displayed strong concern for not imposing too much on their friend's autonomy and for protecting both parties' positive face. Hence, people expressed greater approval of their friend and rated themselves as less likely to persist if their friend resisted when asking favors than when pursuing other goals. When enforcing unfulfilled obligations (e.g., a friend failed to exchange class notes), however, people displayed more concern about the primary goal of seeking compliance and were less concerned about face concerns — except wanting to maintain their own autonomy. In this context, people expressed less approval and exerted greater pressure for their friend to comply; they did not provide numerous reasons why their friend should fulfill the obligation, but they indicated a likelihood of being persistent.

Table 12.4 summarizes how politeness theory has been extended by Wilson and colleagues (Cai & Wilson, 2000; Wilson & Kunkel, 2000). Four perceptions underlie the definition of a goal involved in "asking a favor": A speaker claims to be in need of assistance, there is an assumption that the target is both willing and able to provide assistance, the target is not strictly obligated to comply, and the target would not offer, or know to offer, assistance unless he or she is asked. Given these parameters, asking for a favor is a threat to the target's negative face since by definition the request is an imposition to the target, who is less likely to benefit from helping the agent. Asking for a favor also poses a threat to the agent's own face, because he or she is communicating the fact that he or she cannot achieve a particular goal without another person's assistance; there is also a threat to the speaker's negative face since he or she could be indebted to the person fulfilling the request for assistance.

On the other hand, enforcing an obligation usually involves strong feelings of rights on the part of the agent to force a person to fulfill an obligation to which they should have already complied (pay the phone bill on time, etc.). There is usually less concern about imposing on the target's negative face (compared to asking for a favor) because the agent has a right to make the request. There is less concern about incurring a debt because the target is already obligated and no future compensation or compromises are needed. Because they are in the right in enforcing others to fulfill

Table 12.4

IMPORTANCE OF FACE CONCERNS FOR COMPLIANCE-GAINING GOALS: ASKING FOR FAVORS AND ENFORCING OBLIGATIONS, AND GIVING ADVICE AND ASKING FAVORS

	Influence Goals
Goals/Concerns	Asking for a Favor vs. Enforcing an Obligation
How important is it to (or likely you'd)	
Gain compliance?	More important when enforcing an obligation
Protect target's negative face?	More important when asking for a favor
Protect target's positive face?	More important when asking for a favor
Threaten target's positive face?	More important when enforcing an obligation
Protect own negative face?	More important when asking for a favor*
Protect own positive face?	More important when asking for a favor
Perform a face-threatening act?	More likely when enforcing an obligation
Persist in influencing other?	More persistence when enforcing an obligation
Pressure target to comply?	More likely when enforcing an obligation
Provide more reasons?	More reasons when asking for a favor**
Approve of target?	More important when asking for a favor
	Influence Goals
Goals/Concerns	Giving Advice vs. Asking for a Favor
How important is it to (or likely you'd)	
Protect target's negative face?	More important when asking for a favor
Protect target's positive face?	More important when giving advice
Protect own negative face	More important when asking for a favor
Protect own positive face (lazy)?	More important when asking for a favor
Protect own positive face (nosy)?	More important when giving advice
Offer other-focused reasons?	More other-focused reasons when giving advice
Offer self-focused reasons?	More self-focused reasons when asking for a favor

Top panel is adapted from Cai & Wilson (2000); bottom panel is adapted from Wilson & Kunkel (2000).

*Ratings for protecting own negative face as a more important concern when asking for favors was true for Japanese participants, but not Americans.

**There were no significant differences for the number of reasons given when asking for favors and enforcing an obligation.

their obligations and the focus is on why the target has failed, so far, to fulfill obligations, there is little need to worry about protecting one's face. They would also be more likely to confront or have a direct discussion with a person who had failed in an obligation (vs. asking a favor) — this is called *performing a face-threatening act*. Overall, then, there is a greater need to protect the positive and negative face concerns for both agent and target when the agent asks for a favor, a greater focus on seeking approval from the target, and more compelling reasons to convince a person to perform a favor, compared to fulfilling an obligation. There is a greater need to gain compliance, to be persistent, apply pressure, threaten the target's positive face, and perform a face-threatening act when enforcing an obligation (compared to asking for a favor).

Wilson and Kunkel (2000) compared and contrasted the goals of giving advice and asking for a favor. When giving advice, one runs the risk of threatening the positive face of the target, because advice-giving assumes that the agent perceives that the target is not engaged in an effective course of action and lacks the foresight, ability, or competence to know what to do and how to do it. Giving advice also is a threat to the agent's positive face, since an advice-giver runs the risk of being perceived as a nosy individual. Thus, advice-givers should consider protecting the image of the target and self. Also, when trying to get others to take advice, one focuses on reasons that benefit the target (the other-focused reasons listed in Table 12.4); when focusing on asking for a favor, the agent usually relies on reasons that justify why he or she needs assistance (the self-focused reasons in Table 12.4). Further, when asking for a favor from others, the agent is motivated to protect his or her own image as not being lazy or incompetent at performing his or her own work in achieving goals, and has to ensure that he or she is not making an imposition on the target (while in advice-giving the target is free to dismiss the advice and take no action at all).

In sum, communicators often rely on the assumption of politeness theory when engaging in compliance-gaining activity. Over the years there has been impressive support for the Brown and Levinson work on politeness, but the model is not complete unless one adds a wider, more exhaustive number of image or interactional constraints important for different goals.

Attribution Theory Revisited

Attribution theory, discussed in Chapter 2 and other chapters, is also relevant to the area of compliance-gaining messages. Earlier chapters referenced how women constructed messages rejecting offers to go on dates by claiming causes that were uncontrollable, unstable, and impersonal (e.g., she had to study for finals) in order to avoid hurting a person's feelings and to better cope with an uncomfortable situation. Similarly, attributions about the causes of relational problems had an impact on de-escalating or terminating relationships, accepting apologies, and using relational dissolution tactics. Sillars (1980; Chapter 13) found that attributions of the causes for relational conflict play a role in how roommates cope with conflict.

One additional example of the importance of attribution theory should be added here. Wilson, Cruz, Marshall, and Rao (1993) investigated how individuals try to convince someone who is resistant to the compliance request. Wilson and colleagues convinced students to be confederates and act as if they signed up to participate in an experiment for extra credit. They were to be called by other students ("helpers") who were led to believe that they were helping the experimenter remind participants to show up for the experiment on time. The confederates, however, rehearsed reasons for not participating, saying things like "My bad knee is really acting up. I'm in too much pain right now to make it to the experiment" or "I won't be able to make it. My boss scheduled me to work during that time." The reasons for failing to fulfill an obligation vary along several of the fundamental attribution dimensions (stable vs. unstable, internal vs. external, and controllable vs. uncontrollable).

Wilson and his colleagues reasoned that when the helpers called to remind the confederates of their obligation, they used compliance-gaining tactics to convince the confederates to fulfill their obligation. Further, different types of causes should impact on the helper's use of tactics. When confederates used causes for failing to fulfill the obligation that were unstable, internal, and controllable, helpers persisted longer, denied the validity of obstacles more (obstacles being the reasons why the confederate couldn't attend the experimental session), used guilt and altruism appeals more frequently, and perceived the confederate as more sincere (compared to when stable, external, and uncontrollable reasons were given). Thus, for example, trying to escape from an obligation by using the excuse of celebrating one's twenty-first birthday or going to happy hour with friends prompts others to be persistent, use guilt, and counter the validity of the reasons. Less persistence and fewer emotional attempts were used on the person who used external, stable, and uncontrollable reasons ("I won't be able to make it now because I have to work" or "I had to find a second job because I lost my financial aid").

COMPLIANCE-RESISTING TACTICS

We often resist compliance, and some people are naturally very good at avoiding saying "yes," whereas others agree to too many requests. Oddly, only a handful of studies have systematically examined how people refuse date offers (Folkes, 1982), refuse to fulfill an obligation (Wilson et al., 1993), resist teachers (Lee, Levine, & Cambra, 1997), resist pressure to smoke (Reardon, Sussman, & Flay, 1989), resist sex (Afifi & Lee, 2000), or refuse general compliance-gaining requests (McLaughlin, Cody, & Robey, 1980; McQuillen, 1986; White, Pearson, & Flint, 1989).

McLaughlin et al. (1980) argue that people resist complying to others' requests by using one or more of four strategic approaches: nonnegotiation, negotiation, identity management, and justification resistance. A **nonnegotiation strategy** involves tactics whereby the individual flatly and undeniably refuses to comply (as the neighbor did when Frank was trying to find someone to take care of the dog). **Negotiation strategies** involve compromises so that both individuals accommodate each other. **Identity management strategies** are geared to make the requestor feel bad, guilty, or negative for having asked for compliance. **Justification resistance strategies** involve giving presumably good and convincing reasons for not complying with the request. McLaughlin et al. found that certain resistance strategies pose risks in relational maintenance; hence, harsh strategies like nonnegotiation are not used among intimates (same age group).

Hullett and Tamborini (2001) noted that **compliance resistance** messages vary in intensity (negative valence) and the intensity with which people resist compliance has a significant impact on violation of expectations, a negative impact on evaluation of the interaction, and a negative impact on intention to pursue (to be persistent). In this study the authors had people imagine that their fiancée had asked them to move to a dream job (for the fiancée to another location 1,000 miles away). They found that the following resistance tactics reflect the least intensity, to the most intensity, in rejecting the request:

> *Negotiation:* "Why do you think we should move rather than stay? How about we sit down and discuss the pluses and minuses of staying versus moving? Maybe we could find some sort of compromise."
>
> *Justification:* "I'm not sure that's such a good idea. I think we'd be better off if we stayed here closer to home. Besides, you'll probably wind up liking the jobs in this area better. And I'll probably do better job-wise here."
>
> *Identity Management:* "I'm really shocked. I can't believe you'd ask me to move away from here. I would never ask you to make such a move."
>
> *Nonnegotiation:* "Absolutely not. I refuse to move away from here, and that's that."

Hullett and Tamborini (2001) found that strongly voiced resistance strategies like nonnegotiation prompted people to feel their expectations were violated ("I am surprised at how strongly he resisted — he won't even talk about it"), to rate the encounter as unpleasant, and to decide not to pursue further compliance attempts.

In a fascinating study on family influence patterns, White et al. (1989) found that adolescents were more likely to use justification resistance strategies on their fathers and use more identity management strategies on their mothers. This may be due to gender stereotyping. Fathers may emphasize reasons, explanations, and facts, and children may know that justification resistance strategies may be more effective on fathers than other tactics. Traditionally women nurture children, but adolescents are involved with seeking their own identities, hoping for autonomy and independence. Hence, to separate themselves from their nurturer, they use what is normally a negative tactic ("I can't believe you'd ask me that!"). Adolescent boys relied on more nonnegotiation and negotiation strategies, which are less emotional and characteristic of less maturity (White et al., 1989). Adolescent girls, however, relied on identity management, especially when the target was their mothers. Because girls mature faster than boys, girls were more likely (and at an earlier age than boys) to try to establish parameters about what can and cannot be asked through emotional resistance tactics.

Finally, White and colleagues found that a good deal of reciprocity occurs in parental compliance-gaining with adolescent use of compliance resistance. When mothers or fathers used blunt, harsh tactics such as personal rejection (involving acting cold and withholding affection until the person gives in) or when fathers used nonnegotiation (being persistent until the other person gives in, arguing until the other person gives in), adolescents countered by using nonnegotiation compliance-resisting strategies.

Compliance resistance includes reason-giving (justification), flat denials of non-negotiating, manipulating the identity of the agent, and negotiating a solution. There is some evidence that we avoid negative strategies on close intimates, and we probably use tactics geared to be effective on particular individuals (giving reasons to fathers, for example). Further, many compliance-gaining strategies foster a reciprocal or matched response, with nonnegotiation and personal rejection strategies prompting nonnegotiation resistance strategies. However, adolescents clearly have more than one goal in mind when they use resistance strategies — resist compliance and build independence and autonomy. The study by White and colleagues implies that boys focus on resisting compliance and girls emphasize both goals.

CULTURE AND COMPLIANCE

Several studies have proposed and tested cultural differences in compliance-gaining, and most of these have focused on comparing Americans with collectivist cultures along the Pacific Rim. Burgoon, Dillard, Doran, and Miller (1982), Ting-Toomey (1985), and Hirokawa and Mirahara (1986) compared the behaviors of Japanese and American managers. Kim and Wilson (1994) compared Koreans and Americans, and other recent projects assessed compliance-gaining in classrooms (Lu, 1997) and compliance-resisting in the multicultural classroom (Lee et al., 1997). Burgoon and colleagues found that Japanese people used a wider range of tactics than did Americans and were substantially more likely to use positive-oriented tactics like Promise, Positive Expertise, and Positive Esteem. Ting-Toomey (1985) similarly argued that Japanese people try to avoid the appearance of conflict, and Americans do not. One of the fundamental differences between cultures is that Americans readily rely on and expect a confrontation of ideas, debating ideas, reasons, and arguments, whereas members of the Japanese culture value covert communication codes and strategies that are indirect and subtle (Chapter 3). In the Cai and Wilson (2000) study mentioned earlier, individuals in the United States were more intent on gaining another person's compliance, were more likely to be persistent, and communicated more reasons than did

Japanese individuals. Japanese individuals were more concerned with protecting the positive face concerns of the target of compliance than were Americans.

Hirokawa and Mirahara (1986) found that American managers relied on reward and punishment tactics, whereas Japanese managers relied on tactics based on altruism. Specifically, Americans relied heavily on Direct Request (or Ask in the persuasion schema), followed by Promise, Ingratiation, Disguised Request, and Explanation. Japanese managers relied on Altruism, Duty, Promise, Explanation, Favor, Direct Request, and several tactics designed to build positive feelings (positive esteem, positive moral appeal, and allurement). Many of these differences deal with the emphasis on collectivism in Japan and individualism in America. Americans prosper as individuals and use tactics that promote the individual and give rewards to the individual (Promises and Ingratiation). Japanese managers use more tactics that deal with helping the company and workers: Altruism ("For the sake of the company, please share your ideas and suggestions with us") and Duty ("Remember that it is your duty to suggest how we can improve the overall performance of the company").

In a theoretically rich and detailed analysis, Kim and Wilson (1994) compared how and why Koreans and Americans use requests. Both native-speaking Koreans and Americans rated the likelihood of using tactics and rated the importance of five conversational constraints:

1. Clarity (the importance of making one's intention clear and explicit when making a request verbally)
2. Minimizing imposition (making sure that one's verbal message avoids imposing on the hearer's autonomy or interfering with the hearer's freedom of action)
3. Consideration for the other's feelings
4. Risking disapproval for the self (the desire to avoid negative evaluation by the conversational partner)
5. Effectiveness in achieving one's goal

Kim and Wilson found that Americans rated all tactics as "clearer" than did Koreans and identified more tactics that would likely be used. Koreans rated most tactics as imposing more on the hearer and as showing less consideration for the hearer's feelings than did Americans. The authors concluded that Koreans are more responsive to and concerned with the relational aspects and consequences of making requests than are Americans. Further, Americans rated Direct Request as the most effective tactic, and Americans saw a high correlation between clarity and effectiveness. Koreans rated Direct Request as the least effective tactic and saw a high correlation between effectiveness with minimizing imposition, avoiding hurting the hearer's feelings, and not devaluing the hearer — constraints Americans saw as unrelated to effectiveness. In sum, collectivists (Koreans, Japanese) tend to place more emphasis on the feelings of the interactants and working toward collective goals, whereas Americans tend to emphasize clarity and accomplishing the instrumental goal, with much less emphasis placed on relational secondary goals.

The collectivist and individualistic orientations are also observed among Chinese and American professors (Lu, 1997). American professors prefer reward tactics and other pro-social tactics and are more direct in making their intentions clear ("For those of you motivated enough to read Chapter 15, I will have extra credit items for the test"). Chinese professors use more tactics and a wider range of tactics when trying to influence others. They tend to emphasize their status or position and use three common themes of controlling the classroom, including the individual's "authority" position, his or her interest in teaching "morality," and "modeling." Students who are from collectivist cultures also use fewer compliance-resisting tactics and are less likely to refuse requests made by their teachers or professors (Lee et al., 1997).

Culture has a profound impact on how people resist compliance, as well as on gaining it. For example, Bresnahan, Ohashi, Liu, Nebashi, and Liao (1999) found that Chinese in Singapore reacted different to favors made by friends than Chinese in Taiwan. Singapore Chinese indicated that they would comply with a friends' request, while Taiwan Chinese indicated that they would refuse a moderate to large request made by a friend. However, the Taiwan Chinese indicated that they would find an indirect way of refusing to comply, opting to express their refusal in "several strategies deep so that the illocutionary force of their refusal would be distanced and softened" (Bresnahan et al., 1999, p. 355). Chinese who rated "independent self-construal" as high were more likely to directly refuse to comply with a friend's request than those who did not rate "independence" high. Also, men were more compliant than women. This study adds to a list of studies demonstrating a felt obligation to comply within a collectivist culture, and to be indirect when refusing a friend's request.

CHAPTER SUMMARY

This chapter focused on how and why people try to gain compliance from others in order to achieve instrumental goals. The first part of the chapter focused on the psychological principles underlying why people agree to requests, including anchoring, reciprocity, liking, commitment, scarcity, authority, and social proof. The second half of the chapter focused on compliance-gaining and compliance-resistance messages. We discussed three common typologies of messages and discussed the resistance hypothesis and urgency hypothesis. The selection of compliance-gaining messages depends on a number of factors, including the relative amount of power each person has in the relationship, politeness, and a number of image concerns, attributions, and culture. Compliance-resistance strategies, like their compliance-gaining counterparts, vary from relatively polite to face threatening and highly negative; the latter are used when there is some urgency and are used to resist compliance aggressively, operating to reduce the likelihood that the agent will use more compliance-gaining attempts.

KEY TERMS

▼

activation of impersonal
   commitments, p. 380
activation of personal
   commitments, p. 380
anchoring, p. 365
authority principle, p. 373
commitment principle, p. 370
   foot-in-the-door, p. 370
   lowball, p. 370
compliance-gaining messages, p. 364
compliance resistance, p. 395
   identity management strategy, p. 395
   justification resistance strategy, p. 395
   negotiation strategy, p. 395
   nonnegotiation strategy, p. 394

contrast, p. 365
indebtedness, p. 369
perceptual contrast, p. 365
persuasion schema, p. 383
psychological reactance, p. 375
punishment, p. 378
reciprocity principle, p. 366
   door-in-the-face, p. 368
   reciprocal concessions, p. 368
resistance hypothesis, p. 387
rewarding activity, p. 378
scarcity principle, p. 374
self-perception, p. 371
social proof principle, p. 372
urgency hypothesis, p. 388

EXERCISES FOR FURTHER DISCUSSION

▼

1. Movies often deal with power and influencing others. Some movies over the years that have done this include *Tin Men, Wall Street, Glengarry Glen Ross, The Godfather, The Untouchables.* Discuss the role of powerful people in these films, and identify the tactics used to win over individuals and gain compliance.

2. Access cable TV and sample shows from the 1950s (e.g., "Leave it to Beaver") through the 1990s (e.g., "Full House," "Family Matters"). Compare and contrast how families communicated via compliance requests and compliance resistance over the years. Were family members more polite in earlier decades?

3. This chapter suggests that people typically begin their compliance-gaining attempts with polite strategies and, if unsuccessful, move to more direct and impolite forms of communication. Can you think of situations in which being polite does not help you achieve your instrumental goals, or is being polite always a good policy?

4. Review the discussion of reciprocity, thinking about whether or not you were trained to reciprocate by people in authority.
   a. Do you agree that reciprocity is an important social norm and that people who violate it will eventually become friendless?

b. Have you ever terminated or de-escalated a friendship with someone who failed to live up to your expectations of reciprocity?

c. Have you ever been in a relationship in which you think you did not live up to someone else's expectations of reciprocity?

5. Review the section on lowballing.

a. Have you ever been in a situation where you think you were lowballed? If yes, how did you handle the situation?

b. If this type of situation occurred again, how would you handle it, based on the information presented in this chapter?

6. Watch a home shopping program or go to a store where the salespeople work on commission and sell aggressively. After watching the show or browsing in the store, write a few paragraphs in which you try to identify the compliance principles used by the salespeople.

a. What compliance principles were used most frequently?

b. Did you find any compliance principles that could be added to those listed in this chapter?

c. Which compliance principles were the most effective, and why?

7. List the compliance principles that you think you use in your relationships.

a. Which principle do you use most often with family members?

b. Which principle do you use most often with friends?

c. Which principle do you use most often in romantic relationships?

d. If you use different principles in different relationships, why do you do so?

e. Which compliance principles are most effective for you?

8. Which compliance principles would you use to pursue each of the following goals? Discuss your answers with other class members, justifying the tactics you chose.

a. To convince a professor to write a recommendation for you

b. To convince a friend to take you to the airport

c. To convince a stranger to buy raffle tickets from your school or church group

d. To sell a used car to a stranger

e. To convince someone in your family to loan you some money

f. To convince an acquaintance to loan you notes for a class you missed

g. To borrow some CDs or tapes from your roommate for a trip you are going on

h. To convince your partner to go to a party that you want to go to rather than one that he or she wants to go to

i. To convince your neighbor to start recycling

9. Write a short paragraph in which you describe how the men you know shop and what sorts of sales tactics seem to be most effective in getting them to buy. Now write the same type of paragraph on how the women you know shop.

a. Who shops more frequently, the men or the women?

b. Who spends more money when they shop?

   c. Do you think men and women shop for the same reasons? What are their reasons?

   d. What sorts of sales tactics are most effective for the men?

   e. What sorts of sales tactics are most effective for the women?

   f. What sorts of sales tactics would be most effective for a couple shopping together?

10. Most people feel that it is ethically wrong to manipulate other people. We feel that we have a right to know when we are being influenced and a right to defend ourselves against influence.

   a. Do any tactics described in this chapter violate this ethical principle?

   b. Are there any tactics that you would not use because they appear to be unethical?

   c. Can you think of some guidelines that you would use in deciding when and how to use the tactics discussed in this chapter?

SUGGESTED READING

▼

GENERAL COMPLIANCE PRINCIPLES

Cialdini, R. B. (1993). *Influence: Science and practice* (3rd ed.). New York: Harper-Collins. This popular book first appeared in the early 1980s and is already in its third edition. Cialdini provides a plethora of examples on the use and misuse of the principles of compliance.

LOWBALLING

Cialdini, R. B., Cacioppo, J. T., Bassett, R., & Miller, J. A. (1978). Lowball procedure for producing compliance: Commitment then cost. *Journal of Personality and Social Psychology, 36,* 463–476. This study was the first study demonstrating the importance of the lowball procedure in gaining compliance from others. Prior to this publication, the term *lowball* was used only in reference to sales tactics. Cialdini and others demonstrated that the principle of lowballing helps to gain compliance in non-sales encounters as well.

FOOT-IN-THE-DOOR

Dillard, J. P., Hunter, J. E., & Burgoon, M. J. (1984). Sequential-request persuasive strategies: Meta-analysis of foot-in-the-door and door-in-the-face. *Human Communication Research, 10,* 461–488.

SCARCITY

Brehm, S. S., & Brehm, J. W. (1981). *Psychological reactance: A theory of freedom and control*. Orlando, FL: Academic. The Brehm and Brehm research team spent two decades conducting research on psychological reactance. Chapters detail male and female differences in psychological reactance and detail the importance of this compliance principle in legal, interpersonal, and consumer settings.

Gladue, B. A., & Delaney, H. J. (1990). Gender differences in perception of attractiveness of men and women in bars. *Personality and Social Psychology Bulletin, 16*, 378–391. A clever study by Gladue and Delaney demonstrated that the effect of looking prettier at closing time was not related to the amount of alcohol consumed, among other factors.

REFERENCE LIST

▼

Abrahams, M. F., & Bell, R. A. (1994). Encouraging charitable contributions: An examination of three models of door-in-the-face compliance. *Communication Research, 21*, 131–153.

Aikawa, A. (1988). Relative weight of the recipient's benefits and the donor's costs in determining the magnitude of indebtedness. *Japanese Journal of Psychology, 58*, 366–372.

Aikawa, A. (1990). Determinants of the magnitude of indebtedness in Japan: A comparison of relative weight of the recipient's benefits and the donor's costs. *Journal of Psychology, 124*, 523–533.

Afifi, W. A., & Lee, J. W. (2000). Balancing instrumental and identity goals in relationships: The role of request directness and request persistence in the selection of sexual resistance strategies. *Communication Monographs, 67*, 284–305.

Bacharach, S. B., & Lawler, E. J. (1981a). *Power, tactics, and outcomes*. San Francisco: Jossey-Bass.

Bacharach, S. B., & Lawler, E. J. (1981b). Power and tactics in bargaining. *Industrial and Labor Relations Review, 34*, 219–233.

Baxter, L. A. (1984). An investigation of compliance-gaining as politeness. *Human Communication Research, 10*, 427–456.

Bell, R. A., Abrahams, M. F., Clark, C. L., & Schlatter, C. (1996). The door-in-the-face compliance strategy: An individual differences analysis of two models in an AIDS fundraising context. *Communication Quarterly, 44*, 107–124.

Bell, R. A., Cholerton, M., Davison, V., Fraczek, K. E., & Lauter, H. (1996). Making health education self-funding: Effectiveness of pregiving in an AIDS fundraising/education campaign. *Communication Quarterly, 8*, 331–352.

Bell, R. A., Cholerton, M., Fraczek, K. E., Rohlfs, G. S., & Smith, B. A. (1994). Encouraging donations to charity: A field study of competing and complementary factors in tactic sequencing. *Western Journal of Communication, 58*, 98–115.

Bisanz, G. L., & Rule, B. G. (1989). Gender and the persuasion schema: A search for cognitive invariants. *Personality and Social Psychology Bulletin, 15*, 4–18.

Bisanz, G. L., & Rule, B. G. (1990). Children's and adult's comprehension of narratives about persuasion. In M. J. Cody & M. L. McLaughlin (Eds.), *The psychology of tactical communication* (pp. 48–69). Clevedon, England: Multilingual Matters.

Blake, R., Rosenbaum, M., & Duryea, R. (1955). Gift-buying as a function of group standards. *Human Relations, 8*, 61–73.

Boster, F. J. (1995). Commentary on compliance-gaining message behavior research. In C. Berger & M. Burgoon (Eds.), *Communication and social influence processes* (pp. 91–113). East Lansing: Michigan State University Press.

Boster, F. J., Kazoleas, D., Levine, T. R., Rogan, R., & Kang, K. H. (1995). The impact of power and message content on bargaining success. *Communication Reports, 8*, 136–144.

Boster, F. J., Levine, T. R., & Kazoleas, D. C. (1993). The impact of argumentativeness and verbal aggressiveness on strategic diversity and persistence in compliance-gaining behavior. *Communication Quarterly, 41*, 450–474.

Boster, F. J., & Stiff, J. B. (1984). Compliance gaining message selection behavior. *Human Communication Research, 10*, 539–556.

Bresnahan, M. J., Ohashi, R., Liu, W. Y., Nebashi, R., & Liao, C. C. (1999). A comparison of response styles in Singapore and Taiwan. *Journal of Cross-Cultural Psychology, 30*, 342–358.

Burger, J. M. (1986). Increasing compliance by improving the deal: The that's-not-all technique. *Journal of Personality and Social Psychology, 31*, 277–283.

Burgoon, M., Dillard, J. P., Doran, N. E., & Miller, M. D. (1982). Cultural and situation influences on the process of persuasive strategy selection. *International Journal of Intercultural Relations, 6*, 85–100.

Cai, D. A., & Wilson, S. R. (2000). Identity implications of influence goals: A cross-cultural comparison of interaction goals and facework. *Communication Studies, 51*, 307 328.

Chaiken, S. (1979). Communicator physical attractiveness and persuasion. *Journal of Personality and Social Psychology, 37*, 1387–1397.

Cialdini, R. B. (1993). *Influence: Science and practice* (3rd ed.). New York: HarperCollins.

Cialdini, R. B. (1994). Interpersonal influence. In S. Shavitt & T. C. Brock (Eds.), *Persuasion: Psychological insights and perspectives* (pp. 195–218). Boston: Allyn and Bacon.

Cialdini, R. B., & Ascani, K. (1976). Test of a concession procedure for inducing verbal, behavioral, and further compliance with a request to give blood. *Journal of Applied Psychology, 61*, 295–300.

Cialdini, R. B., Cacioppo, J. T., Bassett, R., & Miller, J. A. (1978). Low-ball procedure for producing compliance: Commitment then cost. *Journal of Personality and Social Psychology, 36*, 463–476.

Cialdini, R. B., & Trost, M. R. (1998). Social influence: Social norms, conformity, and compliance. In S. T. Fiske & D. T. Gilbert (Eds.), *The handbook of social psychology* (Vol. 2, 4th ed., 151–192). Boston: McGraw-Hill.

Clark, R. A. (1979). The impact of self-interest and desired liking on selection of persuasive strategies. *Communication Monographs, 46*, 257–273.

404

Cody, M. J., Canary, D. J., & Smith, S. W. (1994). Compliance-gaining goals: An inductive analysis of actor's goal types, strategies and successes. In J. A. Daly & J. Weimann (Eds.), *Communicating strategically* (pp. 33–90). Hillsdale, NJ: Erlbaum.

Cody, M. J., Seiter, J., & Montagne-Miller, Y. (1995). Women and men in the marketplace. In P. Kalbfleisch & M. J. Cody (Eds.), *Gender, power, and communication in human relationships* (pp. 305–328). Hillsdale, NJ: Erlbaum.

Craig, R. T., Tracy, K., & Spisak, F. (1986). The discourse of requests: Assessment of a politeness approach. *Human Communication Research, 12,* 437–468.

Cupchik, G. C., & Leventhal, H. (1974). Consistency between expressive behavior and the evaluation of humorous stimuli: The role of sex and self-observation. *Journal of Personality and Social Psychology, 30,* 429–442.

deTurck, M. D. (1985). A transactional analysis of compliance-gaining behavior: Effects of noncompliance, relational contexts and actor's gender. *Human Communication Research, 12,* 54–78.

deTurck, M. (1987). When communication fails: Physical aggression as a compliance-gaining strategy. *Communication Monographs, 54,* 106–112.

Driscoll, R., Davies, K. E., & Lipetz, M. E. (1972). Parental interference and romantic love: The Romeo and Juliet effect. *Journal of Personality and Social Psychology, 24,* 1–10.

Falbo, T. (1977). A multidimensional scaling of power strategies. *Journal of Personality and Social Psychology, 35,* 537–547.

Folkes, V. S. (1982). Communicating the causes of social rejection. *Journal of Experimental Social Psychology, 18,* 235–252.

French, J. P. R., Jr., & Raven, B. (1959). The bases of social power. In D. Cartwright & A. Zander (Eds.), *Group dynamics* (pp. 607–623). New York: Harper and Row.

Gladue, B. A., & Delaney, H. J. (1990). Gender differences in perception of attractiveness of men and women in bars. *Personality and Social Psychology Bulletin, 16,* 378–391.

Greenberg, M. S. (1980). A theory of indebtedness. In K. J. Gergen, M. S. Greenberg, & R. H. Willis (Eds.), *Social exchange: Advances in theory and research* (pp. 3–26). New York: Plenum.

Greenberg, M. S., & Westcott, D. R. (1983). Indebtedness as a mediator of reactions to aid. In J. D. Fisher, A. Nadler, and B. M. DePaulo (Eds.), *New directions in helping: Vol. 1. Recipient reactions to aid* (pp. 85–112). New York: Academic.

Guadagno, R. E., Asher, T., Demaine, L. J., & Cialdini, R. E. (2001). When saying yes leads to saying no: Preference for consistency and the reverse foot-in-the-door effect. *Personality and Social Psychology Bulletin, 27,* 859–867.

Hale, J. L., & Laliker, M. (1999). Explaining the door-in-the-face: Is it really time to abandon reciprocal concessions? *Communication Studies, 50,* 203–210.

Hirokawa, R. Y., & Mirahara, A. (1986). A comparison of influence strategies utilized by American and Japanese organizations. *Communication Quarterly, 34,* 250–265.

Hocking, J. E., Margreiter, D. G., & Hylton, C. (1977). Intra-audience effects: A field test. *Human Communication Research, 3,* 243–249.

Howard, J. A., Blumstein, P., & Schwartz, P. (1986). Sex, power, and influence tactics in intimate relationships. *Journal of Personality and Social Psychology, 51,* 102–109.

Hullett, C. R., & Tamborini, R. (2001). When I'm within my rights: An expectancy-based model of actor evaluative and behavioral responses to compliance-resistance strategies. *Communication Studies, 52*, 1–16.

Hunter, J. E., & Boster, F. J. (1987). A model of compliance-gaining message selection. *Communication Monographs, 54*, 63–84.

Kellermann, K., & Shea, B. C. (1996). Threats, suggestions, hints and promises: Gaining compliance efficiently and politely. *Communication Quarterly, 44*, 145–165.

Kim, M. S., & Wilson, S. R. (1994). A cross-cultural comparison of implicit theories of requesting. *Communication Monographs, 61*, 210–235.

Kraut, R. E. (1973). Effects of social labeling on giving to charity. *Journal of Experimental Social Psychology, 9*, 551–562.

Lee, C. R., Levine, T. R., & Cambra, R. (1997). Resisting compliance in the multicultural classroom. *Communication Education, 46*, 29–43.

Leventhal, H., & Cupchik, G. C. (1975). The informational and facilitative effects of an audience upon expression and evaluation of humorous stimuli. *Journal of Experimental Social Psychology, 11*, 363–380.

Leventhal, H., & Cupchik, G. C. (1976). A process model of humor judgment. *Journal of Communication, 26*, 190–204.

Leventhal, H., & Mace, W. (1970). The effect of laughter on evaluation of a slapstick movie. *Journal of Personality, 38*, 16–30.

Levine, T. R., & Boster, F. J. (2001). The effects of power and message variables on compliance. *Communication Monographs, 68*, 28–48.

Lim, T. S., & Bowers, J. W. (1991). Facework: Solidarity, approbation, and tact. *Human Communication Research, 17*, 415–449.

Lu, S. (1997). Culture and compliance gaining in the classroom: A preliminary investigation of Chinese college teachers' use of behavior alteration techniques. *Communication Education, 46*, 11–43.

Marwell, G., & Schmitt, D. R. (1967). *Dimensions of compliance-gaining behaviors: An empirical analysis. Sociometry, 30*, 350–364.

McLaughlin, M. L., Cody, M. J., & Robey, C. S. (1980). Situational influences on the selection of strategies to resist compliance-gaining attempts. *Human Communication Research, 7*, 14–36.

McQuillen, J. S. (1986). The development of listener-adapted compliance-resisting strategies. *Human Communication Research, 12*, 359–375.

Miller, G. R., Boster, F., Roloff, M., & Seibold, D. (1977). Compliance-gaining message strategies: A typology and some findings concerning effects of situational differences. Communication *Monographs, 44*, 37–51.

O'Hair, H. D., & Cody, M. J. (1994). Everyday deception. In W. R. Cupach & B. Spitzberg (Eds.), *The dark side of interpersonal communication* (pp. 181–213). Hillsdale, NJ: Erlbaum.

O'Keefe, D. J., & Figge, M. (1997). A guilt-based explanation of the door-in-the-face influence strategy. *Human Communication Research, 24*, 64–81.

O'Keefe, D. J., & Figge, M. (1999). Guilt and expected guilt in the door-in-the-face technique. *Communication Monographs, 66*, 312–324.

Pennebaker, J. W., Dyer, M. A., Caulkins, R. S., Litowitz, D. L., Ackreman, P. L., Anderson, D. B., & McGraw, K. M. (1979). Don't the girls get prettier at closing time: A country and western application to psychology. *Personality and Social Psychology Bulletin, 5*, 122–125.

Reardon, K. K., Sussman, S., & Flay, B. R. (1989). Are we marketing the right message? Can kids "just say 'no' to smoking"? *Communication Monographs, 56*, 307–324.

Rule, B. G., & Bisanz, G. L. (1987). Goals and strategies of persuasion: A cognitive schema for understanding social events. In M. Zanna, J. Olsen, & P. Herman (Eds.), *Social influence: The Fifth Ontario Symposium on Personality and Social Psychology* (pp. 185–206). Hillsdale, NJ: Erlbaum.

Rule, B. G., Bisanz, G. L., & Kohn, M. (1985). Anatomy of a persuasion schema: Targets, goals, and strategies. *Journal of Personality and Social Psychology, 48*, 1127–1140.

Sanders, R. E., & Fitch, K. L. (2001). The actual practice of compliance-seeking. *Communication Theory, 11*, 263–289.

Seibold, D. R., Cantrill, J. G., & Meyers, R. A. (1994). Communication and interpersonal influence. In M. L. Knapp & G. R. Miller (Eds.), *Handbook of interpersonal communication* (2nd ed., pp. 542–588). Newbury Park, CA: Sage.

Sillars, A. L. (1980). Attributions and communication in roommate conflicts. *Communication Monographs, 47*, 180–200.

Thibaut, J., & Kelly, H. (1959). *The psychology of groups.* New York: Wiley.

Ting-Toomey, S. (1985). Toward a theory of conflict and culture. In W. B. Gudykunst & S. Ting-Toomey (Eds.), *Communication, culture, and organizational processes* (pp. 71–86). Beverly Hills, CA: Sage.

Tracy, K., & Baratz, S. (1994). The case for case studies of facework. In S. Ting-Toomey (Ed.), *The challenge of facework: Cross-cultural and interpersonal issues* (pp. 287–305). Albany: State University of New York Press.

Wheeless, L. R., Barraclough, R., & Stewart, R. (1983). Compliance-gaining and power in persuasion. In R. N. Boston (Ed.), *Communication reviews and commentaries* (pp. 105–145). Newbury Park, CA: Sage.

Whatley, M. A., Webster, J. M., Smith, R. H., & Rhodes, A. (1999). The effect of a favor on public and private compliance: How internalized is the norm of reciprocity? *Basic and Applied Social Psychology, 21*, 251–259.

White, K. D., Pearson, J. C., & Flint, L. (1989). Adolescents' compliance-resistance: Effects of parents' compliance strategy and gender. *Adolescence, 24*, 595–621.

Wilson, S. R. (1992). Face and facework in negotiation. In L. L. Putnam & M. E. Roloff (Eds.), *Communication and negotiation* (pp. 176–205). Newbury Park, CA: Sage.

Wilson, S. R., Aleman, C. G., & Leatham, G. B. (1998). Identity implications of influence goals: A revised analysis of face-threatening acts and application to seeking compliance with same-sex friends. *Human Communication Research, 25*, 64–96.

Wilson, S. R., Cruz, M. G., Marshall, L. J., & Rao, N. (1993). An attributional analysis of compliance-gaining interactions. *Communication Monographs, 60*, 352–372.

Wilson, S. R., & Kang, K. H. (1991). Communication and unfulfilled obligations: Individual differences in causal judgments. *Communication Research, 18*, 799–824.

Wilson, S. R., & Kunkel, A. W. (2000). Identity implications of influence goals: Similarities in perceived face threats and facework across sex and close relationships. *Journal of Language and Social Psychology, 19*, 195–221.

Wiseman, R., & Schenck-Hamlin, W. J. (1981). A multidimensional scaling validation of an intuitively derived set of compliance-gaining strategies. *Communication Monographs, 48*, 251–270.

Wosinska, R., Cialdini, R., Reykowski, J., & Barrett, D. W. (Eds.). (1999). *The practice of social influence in multiple cultures.* Mahwah, NJ: Erlbaum.

C H A P T E R   1 3

MANAGING

INTERPERSONAL

CONFLICT

WHY STUDY CONFLICT?

DEFINING CONFLICT

CONFLICT STYLES

CHOICES IN MANAGING CONFLICT
Confront or Avoid?
Cooperate or Compete?

CONFLICT STRATEGIES AND PATTERNS
Conflict Strategies
Conflict Patterns

MANAGING RELATIONAL PROBLEMS

CONSEQUENCES OF CONFLICT
BEHAVIORS
Attributions
Relational Consequences

CHAPTER SUMMARY

Jason and Scott thought it would be good to share an apartment. They liked the same kinds of music, they seemed to have the same values, and they could cut down on rent if they shared an apartment.

After a few weeks, things clearly weren't going as well as they had first thought. Jason often studied in the evening, typically in the living room. Scott didn't go to school, so he spent his evenings working out at the gym or going out on dates. Eventually, Scott became increasingly annoyed that Jason would never take out the trash. Two or three bags of trash would pile up at the kitchen entry, and Jason didn't even seem to notice. At first Scott said nothing. Then after a few weeks, Scott asked Jason to take out his trash every day. Jason agreed, but he often forgot, which only made Scott more unhappy about the situation.

One night Scott almost fell over the bags of trash set in the hall. This time, Scott decided to confront Jason. Scott said, "Look, you may enjoy living like a pig, but I can't. So if you don't throw this trash out now, I'm gonna toss it in your room."

Jason wasn't about to be pushed around: "If you touch my room, I'll knock you flat."

Scott jumped up, grabbed the trash bags, and smashed them above Jason's bed.

Jason was shaking, "That does it — I'll get you back for this, believe me."

Scott mocked him. "Your threats are nothing but idle chatter."

On those words, the two began fighting, although not very well. The only thing they managed to do was put a hole in one wall, tear some curtains, and break a large window.

The next morning, Jason and Scott left the apartment. They forfeited that month's rent and their security deposit due to the damage caused by the fight.

This story illustrates a few aspects of interpersonal conflict. First, it shows that a particular conflict probably is not an isolated event. The issues at conflict between Jason and Scott occurred over several months. Second, conflicts may never be resolved. Instead, it is probably healthier to think of managing conflict over time. Obviously Jason and Scott didn't manage their conflict very well. Finally, the example illustrates that people choose the way they respond to one another and that these responses often depend on what the other person has done.

WHY STUDY CONFLICT?

Several good reasons exist for studying conflict. A primary reason is to avoid the type of escalation to violence that Jason and Scott experienced. Instead of managing conflict through communicative means, people sometimes resort to physical violence or verbal abuse. Estimates are that approximately 20% of married people and 35% of dating couples have experienced some kind of physical or verbal abuse within the previous year (Marshall, 1994; Spitzberg, 1997). This chapter reveals more productive ways to manage interpersonal conflicts.

A second reason is that conflict interactions are often confusing — both mentally and emotionally. When people are involved in conflict, they tend to engage in biases that grossly distort what both parties are saying and meaning to say (Sillars, Roberts, Leonard, & Dun, 2000). Moreover, negative arousal often increases during conflict, meaning that people sometimes feel overwhelmed and even confused about what is occurring (Gottman, 1994). Finally, the structure of conversation during conflict is very difficult to ascertain, and people forget the initial reason that they began the argument (Sillars & Weisberg, 1987). By knowing that conflict is a confusing type of communication interaction, students can prepare for how they want to manage themselves strategically.

A third reason for studying conflict is to help you achieve your personal goals (Ohbuchi & Tedeschi, 1997). Jason and Scott failed to achieve what they wanted (friendship and saving money), in part because they cut off communication with each other. We are not saying that applying particular communication skills will solve all your interpersonal problems (Sillars & Weisberg, 1987). We do contend that learning more about communication in conflict should better enable you to achieve your goals, even in emotionally charged situations. Research shows that people who think about their communication during conflict are more likely to engage in integrative strategies, which tend to be productive (e.g., Yovetich & Rusbult, 1994). By considering the role of communication before speaking, people can increase their abilities to use the most appropriate and most effective communication strategies for managing conflict situations.

According to Deutsch (1973), conflict can be productive if managed properly. Conflict between family members, friends, lovers, and others can help the parties clarify their personal and relational goals. Conflict can also lead to the generation of new ideas and creative alternatives. Encouraging disagreement can promote effective decision-making, but disallowing conflict can lead to poor decisions and relational dissatisfaction (e.g., Kurdek, 1994). In addition, interpersonal conflict can help people manage their lives better. You may some day be faced with a friend who wants to leave a party after having had too much to drink; it is very possible that the only way your friend will live to see tomorrow is through confrontation with you.

A final reason to study conflict is that it is a natural and inevitable event (Hocker & Wilmot, 1991). Benoit and Benoit (1990) report that on average, a person has seven conflicts a week, mostly among relatives, friends, and lovers with whom they've argued before (86% of conflicts are of this type). Conflict is natural and inevitable simply because people are not mere clones of one another. We each have our unique combination of beliefs, behaviors, and goals, which will inevitably conflict with other people's beliefs, behaviors, and goals.

DEFINING CONFLICT

Conflict has been defined in various ways (Canary, Cupach, & Messman, 1995). In this text we define **conflict** as any disagreement between interdependent parties who perceive that they have incompatible goals (Cahn, 1992; Hocker & Wilmot, 1991; Putnam & Poole, 1987). The key terms in this definition are *disagreement, interdependent,* and *perceived incompatible goals.* Interpersonal conflict occurs when there is some expression of disagreement, either verbal or nonverbal, between two people. When a person experiences internal conflict without expressing disagreement with others, this is known as **intrapsychic conflict,** not interpersonal conflict (Deutsch, 1973). Later in this chapter we describe various strategies and tactics that people use to express disagreement.

Interdependence means that the people in conflict depend on one another to accomplish their goals. You must coordinate behaviors in order to achieve your goals, but during conflict, the person with whom you must coordinate actions appears to block your goals. Probably the most important aspect of the definition concerns how goals might be perceived as incompatible. Goals may not in fact be incompatible; what really matters is that the parties in conflict perceive them as incompatible.

Other features of goals in conflict should be mentioned. Sillars and Weisberg (1987) note that "in many conflicts, goals are quite complex and ephemeral" (p. 141). One reason is that goals change as the conflict progresses. Hocker and Wilmot (1991) identify three types of goals: *prospective goals* are the goals you initially have when entering the conflict episode, *transactive goals* are those that emerge during the interaction, and *retrospective goals* refer to how you look back at the interaction to make sense of it. For example, you might have the prospective goal of getting your roommate to give up the apartment on certain nights so that you have more privacy. Your roommate disagrees, and during the conflict you discover that your roommate doesn't go out due to shyness. Your goal might then change to persuading your roommate to go to a party with you. After the conversation, you might retrospectively decide that your goal was to help your roommate be less of a homebody. The point is that when you engage in conflict, your objectives may change. People who recognize the changing nature of goals can adapt their messages to achieve these goals.

Another factor that complicates conflict is that people have several goals at once (Ohbuchi & Tedeschi, 1997). It is likely that no one single issue is relevant at a given moment of the conflict episode. For example, imagine that you need to type a report for a class, but your significant other wants to go out and makes a point of it. Your instrumental goal of completing your assignment conflicts with your partner's goal of going out. Yet at the same time you want to maintain the relationship (a second important goal), and you would prefer to get away from your homework as well.

CONFLICT STYLES

Are people consistent in their use of conflict behaviors? Researchers who examine conflict styles have addressed this issue. Investigations on the topic, by such researchers as Berryman-Fink and Brunner (1987), Kilmann and Thomas (1977), and Rahim (1986), have revealed five styles that people may use.

Perhaps the best way to explain the five styles of conflict is to place them on a graph that reflects the degrees to which an individual is concerned for others and for himself or herself. In addition, these styles are said to vary according to their degree of cooperation and assertiveness. Figure 13.1 shows the placement of the five styles according to these concerns.

As Figure 13.1 indicates, a person who has a low concern for others and a high concern for self will likely have a **competing style.** This style is assertive, without real consideration for others' outcomes. By contrast, a person can have a high concern for others but a low concern for self. This person would be cooperative and unassertive, characteristic of an **accommodating style.** An individual could have a high concern for both self and others, reflected in being assertive and cooperative. This is the **collaborating style.** Some people have little concern for themselves or others in conflicts. This lack of concern is seen in little assertiveness and little cooperation. Because such persons prefer to withdraw from the situation, this is referred to as the **withdrawing style.** Finally, some people have a moderate amount of concern for self and others. Accordingly, they show moderate amounts of assertiveness and cooperation. They are described as having a **compromising style.**

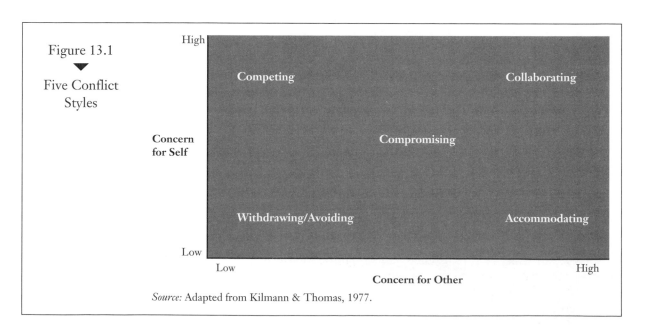

Figure 13.1

▼

Five Conflict Styles

Concern for Self

High

Low

Competing

Collaborating

Compromising

Withdrawing/Avoiding

Accommodating

Low   Concern for Other   High

Source: Adapted from Kilmann & Thomas, 1977.

Avoidance can be quite functional in selected contexts. Kim and Leung (2000) noted how in collectivistic cultures especially, indirect methods for managing conflict reflect a high concern for other. Likewise, individuals in Separate marriages prefer to avoid the discussion, a point we take up later in this chapter.

Overall then, which style is best? According to Hocker and Wilmot (1985), there is no simple answer. Rather, there are advantages and disadvantages to using each of these styles. Table 13.1 lists some of them.

Conflict styles describe how people tend to behave in general. Styles are useful because they let us see how we tend to behave in response to conflict. Moreover, the advantages and disadvantages of these styles are clear.

Table 13.1
ADVANTAGES AND DISADVANTAGES OF THE FIVE CONFLICT STYLES

Style	Advantages	Disadvantages
Competing	Useful if instrumental goal is more important than relational or self-presentational goal; helpful if quick decisions are needed	Can hurt relational and self-presentational goals; can lead to escalation of conflict or avoidance by the other person
Accommodating	Can show reasonableness; can improve relationships, especially with superiors; can keep another from harming you	May communicate lack of power; ignores relational issues; requires sacrifice of instrumental goals
Collaborating	Can satisfy both parties; promotes creative solutions and commitment to them; enhances relational and instrumental goals; works well in long-term associations	Requires much energy, perhaps too much for a given goal; can be frustrated if not reciprocal; can be faked
Withdrawing	Acknowledges that some goals are not worth fighting for; protects against possible harm; appropriate if relationship is short-term	May be perceived as weak or uncaring; abandons goals; reinforces idea that conflict is unnatural and should be avoided at all costs
Compromising	Can let both parties accomplish some goals in an efficient manner; maintains most relational goals; seems reasonable to most people	Easy but may be counter-productive; requires sacrifice of both parties' goals to some degree; hampers use of creative alternatives

Source: Adapted from Hocker & Wilmot, 1985.

414

Beyond tendencies to behave in a particular way, people's spontaneous and real-time choices during conflict more directly affect how they manage conflict. These choices also lead to the use of particular strategies for managing conflict.

CHOICES IN MANAGING CONFLICT

Confront or Avoid?

Perhaps the first choice people make during conflict is whether to confront or avoid the other person (e.g., Sillars & Wilmot, 1994). Imagine that you are waiting in your car at an intersection and the driver in front of you hasn't noticed that the traffic light has turned green. Should you confront the other driver (honk your horn), or should you avoid a conflict and wait quietly?

Several factors determine whether or not you confront or avoid the person. The first concerns your immediate physiological state. That is, if you are feeling stressed because you are running late, or depressed because the winter has been dragging on, or even stifled because of the pollution and heat of the city, you are primed to act aggressively toward others (Berkowitz, 1993). In such conditions, you would likely confront another person.

Several factors determine whether you confront or avoid conflict with someone. Do you believe you are right to pursue your goal? How important is the goal to you? What is your status relative to the person you would be confronting? What public image do you want to present?

Michael Weisbrot/Stock, Boston

Second, people determine the extent to which they have a "right to persuade" (Cody, McLaughlin, & Schneider, 1981). If you believe that you have a right to pursue your goal, you will be more likely to confront the individual than if you are unsure about having the right to persuade. For example, if you noticed that the person in the car in front of you was reading a newspaper, putting on lipstick, or talking on a cell phone, you would probably feel within your rights to honk your horn. But if you see a group of children crossing in front of the other car, you wouldn't feel within your rights to honk your horn.

Another factor that determines whether you confront or avoid the other is how important the goal is to you. If you were late for an important meeting or a job interview, you would probably be less patient than if you were on your way to a party.

Status also affects the decision to confront or avoid. People tend not to confront those who have higher status but do tend to confront those with the same or lower status (see, for example, Putnam & Wilson, 1982; Chapter 12). Accordingly, you may not disagree with your supervisor about critical comments about your work, but you would be less willing to take the same criticism from a co-worker.

As Chapter 6 showed, self-presentation concerns how we groom our public image. Accordingly, the decision to confront or avoid the other person is affected by which public image we want to present. Recall that some people want to appear likable, so they ingratiate, whereas others want to appear dangerous, so they intimidate. Your various self-presentation goals likely affect your decision to confront or avoid conflict with others. If someone publicly challenges your integrity, competence, or even likability, you may decide to confront them ("How dare you question my intelligence!").

Next, some people believe that they can solve their interpersonal problems, and individuals with such beliefs are more likely to confront others in a cooperative fashion (vs. people who do not believe that they have as much control over their personal problems) (Canary, Cunningham, & Cody, 1988; Caughlin & Vangelisti, 2000).

Finally, relational history affects your decision to confront or avoid. Sillars, Pike, Jones, and Redmon (1983) found that for some couples (Independents, see Chapter 10), satisfaction increases as their level of confrontation increases; but for other couples (Separates, see Chapter 10), satisfaction decreases as their level of confrontation increases. Also, as you get to know someone, your confidence in making attributions about that person's behavior increases. A particular kind of silent response, a shrug of the shoulder, or a lukewarm "yes" is more readily interpreted by people who know one another well than by acquaintances. As you learn to interpret the other's nonverbal messages, you may become more likely to confront the other on the basis of those nonverbal cues.

Cooperate or Compete?

A second choice that you face when a conflict arises is whether to be cooperative or competitive. Again, several factors are decisive. They include perceived threat, reciprocity, and responses to inappropriate behavior. Research indicates that people who believe that their personal rights are being violated are more likely to lash out than those who do not see their rights as jeopardized. For example, people are more likely to use such competitive behaviors as shouting and sarcasm if they perceive that they are personally attacked (Canary et al., 1988).

Reciprocity affects your decision to cooperate or compete. As you may recall from earlier chapters, reciprocity refers to the way that dyadic partners mirror each other's behavior. As in self-disclosure, where one person tends to disclose at the same level of intimacy as the partner, reciprocity has a strong effect on selection of conflict behavior. Sillars (1980b), for example, found strong associations between one person's conflict behavior and the partner's conflict interaction. In addition, Burggraf and Sillars (1987) found that reciprocity had more of an effect on conflict behavior than did relationship type or gender. Simply stated, people treat others as they are treated themselves, especially during conflict. So when someone threatens you, the urge is to challenge back; when someone is patient and discloses feelings, the tendency is to offer disclosure in return (Burggraf & Sillars, 1987; Sillars, 1980b). In addition, the reciprocation of negative conflict messages is a distinguishing feature of dissatisfied (vs. satisfied) couples (Gottman, 1994).

Finally, certain kinds of inappropriate communication prompt negative reactions. Benoit and Benoit (1990) indicate that people are often drawn into a competitive mode when they are faced with insults, accusations, commands, or refusals of requests. Such messages prompt conflict; they are illustrated in Table 13.2.

Decisions to confront or avoid and to cooperate or compete have important implications for managing interpersonal conflict. First, and most important, these strategic decisions are under the control of the communicators. People choose whether or not to engage in conflict, and they decide whether or not to cooperate with each other. Granted, these choices happen almost instantly and are often made

Table 13.2
MESSAGES THAT PROMPT CONFLICT

Message	Type
"I don't like your singing."	Insult
"You acted silly at the party."	Insult
"You never clean up like you used to."	Accusation
"We're broke because you spend too much."	Accusation
"Stop talking with your mouth full."	Command
"Tell me when you won't be busy."	Command
"I can't see you because I'm too busy."	Refusal
"You'll just have to type this yourself."	Refusal

Source: Adapted from Benoit & Benoit, 1990.

in a state of emotional upset. Nevertheless, these choices are ours to make, and we must accept responsibility for our conflict behaviors.

In addition, these choices are important because they lead to the use of strategies that reflect these decisions. If you decide to avoid the issue, you will probably engage in behaviors designed to minimize the conflict. If you decide to confront the person, you can do so in degrees of cooperation or competition. Several researchers (e.g., Cupach, 1982; Putnam & Wilson, 1982; Sillars, Coletti, Parry, & Rogers, 1982) cite three basic conflict strategies that reflect decisions to avoid, to cooperate, and to compete. Other researchers (e.g., van de Vliert & Euwema, 1994) report that four strategies emerge from the consideration of the two dimensions. They call these approaches *negotiation* (direct/cooperative), *nonconfrontation* (indirect/cooperative), *direct fighting* (direct/competitive), and *indirect fighting* (indirect/competitive).

CONFLICT STRATEGIES AND PATTERNS

Conflict Strategies

If you decide to avoid the conflict issue, you will likely use the **avoidance strategy.** Avoidance is intended to distract attention from the conflict. Table 13.3 offers examples of avoidance tactics.

If you want to engage the other person in a cooperative manner, you would likely rely on an **integrative strategy.** Integrative behaviors are those that manage the conflict by taking into account both parties' needs and wants; they attempt to integrate both person's resources and goals. Table 13.4 provides examples of integrative behaviors.

If you want to engage the other person in a competitive manner, you would probably use a **distributive strategy.** From a competitive posture, you distribute the resources and goals in a win-lose attitude, and you try to win as much as possible regardless of the other's expense. Table 13.5 offers examples of distributive behaviors.

These tactics seldom occur in isolation. An individual rarely walks up to his or her partner, blurts out a disclosure or a prescription, and then leaves. Instead, an individual perceives that a valued goal is blocked and then decides whether to engage the partner in a conversation. Then these tactics unfold in various ways. A discussion of the various ways in which conflicts unfold can reveal additional insights about the communicative aspects of conflict.

Conflict Patterns

Conflict tactics unfold along several organizational patterns or dimensions (Sillars & Wilmot, 1994). These dimensions each reflect how specific instances of avoidance, integrative, and distributive tactics occur during interaction. The five dimensions that these analysts discuss are variety, continuity, symmetry, stationarity, and spontaneity.

Table 13.3
AVOIDANCE TACTICS

Tactic	Description	Example
Direct denial	The communicator flatly denies that there is a problem.	"No, dear, nothing is wrong."
Evasion	The communicator tries to imply that the problem lies elsewhere.	"I can see how other couples have that problem."
Topic shift	The communicator simply changes the subject.	"That's interesting. Now as I was saying yester- day . . . "
Stalling	The communicator tries to delay or postpone discussion.	"It's too late to talk about that now."
Abstract remark	The communicator shifts the focus to a level that is removed from the issue.	"You say I'm impatient. Well, patience is a virtue that everyone needs to work at."
Procedural remark	The communicator focuses on manner rather than the conflict issue.	"I can't talk to you when you're like this."
Irrelevant remark	The communicator makes a statement that has little or no bearing on the conflict issue.	"There's a fly on the wall."

Source: Adapted from Cupach, 1982; Hocker & Wilmot, 1991; Sillars et al., 1982.

Variety refers to how flexible people are during conflict. A lack of flexibility tends to occur among couples who are dissatisfied (Gottman, 1994; Sillars & Wilmot, 1994). Ting-Toomey (1983), for example, found that dissatisfied couples lapse into the same rigid patterns of defensive communication. Unhappy couples consistently responded to confrontational remarks and complaints with similar defensive statements. Many studies have found that, for people in dissatisfying relationships, negative, distributive behavioral cycles are hard to break (Gottman, 1994). However, using a variety of conflict behaviors, particularly integrative responses, breaks the rigidity of the conflict interaction and increases the likelihood of productive conflict management.

Table 13.4
INTEGRATIVE TACTICS

Tactic	Description	Example
Descriptive statement	The communicator offers a factual explanation.	"There are three bags of trash in the hallway."
Disclosure	The communicator discloses personal feelings about the topic.	"I get very anxious when you speed like this."
Soliciting disclosures	The communicator asks the other person to disclose personal feelings.	"Please tell me what you're thinking."
Understanding and concern	The communicator demonstrates understanding and caring.	"I realize that this must be a tough decision for you."
Supportive remark	The communicator backs up the other person's point of view.	"I can see now what you meant."
Concession	The communicator conveys willingness to give in a little.	"OK, I'll try to drive more carefully from now on."
Acceptance of responsibility	The communicator accepts responsibility for part of the conflict.	"You're right — I can't manage money very well."
Common ground	Both communicators try to find a mutually satisfying solution.	"Can we agree on our major goals?"

Source: Adapted from Cupach, 1982; Hocker & Wilmot, 1991; Sillars et al., 1982.

Continuity refers to the range of topics covered during conflict. Intense conflicts about the same important relational issues (such as not trusting the partner or not showing affection) are unhealthy (Sillars & Wilmot, 1994). At the same time, a conflict episode that entails many different topics (ranging from talking too much and eating habits to lack of trust and affection) reflects a dysfunctional relationship. For example, you may have been involved in a conversation where the parties couldn't focus on a single issue long enough to reach agreement or even understand each other. Or you may have felt the frustration of dealing with the same issue over and over again with a roommate ("I can't believe these dishes are still here!"). People in

Table 13.5
DISTRIBUTIVE TACTICS

Tactic	Description	Example
Personal criticism	The communicator faults the other person's character.	"You idiot! You don't think before you open your mouth."
Rejection	The communicator dismisses the other person's ideas.	"No way — that's out of the question."
Threat	The communicator warns of punishment if argument fails.	"If you don't throw out that trash, I'll toss it in your room."
Blame	The communicator attributes the entire conflict to the other person.	"It's your fault we're having this problem."
Hostile remark	The communicator tries to intimidate.	"Who the hell do you think you are?"
Shouting	The communicator tries to overcome the other person through sheer volume.	"DON'T YOU SHOUT AT ME!"
Sarcasm	The communicator uses intonation to convey that a statement is to be interpreted as its opposite.	"You sure looked macho on that mechanical bull."
Prescription	The communicator tells the other person what to do.	"You should stop thinking only of yourself — people might start liking you more."

Source: Adapted from Cupach, 1982; Hocker & Wilmot, 1991; Sillars et al., 1982.

satisfying relationships tend to develop their ideas before moving on to new issues. And satisfied couples avoid raising the same tired issues over and over again.

Symmetry refers to reciprocity of behavior, or mirroring the other's conflict. Symmetry references a quid pro quo (treat others as they treat you). Satisfied couples tend to reciprocate integrative behaviors but not distributive behaviors (Sillars & Wilmot, 1994). For instance, Ting-Toomey (1983) found that satisfied couples engaged in symmetrical sequences of verbal teasing, confirmation, and description dur-

Calvin and Hobbes, copyright Bill Watterson. Distributed by Universal Press Syndicate. Reprinted with permission. All rights reserved.

Calvin and Hobbes reciprocate each other's conflict behaviors. One of the ways to avoid getting locked into a dysfunctional symmetrical pattern is not to reciprocate distributive tactics.

ing their conflict management discussions. Dissatisfied couples reciprocated defensive statements (Son: "There's no way I could have been out all last night." Father: "I doubt that." Son: "Well, I'm sure of it!" Father: "Don't lie to me!").

Some of the most damaging symmetrical patterns were proposal-counterproposal, complaint-complaint, and metacommunication-metacommunication (Gottman, 1982). Consider the following proposal-counterproposal sequence:

Brad: Let's order some Chinese food and rent a video.
Tracy: No, let's do Italian and go dancing.
Brad: Let's invite Ted and Lisa to join us.
Tracy: No, let's go alone.

or the following more explosive exchange:

Brad: You can leave me alone any time you want.
Tracy: It's my house, so you check out.
Brad: Then you can go to hell.
Tracy: After you.

According to Gottman, partners should at least acknowledge and sincerely validate the other person's point before offering a counterproposal.

Cross-complaining can be common but destructive. For example,

Tracy: You didn't clean the kitchen like I asked.
Brad: So? You didn't wash the clothes.

or

Brad: I don't like your hair like that.
Tracy: You're no movie star either.

Metacommunication exchanges refer to reciprocating talk about talk. Metacommunication can be functional, when it is said with positive emotional overtones. Or it can be dysfunctional, when people respond to each other in negative and defensive ways. Consider the following symmetrical exchange involving negative metacommunication:

Tracy: What do you mean by "be good"?
Brad: Why do you ask?
Tracy: I wouldn't ask if I didn't have a reason.
Brad: That's not a valid argument.
Tracy: Why not? It seems logical to me!
Brad: Logic and validity aren't the same thing.
Tracy: I should give you a few lessons in logic.

By this time, Tracy and Brad have forgotten the real issue they were discussing and are wrapped up in their metacommunicative exchanges.

Although these examples reflect dysfunctional patterns, you can also use reciprocation to "guide the process in a potentially productive . . . direction" (Krueger & Smith, 1982, p. 131). As Burggraf and Sillars (1987) note, it is difficult to engage in competitive, distributive confrontations with someone who offers cooperative, integrative behaviors. Accordingly, one method for breaking a destructive symmetrical pattern is simply to refrain from reciprocating distributive tactics. The box "Conflict Is Deadly in *The War of the Roses*" provides a realistic example of what can happen when partners continue to reciprocate negative behaviors.

In addition, couples go through phases of conflict, a feature referred to as **stationarity** (Sillars & Wilmot, 1994). This means that within a discussion, the conversation goes through clearly different phases. Accordingly, people experience phases of conflict escalation and de-escalation. For example, some dyads begin with integrative messages, then move to more distributive tactics, then return to cooperative behaviors, perhaps because the conflict becomes too emotionally intense. Other dyads might begin and end their discussions with avoidant messages — talking about other people, denying that a problem exists, or shifting from topic to topic, not experiencing any phases of conflict escalation or de-escalation. Gottman and Krokoff (1989)

CONFLICT IS DEADLY IN *THE WAR OF THE ROSES*

In the film *The War of the Roses*, we see the serious damage that can result from an unremittingly competitive approach to managing conflict. Oliver Rose is a professional, and his wife, Barbara, is a homemaker who later begins a business of her own. With his income, they purchase a large house, which she makes elegant through years of hard work. Though initially happy, the Roses ultimately grow apart.

Barbara wants a divorce and the house, but Oliver refuses to relinquish it. The house becomes a trophy to be won. To manage the impasse, the Roses decide to divide the house into three zones — an area for each of them, plus a neutral zone. When his lawyer suggests that Oliver give Barbara the house, Oliver insists that he must win. His lawyer advises, "Oliver, there is no winning this, only degrees of losing." But Oliver misses the point — that using a distributive strategy is counterproductive — and responds, "I got more square footage." For Oliver the house is a battleground, and the outcome of the conflict is measured by the territory occupied.

The Roses then escalate their negative behaviors to the point of violence. Oliver ruins a party that Barbara throws for her clients; she reciprocates by destroying his sports car with her truck. He dismantles her oven; she in turn demolishes their prized porcelain collection, which she also loves but values more as a means of hurting Oliver. Despite attempts to manage the conflict in a cooperative fashion, these people cannot resist the urge to reciprocate negative behaviors, and that mishandling of interpersonal conflict ultimately costs them their lives.

Throughout *The War of the Roses*, both parties consciously decide to escalate the conflict. Neither one is willing to back down, so both end up losing. A great many people decide to manage conflict in the same destructive manner, partly due to the shortsighted belief that winning is a major goal in itself.

---

noted that another common pattern begins with hostility and concludes with the partners avoiding each other.

Phases of conflict behavior are not limited to a single event. Rather, stationarity can also be observed across conflict episodes (Sillars & Wilmot, 1994). Although particular couples can engage in various phases within a given encounter, their tactical patterns are similar in different conflict encounters. So, for example, two people might begin every conflict with calm disclosures about their desired goals, which then gradually escalate into reciprocations of blaming and ridicule. Next, one person realizes that the conflict is destructive and offers a conciliation tactic ("I'm sorry; I'll try to be more considerate"). The couple then goes out to dinner, during which they disclose their true feelings. Clearly there are changes in the phases of conflict within one episode. But if this couple engages in the same tactical pattern of disclosure-blaming-conciliation-disclosure in every conflict episode, these people enact predictable conflict phases across episodes.

Spontaneity refers to the extent to which the parties in conflict are not being overly strategic and guarded in what they say (Sillars & Wilmot, 1994). You may have been involved in a conflict where you measured the effect of each and every word before it was spoken. The reason for this could be that the issue was very important or you didn't feel comfortable expressing your true feelings, or perhaps you felt intimidated by your partner.

Conversely, you may have observed a conflict where the other person plainly vented hostile feelings without thinking about the devastating effects of such "open and honest" communication. Clearly, being either overly cautious or careless about managing conflict may be unproductive. According to Sillars and Wilmot, "Ideally, one would be spontaneous enough to be responsive enough to be collaborative, but strategic enough to modify destructive patterns when they arise" (p. 24).

In sum, five organizational properties help us understand conflict messages: variety, continuity, symmetry, stationarity, and spontaneity (Sillars & Wilmot, 1994). Each property helps us observe how conflict tactics are exchanged and even how they may be modified.

MANAGING RELATIONAL PROBLEMS

Relational problems are inevitable. Some of these problems are resolved quickly; others take months or even years to manage. Responses to relational problems are important because such problems constitute an important conflict domain.

Rusbult (1987) has identified four general responses that people use in dealing with problems in relationships. These responses vary in terms of how passively or actively they confront the problem, and in terms of how constructive or destructive they are. (You will probably notice that these response types coincide with the strategic decisions that people consider when managing conflict in general.) The first response type is **exit,** which is a passive and destructive response. Using exit, the couple separates formally, or the individuals think about or threaten leaving (see also Chapter 11). The second approach is voice. **Voice** is an active and constructive response that includes such actions as discussing problems and suggesting solutions. The third approach is **loyalty,** which reflects a passive and constructive response. With loyalty, the person decides to wait and hope that things work out. Or loyalty could be shown in supporting the partner in the face of personal criticism. Finally, a person can use neglect. **Neglect** includes several active and destructive behaviors — avoid the partner, refuse to discuss the relational problems, and perhaps show hostility. Consider the following true scenario:

Sheila has been married for about twenty years to Doug. She is moderately satisfied with her marriage and her family, but Doug is very controlling: He monitors her communication with other people; he reads her mail and listens on the extension when she receives phone calls (even from her daughter); and he never allows Sheila to go out

Gatewood/The Image Works

Discussing the problem (voice) is one of several options people have when they encounter problems in their relationships. The other options include separating (exit), staying with the partner and hoping things will work out (loyalty), or making the present situation more difficult for the partner (neglect).

alone. Nor does he let her drive the family car. Sheila sacrificed her career in teaching to be with Doug, and she continues to be primarily responsible for raising their four children (three of whom still live at home). Doug, however, enjoys a different life. He goes out whenever and with whomever he pleases, and he refuses to answer to Sheila. Because of his carousing, the family budget is always tight. Often Sheila must ask Doug for money to purchase groceries for the household. But the cash is low, even for groceries. Every month or so they have the same conflict: She must buy the groceries, but there is not enough money to purchase what the family would like to eat. Doug gets very upset, criticizes Sheila, and demands that she "find some way" to make ends meet. In a word, Doug responds to this ongoing problem by using neglect. What is Sheila's response to Doug? She displays loyalty.

Rusbult (1987) has demonstrated that the use of the four responses to relational problems is tied to a person's commitment to the relationship. *Commitment* concerns the extent to which partners want to continue their relationship indefinitely, involving beliefs regarding one's emotional ties to the partner (Rusbult, Olson, Davis, & Hannon, 2001). For Rusbult and colleagues, commitment results from a combination of satisfaction with the relationship (i.e., the extent to which one's partner compares favorably to one's ideal mate), the amount of investment already made in the relationship (such as money and emotional energy), and the lack of quality of alternatives (i.e., the extent to which one's partner compares favorably to other potential partners or to activities — e.g., traveling — not undertaken due to the relationship).

In the scenario presented, why does Sheila respond to her relational problems with loyalty? Part of the reason is that she has invested so much in this relationship — her career, her time raising the children, her friendships. Another reason is that she has no alternatives. She has no income, no job prospects, no conceivable way to meet others, and no transportation. Her options are very limited. And as Sheila gets older, her costs become more reason to stay in the relationship (see Rusbult, Johnson, & Morrow, 1986b).

If Sheila had more options — if only a few friends could offer her support — what might her approach be to this situation? Sheila would probably use voice. Table 13.6 indicates when people theoretically use exit, voice, loyalty, and neglect, depending on the combination of commitment factors. It predicts that Sheila would threaten to leave or actually leave the relationship (that is, use exit) if she were dissatisfied with her partner, did not have much invested in the relationship, and had other friends, activities, or even lovers. Sheila might use neglect if she were dissatisfied, had little invested, but felt that she had nowhere else to turn.

Rusbult, Johnson, and Morrow (1986a) found that the use of voice in mild relational problems helped stabilize the relationship. Moreover, voice and loyalty have been positively related to commitment (Rusbult, 1987). However, as might be expected, the use of exit and neglect were negatively associated with commitment and satisfaction. Women also reported using voice for mild problems and loyalty for all kinds of problems more than men did (Rusbult et al., 1986a). These authors also found that men reported using neglect more often than women did, though most of the research in close relationships shows that women are more competitive (perhaps due to feeling being taken for granted or being treated inequitably) (Canary et al., 1995).

Table 13.6			
TYPICAL RESPONSES TO RELATIONAL PROBLEMS			
Likely Response	Properties of Commitment		
	Satisfaction	*Investment*	*Alternatives*
Exit	Low	Low	High
Voice	High	High	High
Loyalty	High	High	Low
Neglect	Low	Low	Low

Source: Adapted from Rusbult, 1987. Reprinted by permission of Sage Publications, Inc.

Other research has found that the exit-voice-loyalty-neglect typology is associated with certain irrational beliefs that college students have about their romantic relationships (Metts & Cupach, 1990): (1) that disagreement is destructive (it's not okay to disagree); (2) that partners are expected to be mindreaders (your partner should be able to know your thoughts and feelings without your voicing them); (3) that partners cannot and do not change; (4) that the relationship must achieve sexual perfection (your sex life with your partner must be the best there is); and (5) that men and women are different (hence they cannot agree on anything).

Metts and Cupach (1990) found that each of these irrational beliefs correlated positively with a participant's use of exit and neglect and negatively with use of voice. For example, if you believed that your partner could not change an aspect of his or her behavior, you would see no reason to express your concern over the issue. Metts and Cupach also found that exit and neglect correlated negatively with relational satisfaction, whereas voice correlated positively. Clearly the use of the various methods for dealing with relational problems reflects, as well as affects, the nature of a relationship.

CONSEQUENCES OF CONFLICT BEHAVIORS

The premises of attribution theory were presented in Chapter 2, and throughout this book we have discussed the importance of attributions in assessing other people's behavior. As you might imagine, how communicators manage conflict radically affects the way in which their partners view them. In addition to attributions, we address the powerful effects that conflict has on people's relationships.

Attributions

People attribute the causes of events to external (situational) versus internal (dispositional) factors. So, for example, you might believe that the cause of a conflict is external (e.g., he is under a lot of stress right now; she didn't make the swimming team; his wife just left him), or you might attribute the cause of the conflict to be an internal factor (he is impatient and short-tempered; she is a witch). In a general self-serving manner, negative (distributive) behaviors tend to be attributed to the internal properties of the other person, whereas positive (integrative) behaviors tend to be attributed to oneself (see Bradbury & Fincham, 1990).

In a study of college roommates, Sillars (1980a) found that the use of both distributive and avoidance behaviors was positively related to believing that the other person (in this case a roommate) was the cause of the conflict, whereas integrative behaviors were positively associated with believing that you were the cause of the conflict. Of course, the irony is that when distributive behaviors are used, both partners see the other as the cause of a conflict. In the example at the beginning of the chapter, Jason saw Scott's attitude as the cause of the conflict, and Scott saw Jason's lack of cleanliness as the cause.

428

Other causal factors that affect how we perceive conflict are stability and globality (Bradbury & Fincham, 1990). **Stability** refers to the consistency of a conflict over time, and **globality** refers to the number of issues that are in conflict. Research concerning these causal dimensions reveals that perceptions of stability and globality of a conflict's causes are positively related to negative behaviors. Sillars (1980a) also found that stability was positively associated with the use of avoidance tactics ("If he's a slob, why try to change him?").

Karen was the copyeditor of a small magazine. According to Karen, the editor, Mark had goals that conflicted with most of the staff — especially the women. Mark consistently made rude, sexual remarks to many of the women on staff. In addition, he would ask for their ideas about articles, but he would never use them. Because he was disorganized, the magazine copy would be rushed at the last possible minute to Karen, who would have to work all night to meet the deadline. Karen concluded that Mark's "professional and sexual immaturity" was the cause of all the magazine's problems. Karen also concluded that the magazine was a success due to her diligence and editing skills. Mark attributed the success of the magazine to his creativity and hard work.

STUDENT AS OBSERVER: ATTRIBUTING CONFLICT

Although this project can be done alone, it also can be quite effective when working in pairs. Note that it will require honest disclosure if done in pairs. The goal is to have you locate the types of attributions you make about the conflicts you experience.

1. Write a paragraph that describes a recent conflict you have been involved in.
2. What was the event or behavior that began the conflict?
3. As best as you can, recall and write what occurred in order. How did you respond? How did the other person respond next? Continue recalling and writing the exact exchanges.
4. Label both people's behavior using the tactics reported in Tables 13.3, 13.4, and 13.5.
5. What was the primary cause or explanation for this conflict?
6. Look at the nature of the primary cause:
   a. Was it internal or external? Stable or unstable? Global or isolated?
   b. Do you think the other person would make similar attributions about the conflict?
   c. Does the way in which the conflict was resolved affect the way you make attributions about the conflict's causes? How?
7. Generate other explanations of the cause for the conflict that are more positive.
8. Do you think that these alternative explanations might have led you to select different conflict management behaviors?

He realized that he had a few conflicts with the staff, but problems with his staff were seen as part of the pressure to meet deadlines, and they were isolated issues that changed from staff member to staff member.

Compared to satisfied couples, dissatisfied couples perceive the causes of negative events as internal to the partner, stable, and global; but dissatisfied couples perceive the cause of positive events as external to the partner, unstable, and less global (Fincham, Bradbury, & Scott, 1990). In the story just presented, Karen attributed the causes of her conflict to Mark, and these attributions were internal, stable, and global. But Mark perceived the causes of conflict with his staff as external (deadlines) and isolated (varying from person to person).

Several reasons explain why people tend to blame others for their negative encounters. People cannot know their partners' motives (Thomas & Pondy, 1977). In this light, we cannot experience the external demands other people are experiencing. In addition, people are focused more on the partner than on themselves during interaction, and this external focus leads to overattributing responsibility to the partner (Storms, 1973). That is, the cause for the partner's behavior is seen as internal, but the causes for our own behavior are seen as more external. A final reason we attribute the causes of negative conflicts to others is the self-serving bias — we do not want to believe that we are capable of negative actions, so we attribute the causes to others ("I don't want to call you all those nasty names, but you force me to every time you get me so upset"). Again, the irony is that both parties to the conflict are making similar attributions (it's the other guy's fault).

Relational Consequences

Besides affecting causal attributions, conflict messages affect fundamental relational features. One very important relational feature is satisfaction. The research findings reveal that, in general, integrative tactics are positively associated with relational satisfaction, but distributive and avoidant tactics are negatively associated with relational satisfaction (e.g., Sillars, 1980a). Researchers have also found that the use of integrative behaviors appears to be linked to increases in trust, commitment to the relationship, and cooperation (e.g., Canary & Cupach, 1988; Canary & Spitzberg, 1989; Sillars et al., 1983).

Gottman and Krokoff (1989) obtained an interesting result. These authors found that expressions of conflict, including showing anger, were negatively associated with relational satisfaction when conflict and satisfaction were measured at the same time. But reports of satisfaction taken three years later were positively associated with the previous confrontational conflicts and were negatively associated with whining and withdrawal (especially when the husband whines or withdraws). Gottman and Krokoff suggest that husbands should express their feelings openly and that wives should encourage such expressions and discourage avoidance to keep a relationship satisfactory in the long run. However, in a study of lesbian, gay male, and heterosexual couples, Kurdek (1994) found that confrontational remarks were negatively related to relational stability and satisfaction measured one to two years later, regardless of couples' sexual preference.

When does the expression of anger appear to function positively for the partners? The answer probably lies in the way in which relational partners interpret expressions of anger. It appears that conflict behaviors are first interpreted during the conflict episode, and these interpretations then affect the character of the relationship. More specifically, people determine how satisfied they are with the conversation and how competently their partners managed the conflict. These episode-specific judgments then affect the character of the relationships, as several studies have found (for reviews of this phenomenon, see Canary, Cupach, & Serpe, 2001; Spitzberg, Canary, & Cupach, 1994).

That evaluations of the partner's conflict behavior affect relational outcomes has two implications. First, in most of these studies, appropriateness and effectiveness are used as criteria to judge the acceptability of the partner's conflict behavior (see also Chapter 16). It is not enough that the partner is appropriate; he or she should also be effective. Likewise, even though the partner may be effective, the person could still violate relational rules (perhaps through the use of distributive tactics) and thus be seen as inappropriate. Both appropriateness and effectiveness are criteria we use to judge others' conflict messages. Second, behaviors that contribute to these competence criteria may change from relationship to relationship. What is appropriate and effective in one conflict may not be in another.

Nevertheless, in most relationships and for most of the time, distributive conflict behaviors are viewed as incompetent, as reflecting stable and global problems, and as leading to loss of satisfaction with the partner and increased thoughts about separation and (if married) divorce; avoiding the partner also tends to be associated with perceptions of incompetence and declines in relational satisfaction; and integrative conflict behaviors are positively associated with perceptions of competence and relational satisfaction (e.g., Canary et al., 2001; Gottman, 1994; Kurdek, 1994). In brief, if you had to place a strategic bet, you would do well to engage in cooperative behavior.

CHAPTER SUMMARY

Conflict may lead to productive or destructive outcomes, depending on the communication behaviors used. Individuals have conflict styles, or tendencies to respond to conflict. Each style has its advantages and disadvantages. In specific conflicts, however, communicators must decide how they want to deal with the conflicts at hand. Their decisions to confront or avoid and to cooperate or compete lead them to initiate particular strategies — integrative, distributive, and avoidance strategies. These strategies are reflected in specific conflict tactics and patterns of interaction. The literature suggests that people in functional relationships do not reciprocate negative, distributive tactics; they are moderately spontaneous; and they do not fix on a single issue or discuss many different issues in a given conflict.

The causes of negative conflicts are generally attributed to the partner, and dissatisfied couples see these conflicts as internal to the partner, stable, and global. In general, integrative tactics are associated positively with relational satisfaction, and distributive and avoidance tactics are associated negatively with relational satisfaction. In addition, people assess their partners' conflict behaviors according to standards of appropriateness and effectiveness, and these evaluations also affect the relationship. Although the relationship is affected by conflict messages and attributions about the conflict, the nature of the relationship (satisfying versus dissatisfying, high or low in trust, etc.) probably then leads to the choices of communication behavior in future conflicts.

KEY TERMS

▼

accommodating style, p. 412
avoidance strategy, p. 417
collaborating style, p. 412
competing style, p. 412
compromising style, p. 412
conflict, p. 411
continuity, p. 419
distributive strategy, p. 417
exit, p. 424
globality, p. 428
integrative strategy, p. 417

intrapsychic conflict, p. 411
loyalty, p. 424
metacommunication, p. 422
neglect, p. 424
spontaneity, p. 424
stability, p. 428
stationarity, p. 422
symmetry, p. 420
variety, p. 418
voice, p. 424
withdrawing style, p. 412

EXERCISES FOR FURTHER DISCUSSION

▼

1. Examine the advantages and disadvantages of the various conflict styles described in Table 13.1.
   a. Can you think of any advantages and disadvantages that you would add to this table?
   b. What style do you use most frequently in your personal relationships?
   c. What are the advantages and disadvantages of the style you use?
2. Working with another person in your class, role-play how you would respond to each of the messages presented in Table 13.2. Now switch roles and allow the other class member to respond to you. After completing the role playing, revise each of the messages to be less threatening; then repeat the role playing and see if you were effective.

3. Review the discussion of the strategies of avoidance, integrative, and distributive tactics.
    a. What are the advantages and disadvantages of each?
    b. Do you think that people decide to use these strategies during conflict, or do they just occur?
    c. If you were to choose one of these strategies as a way of handling all conflicts, which one would you choose? Try to justify your choice by providing examples of how it would be effective in a range of situations.
4. Note the various ways in which conflict unfolds according to patterns of variety, continuity, symmetry, stationarity, and spontaneity.
    a. Does one of your relationships involve the use of any of these patterns?
    b. Do you think you can recognize such patterns of conflict as they unfold?
5. Using Rusbult's typology of exit-voice-loyalty-neglect, examine the communication behavior of a television character's way of handling relational troubles (a soap opera character would work well for this exercise).
    a. Do this character's behaviors fit within Rusbult's typology?
    b. Do the character's responses to relational problems seem realistic?
    c. In what ways do the character's behaviors differ from the ones you and your friends use? Why do you think you might use different behaviors?
6. Try to identify rules that you have for managing conflict. These might not be rules that you have consciously articulated before but just ideas that govern your sense of fair play. Working with a group of class members, discuss the rules you came up with, and see if you can agree on five rules that all of you would use to govern conflict.

SUGGESTED READING

▼

REVIEWS

Cahn, D. (1992). *Conflict in intimate relationships*. New York: Guilford. Cahn reviews research findings and methods used from different theoretical perspectives. Cahn emphasizes marital conflict and mediation.

Gottman, J. M. (1994). *What predicts divorce*. Hillsdale, NJ: Erlbaum. A very intriguing, though technical, portrayal of how negative conflict behaviors lead to hostile attributions, which then lead to relational instability.

STRATEGIES AND TACTICS

Sillars, A. L., & Wilmot, W. W. (1994). Communication strategies in conflict and mediation. In J. Wiemann & J. Daly (Eds.), *Communicating strategically: Strategies in interpersonal communication*. Hillsdale, NJ: Erlbaum. As the title indicates, various approaches for managing conflict are reviewed. Major sections on various structural features of conflict patterns and on mediation are included.

ATTRIBUTIONS IN CONFLICT

Bradbury, T. N., & Finchman, F. D. (1990). Attributions in marriage: Review and critique. *Psychological Bulletin, 107*, 3–33. This article extensively reviews how people make attributions in marriage. Emphasis is placed on how people make different kinds of attributions about conflicts depending on whether they are in a satisfying or unsatisfying marriage.

Sillars, A. L. (1980). Attributions and communication in roommate conflicts. *Communication Monographs, 47*, 180–200. An interesting study is conducted on how roommate attributions are linked to their communication behavior. Cooperative and competitive behaviors were found to differ according to the types of attributions made about the conflict.

RECENT RESEARCH

Two issues of the *Journal of Social and Personal Relationships* were devoted to the topic of relationship conflict. To read some of the latest research on the topic, readers are advised to look at these: *Journal of Social and Personal Relationships, 17* (4–5), pp. 475–704.

REFERENCE LIST

▼

Benoit, P. J., & Benoit, W. E. (1990). To argue or not to argue. In R. Trapp & J. Schuetz (Eds.), *Perspectives on argumentation: Essays in honor of Wayne Brockriede* (pp. 55–72). Prospect Heights, IL: Waveland.

Berkowitz, L. (1993). Towards a general theory of anger and emotional aggression: Implications of the cognitive-neoassociationistic perspective for the analysis of anger and other emotions. In R. S. Wyer, Jr. & T. K. Srull (Eds.), *Perspectives on anger and emotion: Advances in social cognition* (Vol. VI, pp. 1–46). Hillsdale, NJ: Erlbaum.

Berryman-Fink, C., & Brunner, C. C. (1987). The effects of sex of source and target on interpersonal conflict management styles. *Southern Speech Communication Journal, 33*, 38–48.

Bradbury, T. N., & Fincham, F. D. (1990). Attributions in marriage: Review and critique. *Psychological Bulletin, 107*, 3–33.

Burggraf, C. S., & Sillars, A. L. (1987). A critical examination of sex differences in marriage. *Communication Monographs, 54*, 276–294.

Cahn, D. (1992). *Conflict in intimate relationships.* New York: Guilford.

Canary, D. J., Cunningham, E. M., & Cody, M. J. (1988). Goal types, gender, and locus of control in managing interpersonal conflicts. *Communication Research, 15*, 426–446.

434

Canary, D. J., & Cupach, W. R. (1988). Relational and episodic characteristics associated with conflict tactics. *Journal of Social and Personal Relationships, 5,* 305–322.

Canary, D. J., Cupach, W. R., & Messman, S. J. (1995). *Relationship conflict: Conflict in parent-child, friendship, and romantic relationships.* Thousand Oaks, CA: Sage.

Canary, D. J., Cupach, W. R., & Serpe, R. (2001). A competence-based approach to examining interpersonal conflict: Test of a longitudinal model. *Communication Research, 28,* 79–104.

Canary, D. J., & Spitzberg, B. H. (1989). A model of the perceived competence of conflict tactics. *Human Communication Research,* 15, 630–649.

Canary, D. J., & Spitzberg, B. H. (1990). Attribution biases and associations between conflict strategies and competence outcomes. *Communication Monographs, 57,* 139–151.

Caughlin, J. P., & Vangelisti, A. L. (2000). An individual difference explanation of why married couples engage in demand/withdrawal pattern of conflict. *Journal of Social and Personal Relationships, 17,* 523–551.

Cody, M. J., McLaughlin, M. L., & Schneider, M. J. (1981). The impact of intimacy and relational consequences on the selection of interpersonal persuasion strategies: A reanalysis. *Communication Quarterly, 29,* 91–106.

Cupach, W. R. (1982). *Communication satisfaction and interpersonal solidarity as outcomes of conflict message strategy use.* Paper presented at the International Communication Association conference, Boston.

Deutsch, M. (1973). *The resolution of conflict: Constructive and destructive processes.* New Haven, CT: Yale University Press.

Fincham, F. D., Bradbury, T. N., & Scott, C. K. (1990). Cognition in marriage: Retrospect and prospect. In F. D. Fincham & T. N. Bradbury (Eds.), *Cognition in marriage: Basic issues and applications* (pp. 118–119). New York: Guilford.

Gottman, J. M. (1982). Emotional responsiveness in marital conversations. *Journal of Communication, 32,* 108–120.

Gottman, J. M. (1994). *What predicts divorce? The relationship between marital processes and marital outcomes.* Hillsdale, NJ: Erlbaum.

Gottman, J. M., & Krokoff, L. J. (1989). Marital interaction and satisfaction: A longitudinal view. *Journal of Consulting and Clinical Psychology, 57,* 47–52.

Hocker, J. L., & Wilmot, W. W. (1985). *Interpersonal conflict* (2nd ed.). Dubuque, IA: Brown.

Hocker, J. L., & Wilmot, W. W. (1991). *Interpersonal conflict* (3rd ed.). Dubuque, IA: Brown.

Kilmann, R. H., & Thomas, K. W. (1977). Developing a forced-choice measure of conflict-handling behavior: The MODE instrument. *Educational and Psychological Measurement, 37,* 309–325.

Kim, M-S., & Leung, T. (2000). A multicultural view of conflict management styles: Review and critical synthesis. In M. E. Roloff (Ed.), *Communication yearbook 23* (pp. 227–269). Thousand Oaks, CA: Sage.

Krueger, D. L., & Smith, R. (1982). Decision-making patterns of couples: A sequential analysis. *Journal of Communication, 32,* 121–134.

Kurdek, L. A. (1994). Conflict resolution styles in gay, lesbian, heterosexual nonparent, and heterosexual parent couples. *Journal of Marriage and the Family, 56,* 705–722.

Marshall, L. I. (1994). Physical and psychological abuse. In W. R. Cupach & B. H. Spitzberg (Eds.), *The dark side of interpersonal communication* (pp. 281–311). Hillsdale, NJ: Erlbaum.

Metts, S., & Cupach, W. R. (1990). The influence of relationship beliefs and problem-solving responses on satisfaction in romantic relationships. *Human Communication Research, 17*, 170–185.

Ohbuchi, K-I., & Tedeschi, J. T. (1997). Multiple goals and tactical behaviors in social conflicts. *Journal of Applied Social Psychology, 27*, 2177–2199.

Putnam, L. L., & Poole, M. S. (1987). Conflict and negotiation. In F. M. Jablin, L. L. Putnam, K. H. Roberts, & L. W. Porter (Eds.), *Handbook of organizational communication: An interdisciplinary perspective* (pp. 549–599). Newbury Park, CA: Sage.

Putnam, L. L., & Wilson, C. E. (1982). Communication strategies in organizational conflicts: Reliability and validity of a measurement scale. In M. Burgoon (Ed.), *Communication yearbook 6* (pp. 629–652). Newbury Park, CA: Sage.

Rahim, M. A. (1986). *Managing conflict in organizations*. New York: Praeger.

Rusbult, C. E. (1987). Responses to dissatisfaction in close relationships: The exit-voice-loyalty-neglect model. In D. Perlman & S. W. Duck (Eds.), *Intimate relationships: Development, dynamics, and deterioration* (pp. 209–237). Newbury Park, CA: Sage.

Rusbult, C. E., Johnson, D. J., & Morrow, G. D. (1986a). Impact of couple patterns of problem solving on distress and nondistress in dating relationships. *Journal of Social and Personal Relationships, 50*, 744–753.

Rusbult, C. E., Johnson, D. J., & Morrow, G. D. (1986b). Predicting satisfaction and commitment in adult romantic involvements: An assessment of the generalizability of the investment model. *Social Psychological Quarterly, 49*, 81–89.

Rusbult, C. E., Olsen, N., Davis, J. L., Hanson, P. A. (2001). Commitment and relationship maintenance mechanisms. In J. H. Harvey & A. Wenzel (Eds.), *Close romantic relationships: maintenance and enhancement* (pp. 87–113). Mahwah, NJ: Erlbaum.

Sillars, A. L. (1980a). Attributions and communication in roommate conflicts. *Communication Monographs, 47*, 180–200.

Sillars, A. L. (1980b). The sequential and distributional structure of conflict interactions as a function of attributions concerning the locus of responsibility and stability of conflicts. In D. Nimmo (Ed.), *Communication yearbook 4* (pp. 217–235). New Brunswick, NJ: Transaction Books.

Sillars, A. L., Coletti, S. F., Parry, D., & Rogers, M. A. (1982). Coding verbal conflict tactics: Nonverbal and perceptual correlates of the "avoidance-distributive-integrative" distinction. *Human Communication Research, 9*, 83–95.

Sillars, A. L., Pike, G. R., Jones, T. S., & Redmon, K. (1983). Communication and conflict in marriage. In R. N. Bostrom (Ed.), *Communication yearbook 7* (pp. 414–429). Newbury Park, CA: Sage.

Sillars, A. L., Roberts, L. J., Leonard, K. E., & Dun, T. (2000). Cognition during marital conflict: The relationship of thought and talk. *Journal of Social and Personal Relationships, 17*, 479–502.

Sillars, A. L., & Weisberg, J. (1987). Conflict as a social skill. In M. E. Roloff & G. R. Miller (Eds.), *Interpersonal processes: New directions in communication research* (pp. 140–171). Newbury Park, CA: Sage.

Sillars, A. L., & Wilmot, W. W. (1994). Communication strategies in conflict and mediation. In J. Wiemann & J. Daly (Eds.), *Communicating strategically: Strategies in interpersonal communication* (pp. 163–190). Hillsdale, NJ: Erlbaum.

436

Spitzberg, B. H. (1997). Violence in intimate relationships. In W. R. Cupach & D. J. Canary (Eds.), *Competence in interpersonal conflict* (pp. 174–201). New York: McGraw-Hill.

Spitzberg, B. H., Canary, D. J., & Cupach, W. R. (1994). A competence-based approach to the study of interpersonal conflict. In D. Cahn (Ed.), *Conflict in intimate relationships* (pp. 183–202). Hillsdale, NJ: Erlbaum.

Storms, M. D. (1973). Videotape and the attribution process: Reversing actor's and observers' points of view. *Journal of Personality and Social Psychology, 27,* 165–175.

Thomas, K. W., & Pondy, L. R. (1977). Toward an "intent" model of conflict management among principal parties. *Human Relations, 30,* 1089–1103.

Ting-Toomey, S. (1983). An analysis of verbal communication patterns in high and low marital adjustment groups. *Human Communication Research, 9,* 306–319.

van de Vliert, E., & Euwema, M. C. (1994). Agreeableness and activeness as components of conflict behaviors. *Journal of Personality and Social Psychology, 66,* 674–687.

Yovetich, N. A., & Rusbult, C. E. (1994). Accommodation behaviors in close relationships: Exploring the transformation of motivation. *Journal of Experimental Social Psychology, 30,* 138–164.

CHAPTER 14

INTERPERSONAL

GOALS OVER TIME

INTERPERSONAL RELATIONSHIPS IN FAMILIES AND BEYOND

Attachment Theory

Intergenerational Solidarity Theory

A Comment on Families

Turning Points in Family Relationships

Consequences of Divorce

Turning Points after Divorce

Communication Processes in Becoming a Family

Socioemotional Selectivity Theory

SELF-PRESENTATION IN LATER YEARS

Self-Presentation and Negotiated Identities in Intergenerational Conversations

INTERGENERATIONAL FRIENDSHIPS

Friends and Mentors

CHAPTER SUMMARY

Sean:	Which one [job] did you take?
Will:	It's over at McNeil. It's one of the jobs the professor set up. I haven't told him yet. But I, I went down there and met my boss, my new boss. He seemed like a good guy.
Sean:	Is that what you want?
Will:	Yeah, you know. I think so.
Sean:	Good for you. Congratulations.
Will:	Thanks.

[Pause]

Sean:	Time's up.

[Pause]

Will:	So, that's . . . that's it. We're done?
Sean:	Yeah, that's it. You're done. You are a free man.
Will:	Ah, you know, I just want you to know, Sean . . .
Sean:	You're welcome, Will.

[Pause]

Will:	So, I, I hope we can keep in touch. . . .
Sean:	Me too. I plan on traveling around a bit and it will be hard. But I have an answering machine here at the college that I will be checking in with. Call that and I'll call you right away. [Pause] Well, I figure I'll put my money back on the table and see what kind of cards I get. You do what's in your heart, son. You will be fine.

[The two men hug.]

Will:	Thank you, Sean.
Sean:	Thank you, Will.

From *Good Will Hunting*, American film, 1999

This chapter reviews the literature on the importance of interpersonal goals spanning the 80+ years many of you will be living. Most of us start life in a family and our parents have a strong impact on our interpersonal relationships, as well as on our sense of family solidarity that will influence our behavior of giving and receiving assistance to family members for years to come. In this chapter we will also focus attention on a number of turning points in relationships with parents. One such event is parental divorce, which has a negative impact on children, especially daughters. We will see in this chapter that when so-called blended families are created, communication is fundamentally important over time as they become a family. Another important aspect of aging deals with how interpersonal goals change over the life span, with people focusing on quality interpersonal relationships and minimizing negative feelings as they get older. The last two sections of this chapter address the issue of self-presentation during an intergenerational conversation, and the value of intergenerational friendships and mentoring.

Throughout this chapter, many of the theories and communication processes discussed in earlier chapters will be discussed again, such as communication accommodation theory, self-presentation theory, friendship formation, and turning points. However, there are several unique aspects of studying interpersonal goals over the life span: We study how fathers and mothers influence children, how families form feelings of solidarity that influence their behavior for decades, what people value in life as they age, how people change their relationships and identities with parents as they age, and how people cope with their parents' divorce as well as with their own divorce.

INTERPERSONAL RELATIONSHIPS IN FAMILIES AND BEYOND

Attachment Theory

When we grow up, we learn a certain style of attachment with our parents or caregivers. According to Bowlby (1969), Ainsworth, Blehar, Waters, and Wall (1978), and Hazan and Shaver (1987), three **attachment styles** are developed in early infancy: secure, anxious/ambivalent, and avoidant. These styles continue to have an impact on us throughout our early adult years, influencing our interpersonal relationships, our ability to be and stay in love, and our skills in coping with conflict. When we are young, we are completely dependent on our parents' behavior, and their treatment of us is pervasive, continuous, and unchallenged for several years. We learn a system of "bonding" with others at an early age, and this style of bonding (or attachment) continues, for years, to influence our selection of dates, ideas about love, friendship, trusting others, and so forth.

The bonding developed with parents and caregivers depends on a complex set of factors including the parents' caregiving ability, the child's temperament, and the family environment (Rosen & Rothbaum, 1993). Thus divorce itself does not cause any one particular attachment style to be instilled in children (but see below regarding effects of divorce). Hayashi and Strickland (1998) found that the most important predictor of feeling secure in a romantic relationship as an adult is whether the person grew up with at least one accepting parent who encouraged independence. College students reported more fear of being abandoned if their parent or parent-substitute was rejecting or overprotective, or if their biological parents argued frequently. Roughly 55% to 65% of college students report being "secure," 20% to 30% are "avoidant," and roughly 10% to 20% are "anxious/ambivalent."

Hazan and Shaver (1987) provide a simple way of identifying attachment styles. Table 14.1 lists the possible responses to these researchers' single question: "Which of the following best describes your feelings?" Collins and Read (1990) and Bartholomew (1990; Bartholomew & Horowitz, 1991; Guerrero, 1996; Scharfe & Bartholomew, 1995) provide additional measurement methods.

Secure people are described as being comfortable with intimacy and closeness, prepared to trust and depend on others, and able to acknowledge distress and ask for support (Ognibene & Collins, 1998). They also view themselves as more likable, lovable, good-natured, and friendly, and they see significant others as being generally well intentioned, reliable, and trustworthy. They recall positive experiences of their early family relationships (Feeney & Noller, 1990). If you selected Option 1 in Table 14.1, you are a secure type.

Table 14.1
HAZAN AND SHAVER'S ATTACHMENT STYLE MEASURE

Question: Which of the following best describes your feelings?

1. I find it relatively easy to get close to others and am comfortable depending on them and having them depend on me. I don't often worry about being abandoned or about someone's getting too close to me.
2. I am somewhat uncomfortable being close to others; I find it difficult to trust them, difficult to allow myself to depend on them. I am nervous when anyone gets too close, and love partners often want me to be more intimate than I feel comfortable being.
3. I find that others are reluctant to get as close as I would like. I often worry that my partner doesn't really love me or won't want to stay with me. I want to merge completely with another person, and this desire sometimes scares people away.

Source: Hazan & Shaver, 1987, p. 515, Table 2. Used with permission from the American Psychological Association.

442

If you selected Option 2 in Table 14.1, you are an **avoidantly** attached person who hides feelings of insecurity. You fear intimacy, dismiss distress, and find it difficult to depend on others. Avoidant people often do not trust others, and they prefer independence, self-reliance, and emotional distance. They are more likely to report childhood separation from their mothers and to express mistrust of others (Feeney & Noller, 1990). Because avoidant people place less emphasis on relational closeness, it is not surprising that avoidant men display less distress and unhappiness when relationships end (Simpson, 1990).

Other children grow up with a certain amount of anxiety because they are afraid of being abandoned and need reassurances from others (Option 3). The **anxious/ ambivalent** individual is fairly comfortable with closeness but is worried about being abandoned and unloved (Collins & Read, 1990). Anxious individuals experience more emotional highs and lows in their relationships, experience more jealousy, and are more obsessively preoccupied with their partners. They report a desire for a deep commitment in relationships (Feeney & Noller, 1990).

Attachment styles are related to how we cope with conflict, behave nonverbally during interactions, fall in love, date, and form satisfying relationships. Both Levy and Davis (1988) and Pistole (1989) found secure types reported more reliance on compromising and integrative tactics (see Chapter 13 for definitions) compared to both avoidant and anxious/ambivalent individuals. Levy and Davis (1988) also found that anxious/ambivalent types relied on more "dominating" tactics in conflict, but Pistole (1989) found that anxious/ambivalents were more obliging. One way to interpret the use of both dominating tactics (Levy & Davis, 1988) and obliging tactics (Pistole, 1989) rests in the fact that anxious individuals experience more emotional highs and lows in their relationships; hence they may be more obliging or more dominating, depending on the current status of the relationship. Among newlyweds, Senchak and Leonard (1992) found that secure individuals relied less on withdrawal and verbal aggression than others.

Attachment styles are related to nonverbal expressions as well. Guerrero (1996) sampled couples, videotaped their interactions, and had coders assess the extent to which individuals displayed intimacy and involvement. The couples represented four attachment styles, including secure, preoccupied (similar to the anxious/ambivalent style), and two avoidant styles — fearful avoidant and dismissive. Individuals with preoccupied styles are affiliative and needy in their relationships; they crave attention and love. People who exhibit the two types of avoidant styles differ in their motivation. Fearful avoidant individuals seek relational intimacy, but fear rejection and distrust others. Dismissive individuals are self-reliant and indifferent — they neither desire nor fear close attachments, and they are unmotivated to work on relationships. Guerrero found that secure and preoccupied (anxious/ambivalent) people displayed greater trust/receptivity, eye gaze, facial pleasantness, and general interest in others, and they were more attentive than either fearful avoidant or dismissive people. Preoccupied individuals also engage in more in-depth conversations than dismissive individuals. Fearful avoidant people sat farthest from others and displayed, as do others high in anxiety, low levels of speech fluency and longer response latencies. Both pre-occupied and fearful avoidant people were the most "vocally nervous."

Guerrero (1996) not only demonstrated how attachment styles are related to communication performance, the results also suggested how styles might be related to maintaining and reinforcing beliefs about others. That is, avoidant individuals (both dismissive and fearful avoidant) communicate low levels of attentiveness, interest, and positive affect. If partners matched or reciprocated these levels, avoidant individuals — because of their own styles of communicating — would create and maintain a world in which they saw others as inattentive, negative, and uninterested in them. This is a form of self-fulfilling prophecy, which was discussed in Chapter 2.

Levy and Davis (1988) found that secure types were more likely to experience eros love (erotic love based on attraction) and agape love (selfless love, see Chapter 10), and they were less likely to report experiencing ludus love (game playing, related to relational dissatisfaction). Avoidant types, however, were more likely to report ludus love, and anxious/ambivalent individuals were more likely to experience mania love (obsessive, high need for attention and affection). Collins and Read (1990) reported that secure types also engaged in less "game playing" (ludus) and were more selfless in "loves." Levy and Davis (1988) also found that secure types score higher on all three aspects of love as measured by Sternberg's (1986) scale; secure types scored high on intimacy, high on passion, and high on commitment.

Attachment styles are also related to who interacts with whom, how the interactions unfold, who dates whom, and who marries whom (Collins & Read, 1990; Feeney & Noller, 1996; Le Poire et al., 1997; Le Poire, Shepard, & Duggan, 1999; Senchak & Leonard, 1992; Simpson, 1990). It appears that secure people largely date and marry other secure people, and that insecure people (either anxious/ambivalent or avoidant) date and marry other insecure people. Secure people also reported higher relational satisfaction (Pistole, 1989).

Finally, the attachment styles instilled and maintained in us when we are young can continue to influence us later in life when we and our parental caregivers age. Cicirelli (1991; 1993; see Williams & Nussbaum, 2001) advanced a **life-span attachment theory,** which holds that while it is true we leave home and become more autonomous and less dependent on parents, attachment styles developed early in life are important both when we communicate with our older parents and when parents and their adult children turn to each other in times of need. First, as children move out of the house and away from the parents, a mechanism of symbolic attachment emerges, and through this symbolic representation the adult child can engage in imagined conversation with the parental caregiver and sustain the attachment style; for example, gain a feeling of comfort, support, and closeness if the style developed was a secure style. The imagined conversation, coupled with actual conversations, e-mail, phone contact, and letters and evoked memories of growing up sustain a particular attachment style.

Second, as family members age, they continue to have needs that other family members help to satisfy. Parents continue to provide assistance and aid to adult children for decades and through a number of turning points (see below: "Turning

Points in Family Relationships" and "Turning Points after Divorce") — when the adult child is married, when the grandchildren are born, and so forth. Later in life, adult children are called upon to be the caregivers of the parents. It is expected that children will provide assistance to their parents, especially when they are aged and become increasingly dependent. A substantial body of literature on the support giving between parents and children provides strong support for *lagged reciprocity* — defined as support given to the older parent(s) as part of the fulfillment of an obligation to repay a social debt based on the parents' earlier investments in the child (Silverstein, Conroy, Wang, Giarrusso, & Bengston, 2002). There are three explanations for the reciprocity in parent-child support. First, social exchange scholars have long advocated that the norm of reciprocity is a principle of obligation to repay that includes the exchange of assets, services, and/or sentiments (see Silverstein et al., 2002). Approval, affirmation, and social support are to be reciprocated just as favors, loans, and more tangible gifts are to be repaid later. This application of social exchange theory involves two predictions: (1) adult children should repay parents for support given to them earlier in life, and (2) the repayment to parents should be proportional to what they received. This is the *return on investment* model of intergenerational support.

A second model of intergenerational support is called the *insurance policy* model, and it holds that support received by the child earlier in life is repaid or recovered by the parent under conditions of need. Antonucci (1990) uses a bank metaphor in her work arguing that a support bank symbolically serves as a repository of equity parents pay into using both economic, tangible investments as well as emotional and affective contributions. Adult children can repay the parents at any time, but especially do so when the parents have needs. At any one time, there may be (and will be) an imbalance in the bank, a situation of inequity, depending upon the timing and type of need being fulfilled. The insurance model holds that children's return of support for the parents would be (1) proportional to the perceived contributions they received, and (2) paid back when the parents were in their greatest need.

Both of the above models rely on social exchange theory. The third model relies on the pure altruistic feelings family members have for one another to provide support for one another when a person is in need. According to the *altruism* model, adult children will provide support for aging parents regardless of how much or how little the parents invested in the children during earlier years. More support would be given to parents when they are frail, extremely sick, or extremely old; that is, help is offered to those in need.

Silverstein and colleagues (2002), using a unique data set tracking multiple generations over years, found support for each of the models, but at different times in the life span. Strong support was obtained for the return on investment model: Children who spent more time in shared activities with the parents in 1971 returned more support to the parents later in life. Support was also obtained for the insurance policy model in that financial assistance invested in the child earlier in life was repaid to the parents when the parents were aging. The reason for this is that the parents most likely to provide support early in the child's life may have financial resources to maintain financial independence until very late in life. Finally, the most consistent finding was that the amount of support provided to parents increased with age — even when the early parent-child relationship was emotionally distant and parents had committed neither time nor financial support to the child. When parents were sufficiently old and needy, the adult children provided assistance.

In sum, when we are very young, we learn to bond with or attach to others. Secure types, the most common among college students, grew up in supporting environments, recalling positive experiences and positive interactions with at least one caregiver. They learned to trust and depend on others, and they give and seek more social support in times of stress. Attachment styles are related to different styles of love. The life-span attachment theory extends this to child-parent attachment over decades, with parents providing more support for their children receiving more support in return, and with parents being helped by children as age increases.

Intergenerational Solidarity Theory

Intergenerational solidarity theory focuses on the process of communication among family members and the level of closeness among family members experienced in daily life. A sense of familial identity is created and maintained, family members engage in particular roles, enact particular behaviors, and participate in a familiar family life. Family solidarity is maintained for a long period of time, influencing individuals for decades. For example, the extent to which children are integrated into the activities at home and with family networks can have a significant effect on the child's level of self-esteem for over two decades (Yabiku, Axinn, & Thornton, 1999).

A particular model of intergenerational solidarity advocated by Vern Bengtson and his colleagues has received considerable attention over the years (Bengtson, 2001; Bengtson & Roberts, 1991; Lawton, Silverstein, & Bengtson, 1994; Parrott & Bengtson, 1999; Roberts & Bengtson, 1990; Silverstein & Long, 1998; Whitbeck, Hoyt, & Huck, 1994). The construct *solidarity* consists of six dimensions or perceptions (see Bengtson & Roberts, 1991).

The first is **associational solidarity** and involves (1) the frequency of intergenerational contact (e-mail, mail, telephone, face-to-face) and (2) types of common activities shared between family members (vacations, special occasions, etc.). The second, **affectual solidarity,** involves (1) feelings of affection, warmth, closeness, understanding, trust, and so forth, each member feels for the other and (2) perceived reciprocity of feelings experienced among family members. **Consensual solidarity** involves (1) the amount of agreement among family members in terms of specific values, attitudes, and beliefs and (2) ratings of perceived similarity in specific values, attitudes, and beliefs. **Functional solidarity** involves (1) the frequency of intergenerational exchanges of assistance (financial, physical, emotional) and (2) perceived reciprocity of exchanges. Functional solidarity can be "high" to the extent to which family members give assistance and provide resources to one another; and functional solidarity can also be described as "balanced" (or, conversely, "imbalanced") if there is reciprocity in the exchange of assistance and resources are equal and equitable, although different resources (money, love, emotional support, etc.) could be exchanged by different

446

people at different times. What is important is the perception that the exchanges of assistance and resources are balanced. **Normative solidarity** taps into the perceptions of the strength of the commitment to familial roles by having family members (1) rate the importance of family roles and (2) rate the strength of family obligations. Finally, **structural solidarity** involves (1) the extent to which family members live close to one another, (2) the number of family members there are, and (3) the health of the family members. Structural solidarity is high when there is an increased opportunity for routine or frequent intergenerational interactions — there are a number of family members, many living near one another, and many who are sufficiently healthy to interact.

Bengtson and his colleagues have proposed a theory of intergenerational solidarity that they have been developing, for years. In Bengtson's model (see Bengtson & Roberts, 1991) *normative solidarity* plays an extremely important role. Some families develop a strong commitment to the family unit and feel committed to performing their roles as grandmother, grandfather, father, mother, and so on. Previous communication coupled with frequency of contact help to instill a strong sense of familism in the younger family members. The first proposition of the theory simply states that when parents and children develop a strong sense of normative solidarity (a strong sense of norms of familism), there will be a high degree of parent-child affect and association (*affectual solidarity* and *associational solidarity*). That is, in families with a strong commitment to one another and to the family unit and family roles, there exists an increased feeling of warmth, affection, trust, and respect, as well as more frequent contact through face-to-face meetings, telephone, or mail. In families where there is a weaker commitment to the family unit and to family roles, there is less warmth, affection, trust, and respect, and less frequent associations. When there exist high levels of normative solidarity, high levels of affectual solidarity, and high levels of associational solidarity, then there is likely to be increased *consensual solidarity*, wherein family members share similar values, attitudes, and beliefs.

The second important proposition of the Bengtson model is that perceptions of balance in intergenerational exchanges have a positive impact on feelings of parent-child affection (affectual solidarity) and on future interaction (associational solidarity). Thus, when exchanges in money, assistance, and social support are balanced and family members reciprocate these resources, affection for others is increased and frequency of contact is increased. Alternatively, when these resources are not shared in a balanced manner, and there is less reciprocity, then there is less affection and infrequent contact between family members.

The third proposition states that when there is a greater opportunity for intergenerational interaction, there will be greater association between parent and child. When structural solidarity is high, as when family members live close to one another, family members are healthy, and there are a number of family members with which to interact, then there will be an increase in actual, real interactions. On the other hand, when a generation ages sufficiently to become less able to travel and/or more family members move to various locations, and there is less of an opportunity for interaction, there will be a significant decrease in actual associations between family members. Hopefully, training older individuals to use the Internet will help to make them more connected with family members and enable them to associate with family members despite long distances and the decrease in mobility people experience as they age (Cody, Dunn, Hoppin, & Wendt, 1999).

The fourth proposition states that affection between child and parent will result in more frequent contact between adult children and parents (affectual solidarity is related to associational solidarity). Further, affection for one family member is likely to be mutually reciprocated and mutually reinforcing; the more affection the child feels and communicates to the parent, the more the parent will feel and communicate affection for the child. The love one gives is equal to the love one receives (to paraphrase the Beatles). On the other hand, when, in some families, there is little felt affectual solidarity, there is less motivation to maintain high levels of associational solidarity.

Several studies have found that familism (normatively solidarity) and affectual solidarity influence the amount of instrumental assistance (transportation, health care assistance when parents are ill) and emotional support (Parrott & Bengtson, 1999; Whitbeck et al., 1994). A history of an affectionate relationship with a parent was associated with more overall support given to the parent, more expressive forms of support, and to equitable and reciprocal exchanges of support (Parrott & Bengtson, 1999). Not surprisingly, high affection in the past is often related to more support in the present. However, when the adult children had little affection for their parents, they were more likely to become involved in obligatory exchanges that helped the ailing or sick parent in time of need. However, in some families adult children may develop a strong sense of familism (normative solidarity), and they would feel obligated to help their fathers in a time of need, even if they received little financial or expressive support from their fathers during earlier years. In this situation, some adult children gave help and assistance to their aging father that exceeded what they had received from the father. Fortunately, Parrott and Bengtson (1999) found that earlier conflicts between the adult child and parent did not interfere with the amount or type of help and support given later in life. Most of the conflict episodes were set aside and not used when making decisions to offer support, or to withhold support.

Lawton and colleagues (1994) found a reciprocal association between affection with mother and frequency of contact with mother (especially if living close at hand); that is, the more mothers and adult children see each other, the greater affection they have for one another. Reciprocal effects were not observed for fathers, however. Increased feelings of affection for father did not translate into increased contact for fathers as it did for mothers. There could be two reasons for this outcome. First, mothers may view the frequency of contact as a test of the quality of the relationship and are likely to be motivated to reinforce the quality of the relationship and the amount of affect in the relationship more consistently than fathers, and this role as a "kin keeper" is one "traditionally adopted by female family members" (Lawton et al., p. 66). Father–adult child interactions may be more instrumental and less relationally driven for fathers and for the adult child. Second, parental divorce has a devastating impact on the father–adult child relationship. Divorce not only reduces affection (for both parents), but also reduces affection for fathers over time due to decrease in contact (also see below: "Consequences of Divorce").

Intergenerational solidarity theory provides a framework for viewing relationships between family members over decades, and helps to explain affect, contact, providing instrumental aid and assistance to one another, and shared values, attitudes, and beliefs among family members. As a general rule, family members offer assistance (functional solidarity) to others when affectual solidarity and normative solidarity is high. Associational solidarity is high when affectual solidarity is high and when there is an increased opportunity for contact (structural solidarity is high).

A Comment on Families

Families are based on biological ties, or kinship. However, some groups have a much more expansive idea of what constitutes a family. For many people the family is the most important group, but this group is embedded in a larger network of relationships. Research indicates that various ethnic groups utilize these social networks differently. African Americans, for example, are much more likely to define the boundaries of their families flexibly to include *fictive kin* (referred to in different communities as "play" relatives or "godmother" and "godfather") and to upgrade more distant kin into the status of primary kin (see Johnson, 1999; Johnson & Barer, 1995). For some African Americans, the expanded definition of *family* to include various nieces, nephews, and unrelated adults such as aunts, means that members in such communities can significantly increase the number of family members who can be called upon to help older individuals. In fact, Johnson and Barer (1995) found that nearly half of all African American individuals who were childless could call upon nephews and others as family members to help them. Being integrated into a social network can have a positive impact on one's well-being and health, and reduce the risks of becoming lonely (Bondevik & Skogstad, 1998; Lennartsson, 1999). A new trend in the fields of communication and gerontology is to examine less traditional families (see the section "Communication Processes in Becoming a Family" later in this chapter; see also Allen & Demo, 1995; Allen & Olson, 2001; Kurdek, 1998; Roe & Minkler, 1999).

Turning Points in Family Relationships

The relationships we have with our mothers and fathers are unique, for many reasons. Most obviously, most of us will experience a range of intensely felt emotions over the years spanning birth to adulthood, including pride, anger, shame, joy, disappointment, and more. Second, we learn styles of attachment from parents (or the main caregiver), and these attachment styles remain with us for years as discussed earlier in the chapter. Third, we have expectations about the quality or closeness of our relationships with our parents that are largely due to societal expectations, media portrayals, and social comparisons with others who may have better or worse relationships with their parents than we do with ours. We may have a sense of pride due to the fact that we have a close, positive, and quality relationship with one or more parent, or we may experience a sense of disappointment if such a relationship is elusive, yet others have it. Fourth, relationships with parents are complex and enduring. Conflicts we have with friends, co-workers, and neighbors may result in an end to a relationship and termination of all contact. Some families who experience severe conflict may also witness a termination of contact lasting years, even decades, but there are expectations of resuming contact with family members, and many probably do.

There are turning points in family relationships, just as there are in other interpersonal relationships. Golish (2000) identified 10 common turning points in her study of parent–adult child relationships. Most young adults experienced 3.5 turning points with mothers and 3.6 turning points with fathers, although some young adults reported no events that altered their relationships with parents, and others reported as many as nine events that altered their relationships with parents. Turning points are important, because they mark a point in time in which the closeness of one's relationship to a parent changes, and there may be a comparable change in one's role (treated more as an adult, given greater autonomy, and so forth). These are times when an individual's image with their parents is likely to change. In the eyes of one's parents, a person can become more mature and competent, increase or decrease likability, become more, or less, dedicated and worthy, and so on.

The most common turning point was *physical distance*, which included moving out of the home or further away from the parents. This turning point was more likely to alter the relationship with the mother, who is the primary caregiver. For most people, this turning point altered the relationship with mothers more than with fathers. Typically, relational closeness is reduced, as there is less daily or weekly contact. However, parents may treat their adult child as more of an adult, more independent.

The second common turning point was *times of crises*, which included disruptions in normal family life, such as getting a divorce, illness and/or death in the family, unemployment, threats to safety, and conflict between parents (or one of them) and a person's spouse. During these crisis moments, some young adults felt closer to their parents, and those who felt closer also experienced a feeling of gratitude and appreciation for one's parents. When crisis moments resulted in a loss of closeness, a sense of loss and uncertainty were also experienced.

The third common turning point was called *communication* and refers to a change in the young adult's routine or habitual interactions with parents. These turning points involved the realization that one's parents were listening more to their children, involving their children in decision-making, spending more time communicating, communicating honestly, and communicating respect of their differences.

The fourth common turning point was called *rebellious teenager*, which involved a young adult expressing a need for more autonomy and independence, experimenting with adult activities (alcohol, etc.), and altering one's role in the family, such as taking care of younger siblings. These turning points were more likely to affect the person's relationship with the mother, who often is the disciplinarian and manages household duties and family rules.

The fifth common turning point was called *engagement/marriage*, which included events in which the young adult commits to a serious relationship with another person. Depending on the parents' acceptance or rejection of the young adult's choice for marriage, there could be an increase or a decrease in closeness. On the other hand, a person's wedding day is often a time of increased closeness between parents and the young adult. Engagement or marriage to another often prompted the parents to treat their former adolescent as a more autonomous, independent, maturing adult.

The sixth common turning point involved having *children*, and a new child introduced into the family usually prompted an increase in closeness between parents (now grandparents) and their children for two reasons. First, grandparents desire to see their grandchild and, secondly, parents often depend on their grandparents in helping to take care of the new infant.

The seventh common turning point involved *activities together* shared by parents and children. These events included family vacations, attending sporting events together, spending more time together, and doing things together around the house or family business. Sharing special events and emotions, or working on tasks together reflects a time of increased closeness, especially in relationships with fathers. Mothers, according to Golish (2000), often expressed affection toward their children by talking, hugging, and kissing, while fathers showed greater closeness and affection by taking the child or children out to events (also see below regarding the gendered closeness perspective).

Three turning points identified by Golish (2000) were less frequently reported by respondents, compared to the seven just listed. The eighth turning point described was called *feelings of jealousy*, and involved the fact that as some people grow up they experience jealousy over how parents treat a sibling, and the jealous individual would similarly feel resentment and alienation from the parents. The ninth turning point, *alcohol/abuse*, describes a point in the relationship in which a person, usually the father, used or abused alcohol and this caused a change in family relationships. During this turning point, young adults experienced greater closeness with their mothers. The final turning point, *dating/cohabitation*, involved the young adult engaging in a serious dating relationship or cohabitation with someone. Involvement in a serious relationship with another could increase or decrease closeness with parents, depending on whether the father and/or mother approved or disapproved of the relationship; cohabitation usually resulted in a marked decrease in closeness with one's parents.

Golish (2000) also identified seven patterns of closeness in adult child–parent relationships. The most common pattern was the *single major disruption*. This pattern was characterized as a significant drop in closeness and a slow increase after the disruption, which was often a time of teenage rebellion, cohabitation, marrying someone the parents disapproved of, total lack of communication, sibling jealousy, death in the family, or a major fight. Eventually the adult child was able to reestablish much, but maybe not all, of the closeness experienced earlier. The *sustained, low to moderate degree of closeness* pattern was characterized as a low to moderate level of closeness with a parent, which only slightly increased or decreased over time. This pattern usually involved the relationship with one's father, since fathers are less likely to be the primary caregiver and are at home less. The *sustained, high degree of closeness* pattern often involved the relationship with one's mother, although some fathers also sustained high levels of closeness over time. The fourth pattern, *gradual increases in close-ness*, occurred when adult children realized that they experienced greater closeness with parents as they aged and matured (perhaps when parents were more established in their careers). The fifth pattern, *irregular cycle*, involved a dramatic series of ups and downs in the quality of the relationship as some events brought the child and parent closer together and some pulled them further apart. According to Golish, adult children who have a need to please their parents are more likely to experience this pattern than others; and the ups and downs reflect felt approval and disappoint-ment from one's parent. Finally, some adult children experience a *gradual decrease in closeness* as they slowly drift away from their parents, as time passes, as contact with them is lost, and as parents become less active or ill.

We should also note that there is growing evidence that mothers and fathers do not communicate affection in the same way. As noted earlier, mothers show affection by nonverbal and verbal strategies, while fathers show affection by attending events with the children. Morman and Floyd (1999; Floyd, 1995, 1996a, 1996b; Floyd & Parks, 1995) have argued in favor of a **gendered closeness perspective** of affection that holds that women express affection and closeness by use of overt tactics such as direct verbal statements and nonverbal expressions (hugging, kissing, saying "I love you"), while men communicate affection or closeness by sharing activities and involv-ing instrumental support (helping to fix or repair objects, helping a child achieve his or her goals) — being dependable, helpful, but detached. Morman and Floyd (1999) in fact found that both fathers and their sons communicated affection primarily through engaging in supporting actions, rather than by verbal expressions of affection or nonverbal expressions of affection. Cicirelli (1981, 1995) also found that when giv-ing assistance to aging parents, men prefer to engage in supporting activities and in-strumental support (helping to repair things, provide transportation, focus on bu-reaucratic and financial institutions for the aged parents), rather than show affection via emotional support, or personal care, which are needs women adult children fulfill, a finding that parallels the gendered closeness perspective.

More recently, Floyd and Morman (2000) found that the affection the son received from the father is systematically related to affection returned to the father from the son, and the amount of affection given and received corresponded to higher ratings of closeness, involvement, and satisfaction. Updegraff, Madden-Derdich, Estrada, Sales, and Leonard (2002) found that acceptance and open communication with one's father was significantly related to the adolescent boy's ability and skill in developing friend-ship intimacy, indicating that boys benefit from the opportunity to develop interper-sonal skills in their father-son interactions. However, these effects were found for Eu-ropean American families, but not necessarily for Latino American families, where the adolescent boys learn from being in a larger group setting (larger families).

Consequences of Divorce

Divorce disrupts the lives of the children, who may or may not cope adequately with changes in relationships. Parental divorce may affect family members in five possible ways. First, the children of divorced parents may be adversely influenced by parental divorce. Research indicates that children from divorced families lack trust in others, or, at least, claim to be less optimistic about their ability to trust a future spouse (Franklin, Janoff-Bulman, & Roberts, 1990; Jacquet & Surra, 2001; Sun, 2001). Second, the children from divorced families may be hesitant to show much commitment to a serious relationship for fear that it would not last (Wallerstein & Blakeslee, 1989). However, fear of commitment may dissipate as time passes (see Jacquet & Surra, 2001). Third, children from divorced families may be ambivalent about dating and falling in love; with the ambivalence stemming from the contradictory needs of attention and affection, on one hand, and fear of betrayal and abandonment on the other. Fourth, children from divorced families report less satisfaction and less happiness in general, and less satisfaction is derived from friendships, family life, and community (Allison & Furstenberg, 1989; Amato, 1999; Glenn & Kramer, 1985; Jacquet & Surra, 2001). Fifth, children of divorced parents may expect more conflict, negativity, and relational problems than children from intact families.

In one of the more recent studies of the effects of parental divorce on premarital young adults, Jacquet and Surra (2001) found that women from divorced families differ substantially from women from intact families (also see Sun, 2001). According to Jacquet and Surra, women from divorced families rated trust in their partner's benevolence lower than did other women, reported greater ambivalence in becoming involved with their dating partner, and reported more conflict and negativity than did women from intact families. They also rated satisfaction lower when dating casually, but not if they were seriously dating or privately committed to their partners. Women from divorced families also reported that they valued consistency of commitments less than did women from intact families. Finally, women from divorced families may experience love during casual dating relationships differently from those from intact families. Specifically, women from divorced families rated "passionate" love higher in casually dating relationships, but not "friendship-based" love. Passionate love is fueled by strong feelings, excitement, vulnerability, and by an intense longing for another person. Friendship-based love is based on companionate, affectionate, comfortable love (Grote & Friese, 1994; Hatfield & Sprecher, 1986). Jacquet and Surra (2001) argued that women from divorced families were more strongly affected by parental divorces than men because women are socialized to assume the role of maintaining relationships and their parents' divorce demonstrated how fragile and difficult relational maintenance can be. They have learned to be more careful and cautious when pursuing their own relationships.

While men from divorced families did not differ significantly from men in intact families, Jacquet and Surra (2001) found that men rated conflict, negativity, and ambivalence higher, and trust lower, when they were paired with women from divorced families. The authors argued that this may occur because the men may have become sensitive to the women's negativity, conflict, and ambivalence and may have become wary of trusting women who are ambivalent and cautious about trust themselves.

Parental divorce may significantly alter the relationships children have with their parents. Aquilino (1994) found that divorce could disrupt child-parent relationships in two ways. First, living in a mother-custody family following divorce resulted in less of an opportunity to provide financial assistance to adult children. This is because many noncustodial fathers make few if any payments for children after the age of 18, and the salaries for single-mother workers are limited. On the other hand, custodial fathers can provide greater financial assistance later in life, and adult children of custodial fathers were likely to have long-term relationships with their fathers. The second disruption was that "becoming the non-custodial parent after divorce has extremely negative consequences for long-term father-child relations" (Aquilino, 1994, p. 309). The father-child relationship usually suffered.

Turning Points after Divorce

Many of the readers of this book will have to survive a divorce. As discussed in the chapter on relational de-escalation, breaking up with an intimate partner can be a very emotional experience, and sometimes a devastating one. Divorcing and the aftermath of divorce is one of the most traumatic experiences people will ever experience. Using a sample of divorced couples that had at least one child, Graham (1997) examined the processes of coping with divorce over time in order to provide a better understanding of the changes individuals experience over time and their feelings and sense of commitment to the newly defined relationship with their ex-partner. Because a child is involved and both partners should arrange a way to raise the child(ren) collaboratively, there should be some commitment or maintenance to maintaining a viable post-divorce relationship. That is, the parents have to "uncouple without unfamilying" (Ahrons & Rodgers, 1987). No single theory in communication or psychology can explain processes such as coping with divorce, because family members must negotiate changes with two formally married individuals and their children. Also, new step-parents are involved in changes over time, along with a change in maturation in all family members.

Graham identified 11 common turning points in the post-divorce process. Table 14.2 is based on Graham's work. Note that not all divorced individuals experience these turning points in the same chronological order, and that the typical divorced individual experienced four of these turning points. The most common turning point is the *well-functioning bi-nuclear family*, which involves "settling in" (Graham, 1997, p. 354) to a new arrangement and reflects a positive relationship in which participants focus on successful co-parenting events and help to satisfy children's needs and maintain normative relationships between members of the nuclear family and the extended family. The second most common turning point, the *dysfunctional former spousal relationship*, reflects continued fighting and conflict, including hurtful disclosures and legal actions and disputes over child rearing and finances. Obviously, actions taken and communications made during this phase reduce any feelings of commitment to maintaining a post-divorce relationship. The third most common turning point is the *life-improving events* and is marked by a return to happiness, an appreciation for one's freedom, a sense of hope, and an improvement in personal and instrumental goals. Two turning points deal with the respective remarriages of the two spouses. A sixth

Table 14.2
POSSIBLE TURNING POINTS IN POST-DIVORCE RELATIONSHIPS

Well-Functioning Bi-nuclear Family

Characterized by: Successful co-parenting. Children realize divorced life will be OK. New life settles into a routine. Noncustodial parent moves closer to help with co-parenting, visiting. New roles are defined. Typical family events are celebrated: birthdays, graduations, etc. Family and friends' deaths jointly mourned.

Dysfunctional Former Spousal Relationship

Characterized by: Custody battles. Parenting disagreements. Hurtful disclosures. Legal problems due to financial disagreements. Conflict and fighting. Steady decline in relationship.

Life-Improving Events

Characterized by: Sense of hope for the future. Laughter returns, one experiences self-sufficiency and has self-affirming moments, appreciates freedom, buys home, returns to school, achieves financial stability, receives promotions, and experiences success in career.

Remarriage — Self and Re-marriage — Former Spouse

Characterized by: Falling in love with a new partner, remarriage.

Parent-Child Problems

Characterized by: Former spouse disappoints child, hits child; parent or step-parent conflict occurs or escalates; loss of control over child.

Emotional Divorce

Characterized by: Former spouse begins to date, realization that there is no future in the relationship, division of property, letting go of the previous relationship.

Relocation

Characterized by: Former spouse moves away, parent and child move away, former spouse threatens to move away, new job prompts move.

Personal Hardships

Characterized by: Financial troubles, health problems, and feelings of failure.

Participant's 2nd Marriage Ends or Former Spouse's 2nd Marriage Ends

Source: Adapted from Graham (1997).

turning point is the *parent-child problems* phase, in which the former spouse disappoints the children, conflicts emerge among family members, children rebel, and/or there is a loss of control over the children.

One exceptionally important turning point is an *emotional divorce* phase that deals with the realization that there is no future in the relationship, the partner is dating, property is divided, and there is a sense of "letting go." The *relocation* turning point involves one (or both) individuals moving to a new location. *Personal hardships* involve a phase in which individuals experience financial difficulties, feelings of failure, and health and physical problems. For a few of the individuals in this study, second marriages ended in divorce for themselves or for their partners.

Turning points like life-improving events and well-functioning bi-nuclear family involved events that were most personally gratifying to the divorced parent, and were also associated with commitment to keeping a positive co-parenting relationship with the former spouse; followed by remarriage (self or former partner), which is a time when individuals may be on gracious good behavior. The most devastating episodes in terms of maintaining commitment involved the *participant's 2nd marriage ends*, emotional divorce, dysfunctional former spousal relationship, and parent-child problems, which disrupted a continuity in child rearing and blocked the individual from progressively moving forward to achieve personal goals.

Communication Processes in Becoming a Family

After divorce and remarriage, many people will confront the situation of blending or melding together two families into one, as popularized on "The Brady Bunch." Baxter, Braithwaite, and Nicholson (1999) and Braithwaite, Olson, Golish, Soukup, and Turman (2001) have studied the communication dynamics involved when blended families engage in the process of becoming a family. There is no one clear pathway to becoming a new family. When a new family is assembled and a step-parent and step-children are melding into a new "Brady Bunch," the blended family must manage issues dealing with boundaries, conflicts over loyalties, solidarity, and adaptation to changes. One of the first critical adjustments to be made deals with members of the family establishing and maintaining a set of appropriate boundaries within the family, and in regard to the new custodial role of the step-parent. Secondly, matters of conflict over loyalty toward the noncustodial parent who is without a family and the new step-parent must be addressed. There is also a question as to whether or not step-siblings will behave competitively or collaboratively, and whether or not they accept the new family arrangement. The issue of creating a sense of solidarity within the blended family is complex. Typically a sense of normative solidarity is instilled in the children via communication and interactions with parents and grandparents, and the divorce/remarriage now may increase uncertainty about obligations, decrease contact with the noncustodial parent and one set of grandparents, and so forth. Clearly, feelings of closeness and connectedness may take some time to develop due to the lack of family history and, perhaps, the temporary nature of the relationships of step-siblings who may only be living together for a limited number of years.

Braithwaite and colleagues, in their sample of families studied over four years, found that the process of becoming a family involved five trajectories. The *accelerated trajectory* represented the largest number of families and reflected a pattern of quickly reaching, and sustaining, a sense of "feeling like a family." This trajectory represented 30% of the families studied. For this group, family members adopted traditional family roles early, and sought to meet the expectations of being a traditional family. By the second year, these family members formed and adopted to family rituals and norms, taking family vacations, sharing holiday rituals, and engaging in recreational activities. Role conflicts were resolved by year three, and feelings of security were expressed in year four.

A *prolonged trajectory* was one in which it took years before the members in the family had a sense of "feeling like a family." This trajectory represented 26% of the families studied. Poor family solidarity was experienced in year one, and role relationships were ambiguous, resulting in discomfort and awkwardness and a desire to cling to the past. It was not until year two that there were signs of trust, solidarity, and acceptance. Family roles were eventually defined by the end of year two. By the time year three ended, norms, roles, and rituals had been adopted, and solidarity continued to improve. Despite the fact that members in the prolonged trajectory never described themselves, or compared themselves to a traditional family (as was done in the accelerated trajectory), members in these blended families achieved relatively high levels of satisfaction. They did so largely because they were willing to negotiate family-specific roles, norms, boundaries, and expectations, despite the uncertainty and awkwardness of the first year.

The *declining trajectory* represented only three of the families studied, and they started at a high level of "feeling like a family," which disintegrated over time. This trajectory represented 6% of the families studied. These family members expressed high expectations for forming a new family, and experienced high solidarity and well-defined family roles and family rituals in the first year. However, after a "honeymoon" period, instability surfaced as individuals experienced loyalty conflicts ("I resented calling my step-mother 'Mom' because she wasn't"), and divisions formed based on bloodlines, with people from one bloodline being treated differently than the other. These divisions grew in year two, with some family members avoiding communication with others. In years three and four more family members moved out. What had begun optimistically was undermined by loyalty conflicts, strained family roles, and divisive family ties.

The *stagnating trajectory* represented families in which people started living together, but no "feeling like a family" developed. This trajectory represented 13% of the families studied. There seems to be a true lack of communication in these families — in some, the parents got married and told the children afterwards that they were married and that the children "would have to deal with it." Family members in this trajectory expressed a sense of "manufactured" family solidarity and "going through the motions" (Braithwaite et al., 2001, p. 236). Roles were poorly defined and loyalty conflicts were strongly felt, and children expressed a preference in the parent-child bonds, rituals, and norms of the old family. In these families, some sense of family solidarity would periodically surface when family members rallied around another in times of need; but the children resented being ignored in decision-making, parents not listening, and parents not allowing for an adjustment to the idea of marriage before "being thrown together."

The *high-amplitude turbulent trajectory* represented families that exhibited high and low "feelings of being a family" over the four-year period. This trajectory represented 21% of the families studied. This group of family members also had an unrealistic expectation about being a traditional family, which developed quickly, but individuals expressed uncertainty about how to carry out their new role as mother, sister, etc. Braithwaite and colleagues (2001) aptly described it: "The second year brought with it increased instability, chaotic household boundaries, and unmet expectations of perceived family roles and norms. . . . Family members began moving in and out of households as a result of conflict" (p. 239). Over the next several years, potential family members coped with this situation in one of two ways. Some family members experienced intense conflicts and negative cyclical behavioral patterns, described the situation as hopeless, and desired to avoid confronting the problems with the families. Avoiding problems resulted in the problems continuing, along with less satisfying relationships and little sense of "feeling like a family." On the other hand, some individuals engaged in an attempt to create and maintain open lines of communication, confront problems, and work toward resolution. At least some of the latter achieved some sense of family solidarity from time to time.

Four of the most important lessons to be learned about how to "become a family," include (see Braithwaite et al., 2001):

1. "First, in terms of family boundaries, our results revealed that individuals who experienced the more constructive trajectories were more likely to describe successful and flexible boundary management. For many of these families, it meant the ability to negotiate movement of blended family members from one household to another due to shared custodial parental or extended family relationships" (p. 241).

2. The development of family solidarity was also critical in forming successfully blended families. Solidarity formed in both the accelerated and prolonged trajectories, representing 56% of the families studied. In the remaining three groups ". . . the push for family solidarity seemed to cause more tension and conflict as family members strove to be what they were not" (p. 242).

3. The ability to adapt to changes, to family roles, and to changes in how roles were to be played out also weighed in as critical. In most of the trajectories reported, the pressure to conform to a traditional role and to traditional norms often met with resentment, while openness to adapting roles and norms for a particular family helped family members to become a family.

4. "Blended families that were characterized by flexibility, open communication, and constructive conflict management were able to handle almost anything that occurred" (p. 243).

Socioemotional Selectivity Theory

As individuals age, one of the most important changes in interpersonal relations rests in the fact that social networks become smaller as individuals place greater emphasis on a select number of friends who are emotionally important to the individual. This theory is called the **socioemotional selectivity theory** (Carstensen, 1993, 1995; Carstensen & Lang, 1997; Lang, Staudinger, & Carstensen, 1998). Socioemotional selectivity theory argues that as individuals become older they begin to sense that the future is limited. Sensing a more limited future, they become more selective in which goals are important to pursue, and prioritize activities, including interactions with friends, along emotional lines in order to derive emotional gratification (more so than younger people). They change how many friends to retain in one's social network, and exert more control over emotional expressions. First, they shift focus away from long-term or long-range goals, and focus more attention on short-term goals that may bring more immediate emotional gratification. Achieving instrumental goals of getting a better job, learning a skill, or traveling the world become less important relative to deriving satisfaction from a select number of intimate, meaningful, and emotionally charged relationships. Younger people may place greater emphasis on being popular and having lots of friends, but an older individual has fewer "peripheral social friends" and a number of quality friends (Fung, Carstensen, & Lang, 2001). Fredrickson and Carstensen (1990) found that perceptions of limited future orientation was associated with spending time with emotionally close partners, and Carstensen and Charles (1994, 1998), Lang and Carstensen (1994), and Lang, Staudinger, and Carstensen (1998) found that the smaller social networks of older people are marked by salient emotional memories of interactions with these selected few individuals, and with strong feelings of social embeddedness (satisfaction with friends, family members, and important relationships, and expressions of tenderness).

One of the important social and health-related aspects of the socioemotional selectivity theory deals with how older people cope with negative affect and control emotions. Confronted with limited time and a motivation to prioritize events and relationships in one's life, older people are more likely to avoid potentially negative events and select to be with well-known social partners who are rewarding, personally and emotionally. As people age, they maintain a more positive (rather than negative) outlook on life that is fairly stable over time; however, people experience fewer negative emotions and report fewer intensely negative feelings as they age (see Charles, Reynolds, & Gatz, 2001). Older adult couples express fewer negative emotions such as anger and disgust, compared to middle-aged individuals, and report less negative affect when discussing conflicts with others (Carstensen & Charles, 1998; Carstensen, Graff, Levenson, & Gottman, 1996; Levenson, Carstensen, & Gottman, 1994). Charles and colleagues (2001) argued that an avoidance of negative affect may enable older adults to control their emotions and to respond less intensely when physiologically aroused (Levenson, Carstensen, Friesen, & Ekman, 1991), which promotes a greater sense of well-being that can be linked to healthier outcomes.

The socioemotional selectivity theory helps to explain a number of changes for individuals and couples as they age. For example, couples who have been married for forty years or more indicate that they are able to minimize the amount of conflict in the marriage as time passes, while intensely experienced conflict from earlier years of marriage (parenting and in-law troubles) were viewed in the past, having no influence on the present day experiences of the couple (Dickson et al., 2002). Carstensen, Gottman, and Levenson (1995) found that older couples were more affectionate during conflict resolution than were mid-life couples. Further, husbands become more affiliative and expressive, as they focus less on career goals and instrumental goals, and more on relational goals and family relations, while mothers can spend less time and energy on family goals (insofar as the children are more mature and have moved on to college and careers) (Keith, Wacker, & Schafer, 1991). Older and remarried couples also valued more autonomy both within the marriage and outside the marriage, valuing the freedom to pursue a number of personally and mutually gratifying types of relationships which emphasize intimacy and togetherness (Allen, Boucom, Burnett, Epstein, & Rankin-Esquer, 2001). Projects like these highlight that the quality relationships pursued by individuals as they age can be found both within the family and as a complement to the family — in church, the community, and various organizations women and men join.

On the other hand, individuals who are without partners in the later years are significantly lonelier than others (Huyck, 2001; Peters & Liefbroer, 1997). In fact, research indicates that the older individual experiencing the greatest amount of loneliness is an individual who has experienced a second dissolution in the last ten years. Further, men who are living without a partner experienced significantly more loneliness than women who were living without a partner (Peters & Liefbroer, 1997). Given that older individuals are focused more on quality relationships at this stage of their lives, the fact that men and those from a second dissolution are lonely indicates that they are lonely at possibly the worst time. They are motivated to have quality relationships, but have far less contact with others than expected.

Besides the experience of loneliness, many of the elderly, when frail, will develop what is referred to as **geriatric depression** (see www.Stanford.Edu/~yesavage/ GDS.html, www.Ec-online.net/Knowledge/SB/Sbdepressionoverview.html, www .psychologynet.org/geriatric.html, www.psychom.net/depression.central.elderly.html). Geriatric depression usually occurs among elderly who have realized that they can no longer continue to do the mental and physical tasks they once could. Often they are frail, living in assisted-living facilities, have experienced multiple life changes, and have diminished personal resources. Depression is a disease different from dementia and it is a treatable illness. However, until it is treated, a depressed individual finds no comfort or support from her or his interactions with others, withdraws from contact with others, lacks hope in the future, is dissatisfied and inconsolable, worries constantly, cannot make decisions, and suffers from impaired concentration. Older individuals who are healthy and not depressed follow a pathway to aging successfully, as discussed earlier with the socioemotional selectivity theory. However, older individuals suffering from geriatric depression often experience a decline in health due to poorer eating habits, tension and irritability, and abuse of alcohol.

SELF-PRESENTATION IN LATER YEARS

Self-Presentation and Negotiated Identities in Intergenerational Conversations

In earlier chapters we discussed how individuals presented a self to others, creating, maintaining, and defending an image of the self as competent, likable, dedicated, weak, or intimidating. We continue to create, maintain, and defend public images throughout our lives. As people age, however, there are threats to their public image: The perception and stereotype of "older" people is that they are less competent and less self-reliant (Martin, Leary, & Rejeski, 2000). As discussed in Chapter 6, which focussed on self-presentation, our public images or identities often emerge through interactions with others, who can confirm the image we are hoping to establish, reject our attempt to promote a particular image, or work with us to modify a particular self-presentation.

All people — young, middle aged, or old — present particular public images to different audiences, as we described in the research on how politicians and celebrities present themselves as likable, worthy, and competent in Chapter 6. Shows like "The Sopranos" show older people as intimidators, as likable, or as competent. Shows like "Frasier," in fact, raise issues about how older people are treated. Frasier's father defends himself quite frequently from his sons' attempts to look after him and care for him — he resists their attempts to make him dependent.

While "Frasier" is just a television show, the truth is that when younger people meet an older person, they may think about the older person in certain stereotypical ways and behave in ways that help fulfill their stereotypes. A model of intergenerational communication, called the **Communication Predicament of Aging Model,** has been advanced that explains this process (Coupland, Coupland, Giles, & Henwood, 1988; Giles & Williams, 1994; Harwood, 1998; Harwood & Giles, 1996; Harwood, Mckee, & Lin, 2000; Harwood & Williams, 1998; Ryan, Hummert, & Boich, 1995). First, the model holds that younger individuals have well-defined stereotypes of older individuals, believing that they would be frail, weak, slow, and so forth. When they meet and talk to older people, their stereotyped expectations negatively impact on their interactions with older people because they behave in ways that anticipate slow, hard-of-hearing individuals and the actions of older people may fulfill the self-prophecy (older individuals do in fact act older). In some cases an older person may accept the definition of old being foisted on him or her by the younger individual, and may not be aware it is happening. It is also possible that the older person's stereotype of young people may have a significant impact on the interaction, but much of the research looks at how older people are treated and how they react.

You will recall that the Communication Accommodation Theory, which was discussed in Chapter 4, asserts that we may converge our communicative behaviors when we are motivated to be liked by our partner, when we want to be efficient, seek oneness, and so on. On the other hand, we diverge our communicative behavior when we want to contrast our self-image from that of the partner, when we dissociate from the partner, and so forth. If young people have a negative stereotype of older persons, then young people will diverge by restricting the topics for discussion, asking more questions, speaking loudly, slowly, and in a more exaggerated manner, and include more patronizing speech. Mulac and Giles (1996) (also see Williams & Nussbaum, 2001) coined the term **instant aging** to denote the situation in which, when certain conversational behaviors are engaged in, the older person can be induced to act, think, and feel older than he or she is in reality. Some individuals may treat an older person as if the older person were feeble, weak, dependent — like a baby. This is called *patronizing talk* (see the box "What Is Patronizing Talk?"). A younger person may say, "Do you need help with that?" "Do you feel better today?" or "You can do this, yes you can. Try harder," and the like, and communicate a low level of expectation of strength or competence. Conversations may center on themes stereotypical of aging: immobility, economic hardship, illness, and so forth. On the other hand, a young person in a conversation with an older person may actually, and intentionally, act younger than he or she is in order to increase liking from the older person (Williams & Nussbaum, 2001). This is done by portraying an image of being nice, youthful, energetic, clean cut — a censored version for the older conversational

WHAT IS PATRONIZING TALK?

Researcher studies how people talk down to the elderly.

By ROGER MARTIN (12/6/1996)

The sound of baby talk spooned out with bites of food at a nursing home is unforgettable: "That's my girl. Not much left."

Baby talk is just one of four ways we talk down to aging people, according to a paper published recently in the *International Journal of Psycholinguistics* by a KU faculty member and a colleague at McMaster University, Hamilton, Ontario. Two of those patronizing speech forms are more caring and two are less so, according to the paper by Mary Lee Hummert, KU associate professor of communication studies and research associate at the KU Gerontology Center, and colleague Ellen Ryan. Two try to control the elder, while the other two do not.

"I hate to say these are the only forms of patronizing speech," Hummert said, "but they're probably the major ones." Baby talk is both caring and controlling, Hummert said. It's high-pitched and

(Continued)

462

(Box continued from previous page)

exaggerated. The vocabulary is simple. It employs "minimizing terms," like "not much left," as a way of downplaying how much is left to eat. Terms of endearment, like "Honey," are also part of it. Hummert conceded that "there is research that shows some individuals in nursing homes respond positively to this. They focus more on the warmth and caring than on the control."

A second kind of condescending talk or behavior is high in caring too, but low in control, Hummert said. The paper speaks of a nursing home caregiver named Dolly who sees a resident and says, "Hi, little peach," then hugs her. A male resident walks by and kisses the other resident. Dolly says, "Isn't that cute? Look at that. Poor little things."

The nurse isn't trying to control behavior, Hummert wrote, but her "hug may be interpreted by the resident as patronizing, as may her observation of the intimate moment with the other resident." Hummert brands high-caring, low-controlling talk "overly personal." The caregiver may unknowingly ask questions that are too intimate, such as "How did you feel when your husband died?"

Caring is less evident in two other forms of patronizing talk, she said. One, "directive talk," is controlling. For example, an attendant says, "Finish your breakfast," with no softening of the voice. Directive talk is full of orders. Negatives like "don't" or "cannot" are sprinkled in. An angry, disdainful tone implies that the elder is obstinate, unruly or stupid. "Of course there are situations in which being directive is appropriate," Hummert said.

The second kind of uncaring talk doesn't seek control, Hummert said. "Superficial talk" shows little regard for an elder's concerns. An older man complains to a doctor that he has no sexual yearnings, for example, but the doctor quickly switches the conversation to the patient's prostate.

Superficial talk may take the form of two speakers discussing a person as "he" or "she" although the person is present. Superficial talk, Hummert wrote, ignores the person's interests or presence.

Affirming talk is the best kind. It requires asking questions that really are questions, not orders in disguise. It means listening deeply — and not preparing answers before a speaker finishes. It strikes a balance between care and control. It means saying "I think," not "you should."

Hummert said it's a style of talking and listening that would benefit everyone.

partner (Williams & Nussbaum, 2001). In this situation, the younger person would be portraying an image of a youthful person that the older person prefers to hear.

During conversations, older individuals can use several conversational techniques either to identify their age for others, or to protect against threatened identities (when they do not want to adopt the position of "an old person"). There are several reasons for making these statements so that others know one's age. First, the information provides a way to have a conversation by allowing both partners to compare and contrast social worlds: the way things were in the 1950s or 1960s to the 1990s and 2000s. Second, it helps to reduce uncertainty when an older person and a younger person meet — it provides a rough approximation of the older person's age and the younger person does not have to ask. They can ask questions about the 1950s, 1960s, or the American Depression without wondering if the older person represented the various historical eras. Finally, some of these statements are used as a self-handicapping tactic (see Chapter 6 on self-presentation). Claiming to be old helps set up low expectations for the interaction, which may reduce anxiety on the part of the older individual, who might be able to maintain some amount of self-esteem and competence despite being old (also see Martin et al., 2000).

First, older people (65+) let it be known through their conversations that they are old (Coupland, Coupland, & Giles, 1991; Coupland et al., 1988). The older a person is, the more likely it is for them to receive a gratifying, positive comment: "87 years old. That's great," "You don't look it," "Marvelous." A second approach is the age-related category or role reference that is used when a person uses roles or categories to refer to self or other. A person may say, "We pensioners . . ." or "We retired engineers . . ." and claim he or she is a member of a particular group. A person may also self-categorize him- or herself in terms of health or a physical impairment with statements like "I've been a widower for five years," and "Oh, I just don't get around like I used to." An older person may use such statements as self-handicapping, in the sense that they are communicating to others that others should not expect much out of them — thus, if the conversation flows well he or she can claim to have successfully achieved a good conversation despite his or her limitations.

Three other ways to identify one's age to others are *temporal framing process, self-association with the past,* and *recognizing historical, cultural, or social change.* In the first of these, an individual tells part of his or her life story and judging his or her age is relatively easy: "I retired in 1983 and my partner died in 1990." The second links the individual to a particular group or event in history, making his or her approximate age be known: "Yeah, I was one of those 19-year-olds sent off to 'Nam." The third links the speaker to another era, recognizing that historical, cultural, and social changes have been made over the years: "Oh, yes. My first truck had running boards . . . but I guess you can say that about new trucks today," "We danced to psychedelic music — with light shows and everything. I had a lava lamp in my living room!"

During some conversations an older person may not want others to think of him- or herself as old, since we do in fact live in an ageist society and some of the tactics listed earlier, like the self-handicapping age identity in relation to health or physical impairment, can lead to the older person being treated as if he or she were old, and facilitates a self-fulfilling prophecy. As Williams and Nussbaum (2001, p. 137) aptly question: "Can older people maintain positive self-esteem in the face of threats to a positive image of the aging self, and if so how do they achieve this?"

Martin et al. (2000) discuss several tactics used by older individuals to avoid the appearance of old age. People with a hearing loss, for example, can pretend to hear, nod, act pleasant, and agree to what is being said in order to pass for people who have normal hearing. People who tire easily can take multiple pauses or stops to listen to music, watch the sunset, smell the flowers, and so on, to hide the fact that they are tired. People may use an excuse such as being too tired, being interrupted by noisy neighbors, or being too busy in order to avoid the fact that they experience a loss in memory. Williams and Nussbaum (2001, pp. 139–144) also identified several tactics an older person can use to avoid being cast in a negative light because of age, or use age to one's advantage:

1. The *denial of personal disadvantage* is defined as perceiving discrimination at the societal level, but denying its occurrence at the personal level. An older person may concede that as a group millions of older people are in fact slower, less competent, and so forth, but that the stereotype does not apply to him or her.

2. The *discourse of self-exception* involves identifying that there are subgroups of incompetent old people with which the old person is not associated. Thus one person can dissociate him- or herself from "those geriatrics" or "those crotchety complainers," and so on. Actually, young people may engage in the same behavior, by dissociating themselves from undesirable groups of young people.

3. A third tactic of protecting self-esteem is a form of self-stereotyping by which an older person attempts to portray him- or herself in a positive light. A person can portray him- or herself as a *survivor*, and focus on the obstacles he or she overcame in order to make various achievements over time.

The stereotypes of both younger people of old people and older people of young people can profoundly influence the nature of a conversation between generations, and unless the first conversation is pleasant, it is unlikely that a friendship would follow. Harwood et al. (2000) found that intergenerational conversations fell into one of three categories. First, young and older individuals engaged in a mutually positive conversation in which the old person provided information and wisdom and may have felt younger as a product of this interaction. Second, conversations took place in which one party felt some disconnection or distance from the other or the positivity was not mutual or reinforced. Third, conversations took place in which the younger person displayed considerable negativity and the attempts by the older person to help the younger person engage in a positive interaction failed. Some younger people were unable to maintain a positive, competent conversation with an older individual. Part of this difficulty may stem from the fact that our society largely segregates and isolates young people from older people, thus limiting young people's access to potential friends who might be older.

INTERGENERATIONAL FRIENDSHIPS

Friends and Mentors

In many ways intergenerational friendships are not very different from peer-age friendships (Bettini & Norton, 1991; Holladay & Kerns, 1999; Williams & Nussbaum, 2001). There appear to be two important differences. First, there is greater intimacy and emotional involvement in same-age friendships, relative to intergenerational friendships. Second, intergenerational friendships are more likely to be characterized as an advice-giving, care-taking relationship in which the older partner gives advice, provides more information than the younger person, and provides guidance.

There are two important psychological benefits that may be derived from participating in and maintaining successful intergenerational friendships. First, older individuals can gain a sense of gratification by being in the role of an adviser or mentor, may feel they can (continue to) make a contribution to society, and perhaps can be made to feel younger. Younger individuals can gain a sense of gratification by having a more experienced, more informed, and perhaps wiser individual confirm their identities, approve and give advice on what they are doing in life and in their careers, as well as their plans and strategies for the future (relative to the advice of a same-age friend) (see Bettini & Norton, 1991; Holladay & Kerns, 1999). Matthews (1986) also noted that many "age-discrepant" friendships may occur when most of us have launched a career and enter into middle-aged years. This is because we meet more and more people through work, church, and various groups to which we belong, and age differences are relatively less important than when we are young. That is, there is a strong bias against age-discrepant friendships of either the same sex or opposite sex when a person is young, and a friendship between an 18-year-old and a 28-year-old may seem nonnormative. On the other hand, a friendship between a 28-year-old and 38-year-old, or a 40-year-old and a 60-year-old is less nonnormative.

Bettini and Norton (1991) found that older adults (at least 80 years old) meet younger friends through contact with their children and grandchildren and through church activities. Young individuals meet older friends through contact with their parents. Older individuals felt there was a difference in equality in their intergenerational friendships, but younger individuals reported the qualities and characteristics of intergenerational friendships to be the same as in peer-age friendships.

Holladay and Kerns (1999) studied both casual friendships and close friendships people report having with both same-age peers and age-discrepant peers. They found that an age-discrepant friend was more than twice as likely to be considered a "close friend," rather than a "casual friend." Further, both close and casual age-discrepant friendships were more likely to be friendships with people of the same sex, not opposite sex. The qualities of the friendships also varied as a function of the type of friendship studied. Same-age peer close friendships received higher ratings than age-discrepant close friendships in companionship, satisfaction, intimacy, nurturance, and reliable alliance (dealing with the perception that the friendship will continue for years). The authors concluded that the same-age close relationships were experienced more intensely than age-discrepant relationships. On the other hand, there were no significant differences in perceived conflict, amount of instrumental aid given (dealing with helping others get things done in general, at school, home, work, etc.), antagonism, affection, admiration, or relative power. Among casual friends, only one quality was rated significantly different between same-age peer and age-discrepant

466

peer friendships: admiration ("this person respects me, admires me"). There is greater admiration in age-discrepant casual friendships.

A limitation to survey projects like the ones mentioned here is that they fail to study the dynamics of changes that occur in friendship over time. We all know that a best friend in high school may be a casual friend today, or that a person in your community slowly became a friend, then became a mentor, from whom you then became estranged, and to whom you returned to being a friend later. As stated in the wonderful movie *Stand By Me*, "friends are like so many waiters coming and going from our lives." Some scholars have made a distinction between friends (who share emotional experiences, help one another, collaborate on goals, provide feedback, assistance, and advice, and to whom one can easily seek assistance), and mentors (where one person who has accomplished particular goals or reached a particular status coaches, advises, and provides guidance to another, usually younger, protégé). The truth, however, is that some

INTERGENERATIONAL FRIENDSHIP FORMATION IN *GOOD WILL HUNTING*

While the romance story between Will Hunting (Matt Damon) and Skylar (Minnie Driver) is memorable, cute, and charming, the main relationship in the movie *Good Will Hunting* that drives changes in character development is the relationship between Will Hunting and his therapist, Sean McGuire (Robin Williams). Will is an angry, cynical, deviant young man who is a genius in mathematics. After manipulating other therapists, a college math professor who is assisting Will takes Will to see Sean, an old college friend who teaches at a Boston community college.

First Session   During the first session, Sean initiates a conversation and attempts to find commonality between the two "Southies" (people who grew up in South Boston). Will ignores this and, in trying to control the conversation, talks about whether Sean bought each book in his office separately, or bought a kit. As the two talk about books, the therapist, Sean, is still attempting to find commonalities. Will verbally rejects the books and recommends a better history book, which prompts Sean to counter with his own recommendation, as the two men engage in verbal sparring. Will notices Sean's art, which he critiques; the fact that he believes he has found a weakness in Sean excites and interests Will, who pushes on the point that Sean has met "the wrong woman." Sean is angered. There is a reversal in roles, in which the patient has found the weakness and raw, unresolved issues of the therapist. But Sean agrees to be Will's therapist.

Next Two Sessions   Will does not have to speak, and so they are involved in a competition. Eventually, Will talks first, and tells a joke. Feeling vulnerable, Will announces that he has had sex, and has dated a wonderful woman the week before. Will, the patient, is finally engaging in self-disclosure. However, he self-presents an image of himself as being in control and not really caring about her—he claims not to have called her (Skylar) out of concern that he might find her not to be as perfect as he had first thought. At this point the therapist rejects this claim, saying, in essence, that Will is avoiding intimacy for fear that she would not find him perfect. After a lecture about going through life avoiding intimacy, the two men are silent. Sean then decides to reciprocate Will's self-disclosure and reveals personal, intimate information about his wife. The two talk. Will asks if Sean thinks about remarrying, and he cleverly uses Sean's own advice on Sean, that Sean is avoiding meeting new people and will go through life not meeting anyone.

Will takes to heart Sean's advice, and he decides to go visit the girl he dated, but never called. Will and Skylar spend more time together, and the relationship blossoms.

Fourth Session   Will tells Sean he's read Sean's book and they talk about counseling veterans and Sean explains he gave it up when his wife was getting sicker and sicker. Sean tells the story of missing the World Series because he was madly in love with his girlfriend and gave up the ticket as he told his friends, "Sorry, guys. I've got to go see about a girl." During this session the two men emotionally bond over baseball, and the excitement of a World Series won in the twelfth inning. Will, it appears, is impressed that a person would make a sacrifice in this way.

Later . . .   Sean and the math professor are arguing when Will overhears and enters the room. Sean and Will share stories about being physically abused when young, and Will announces that he broke off his relationship with Skylar. Sean repeats that it is not Will's fault, and Will eventually cries and the two men hug.

Will decides to change his life. He accepts a job (see the story at the beginning of the chapter). His friends give him a car for his twenty-first birthday and he leaves a note for the therapist, "I've got to go see about a girl."

The lives of both men are changed for the better after working through the defense mechanisms both had constructed, by self-disclosing, by emotionally sharing, and by giving and accepting advice. Some intergenerational relationships can become friendships, and both individuals may benefit interpersonally.

casual friendships can develop into mentoring relationships, and some mentoring relationships can develop into friendships, with less of a coaching or advising role.

Mentoring relationships are an extremely important intergenerational form of relationship. Individuals who mentor and help one another do in fact form emotional bonds (see Bell, Golombisky, Singh, & Hirschmann, 2000). Research indicates that individuals who are mentored (compared to those who do not have mentors) advance more quickly on the job, achieve higher incomes and benefit professionally (Hill, Bahniuk, & Dobos, 1989; Peluchette & Jeanquart, 2000; Whitely, Dougherty & Dreher, 1991, 1992). Kalbfleisch (2002) reviewed elements of successful mentoring

468

and offered particular advice on seeking and maintaining a mentor. First, an older, more advanced, individual is more likely to agree to be a mentor if the protégé (one seeking the mentor) develops a relationship with the mentor prior to asking the mentor to formally agree to be the mentor. The people you want most to be your mentor are probably too busy to agree to do so, and accepting the label of *mentor* carries with it some risks for the mentor-to-be, including a loss of time, giving one's knowledge and perhaps secrets away for free, placing trust in another person (who may actually be a rival or competitor later in life), and being responsible if she or he gives poor advice. Also, there are many others who might ask the person to be a mentor. Thus, a mentor is likely to reject the request to be a mentor until some amount of trust and likability is established. It also improves your chance of securing a particular person as a mentor if

STUDENT AS OBSERVER: INTERGENERATIONAL FRIENDSHIP AND FAMILY SOLIDARITY, HOLLYWOOD STYLE

Option 1. A number of movies portray interactions between older individuals and younger ones. This happens in movies like *Good Will Hunting*, *As Good As It Gets*, *The Color of Money*, and many more. Watch a movie that features a friendship that you believe is an intergenerational friendship. Given what you know about friendship formation (see text in this chapter and in earlier chapters), write an analysis of how the friendship formed, and why. Use the box "Intergenerational Friendship Formation in *Good Will Hunting*" as an example. Your analysis probably will include the topics of self-disclosure, reciprocity, emotional bonding (sharing feelings), sharing activities, cooperative action, and assisting one another in pursuing goals.

Option 2. The classic movie *The Godfather* contains much information about intergenerational solidarity. When you watch this movie, you will see that there is a good deal of normative solidarity in that there is a strong sense of commitment to family and family relationships. There is also a strong sense of structural solidarity in that there is plenty of opportunity for family (and extended family members and fictive kin relations) to meet, talk, get together (there are many family members, many who are living relatively close to one another, who are healthy and can get together). There is a strong sense of functional solidarity in that there is an expectation that family members help one another. There is a strong sense of consensual solidarity in that family members share the same values, beliefs, and attitudes. There is a strong sense of affectual solidarity as well: Family members are mutually affectionate, close, and warm, even when they have verbal disagreements. Finally, there exists a high amount of associational solidarity — there are many family gatherings, and families (extended family and fictive kin) gather for celebrations — weddings, birthdays, and so forth.

First, watch *The Godfather* and make observational notes about scenes or interactions in the movie that illustrate each of the six types of family solidarity discussed in this box. Then compile your notes into a short report of no more than three pages long, describing how the Corleone family stays together.

a mutual friend, a friend of the individual, or a person who has credibility to the individual asks him or her to be your mentor. Also, keep in mind that male protégés prefer male mentors and female protégés prefer female mentors. Because of the power of the mentor over the protégé, and the protégé's dependence on the mentor, it is largely the responsibility of the protégé to resolve conflicts, engage in maintenance and repair strategies, and monitor self-presentational goals; this is especially true if the mentor has assisted the protégé in achieving his or her goals.

CHAPTER SUMMARY

We start life in a family and our parents have a strong impact on our interpersonal relationships. Mothers and fathers have a strong impact on the development and maintenance of our attachment styles and how we construct friendships with others — our age and older. Our families also instill in us a sense of family solidarity, which has a strong impact on our relationships with other family members, including giving and receiving support, for decades. Parental divorce may have a significant impact on children, fostering caution and lack of trust among children, especially daughters. The ability of sons to develop close intimate ties with others is strongly influenced by their fathers' expressions of affection and support. As people age, they become more selective in pursuing goals, placing more emphasis on quality, meaningful relationships with fewer people, and minimizing negative feelings and conflict.

Turning points are important in terms of changing relational definitions with parents, coping with divorce, and with "becoming a family" when parents remarry. Stereotypes of others based on age may make it difficult for individuals to engage in quality, satisfying relationships with people of an older generation. However, there are benefits to establishing and maintaining a friendship or mentoring relationship with an older individual, usually of the same gender, who can give advice about career and personal choices about one's life at work, church, or in a community.

KEY TERMS

affectual solidarity, p. 445
anxious/ambivalent, p. 442
associational solidarity, p. 445
attachment styles, p. 440
avoidant, p. 442
Communication Predicament
  of Aging Model, p. 460
consensual solidarity, p. 445
functional solidarity, p. 445

gendered closeness perspective, p. 451
geriatric depression, p. 459
instant aging, p. 461
intergenerational solidarity theory, p. 445
life-span attachment theory, p. 443
normative solidarity, p. 446
secure, p. 441
socioemotional selectivity theory, p. 458
structural solidarity, p. 446

EXERCISES FOR FURTHER DISCUSSION

▼

1. Answer the questions in Table 14.1. Are you a secure, anxious/ambivalent, or avoidant type? Answer the questions in Table 14.1 for your mother and father — which attachment type best describes them? What do you think is the relationship between your attachment style and your parents? Do you express a certain form of love? Contact your parents and ask them the questions in Table 14.1 to confirm what you believe are their styles. Do their answers support or contradict what is written in the text?

2. Do you believe there are high levels of intergenerational solidarity among family members in your family? Would your brothers, sisters, parents and grandparents agree or disagree? Is there a high level of affective solidarity? How important is it to have the family gather to celebrate events? Is there an expectation that family members will help one another?

3. Write out what you think are the turning points in your relationship with your mother and your father. What are the events that changed, for better or worse, the quality of the relationship and your sense of closeness to each of them. How do these compare with the ones listed in the text (if at all). Interview one of your parents and ask him/her to make a list of turning points. Spend time discussing what each person wrote as a turning point to see if you agree and share the same perceptions of how your relationship has changed or stayed the same.

4. Interview your grandparents. Ask them how important each of the goals are that we listed in Chapter 1 (Tables 1.1, 1.2, and 1.3) — how important are self-presentational goals? Relational goals? Instrumental goals? Today and when they were your age? The socioemotional selectivity theory would predict that relational goals are more important than self-presentational goals or instrumental goals. Also, ask them how they dealt with conflict when they were first dating, and how they deal with conflict today. Research described in the text suggests that they would say there is very little conflict in their married lives today, as they focus on positive aspects of life and minimize negative aspects.

5. Talk to a person who is older than you by one generation (twenty years or so). When you have this conversation, are you able to avoid using stereotypes? How does the older individual present him/herself? Do they identify their age group (see text), and/or do they characterize aging as a negative thing (less competent, more dependent) or as a positive thing (being a survivor, lots of experience)?

SUGGESTED READING

▼

ATTACHMENT STYLE

Cassidy, J., & Shaver, P. R. (Eds.). (1999). *Handbook of attachment: Theory, research, and clinical applications*. New York: Guilford.

Feeney, J., & Noller, P. (1996). *Adult attachment*. Thousand Oaks, CA: Sage.

BECOMING A FAMILY

Braithwaite, D. O., Olson, L. N., Golish, T. D., Soukup, C., & Turman, P. (2001). "Becoming a family": Developmental processes represented in blended family discourse. *Journal of Applied Communication Research, 29,* 221–247.

COMMUNICATION PREDICAMENT OF AGING MODEL

Harwood, J., Mckee, J., & Lin, M. C. (2000). Younger and older adults' schematic representations of intergenerational communication. *Communication Monographs, 67,* 20–41.

Ryan, E. B., Hummert, M. L., & Boich, L. H. (1995). Communication predicaments of aging: Patronizing behavior toward older adults. *Journal of Language and Social Psychology, 13,* 144–166.

INTERGENERATIONAL SOLIDARITY THEORY

Bengtson, V. L., & Roberts, R. E. L. (1991). Intergenerational solidarity in aging families: An example of formal theory construction. *Journal of Marriage and the Family, 53,* 856–870.

SOCIOEMOTIONAL SELECTIVITY THEORY

Carstensen, L. L. (1993). Motivation for social contact across the life span: A theory of socioemotional selectivity. In J. Jacobs (Ed.), *Nebraska symposium on motivation: Developmental perspectives on motivation* (Vol. 20, pp. 209–254). Lincoln: University of Nebraska Press.

REFERENCE LIST

▼

Ahrons, C. R., & Rodgers, R. H. (1987). *Divorced families: A multidisciplinary developmental view.* New York: Norton.

Ainsworth, M. D. S., Blehar, M. C., Waters, E., & Wall, S. (1978). *Patterns of attachment: A psychological study of the strange situation.* Hillsdale, NJ: Erlbaum.

472

Allen, E. S., Boucom, D. H., Burnett, C. K., Epstein, N., & Rankin-Esquer, L. A. (2001). Decision-making power, autonomy, and communication in remarried spouses compared with first-married spouses. *Family Relations, 50*, 326–334.

Allen, K. R., & Demo, D. H. (1995). The families of lesbians and gay men: A new frontier in family research. *Journal of Marriage and the Family, 57*, 111–127.

Allen, W. D., & Olson, D. H. (2001). Five types of African-American marriages. *Journal of Marital and Family Therapy, 27*, 301–314.

Allison, P. D., & Furstenberg, F. F., Jr. (1989). How marital dissolution affects children: Variations by age and sex. *Developmental Psychology, 25*, 540–549.

Amato, P. R. (1999). Children of divorced parents as young adults. In M. E. Hetherington (Ed.), *Coping with divorce, single parenting, and remarriage: A risk and resiliency perspective* (pp. 147–164). Mahwah, NJ: Erlbaum.

Antonucci, T. (1990). Social supports and social relationships. In R. H. Binstock and L. K. George (Eds.), *Handbook of aging and the social sciences* (3rd ed., pp. 205–226). New York: Academic.

Aquilino, W. S. (1994). Impact of childhood family disruption on young adults' relationships with parents. *Journal of Marriage and the Family, 56*, 295–313.

Bartholomew, K. (1990). Avoidance of intimacy: An attachment perspective. *Journal of Social and Personal Relationships, 7*, 147–178.

Bartholomew, K., & Horowitz, L. M. (1991). Attachment styles among young adults: A test for a four-category model. *Journal of Personality and Social Psychology, 61*, 226–244.

Baxter, L. A., Braithwaite, D. O., & Nicholson, J. (1999). Turning points in the development of blended family relationships. *Journal of Social and Personal Relationships, 16*, 291–313.

Bell, E., Golombisky, K., Singh, G., & Hirschmann, K. (2000). To all the girls I've loved before: Academic love letters on mentoring, power and desire. *Communication Theory, 10*, 27–48.

Bengtson, V. L. (2001). The Burgess Award Lecture: Beyond the nuclear family: The increasing importance of multigenerational bonds. *Journal of Marriage and the Family, 63*, 1–16.

Bengtson, V. L., & Roberts, R. E. L. (1991). Intergenerational solidarity in aging families: An example of formal theory construction. *Journal of Marriage and the Family, 53*, 856–870.

Bettini, L. M., & Norton, M. L. (1991). The pragmatics of intergenerational friendships. *Communication Reports, 4*, 64–72.

Bondevik, M., & Skogstad, A. (1998). The oldest old, ADL, social network, and loneliness. *Western Journal of Nursing Research, 20*, 325–343.

Bowlby, J. (1969). *Attachment and loss: Vol 1. Attachment*. New York: Basic Books.

Braithwaite, D. O., Olson, L. N., Golish, T. D., Soukup, C., & Turman, P. (2001). "Becoming a family:" Developmental processes represented in blended family discourse. *Journal of Applied Communication Research, 29*, 221–247.

Carstensen, L. L. (1993). Motivation for social contact across the life span: A theory of socioemotional selectivity. In J. Jacobs (Ed.), *Nebraska symposium on motivation: Developmental perspectives on motivation* (Vol. 20, pp. 209–254). Lincoln: University of Nebraska Press.

Carstensen, L. L. (1995). Evidence for a life-span theory of socioemotional selectivity. *Current Directions in Psychological Science, 4*, 51–56.

Carstensen, L. L., & Charles, S. T. (1994). The salience of emotion across the adult life span. *Psychology of Aging, 9*, 259–264.

Carstensen, L. L., & Charles, S. T. (1998). Emotion in the second half of life. *Current Directions, 7*, 144–149.

Carstensen, L. L., Gottman, J. M., & Levenson, R. W. (1995). Emotional behavior in long-term marriage. *Psychology and Aging, 10*, 140–149.

Carstensen, L. L., Graff, J., Levenson, R. W., & Gottman, J. M. (1996). Affect in intimate relationships: A developmental course of marriage. In C. Magai & S. H. McFadden (Eds.), *Handbook of emotion, adult development, and aging* (pp. 227–247). New York: Academic.

Carstensen, L. L., & Lang, F. R. (1997). Social relationships in context and as context: Comments on social support and the maintenance of competence in old age. In S. Willis & K. W. Schaei (Eds.), *Societal mechanisms for maintaining competence in old age* (pp. 207–222). New York: Springer.

Charles, S. T., Reynolds, C. A., & Gatz, M. (2001). Age-related differences and change in positive and negative affect over 23 years. *Journal of Personality and Social Psychology, 80*, 136–151.

Cicirelli, V. G. (1981). *Helping elderly parents: Role of adult children*. Boston: Auburn House.

Cicirelli, V. G. (1991). Attachment theory in old age: Protection of the attached figure. In K. Pillemer & K. McCartney (Eds.), *Parent-child relations throughout life* (pp. 2–42). Hillsdale, NJ: Erlbaum.

Cicirelli, V. G. (1993). Attachment and obligation as daughters' motives for care giving behavior and subsequent effect on subjective burden. *Psychology of Aging, 8*, 144–155.

Cicirelli, V. G. (1995). *Sibling relationships across the life span*. New York: Plenum.

Cody, M. J., Dunn, D., Hoppin, S., and Wendt, P. (1999). Silver surfers: Assessing the consequence of Internet connectivity among adult learners. *Communication Education, 48*, 269–286.

Collins, N. L., & Read, S. J. (1990). Adult attachment: Implications for explanation, emotion and behavior. *Journal of Personality and Social Psychology, 58*, 644–663.

Coupland, N., Coupland, J., & Giles, H. (1991). *Language, society, and the elderly: Discourse, identity and ageing*. Oxford, England: Basil Blackwell.

Coupland, N., Coupland, J., Giles, H., & Henwood, K. (1988). Accommodating the elderly: Invoking and extending a theory. *Language and Society, 17*, 1–41.

Dickson, F. C., Hughes, P. C., Manning, L. D., Walker, K. L., Bollis-Pecci, T., & Gratson, S. (2002). Conflict in later-life, long-term marriages. *Southern Communication Journal, 67*, 110–121.

Feeney, J. A., & Noller, P. (1990). Attachment style as a predictor of adult romantic relationships. *Journal of Personality and Social Psychology, 58*, 281–291.

Feeney, J. A., & Noller, P. (1996). *Adult attachment*. Thousand Oaks, CA: Sage.

Floyd, K. (1995). Gender and closeness among friends and siblings. *Journal of Psychology, 129*, 193–202.

Floyd, K. (1996a). Brotherly love I: The experience of closeness in the fraternal dyad. *Personal Relationships, 3*, 369–385.

Floyd, K. (1996b). Communicating closeness among siblings: An application of the gendered closeness perspective. *Communication Research Reports, 13*, 27–34.

Floyd, K., & Morman, M. T. (2000). Affection received from fathers as a predictor of men's affection with their own sons: Tests of the modeling and compensation hypotheses. *Communication Monographs, 67,* 347–361.

Floyd, K., & Parks, M. R. (1995). Manifesting closeness in the interactions of peers: A look at siblings and friends. *Communication Reports, 8,* 69–76.

Franklin, K. M., Janoff-Bulman, R., & Roberts, J. E. (1990). Long-term impact of parental divorce on optimism and trust: Changes in general assumptions or narrow beliefs. *Journal of Personality and Social Psychology, 59,* 743–755.

Fredrickson, B., & Carstensen, L. L. (1990). Choosing social partners: How old age and anticipated endings make people more selective. *Psychology and Aging, 5,* 163–171.

Fung, H. H., Carstensen, L. L., & Lang, F. R. (2001). Age-related patterns in social networks among European Americans and African Americans: Implications for socioemotional selectivity across the life span. *International Journal of Aging and Human Development, 52,* 185–206.

Giles, H., & Williams, A. (1994). Patronizing the young: Forms and evaluations. *International Journal of Aging and Human Development, 39,* 33–53.

Glenn, N. D., & Kramer, K. B. (1985). The psychological well-being of adult children of divorce. *Journal of Marriage and the Family, 47,* 905–912.

Golish, T. D. (2000). Changes in closeness between adult children and their parents: A turning point analysis. *Communication Reports, 13,* 79–97.

Graham, E. E. (1997). Turning points and commitment in post-divorce relationships. *Communication Monographs, 64,* 350–368.

Grote, N. K., & Frieze, I. H. (1994). The measurement of friendship-based love in intimate relationships. *Personal Relationships, 1,* 275–300.

Guerrero, L. K. (1996). Attachment-style differences in intimacy and involvement: A test of the four-category model. *Communication Monographs, 63,* 269–292.

Harwood, J. (1998). Younger adults' cognitive representations of intergenerational conversations. *Journal of Applied Communication Research, 26,* 13–31.

Harwood, J., & Giles, H. (1996). Reactions to old people being patronized: The roles of response strategies and attributed thoughts. *Journal of Language and Social Psychology, 15,* 395–421.

Harwood, J., Mckee, J., & Lin, M. C. (2000). Younger and older adults' schematic representations of intergenerational communication. *Communication Monographs, 67,* 20–41.

Harwood, J., & Williams, A. (1998). Expectations for communication with positive and negative subtypes of older adults. *International Journal of Aging and Human Development, 47,* 11–33.

Hatfield, E., & Sprecher, S. (1986). Measuring passionate love in intimate relationships. *Journal of Adolescence, 9,* 383–410.

Hayashi, G. M., & Strickland, B. R. (1998). Long-term effects of parental divorce on love relationships: Divorce as attachment disruption. *Journal of Social and Personal Relationships, 15,* 23–38.

Hazan, C., & Shaver, P. R. (1987). Romantic love conceptualized as an attachment process. *Journal of Personality and Social Psychology, 52,* 511–524.

Hill, S. E. K., Bahniuk, M. H., & Dobos, J. (1989). The impact of mentoring and collegial support on faculty success: An analysis of support behavior, information adequacy, and communication apprehension. *Communication Education, 38,* 15–33.

Holladay, S. J., & Kerns, K. S. (1999). Do age differences matter in close and casual friendships? A comparison of age discrepant and age peer friendships. *Communication Reports, 12,* 101–114.

Huyck, M. H. (2001). Romantic relationships in later life. *Generations,* Summer, 9–17.

Jacquet, S. E., & Surra, C. A. (2001). Parental divorce and premarital couples: Commitment and other relationship characteristics. *Journal of Marriage and the Family, 63,* 627–638.

Johnson, C. L. (1999). Fictive kin among oldest old African Americans in the San Francisco Bay area. *Journal of Gerontology, 54B,* S368–S375.

Johnson, C. L., & Barer, B. M. (1995). Childlessness in late late life: Comparisons by race. *Journal of Cross Cultural Gerontology, 9,* 289–306.

Kalbfleisch, P. J. (2002). Communicating in mentoring relationships: A theory for enactment. *Communication Theory, 12,* 63–69.

Keith, P. M., Wacker, R. R., & Schafer, R. B. (1991). Equity in older families. In M. Szinovacz, D. J. Ekerdt, & B. H. Vinick (Eds.), *Families and retirement* (pp. 189–201). Newbury Park, CA: Sage.

Kurdek, L. A. (1998). Relationship outcomes and their predictors: Longitudinal evidence from heterosexual married, gay cohabitating and lesbian cohabitating couples. *Journal of Marriage and the Family, 60,* 553–568.

Lang, F. R., & Carstensen, L. L. (1994). Close emotional relationships in late life: Further support for proactive aging in the social domain. *Psychology and Aging, 9,* 315–324.

Lang, F. R., Staudinger, U. M., & Carstensen, L. L. (1998). Perspectives on socioemotional selectivity in late life: How personality and social context do (and do not) make a difference. *Journal of Gerontology, 53B,* 21–30.

Lawton, L., Silverstein, M., & Bengtson, V. L. (1994). Affection, social contact, and geographic distance between adult children and their parents. *Journal of Marriage and the Family, 56,* 57–68.

Lennartsson, C. (1999). Social ties and health among the very old in Sweden. *Research on Aging, 21,* 657–681.

Le Poire, B. A., Haynes, J., Driscoll, J., Driver, B. N., Wheelis, T. F., Hyde, M. K., Prochaska, M., & Ramos, L. (1997). Attachment as a function of parental and partner approach-avoidance tendencies. *Human Communication Research, 23,* 413–441.

Le Poire, B. A., Shepard, C., & Duggan, A. (1999). Nonverbal involvement, expressiveness and pleasantness as predicted by parental and partner attachment style. *Communication Monographs, 66,* 293–311.

Levenson, R. W., Carstensen, L. L., Friesen, W., & Ekman, P. (1991). Emotion, physiology, and expression in old age. *Psychology and Aging, 4,* 425–437.

Levenson, R. W., Carstensen, L. L., & Gottman, J. M. (1994). Influence of age and gender on affect, physiology, and their interrelations: A study of long-term marriages. *Journal of Personality and Social Psychology, 67,* 56–68.

476

Levy, M. B., & Davis, K. E. (1988). Love styles and attachment styles compared: Their relations to each other and to various relationship characteristics. *Journal of Social and Personal Relationships, 5*, 439–471.

Martin, K. A., Leary, M. R., & Rejeski, W. J. (2000). Self-presentational concerns in older adults: Implications for health and well-being. *Basic and Applied Social Psychology, 2*, 169–179.

Matthews, S. H. (1986). *Friendships through the life course: Oral biographies in old age.* Beverly Hills: Sage.

Morman, M. T., & Floyd, K. (1999). Affectionate communication between fathers and young adult sons: Individual- and relational-level correlates. *Communication Studies, 50*, 294–309.

Mulac, A., & Giles, H. (1996). "You are only as old as you sound": Perceived vocal age and social meanings. *Health Communication, 8*, 199–215.

Ognibene, T. C., & Collins, N. L. (1998). Adult attachment styles: Perceived social support and coping strategies. *Journal of Social and Personal Relationships, 15*, 323–345.

Parrott, T. M., & Bengtson, V. L. (1999). The effects of earlier intergenerational affection, normative expectations, and family conflict on contemporary exchanges for help and support. *Research on Aging, 21*, 73–105.

Peluchette, J. V., & Jeanquart, S. (2000). Professionals' use of different mentor sources at various career stages: Implications for career success. *Journal of Social Psychology, 140*, 549–564.

Peters, A., & Liefbroer, A. C. (1997). Beyond marital status: Partner history and well-being in old age. *Journal of Marriage and the Family, 59*, 687–699.

Pistole, M. C. (1989). Attachment in adult romantic relationships: Style of conflict resolution and relationship satisfaction. *Journal of Social and Personal Relationships, 6*, 505–510.

Roberts, R. E. L., & Bengtson, V. L. (1990). Is intergenerational solidarity a unidimensional construct? A second test of a formal model. *Journal of Gerontology, 45*, S12–S20.

Roe, K. M., & Minkler, M. (1999). Grandparents raising grandchildren: Challenges and responses. *Generations*, Winter, 25–32.

Rosen, K. S., & Rothbaum, F. (1993). Quality of parental care giving and security of attachment. *Developmental Psychology, 29*, 358–367.

Ryan, E. B., Hummert, M. L., & Boich, L. H. (1995). Communication predicaments of aging: Patronizing behavior toward older adults. *Journal of Language and Social Psychology, 13*, 144–166.

Scharfe, E., & Bartholomew, K. (1995). Accommodation and attachment representations in young couples. *Journal of Social and Personal Relationships, 12*, 389–401.

Senchak, M., & Leonard, K. E. (1992). Attachment styles and marital adjustment among newlywed couples. *Journal of Social and Personal Relationships, 9*, 51–64.

Silverstein, M., Conroy, S. J., Wang, H., Giarrusso, R., & Bengtson, V. L. (2002). Reciprocity in parent-child relations over the adult life course. *Journal of Gerontology, 57B*, S3–S13.

Silverstein, M., & Long, J. D. (1998). Trajectories of grandparents' perceived solidarity with adult grandchildren: A growth curve analysis over 23 years. *Journal of Marriage and the Family, 60*, 912–923.

Simpson, J. A. (1990). Influence of attachment styles on romantic relationships. *Journal of Personality and Social Psychology, 59*, 971–980.

Sternberg, J. (1986). A triangular theory of love. *Psychological Review, 93*, 119–135.

Sun, Y. (2001). Family environment and adolescents' well-being before and after parents' marital disruption: A longitudinal analysis. *Journal of Marriage and the Family, 63*, 697–713.

Updegraff, K. A., Madden-Derdich, D. A., Estrada, A. U., Sales, L. J., & Leonard, S. A. (2002). Young adolescents' experiences with parents and friends: Exploring the connections. *Family Relations, 51*, 72–80.

Wallerstein, J. S., & Blakeslee, S. (1989). *Second chances: Men, women, and children a decade after divorce*. New York: Ticknor & Fields.

Whitely, W., Dougherty, T. W., & Dreher, G. F. (1991). Relationship of career mentoring and socioeconomic origin to managers' and professionals' early career progress. *Academy of Management Journal, 34*, 331–351.

Whitely, W., Dougherty, T. W., & Dreher, G. F. (1992). Correlates of career-oriented mentoring for early career managers and professionals. *Journal of Organizational Behavior, 13*, 141–154.

Whitbeck, L., Hoyt, D. R., & Huck, S. M. (1994). Early family relationships, intergenerational solidarity, and support provided to parents by their adult children. *Journal of Gerontology, 49*, S85–S94.

Williams, A., & Nussbaum, J. F. (2001). *Intergenerational communication across the life span*. Mahwah, NJ: Erlbaum.

Yabiku, S. T., Axinn, W. G., & Thornton, A. (1999). Family integration and children's self-esteem. *American Journal of Sociology, 104*, 1494–1524.

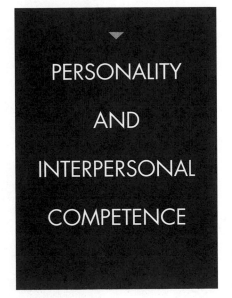

PERSONALITY

AND

INTERPERSONAL

COMPETENCE

In our final part, we look at the important issue of interpersonal communication competence. Chapter 15 on personality and interpersonal communication discusses eight important types of personality constructs that are directly relevant to interpersonal communication. Chapter 16, our final chapter, presents criteria that we can use for measuring competence and includes a self-test so you can practice assessing your own level of interpersonal competence. The chapter concludes with a review of the book, looking at all the issues — fundamentals, self-presentation, relational development, instrumental objectives, and personality — in terms of their applications for interpersonal competence.

C H A P T E R   1 5

INDIVIDUAL

DIFFERENCES AND

INTERPERSONAL

COMMUNICATION

THE IMPORTANCE OF KNOWING
ABOUT INDIVIDUAL DIFFERENCES

FACTORS AFFECTING INDIVIDUAL
DIFFERENCES
Machiavellian Behavior
Self-Monitoring Behavior
Locus of Control
Cognitive Complexity
Argumentativeness
Communication Apprehension
Loneliness

CHAPTER SUMMARY

After a vigorous game of racquetball, Gordon Gekko and Bud Fox were in the locker room when Gekko shared some of his philosophy of life and business:

"I don't throw darts at a board. I bet on sure things. Read Sun Tzu, *The Art of War*. Every battle is won before it's ever fought. Think about it. [Pause.] You're not as smart as I thought you were, buddy-boy. Have you ever wondered why the fund managers can't beat the S&P 500? Because they're sheep, and sheep get slaughtered. I've been in this business since '69. Most of these Harvard MBAs — they don't amount to [beans]. Give me a guy who is poor, smart, and hungry — and no feelings! You win a few, you lose a few, but you keep on fighting. And if you need a friend, get a dog. It's trench warfare out there, pal."

Later, Gekko also parts with advice to the stockholders at Teldar:

"Greed, for lack of a better word, is good. Greed is right. Greed works. Greed clarifies and cuts through and captures the essence of the evolutionary spirit. Greed in all its forms — greed for life, for money, for love, for knowledge — has marked the upward surge for mankind, and greed — you mark my words — will save not only Teldar Paper but that other malfunctioning corporation called the USA."

Communicators differ greatly in their goals, plans, and styles of communicating. For example, our scenario, adapted from the movie *Wall Street*, dramatizes how one person, Gekko, is driven by the need to compete and win, even if he has to lie, cheat, and violate laws to do so. We call this type of person a *Machiavellian*, a term synonymous with manipulator. The movie illustrates how Gekko uses communication to manipulate others so that he can achieve his goals. Gekko seduces the young Bud Fox to join the world of ethics-free affluence. Gekko rewards Fox with riches and beautiful women, shows him the "good life" at the finest restaurants, and confides in him as if Bud Fox were a good friend. However, Gekko also challenges and berates Bud Fox ("You're not as smart as I thought you were, buddy-boy"), manipulating Fox into wanting to do more and more to appease Gekko. Eventually Bud Fox engages in more frequent, and more blatant, unethical actions. Greed conquers. Communicators who place so much emphasis on being competitive and on winning use communication much differently than other types of communicators.

In this chapter we first look briefly at why it is important in interpersonal communication to be aware of individual differences. Then we review research on eight factors affecting individual differences: Machiavellian behavior, self-monitoring behavior, locus of control, cognitive complexity, argumentativeness, communication apprehension, and loneliness. We selected these factors because they have been studied carefully and thoroughly over the years and each plays an important role in interpersonal communication.

THE IMPORTANCE OF KNOWING ABOUT INDIVIDUAL DIFFERENCES

Anyone who wants to understand interpersonal communication needs to be aware of the important ways in which people differ. Although this chapter is placed late in our book, individual differences have been discussed throughout the various sections. *Individual differences* is a term that incorporates personality types (Machiavellian, self-monitors, etc.) and different styles of behaving that are "relatively enduring way[s] in which one individual differs from others" (Guilford, 1959, p. 6; see also Daly & Bippus, 1998). Individual differences influence which goals people find important. Some people value winning and being successful in achieving instrumental goals, and they place very little emphasis on friendship, love, and relational goals. Individual differences are associated with different skills and abilities — some people find it easier to adapt to different environments, some read (decode) nonverbal behaviors of others more accurately than do others, and some are better performers and speakers than others.

In this chapter, we emphasize the fact that individual differences among communicators affect the routine or typical way in which people communicate. Recall from Chapter 6 that we present an image of ourselves to others without thinking about our self-presentation. Some people want others to like them and engage in behaviors geared to ingratiate. Others want to self-promote and use name dropping, brags, and self-bolstering statements. We do this naturally, typically, and routinely without thinking about what we are doing (unless something activates a need to monitor the self-presentation). Because of this predisposition to ingratiate, self-promote, and so forth, many of the communicative behavioral patterns are overlearned, meaning that it is hard to change our style (see Godfrey, Jones, & Lord, 1986). Knowing an individual's personality type or style means that you can better understand why a person is behaving the way he or she is, predict how they will respond to events and messages, and, we hope, better adjust your message to him or her in order to achieve your goals.

There are important reasons why students of interpersonal communication should learn about individual differences. First, when people are attracted to others, they often assume similarity between themselves and the people to whom they are attracted. We engage in wishful thinking in that we assume the attractive other person is just like we are and that we share many beliefs, attitudes, and experiences. This is often false. We might have some things in common with an attractive potential partner, but he or she may be very, very different from us, or from what we initially believe he or she is like. Knowing about different personality types and differences is important.

Second, although opposites might be attracted to each other, those who stay together the longest have things in common. Certain individual styles are related to staying together longer (e.g., low self-monitors), whereas others are not related to long-term, stable, intimate relationships (e.g., also see section on attachment styles in Chapter 14). Knowing how similar or different you are to others is an important element in interpersonal communication.

A third issue deals with change. When dating others, we may believe that we can change some of the behaviors they engage in or encourage them to do something new. Some changes are unlikely, however, because a person's style of communicating has been shaped by years of practice, feedback, refinement, and repeated performances. Although people can learn new skills and adapt to new situations and roles, most personality types reflect certain presentational styles or communication patterns that are the product of years of experiences and rewards. You won't be able to make a verbally assertive or aggressive person nicer in a matter of a few months. You probably won't be able to make a shy person more talkative. If your goal is to form a satisfying long-term relationship, it is in your best interest to emphasize similarities and commonalities and not to plan or hope to change your partner.

In sum, knowledge of individual differences increases our ability to understand others, to predict their behavior, and perhaps to better adjust our messages to improve our own ability to achieve goals. Within interpersonal relationships, knowledge of individual differences helps us to know others for whom they really are (not our wishful thinking of assuming similarity), to assess our compatibility, and to determine whether or not we can change our dating partners in any realistic way.

FACTORS AFFECTING INDIVIDUAL DIFFERENCES

Machiavellian Behavior

Niccolò Machiavelli in 1513 wrote *The Prince*, which detailed how to achieve and retain power through deception, exploitation, and cruelty. Christie and Geis (1970) developed a test of **Machiavellianism** that measures a person's general tendency to be manipulative. However, over the years, people have raised questions about the accuracy of such a test. Hunter, Gerbing, and Boster (1982) argue that the tendency to be manipulative is not measured with a single set of questions. Rather, at least four different beliefs are involved in a Machiavellian orientation. Further, at the core of this personality type is the very high need to compete. In fact, manipulative characters are more likely to have come from families with intense sibling rivalry that encourages "beating out" the rival.

Table 15.1 presents items that measure four aspects of the Machiavellian orientation: attitude toward deceit, attitude toward flattery, beliefs concerning immorality, and cynicism. A Machiavellian would answer "true" to the sample items for flattery and cynicism, and "false" to the sample items for deceit and immorality; that is, a

<table>
<tr><td colspan="2" align="center">Table 15.1</td></tr>
<tr><td colspan="2" align="center">SAMPLE ITEMS FROM A MACHIAVELLIANISM SCALE</td></tr>
<tr><td>Topic</td><td>Sample Items</td></tr>
<tr><td>Deceit</td><td>• There is no excuse for lying to someone else.
• Honesty is the best policy in all cases.</td></tr>
<tr><td>Flattery</td><td>• It is wise to flatter important people.
• The best way to handle people is to tell them what they want to hear.</td></tr>
<tr><td>Immorality</td><td>• Most people who get ahead in the world lead clean, moral lives.
• Most people are basically good and kind.</td></tr>
<tr><td>Cynicism</td><td>• Anyone who trusts anyone else completely is asking for trouble.
• It is safest to assume that all people have a vicious streak that will come out if given the chance.</td></tr>
</table>

Source: Adapted from Hunter et al., 1982. Copyright by the American Psychological Association. Adapted by permission.

Machiavellian is highly cynical, has a positive attitude toward deceit and flattery, and believes that people are basically immoral. You may also take the complete test on-line at www.salon.com/books/it/1999/09/13/machtest, where high scorers are referred to as cutthroat, charming, confident and glib, arrogant, calculating, and prone to manipulation and exploitation. Low scorers are referred to as pussy cats and are also described as dependent and submissive.

Machiavellians (called *high Machs*) are more interested in pursuing (and achieving) their own personal goals, whereas *low Machs* focus on both personal and relational goals. High Machs prefer to win, sometimes at any cost; low Machs place more emphasis on maintaining interpersonal relations, perhaps giving less importance to winning if doing so embarrasses a friend or lessens a friendship. In fact, recent research on bargaining indicates that low Machs reciprocate trust during negotiations, while high Machs "overwhelmingly defect when it is to their advantage" to win larger rewards at bargaining tasks (Gunnthorsdottir, McCabe, & Smith, 2002, p. 49). Additional research over the years indicates that high Machs are more manipulative, more exploitive, and lie more often than low Machs (Cherulnik, Way, Ames, & Hutto, 1981; Vecchio & Sussmann, 1991; Wilson, Near, & Miller, 1998; Znakov, 1995). Other studies indicate that high Machs have unethical inclinations, accept kickbacks and rate ethical issues as less serious, compared to low Machs (Hegarty & Sims, 1978, 1979; Jones & Kavanaugh, 1996; Singhapakdi & Vitell, 1990).

Merrill, Lorimor, Thornby, and Vallbona (1998) found that senior medical students scoring high on Machiavellianism showed negative attitudes toward their patients, while senior medical students who had low scores on Machiavellianism and high scores on self-monitoring (see the next section) displayed a more positive orientation toward patients. As a general rule, low Machs are more likely to focus on interpersonal and relational goals than high Machs.

Here is a brief list of some relevant research findings (see Steinfatt, 1987):

1. High Machs place emphasis on winning over the maintenance of interpersonal relations.

2. High Machs manipulate others and change manipulative tactics quickly as a situation unfolds. For example, high Machs can switch easily during games and bargaining contexts so fast and so easily that they sometimes adamantly advocate a position that they had rejected only a few minutes earlier. Emotions are easily manipulated as well — a high Mach may be friendly one minute, make you feel guilty the next minute, and then use a threat to get you to do something. This adaptability and ability to manipulate emotions makes it easier for high Machs to lie more convincingly (DePaulo & Rosenthal, 1979; Exline, Thibaut, Hickey, & Gumpert, 1970; Geis & Moon, 1981).

3. High Machs are also better at bargaining because they look for ways to bargain effectively as the session progresses, show great flexibility in their behaviors, use emotional appeals, and enjoy the experience of bargaining. In some situations, high Machs are better salespersons than low Machs (Ricks & Fraedrich, 1999).

4. During encounters, low Machs focus on how people in the situation differ from each other, whereas high Machs focus on how people in the situation differ from themselves, looking for weaknesses to exploit.

5. High Machs are more resistant to social influence than low Machs; high Machs are less likely to change their beliefs just to please someone else or due to social pressures.

6. High Machs are more effective when the situation is unstructured (no time constraint, no limits placed on behaviors or roles, etc.), communication is face-to-face, and interpersonal manipulation is allowed. However, if high Machs had to send messages and memos through a formalized chain of command, they would be no more effective than low Machs.

7. High Machs tend to have fewer close friends than low Machs. Further, high Machs tend to prefer friends who are substantially lower than themselves in Machiavellian beliefs, possibly because low-Mach friends may be more easily influenced and may be naive and fail to understand the full range of a high Mach's manipulative behavior. However, even though high Machs may not have other high Machs as friends, they have a good deal of respect for other high Machs (who are other winners).

The implications of the research are that most of us like having a highly Machiavellian friend or co-worker, as long as we are both working toward the same goals. Otherwise, if we had to compete against a highly Machiavellian individual, we would be startled by their assertiveness and their ability to lie and change emotional appeals. If you want a long-term, stable, trusting relationship with another, you are better off with a low to mid-range Machiavellian.

Self-Monitoring Behavior

Self-monitoring is a personality construct that is intimately linked to a person's view of the self. High self-monitors pay close attention to their own behavior and to that of others in social situations, and they behave appropriately for a given situation. They are social chameleons who routinely blend in with their current environment. Snyder (1987) refers to the high self-monitor as a person who presents a pragmatic conception of the self that defines his or her identity in terms of specific social situations and roles. High self-monitors have acting ability, enjoy being at the center of attention, and can deceive by acting friendly even with people they dislike. Read each statement in Table 15.2 and state whether it is basically true or false with respect to you — the more often you answer "yes," the more likely it is that you are a high self-monitor.

Whereas the high self-monitor presents a pragmatic view of the self, the low self-monitor presents a view of the self that is principled, defining his or her identity in terms of personal characteristics and attributes. The self is a coherent identity of at-

---

Table 15.2
SAMPLE ITEMS FROM A SELF-MONITORING SCALE

1. I would probably make a good actor.
2. I have considered being an entertainer.
3. I can look anyone in the eye and tell a lie with a straight face (if for the right end).
4. In different situations and with different people, I often act like very different people.
5. I can make impromptu speeches even on topics about which I have almost no information.
6. I guess I put on a show to impress or entertain others.
7. I'm not always the person I appear to be.
8. I may deceive people by being friendly when I really dislike them.

Source: Adapted by permission from Snyder & Gangestad, 1986. Copyright by the American Psychological Association.

tributes, values, and attitudes that are held as enduring "for all time and for all places," unchanging as the communicator moves from situation to situation. A low self-monitor might say, "I am friendly, I am even-tempered, I am reliable," and so on, as if immutable. Low self-monitors have a rich and accessible knowledge of themselves, and they "choose words and deeds that accurately reflect their underlying beliefs, attitudes, and dispositions" (Snyder, 1987, p. 50).

Principled individuals are likely to maintain strong ethical standards, rejecting goals and situations in which they cannot "be themselves" and the use of tactics that they consider manipulative. In fact, Smith, Cody, LoVette, and Canary (1990) found that low self-monitors, especially males, rejected the use of emotional manipulations (putting on a happy face, pouting, sulking, etc.) and the use of pressure or force, relying instead on direct requests and logic. Let us review the relevant features of self-monitoring (see Snyder, 1987; Snyder & Gangestad, 1986):

1. In social situations, high self-monitors focus their efforts on reading and interpreting what is occurring around them to help them choose their own self-presentations and predict other people's intentions. Low self-monitors behave in ways compatible with their notion of their "true self" and accept people at face value.

2. High self-monitors are skilled "impression managers," displaying high levels of acting ability, flexibility, and adaptability. They have groomed these skills over the years to provide presentations of the self that are appropriate for the situations in which they find themselves, but they may communicate little about their private beliefs, feelings, or intentions. Low self-monitors present themselves in ways that reflect their true, authentic attitudes, values, and beliefs.

3. During conversations, high self-monitors are more highly motivated than low self-monitors to work on ensuring that the conversation is smooth-flowing, prompting others to talk about themselves, conveying an immediate sense of closeness or intimacy, using humor, reciprocating self-disclosures, and employing other skills to keep the conversation going.

4. High and low self-monitors differ in social participation. High self-monitors typically select specific friends for particular activities, and usually only for those selected activities. So high self-monitors have certain friends they go to football games with and others with whom they play golf, who are different from their tennis partners, etc. Further, these different friends may be separated by large geographic distances and may rarely (if ever) interact. In short, high self-monitors segment their social life. Low self-monitors share a wide range of activities with the same friend or group of friends. When asked to list whom they select for leisure activities and why, high self-monitors indicate that they prefer to play tennis with "good" tennis players and dance with "good" dancers. High self-monitors prefer to engage in activities with experts, thereby comparing their own abilities with experts and improving on these skills. Low self-monitors prefer to engage in activities with the people they like.

5. Although most high self-monitors have low self-monitors as casual friends, they prefer other high self-monitors as close friends; high self-monitors feel more comfortable with other people who understand and prefer the life of diversity. Low self-monitors prefer other low self-monitors as both casual and close friends. However, because friendships are intimately linked to specific activities, it is far easier (and more likely) for high self-monitors to replace friends to play tennis with, dance with, and so on. As high self-monitors' skills improve, they "trade up" to better experts in tennis, dancing, and so forth.

6. Low and high self-monitors differ in both the selection of dates and in the quality of the friendships they forge. High self-monitoring males spend more time studying a potential date's physical characteristics; in fact, when given the choice, the high-self-monitoring male would select a date with a beautiful woman even after she was described as "moody, withdrawn, and self-centered." Low self-monitoring men focused more on the potential date's psychological characteristics. High self-monitors date exclusively for briefer periods of time (relative to low self-monitors), date more different people in a year, have sex with more people in a year, and have more one-night stands than low self-monitors (especially low-self-monitoring females).

Low self-monitors view friendship "in terms of an affect-based orientation, a definite sense of depth of friendship, considerable conception of compatibility and endurance beyond the present context, and much evidence of a conception of nurturance and sympathy within friendship" (Snyder, 1987, p. 68). High self-monitors view friendship as an activity-based orientation, with a "somewhat shallow sense of friendship, little conception of compatibility beyond [the here and now], and little conception of nurturance" (p. 68).

Some of us like high self-monitors as friends because they are adaptable and flexible in their behaviors — they can be good actors, they fit in well and gracefully in different situations, and they are motivated to improve on their abilities. However, the relatively low level of commitment on the part of high-self-monitoring individuals means that it is easier for them to de-escalate or terminate one relationship and start new ones at the same time. Low self-monitors adopt a committed orientation in dating relationships. They prefer to spend time with their current dating partner, are more likely to date others exclusively and for longer periods of time, and date fewer people over the years. If you are a low self-monitor, you are probably more compatible with other low self-monitors.

Locus of Control

The concept of **locus of control** stems from work initiated by Rotter (1966), who argued that behavior is a function of expected reinforcement, the value of that reinforcement, and the situation, as defined by the person (Steinfatt, 1987). As people mature, they learn that they receive reinforcements for behaviors. If people behave in a certain way, receive reinforcement, and believe that their behavior caused the reinforcement, they have developed an internal locus-of-control orientation. People who have developed an internal orientation believe that their achievements will be rewarded, that they can have an impact on the world and help shape their own destinies. Internals believe that control of their behaviors stems from their own motivations, abilities, and achievements and that their behaviors are the cause of the reinforcements. By contrast, people who have developed an external locus-of-control orientation have little hope of controlling outcomes, feel that effort is not necessarily rewarded (one has to be in the right place at the right time to get rewards), and believe that their behavior is not motivated internally but rather that they are responding to external pressures.

Rotter (1982) developed a scale that measures one's general locus of control, and this locus-of-control measure also appears at www.queendom.com/tests/personality/lc_access.html, www.dushkiin.com/connectext/psy/ch11/survey11.mhtml, and hsc.usf.edu/~kmbrown/Locus_of_Control_Construct.htm. Table 15.3 presents some of the items that are used to measure the locus-of-control orientation for an important domain in interpersonal communication: affiliation. Other scholars have developed a measure of locus of control for one's health, and the reader who is interested in this topic is referred to http://hsc.usf.edu/~kmbrown/Locus_of_Control_Overview.htm. A related construct is called *self-efficacy* (discussed in earlier chapters) and deals with the extent to which individuals believe they have the knowledge, ability, and resources to control outcomes in their lives — that they have the ability to quit smoking, improve their grades, and achieve various personal, relational, and instrumental goals. A very informative Web site on self-efficacy is maintained by a community of on-line scholars (www.emory.edu/EDUCATION/mfp/effpage.html#top).

Look at the items listed in Table 15.3. If you have an internal locus of control, you would strongly agree with the items listed for ability and effort — you would agree that you have both the ability to engage in the behaviors and that you will make an effort to engage in the behaviors. Internals believe that they earn rewards because they have the ability to earn them and made the effort to do so. Externality, however, is derived from the belief that rewards are obtained either because of luck or something else external to the individual.

Research indicates that locus of control has a very strong impact on goals and communication (Canary, Cody, & Marston, 1986; Canary, Cunningham, & Cody, 1988; Lefcourt, 1982; Lefcourt, Von Bayer, Ware, & Cox, 1979; Lefcourt, Martin, Fick, & Saleh, 1985; Steinfatt, 1987).

1. Compared to externals, internal locus-of-control communicators are more willing to enter into a wider range of influence goals, rated goals as easier to imagine, claimed greater confidence, and indicated that they would be more persistent when attempting to influence others.

2. Internals are more resistant to influence and pressure than externals.

3. Internals employ personal powers of persuasion when attempting to influence others.

Table 15.3
SAMPLE ITEMS FROM A LOCUS-OF-CONTROL SCALE FOR AFFILIATION

Component	Sample Items
Ability	• It seems to me that getting along with people is a skill. • Having good friends is simply a matter of one's social skill. • I feel that people who are often lonely are lacking in social competence.
Effort	• Maintaining friendships requires real effort to make them work. • In my case, success at making friends depends on how hard I work at it. • If I didn't get along with others, it would tell me that I hadn't put much effort into the pursuit of social goals.
Context	• My enjoyment of a social occasion is almost entirely dependent on the personalities of the other people who are there. • Some people can make me have a good time even when I don't feel sociable. • No matter what I do, some people just don't like me.
Luck	• Making friends is a funny business; sometimes I have to chalk up my successes to luck. • In my experience, making friends is largely a matter of having the right breaks. • Often chance events can play a large part in causing rifts between friends.

Source: Adapted from Lefcourt et al., 1979. Used with permission of the authors.

Internals employ rationality (reasons, evidence), dyad-oriented tactics, and the manipulation of positive (but not negative) emotions when persuading others (Canary et al., 1986). At work, internals use more personal powers of persuasion, meaning that they worked with employees on improving performance, set goals and schedules, and praised employees to encourage performance (Goodstadt & Hjelle, 1973). Externals employ more threats to convince others to work. What explains this? Internals and externals employ tactics that are compatible with their own view of why people are rewarded. Externals believe that behaviors, and rewards for those behaviors, are caused externally by the context or by luck. To prompt workers to work more, externals try to apply external pressure on them (threats). Internals believe that the individuals' own behaviors cause the rewards to be given; the philosophy is to communicate to workers that hard work is noticed and rewarded. Hence externals apply external pressure on workers, whereas internals use a set of tactics designed to create a reward system (Goodstadt & Hjelle, 1973).

External and internal locus-of-control individuals are fundamentally incompatible. Externals believe that outcomes and rewards are derived by fate, luck, or chance happenings. Hence, they are motivated to "get by" rather than "get ahead" or make things happen. Externals might view internals as pushy, and internals might view externals as unmotivated.

Cognitive Complexity

Communicators differ substantially in the extent to which they have developed detailed ways of viewing and describing objects and people around them. This is known as **cognitive complexity.** Eskimos, for example, have many ways to describe snow and Americans have many ways to describe automobiles. People also differ in their ability to characterize people and to differentiate among different types of people. When asked to write out descriptions of one's friends, some can provide very detailed, thorough, and complex descriptions, noting the friends' habits, beliefs, mannerisms, ways of treating others, traits, and personality characteristics. People who provide such detailed descriptions are considered to be cognitively complex because they have developed, and use, a "relatively differentiated, abstract, and organized system of interpersonal constructs" (Burleson, 1987, p. 308). Some other people can provide only minimal descriptions of a person's characteristics ("He is big, tall. He runs fast. He's a good dancer.").

Descriptions people make of others vary along three criteria: (1) The number of constructs or terms used to describe people (called *interpersonal construct differentiation*); (2) the abstractness of these constructs (concrete, physical descriptions are low in abstractness; describing values and ethical principles would be highly abstract); and (3) the degree of organization of the constructs (merely listing features reflects a low level of organization). Most research in the area of cognitive complexity has relied on construct differentiation (Applegate, 1982; Burleson, 1984, 1987; Sypher & Applegate, 1984).

People with well-defined systems for characterizing others display several social perception skills (Burleson, 1987), including the ability to infer multiple causes for and consequences of the actions of others, to recognize and understand other people's emotional states, to reconcile and integrate potentially inconsistent information about others, to avoid making simplistic, global evaluations of others, and to convey and understand the cognitive, emotional, and motivational aspects of other people's perspectives. Because of these skills, cognitively complex people are more likely to employ *person-centered* messages when communicating with others. In person-centered speech, the communicator is able to construct and communicate a message that takes into consideration the perspective of the target; the target's values, beliefs, and emotional needs are incorporated into the communicator's message, thus making the communicator more effective at persuasion in conflict episodes and when comforting others.

Table 15.4 presents an example of what we mean by different levels of **perspective taking** (Delia, Kline, & Burleson, 1979). There are nine levels that span from inability or lack of taking the receiver's perspective (levels 0, 1, and 3) to full accommodation of the receiver's perspective. Cognitively complex communicators employ higher levels of other-perspective-taking, person-centered messages, and comforting messages when pursuing their relational and instrumental goals.

This personality variable has been shown to be important in achieving goals and in maintaining interpersonal relationships. Burleson and Caplan (1998, p. 255) concluded that "cognitively complex actors are more interpersonally effective in a variety of social contexts than their less complex counterparts." Studies demonstrate that more complex children are popular and better liked in school by peers, and they form more reciprocated friendships with others (relative to their low complex peers). Among friends and dating partners, there is a preference to be with similar others — more complex are attracted to others who are complex, the less complex are more attracted to those with lower levels of complexity (see Burleson & Caplan, 1998).

Table 15.4

LEVELS OF PERSPECTIVE TAKING

I. No Discernible Recognition of and Adaptation to the Target Perspective
    0. No statement of desire or request; no response given.
    1. Unelaborated request
        a. "Mommy, can I have someone over to sleep on my bed?" "Could I have a party please?"
        b. "Could you please take care of this puppy?" "Could you keep this dog?"
    2. Unelaborated statement of personal desire or need. This level also includes pleas, begging, or a repeated statement of the request or personal need.
        a. Simple statement of desire: "I want a party. Can I have one?" "I would enjoy a party."
        b. Please: "Please, pretty please and sugar on top?" "I'd tell her. Please, Mommy, it really means a lot. Please." "Oh, please don't say no."

II. Implicit Recognition of and Adaptation to the Target's Perspective
   3. Elaboration of the necessity, desirability, or usefulness of the persuasive request.
       a. Elaboration of persuader's need: "I've never had this before or anything so why don't you let me really have a party 'cause I've been wanting to do this for a long time." "Well, I'm going away pretty soon and I think it's really important to me to have a slumber party because I won't be here that much longer."
       b. Elaboration of need from the perspective of an involved party other than the persuader or target: "Would you keep this dog safe so he won't run out in the street and would you keep it in your house so it won't be scared and fight with the other dogs?" "My friends like me a lot. They would like to have a party and want you to let them come over. They'll be really disappointed if they can't 'cause they've been wanting to come over for a long time." "This dog is really skinny and he doesn't have any place to go."
   4. Elaboration of persuader's or persuasive object's need plus minimal dealing with anticipated counterarguments.
       a. Request refutes anticipated counterargument. "This is a lost puppy. Could you maybe keep it for a day or two 'cause I can't keep it at my house?" "Will you please keep this dog for me 'cause my Mom won't let me keep it?"
       b. Request is limited or altered to become more acceptable: "This poor puppy, he's been lost and he's hungry. Will you keep this dog while I try to find its owner?" "Mom, could I have a slumber party for my birthday and *just* invite about five girls?"
       c. Appealing to general principles: "I think that you should give me more responsibility by letting me have the party." "It's part of humanity you know. You have to take something."
   5. Elaborated acknowledgment of and dealing with multiple anticipated counterarguments.
       a. Refuting anticipated counterarguments: "Hi, I just found this puppy on the street and he didn't have a collar. If I took it home I know my father and mother wouldn't let me keep him because we already have a big dog. My father would have to get it shots, and we really don't have any place to keep him. Our dog would probably hurt the puppy. So could you keep him?"
       b. Alleviating effects of anticipated counterarguments: "It's big enough to stay outside and you only have to feed him and water him and that doesn't take all day." "And I'd make sure everything's cleaned up and I'd pay for all the food. And there wouldn't be any beer." "Mother,

(Continued)

(Table continued from previous page)

can I have six kids over? We'll make up our sleeping bags and we'll fix our own popcorn." "There wouldn't be a lot of running around and there would only be about five people. I'd tell her what kind of entertainment we were going to have to show that we'd stay out of trouble."

III. Explicit Recognition of and Adaptation to the Target's Perspective

    6. Truncated efforts to demonstrate relevant consequences to the target of accepting (or rejecting) the persuasive request.

        a. General advantage to anyone granting this request: "You know, a dog's a good playmate for kids." "It would be good for you to have a dog around as protection or a friend."

        b. Bribes: "If you let me have a party, I'll make something that my father likes to eat." "If you keep the puppy, I'll wash your car every day."

    7. Elaboration of specific consequences of accepting (or rejecting) the persuasive request to one with characteristics of the target.

        a. "You look kind of lonely. This dog would be a good companion, somebody to talk to and everything." "You need a watchdog around here because there have been some break-ins around here. This dog might be able to help you."

        b. "You've been saying you wanted to get to know my friends better. If you let me have a party, you can get to know them."

    8. Demonstrable attempts by the persuader to take the target's perspective in articulating an advantage or attempts to lead the target to assume the perspective of the persuader, another person, or the persuasive object.

        a. Demonstrable attempts to take the target's perspective in articulating an advantage: "If I were you and I lived alone, I'd like a good watchdog like this one."

        b. Leading the target to take the perspective of an involved party: "I'd tell her how he might have an owner and if she was in the same situation, if she had lost her puppy, she would want somebody to take care of it for her." "If you were out in the cold and everything, wouldn't you want somebody to come and pick you up and give you a home? That's what this puppy wants."

COGNITIVE COMPLEXITY AS A PERSONALITY TYPE

Individuals scoring high on cognitive complexity have the ability to analyze a situation or goal and break it down into many smaller elements, explore those elements and the relationships between elements, and devise a plan of action suitable and refined for the particular elements (persons, time constraints, resources, etc.) involved. They can think in multidimensional ways. Research summarized in Streufert and Swezey (1986) provide a number of conclusions of relevance to communication, interpersonal relationships, and managing others:

Attraction: People of high complexity tend to be attracted to each other and to less complex people, while people of lower complexity are usually attracted only to each other based on similar content (e.g., similar attitudes).

Communication: Complex persons are often more effective at a communication-dependent task. They are more resistant to persuasive attacks if inoculated (e.g., have been trained in counter-arguments).

Creativity: Flexibly complex persons are often able to generate more novel, unusual, and potentially remote views and actions.

Flexibility: Complex persons are often more flexible in thinking, and may demonstrate more fluency of ideas in creativity.

Information: Complex people tend to be more open to new information, rely more on their own integrative efforts than new information, seek more novel information, search across more categories of information, and be less externally information bound. They tend to take in more information and form more well-rounded impressions than less complex persons.

Problem Solving: Complex people tend to search for more different kinds of information when faced with a decision problem. They are often less certain after a decision, especially if verification is unavailable.

Strategic Planning: Complex individuals are often better strategic planners due to consideration of more information, from more perspectives, and greater flexibility in considering alternatives. They usually develop more inclusive long-range goals, consider a wider range of implications, and develop more complex strategies.

Source: Streufert, S., & Swezey, R.W. (1986). Complexity, managers, and organizations. New York: Academic Press. Adapted from: www.css.edu/users/dswenson/web/COGCOMPX/HTM

Argumentativeness

Infante (1987; Infante, Chandler, & Rudd, 1989; Infante & Rancer, 1982; Infante, Trebling, Shepard, & Seeds, 1984; Infante & Wigley, 1986; Rancer, 1998) proposes that people vary in the degree to which they are argumentative. Argumentativeness is seen as the motivation to defend one's own view and attack the position of others. It also reflects a lack of motivation to avoid arguments. Accordingly, Infante and Rancer (1982) offer a measure of argumentativeness that is composed of two factors, approaching arguments and avoiding arguments. Table 15.5 presents examples. The measure can also be found at http://www.hksrch.com/hk/quiz/argue.htm.

Argumentativeness is a characteristic of someone who likes to confront others' ideas. For example, Rancer and Infante (1985) found that for highly argumentative people, motivation to argue was increased when the conversational partner was also thought to be highly argumentative. But those who were low in argumentativeness were not motivated to argue regardless of the conversational partner's degree of argumentativeness. Thus argumentative people enjoy debating other argumentative people.

It is important to distinguish argumentativeness from verbal aggressiveness. **Verbal aggressiveness** refers to the tendency to attack the self-concept of the partner verbally with the intention of causing hurt (Infante & Wigley, 1986). Argumentativeness and verbal aggression are different in their locus of attack. That is, an argumentative person attacks the partner's ideas, but a verbally aggressive person attacks the

---

Table 15.5
SAMPLE ITEMS FROM AN ARGUMENTATIVENESS SCALE

1. Arguing over controversial issues improves my intelligence.
2. I enjoy avoiding arguments.
3. I am energetic and enthusiastic when I argue.
4. Once I finish an argument, I promise that I will not get into another.
5. I have a pleasant, good feeling when I win a point in an argument.
6. When I've finished arguing with someone, I feel nervous and upset.
7. I enjoy a good argument over a controversial issue.
8. I enjoy defending my point of view on an issue.
9. I feel refreshed to do well in an argument.
10. I have the ability to do well in an argument.

Source: Adapted from Infante & Rancer, 1982. Used with permission of the authors.

When people cannot present or defend arguments, they tend to lash out in aggressive ways, or say nothing.

Freda Leinwand/Monkmeyer

partner. Infante, Sabourin, Rudd, and Shannon (1990) identified ten types of verbally aggressive behavior: character attacks (making unfavorable remarks about the partner's character), competence attacks (attacking the person's ability to be a good partner), background attacks (attacking the person's upbringing), criticism of physical appearance, maledictions (wishing evil for a person), teasing, ridicule, threats, swearing, and nonverbal emblems (using facial expressions, gestures, and eye behaviors to attack another).

Studies indicate that argumentativeness is either unrelated to verbal aggressiveness or that being argumentative can actually decrease the tendency to be aggressive. Infante and Wigley (1986) found that argumentativeness was unrelated to verbal aggressiveness. Similarly Infante and co-workers (1984) found that highly argumentative people were unlikely to revert to aggressive communication when confronted with a stubborn roommate. Infante, Chandler, and Rudd (1989), in fact, found support for a "skill deficiency model" of interpersonal violence. This means that interpersonal violence is partly due to an inability to present one's ideas. These researchers found that violent marriages were characterized by lower self-reported argumentativeness and higher reports of spousal verbal aggressiveness.

Argumentativeness appears to be related to constructive outcomes, and aggressiveness is linked to negative outcomes (such as abuse). A growing body of evidence supports the "argumentative skill deficiency model of intrafamily violence," indicating that those who cannot present, defend, and counterargue verbal arguments are the ones who lash out in aggression and violence. According to Infante, Riddle, Horvath, and Tumlin (1992), people resort to the use of aggressive behavior in order to reciprocate hurt or disdain for the partner or to vent anger. They may also behave aggressively when they are unable to think of an effective argument or when a rational conversation degenerates into a fight. Some people are taught to handle conflict with aggression. Some people are aggressive because something in the present situation triggers an aggressive reaction to a previous unresolved hurt. Some people imitate action seen on TV. Two other reasons deal with the motive to appear tough, like an intimidator, or simply to be mean-spirited or vindictive. These authors found that four of these motivations distinguished the most aggressive persons from the least aggressive ones: wanting to appear tough, degenerating from rationality to aggression, wanting to be mean, and disdain for the partner.

Some differences in argumentativeness due to culture have been found. Rancer (1998) reports that Americans are more argumentative than Japanese, and American women are more argumentative than Korean women (but there is no significant difference among men). Norwegian and Finnish samples score higher on argumentativeness than Americans.

Semic and Canary (1998) examined how friends developed points of arguments during interactions. They discovered that high/high argumentative dyads (i.e., where both people are highly argumentative) had the highest proportion of completed, developed arguments (a warrant plus a claim); and high/low argumentative dyads had the lowest proportion of developed arguments (they asserted their views without evidence or backing, interrupted the other person, and so forth). Looking only at one member of the dyad revealed no relationship between argumentativeness and the development of arguments; rather, friends reciprocated each other's behaviors. Some partners would either increase or decrease argument development in order to match their partner's level of argument development.

There are several important implications for interpersonal relationships. People who score high on argumentativeness and low on aggression are perceived as more competent, and hence more likable, and they score higher on self-esteem. One study found that marital satisfaction was highest when husbands and wives did not have similar scores on argumentativeness — in traditional marriages, the husband's score is somewhat higher than the wife's (Rancer, 1998). Another study found that husbands were more satisfied with their marriages when their wives were high in argumentativeness (Rancer, 1998). Combined, these studies indicate that couples are happy and satisfied when husbands score somewhat higher than wives, who are moderate in levels of argumentativeness. People who score very low on argumentativeness are likely to give in during family discussions and at some point in time lash out in aggression when frustrated. Rancer, Infante, and colleagues propose teaching family members to be more skilled in argument and conflict management as one way to help the low argumentative/high aggressive family member.

Communication Apprehension

Many individuals suffer from high levels of anxiety over how they might be evaluated in a given situation or how they might behave. This is referred to as **communication apprehension.** There appears to be a strong genetic influence on scores on communication apprehension (Beatty, McCroskey, & Heisel, 1998) as well as general social anxiety (Beatty, Heisel, Hall, Levine, & LaFrance, 2002), indicating that some people are born more anxious than others, and are likely to have more anxiety about speaking in public, entering into situations involving communication, and anticipating how they will be judged or evaluated because of their communication skills or performance. Anxious and nonanxious individuals differ significantly in both social relations and in communicative behaviors (Daly, McCroskey, Ayres, Hopf, & Ayres, 1997; Daly & Stafford, 1984; McCroskey, 1982; McCroskey & Beatty, 1998).

1. *Social Skills.* Anxious individuals date less often and possess fewer social skills than nonanxious individuals. They rate themselves lower in physical attractiveness. Anxious individuals are more likely to date one person exclusively for a relatively long time and are not likely to accept blind dates. Anxious individuals have fewer friends, are shy and conformist, and are less likely to accept a position of leadership in a group. They are not as capable in constructing strategies for making friends.

2. *Behaviors.* Anxious individuals are much more likely to display their anxiety via nonverbal behaviors: greater body tension, greater disinterest, less eye contact, more fidgeting, less nodding, more leaning away from others, less facial pleasantness, and greater space needs.

3. *Conversation Skills.* Anxious individuals speak less frequently and more briefly than nonanxious communicators. They are less likely to interrupt others effectively and are relatively ineffective in initiating or controlling a conversation. Anxious communicators are more likely to speak with disfluencies, make speech errors, and exhibit more nervous smiling, more frequent silences, more verbal repetitions, and longer latencies. They recall fewer previous interactions and make more mistakes in what they recall.

Very high levels of anxiety or apprehension are detrimental to the communicator's personal life, often limiting the ability to achieve instrumental goals. Some campuses or schools have developed programs for anxiety desensitization that enable students to cope more effectively with high levels of anxiety that interfere with daily life. At a minimum, communicators who suffer from high levels of communication apprehension should concentrate on developing the social skills necessary to meet people, make friends, and achieve interpersonal goals. As McCroskey and Beatty (1998) note, training can be implemented to help reduce the negative effects of high levels of communication apprehension, but forcing apprehensive individuals to speak in public is "very likely to reinforce and strengthen the CA [communication apprehension] response" (p. 228). Cross-cultural comparisons and issues are reported in Klopf (1997). Additional information about communication apprehension can be found at www.mhhe.com/socscience/speech/commcentral/mgcomap.html.

Loneliness

Loneliness refers to the pain experienced due to the discrepancy between desired and actual social contacts (Bell, 1985; Spitzberg & Canary, 1985; Zakahi & Duran, 1985). Loneliness is a pervasive problem in society, and there are a number of Web sites offering information about loneliness as well as advice on how to reduce loneliness (see www.couns.uiuc.edu/Brochures/loneliness.htm, www.ub-counseling.buffalo.edu/loneliness.shtml, www.crha-health.ab.ca/hlthconn/items/lon-oa.htm, www.solosingls.com/sslonelygoalset.htm, www.counsel.ufl.edu/selfHelp/dealingWithLoneliness.asp, www.counseling.swt.edu/overcoming_loneliness.htm). The University of Illinois Web site, for example, takes the position that the experience of loneliness should be viewed as a signal or indicator that a person's important needs are not being met, and that accurate and realistic plans should be taken to end loneliness. The bad news is that many people experiencing loneliness also feel depressed, angry, afraid, and misunderstood, they become very critical of themselves, and they engage in self-pity. This negative psychological frame of mind is associated with (a) greater difficulty in taking social risks and initiating communication with others (including phone calls, introducing one's self to others, participating in groups, or enjoying parties) and less assertive behavior, (b) reduced skills in self-disclosure and a tendency to approach social encounters with mistrust and cynicism, and (c) increased negative thoughts and expectations about self and others and the tendency to think that others will reject them (even before trying to meet and talk to them) (www.couns.uiuc.edu/Brochures/loneliness.htm). They also spend time worrying (see the box "How Highly 'Apprehensive' Worriers Differ from 'Normal' Nonworriers").

Practical advice on ending loneliness is available at most university counseling offices and Web sites (see the ones listed in the preceding paragraph) and some health organizations. This is because lonely students have more restless sleep than nonlonely ones, and a lifetime of loneliness is related to health problems like high blood pressure and chronic sleep dreprivation (www-news.uchicago.edu/releases/00/000807.loneliness.shtml). This practical advice includes suggestions for personal changes (setting personal goals in skills to achieve), seeking contact with others and spending time with others, expanding one's social network and reflecting back on quality friendships and valuing the friends one has (as opposed to wishing or dreaming that some marvelous romantic relationship will one day take place, ending your loneliness, or becoming overly committed to only one person, hoping that one other person can solve a person's feelings of loneliness) (www.couns.uiuc.edu/Brochures/loneliness.htm).

Unless changes are made in knowledge of social skills and in implementing the skills in order to achieve goals, lonely individuals are likely to stay lonely. This is

HOW HIGHLY "APPREHENSIVE" WORRIERS DIFFER FROM "NORMAL" NONWORRIERS

Our text says a good deal about highly apprehensive individuals and lonely individuals. As the following newspaper article suggests, people who are chronic worriers are also probably highly apprehensive and probably more lonely than nonworriers. Chronic worriers apparently think much differently from nonworriers.

How to help the chronic worrier? Besides seeking counseling, the article recommends two ways. First, it is unproductive to worry all the time, so one recommendation is to set aside a certain time to worry. The second recommendation involves interpersonal communication — being assisted by friends who communicate social support and who help the worrier understand what is and isn't worth worrying about.

We all know them: the walking worried. The worry warts of the world. The woe-is-me, hand-wringing . . . well, you get the idea.

Generally, chronic worriers have been considered somewhat annoying people who could stop worrying if they wanted but who instead get a perverse pleasure from it.

That view may be unsympathetic. In recent years, chronic worriers have attracted greater interest among psychologists, who now believe that extreme worrying is an addictive thought pattern that can lead to serious mental and physical consequences. But they also say it is something that can be successfully treated with hard work.

"In therapy it has always been considered as not very serious and that there was not much you could do about it," says Dr. Gary Emery, a worry expert and director of the Los Angeles Center for Cognitive Therapy. "Surprisingly, for how prevalent it is and how much suffering it causes, it hasn't been studied much."

Experts' efforts over the last decade have been devoted to defining chronic or obsessive worrying. After all, everyone worries. But what is the difference between worrying a little and worrying a lot?

A chronic worrier, Emery says, is "someone who has a morbid preoccupation with what can go wrong. Chronic worrying is unrealistic in the sense that it's unhelpful and it's counterproductive. It's realistic in the sense that what you're worried about could actually happen. It's not paranoia like, "The CIA is after me." . . .

In a recent study, [Michael Vasey at Ohio State University] looked at 48 college students, half of whom were found to be chronic worriers. When asked what worried them, both groups gave similar responses: academic success, relationships, and health.

The students were then asked, "What is it about getting good grades that worries you?" And this is where the differences stood out. Worriers produced much longer lists of possible consequences.

(Continued)

(Box continued from previous page)

For example, chronic worriers saw a stronger likelihood that not getting good grades would eventually result in pain, physical deterioration, and death. To a nonworrier, the result might be unhappiness and strain, but nothing beyond that. . . .

[Vasey] was stunned to see how large a role worrying seemed to play in some people's lives. The worriers in his group said they spent at least half of their waking hours worrying. In contrast, the others said they worry less than 10% of each day. . . .

But worriers can learn to break the habit, experts point out. . . .

"The problem is that people worry any place and every place, but . . . never get past that initial stage of thinking about what may go wrong," Vasey says. "But if you devote enough time to it [in one sitting], then maybe you can begin to come up with solutions." . . .

The key to giving up the worry habit is realizing that worrying doesn't help, Emery says.

"It comes from the insight that it's a waste of time. . . . It doesn't solve things. It's a substitute for action. When people realize this, they can let go of it." . . .

Some people find it helps to ask themselves, "What is the worst thing that can happen?" he says — and to realize that almost none of those "worst things" happen.

According to Vasey, people who cope well with worries often do so because they ask other people, "Do you think I should be worried about this?"

"When someone says, 'I think you're overreacting,' most people can use this information to stop worrying," he says. "But serious worriers are probably going to need more help than that."

From Shari Roan, "Oh, No! *Now* What Could Go Wrong?" Copyright 1993, *Los Angeles Times.* Reprinted by permission.

because they actually engage in behaviors that perpetuate their loneliness. Bell and Roloff (1991) found that loneliness was negatively correlated with choosing situations in which a person might find potential partners. They also found that it was negatively associated with disclosures about one's personality and about one's activities and interests — lonely individuals do not disclose or reveal information that is highly personal, preferring nonintimate revelations such as demographics (age, place of birth, etc.). Hawken, Duran, and Kelly (1991) found that lonely individuals failed to develop rapport with their roommates, failed to maintain composure in social settings, made inappropriate self-disclosures, and experienced a limited range of social contacts (fewer kinds of friends and acquaintances). Similarly, Solano, Batten, and Parrish (1982) found that lonely people disclosed less intimate topics to a member of the opposite sex than non-lonely people did.

The fact that lonely individuals behave differently than non-lonely ones may help to explain research on loneliness and Internet use. Ideally, any person, even a lonely one, can go on-line and disclose a true inner self to others while on-line, and make friends on-line (see McKenna, Green, & Gleason, 2002). However, for some lonely individuals going on-line and spending time on-line may or may not reduce their feelings of loneliness: It depends on what they do and how they communicate with others on-line. One study found that uses of and the consequences of being on-line was an extension of the users' personalities — extraverted individuals and those with a good deal of social support benefited more from being on-line than introverts and those lacking social support (Kraut et al., 2002). Another study found that being on-line can effectively reduce "social loneliness" (number and type of contact) of users, but not the "emotional loneliness" (feelings of closeness and emotional bonding) (Moody, 2001). Simply being on-line frequently will not reduce feelings of loneliness.

Margulis, Derlega, and Winstead (1984) suggested four conditions that underlie the experience of loneliness: (1) the unavailability of a person or group to help the individual achieve valued goals; (2) the belief that this unavailability will continue for some time; (3) the unavailability of a companion, friend, or acquaintance for extremely important or publicly expected occasions (holidays, weddings, formal dinners, etc.); and (4) a steady desire, unsatisfied over an extended period of time, to have such a social partner.

Joel Gordon

Both communication apprehension and loneliness reflect a limited social environment. To be emotionally healthy, people in such circumstances must work at developing skills that will let them communicate and connect with others.

There are two kinds of loneliness, situational and chronic. Situational loneliness is the temporary loneliness that people experience now and then. Chronic loneliness tends to be severe and lasts months and perhaps even years. Chronic loneliness, much more than situational loneliness, has been associated with dysfunctional social behaviors. For example, Spitzberg and Canary (1985) found that chronically lonely people are seen as less communicatively competent than situationally lonely and non-lonely people.

Why do some people become chronically lonely and other people experience only transient situational loneliness? Spitzberg and Canary (1985) feel that chronic loneliness is explainable in terms of attribution theory.

> Persons who attribute loneliness to unstable, external, and controllable causes are more likely to take steps to remedy their loneliness than those who attribute loneliness to stable, internal, and uncontrollable causes. Furthermore, chronically lonely people are much more likely than situationally lonely people to attribute their loneliness to stable, uncontrollable causes. (p. 389)

Imagine that you move to a new city because you change jobs or transfer to a new university. This may well involve losing touch with valued friends and family and even a breakup with a romantic partner. You feel the loss of these relationships, but you attribute that feeling to factors that are external, unstable, and controllable. That is, the move, not your specific actions, caused the loss of friendships; and this type of change is unusual, rather than a stable, recurring process. Basically you believe that your ability to meet and gain new friends is something that you can control. Given this scenario, you probably are experiencing situational loneliness and will make new friends in time. Chronically lonely people, by contrast, see their loneliness as something that will not end, due in part to their character, previous experiences, and lack of social skills.

Over time, as the experience of loneliness progresses, the chronically lonely person's social skills worsen, even atrophy, and the lonely person may give up on interpersonal goals. Segrin's (1998) review of the research reveals that chronically lonely people engage in behaviors and hold onto beliefs that prevent them from establishing relationships. For instance, chronically lonely people (versus situationally lonely and other people) make fewer references to their partners, appear less involved nonverbally in conversation (e.g., offer fewer back-channels), demonstrate less attention in their partner, self-disclose less, and talk less in general (Segrin, 1998, p. 229, also see Bell, 1985). Chronically lonely individuals also adopt a negative view of themselves and others — they make more negative ratings of people they have just met, have less trust in others, and make more negative, cynical attributions about the behavior of others. To change and become less lonely, the chronically lonely must fight against both a lack of social skills and a cynical belief system about others and relationships.

Table 15.6

SAMPLE ITEMS FROM THE REVISED UCLA LONELINESS SCALE

1. I lack companionship.
2. There is no one I can turn to.
3. I am no longer close to anyone.
4. My interests and ideas are not shared by the people around me.
5. I feel left out.
6. My social relationships are superficial.
7. No one really knows me well.
8. I feel isolated from others.
9. I am unhappy being so withdrawn.
10. People are around me but not with me.

Source: Adapted from Russell et al., 1980. Used with permission of the author.

Table 15.6 presents sample items from the Revised UCLA Loneliness Scale (Russell, Peplau, & Cutrona, 1980), the most popular measure of loneliness. If the items apply to you over the past two weeks, you are facing situational loneliness. If they apply over the past two years, chronic loneliness is a possibility. Regardless, you should understand that the remedy for loneliness is communicating with others. Eight steps for developing friendships are offered on Web sites devoted to this question: (1) Remind yourself that loneliness will not last forever; (2) look at your daily schedule and find ways to do things with other people; (3) engage in activities that are of genuine interest to you, where you can meet people with common interests; (4) make use of campus and community resources and join groups and sign up for excursions, and more [but avoid cult groups who prey upon lonely individuals]; (5) work at developing social skills and communication skills, and practice getting to know others and letting them get to know you; (6) keep an open mind in meeting each person and don't prejudge them based on previous experiences or stereotypes; (7) let interpersonal relationships develop slowly and naturally (don't rush to intimacy in order to end loneliness); and (8) value each friendship for the positive uplifting feature each one provides, value the unique characteristics of each friend, male or female, same age or age-discrepant, casual, close, or intimate. Stop believing that only a romantic relationship will end loneliness. These recommendations are found on-line at www.couns.uiuc.edu/Brochures/loneliness.htm. Helpful links to information about loneliness are provided in the box "Loneliness: Helpful Links"

LONELINESS: HELPFUL LINKS

The Psychological Self-Help [http://mentalhelp.net/psyhelp/chap6/chap6m.htm]. Contains an excellent summary of loneliness and self-help techniques you can use to overcome it.

The University of Illinois at Urbana-Champaign Counseling Center [http://www.couns.uiuc.edu/Brochures/loneline.htm]. Contains some good tips to help alleviate loneliness.

Solitude-Loneliness [http://www.annabelle.net/topics/solitude-loneliness.html]. This Web page gives you additional definitions and ideas about loneliness. Traces back ideas from the time of Aristotle to Mother Teresa.

What Should I Do? [http://www.whatshouldido.com/lonely.shtml]. This Web page offers good advice for people who feel lonely, especially for those people who are suffering from homesickness as well.

Love and Loneliness [http://www.geocities.com/a_lonely0us/love_lost.htm]. A Web page developed for those looking for more information on love and loneliness.

Psychcentral.com [http://psychcentral.com/]. This is Dr. John Grohol's Mental Health Page, a personalized one-stop index for psychology, support, and mental health issues, resources, and people on the Internet.

Philosophy and Self-Help Site [http://www.primechoice.com/philosophy/shelp/soskill.htm]. This is a site to help you build your social skills.

If you need information, support, or help for an emotional problem please check out the following sites:

Befrienders International [http://www.befrienders.org/mainindex.htm]

Mentalhealth.org [http://www.mentalhealth.org/]

The Samaritans [http://www.samaritans.org.uk/]

Social Anxiety Support [http://www.socialanxietysupport.com/]

Berent Associates — Center for Shyness and Social Therapy [http://www.social-anxiety.com/]

Others located on-line at http://web.aces.uiuc.edu/loneliness/links.htm

Adapted from: http://web.aces.uiuc.edu/loneliness/links.htm

(at least for those in North America or countries similar to North American countries). Not all people cope the same way with loneliness. North Americans rely more on social support groups to cope with loneliness, relative to South Asian or West Indian peoples, who are more likely to reflect on the causes of loneliness, seek more activity, and to rely on religion than do individuals in North America (Rokach, 1999).

STUDENT AS OBSERVER EXERCISE: PERSONALITIES ON TELEVISION'S "SEINFELD"

The television show "Seinfeld" airs in syndication routinely. The show was (and is) popular in part because of the distinct personalities of the characters. Recall the show (or watch some episodes of the show) and write a brief statement about each character's personality. That is, answer these questions:

George

Is George a high or low Mach? Why do you say this? Or, give an example.

Is George a high or low self-monitor? Why do you say this? Or, give an example.

Is George an internal locus of control person or an external locus of control person? Why do you say this? Or, give an example.

Is George a cognitively complex individual, or cognitively simple individual? Why do you say this? Or, give an example.

Is George a person who is high or low in argumentativeness? Why do you say this? Or, give an example.

Is George a person who is high or low in communication apprehension? Why do you say this? Or, give an example.

Is George a lonely individual? Why do you say this? Or, give an example.

Answer the same questions for Elaine, Jerry, and Kramer.

CHAPTER SUMMARY

Machiavellians are well equipped to manipulate others and occasionally lie and manipulate emotions so as to compete better and win. On the other hand, self-monitoring individuals vary fundamentally in the presentation of self in everyday life. High self-monitoring individuals adapt to groom public images so that they fit in appropriately to the situation, and they seek out new people to date and experts in various areas of play, leisure, and work. Internal locus-of-control individuals have higher confidence in influencing others than people with an external locus of control, and they employ more tactics, including rationality and persistence, to influence others. Cognitive complexity, the ability of individuals to describe the people they know, is strongly related to the ability of the communicator to employ messages that adopt the receiver's perspective, thus helping achieve various relational and instrumental goals. For these personality types, similarity in behaviors and scores probably increases compatibility.

Argumentative individuals seek and obtain satisfaction from oral argument and from the mental work involved in researching evidence, using logic, and applying their minds. Those who lack a skill in arguing reasonably often lash out in aggression; hence the importance of training. People suffering from communication apprehension and loneliness have constructed for themselves a limited social environment. Interpersonal communication can help them overcome these barriers.

KEY TERMS

▼

argumentativeness, p. 496
cognitive complexity, p. 491
communication apprehension, p. 499
locus of control, p. 488
loneliness, p. 500

Machiavellianism, p. 483
perspective taking, p. 492
self-monitoring, p. 486
verbal aggressiveness, p. 496

EXERCISES FOR FURTHER DISCUSSION

▼

1. List the three goals that you consider the most important for you to achieve. Then outline a plan for achieving each of those goals.
   a. Will your personality help you achieve these goals?
   b. What individual resources do you need to achieve your goals that you don't already have? How might you go about obtaining those resources?

c. Discuss your plan with someone who knows you well, and see if that person thinks your plans sound workable, given your personality.

2. Review the material in Chapter 6 on self-presentation styles (ingratiators, intimidators, exemplifiers, supplicators, self-promoters). List the personality constructs (or individual differences) discussed in this chapter, and write next to each the self-presentation style (or styles) that you believe the personality type would most likely use. Compare your answers with those of other class members.

3. Think about your own reactions to the personality constructs discussed in this chapter.
    a. Do you personally know individuals whom you would identify as cognitively complex? Lonely? Apprehensive? Argumentative?
    b. Which of the personal styles discussed do you find most appealing?
    c. How would you describe yourself in terms of the personality constructs presented?

4. Write a short paragraph in which you describe one of your favorite television or movie characters in terms of the personality constructs presented in this chapter.

5. Speculate on the relationship between personality construct and relational decay, disengagement, and adjustment.
    a. What personality construct do you think would stay in a relationship the longest? Why?
    b. What personality construct would work the hardest to keep a relationship going? Why?
    c. What personality construct would be most likely to initiate a breakup? Why?
    d. What type of disengagement tactic (manipulation of negative feelings, positive tone, de-escalation, etc.) would each personality construct use?

6. Consider the relationship you have with your family in terms of the personality constructs that you identified in yourself.
    a. Are you similar to or different from your brothers and sisters?
    b. Was there a lot of sibling rivalry in your family? If so, what effect do you think it had on your personality?
    c. Do you think your personality is similar to that of one of your parents? If so, in what ways do you try to adjust your personality to either be more or less like that parent?

SUGGESTED READING

▼

SELF-MONITORING

Snyder, M. (1987). *Public appearances, private realities: The psychology of self-monitoring.* New York: Freeman. Snyder reviews his fifteen years of research on self-monitoring. Chapters include discussions of measuring the high and low self-monitoring individual, dating preferences, preferences for being in (or avoiding) situations, and behaviors that are displayed by high and low self-monitors during interactions.

MACHIAVELLIANISM

Christie, R., & Geis, F. L. (Eds.). (1970). *Studies in Machiavellianism.* Orlando, FL: Academic. Christie and Geis present the classic works on the Machiavellian construct in this volume. An excellent reference to learn more about Machiavellianism.

Steinfatt, T. M. (1987). Personality and communication: Classical approaches. In J. C. McCroskey & J. Daly (Eds.), *Personality and interpersonal communication* (pp. 42–128). Newbury Park, CA: Sage. Steinfatt's extensive review of "classic" personality constructs includes material more contemporary than the Christie and Geis volume and includes more material on Machiavellianism and tactics of manipulation.

LOCUS OF CONTROL

Lefcourt, H. M. (1982). *Locus of control: Current trends in theory and research* (2nd ed.). Hillsdale, NJ: Erlbaum. Lefcourt and his students review two decades of research on locus of control, with attention given to its measurement and its importance in interpersonal and marital contexts.

COGNITIVE COMPLEXITY

Applegate, J. L. (1982). The impact of construct system development on communication and impression formation in persuasive contexts. *Communication Monographs, 49,* 277–289. Applegate's well-written paper on impression formation is recommended for its review of the literature on cognitive complexity and its clearly written description of a coding system demonstrating the complexity of impressions people make on others.

ARGUMENTATIVENESS

Infante, D. A., & Rancer, A. S. (1982). A conceptualization and measure of argumentativeness. *Journal of Personality Assessment, 46,* 72–80. Infante and his students have devoted two decades of research to the issues of argumentativeness versus other constructs (e.g., assertiveness). This 1982 study provides a well-written rationale for this line of research and an examination of how to measure the construct.

COMMUNICATION APPREHENSION

Daly, J. A., McCroskey, J. C., Ayres, J., Hopf, T., & Ayres, D. M. (1997). *Avoiding communication: Shyness, reticence, and communication apprehension* (2nd ed.). Cresskill, NJ: Hampton. Daly and his colleagues review different constructs and measures of communication avoidance, based on lack of skills, low esteem, and negative affect, and also focusing on measurement issues and solutions.

LONELINESS

Segrin, C. (1998). Interpersonal communication problems associated with depression and loneliness. In P. A. Anderson & L. K. Guerrero (Eds.), *Handbook of communication and emotion: Research, theory, application, and contexts* (pp. 215–242). San Diego, CA: Academic. Chris Segrin offers an extensive review of the research on loneliness and depression, including theoretical explanations and communication behaviors.

REFERENCE LIST

▼

Applegate, J. L. (1982). The impact of construct system development on communication and impression formation in persuasive contexts. *Communication Monographs, 49,* 277–289.

Beatty, M. J., Heisel, A. D., Hall, A. E., Levine, T. R., & LaFrance, B. H. (2002). What can we learn from the study of twins about genetic and environmental influences on interpersonal affiliation, aggressiveness, and social anxiety? A meta-analytic study. *Communication Monographs, 69,* 1–18.

Beatty, M. J., McCroskey, J. C., & Heisel, A. D. (1998). Communication apprehension as temperamental expression: A communibiological paradigm. *Communication Monographs, 65,* 197–219.

Bell, R. A. (1985). Conversational involvement and loneliness. *Communication Monographs, 52,* 218–235.

Bell, R. A., & Roloff, M. E. (1991). Making a love connection: Loneliness and communication competence in the dating marketplace. *Communication Quarterly, 39,* 58–74.

Burleson, B. R. (1984). Comforting communication. In H. E. Sypher & J. L. Applegate (Eds.), *Communication by children and adults* (pp. 63–104). Newbury Park, CA: Sage.

Burleson, B. R. (1987). Cognitive complexity. In J. C. McCroskey & J. A. Daly (Eds.), *Personality and interpersonal communication* (pp. 305–349). Newbury Park, CA: Sage.

Burleson, B. R., & Caplan, S. E. (1998). Cognitive complexity. In J. C. McCroskey, J. A. Daly, M. M. Martin, & M. J. Beatty (Eds.), *Communication and personality: Trait perspectives* (pp. 233–286). Cresskill, NJ: Hampton.

Canary, D. J., Cody, M. J., & Marston, P. J. (1986). Goal types, compliance-gaining, and locus of control. *Journal of Language and Social Psychology, 5,* 249–303.

Canary, D. J., Cunningham, E. M., & Cody, M. J. (1988). Goal types, gender, and locus of control in managing interpersonal conflict. *Communication Research, 15,* 426–446.

Cherulnik, P. D., Way, J. H., Ames, S., & Hutto, D. B. (1981). Impressions of high and low Machiavellian men. *Journal of Personality, 49,* 388–400.

Christie, R., & Geis, F. L. (Eds.). (1970). *Studies in Machiavellianism.* Orlando, FL: Academic.

Daly, J. A., & Bippus, A. (1998). Personality and interpersonal communication. In J. C. Mc-Croskey, J. A. Daly, & M. Martin (Eds.), *Communication and Personality* (pp. 1–40). Cresskill, NJ: Hampton.

Daly, J. A., McCroskey, J. C., Ayres, J., Hopf, T., & Ayres, D. M. (Eds.). (1997). *Avoiding communication: Shyness, reticence, and communication apprehension* (2nd ed.). Cresskill, NJ: Hampton.

Daly, J. A., & Stafford, L. (1984). Correlates and consequences of social-communicative anxiety. In J. A. Daly & J. C. McCroskey (Eds.), *Avoiding communication: Shyness, reticence, and communication apprehension* (pp. 125–144). Newbury Park, CA: Sage.

Delia, J. G., Kline, S. L., & Burleson, B. R. (1979). The development of persuasive communication strategies in kindergartners through twelfth-graders. *Communication Monographs, 46,* 241–256.

DePaulo, B. M., & Rosenthal, R. (1979). Telling lies. *Journal of Personality and Social Psychology, 37,* 1713–1722.

Exline, R. V., Thibaut, J., Hickey, C. B., & Gumpert, P. (1970). Visual interaction in relation to Machiavellianism and an unethical act. In R. Christie & F. Geis (Eds.), *Studies in Machiavellianism* (pp. 53–77). New York: Academic.

Geis, F. L., & Moon, T. H. (1981). Machiavellianism and deception. *Journal of Personality and Social Psychology, 41,* 766–775.

Godfrey, D. K., Jones, E. E., & Lord, C. G. (1986). Self-promotion is not ingratiating. *Journal of Personality and Social Psychology, 50,* 106–115.

Goodstadt, B. E., & Hjelle, L. A. (1973). Power to the powerless: Locus of control and the use of power. *Journal of Personality and Social Psychology, 27,* 190–196.

Guildford, J. P. (1959). *Personality.* New York: McGraw-Hill.

Gunnthorsdottir, A., McCabe, K., & Smith, V. (2002). Using the Machiavellianism instrument to predict trustworthiness in a bargaining game. *Journal of Economic Psychology, 23,* 49–66.

Hawken, L., Duran, R. L., & Kelly, L. (1991). The relationship of interpersonal communication variables to academic success and persistence in college. *Communication Quarterly, 39,* 297–308.

Hegarty, W. H., & Sims, Jr., H. P. (1978). Some determinants of unethical decision behavior: An experiment. *Journal of Applied Psychology, 63,* 451–457.

Hegarty, W. H., & Sims, H. P., Jr. (1979). Organizational philosophy, policies, and objectives related to unethical decision behavior: A laboratory experiment. *Journal of Applied Psychology, 64,* 331–338.

Hunter, J. E., Gerbing, D. W., & Boster, F. J. (1982). Machiavellian beliefs and personality: Construct invalidity of the Machiavellianism dimension. *Journal of Personality and Social Psychology, 43,* 1293–1305.

Infante, D. A. (1987). Aggressiveness. In J. C. McCroskey & J. A. Daly (Eds.), *Personality and interpersonal communication* (pp. 157–192). Newbury Park, CA: Sage.

Infante, D. A., Chandler, T. A., & Rudd, J. E. (1989). Test of an argumentative skill deficiency model of interspousal violence. *Communication Monographs, 56,* 163–177.

Infante, D. A., & Rancer, A. S. (1982). A conceptualization and measure of argumentativeness. *Journal of Personality Assessment, 46,* 72–80.

Infante, D. A., Riddle, B. L., Horvath, C. L., & Tumlin, S. A. (1992). Verbal aggressiveness: Messages and reasons. *Communication Quarterly, 40,* 116–126.

Infante, D. A., Sabourin, T. C., Rudd, J. E., & Shannon, E. A. (1990). Verbal aggression in violent and nonviolent marital disputes. *Communication Quarterly, 38,* 361–371.

Infante, D. A., Trebling, J. D., Shepard, P. E., & Seeds, D. E. (1984). The relation of argumentativeness to verbal aggression. *Southern Speech Communication Journal, 50,* 67–77.

Infante, D. A., & Wigley, C. J. (1986). Verbal aggressiveness: An interpersonal model and measure. *Communication Monographs, 53,* 61–69.

Jones, G. E., & Kavanaugh, M. J. (1996). An experimental examination of the effects of individual and situational factors on unethical behavioral intentions in the workplace. *Journal of Business Ethics, 15,* 511–523.

Klopf, D. W. (1997). Cross-cultural apprehension research: Procedures and comparisons. In J. A. Daly, J. C. McCroskey, J. Ayres, T. Hopf, & D. M. Ayres (Eds.), *Avoiding communication: Shyness, reticence, and communication apprehension* (pp. 269–284). Cresskill, NJ: Hampton.

Kraut, R., Kiesler, S., Boneva, B., Cummings, J., Helgeseon, V., & Crawford, A. (2002). Internet paradox revisited. *Journal of Social Issues, 58,* 49–74.

Lefcourt, H. M. (1982). *Locus of control: Current trends in theory and research* (2nd ed.). Hillsdale, NJ: Erlbaum.

Lefcourt, H. M., Martin, R. A., Fick, C. M., & Saleh, W. E. (1985). Locus of control for affiliation and behavior in social interactions. *Journal of Personality and Social Psychology, 48,* 755–769.

Lefcourt, H. M., Von Bayer, C. L., Ware, E. E., & Cox, D. J. (1979). The Multidimensional-Multiattributional Scale: The development of a goal-specific locus of control scale. *Canadian Journal of Behavioral Science, 11,* 286–304.

Margulis, S. T., Derlega, V. J., & Winstead, B. A. (1984). Implications of social psychological concepts for a theory of loneliness. In V. J. Derlega (Ed.), *Communication, intimacy, and close relationships* (pp. 133–160). Orlando, FL: Academic.

McCroskey, J. C. (1982). Oral communication apprehension: A reconceptualization. In M. Burgoon (Ed.), *Communication yearbook 6* (pp. 136–170). Newbury Park, CA: Sage.

McCroskey, J. C., & Beatty, M. J. (1998). Communication apprehension. In J. C. McCroskey, J. A. Daly, M. M. Martin, & M. J. Beatty (Eds.), *Communication and personality: Trait perspectives* (pp. 215–232). Cresskill, NJ: Hampton.

McKenna, K. Y. A., Green, A. S., & Gleason, M. E J. (2002). Relationship formation on the Internet: What's the big attraction? *Journal of Social Issues, 58,* 9–31.

Merrill, J. M., Lorimor, R. J., Thornby, J. I., & Vallbona, C. (1998). Medical manners: Medical students' perceptions of their own. *Southern Medical Journal, 91,* 256–260.

Moody, E. J. (2001). Internet use and its relationship to loneliness. *CyberPsychology & Behavior, 4,* 393–401.

Rancer, A. S. (1998). Argumentativeness. In J. C. McCroskey, J. A. Daly, M. M. Martin, & M. J. Beatty (Eds.), *Communication and personality: Trait perspectives* (pp. 149–170). Cresskill, NJ: Hampton.

Rancer, A. S., & Infante, D. A. (1985). Relations between motivation to argue and the argumentativeness of adversaries. *Communication Quarterly, 33,* 209–218.

Ricks, J., & Fraedrich, J. (1999). The paradox of Machiavellianism: Machiavellianism may make for productive sales but poor management reviews. *Journal of Business Ethics, 20,* 197–205.

Rokach, A. (1999). Cultural background and coping with loneliness. *The Journal of Psychology, 133,* 217–229.

Rotter, J. B. (1966). Generalized expectancies for internal vs. external locus of control of reinforcement. *Psychological Monographs, 80* (Whole No. 609).

Rotter, J. B. (1982). *The development and applications of social learning theory.* New York: Praeger.

Russell, D., Peplau, L. A., & Cutrona, C. E. (1980). The Revised UCLA Loneliness Scale: Concurrent and discriminant validity evidence. *Journal of Personality and Social Psychology, 39,* 472–480.

Segrin, C. (1998). Interpersonal communication problems associated with depression and loneliness. In P. A. Anderson & L. K. Guerrero (Eds.), *Handbook of communication and emotion: Research, theory, application, and contexts* (pp. 215–242). San Diego: Academic.

Semic, B. A., & Canary, D. J. (1998). Trait argumentativeness, verbal aggressiveness, and minimally rational argument: An observational analysis of friendship discussions. *Communication Quarterly, 45,* 355–379.

Singhapakdi, A., & Vitell, S. J. (1990). Marketing ethics: Factors influencing perceptions of ethical problems and alternatives. *Journal of Macro-marketing, 10* (Spring), 4–18.

Smith, S. W., Cody, M. J., LoVette, S., & Canary, D. J. (1990). Self-monitoring, gender, and compliance-gaining goals. In M. J. Cody & M. L. McLaughlin (Eds.), *The psychology of tactical communication* (pp. 91–135). Clevedon, England: Multilingual Matters.

Snyder, M. (1987). *Public appearances, private realities: The psychology of self-monitoring.* New York: Freeman.

Snyder, M., & Gangestad, S. (1986). On the nature of self-monitoring: Matters of assessment, matters of validity. *Journal of Personality and Social Psychology, 51,* 125–139.

Solano, C. H., Batten, P. G., & Parrish, E. A. (1982). Loneliness and patterns of self-disclosure. *Journal of Personality and Social Psychology, 43,* 524–531.

Spitzberg, B. H., & Canary, D. J. (1985). Loneliness and relationally competent communication. *Journal of Social and Personal Relationships, 2,* 387–402.

Steinfatt, T. M. (1987). Personality and communication: Classical approaches. In J. C. McCroskey & J. A. Daly (Eds.), *Personality and interpersonal communication* (pp. 42–128). Newbury Park, CA: Sage.

Streufert, S., & Swezey, R. W. (1986). *Complexity, managers, and organizations.* New York: Academic.

Sypher, H. E., & Applegate, J. L. (Eds.). (1984). *Communication by children and adults.* Newbury Park, CA: Sage.

Vecchio, R. P., & Sussmann, M. (1991). Choice of influence tactics: Individual and organizational determinants. *Journal of Organizational Behavior, 12,* 73–80.

Wilson, D. S., Near, D. C., & Miller, R. R. (1998). Individual differences in Machiavellianism as a mix of cooperative and exploitative strategies. *Evolution and Human Behavior, 19,* 203–212.

Zakahi, W. R., & Duran, R. L. (1985). Loneliness, communicative competence, and communication apprehension: Extension and replication. *Communication Quarterly, 33,* 50–60.

Znakov, V. V. (1995). Machiavellianism and the fib phenomenon. *Voprosy Psychologii, 6,* 59–70.

CHAPTER 16

IMPLICATIONS FOR

INTERPERSONAL

COMMUNICATION

COMPETENCE

A COMPONENT MODEL OF COMPETENCE

Motivation

Knowledge

Skill

CRITERIA FOR ASSESSING COMPETENCE

Adaptability

Conversational Involvement

Conversational Management

Empathy

Effectiveness

Appropriateness

ASSESSING YOUR OWN INTERPERSONAL COMMUNICATION COMPETENCE

IMPLICATIONS FOR COMPETENCE: A REVIEW

Fundamentals of Communication
    Competence

Competence in Self-Presentation

Competence in Relational Development

Competence in Instrumental Objectives

Personality and Competence

FINAL COMMENTS

It was my first job interview after completing my Ph.D. I had trouble falling asleep because I was excited about the possibility of working at a major university. After four hours of counting backward, sleep came.

The hotel operator forgot to deliver the wake-up call. So when the phone finally rang in the morning, it was the department chair's loud voice wondering, "Hello, are you ready yet? I am waiting for you in the lobby." Ten minutes later, unshaved and without umbrella, I greeted the chair. I felt good about getting ready in ten minutes, but the chair didn't seem to have enjoyed his wait.

Having no time for breakfast, I was glad for the coffee in the faculty lounge. "Sugar?" the chair asked. I nodded yes. "That is a very special sugar container," said the chair. "Our wonderful secretary for over thirty years gave us this splendid present just last month." That was the first time the chair smiled, recollecting his life-long co-worker. I noticed the other dozen or so faculty members were smiling too. I attempted to return their sugar container.

Without apparent cause, the container flew from my hands to the center of the faculty lounge, where it crashed into a thousand pieces of glass intermingled with white sugar. Broken were thirty years of memories. And next to those memories, my future was relatively unimportant. After several gasps and an awkward silence, the chair announced, "The presentation begins in five minutes. Be sure to take your umbrellas because it's starting to rain."

The presentation began well, then slowly fell apart. I had difficulty articulating some of my ideas because the topic I had chosen was rather esoteric. At one point during the presentation, it was clear that the entire audience was bored. Still, I was determined to present all my ideas. The question-and-answer session also went very poorly. My attempts to evade questions I couldn't answer only generated direct and vicious follow-up questions. Afterward, only one person complimented me: "That was interesting," was all he said.

Being interpersonally competent seems easy for some people. Some people appear at ease no matter where they are. They know how to act and what to say. They seem genuinely involved in the conversation, control the pace and tenor of the conversation, change topics without offending others, and listen well. Other people are less competent at times. They don't know how to act or what to say. Instead of showing genuine interest in what someone has to say, they focus on themselves, ingratiate, or withdraw.

Communication scholars have spent considerable energy researching the idea of **communication competence** (Bostrom, 1984; Cegala, 1991; Duran, 1983; McCroskey, 1982; Parks, 1994; Pearce & Cronen, 1980; Rubin, 1985; Spitzberg & Cupach, 1984; Wiemann & Backlund, 1980). This research suggests that communication competence is determined by both conversational partners, involves knowing how to communicate, references actual communication behavior, and takes into account the communicator's success at achieving his or her goals.

The energies spent to investigate communication competence are justified. Spitzberg and Cupach (1989) show that a lack of communication competence is linked to mental illness, depression, anxiety, shyness, loneliness, developmental disorders, academic problems, sexual offenses, and drug abuse. Communication competence, by contrast, is positively associated with having friends and the ability to function personally.

A COMPONENT MODEL OF COMPETENCE

Perhaps the most comprehensive theory of communication competence is that of Spitzberg and Cupach (1984). Part of their theory is a *component model*. According to these scholars, evaluation of competence occurs in three components: motivation, knowledge, and skill.

Motivation

Spitzberg and Cupach (1984, 1989) conceive of motivation as an individual's approach or avoidance orientation in various social situations. For a variety of reasons, individuals are drawn to particular social episodes (approach) and are discouraged from engaging in other social episodes (avoidance).

We know that goals motivate individuals to act (Berger, 1997; Chapter 1). Interpersonal goals refer most generally to self-presentation, relational, and instrumental objectives. At the less abstract (basic) level, goals are more specific regarding what the communicator wants and with whom. Self-efficacy (Bandura, 1989) alters whether a person approaches or avoids a particular kind of interaction goal. In other words, an individual's confidence in being successful in a particular type of interaction increases the likelihood that the person will approach that particular type of interaction. Conversely, if the person lacks confidence regarding success or believes that he or she will fail, the person will likely avoid pursuing those goals.

You may ask yourself about your motivation for various self-presentation, relational, and instrumental goals. Knowing your own motivation for personal goals is vital to understanding your behavior. Of course, this does not imply that you take stock of your wants and impulses before every conversation. It does mean, however, that you have a set of values that indicate what is important in life. Knowing what you want and how much you are willing to sacrifice to get it will guide your interpersonal contacts and communication.

Knowledge

In addition to motivation, the communicator must know how to act. Spitzberg and Cupach (1984) observe that once an individual decides to pursue a conversational goal, the usual kinds of interaction for that situation are imagined, and applicable schema or plans are analyzed and adopted. As mentioned in Chapter 1, goals lead to plans for action. Once you are motivated toward a goal, you begin constructing plans to obtain it. Previous experience informs your knowledge of what constitutes a workable plan, and you tend to adopt plans that have worked in similar situations instead of recreating new plans for each situation (Berger, 1997; Berger & Jordan, 1992). In this vein, competence would entail having a repertoire of plans that can be used to achieve valued goals.

Greene (1984) calls knowing how to act **procedural knowledge.** Procedural knowledge refers to the ways people read social situations and decide on a course of action that yields desired outcomes. According to Greene, people recall procedural knowledge obtained from previous experience and watching others and within moments make a decision as to how to behave. Of course, people know how to behave in many situations, so the process of assembling the best action procedure requires almost no time. People may have learned procedural knowledge from many sources, including a prototype of interpersonal competence (Pavitt & Haight, 1985). A prototype is a model representative. Accordingly, you may observe different prototypes that indicate to you what action should be performed in social situations. In novel situations, you must work harder to construct an appropriate plan of action (Greene, 1984).

Skill

The third component in Spitzberg and Cupach's (1984) model is skill. In this model, *skills* refer to behaviors actually performed. Spitzberg and Cupach review several studies showing that a person may be motivated to act and know how to act but may not actually behave as desired. How many times have you been motivated to perform well and knew how, but you failed to enact the behavior as you wished?

Recall the story at the beginning of this chapter. The candidate for the university position was quite motivated and knowledgeable about how to communicate in an interview setting. But the candidate lacked some basic social skills that day. First, although he made his prospective chair wait for ten minutes, he did not apologize for his failure to be prompt. Second, he dropped the valued sugar container, obviously because he was not careful to hold it firmly. He had forgotten his umbrella, so you can imagine that the day was filled with awkward requests to borrow or share someone's umbrella. Finally, he had several problems delivering his speech and did not adjust to the audience even though he realized they were bored. Such incompetent behaviors are often attributed to jerks.

CRITERIA FOR ASSESSING COMPETENCE

How do you know when someone is communicatively competent? The answer depends on the standards for evaluation that you use. The following six criteria for assessing competence have received much theoretical and empirical attention for several years. All of the criteria apply to interpersonal contexts; furthermore, they are representative of the competence literature. Finally, each of these criteria is relevant to the goals-based view offered in this book. The criteria are adaptability, conversational involvement, conversational management, empathy, effectiveness, and appropriateness.

Adaptability

According to Spitzberg and Cupach (1989), **adaptability** (or flexibility) is the most commonly cited standard for judging competence. *Communicative adaptability* refers to the ability to change behaviors and goals to meet the needs of the interaction (Duran, 1983). As several studies have shown, being adaptable is important to interpersonal competence. For example, Lakey and Canary (2001) found that being sensitive to the other person's goals is positively linked to their being rated as communicatively competent.

According to Duran (1991), adaptability comprises six factors: social experience, social composure, social confirmation, appropriate disclosure, articulation, and wit. Social experience refers to having participated in various social interactions, which allows people to develop a set of communication strategies and skills. From the repertoire they have developed, people can select the most optimal communication behaviors. Social composure refers to keeping calm. The ability to keep calm is related to the ability to perceive situations accurately (Duran, 1991). Social confirmation refers to acknowledgment of the partner's self-presentation efforts. Understanding the partner's self-presentation goals helps the communicator adapt. Appropriate disclosure refers to being sensitive to the amount and type of information presented to the partner (see also Chapter 7). Articulation refers to the ability to express ideas through language. Developing a range of verbal skills allows people to express their ideas to various conversational partners. Finally, Duran (1991) states that the ability to use humor assists in adapting to the social situation. A person's humor can make dull interactions brighter. Wit can also ease tensions between people and alleviate embarrassment.

Conversational Involvement

A second standard for assessing communication competence is **conversational involvement.** Cegala (1991) reports that being involved in the conversation is critical to communication competence. Conversational involvement represents a behavioral as well as a cognitive activity. In other words, communicators must be cognitively involved in the conversation and demonstrate their involvement through their interaction behaviors (head nods, vocal cues, etc.).

According to Cegala (1984), conversational involvement is assessed according to the factors of responsiveness, perceptiveness, and attentiveness. Responsiveness refers to such behaviors as knowing what to say, understanding what your role is, and feeling part of the interaction. Perceptiveness concerns being aware of how others perceive you, how others respond to you, and how observant you are of others. Attentiveness refers to listening carefully to others, focusing on the conversation, and not being preoccupied with your own thoughts. The conceptual opposite of involvement is being overly concerned with yourself in interaction—what Vangelisti, Knapp, and Daly (1990) call **conversational narcissism.** In sum, you are said to be conversationally involved to the degree that you are cognitively and behaviorally responsive, perceptive, and attentive to your conversational partner.

Conversational Management

Conversational management concerns how communicators regulate their interactions (Wiemann & Backlund, 1980). Skilled interactants understand their role in managing interaction. Managing conversations also implies that people do not adapt to social situations only; they also control them. Accordingly, competence is assessed in terms of who controls the interaction ebb and flow and how smoothly the interaction proceeds.

The conversational ebb and flow is witnessed in such activities as turn taking and yielding, topic shifts and extensions, asking questions, intonation, nodding, interrupting, and the like (Spitzberg & Cupach, 1984, p. 138). Conversational turn taking and yielding simply refer to how communicators alternate at speaking (only one communicator tends to talk at one time). How topics proceed and change is a matter of conversational management. In addition, people indicate where attention should be directed by asking questions, varying the intonation in their voice, nodding their heads, and even interrupting one another.

Empathy

For many years now, researchers have known that empathy is an important skill in interpersonal communication (e.g., Keefe, 1976). **Empathy** refers to the ability to show your conversational partner that you understand his or her situation and that you share his or her emotional reactions to it (Gladstein, 1986). Empathy should not be confused with sympathy; sympathy is feeling sorry for another person to the extent that you want to help the person (Wispe, 1986). Empathy need not necessarily lead to helping the other person (Gladstein, 1986; Miller, Stiff, & Ellis, 1988).

According to Gladstein (1986), empathy entails both cognitive understanding (also called role taking or perspective taking) and feeling parallel emotions (also called emotional contagion). Empathy involves a process of suspending your own attitudes and values about a particular event and allowing the conversational partner's experience to guide your thoughts and feelings. Thus empathy involves putting aside your attitudes, adopting the perspective of your conversational partner, and feeling the emotions that he or she feels (Gladstein, 1986; Keefe, 1976). Of course, empathy may involve positive or negative emotional responses and may even lead to occupational burnout in environments where people work with others' stressful situations (Miller et al., 1988).

Effectiveness

Effectiveness refers to achieving the objectives you have for your conversations. According to Parks (1994), communication competence refers to the degree to which

Appropriateness and effectiveness are two fundamental criteria for assessing communication competence. If you can achieve your goals (effectiveness) without violating what other people expect of you (appropriateness), you are seen as competent.

Barbara Ries/Photo Researchers

you achieve your personal goals in a given situation without jeopardizing other important secondary goals. For example, your conversational goal may be to obtain a particular two-week vacation so that you can visit some high school friends. Accordingly, you would judge the quality of the exchange with the supervisor by your degree of success at obtaining the vacation time you wanted. But you would not want to risk other important goals (salary increases, being perceived as a loyal worker, etc.).

If communication is assessed according to the standard of effectiveness, certain communication behaviors would appear to be more competent than others. For example, asserting your desires in conflict, being persistent in compliance-gaining situations, and directly or indirectly obtaining the information you want are communication behaviors that function primarily to achieve personal goals.

Appropriateness

Spitzberg and Cupach (1984) define communication competence as the degree to which the communicator's goals are achieved through appropriate interaction. **Appropriateness** refers to upholding the expectations for a given situation. According to Spitzberg and Cupach, appropriateness is one of two fundamental criteria for determining competence. Effectiveness, already discussed, is the other criterion.

It is certainly possible for a person to be appropriate but not effective, or to be effective but inappropriate (Spitzberg, Canary, & Cupach, 1994). For example, in a conflict situation, it is possible to agree with the other person to the extent that you never argue for your own position. In this instance, you could meet the criterion of appropriateness, but in doing so sacrifice your primary goal. By contrast, you could be overly competitive in your use of conflict strategies. In this instance, you may achieve your primary goal, but at the expense of violating the expectations others have of you. According to Spitzberg and Cupach (1984) and Spitzberg et al. (1994), both appropriateness and effectiveness contribute to competence in communicating.

ASSESSING YOUR OWN INTERPERSONAL COMMUNICATION COMPETENCE

Using Spitzberg and Cupach's components, we can more precisely assess communicator competence according to each of the six competence criteria. For the purposes of this book, we limit the evaluation of interpersonal competence to you. Answer each of the items in Table 16.1 to assess how well you believe you fare on each of the criteria according to your motivation, knowledge, and skill. Many other measures of competence that have established reliability and validity are reviewed by Spitzberg and Cupach (1989). However, the items in Table 16.1 apply to the concepts we have presented in this chapter. After looking at the criteria of motivation, knowledge, and skill, use Table 16.1 to expand your self-evaluation by means of the subscale scores, which profile your competence according to adaptability, involvement, conversational

Table 16.1

EVALUATION OF INTERPERSONAL COMMUNICATION COMPETENCE

Instructions: Answer each item honestly as it currently applies to you in typical conversations with others. Use a 5-point scale for your responses. Write 5 if you *strongly agree*, 4 if you *slightly agree*, 3 if you are *unsure*, 2 if you *slightly disagree*, and 1 if you *strongly disagree*.

_____ 1. I want to adapt my communication behavior to meet others' expectations.

_____ 2. I have enough knowledge and experiences to adapt to other people's expectations.

_____ 3. I use a wide range of behavior, including self-disclosure and wit, to adapt to others.

_____ 4. I want to be involved in the conversations I have with other people.

_____ 5. I know how to respond to others because I am perceptive of social situations and attentive to others' behaviors.

_____ 6. I show my involvement in conversation both nonverbally and verbally.

_____ 7. I want to make my conversations with others go smoothly.

_____ 8. I know how to change topics and control the basic tenor of the conversations I have with others.

_____ 9. It is easy for me to manage conversations the way I want them to proceed.

_____ 10. I want to understand other people's viewpoints and emotions.

_____ 11. Truly understanding another person means both taking the role of that person and feeling the feelings that the person feels.

_____ 12. I demonstrate my understanding of others by reflecting their thoughts and feelings to them.

_____ 13. I am motivated to obtain the conversational goals I set for myself.

_____ 14. Once I set a goal for myself that involves another person, I know the steps to take to achieve it.

_____ 15. I achieve my interpersonal goals.

_____ 16. I want to communicate with others in an appropriate manner.

_____ 17. I am aware of the rules that guide social behavior.

_____ 18. I act in ways that meet situational demands for appropriateness.

Scoring: To assess *motivation*, add items 1, 4, 7, 10, 13, and 16. To assess *knowledge*, add items 2, 5, 8, 11, 14, and 17. To assess *skill*, add items 3, 6, 9, 12, 15, and 18. *Adaptability* subscale = 1, 2, 3; *involvement* subscale = 4, 5, 6; *conversation management* subscale = 7, 8, 9; *empathy* subscale = 10, 11, 12; *effectiveness* subscale = 13, 14, 15; *appropriateness* subscale = 16, 17, 18. *Overall* self-evaluation = 1–18 (possible range = 18 to 90 points).

To interpret your score, divide the score by the number of items in each subscale. For example, a motivation subscale score of 26 should be divided by six (the number of items in the subscale), which would give a score of 4.33. Next, look at the response categories associated with each number (where 1 = *strongly disagree* and 5 = *strongly agree*). Using the same example, a score of 4.33 indicates that the person is motivated. Scores above 4 are very strong, and scores below 3 indicate areas that could use attention (to increase your competence in specific areas).

STUDENT AS OBSERVER: ASSESS YOUR INTERPERSONAL COMPETENCE

Complete the self-evaluation of interpersonal communication competence in Table 16.1.

How did you score yourself in terms of motivation? Knowledge? Skill?

In what ways do you think you are already a competent communicator? What is your greatest strength?

In what ways do you think you could improve as a competent communicator?

Ask someone who knows you whether your answers are actually what other people might think.

Note the discrepancies, if any, between this person's assessments and yours.

management, empathy, effectiveness, and appropriateness. Finally, you can obtain a very general measure of your competence by simply summing all the items.

IMPLICATIONS FOR COMPETENCE: A REVIEW

Throughout this book we have presented many communication strategies, tactics, and other behaviors that are functionally related to people's goals. Research has shown which behaviors are more or less related to successful outcomes. We are aware that many of these communication behaviors seem new or even strange to you. You may have responded, "I could never do this" or "I can't imagine saying that." Nevertheless, by presenting these various communication strategies, tactics, and behaviors, we hope to increase your range of communication options.

Moreover, throughout this book we have framed the material within the context of the communicator's goals. Although this focus coincides with our view of communication, it may give the impression that once you establish your goals, know how to enact the plans to achieve your goals, and engage in certain communication strategies, you should be effective in getting what you want. We want to dismiss such a simple conceptualization of the communication process. Instead we stress that in interpersonal interaction, two people are constructing goals and plans, two people have various motivations for their desires, two people are presenting a public image of who they are, two people are attempting to define their relational desires, and two people have instrumental objectives that may correspond to or conflict with each other's instrumental objectives. In addition, as Chapters 15 and 16 suggest, these two people may have various individual differences that complicate the goals-plus-communication model. In other words, we assume that two people have the right to set each of their goals and to pursue them interdependently with others.

Finally, throughout this book we have attempted to present theory and research that show how we can be more competent interpersonal communicators. Each discussion has implications for interpersonal communication competence. Table 16.2 summarizes these implications, and we discuss them in the remainder of this chapter.

Table 16.2

SUMMARY OF IMPLICATIONS
FOR COMMUNICATION COMPETENCE

Competent communicators . . .

1. Know their self-presentation, relational, and instrumental goals.
2. Realize that optimal competence involves achieving their primary goals without sacrificing their important secondary goals.
3. Appreciate that culture influences the ways in which people think and communicate.
4. Acknowledge that their own perceptions are biased.
5. Understand that other people perceive them differently than they perceive themselves.
6. Realize that conversation requires cooperation for it to be productive.
7. Know that messages are communicated through multiple channels.
8. Are aware of the communication behaviors that reflect their self-presentations.
9. Carefully select how they self-disclose to others.
10. Know how to recover from inevitable social failings.
11. Anticipate variation in the progression of intimacy.
12. Realize that communication is necessary for maintaining close relationships.
13. Recognize that strategic communication accompanies relational dissolution.
14. Understand the principles that motivate people to comply to other's influence attempts.
15. Use various compliance-gaining strategies to achieve their instrumental goals.
16. Choose productive conflict messages over destructive conflict messages.
17. Are sensitive to the manner in which conflict progresses and alter behaviors to make their conflicts more productive.
18. Acknowledge that people change radically over the life-span, and their communication reflects such changes.
19. Understand that individuals have different personalities that play out in their communication behaviors.

The authors wish to thank Sandi Lakey for her help in suggesting and constructing this table.

Fundamentals of Communication Competence

This book opened with a presentation of concepts fundamental to communication. Chapter 1 discussed how important interpersonal communication is to achieving your self-presentation, relational, and instrumental goals. One clear implication is that competent communicators are aware of their self-presentation, relational, and instrumental goals that they attempt to achieve interpersonally. In addition optimal competence refers to achieving your main goals without sacrificing your less important goals (Parks, 1994). Recall that two people make up a relational system; in other words, two individuals' goals are involved in interaction. Accordingly, assessments of competence must account for both parties, not just one person's behavior (Spitzberg & Cupach, 1984, 1989).

Chapter 2 discussed several features of perception. From this chapter we see three direct implications for communication competence. First, the cultural context affects our perceptions of other people and their behavior. People are most comfortable in their own cultures and understand behavior in terms of what is normative for that culture. In the extreme, people devalue other cultural practices based on their own cultures, what is known as *ethnocentrism*. Competent communicators avoid being ethnocentric in their appreciation of cultural influences on perception. Second, competent communicators realize in other ways that their perceptions are biased. Given the way that humans selectively interpret messages, the competent communicator does not attempt to delude himself or herself into thinking that he or she sees the social world accurately. Rather, everyone has biases that act as interpretive filters. Third, we realize that other people's perceptions of us may not be accurate. At least we know that other people may have different perceptions of us than the ones we hold ourselves. For example, Chapter 2 discussed how the actor-observer bias works in such a way that we tend to hold other people more responsible for their behaviors, whereas we tend to rely more on situational cues to interpret our own behavior. Likewise, other people probably hold you more responsible for your own communication behavior than you do, and they perceive you in terms of social categories — age, sex, culture, and so forth. Competent communicators realize this and are not surprised when such biases appear to distort people's perceptions of one another.

Chapters 3, 4, and 5 presented many concepts concerning listening and exchanging messages, both verbally and nonverbally. Chapter 3 reveals that different styles for listening exist, and the communicator should be able to choose the style that best matches his or her conversational objective. One clear implication from Chapter 4 is that competent communicators realize that conversation requires cooperation for it to be productive. For example, they know they should fulfill Grice's maxims and align themselves with the conversational partner's message. Chapter 5 illustrated how messages are communicated through multiple nonverbal channels, and a single behavior can contain several meanings. Competent communicators know that nonverbal messages are not easily interpreted, but they remain sensitive to nonverbal signals to infer various plausible meanings.

Competence in Self-Presentation

Chapter 6 noted that self-presentation is so common that you seldom think about it, but you do think about your desired public image when it is called into question. Chapter 6 highlighted the direct self-presentation strategies of ingratiation, intimidation, self-promotion, supplication, and exemplification. You probably learned these concepts for the first time and applied them to yourself. One implication for competence answers this question: What communication behaviors do you choose to develop your public image? Answering this question may reveal to you why you use certain messages rather than others.

Chapter 7 concerned self-disclosure. We implied that self-disclosure is best conceptualized as the decision to reveal something about yourself or to remain private. Factors affecting your decision to disclose or to remain private were emphasized. Chapter 7 also presented research on the consequences of self-disclosure, indicating that you should not disclose a lot of intimate information early in a conversation. In addition, the norm of reciprocity is met by disclosing information about the topic at hand or by reciprocating information at the same level of intimacy. Finally, research suggests that you should avoid disclosing negative aspects of yourself in most encounters. Accordingly, competent communicators carefully select how they self-disclose to others; self-disclosure should be reserved for few situations and a few people.

Chapter 8 discussed communication behaviors used to defend a threatened public image — accounts. Recall that accounts are messages offered in response to a perceived social failure. Excuses attempt to show that the communicator is not to blame for the event. Justifications seek to lessen the impact of the failure event by claiming that the consequences are not important. Concessions involve admitting responsibility for the failure. Apologies admit to the failure and promise to repair the problem. Finally, refusals involve a claim that the event did not occur, denial of the right of the partner to question you about the event, or evasion. Chapter 8 also indicated which of these accounts are seen as effective. Using accounts has several implications for interpersonal competence, including whether or not we should become adept at using them. After all, why should socially competent people learn various ways to recover from social failures? The answer lies in the fact that we all fail occasionally. Thus competent communicators know how to use accounts to recover from social failings.

Competence in Relational Development

Relational development is seen as the outcome of people's goals to escalate (Chapter 9), maintain (Chapter 10), and de-escalate or terminate (Chapter 11) their relationships. These chapters imply that there is no one correct way to pursue your relational goals. Relationships develop in many different ways, and they are maintained successfully according to the relational definitions the partners choose to adopt. In addition, people consider many factors and communication approaches when de-escalating a relationship.

LESSONS FROM *THE JERK*

Many critics hold that the primary function of comedy is to ridicule ourselves so that we can learn from our shortcomings. And many of the best comedians are fine instructors in human error. If we pay attention to what comedians tell us, we might gain insights about our foolish behaviors, to remedy them.

In *The Jerk*, Steve Martin portrays a simpleminded person who doesn't seem to have a clue about how to present himself, how to develop a relationship, or how to succeed in business. Martin plays Navan Johnson, a rhythmless white man raised by a black family. Late one night, Navan hears some elevator music that inspires him to seek his own identity. So he hitchhikes to the big city and takes a job at a gas station.

One day Navan is talking with the owner of the station, Mr. Artunian, when a van arrives delivering phone books.

Navan: The new phone book is here! The new phone book is here!
Artunian: *(sarcastically)* I wish I could get that excited about nothing.
Navan: Nothing! Are you kidding? *(he reads)* Page 73: "Johnson, Navan R. I'M SOMEBODY NOW. Millions of people look at this book every day! This is the kind of spontaneous publicity — your name in print — that MAKES people. Things are going to start happening to me now!"

Indeed they do start happening. He meets Marie (played by Bernadette Peters) and attempts to ask her on a date, but all he can do is mumble the words. She tells him to stomp his feet "once for no, twice for yes." He stomps twice and they meet the next day.

Navan: Are you a model?
Marie: No, I'm a cosmetologist.
Navan: Really? That's unbelievable. That's impressive. It must be tough to handle weightlessness. Do you have a boyfriend?
Marie: Sort of.
Navan: Do you think, the next time you make love to your boyfriend you could think of me?
Marie: I haven't made love to him yet.
Navan: That's too bad. Do you think it's possible that someday you could make love to me and think of him?
Marie: Who knows — maybe you and he could make love and you could think of me.
Navan: I'd just be happy to be in there somewhere.

Marie and Navan continue seeing each other, and Navan decides to propose marriage. Navan is in a bathtub and calls out to Marie as she is gathering her things to leave him:

(Continued)

530

(Box continued from previous page)

Navan: Honey, guess what! I wrote a song for you this morning:

                Oh, I'm picking out a thermos for you.
                    Not an ordinary thermos for you.
                But the extra best thermos you can buy,
                    with vinyl and stripes and a cup built right in.
                I'm picking out a thermos for you
                    and maybe a barometer too.
                And what else can I buy so on me you'll rely?
                    A rear end thermometer too!

        Honey, there's a question I've been wanting to pop, but I've been afraid you'd say no. But this seems like the right time and place, so here goes: Honey, will you marry me?

The dog then barks twice, and Navan mistakes that for a yes. He shouts "Yahoo!" But during the proposal, Marie had slipped out the front door.

In the remainder of the film, Navan earns millions of dollars through luck and loses it because of ineptitude. But because he remembered to send a few dollars home each week, he salvages some of his wealth. The film concludes as it began, with Navan back on the farm, not quite keeping time to a favorite family hymn.

We can see from excerpts of dialogue how Navan presented himself — as a jerk. His first date and proposal to Marie are examples of how not to present yourself and develop a relationship. The fact that he didn't save any substantial amounts of money and lost a fortune overnight also indicate his incompetence.

The Jerk exaggerates people's incompetent behaviors — or does it? Can you think of other comedians who offer insights about people by making fun of their incompetence? What would they have us laugh at? What can we learn from their insights?

Chapter 9 focused on relational escalation. Recall that people are attracted to others for a variety of reasons. Chapter 9 also showed that research suggests that the escalation of relationships progresses with increases and decreases of intimate messages. Finally, Chapter 9 reviewed turning points. The literature shows that some couples escalate their relationships quickly through a few relational turning points, whereas other couples experience more turning points and take longer to commit to each other. One implication for competence is that you should anticipate variation in the progression of intimacy. Some relationships escalate to intimacy more quickly than others; some relationships involve different types of love; and there are periods when the relationship does not escalate but shelters ordinary conversations and conflict.

Chapter 10 presented several strategies people use to maintain their personal relationships: positivity, openness, assurances, social networks, and sharing tasks. Each strategy has been shown to be effective in preserving both romantic and nonromantic relationships. The implication is to recognize that communication is required to maintain close relationships. When we think of relational maintenance processes, we should think of fluctuations in relational properties (such as intimacy and trust, or in terms of dialectics) and recognize that we use communication strategies to keep our relationships within a desired range of fluctuation.

Chapter 11 focused on various issues and communication behaviors associated with relational de-escalation and termination. Five strategies people use in de-escalating or terminating their relationships were discussed: positive tone (emotional attempts not to hurt the rejected partner), de-escalation tactics (reasons for de-escalation without alleviating the partner's hurt feelings), withdrawal or avoidance (avoiding the partner), justification tactics (citing positive consequences of disengaging or negative consequences for not disengaging), and negative identity or manipulation tactics (showing little regard for the partner thereby arousing feelings that lead to a quick end). Discussing the ways in which people can competently de-escalate or terminate a relationship sounds cold and ruthless. Still, we need to recognize that most of our relationships require some kind of communication to bring about separation, and Chapter 11 indicated when people use these various de-escalation strategies.

Competence in Instrumental Objectives

We all have personal goals regarding self-advancement, or instrumental objectives. You may need a favor from someone or some material assistance (e.g., a car loan or a ride to the airport). Chapters 12, 13, and 14 discussed principles related to gaining such compliance from others and how to manage situations in which you perceive your goals are blocked.

Chapter 12 reviewed rules that associate the success of interpersonal influence attempts with underlying principles. These rules involved anchoring and contrast effects, reciprocity, commitment, liking, social proof, authority, and scarcity. The implication of these rules is that competent communicators understand the principles that motivate people to comply with others' influence attempts. Also, Chapter 12 discussed some of the various ways in which people use communication to obtain compliance from others and reviewed several forms of compliance-gaining messages. It strongly suggested that compliance-gaining behaviors vary in terms of their perceived appropriateness and effectiveness. For instance, people tend to seek compliance by using indirect methods or simple requests, and they escalate to more elaborate and negative messages if they do not initially achieve compliance. The many strategic orientations that we discussed indicated that you should have an array of compliance-gaining strategies and tactics at your disposal.

Chapter 13 discussed the manner in which conflict is managed. At least two implications arise from this chapter. First, competent communicators choose productive over destructive conflict strategies. Integrative behaviors are cooperative, seek areas of mutual agreement, and tend to be the most productive means of managing conflict. Distributive tactics are competitive and seek self-advancement, even at the partner's expense. Avoidance tactics minimize the conflict. Each strategy has advantages and disadvantages, and the communicator must choose the most effective strategy in a given conflict episode. Chapter 13 shows that these strategies unfold in different patterns. These patterns can be characterized according to their variety, continuity, symmetry, stationarity, and spontaneity. In this light, the competent communicator is sensitive to the manner in which his or her communication progresses during conflict and alters his or her behavior to make the conflict episode more productive.

Chapter 14 discussed how people's communication behavior reflects their individual development across the life span. For example, people have different attachment styles that they learned years ago. These attachment styles often affect their communicative behaviors. Also, Chapter 14 discussed how older people engage in self-presentation behaviors that they might be seen as capable. The competent communicator would know to validate these behaviors, thus appearing to be sensitive to the other person's identity management concerns.

Personality and Competence

Chapter 15 indicated that people have various reactions to different social situations and reviewed seven personality factors: self-monitoring, Machiavellianism, locus of control, cognitive complexity, argumentativeness, communication apprehension, and loneliness. This material shows that people vary in their preferred social situations. For example, highly argumentative people enjoy participating in social debates and seek to initiate conversations with others who are also argumentative. In a similar vein, people who are low self-monitors seek relationships with people whose beliefs correspond to their own. In addition, Chapter 15 demonstrated that people communicate differently according to these personality factors. The implication is that we should realize that people vary in their preferred social situations and communication behaviors. Knowing these differences may enable us to communicate with a wider range of people more competently.

FINAL COMMENTS

This book has been about using interpersonal communication to achieve your personal goals. As with all books and studies, you should adapt the principles to your own interpersonal situations and life experiences. Sometimes the principles we present are based on many studies and personal experiences. At other times, they are based on very recent research that has not yet been replicated. Throughout, however, we have presented the best information we knew on the topic. Nevertheless, you must use judgment regarding the practical application of all the material presented in this text.

We hope that this book has increased your interest in studying more about interpersonal communication. Many universities offer graduate courses on the topic of interpersonal communication. These courses will no doubt extend your knowledge and make you aware of other approaches to the topic. Our hope is that this text has whetted your appetite for further inquiry about interpersonal communication processes.

My second and third job interviews gave me other opportunities to improve my "personal marketing skills." I couldn't tell if the first presentation topic was too abstract or if I just could not impart the ideas. So I switched the presentation topic to something less abstract. I also prepared handouts and a relevant cartoon (to lighten the presentation).

My chief concern was running into the unexpected. I learned that when seeking a job, surprise is inevitable. I also learned from my past mistakes. I read a lot before going to bed, not allowing the next day's worries to bother me. I also made sure that the hotel alarm clock was set. And as luck would have it, the hotel operator was fifteen minutes late with the wake-up call for my third (and most important) interview. Regardless, I was ready when the chair walked into the lobby.

I also made sure I had plenty of time for breakfast and coffee. So I felt energetic and awake when I met my future colleagues. I tried to be sensitive to their issues and direct in answering their questions. I believed — correctly — that honesty was essential for our continued working relationship. I must admit to lying to one of the faculty members, however. When asked if I cared for any sugar in my coffee, I smiled and replied, "No, thank you."

KEY TERMS

adaptability, p. 520
appropriateness, p. 523
communication competence, p. 518
conversational involvement, p. 521
conversational management, p. 521

conversational narcissism, p. 521
effectiveness, p. 522
empathy, p. 521
procedural knowledge, p. 519

EXERCISES FOR FURTHER DISCUSSION

1. One of the main ideas in this book has been that knowing our own motivation for personal goals is vital if we are to understand our behavior. Do you agree or disagree with this premise? Discuss why or why not.

2. List five people whom you think of as competent communicators, people who could serve as models for your own interpersonal communication competence.
    a. What behaviors do these people use that make them competent?
    b. What behaviors do they use that you would like to begin to use as well?
3. Review the twenty implications presented in the final section of this chapter (Table 16.2).
    a. Which three of these implications are the most relevant to your life? Why?
    b. Which three of these implications constitute principles that you can adopt for your own interaction behaviors?
4. Look again at the communication competence story presented at the beginning and end of this chapter. Now write a story of your own that shows differences in competent and incompetent communication behaviors.

SUGGESTED READING

▼

Parks, M. R. (1994). Communicative competence and interpersonal control. In M. L. Knapp & G. R. Miller (Eds.), *Handbook of interpersonal communication* (2nd ed., pp. 589–618). Thousand Oaks, CA: Sage. This essay examines competence from the perspective of how one controls oneself at various levels of consciousness. Its point of view corresponds well to the thesis of this book — that people are competent to the extent they achieve personal goals.

Spitzberg, B. H., & Cupach, W. R. (1984). *Interpersonal communication competence*. Newbury Park, CA: Sage. These authors review different conceptualizations of competence. They emphasize various components of competent interaction, stressing that competence is a relational accomplishment.

Spitzberg, B. H., & Cupach, W. R. (1989). *Handbook of interpersonal competence research*. New York: Springer-Verlag. Various measures of competence are reviewed. This is an excellent sourcebook for anyone doing research on the topic.

REFERENCE LIST

▼

Bandura, A. (1989). Self-regulation of motivation and action through internal standards and goal systems. In L. A. Pervin (Ed.), *Goal concepts in personality and social psychology* (pp. 19–85). Hillsdale, NJ: Erlbaum.

Berger, C. R. (1997). *Planning strategic interaction: Attaining goals through communicative action*. Mahwah, NJ: Erlbaum.

Berger, C. R., & Jordan, J. M. (1992). Planning sources, planning difficulty, and verbal fluency. *Communication Monographs, 59,* 130–149.

Bostrom, R. N. (1984). *Communication in competence: A multidisciplinary approach*. Newbury Park, CA: Sage.

Cegala, D. J. (1984). Affective and cognitive manifestations of interaction involvement during unstructured and competitive interactions. *Communication Monographs, 51*, 320–338.

Cegala, D. J. (1991). *Conversational involvement: Ten years later*. Paper presented at the Speech Communication Association convention, Atlanta.

Duran, R. L. (1983). Communicative adaptability: A measure of social communicative competence. *Communication Quarterly, 31*, 320–326.

Duran, R. L. (1991). *Communicative adaptability: A review of conceptualization and measurement*. Paper presented at the Speech Communication Association convention, Atlanta.

Gladstein, G. A. (1986). Understanding empathy: Integrating counseling, developmental, and social psychology perspectives. *Journal of Counseling Psychology, 30*, 467–482.

Greene, J. O. (1984). A cognitive approach to human communication: An action assembly theory. *Communication Monographs, 51*, 289–306.

Keefe, T. (1976). Empathy: The critical skill. *Social Work, 21*, 10–14.

Kelley, H. (1979). *Personal relationships: Their structure and process*. Hillsdale, NJ: Erlbaum.

Lakey, S. G., & Canary, D. J. (2001, May). *Actor goal achievement and sensitivity to the partner as critical factors in understanding interpersonal competence and conflict strategies*. Paper presented at the International Communication Association conference, Washington, DC.

McCroskey, J. C. (1982). Communication competence and performance: A research and pedagogical perspective. *Communication Education, 31*, 1–8.

Miller, K. I., Stiff, J. B., & Ellis, B. H. (1988). Communication and empathy as precursors to burnout among human service workers. *Communication Monographs, 55*, 250–265.

Parks, M. R. (1994). Communicative competence and interpersonal control. In M. L. Knapp & G. R. Miller (Eds.), *Handbook of interpersonal communication* (2nd ed., pp. 589–618). Thousand Oaks, CA: Sage.

Pavitt, C., & Haight, L. (1985). The "competent" communicator as a cognitive prototype. *Human Communication Research, 12*, 225–241.

Pearce, W. B., & Cronen, V. E. (1980). *Communication, action, and meaning*. New York: Praeger.

Rubin, R. B. (1985). The validity of the communication competence assessment instrument. *Communication Monographs, 52*, 173–185.

Spitzberg, B. H., Canary, D. J., & Cupach, W. R. (1994). A competence-based approach to the study of interpersonal conflict. In D. D. Cahn (Ed.), *Conflict in personal relationships* (pp. 183–202). Hillsdale, NJ: Erlbaum.

Spitzberg, B. H., & Cupach, W. R. (1984). *Interpersonal communication competence*. Newbury Park, CA: Sage.

Spitzberg, B. H., & Cupach, W. R. (1989). *Handbook of interpersonal competence research*. New York: Springer-Verlag.

Vangelisti, A. L., Knapp, M. L., & Daly, J. A. (1990). Conversational narcissism. *Communication Monographs, 57*, 251–274.

Wiemann, J. M., & Backlund, P. (1980). Current theory and research in communicative competence. *Review of Educational Research, 50*, 185–199.

Wispe, L. (1986). The distinction between sympathy and empathy: To call forth a concept, a word is needed. *Journal of Personality and Social Psychology, 50*, 314–321.

Name Index

Abbey, A., 123–124, 258
Abrahams, M. F., 369
Abramson, L. Y., 104
Adelman, M. B., 290
Adesman, P., 197
Afifi, W. A., 258, 259, 333, 336, 388, 394
Agostinelli, G., 348
Ahrons, C. R., 453
Aikawa, A., 369
Ainsworth, M. D. S., 440
Aleman, C. G., 391
Alexander, J. F., 250
Allen, E. S., 459
Allen, K. R., 448
Allen, M., 190
Allen, W. D., 448
Allison, P. D., 452
Allspach, L. E., 127
Alt, R., 348
Altendorf, S. M., 342
Altman, I., 180, 181, 250, 263
Amato, P. R., 452
Ames, S., 484
Amirkhan, J., 228
Andersen, J. F., 259
Andersen, P. A., 105, 107, 111, 125, 126, 251, 259, 263, 268, 273
Anderson, C. A., 109
Andrews, S. L., 123
Antonucci, T., 444
Applegate, J. L., 491
Aquilino, W. S., 452–453
Archer, R. L., 179, 184, 193, 194, 272
Argyle, M., 125, 288
Arkin, R. M., 160
Arnett, R., 63
Arnold, C. L., 57, 65
Arnold, J., 141, 167
Ascani, K., 368
Asher, T., 371
Attridge, M., 285
Avolio, B. J., 167
Axinn, W. G., 445
Ayres, D. M., 499
Ayres, J., 287, 288, 499

Bach, K., 82
Bacharach, S. B., 388
Backlund, P., 6, 518, 521
Bahniuk, M. H., 467
Ballard-Reisch, D. S., 286, 303
Bandura, A., 9, 518
Bangerter, A., 140
Banks, S. P., 342, 347, 348
Baratz, S., 390
Barbato, C. A., 95
Barer, B. M., 448
Barker, L., 59

Barnes, M. L., 298
Barraclough, R., 376
Barrett, D. W., 364
Bartholomew, K., 251, 441
Bassett, R., 370
Battaglia, D. M., 325, 336, 337, 352
Batten, P. G., 502
Baumeister, R. F., 168
Bavelas, J. B., 60, 61, 65
Baxter, L. A., 264, 268, 270, 272, 286, 288, 292, 293, 328, 337, 339, 341, 342, 343, 348, 390, 455
Beatty, M. J., 55, 56, 286, 499
Bejlovec, R. A., 348
Belch, C., 127
Bell, E., 467
Bell, R. A., 157, 286, 369, 500, 502, 504
Bell-DeTiene, K., 233
Ben, R. A., 154
Bengtson, V. L., 444, 445, 446, 447
Bennett, M., 219
Benoit, P. J., 410, 416
Benoit, W. E., 410, 416
Berg, J. H., 179
Berger, C. R., 3, 6, 10, 11, 251, 252, 518, 519
Berkowitz, L., 414
Bernasco, W., 318
Bernie, B., 226
Berry, D. S., 117
Berryman-Fink, C., 412
Best, P., 303
Bethea, L. S., 58
Bettini, L. M., 464–465
Bies, R. J., 230
Billig, M. G., 40
Bippus, A., 482
Birdwhistell, R. L., 105
Bisanz, G. L., 376, 383, 384, 386
Black, A., 65
Blake, R., 366
Blakeslee, S., 452
Blanck, P. D., 107
Blehar, M. C., 440
Blumstein, P., 158, 388
Bochner, A. P., 5
Boich, L. H., 460
Bolino, M. C., 168
Bond, M. H., 169
Bondevik, M., 448
Booth-Butterfield, M., 157
Booth-Butterfield, S., 157
Boster, F. J., 380, 389, 390, 399, 483
Bostrom, R. N., 52, 53, 59, 518
Boter, F., 380
Boucom, D. H., 459
Bowers, J. W., 214, 390
Bowlby, J., 440

Boyd, M., 160
Braaten, D. O., 233, 331
Bradac, J. J., 92, 195
Bradbury, T. N., 36, 427, 428, 429
Braithwaite, D. O., 455–457
Brennan, J., 316
Bresnahan, M. J., 398
Brewer, M. B., 168
Brissett, D., 138
Brockriede, W., 5
Brodsky, J., 347
Brosius, H. B., 66
Brown, J. D., 168
Brown, L., 168
Brown, P., 214
Brown, R., 40, 41
Brownell, J., 57
Brunner, C. C., 412
Buerkel-Rothfuss, N. L., 157
Buhrke, R. A., 295
Buhrmester, D., 250
Buk, R., 111
Bull, R., 253
Buller, D. B., 118, 119, 125, 256
Bullis, C., 268, 270
Bundy, R. P., 40
Burdick, C. A., 123
Burger, J. M., 364, 365
Burggraf, C. S., 416, 422
Burgoon, J. K., 5, 13, 30, 31, 32, 118, 119, 121–122, 126, 250, 256, 257
Burgoon, M., 396
Burke, R. J., 191
Burleson, B. R., 289, 491, 492–494
Burnett, C. K., 459
Burns, A. B., 168
Buss, D. M., 163
Buunk, B., 283
Byrne, D., 252, 253, 254
Byrne, P. R., 158

Cacioppo, J. T., 370
Cahn, L. L., 411
Cai, D. A., 396
Cambra, R., 394
Camden, C. T., 110
Campbell, D. M., 81
Campbell, J. D., 4
Canary, D. J., 4, 8, 9, 281, 283, 285, 286, 288, 290, 296, 297, 301, 386, 411, 415, 416, 429, 430, 487, 489, 490, 498, 500, 504, 520, 523
Cantor, N., 9
Cantrill, J. G., 29, 30, 380
Caplan, S. E., 492
Cappella, J. N., 122, 255
Carstensen, L. L., 458, 459

Carter, J. D., 127
Carton, J. S., 127
Cate, R., 269
Caughlin, J. P., 4, 415
Cavanaugh, L. E., 333
Cegala, D. J., 518, 521
Chadiha, L. A., 318
Chaiken, S., 371
Chaikin, A. L., 184, 193, 194, 195, 196
Chandler, T. A., 496, 497
Charles, S. T., 458
Cherulnik, P. D., 484
Cholerton, M., 369
Chovil, N., 65
Christie, R., 483
Christopher, A. N., 230
Cia, D. A., 391, 392
Cialdini, R., 364
Cialdini, R. B., 163, 165, 166, 364, 366,
   367, 368, 370, 372, 373, 374
Cialdini, R. E., 371
Cicirelli, V. G., 443, 451
Clark, A. J., 60, 66
Clark, C. L., 369
Clark, R. A., 11, 376
Clatterbuck, G. W., 252, 255
Cleavenger, D., 167
Clore, G. L., 254
Coakley, C. G., 52, 55, 57, 59
Coates, L., 60
Cochenour, J. J., 116
Cochran, A. T., 30
Cody, M. J., 9, 17, 219, 220, 233, 236,
   328, 329, 331, 337, 339, 341, 342,
   343, 364, 372, 373, 386, 394, 415,
   487, 489
Cole, J., 124
Coleman, M., 157
Collett, P., 105
Colletti, S. F., 417
Collins, N. L., 193, 441, 442, 443
Collins, R. L., 168
Coltrane, S., 290
Conaway, M. S., 59
Conroy, S. J., 444
Conville, R. L., 292, 348
Cook, S. W., 347
Cooker, L. L., 159
Cooper, J., 108
Cooper, P., 67
Cornelius, P. R., 181, 184
Costanza, R., 105
Coupland, J., 460, 463
Coupland, N., 88, 92, 460, 463
Cox, D. J., 489
Cozby, P. C., 186, 193
Cozzarelli, C., 258
Craig, J. M., 124, 258

Craig, R. T., 11, 390
Cramer, L., 283
Crocker, P. E., 168
Cronen, V. E., 518
Cronkhite, G., 5
Cross, S. E., 168
Crouter, A. C., 268
Crow, B. K., 84, 85
Cruz, M. G., 394
Csikszentmihalyi, M., 113
Cunningham, E. M., 415, 489
Cunningham, M. R., 142
Cupach, W. R., 6, 8, 214, 215, 216,
   220–222, 292, 330, 348, 411, 417, 418,
   419, 420, 427, 429, 430, 518, 519, 520,
   521, 523, 527
Cupchik, G. C., 373
Cutrona, C. E., 505

D'Addario, K. P., 115–116
Dainton, M., 4
Daly, J. A., 154, 157, 158, 286, 482, 499,
   521
Dansereau, F., 67
Darby, B. W., 219
Datteri, D. L., 325, 352
Davidson, M., 239
Davies, K. E., 375
Davis, J. L., 425
Davis, K. E., 33, 255, 442, 443
Davison, V., 369
Dean, J., 125
Deaux, K., 168
Dedden, L. A., 163
Delaney, H. J., 375
Delia, J. G., 11, 492–494
Demaine, L. J., 371
Demo, D. H., 448
De Nicholas, M. E., 163, 165
DePaulo, B. M., 110, 168, 483
Derlega, V. J., 105, 183, 184, 190, 193,
   194, 195, 196, 503
deTurck, M. D., 387
Deutsch, M., 410, 411
Dicke, A., 298
Dickson, F. C., 459
Dickson, R., 331
Dickson-Markman, F., 191
Diemer, M. A., 284
Dillard, J. P., 10, 11, 17, 67, 396
Dillman, L., 126
Dindia, K., 179, 180, 184, 190, 191, 281,
   286, 292
Dixon, J. T., 252
Dobos, J. A., 55, 56, 467
Donohue, W., 220
Doran, N. E., 396
Dougherty, T. W., 467

Dreher, G. F., 467
Drentea, P., 318
Drigotas, S. M., 285
Driscoll, R., 375
Driver, R. E., 121
Duck, S. W., 6, 198, 250, 251, 255, 273,
   281, 319, 320, 321, 322, 325
Duggan, A., 443
Dun, T., 410
Dunn, D., 236, 447
Duran, R. L., 500, 502, 518, 520
Duryea, R., 366
Durham, B., 190

Eagly, A. H., 168
Earwaker, D., 219
Edelmann, R. J., 225
Edgley, C., 138
Edwards, R., 59
Ekman, P., 104, 105, 110, 111, 112, 114,
   458
Ellis, B. H., 522
Ellis, D. G., 78, 80, 264
Ellis, J. B., 169
Englehardt, E. E., 8
Epstein, N., 459
Estrada, A. U., 451
Euwema, M. C., 417
Exline, R. V., 483

Faber, J., 138
Fabin, L. A., 317, 318, 347
Falato, W. L., 333
Falbo, T., 376, 380–382, 386
Falk, D. R., 194
Feeney, J. A., 347, 441, 442, 443
Fehr, B., 249, 347
Felmlee, D. H., 319, 327, 347
Felson, R. B., 151
Fick, C. M., 489
Figge, M., 368
Finch, J. F., 163, 166
Fincham, F. D., 283, 427, 428, 429
Fine, M. A., 157, 347
Fiske, S. T., 27, 37
Fitch, K. L., 337, 387
Fitzgerald, N. M., 269
Fitzpatrick, M. A., 27, 179, 180, 184, 302,
   303
Flament, C., 40
Flay, B. R., 394
Fletcher, G. J. O., 283, 325
Flint, L., 394
Flora, J., 316, 325
Floyd, K., 105, 116, 117, 119, 264, 451
Folkes, V. S., 228, 229, 394
Foss, K. A., 78, 79
Foss, S. K., 78, 79

Fraczek, K. E., 369
Fraedrich, J., 483
Fraizer, P. A., 347
Franco, J. N., 184
Franklin, K. M., 452
French, J. P. R., 376, 378–379, 389
Friedman, R. A., 239
Friese, I. H., 452
Friesen, W. V., 104, 110, 111, 112, 114, 458
Fitzpatrick, M. A., 303
Fukuno, M., 223
Fung, H. H., 458
Fuqua, D., 295

Gabriel, H. R., 168
Gaines, C., 59
Gaines, S. O., Jr, 285
Galvin, K. S., 348
Gangestad, S., 63, 486, 487
Ganong, L., 157
Garcia, S. D., 285
Gardner, W. L., 167, 168
Garnick, N. N., 348
Gary, A. L., 193
Gatz, M., 458
Geis, F. L., 483
Gerbing, D. W., 483
Gergen, K. J., 148, 151
Giarrusso, R., 444
Gibson, B., 142
Gilbert, D. T., 161
Gilbert, S. J., 179, 193, 194, 196
Giles, H., 88, 92, 460, 461, 463
Gladney, K., 59
Gladstein, G. A., 522
Gladue, B. A., 375
Gleason, M. E. J., 503
Glenn, N. D., 452
Goby, V. P., 56
Gockel, B., 190
Godfrey, D. K., 159, 482
Gody, M. J., 447
Goffman, E., 12, 138, 214
Golden, A. G., 318
Goldsmith, D., 289
Goldstein, P., 164–165
Golen, S., 69
Golish, T. D., 449–451, 455
Gollwitzer, P. M., 150, 151
Golombishky, K., 467
Gonzales, M. H., 233
Gonzalez, C., 286
Gonzalez, M. C., 157
Goodstadt, B. E., 490–491
Gottman, J. M., 5, 302, 336, 410, 416, 418, 421, 422, 429, 430, 458, 459
Goyner, K., 316

Graft, J., 458
Graham, E. E., 453, 454
Green, A. S., 503
Greenbaum, P. E., 116
Greenberg, M. S., 369
Greenberg, R., 197
Greenberger, D., 282
Greene, J. O., 11, 342, 519
Greene, R. W., 29
Greenfield, S., 252
Greenspan, M., 193
Grice, P. C., 81, 83, 85, 86, 96, 140
Grote, N. K., 452
Guadagno, R. E., 371
Gudykunst, W. B., 87, 88, 94, 168, 192
Guerrero, L. K., 125, 126, 251, 268, 288, 441, 442, 443
Guilford, J. P., 482
Gumpert, P., 483
Gunnthorsdottir, A., 484
Gustafson, T. B., 168

Haas, J. W., 57, 65
Haas, S. M., 286, 290
Hafer, C. L., 158
Hagiwara, S., 224
Haight, L., 519
Halberstadt, A. G., 107, 127
Hale, C., 233
Hale, J. L., 31, 32, 122, 250, 368
Hall, A. E., 499
Hall, E. T., 107
Hall, J. A., 104, 107, 109, 127
Hall, T. J., 196, 288
Halone, K. K., 52, 53, 54, 55, 69
Hamilton, V. L., 224
Hammer, M. R., 264
Hampton, S., 59, 60
Hannon, P. E., 425
Harden, J. M., 10
Harnisch, R. M., 82
Harnish, R. J., 258
Harris, B., 296
Harris, L. M., 151
Harris, M. S., 196
Harrison, D., 191
Harrison, S., 105
Harvey, J. H., 348, 349, 350
Harwood, J., 460, 463
Hatfield, E., 253, 282, 283, 452
Hause, K. S., 286, 296, 297
Hawken, L., 502
Hay, J., 282
Hayashi, G. M., 441
Hays, R., 268
Hazan, C., 440, 441
Heatherington, L., 168
Hecht, M. L., 6, 11, 196, 288, 300, 301

Hegarty, W. H., 484
Hegde, R., 41
Heider, F., 32, 33
Heisel, A. D., 499
Henderson, M., 288
Hendrick, C., 298, 299, 300, 301
Hendrick, S. S., 193, 298, 300, 301
Henley, N. M., 108
Henwood, K., 460
Herman, C. P., 108
Herman, E., 197
Heron, N., 283
Hewitt, J. P., 216
Hickey, C. B., 483
Higgins, E. T., 108
Higgins, R. L., 213
Hill, C., 316, 317
Hill, S. E. K., 467
Hindy, C. G., 347
Hirokawa, R. Y., 396, 397
Hirschmann, K., 467
Hjelle, L. A., 490–491
Hocker, J. L., 10, 410, 411, 413, 418, 419, 420
Hocking, J. E., 373
Hodgins, H., 107, 127
Hogg, M. A., 42
Holladay, S. J., 464–465
Holley, F., 59
Holman, R. H., 113
Holmberg, D., 316
Holmes, J. G., 214, 215, 322
Holtgraves, T., 214, 217, 219
Holtzworth-Munroe, A., 36
Honeycutt, J. M., 29, 30, 55, 68
Hopf, T., 499
Hoppe-Nagao, A., 318
Hoppin, S., 447
Horenstein, D., 179, 194, 196
Horgan, T. G., 127
Horowitz, L. M., 441
Horvath, C. L., 498
Horwitz, M., 40
Hosman, L. A., 194, 195
Howard, J. A., 158, 388
Hoyt, D. R., 445
Huck, S. M., 445
Hughes, D., 270
Hullett, C. R., 395
Hummert, M. L., 460
Hunter, J. E., 380, 483, 484
Hurst, M. H., 198
Huston, T. L., 268, 269–270
Huszti, H. C., 348
Hutto, D. B., 484
Hutton, D. G., 168
Huyck, M. H., 459
Hylton, C., 373

Ide, R., 224
Infante, D. A., 496, 497, 498
Itoi, R., 223

Jablin, F. M., 67, 68
Jackson, S., 80, 81, 82, 83
Jacobs, S., 80, 81, 82, 83
Jacobson, N. S., 36
Jacquet, S. E., 452
Janoff-Bulman, R., 452
Jeanquart, S., 467
Johnson, C. L., 448
Johnson, D., 51, 67
Johnson, D. J., 426
Johnson, M. D., 36
Johnson, M. L., 258, 259
Johnson, P., 92
Johnson, T., 60
Jones, E. E., 13, 33, 34, 143, 152, 154,
   159, 161, 184, 193, 194, 482
Jones, G. E., 484
Jones, S. E., 105, 106, 111
Jones, S. M., 126
Jones, T. S., 303, 415
Jordan, J. M., 519
Jordan, J. V., 168
Jorgensen, P. F., 125
Jourard, S. M, 184
Joyner, K., 333
Jussim, L., 42, 43

Kahn, G. M., 193
Kalbfleisch, P. J., 286, 467
Kalmijn, M., 318
Kaluzny, M., 333
Kamo, Y., 250
Kanagawa, C., 168, 169
Kang, K. H., 389, 390
Kaplan, A. G., 168
Karney, B. R., 36
Kashubeck-West, S., 168
Kavanaugh, M. J., 484
Kazoleas, D. C., 380, 389
Keefe, T., 521, 522
Keith, P. M., 459
Kellermann, K., 6, 34, 86, 387, 388, 390
Kelley, D. L., 31, 225, 239
Kelley, H. H., 9, 33, 250
Kelley, P., 30
Kelly, A. E., 183, 186, 198
Kelly, D., 30
Kelly, H., 389
Kelly, L., 67, 502
Kennedy, D. R., 333
Kenny, D. A., 179, 180, 184
Kerckhoff, A. C., 255
Kerns, K. S., 464–465
Kessler, E. A., 127

Kiewitz, C., 66
Kilmann, R. H., 412
Kim, H., 67
Kim, M. S., 95, 396, 397, 413
Kim, Y. Y., 108, 192
Kirtley, M. D., 55, 63, 65, 66, 68
Kitayama, S., 94, 168
Kline, S. L., 492–494
Klopf, D. W., 192, 500
Knapp, M. L., 104, 107, 109, 264, 265,
   266, 327, 521
Knox, D., 333
Koenig, J. A., 5, 30, 353
Koestner, R., 141
Kohn, M., 383, 384
Koralewski, M. A., 123
Kowalski, K. C., 168
Kowalski, N. P., 168
Kowalski, R. M., 147
Kramer, K. B., 452
Kraut, R., 503
Kraut, R. E., 371
Kreiser, P. O., 154
Krivonos, P. D., 253
Krokoff, L. J., 422, 429
Krueger, D. L., 422
Kunkel, A. W., 391–393
Kurdek, L. A., 327, 410, 430, 448
Kurzweil, N., 296

LaFrance, B. H., 499
Lakey, S. G., 4, 8, 520, 526
Lakoff, G., 39
Laliker, M., 368
LaMar, L., 333
Lambkin, J. K., 30
Lang, F. R., 458
Lang, L. R., 458
Langer, E. J., 6
Lannamann, J. W., 151
Larkey, L. K., 300, 301
Lauter, H., 369
Lavalle, L. F., 4
Lawler, E. J., 388
Lawton, L., 445, 447
Lea, M., 42, 43
Leary, M. R., 147, 197, 460
Leatham, G. B., 391
Leathers, D. G., 118, 323
Leber, D., 318
Lee, C. R., 394, 396, 398
Lee, J. A., 298
Lee, J. W., 388, 394
Lee, L., 348
Lee, S., 168
Lefcourt, H. M., 489, 490
Legg, W. B., 59
Lemery, C. R., 65

Lennartsson, C., 448
Leonard, K. E., 410, 442, 443
Leonard, S. A., 451
Le Poire, B. A., 443
Leung, K., 169, 413
Leung, T., 413
Levenson, R. W., 336, 458, 459
Leventhal, H., 373
Levine, R., 108, 112
Levine, T. R., 54, 62, 81, 168, 380, 389,
   390, 394, 499
Levinger, G., 253
Levinson, S. C., 214
Levy, M. B, 442, 443
Lewis, J. H., 56
Lewis, R. J., 105
Liao, C. C., 398
Liefbroer, A. C., 459
Lim, T. S., 214, 390
Lin, M. C., 460
Liotta, A., 30
Lipetz, M. E., 375
Liska, J., 104
Littlefield, R., 189
Liu, W. Y., 398
Logan, C., 55
Long, J. D., 445
Lord, C. G., 159, 325, 352, 482
Lorimor, R. J., 483
Lo Vette, S., 487
Lu, S., 396, 398
Ludwig, D., 184
Lyman, S. M., 207, 208, 209

Mace, W., 373
Mackey, R. A., 284
Madden-Derdich, D. A., 451
Major, B., 168
Malloy, T. E., 184
Mandelbaum, J., 62
Mann, L., 184
Manning, L. M., 41
Manusov, V., 5, 30, 34–36, 41, 110, 122,
   220, 353
Marcus, C. C., 113
Margreiter, D. G., 373
Margulis, S. T., 183, 503
Markham, S. E., 67
Markus, H., 94, 168
Marsh, P., 105
Marshall, L. I., 410
Marshall, L. J., 394
Marsnik, N. C., 58
Marston, P. J., 300, 301, 489
Martin, J., 189
Martin, K. A., 460, 463
Martin, M. W., 157
Martin, P., 157

Martin, R. A., 489
Martinko, M. J., 167
Marvin, L. E., 116
Marwell, G., 376–380, 386
Mather, J., 167
Mather, R., 141
Matthews, S. H., 464
McCabe, K., 484
McCain, T. A., 252
McCall, G. J., 38
McComb, K. B., 67, 68
McCornack, S. A., 11, 81, 92
McCroskey, J. C., 252, 499, 518
McCullough, M. E., 239
McHale, S. M., 268
Mckee, J., 460
McKenna, K. Y. A., 503
McKillop, K. J., 183, 186, 198
McLaughlin, K., 258
McLaughlin, M. L., 219, 394, 415
McQuillen, J. S., 394
Mearns, J, 347
Mechanic, D., 57
Merbach, N., 348
Merrill, J. M., 483
Merton, R. K., 28
Messman, S. J., 286, 296, 297, 411
Metts, S., 183, 214, 215, 216, 220–222,
    292, 316, 330, 339, 341, 343, 344, 345,
    347, 348, 427
Meyer, S., 57
Meyers, R. A., 380
Miczo, N., 127
Miell, D., 251, 255
Milardo, R. M., 290
Millar, F. E., 4
Miller, C. L., 123
Miller, D. T., 28
Miller, G. R., 251, 255, 380
Miller, H., 141, 160, 167
Miller, J. A., 370
Miller, J. B., 168
Miller, K. I., 522
Miller, L. C., 159, 183, 191, 193
Miller, M. D., 396
Miller, R. R., 484
Minkler, M., 448
Mintz, L. B., 168
Mirahara, A., 396, 397
Mischel, W., 9
Miyake, K., 107
Moeai, J., 327
Monahan, J. L., 37
Monsour, M., 296
Montagne-Miller, Y., 364, 372
Montgomery, B. M., 281, 292
Moody, E. J., 503
Moon, T. H., 483

Morgan, F., 159
Morman, M. T., 116, 451
Morris, D., 105
Morris, G., 327
Morrow, G. D., 426
Morton, T. L., 191, 250
Motley, M. T., 110, 111, 114
Muehlenhard, C. L., 123
Mulac, A., 92, 461
Mullett, J., 65
Munley, M. E., 252
Murray, S. L., 322
Mutsaers, W., 283
Myers, S. A., 286

Nakagawa, G., 63
Nakanishi, M., 192
Naughton, J., 12
Near, D. C., 484
Nebashi, R., 398
Neuberg, S. L., 37
Nichols, R. G., 58
Nicholson, J., 455
Nisbett, R. E., 34
Nishida, T., 192
Noller, P., 347, 441, 442, 443
Norman, N. M., 11, 151
Norton, M. L., 464–465
Nussbaum, J. F., 5, 95, 443, 461, 463, 464
Nyquist, M., 69

Oakes, P. J., 42
O'Brien, B. A., 284
Oetzel, J. G., 94
Ogden, C. K., 78
Ogden, J. K., 184
Ognibene, T. C., 441
O'Hair, H. D., 386
Ohashi, R., 398
Ohbuchi, K. I., 219, 223, 224, 410, 411
O'Keefe, B. J., 11, 92, 93, 94
O'Keefe, D. J., 368
Olson, D. H., 448
Olson, J. M., 158
Olson, L. N., 455
Olson, N., 425
Orbuch, T. L., 316, 348
O'Shaughnessy, M., 105
O'Sullivan, M., 110
O'Sullivan, P. B., 13, 140

Papa, M. J., 57, 65
Pape, C. L., 127
Park, H. S., 168
Parks, M. R., 6, 8, 198, 264, 290, 451,
    518, 527
Parrish, E. A., 502
Parrott, T. M., 445, 447

Parry, D., 417
Passman, J. L., 63
Pasupathi, M., 54, 56
Paulhus, D. L., 169
Pavitt, C., 519
Pearce, W. B., 184, 518
Pearson, J. C., 394
Pecchioni, L. L., 5, 53, 54, 55, 69
Pelligrini, R. F., 109
Peluchette, J. V., 467
Pennebaker, J. W., 183, 375
Peplau, L. A., 316, 317, 505
Perlman, D., 249
Perse, E. M., 95
Pervin, L. A., 9
Peters, A., 459
Petronio, S., 183, 188–189, 190
Pike, G. R., 303, 415
Pistole, M. C., 442, 443
Pittman, G., 272
Pittman, T. S., 13, 143, 152
Planalp, S., 27
Pondy, L. R., 429
Pontari, B. A., 138, 230
Poole, M. S., 411
Postmes, T., 42
Potter, S., 159
Prager, K., 250
Prins, K. S., 283
Putnam, L. L., 411, 415, 417

Rabbie, J. M., 40
Rachal, K. C., 239
Rahim, M. A., 412
Rancer, A. S., 496, 498
Rankin-Esquer, L. A., 459
Rao, N., 394
Raven, B., 376, 378–379, 389
Ravizza, S. M., 11
Rawlins, W. K., 186, 187, 188, 292
Ray, E. B., 59
Read, S. J., 441, 442, 443
Reardon, K. K., 394
Redmon, K., 303, 415
Reicher, S. D., 42
Rejeski, W. J., 460
Remland, M. S., 104
Reykowski, J., 364
Reynolds, C. A., 458
Reynolds, R., 86
Rezabek, L. L., 116
Rhodes, A., 369
Richard, F. D., 325, 352
Richards, I. A., 78
Richardson, K. D., 163
Richendoller, N. R., 63
Ricks, J., 483
Riddle, B. L., 498

Riggio, R. E., 127
Ritchie, L. D., 27
Rivera, S. M., 285
Roach, K. D., 158
Roan, S., 502
Robers, T., 300
Roberts, J. E., 452
Roberts, L. D., 264
Roberts, L. J., 410
Roberts, R. E. L., 445, 446
Robey, C. S., 394
Robinson, J. D., 4
Rochberg–Halton, E., 113
Rodgers, R. H., 453
Rodriguez, J. S., 110
Roe, K. M., 448
Rogan, R., 389
Rogers, G. R., 4
Rogers, M. A., 417
Rogge, R., 36
Rohlfs, G. S., 369
Rokach, A., 507
Roloff, M. E., 286, 380, 502
Roscoe, B., 333
Rosen, K. S., 440
Rosenbaum, M., 366
Rosenberg, K. J., 184
Rosenfeld, H. M., 116
Rosenfeld, L., 183, 185
Rosenthal, R., 28, 29, 107, 110, 483
Rosenwald, G., 5
Ross, L., 34
Rothbaum, F., 440
Rotter, J. B., 488–489
Rowatt, W. D., 142, 168
Rubin, D. B., 28, 29
Rubin, D. L., 59, 60
Rubin, R. B., 95, 157, 518
Rubin, Z., 316, 317
Rudd, J. E., 496, 497
Rule, B. G., 376, 383, 384, 386
Rumsey, N., 253
Rusbult, C. E., 282, 285, 410, 425, 426
Russell, D., 505
Rutt, D. J., 198
Ruusuvuori, J., 57
Ruvolo, A. P., 316, 317, 318, 347
Ruvolo, C. M., 316, 318, 347
Ryan, E. B., 460
Ryska, T. A., 160

Sabourin, T. C., 497
Sachau, D., 142
Sacher, J. A., 347
Safran, C., 327
Saleh, W. E., 489
Sales, L. J., 451

Samter, W., 289
Sanders, R. E., 3, 337, 387
Sato, K., 219
Saunders, K. J., 168
Scharfe, E., 441
Schauss, A. G., 109
Scheflen, A. E., 258
Schenck-Hamlin, W. J., 376
Schlatter, C., 369
Schlenker, B. R., 138, 141, 148, 197, 213, 216, 219, 230, 232, 233
Schmidt, G. W., 168
Schmidt, T. O., 181, 184
Schmitt, D. R., 376–380, 386
Schneider, M. J., 415
Schönbach, P., 208, 210–212, 220
Schutz, A., 163, 165, 166, 168
Schutz, W. C., 250, 254
Schwartz, J., 9
Schwartz, P., 158, 282, 388
Schwarz, J. C., 347
Scott, C. K., 429
Scott, M. B., 207, 208, 209
Searle, J. R., 82
Segrin, C., 10, 104, 127, 316, 504
Seibert, J., 56
Seibold, D. R., 380
Seiter, J., 364, 372
Semic, B. A., 498
Senchak, M., 442, 443
Serpe, R., 430
Shafer, R. B., 459
Shaffer, D. R., 184
Shannon, E. A., 497
Shaver, P. R., 440, 441
Shea, B. C., 387, 388, 390
Shepard, C., 443
Shepard, P. E., 496
Shepard, T., 196, 288
Sheppard, G. J., 92
Shepperd, J. A., 160
Sherman, R. C., 39
Shimizu, L., 327
Sholis, D., 190
Shotland, R. L., 124, 258
Sieburg, E., 85, 86
Sillars, A. L., 95, 303, 393, 410, 411, 414, 415, 416, 417, 418, 419, 420, 422, 423, 424, 427, 428, 429
Silverstein, M., 444, 445
Simpson, J. A., 325, 347, 442, 443
Sims, H. P., 484
Singh, G., 467
Singhapakdi, A., 484
Sitkin, S. B., 230
Skogstad, A., 448
Sleight, C., 67

Smith, B. A., 369
Smith, M., 11
Smith, R. H., 369, 422
Smith, S. W., 9, 386, 487
Smith, V., 484
Snyder, C. R., 213
Snyder, M., 486–488
Solano, C. H., 502
Solomon, D. H., 259
Solowczuk, K., 81
Somera, L., 67
Soukup, C., 455
Spears, R., 42, 43
Spisak, F., 11, 390
Spitzberg, B. H., 6, 410, 429, 430, 500, 504, 518, 519, 520, 521, 523, 527
Sprecher, S., 253, 282, 283, 284, 316, 318, 325, 347, 452
Stafford, L., 283, 286, 288, 290, 301, 499
Staudinger, U. M., 458
Steinberg, M., 251
Steinfatt, T. M., 483, 488, 489
Stern, L. A., 126
Sternberg, J., 443
Sternberg, R. J., 298
Stewart, J., 55, 60, 63
Stewart, R., 376
Stiff, J. B., 67, 380, 522
Stiver, I. P., 168
Stokes, R., 216
Storms, M. D., 429
Strejc, H, 198
Streufert, S., 495
Strickland, B. R., 441
Sugimoto, N., 224
Sun, Y., 452
Sunnafrank, M., 255
Surra, C. A., 269, 270, 452
Surrey, J. L., 168
Sussman, M., 484
Sussman, S., 394
Swann, W. B., 37
Swezey, R. W., 495
Sypher, H. E., 491

Tacey, W. S., 58
Tajfel, H., 40, 42
Takaku, S., 224
Tamborini, R., 395
Tardy, C. H., 183, 195, 198
Tata, J., 224
Taylor, D. A., 180, 263
Taylor, L., 158
Taylor, S. E., 27
Tedeschi, J. T., 151, 410, 411
Thelen, M., 252
Thibaut, J., 389, 483

Thomas, G., 325
Thomas, K. W., 412, 429
Thomas, L. T., 54, 62
Thompson, T. L., 5, 57
Thornby, J. L., 483
Thornton, A., 445
Tice, D. M., 138, 168
Tidwell, L. C., 191, 192
Ting-Toomey, S., 87, 88, 94, 214, 318, 396, 418, 420
Toch, H., 158
Torres, H. I., 81
Traban, C. B., 298
Tracy, K., 9, 11, 12, 390
Trapp, R., 78, 79
Traupmann, J., 282
Travis, S. S., 58
Trebling, J. D., 496
Trees, A. R., 30, 62–63
Tremblay, S. W., 157
Tsang, J., 159
Tumlin, S. A., 498
Turman, P., 455
Turnbull, W., 28
Turner, J. C., 42
Turnley, N. H., 168

Udry, J. R., 316, 333
Uebelacker, L., 168
Updegraft, K. A., 451
Utne, M. K., 282
Utz, S., 265

Vallbona, C., 483
Vandervenken, D., 82
van de Vliert, E., 417
Vangelisti, A. L., 4, 33, 55, 186, 265, 266, 327, 332, 415, 521
Van Lange, P. A. M., 285
Van Lear, C. A., 268
Vanni, D., 347
Van Willigen, M., 318
Van Yperen, N. W., 283
Vaughan, D., 348
Vecchio, R. P., 484

Verette, J. A., 228, 285
Veroff, J., 316, 318
Vitell, S. J., 484
Vogl-Bauer, S., 286
Von Bayer, C. L., 489
Vonk, R., 154

Wacker, R. R., 459
Wagner, F. N., 194
Waldhart, E., 52
Wall, S., 440
Wallace, L. A., 255
Wallerstein, J. S., 452
Walther, J. B., 13, 86, 115–116, 140, 191, 192
Wan, K., 169
Wang, H., 444
Wanzer, J. B., 157, 158
Ware, E. E., 489
Waters, E., 440
Watt, S. E., 42
Way, J. H., 484
Weaver, J. B., 63, 65, 66
Weber, A. L., 348
Weber, M. D., 252
Webster, J. M., 369
Weigel, D. J., 286, 303
Weigold, M. F., 138, 141, 233
Weiner, B., 224, 226, 228
Weiner, J. L., 333
Weir, T., 191
Weisberg, J., 410, 411
Weiss, R. S., 348
Wendt, P., 447
Werking, K. J., 293, 295
Westcott, D. R., 369
Wetherell, M. S., 42
Whatley, M. A., 369
Wheeler, L., 108, 141
Wheeless, L. R., 376
Whitbeck, L., 445, 447
White, C. H., 119
White, G. L., 326
White, K. D., 394, 395, 396
Whitely, W., 467

Wiederman, M. W., 333
Wiemann, G., 66
Wiemann, J. M., 6, 518, 521
Wigley, C. J., 496, 497
Williams, A., 443, 460, 461, 462, 463, 464
Williams, B. A., 264
Williamson, R. N., 303
Wilmot, W. W., 10, 95, 264, 265, 282, 288, 292, 343, 410, 411, 413, 414, 417, 418, 419, 420, 422, 423, 424
Wilson, C. E., 415, 417
Wilson, D. S., 484
Wilson, S. R., 390, 391–393, 394, 396, 397
Winchatz, M. R., 41
Winstead, B. A., 105, 193, 503
Wiseman, R., 376
Wispe, L., 522
Witteman, H., 303
Wittenbaum, G. M., 169
Wolff, F. I., 58
Wolvin, A. D., 52, 57, 59
Wong, P. T. P., 193
Woodall, W. G., 118, 256
Word, C. O., 108
Worthington, E. L., 239
Worthy, W., 193
Wortman, C. B., 152–153, 154, 197
Wosinska, R., 364, 369

Yabiku, S. T., 445
Yik, M. S. M., 169
Yin, Z., 160
Young, S. L., 332
Yovetich, N. A., 410
Yum, Y. O., 285

Zakahi, W. R., 500
Zanna, M. P., 108
Zappa, J., 220
Zebrowitz-McArthur, L., 117
Zediker, K., 60
Zelley, E., 286
Znakov, V. V., 484
Zuckerman, M., 107, 121
Zusman, M. E., 333

Subject Index

Note: The **boldfaced** items are specialized terms that were identified in each of the chapters. Please refer to the page numbers indicated to see their usage.

ability, self-promotion and, 159, 160
abstract remark tactic, 418
acceptance of responsibility tactic, 419
acceptances, 82
accidents
    appeals to, 208, 209, 235
    embarrassment and, 220
accommodating style, in conflict,
    412–413
accounter's dilemma, 234
accounts
    approaches to, 207
    attribution theory and, 225–230
    communication competence and, 528
    concessions, 210, 211, 214
    culture and, 223–225
    defined, 60, 207–208, 239
    in formal settings, 237–238
    functions of, 213–214
    goals achieved through, 214
    impression management and, 232–237
    infidelity and, 220
    listeners and, 60–61
    nonverbal behavior in, 61
    preferred, 216–220
    reactions to, 217–220
    in reality-based television, 227
    in relational disengagement, 348–349,
    353
    Schönbach's expanded typology of,
    210–213
    types of, 61, 208–213
accuracy
    impression management and, 141, 143
    in perception, 25–26, 527
acknowledgments, 82
acquiescence, 293
act, 4
action listening style, 66
**activation of impersonal commit-
    ments,** 380
activation of personal commitments,
    380
active listening, 67–68
actor-observer bias, 34, 527
actors, self-presentation and, 138
actual equity, 326
adaptability, 520
adolescents, compliance-resisting tactics
    of, 395–396
advice
    goals of, 393
    relational maintenance and, 296
affect, listening and, 52

affection. *See also* love
    behaviors communicating, 257
    in parent-child relationships, 447, 451
    relational escalation and, 250
    in relationships, 254–255
affection communication, 116–117
Affection Exchange Theory (AET),
    116–117
affective processes, during listening, 55
affectual solidarity, 445, 446
affinity seeking, 155–158
agape, 299, 300
agentic welfare, 250
aggression
    coping with embarrassment with, 221
    verbal aggressiveness, 496–498
aging. *See also* life span
    self-presentation and, 460–464
    socioeconomic selectivity theory and,
    458–460
alignment, 81
altercasting tactic
    negative, 377
    positive, 377
altruism
    as affinity-seeking strategy, 157
    as compliance-gaining tactic, 378
    intergenerational support model, 444
anchoring, 365–366
anger
    consequences of, 429–430
    in relational disengagement, 346
anthropological attraction research, 252,
    253
antisocial tactics, 285–286
anxious-ambivalent attachment style,
    440–443
anxiousness, 499–500
apologies, 82, 216–217, 218, 528
    benefits of, 232–233
    coping with embarrassment with, 221
    cultural differences, 224–225
    in formal contexts, 237–238
    full-blown, 216–217, 218, 235
    impression management and, 232–237
    perfunctory, 235
    reactions to, 217–219
    relational disengagement and, 331–332
    types of, 209
appeals
    to accidents, 208, 209, 235
    to biological drives, 208–210
    to defeasibility, 209, 210
    to independence, 338

to loyalties, 209, 210
    for suspended judgment, 216
appearance. *See* physical appearance
apprehensiveness
    individual differences in, 499–500
    worrying and, 501–502
appropriateness
    communication competence and, 523
    of disclosure, 520
    norm of, in self-disclosure, 194
approval, of relationships, 319, 328–329
arbitrary nonverbal cues, 104
argumentativeness
    cultural differences in, 498
    individual differences in, 496–498
    scale, 496
    verbal aggressiveness *vs.*, 496–498
argumentative skill deficiency model,
    497–498
articulation, 520
As Good As It Gets, 315, 363
ask tactic, 383–385, 386
assertions, 82
assertion tactic, 380, 381
assertiveness, 12
associational solidarity, 445, 446
associations
    derogatory comments about, 163
    rewarding, 158
    self-presentation through, 163–166
assuming control, 157
assuming equality, 157
assurances, 288–289, 296
attachment styles, 251–252, 440–443
    anxious/ambivalent, 440–443
    avoidant, 440–443
    coping behaviors and, 442
    life-style attachment theory and,
    443–444
    nonverbal communication and,
    442–443
    secure, 440–443
attachment theory, 440–445
attainment, indicators of, 150–151
attention, in courtship behaviors, 258
attentiveness, 521
attitude similarity, 264
    interpersonal attraction and, 254–255
    relational disengagement and, 318
attraction. *See* interpersonal attraction
attractiveness. *See* physical attractiveness
attributional conflict tactics, in disen-
    gagement, 343–345
attribution biases, 34–36

attributions, 32–36
  causal loci, 32
  conflict behaviors and, 427–429
  consensus and, 33–34
  consistency and, 33
  defined, 32
  distinctiveness and, 33
  equity and, 283–285
  errors and biases in, 34–36
  external explanations, 34
  of hurtful messages, 33
  intent and, 32–33
  internal explanations, 34
attribution theory
  communication of accounts and,
    225–230
  compliance-gaining messages and,
    393–394
  defined, 225
  excuse credibility and, 227–230
  hurtful messages and, 332–333
  rejection and, 228–230
  relational disengagement and, 331–333
audience
  reactions of, 139
  self-presentation and, 138–139
authentic ingratiation, 152
authority principle, 373–374
autonomy, 292
aversive stimulation tactic, 377, 378
avoidance
  confrontation *vs.*, 415–417
  coping with embarrassment with, 221,
    222
  relational maintenance and, 297
avoidance strategy, in conflict, 417
avoidance tactics
  in conflict, 418
  in disengagement, 339, 340
avoidant attachment style, 440–443

backchannels, 54, 60
  marriage length and, 56
background attacks, 497
bald on record tactics, in disengagement, 343–345
bargaining
  as compliance-gaining tactic, 380, 381,
    383
  in relational disengagement, 346
basic goals, 9
basking in reflected glory, 165
behavior. *See also* nonverbal communication
  comforting, 289
  interpersonal attraction and, 255–256
  life span effects, 94–95
  listening and, 52, 58

biddings, 82
biological drives, appeals to, 208–210
Bisanz and Rules persuasion schema,
   383–387
blame
  in couple conflicts, 429
  as distributive tactic, 420
blended families, 440, 455–457
blind dates, 231
body language, 105. *See also* nonverbal
   communication
bonding. *See also* attachment styles
  by couples, 316–319
  parent-child, 440–441
  relational escalation stage, 267
boosting, 166
boundary coordination, 188–190
bragging, 159–160
breaking up. *See* relational disengagement
bullies, 146

candor, 188
Casablanca, 315
cascade model, of marital dissolution,
   336
CAT. *See* **Communication Accommodation Theory (CAT)**
categorization, 40–41
causal loci, 32
causes
  attribution theory and, 225–230
  controllable, 226
  external, 226
  impersonal, 226
  internal, 226
  personal, 226
  stable, 226
  uncontrollable, 226
  unstable, 226
change, in interpersonal communication,
   5
channel consistency, 110
channel discrepancy, 110, 121, 323
character attacks, 497
chronemics, 108–109
chronic loneliness, 503–504
clarity, prescription, 230–232
closedness, 292
closeness
  in intergenerational friendships, 465
  patterns of, in parent-child relation-
    ships, 450–451
  perceptions of, 157
  in step-families, 455–457
clothing
  authority principle and, 373–374
  cultural differences, 113
coercive power, 378

cognitive attraction research, 252,
   254–255
cognitive complexity
  defined, 491
  individual differences in, 491–495
  as a personality type, 495
cognitive disclaimers, 216
cognitive processes, 25, 27–42
  attributions, 32–36
  attribution theory, 225–227
  integration of, 42
  interpersonal expectancies, 28–32
  listening and, 52–54
  person perception, 36–39
  stereotypes, 39–42
cognitive valence theory, 125–126,
   259–263
coherence, of self-presentation, 148
coherent topic shifts, 84
collaborating style, in conflict, 412–413
collectivist cultures, 88. *See also* culture
  accounts in, 224–225
  compliance and, 396–398
  self-presentation in, 168–169
color, 109
comfortable self, 157
comforting behaviors, 289
commissives, 82
commitment
  conflict and, 425–426
  relational disengagement and, 325
commitment principle
  compliance and, 369–371
  foot-in-the-door tactic, 370, 371
  low-ball tactic, 370–371
  self-perception and, 371
committed love, 300
common ground, 419
communal welfare, 250
**Communication Accommodation
   Theory (CAT),** 88–92, 461
communication apprehension, 499–500
communication behaviors, in attraction,
   255–256
communication channels, 139–140
  channel consistency, 110
  channel discrepancy, 110, 121, 323
communication competence, 517–532
  communicator training, 57
  component model of, 518–519
  criteria for assessing, 520–523
  defined, 6–7, 518
  ethics and, 8
  fundamentals of, 526–527
  implications of, 525–532
  individual differences in, 517–518
  in instrumental objectives, 531–532
  listening and, 63–65

natural ability and, 159, 160
personality and, 532
in relational development, 528–531
self-assessment of, 523–525
self-handicapping and, 160–161
self-presentation and, 12, 527–528
self-promotion and, 158–159
Communication Predicament of Aging Model, 460
communication skills, competence and, 519
communicative adaptability, 520
communicative functions
affectionate expression, 116–117
conversation management, 121–122
deception, 118–121
defined, 113–114
emotional expression, 114–115
identity management, 117–118
impression formation, 117–118
of nonverbal communication, 113–126
relational messages, 122–126
communicator competence training, 57
companionate love, 300, 301
compatibility postulate, 254–255
compensation, 30, 217
nonverbal communication and, 125–126
competence. *See* communication competence
competence attacks, 497
competing style, in conflict, 412–413
competition
attacking, 163
cooperation *vs.*, 415–417
completion stage, of disengagement, 353
complex plans, 11
compliance, 364–376. *See also* influence
anchors, 365–366
authority and, 373
commitment and, 364, 369–371
contrast effects, 365–366
culture and, 396–398
door-in-the-face, 368
foot-in-the-door tactic, 370
liking and, 371
perceptual contrast, 365–366
physical attractiveness and, 371–372
reciprocal concession, 368
reciprocity principle, 366–369
resistance to, 364
scarcity and, 374–376
social proof and, 372–373
strategies, 30
compliance-gaining messages. *See also* influence
attribution theory and, 393–394

Bisanz and Rule persuasion schema, 383–387
defined, 364, 376
Falbo's power tactics, 380–383
image concerns and, 390–393
Marwell and Schmitt's typology of, 376–380, 386
politeness theory and, 390–393
resistance hypothesis, 387–388
social power and, 388–390
typologies of, 376
urgency hypothesis, 388
use of, 387–394
compliance-resistance, 394–396
identity management strategy, 395–396
justification resistance strategy, 395–396
negotiation strategy, 395–396
nonnegotiation strategy, 395–396
complimenting, 82, 154–155
component model of communication competence, 518–519
compromise
as compliance-gaining tactic, 380, 381
in disengagement, 337, 338
compromising style, in conflict, 412–413
computer-mediated communication, 42–43. *See also* on-line communication
confirming messages in, 86
self-disclosure in, 191–192
conceding control, 157
concern, as integrative tactic, 419
concessions, 61, 216, 528
expanded typology of, 211, 213
functions of, 213–214
as integrative tactic, 419
condemnation of condemners, 209, 210
condolences, 82
confidence
communication competence and, 518
interpersonal attraction and, 256
confirming messages, 85–86
conflict
accommodating style, 412–413
age and, 458–459
attachment styles and, 442
avoidance strategy, 417
behavior consequences, 427–430
collaborating style, 412–413
communication competence and, 531–532
competing style, 412–413
compromising style, 412–413
confrontation *vs.* avoidance, 414–415
continuity pattern, 419–420

cooperation *vs.* competition, 415–417
defined, 411
distributive strategy, 417
escalation of, 410, 421–424
inevitability of, 410–411
integrative strategy, 417
intrapsychic, 411
management of, 414–417, 531–532
in marriage, 459
messages prompting, 416
metacommunication pattern, 422
patterns, 417–424
productive, 410
reasons for studying, 410–411
relational problems, 424–427
relational satisfaction and, 429–430
spontaneity pattern, 424
stationarity pattern, 422–423
strategies, 417
styles, 412–414
symmetry pattern, 420–422
variety pattern, 418
withdrawing style, 412–413
conformity, 155
confrontation, 415–417
confusion, in relational disengagement, 346
congratulations, 82
Conroy, Pat, 281
consensual families, 27
consensual solidarity, 445, 446
consensus, 33–34, 225
consistency
attribution and, 33, 225
high preference for, 371
constatives, 82
content analysis, of Web sites, 142
content listening style, 66
context, pragmatic code and, 80
continuity conflict pattern, 419–420
contrast, 365–366, 369
control
assuming, 157
conceding, 157
locus of, 488–491
personal, 206, 232
relational escalation and, 250
in relationships, 255, 333–336
controllable causes, 226
conventional message design logic, 93
conventional secrets, 186, 187
conversational involvement, 520–521
conversational maxims, 81
conversational narcissism, 521
conversational rule keeping, 157
conversation management, 521
through nonverbal cues, 121–122

conversations
  listener role in, 60–62
  nonverbal cues in, 61
cooperation
  competition *vs.*, 415–417
  lack of, 87
Cooperative Principle, 81–82, 83
  topic focus and, 85
coping skills
  attachment styles and, 442
  embarrassment and, 220–223
  relational disengagement and, 353
cost escalation, in relational disengagement, 343
couples. *See also* courtship; families; love; marriage; relationships; romantic relationships
  attribution biases in, 36
  blame and, 429
  commitment by, 269–272
  conflict patterns, 418
  confrontation decisions by, 415
  infidelity and, 333–336
  likelihood of staying together, 316–319
  marriage satisfaction, 268, 282, 303, 429–430
  openness between, 287–288
  overbenefited partners in, 283
  relationship development, 29–30, 265–271
  self-perception and, 39–42
  social networks, 290
  synchronization of, 266
  types of, 302–304
  underbenefited partners in, 283
courtship. *See also* couples; love; romantic relationships
  behaviors, 257–259
  gender differences, 260–261
  stages of, 258
  turning points in, 269–270
credentialing, 216
cross-sex friendships, 293
culture
  argumentativeness and, 497
  collectivist, 87–88, 168–170, 224–225, 396–398
  Communication Accommodation Theory and, 88–92
  communication of accounts and, 223–225
  compliance and, 396–398
  emblems and, 105
  emotional expression and, 114
  ethnocentrism and, 527
  family definition and, 448
  gestures and, 105

  high-context, 192
  individualistic, 87–88, 94, 169, 224–225, 396–398
  listening styles and, 66–67
  low-context, 192
  Mutual Accommodation Theory and, 91–92
  nonverbal communication and, 111–113
  perception and, 527
  personal space and, 107
  relational maintenance strategies and, 285–286
  relationship escalation and, 250
  schemata and, 26
  self-construal and, 169–170
  self-disclosure and, 192
  verbal communication and, 87–92

date offers, rejection of, 228–230
Dead Poets Society, The, 14
debt tactic, 377
deceit tactic, 380, 381, 386
deception
  behavior, 7
  Cooperative Principle and, 81
  defined, 118
  Interpersonal Deception Theory (IDT), 118–119
  nonverbal communication and, 118–121
  in self-presentation, 143–144
  supplication, 162–163
dedication, self-presentation goals and, 12–13
de-escalation, 315. *See also* relational disengagement
de-escalation messages, 337, 338
defeasibility, appeal to, 209, 210
defense of self, 205–240
  accounts, 207–214
  attribution theory and, 225–230
  culture and, 223–225
  excuses, 206–207
  facework, 214–223
  forgiveness and, 239
  impression management, 232–237
  politeness theory, 214–223
  triangle model of responsibility, 230–232
deficient fit, in self-disclosure, 189
deficit model of listening, 55–56
deindividuation, 42–43
deliberative listening, 67, 68
denial
  of injury, 209, 210
  of intent, 235
  of offenses, 238

  in relational disengagement, 346, 349–351
  types of, 238
  of victim, 209, 210
depression
  geriatric, 459–460
  relational disengagement and, 315–316, 347
  unhealthy relationships and, 333
depth, behaviors communicating, 257
derogatory comments, 163. *See also* hurtful messages
description, 82
  as integrative tactic, 419
descriptive intimacy, 179–180
deviant behavior, 208
dialectical tensions, 292–293
dialogue, 60–62
direct-bilateral disengagement, 341
direct denial tactic, 418
direct fighting, 417
directives, 82
direct requests, 390, 391
direct-unilateral disengagement, 341
disclaimers, 216
disclosure. *See* self-disclosure
disconfirming listening style, 56
disconfirming messages, 85–86
discrimination
  favorable, 41
  in groups *vs.* out groups, 40–41
  negative, 40–41
discussion, in dialectical tensions, 292
disorientation, in relational disengagement, 346
display rules, 111, 114
dispreferred pair parts, 83
disputations, 82
disqualification, disconfirming messages, 86
distal goals, 10
distance zones, 107–108
distinctiveness, attribution and, 33, 225
distress-maintaining bias, 35*f*, 36
distributive conflict strategies, 417, 420
divorce
  attachment styles and, 440–441
  consequences of, 440, 451–453
  rates, 285
  turning points after, 453–455
doctor-patient relationships, 57–59
dominance, relational expectancies, 31*f*
door-in-the-face, 368
dramaturgy, 138–139
Driving Miss Daisy, 294–295
dyadic effect, in self-disclosure, 184
dyadic phase, of disengagement, 319–321

dyad-oriented tactics, 384, 385–386
dynamism, 157

editing, gender differences in, 140
educational contexts, listening in, 59–60
effective listening, 67–69
effectiveness, 522–523
elderly people
    avoiding appearance of age, 463–464
    depression in, 459–460
    identifying age to others, 462–463
    loneliness of, 459
    marriage and, 459
    patronizing talk to, 461–462
    self-presentation of, 460–464
    socioeconomic selectivity theory and,
        458–460
    stereotypes of, 460–464
e-mail, self-presentation goals and, 13
embarrassment
    coping with, 220–223
    cultural differences, 225
    helping others cope with, 221–222
emblems, in nonverbal communication,
    105
emoticons, 115–116
emotion-agent tactic, 380, 381
emotional abuse, 334
emotional alleviation, 224
emotional expression
    facial expressions, 112
    intentionality of, 110
    nonverbal communication and,
        114–115
emotional infidelity, 333
emotional loneliness, 503
emotions
    age and, 458–460
    control of, 228–230
    in relational disengagement, 347
    relational escalation and, 251
    Web site resources, 506
emotion-target tactic, 380, 381
empathic listening, 67
empathy
    apology and, 239
    communication competence and,
        521–522
    coping with embarrassment with, 222
    listening and, 63–65
    measures of, 64–65
employment, listening skills and, 56–57
enhancements, self-presentation and,
    165–166
enjoyment, facilitating, 157
entitlements, self-presentation and, 165
equality, assuming, 157
Equilibrium Theory, 125

equity
    actual, 326
    defined, 283
    in marriage, 283–285, 303
    psychological, 325–326
    relational disengagement and,
        317–318, 325–327
    relational maintenance and, 282–285
    task sharing and, 290, 291, 296
equivocal fit, in self-disclosure, 189
eros love, 298, 299, 300
escalation. *See* relational escalation
escape, coping with embarrassment with,
    221, 222–223
esteem tactic
    negative, 378
    positive, 378
ethics, 8
ethnic similarity, 264
ethnocentrism, 88, 527
evaluative intimacy, 179–180
evasion tactic, 380, 381, 386, 418
event-focused messages, 83–84
event schemata, 27
exchange, communication as, 4
excuses
    attribution theory and, 225–230
    coping with embarrassment with,
        221
    credibility of, 227–228
    defined, 208, 230, 528
    expanded typology of, 211, 213
    external, 61
    focusing on requirements, 206
    in formal contexts, 237–238
    functions of, 213
    impression management and,
        233–237
    personal control and, 206, 232
    personal obligations and, 207, 232
    as preferred accounts, 217
    prescription clarity and, 230–232
    reactions to, 228
    shared on-line, 206–207
    triangle model of responsibility and,
        230–232
    types of, 209, 226–227
exemplifiers
    defined, 145
    self-presentation and, 161–162
    strategies, 144
exit response, in conflict, 424–427
expectancies
    behavior and, 28–29
    interpersonal, 28–32
    in personal relationships, 29–32
experimenting, relational escalation
    stage, 265

expertise tactic, 380, 381
expert power, 379
    authority principle and, 374
    negative tactic, 377, 379
    positive tactic, 377, 379
expressive message design logic, 92
external causes, 226
external excuses, 61
external locus of control, 489–491
extramarital affairs, 283

face
    defined, 214
    management of, 215
    negative, 215
    positive, 214–215
face-threatening acts, 393
facework, 12, 214–223
    defined, 215
    in relational disengagement,
        342–345
facial expressions
    culture and, 111–113
    of emotions, 112
    intentionality of, 110
    as nonverbal cues, 104
facial maturity, 117
facial primary, 104
fairness messages, in disengagement, 337,
    338
fait accompli tactic, 380, 381, 383
Falbo's power tactics, 380–383
families. *See also* parent-child
        relationships
    affinity-seeking behaviors in, 156
    attachment styles, 440–443
    blended, 455–457
    closeness patterns in, 450–451
    cultural definitions of, 448
    identity formation, 445
    intergenerational solidarity theory and,
        445–448
    interpersonal relationships in,
        440–460
    relational schemata, 27
    secrets of, 186, 187
    self-presentation based on, 169
    turning points in relationships, 440,
        448–451
fatalism, 209
fatalistic messages, 337, 338
father-son relationships, 56. *See also*
        parent-child relationships
faux pas, 220
favors
    asking for, 391–393
    rendering, 155
fear, in relational disengagement, 346

feedback
  in active listening, 67–68
  negative, 139
  positive, 139
  self-presentation and, 139, 150
fictive kin, 448
Fitzpatrick's marital typology, 302
flirting
  gender differences, 259, 260–261
  interpersonal attraction and, 256
  interpreting, 258–259
  relational maintenance and, 297
  stages of, 258
foot-in-the-door tactic, 370, 371
forgiveness, 239
freedom
  restriction of, 375
  scarcity principle and, 374, 375
free samples/gifts, reciprocity principle
    and, 367–369
friendliness, self-presentation goals and,
    12
friendships. See also relationships
  age and, 458
  following relational disengagement,
    348
  intergenerational, 464–469
  opposite-sex, 293–297
  platonic, 293–297
  self-monitoring and, 487–488
  turning points in, 268–271
full-blown apologies, 216–217, 218, 235
  relational disengagement and, 331–332
functional solidarity, 445
fundamental attribution error, 34, 35*f*

gays
  infidelity and, 333
  relationship escalation and, 252
gender differences
  in affection displays, 447, 451
  in divorce consequences, 452
  in editing, 140
  in flirting, 259, 260–261
  in modesty, 167–168
  nonverbal sensitivity, 124, 127
  in on-line communication, 140–141,
    142
  in personal ads, 14, 141, 144
  in personal space, 107–108
  in personal Web pages, 167
  in relational disengagement, 318
  in self-disclosure, 185–186, 190–191
  in self-presentation, 140, 141, 167–168
  in touch, 105–107, 258
gendered closeness perspective, 451
general self-disclosure, 193–194

geriatric depression, 459–460
gestures, 105
globality, of conflict, 428
goal-driven behavior, 3–8
goals. See also interpersonal goals
  abstractness of, 9
  account and, 214
  challenging, 9
  clarity of, 9
  communication competence and, 518,
    526–527
  communication events and, 10
  conflict study and, 410
  confrontation and, 415
  immediacy of, 10
  interpersonal conflict and, 411
  multiple, 10
  nature of, 9–11
  plans for action and, 10–11
  pragmatic code and, 80
  for self-presentation, 147–148
  social cognition and, 43–44
  types of, 9–18
  in verbal communication, 77, 80–97
Godfather, The, 468
Gods Must Be Crazy, The, 26
Good Will Hunting, 439, 466–467
grave-dressing phase, of disengage-
    ment, 319–321, 348–353
greetings, 82
Grice's cooperation principle, 81–82, 83
  confirming and disconfirming
    messages, 86
  topic focus and, 85
guilt
  reciprocity and, 368–369
  in relational disengagement, 346

handicapping, 161
handshakes, 111
haptics, 105–107
health care providers, 57–59
healthy relationships, 334
hedging, 216
helplessness, 12
He Said/She Said, 25, 39
high-context cultures, 192
high preference for consistency, 371
"high reward" relationships, 32
hinting tactic, 380, 381, 383, 391
home pages. See also Web sites
  self-presentation in, 140, 142
homogamy, 254
homosexuals
  infidelity and, 333
  relationship escalation and, 252
honesty, in self-disclosure, 196–197

hope, in relational disengagement, 346
hostile remarks, 420
humor
  communication competence and, 520
  coping with embarrassment with, 221,
    222
  obscene jokes, 85
hurtful messages
  attribution theory and, 332–333
  derogatory comments, 163
  intent and, 32
hyperpersonal interaction, 140

iconic nonverbal cues, 104
identification, self-presentation and, 166
identity change stage, of disengage-
    ment, 353
identity management. See also self-
    presentation
  compliance resistance strategies,
    395–396
  goals, 11–13
  indicators of attainment, 149–150
  nonverbal communication and,
    117–118
IDT. See Interpersonal Deception
    Theory (IDT)
illicit ingratiation, 152
illocutionary acts, 82–83
illustrators, in nonverbal communi-
    cation, 105
immediacy
  behaviors communicating, 256
  interpersonal attraction and, 256
  nonverbal communication and, 125
impersonal causes, 226
**impersonal commitments, activation
    of,** 380
imperviousness, 86
implied possible messages, in disengage-
    ment, 338
impression formation, 117–118
impression management, 138, 232–237
  intimidation and, 156
  on-line, 140, 142
  in organizations, 167
  purposes of, 141, 143
  self-monitoring and, 487
incentive value, of ingratiation, 151–152
inclusion
  of others, 157
  relational escalation and, 250
indebtedness, 369
independence appeals, in disengagement
    messages, 338
independent couples, 302, 303
independent self-construals, 94, 169

indicators of attainment, 150–151
indifference, disconfirming messages, 86
indirect-bilateral disengagement, 341
indirect fighting, 417
indirect-unilateral disengagement, 341
individual differences
　argumentativeness, 496–498
　cognitive complexity, 491–495
　communication apprehension,
　　499–500
　communication competence, 517–518
　factors affecting, 483–507
　importance of understanding, 482–483
　interpersonal communication, 481–508
　locus of control, 488–491
　loneliness, 500–506
　Machiavellian behavior, 483–486
　self-monitoring behavior, 486–488
　self-presentation, 168
individualistic cultures, 87–88. *See also*
　culture
　accounts in, 224–225
　compliance and, 396–398
　self-construals in, 94, 169
individuation, 37, 43
infidelity, 333–336
　accounts and, 220
　discovering, 336
　emotional, 333
　sexual, 333
influence, 364–399. *See also* compliance;
　compliance-gaining messages
　communication competence and, 531
　compliance, 364–376
　compliance-gaining messages, 376–387
　compliance-resisting tactics, 394–396
　culture and, 396–398
　types of, 364–365
informality, relational expectancies, 31*f*
ingratiation, as compliance-gaining
　message, 385
ingratiators
　affinity seeking, 155–156
　authentic ingratiation, 152
　complimenting, 153–155
　defined, 143–144
　dilemma, 152–153
　illicit ingratiation, 152
　incentive value of, 151–152
　opinion conformity, 155
　organizations and, 167
　perceived legitimacy of, 153
　rendering favors, 155
　strategies, 144, 151–156
　subjective probability of success, 152
　types of, 151–152
　in Web sites, 142

ingratiator's dilemma, 152–153
in-groups, 40–41
initiating, relational escalation stage, 29,
　265
injury, denial of, 209, 210
instant aging, 461
instrumental goals, 11, 17–18
insurance policy model, of intergenera-
　tional support, 444
integrating, relational escalation stage,
　266
integrative conflict strategies, 417, 419
intensifying, relational escalation stage,
　29, 265–266
intention
　attributions and, 32
　denial of intent, 235
　hurtful messages and, 32
　intentional causes, 226
intentionality, of nonverbal communi-
　cation, 109–111
interact, 4
Interaction Adaptation Theory, 126
interaction patterns, 4
interdependence-autonomy dialectic
　tensions, 292
interdependent self-construals, 94, 169
interethnic/intercultural relationships,
　285, 327–328
intergenerational friendships, 464–469
　formation of, 466–467
　mentoring relationships, 464–469
　stereotypes and, 460
intergenerational solidarity theory,
　445–448
　affectual solidarity, 445, 446
　associational solidarity, 445, 446
　consensual solidarity, 445, 446
　defined, 445
　functional solidarity, 445
　normative solidarity, 446
　structural solidarity, 446
intergenerational support
　altruism model of, 444
　insurance policy model of, 444
　return on investment model of, 444
　social exchange theory and, 444
internal causes, 226
internal locus of control, 489–491
Internet. *See* on-line communication
interpersonal attraction, 249
　behaviors communicating, 257
　research on, 252–256
interpersonal attraction, 252–256. *See*
　also physical attractiveness
　attitude similarity, 254–255
　communication behaviors, 255–256

defined, 252
physical beauty, 253
supportiveness, 253–254
interpersonal communication compe-
　tence. *See* **communication**
　competence
interpersonal conflict. *See* conflict
interpersonal construct differentiation,
　491
Interpersonal Deception Theory (IDT),
　118–119
interpersonal expectancies, 28–32, 44
interpersonal goals, 440–469. *See also*
　goals
　defined, 9
　instrumental, 11, 17–18
　loneliness and, 504
　over time, 440–469
　relational, 11, 13–16
　self-disclosure and, 183
　self-presentation, 11–13
　types of, 11–18
interpersonal needs, relationship escala-
　tion and, 250–251
interpersonal relationships. *See* relation-
　ships
interruptions, 68
intimacy
　apology and, 239
　behaviors communicating, 256–257
　couple satisfaction and, 316
　descriptive, 179–180
　evaluative, 179–180
　increasing, during interaction,
　　256–263
　nonverbal communication and, 125
　openness, 287–288
　reciprocity and, 30
　relational escalation and, 250,
　　256–271
　relational expectancies, 31*f*
intimidators, 156, 158
　defined, 145
　organizations and, 167
　school bullies, 146
　strategies, 144
intrapsychic conflict, 411
intrapsychic phase, of disengagement,
　319–321
intrinsic nonverbal cues, 104
intrusion, in relational disengagement,
　351
intuitive love, 300
invitations, in courtship behaviors, 258
involvement, behaviors communicating,
　256
irrelevant remark tactic, 418

irrelevant responses, 86
issue-focused messages, 83–84

justification messages, in disengagement, 339, 340
justification resistance strategies, 395–396
justifications, 61
    benefits of, 233
    coping with embarrassment with, 221
    defined, 208, 210, 528
    expanded typology of, 212
    functions of, 213–214
    impression management and, 233–237
    loyalties and, 233–234
    reactions to, 217–220

kinesics, 105
knowledge, communication competence and, 519
knowledge structures
    defined, 26–27
    interpersonal expectancies and, 29–30
    stereotypes as, 40

L.A. Story, 14
lagged reciprocity, 444
laissez-faire families, 27
legitimate power, 379–380
lesbians
    infidelity and, 333
    relationship escalation and, 252
liar stereotypes, 118
life span
    attachment theory and, 440–445
    communication behavior and, 94–95
    communication competence and, 532
    divorce consequences, 451–455
    family relationships and, 440–457
    intergenerational friendships, 464–469
    intergenerational solidarity theory and, 445–448
    relationship turning points in, 448–451
    remarriage and, 455–457
    self-presentation and, 460–464
    socioeconomic selectivity theory and, 458–460
life-style attachment theory, 443
likelihood of candor, 188
liking
    behaviors communicating, 256–257
    as compliance-gaining tactic, 377, 378
    referent power and, 378
    self-disclosure and, 193–194, 197
liking principle, 371
listening, 51–70
    accounting and, 60–61
    active, 67–68

affective processes, 55
affinity-seeking through, 157
attentiveness during, 54
cognitive processes in, 52–54
competence and, 65–66
contexts of, 55–60
couple satisfaction and, 318–319
deficit model of, 55–56
definitions of, 51–55
deliberate, 67, 68
disconfirming style, 56
as dyadic, 60–62
in educational contexts, 59–60
effective, 63, 67–69
empathic, 63–65, 67
employment and, 56–57
importance of, 51
improving skills, 69
interruptions and, 68
in marriage, 55–56
in medical contexts, 57–59
message interpretation and, 52
nonverbal behavior during, 54
in organizations, 56–57
processes associated with, 52, 62–66
relational, 53
relationships and, 55–56
retention and, 52
as social support, 62–63
time spent in, 51
verbalizations during, 54
listening styles, 66–67
    action, 66
    content, 66
    cultural differences in, 66–67
    effective, 68
    people, 66
    time-oriented, 66
locus of control
    external, 489–491
    individual differences in, 488–491
    internal, 489–491
    scales, 489–490
logical proof arguments, 236, 238
loneliness
    age and, 459
    chronic, 503–504
    dealing with, 500–501, 505
    defined, 500
    emotional, 503
    individual differences in, 500–506
    on-line communication and, 502–503
    scale of, 504–505
    situational, 503–504
    social, 503
    Web site resources, 506
looking glass self, 38

love. *See also* affection; courtship; romantic relationships
    attachment styles and, 443–444
    behaviors communicating, 257
    relational disengagement and, 316
    romantic relationships, 298–302
love styles, 298–300
love ways, 300–302
low-ball tactic, 370–371
low-context cultures, 192
"low reward" relationships, 32
loyalty
    appeal to, 209, 210
    justifications and, 233–234
    response, in conflict, 424–427
ludus love, 298, 299, 300
lying. *See also* deception
    supplication, 162–163

Machiavellianism, 382, 383, 481
    individual differences and, 483–486
maledictions, 497
mania, 299, 300
manipulation
    in disengagement, 339, 340–341
    goals achievement and, 7
    Machiavellian personality type, 483–486
manner, Cooperative Principle and, 81
marital schemata, 302
marriage. *See also* couples; courtship; love; romantic relationships
    cascade model of dissolution, 56, 336
    communication in, 302–303
    conflict in, 459
    disclosure in, 185, 191
    divorce rates, 285
    equity in, 283–285, 303
    Fitzpatrick's marital typology, 302
    life span and, 95
    listening in, 55–56
    nonverbal communication in, 110
    paths toward, 29–30, 268, 269–270
    relational maintenance in, 303
    roles in, 302
    satisfaction with, 268, 282, 303, 498
    social networks and, 290
    types of, 302–304
    violence in, 497
Marwell and Schmitt's typology, of compliance-gaining messages, 376–380, 386
meaning, semantics and, 77–78
medical contexts, listening in, 57–59
memory, selective attention and, 25
men. *See* gender differences
mentoring relationships, 464–469

message design logics, 92–94
  conventional, 92
  expressive, 92
  rhetorical, 92
meta-analysis, 193
metacommunication conflict pattern,
  422
metaperceptions, 39
mirroring, 38
mistakes, embarrassment and, 220
mixed couples, 302
Möbius syndrome, 124
modesty, gender differences in, 167–168
MOOs, 265
moral appeal tactic, 377, 380
moral pragmatists, 161–162
moral standards, 161–162
motivation
  accounts and, 224
  communication competence and,
    518–519
  defined, 518
  for platonic relationships, 297
  ulterior, 152
motor mimicry, 65
Multi-User Domains (MUDS), 265
mutual accommodation, 92

"naive scientists," 32
natural ability, self-promotion and, 159,
  160
negative discrimination, 40–41
negative face needs, 215
negative identity management, 339,
  340–341
negative statements, about opposing
  groups, 163
negative tactics, 384, 386, 387
negativity bias, 34, 35f
neglect response, in conflict, 424–427
negotiation, as response to conflict, 417
negotiation strategies, for resisting
  compliance, 395–396
neutralization, 292
noncoherent topic shifts, 84–85
nonconfrontation, 417
nonnegotiation strategies, 394–396
non-response (non-accommodation), 125
nonverbal abilities, 126–127
nonverbal communication, 102–128
  in accounting, 61
  affinity-seeking through, 157
  arbitrary, 104
  assurances, 288–289
  attachment styles and, 442–443
  chronemics, 108–109
  conscious, 110
  culture and, 109–113

defined, 104
elements of, 104–109
environment, 109
facial expressions, 104
functions of, 113–126
haptics, 105–107
iconic, 104
importance of, 103
intentionality of, 109–111
intrinsic, 104
kinesics, 105
during listening, 54, 61, 63
misconceptions about, 109–113
motor mimicry, 65
nonverbal abilities, 126–127
physical appearance, 108
proxemics, 107–108
in relational disengagement, 323
social support through, 63
touch diaries, 106
types of, 104
vocalics, 107
nonverbal emblems, 497
nonverbal sensitivity, 127
normative solidarity, 446
norm of appropriateness, 194
norm of reciprocity, 183–184, 194
novelty, 292

obligations
  enforcing, 391–393
  personal, 207, 232
obscene jokes, 85
on-line communication, 42–43. *See also*
  Web sites
  confirming messages in, 86
  deindividuation in, 42–43
  emoticons, 115–116
  excuses, 206–207
  gender differences in, 140–141, 142
  loneliness and, 502–503
  relationship development, 264–265
  self-disclosure in, 191–192
  self-perceptions and, 39
  self-presentation in, 139–140
openness
  affinity-seeking through, 157
  relational maintenance and, 287–288,
    297
openness-closedness dialectic tensions,
  292
opinion conformity, 155
opposite-sex friendships, 293–297
optimism, 157
organizations, listening in, 56–57
other-orientation, in disengagement,
  342
out-groups, 40–41

overbenefited partners, 283, 327
overcompensation, 189

pair parts, 82–83
paralanguage, 107
parent-child relationships. *See also*
  families
  affection in, 447, 451
  closeness patterns in, 450–451
  divorce and, 451–453
  father-son, 56
  intergenerational solidarity theory and,
    445–448
  listening behaviors, 56
  support and reciprocity, 443–445
  turning-points in, 448–451
passion-stability dialectic tensions, 292
patronizing talk, 461–462
people listening style, 66
perceived legitimacy of ingratiation,
  153
perception
  communication competence and,
    526–527
  first impressions, 37
  inaccuracies in, 25–26, 527
  metaperception, 39
  on-line relationships, 39
  person, 36–39
  of relationships, 25
  selective, 25–26
  self-, 37–39, 371
perceptiveness, 521
perceptual contrast, 365–366, 369
performance, self-presentation and, 139
perfunctory apologies, 235
permissions, 82
persistence tactic, 380, 381
personal ads, 137, 140, 141, 144
personal autonomy, affinity-seeking
  through, 157
personal causes, 226
personal control. *See also* control
  excuses and, 206, 232
  in triangle model of responsibility, 232
personal criticism, 420
personal descriptors, 42
personal goals, 3–4. *See also* goals
personalistic self-disclosure, 193
personality
  argumentativeness, 496–498
  cognitive complexity, 491–495
  communication apprehension,
    499–500
  communication competence and,
    517–518, 532
  importance of understanding, 482–483
  individual differences in, 482–506

personality *(cont.)*
  in interpersonal communication,
    481–508
  locus of control, 488–491
  loneliness, 500–506
  Machiavellian behavior, 483–486
  self-monitoring behavior, 486–488
personalized messages, 263
personal obligations
  excuses and, 207, 232
  in triangle model of responsibility, 232
personal relationships. *See* relationships
personal space, 107–108
personal Web pages. *See also* Web sites
  gender differences in, 167
  self-presentation in, 141–143
personal welfare, 250
person-centered messages, 491–492
person perception, 36–39
  defined, 36
  factors affecting, 37
  first impressions, 37
  self-, 37–39
person schemata, 27, 37
perspective taking, 492–494
persuasion schema, 383–387
persuasion tactic, 380, 381, 383
**Petronio's Privacy Boundary Coordi-
  nation theory,** 188–190
physical abuse, 335
physical appearance. *See also* physical
  attractiveness
  attacks, 497
  cultural differences in, 111
  as nonverbal communication, 108
physical attractiveness
  affinity-seeking through, 157
  compliance and, 371–372
  impression formation and, 117
  interpersonal attraction and, 253
  nonverbal communication through,
    108
  scarcity principle and, 375–376
physical environment, 109
physicians, 57–59
platonic relationships, 293–297
  defined, 293
  maintaining, 295–297
  motives for, 297
pluralistic families, 27
politeness theory, 214–223
  compliance-gaining messages and,
    390–393
  disclaimers, 216
  embarrassment, 220–223
  facework and, 214–215
  preferred accounts, 216–220
  relational disengagement and, 342–345

popularity, 372–373
positioning, in courtship behaviors, 258
positive face needs, 214–215
positive-tone messages, in disengagement, 337, 338, 341
positivity, in relational maintenance,
  286–287, 297
positivity bias, 34, 35*f*
postural mirroring, 257
power
  compliance-gaining messages and,
    388–390
  definitions of, 389
  displays, 166
  in relationships, 333–336
power-dependency theory, 389
power distance, 224
power tactics
  Falbo's theory of, 380–383
  social acceptability of, 380, 382, 383
pragma, 299, 300
pragmatic code, 80
pragmatic connectedness, 80
pre-act bounding, 84
predictability-novelty dialectic tensions,
  292
prediction, self-presentation and,
  149–150
preferred accounts, 216–220
preferred pair parts, 82–83
pre-giving tactic, 377, 378
prejudice, 40–41
prescription, as distributive tactic, 420
prescription clarity, in triangle model of
  responsibility, 230–232
primary goals, 10
Prince of Tides, The (Conroy), 281
privacy
  boundary coordination, 188–190
  likelihood of candor and, 188
  tolerance of vulnerability and, 186–188
**Privacy Boundary Coordination
  theory,** 188–190
procedural knowledge, 519
procedural remark tactic, 418
prohibitions, 82
promised friendship messages, 338
promise tactic, 377, 378
  politeness theory and, 391
prospective goals, 411
protective families, 27
prototypes, 37
proxemics
  functions of, 114
  in nonverbal communication, 107–108
proximal goals, 10
psychological equity, 325–326
psychological reactance, 375

public images, 234–237
punishment, 378
punishment avoidance, 224
Pygmalion effect, 28, 29

quality, Cooperative Principle and, 81
quality of outcomes, 389
quantity, Cooperative Principle and, 81
quasi-courtship, 257–259

racial discrimination, 108–109
reality-based television
  accounts in, 227
  listening behaviors in, 61
reason tactic, 380, 381
recall of information, 59
recipient situations, embarrassment and,
  220
reciprocal concession, 368
reciprocity
  compliance-gaining messages and, 386
  compliance-resistance and, 396
  cooperation *vs.* competition and, 416
  lagged, 444
  nonverbal communication and, 125
  norm of, in self-disclosure, 183–184,
    194–195
  parent-child support and, 443–445
  of self-disclosure, 183–184, 194–195
reciprocity principle, 366–368
  door-in-the-face, 368
  guilt and, 368–369
  indebtedness and, 369
  reciprocal concession, 368
  self-presentation theory and, 369
recognition, in courtship behaviors, 258
references, in semantic triangle, 78
referent power, 378
referents, in semantic triangle, 78
reflected appraisals, 38
reflected glory, basking in, 165
reframing, dialectical tensions and, 293
refusals
  defined, 528
  expanded typology of, 212, 213
  impression management and, 236
  reactions to, 219
  types of, 213–214, 238
regrets, 217–219
regulators, in nonverbal communication,
  105
reinforcement
  attraction research, 252, 253–254
  behavior and, 488–489
rejections
  as acknowledgments, 82
  as distributive tactic, 420
  reasons reported for, 228–230

relation, Cooperative Principle and, 81
relational dialectics, 291–293
  defined, 292
  dialectical tensions, 292
  responding to dialectical tensions,
    292–293
relational disengagement, 314–354. *See
  also* relationships
  adjustment to, 348–353
  attribution theory and, 331–332
  barriers to, 285
  cascade model of, 336
  communication competence and,
    531
  consequences of, 345–353
  control issues, 333–335
  coping with, 346–347
  emotional consequences of, 347
  equity and, 325–327
  facework and, 342–345
  factors affecting, 317
  friendship following, 348
  gender difference, 318
  infidelity and, 333–336
  initiation of, 318
  of interethnic/intercultural relation-
    ships, 285–286, 327–328
  media representation of, 315, 352
  phases of, 319–325
  politeness theory and, 342–345
  problem valence and frequency,
    332–333
  reasons for, 315–319, 327–331
  repair strategies, 319, 321, 322–325
  tactics in, 337–342
  termination rates, 316
  themes of, 330
relational escalation, 249–273
  See also relationships
  advantages of, 250–251
  cognitive valance theory and, 259–263
  communication competence and,
    528–531
  couples, 29–30
  disadvantages of, 251–252
  features of, 249–252
  interpersonal attraction and, 252–256
  intimacy and, 256–271
  rate of, 268
  relational development processes,
    263–272
  research on, 267–268
  social penetration theory and, 180–182
  stages of, 265–267
  turning points, 268–271
relational expectancies, 28–32, 30
  measures of, 31*f*
  violation of, 32

relational goals, 11, 13–16
  de-escalating, 16
  escalating, 16
  maintaining, 16
relational listening, 53
  defined, 53
  theoretical model of, 53–54
relational maintenance, 281–305
  culture and, 285–286
  defined, 281–282
  equity and, 281–285
  platonic friendships, 293–297
  reasons for, 282
  relational dialectics, 291–293
  romantic relationships, 298–304
relational maintenance strategies, 285–291
  assurances, 288–289
  openness, 287–288
  positivity, 286–287
  sharing tasks, 290, 291, 296
  social networks, 290
relational messages
  defined, 122
  nonverbal communication and,
    122–126
  synchrony in, 122–123
relational problems. *See also* conflict
  managing, 424–427
relational rewards, 263
relational schemata, 27
relationship development. *See* relational
  escalation
relationship-enhancing bias, 35*f*, 36
relationship fault messages, in disengagement, 338
relationships. *See also* couples; families;
    friendships; romantic relationships
  affectionate communication and,
    116–117
  argumentativeness and, 498
  attachment theory and, 440–445
  communication competence and,
    528–531
  in families, 440–460
  gender and, 124
  intergenerational solidarity theory and,
    445–448
  interpersonal goals and, 13–16
  judgments about behavior of others,
    32–36
  listening and, 55–56
  nonverbal communication in, 122–126
  on-line, 264–265
  paths of, 29–30
  paths toward marriage, 29–30
  perception of, 25
  secrets and, 185–186
  self-disclosure and, 191–192

socioemotional selectivity theory and,
    458–460
  turning points in, 268–271
  unequal, 30
relationship talk tactics, in disengagement, 343–345
relief, in relational disengagement, 346
remediation, coping with embarrassment
  with, 221, 222
rendering favors, 155
repairing relationships, 319, 321, 322–325
requests, 82
requirements, 82, 206
resistance hypothesis, 387–388
resolution, in courtship behaviors, 258
responsibility, acceptance of, 419
responsiveness, 521
retention, listening and, 52–53
retrospective goals, 411
Retrospective Interview Technique (RIT),
    269
return on investment model, of intergenerational support, 444
revenge, 220
revitalization, dialectical tensions and,
    292–293
rewarding activity, 378
rewarding association, 158
reward power, 378
rhetorical message design logic, 93
right to persuade, 415
RIT (Retrospective Interview Technique),
    269
roles
  in marriage, 302
  schemata, 27
  self-presentation and, 138, 166–167
romantic relationships, 298–304. *See also*
    couples; courtship; love; marriage;
    relationships
  behaviors communicating, 257
  communication among marital types,
    302–303
  Fitzpatrick's marital typology, 302
  love styles, 298–300
  love ways, 300–302
rule keeping, conversational, 157
rule violation secrets, 186, 187

sadness, in relational disengagement, 346
sad tale justification, 209, 210
sandbagging, 142–144, 161
sarcasm, 420
satisfaction
  marital, 268, 282, 303, 498
  relational, 268, 282, 302, 316,
    318–319, 429–430
satisfactory fit, in self-disclosure, 189

scapegoating, 209, 210, 218
scarcity principle, 374–376
schadenfreude, 164–165
schemata, 26–27. *See also* cognitive
    processes
  culture and, 26
  defined, 26, 383
  person, 37
  types of, 27
school bullies, 146
scripts, 27, 29, 139
secondary goals, 10
secrets. *See also* privacy
  relationships and, 184–185
  revealing, 183
  suppressing, 183
  taboo, 186, 187, 288
  types of, 186, 187
secure attachment style, 440–443, 445
secure love, 300, 301
seduction behaviors, 258–259
selection, dialectical tensions and, 292
selective attention, 25
selective self-presentation, 13
self-blame, in relational disengagement,
    346
self-concepts
  confirmation of, 158
  development of, 37–38
self-consistency, 141, 143
self-construals, 94
  culture and, 169–170
  independent, 94, 169
  interdependent, 94, 169
self-defense. *See* defense of self
self-descriptors, 42
self-disclosure, 179–198
  affinity-seeking through, 157
  amount of, 193–194
  appropriate, 520
  breadth of, 181
  candor and, 188
  choosing against, 185–186
  communication competence and, 528
  culture and, 192–193
  defined, 179
  depth of, 181, 194–195
  factors affecting, 183–190
  gender differences in, 185–186,
    190–191
  general, 193–194
  goals and, 183
  honesty in, 196–197
  as integrative tactic, 419
  liking and, 193–194, 197
  manner of, 190–197
  in marriage, 185

negative, 196
norm of reciprocity in, 183–184,
    194–195
in on-line relationships, 191–192
perception of, 193–197
personalistic, 193
positive, 196
privacy needs and, 186–190
purposes of, 183
reciprocity of, 183–184, 194–195
relationships and, 191–192
as relationship stage, 29
social penetration theory of, 180–182
student rating of, 196
timing in, 197
types of, 179–180
valence in, 196
vulnerability and, 186–188
self-disconfirming prophecies, 28
self-efficacy
  communication competence and, 518
  of goals, 9
  locus of control and, 489
self-esteem
  relational disengagement, 322
  through opposition to others, 163
self-feeling tactic
  negative, 377, 380
  positive, 377, 380
self-fulfilling prophecies, 28
self-fulfillment, 209, 210
self-glorification, 141, 143
self-handicapping, 160–161
self-identity, 148–150
self-inclusion, 158
self-monitoring, 168, 486–488
self-orientation disengagement, 341–342
self-oriented tactics, 383–385, 386
self-perception, 37–39
  chronic view of self, 37–39
  commitment principle and, 371
  reflected appraisal, 38
self-presentation, 136–170
  affinity-seeking through, 157
  aging and, 460–464
  coherence of, 148
  communication competence and,
    527–528
  confrontation and, 415
  cultural differences, 168–170
  defined, 137–138
  direct strategies of, 151–163
  exaggeration in, 143
  exemplification, 161–162
  gender differences in, 167–168
  goals for, 147–148
  as guide to action, 149

indicators of attainment, 150–151
indirect strategies of, 163–166
individual differences, 168
ingratiation, 151–156
interpersonal, 141–151
intimidation, 156–158
monitoring, 147–148
nature of, 138–141
reciprocity and, 369
roles, 166–167
self-identity and, 148–150
self-promotion, 158–161
strategic, 138
strategics, 144–145
supplication, 162–163
in Web pages, 141–143
self-presentation goals, 11–13
self-promoters, 145
"self-promoter's paradox," 167
self-promotion
  bragging *vs.*, 159–160
  intimidation and, 156
  organizations and, 167
  self-handicapping, 160–161
  self-presentation through, 158–161
  strategies, 144
  in Web sites, 142
self-schemata, 27
semantics, 77–78
semantic triangle, 78
sensitivity
  affinity-seeking through, 158
  communication competence and, 520
  interpersonal attraction and, 256
  nonverbal, 127
separate couples, 302, 303
separate vacations, 318
separation, dialectical tensions and, 292
severity of offense, in relational disen-
    gagement, 343
"Sex and the City," 352
sexual arousal, 258
sexual infidelity, 333. *See also* infidelity
sharing tasks, 290, 291, 296
shouting, as distributive tactic, 420
SIDE (Social Identity model of Deindi-
    viduation Effects), 42–43
similarity
  attitude, 254–255, 264, 318
  attractiveness and, 254–255
  behaviors communicating, 257
  ethnic, 264
  relational disengagement and, 318
simple statement tactic, 380, 381
sin licenses, 85, 216
situational loneliness, 503–504
smiles, 110

smileys, 115
sociability, 252
social categories, 42
social chameleons, 168
social cognition, 25, 44
social composure, 520
social confirmation, 520
social exchange theory, 444
social experience, 520
social loneliness, 503
social networks
    couple satisfaction and, 319
    relational maintenance and, 290
social penetration theory, 180–182,
    263–264
social perception skills, 491–492
social phase, of disengagement, 319–321
social power, 388–390
social principles tactics, 384, 386
social proof principle, 372–373
social support, listening and, 62–63
social validation. *See* social proof principle
socioeconomic selectivity theory,
    458–460
soliciting disclosure, as integrative tactic,
    419
speech acts, 82
speech convergence, 90–91
speech divergence, 91
spontaneity conflict pattern, 424
stability
    of conflict, 428
    dialectical tensions, 292
stabilizing processes, 37
stable causes, 226
stage, self-presentation and, 139
stalling tactic, 418
Stand By Me, 466
stationarity conflict pattern, 422–423
status
    authority principle and, 374
    confrontation and, 415
step-families
    affinity-seeking behaviors in, 156
    communication processes in, 455–457
stereotypes, 39–42
    defined, 39
    discrimination and, 40–41
    image formation and, 117–118
    letting go of, 41–42
    liar, 118
    of older people, 460–464
    prejudice and, 40–41
    usefulness of, 40
storge, 299, 300
storytelling, 5
strategic communication, 6, 25

strategic self-presentation, 138. *See also*
    impression management
strategies, 6, 10–11, 25
structural attraction research, 252,
    255–256
structural solidarity, 446
students
    listening skills of, 59–60
    performance and teacher expectancies,
    28–29
subjective probability of success, 152
subliminal slides, 37
subordinate goals, 9
supplicators
    defined, 145
    organizations and, 167
    self-presentation and, 162–163
    strategies, 144
supportiveness
    affinity-seeking through, 158
    assurances, 288–289
    coping with embarrassment with, 222
    defined, 252
    as integrative tactic, 419
    interpersonal attraction and, 253–254
supraordinate goals, 9
suspended judgment, appeal to, 216
symbols
    meanings of, 5–6
    nonverbal communication through, 113
    in semantic triangle, 78
symmetry conflict pattern, 420–422
sympathy, 65, 521
symptoms, 5
synchronized messages, 264
synchrony, 122–123
syntactic code, 78–80

taboo secrets, 186, 187, 288
taggers, 89
talkativeness, 256
tangential responses, as disconfirming
    messages, 86
task sharing, 290, 291, 296
temperature, behavior and, 109
termination, of relationships, 315. *See also*
    relational disengagement
Terminator 2, 103
test of relationship messages, 338
thanks, 82
thought manipulation tactic, 380, 381
threat tactic, 377, 378, 380, 381, 383
    distributive, 420
    politeness theory and, 390–391
time, as nonverbal communication,
    108–109
time-oriented listening style, 66

timing, of self-disclosure, 197
titles, authority principle and, 373–374
tolerance of vulnerability
    self-disclosure and, 188–190
topic focus, 83–85
topic shading, 84
topic shifts, 84–85, 418
    coherent, 84
    noncoherent, 84–85
    sin licenses and, 85
touch
    in courtship relationships, 258, 268
    gender differences, 105–107, 258
    interpretation of, 258
    as nonverbal communication, 105–107
touch diaries, 106
traditional couples, 302, 303
traditional romantic love, 301
traffic court, excuses and apologies in,
    237–238
transact, 4
transactional analysis, 4–5
transactive goals, 10, 411
traumatic events, 349
triangle model of responsibility, 225–230
    personal control, 232
    personal obligation, 232
    prescription clarity, 230–232
trust, 57
trustworthiness, 158
turning points, 268–271
    activities together, 450
    after divorce, 453–455
    alcohol/abuse, 450
    communication, 449
    dating/cohabitation, 450
    engagement/marriage, 449–450
    in family relationships, 448–451
    having children, 450
    jealousy feelings, 450
    physical distance, 449
    rebellious teenager, 449
    times of crises, 449

ulterior motives, 152
ultimate attribution error, 34, 35*f*
uncertainty, relational escalation and, 251
uncontrollable causes, 226
underbenefited partners, 283
    equity restoration by, 326–327
    relational disengagement and, 317, 326
understanding, as integrative tactic, 419
unhealthy relationships
    control issues, 333–336
    depression and, 333
    infidelity, 333–336
    signs of, 334

unilateral facework tactics, in disengagement, 343–345
unstable causes, 226
urgency hypothesis, 388

vacations, separate, 318
valence
   relational disengagement and, 332
   self-disclosure and, 196
valuative inquiry, 207
variety conflict pattern, 418
verbal aggressiveness, 496–498
verbal communication, 76–97
   codes in, 77–80
   culture and, 87–92

goals and, 80–87
individual factors affecting, 92–96
victim, denial of, 209, 210
violence
   argumentative skill deficiency model of, 497–498
   intimidation and, 156, 158
   in marriage, 497
   self-presentation and, 150
vocalics, 107
voice response, in conflict, 424–427
vulnerability, tolerance of, 188–190

Wall Street, 481
War of the Roses, 422, 423
weakness, supplication, 162–163

Web sites. *See also* on-line communication
   content analysis of, 142
   on emotional problems, 506
   on loneliness, 506
   personal, 141–143, 167
"we-ness," of couples, 316, 319
wit, 520
withdrawal tactics, in disengagement, 339, 340
withdrawing style, in conflict, 412–413
women. *See* gender differences
word order, 78–80
working-through stage, in relational disengagement, 352–353
worrying, 501–502